MW01629309

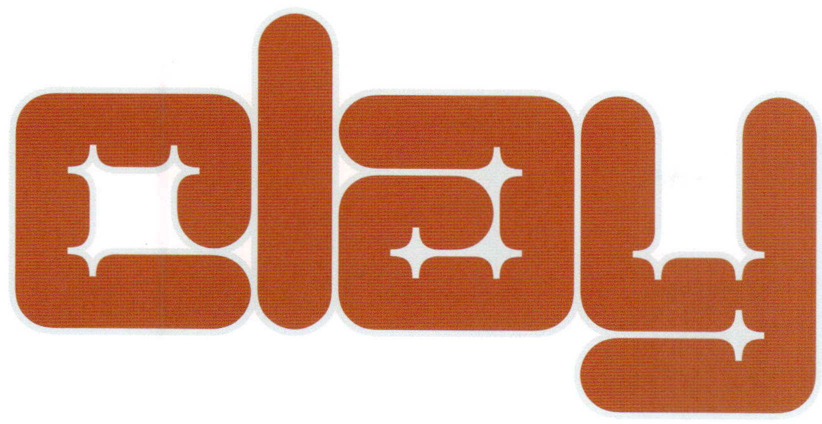
clay

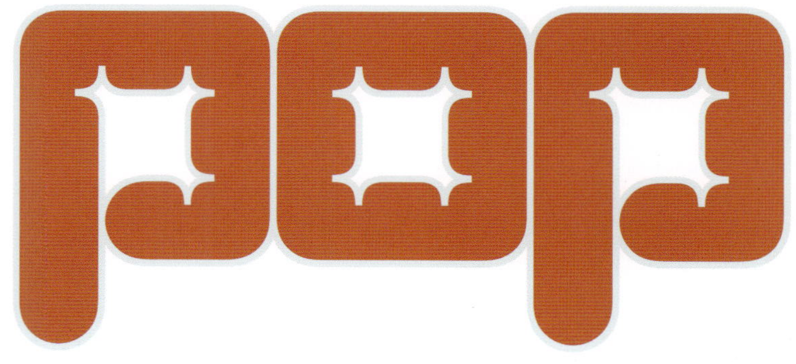
pop

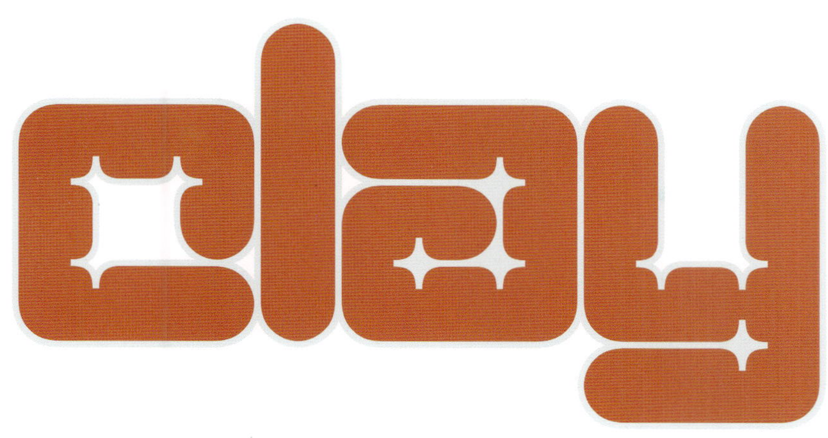

Introduction By Alia Dahl
Essay By Michael Lobel

Jeffrey Deitch

Rizzoli Electa

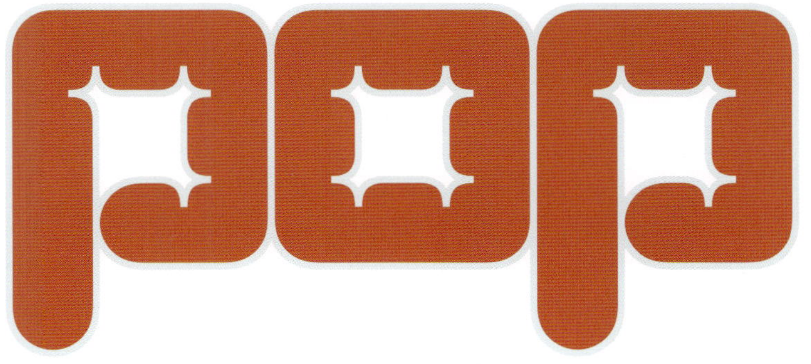

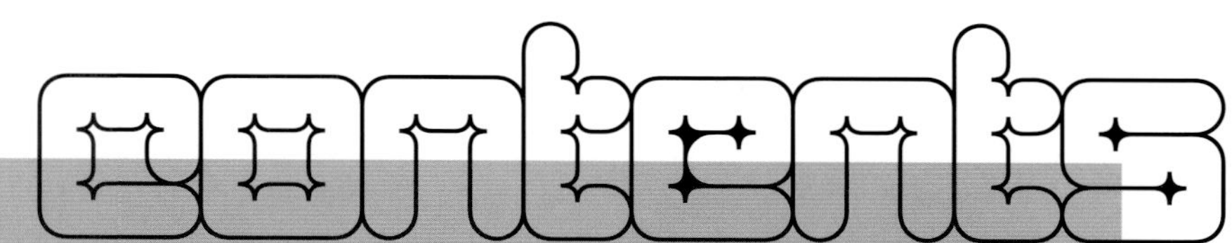
contents

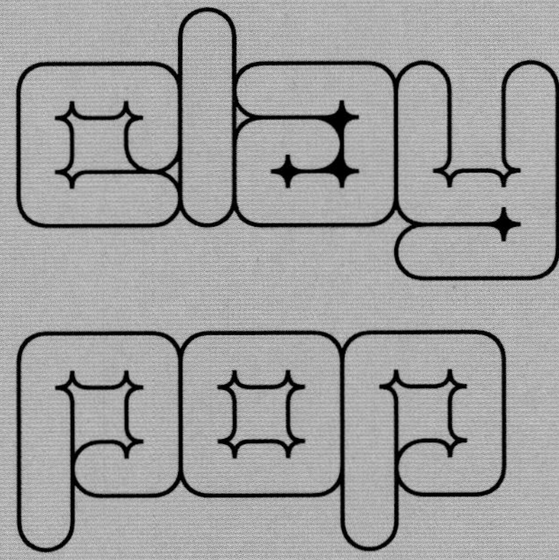

ALIA DAHL

Ceramic is an intuitive and complex medium for art making. To make a successful piece, you need to have both spontaneous creativity and technical discipline. You need to simultaneously think like an artist, scientist, and engineer—and even after that, once you put a clay sculpture in a kiln, you are not guaranteed a final, let alone successful, result. Today a new generation of artists use ceramics to capture their present reality, tackling issues of identity, culture, gender, race, and other social issues. A medium long connected with craft now subverts tradition through its engagement with popular culture. *Clay Pop*, presented at Jeffrey Deitch in New York in 2021, marked the first large exhibition to document this new direction of ceramic sculpture within the Pop art tradition.

Represented in this book is a thriving community of artists that gives a new dimension to Pop art. They reference vintage cartoons, animations, films, billboards, and street signs, alongside contemporary imagery. American Pop artists like Claes Oldenburg and Andy Warhol are as much reference points as advertising, commercials, and global brands. Bright colors and immense scales force you to engage with the work head-on. Some borrowed processes, like stenciling and airbrush, subvert the typically visible artist's hand in ceramic work. Others keep noticeable fingerprints and expressive markings. The artists in this book make radical decisions regarding scale, complexity, glazing techniques, and subject matter.

Several shows provided inspiration for *Clay Pop*. In *Making Knowing: Craft in Art, 1950–2019* at the Whitney Museum of American Art, older-generation ceramicists like Peter Voulkos, Kenneth Price, and Betty Woodman were shown alongside younger artists like Sterling Ruby and Kahlil Robert Irving. The wide variety of ceramics was presented in a nontraditional arrangement: instead of sitting on individual uniform pedestals throughout the room, the sculptures settled on multilevel structures that allowed several vantage points.

Genesis Belanger's solo exhibition at the Aldrich Contemporary Art Museum served as a starting point for this book. Belanger completely connects pop culture and the ceramic world. Imagery like her tape dispenser with a wagging tongue and a delicate feminine hand picking up a phone seem to be pulled from film stills, her imagery concurrently playful, strange, and familiar.

Woody De Othello, an Oakland-based ceramic artist, regularly presents ambitious works in galleries and art fairs, but his presentation in the 2022 Whitney Biennial was particularly impressive. Creating his own assemblage of familiar household items, like a radiator, coffee cup, and stepladder, he anthropomorphizes

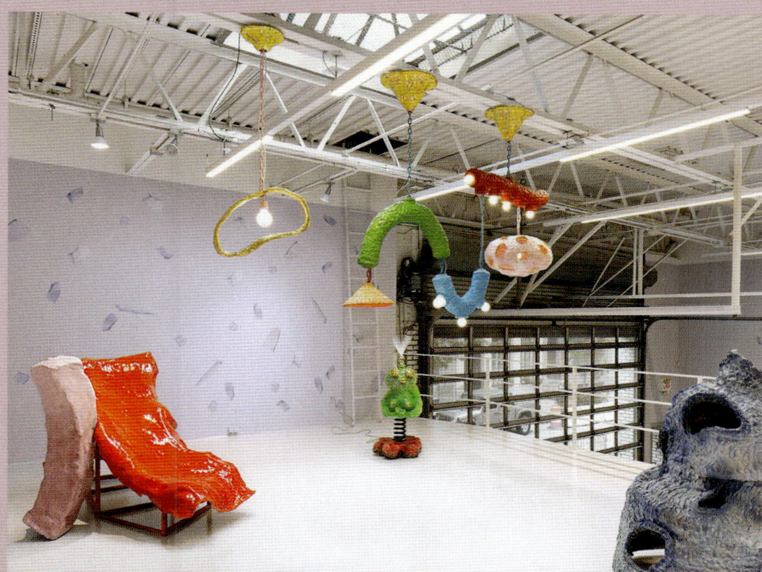

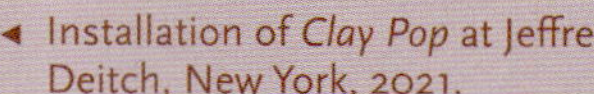

Installation of *Clay Pop* at Jeffrey Deitch, New York, 2021.

the common living room with a wonky twist. De Othello's works emotionally and physically take up space—setting a new direction for ceramic conventions.

Ruby Neri's large-scale female figures twist and leap off the surface of her pots. Alake Shilling, who draws inspiration from vintage cartoons to Walt Disney to natural sea-life forms, sends her ceramic snakes, bunnies, and bears on journeys into new lands. Jessica Stoller challenges traditional ideas of gender and aging with her graceful porcelain sculptures that betray signs of aging such as fine white hairs and delicate wrinkled skin. Trisha Baga challenges our engagement with modern-day technology and celebrity image culture through clay. Elizabeth Jaeger's watching birds and miniature figures on benches give life to intimate interactions on busy city streets. Heidi Lau and Ryan Flores both masterfully engineer large-scale sculptures with complicated glazes, giving a sense of otherworldliness to ambitious structures.

Conversations with some artists led to suggestions of others, leading to a larger global community of ceramicists. Kahlil Robert Irving, based in St. Louis, uses stencil and collage techniques to replicate found materials that divulge complex urban histories. Raven Halfmoon, an Indigenous artist and member of Caddo Nation born in Oklahoma, constructs towering ancestral monuments that command your attention. In London, Lindsey Mendick's sculptures challenge and celebrate culture's idea of beauty flaws. The Japanese artist Masato Mori fuses Japanese figuration with underground graffiti art.

One of the most interesting qualities of this new generation of ceramicists is the deep sense of community. Artists like Grant Levy-Lucero, Bari Ziperstein, Brian Rochefort, and Alake Shilling are based in the Southern California area—a geography with a long tradition of ceramics. Grant Levy-Lucero's vessels present commercial brands in a unique style inspired by hand-painted signs seen throughout Los Angeles. Sharif Farrag's narrative works explore how his multicultural heritage and American upbringing in Los Angeles collide. Over several decades, Magdalena Suarez Frimkess has documented her personal history through small ceramic tiles and freestanding figurative forms with Walt Disney and Popeye cartoon imagery. Alex Anderson reflects on his multiethnic and gay identity through whimsical motifs and gold luster elements. Both Alex Becerra and Melvino Garretti interweave their passion for music and art through intuitive techniques. Seth Bogart's punk and counterculture library books entertain and mystify. The undulating glazes and tactile textures of Brie Ruais's and Brian Rochefort's sculptures replicate surfaces found in nature. Katie Stout's slide, frog rider, and climbing dome make for a lively modern-day ceramic playground. Deep psychological narratives are present in Wade Tullier's surreal sculptures and Keegan Monaghan's discarded everyday household objects. Jennifer Rochlin and Jasmine Little shape their own unique visions of traditional vases with their painterly figurative reliefs and clay etchings. Amia Yokoyama's slimy female figures inhabit a mysterious world full of folklore, while Candice Lin's looming totemic sculptures challenge colonial histories. The sweet figures in Sally Saul's sculptures seem almost human, while Diana Yesenia Alvarado and Bari Ziperstein's works share powerful figurative imagery that demand attention and are rooted in contemporary culture. Coming from a painting background, Dominique Fung gives life to the traditional Chinese ceramic objects depicted in her paintings.

Nothing about the New York *Clay Pop* exhibition was conventional. We knew that the exhibition could not be a predictable sea of white pedestals. The presentation should reflect the unique and varied sculptures and the community making them. We collaborated with the design team Charlap Hyman & Herrero, based in New York, to fulfill our exhibition design vision. I had seen their work previously in a gallery show on the Lower East Side and was astonished: the modest exhibition space was transformed into an Upper East Side funeral parlor complete with curtains and crown molding. Visiting Katie Stout led to another connection to Charlap Hyman & Herrero—Stout was close to one of the founders. Despite the exhibition's early planning stage, Charlap Hyman & Herrero was enthusiastic about this challenge and created their own ceramic world: the multilevel geodesic labyrinth was punctuated with pastel purple paint and hand-drawn ceramic shards. The exhibition's design is reflected on the endpapers in this book.

Charlap Hyman & Herrero's genius design set the stage for an exceptional exhibition. By the time we got to the September opening, there was a pulsating energy around the show. You could see visitors on the main floor and platform ascending and descending between sculptures—looking from above, from the side, sometimes from below. Visitors to the show were contorting themselves to be able to view the work.

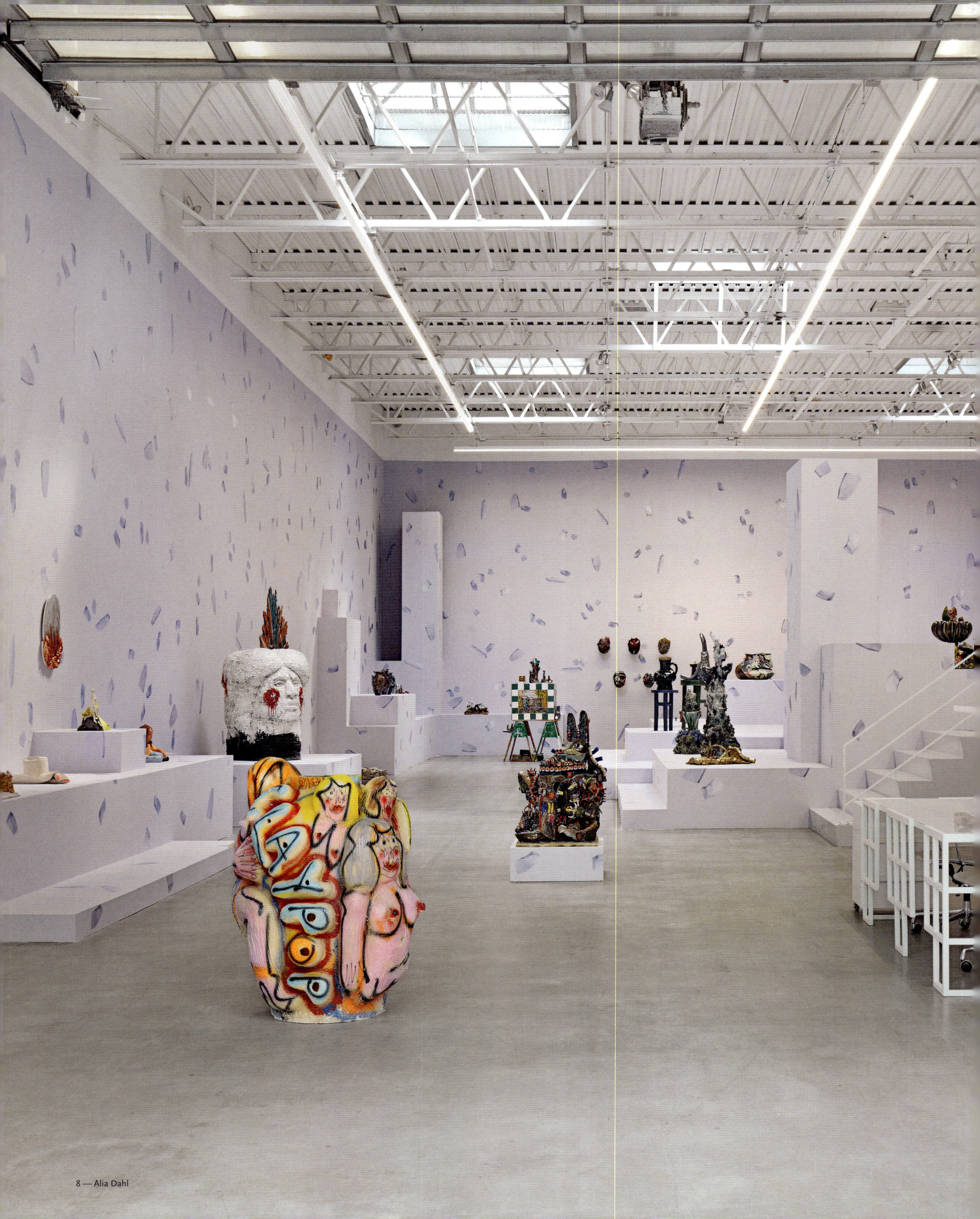

The success of the exhibition led to more conversations around the new generation of ceramics artists, and the inclusion of additional artists in this book. Stephanie Temma Hier fuses traditional paintings with amusing ceramic sculpture. Narumi Nekpenekpen and Jiha Moon's sculptures balance delicate forms with dynamic glazes. Joel Gaitan approaches his terracotta vases with tongue-in-cheek humor. Stephanie H. Shih's ceramic arrangements replicate painting compositions, in which Asian condiments and cooking ingredients are ready to be assembled for a family meal.

In this book, thoughtfully designed by POLYMODE, we've included a selection of recent work by each artist that reflects their engagement with ceramics, particularly within the tradition of Pop art. Each portfolio of images is accompanied by a text describing the artist's practice. An essay by Michael Lobel, professor at the City University of New York and a scholar of Pop art, explores how the global Pop phenomenon challenges assumptions of what art can be, and allows for artists to unleash endless creative possibilities. This book serves as an important document of a community of artists, at a moment of change in how ceramic art is made.

◂ Installation of *Clay Pop* at Jeffrey Deitch, New York, 2021.

diana yesenia alvarado

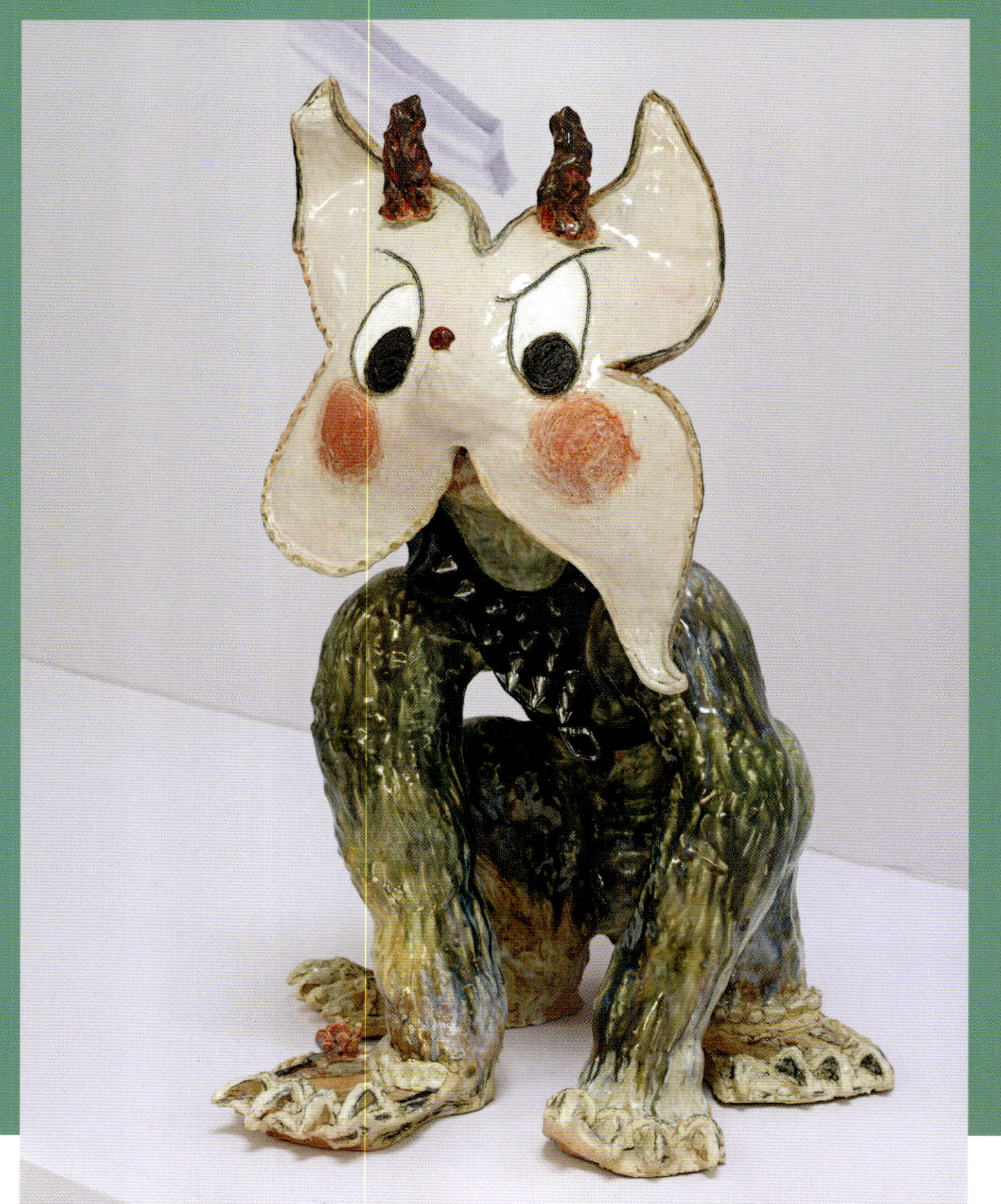

Diana Yesenia Alvarado (b. 1992, Los Angeles) is a multidisciplinary artist whose work foregrounds the visual, cultural, and spiritual idiosyncrasies present in her native hometown of South/East Los Angeles. Working primarily with clay, Alvarado creates hand-built sculptures that can be characterized by their dreamlike glazing, accentuated sartorial details, and animated faces on distorted figures. Her sculptures are typically displayed in a way that combines her connection to domestic space and the environments reminiscent of working-class neighborhoods in Los Angeles—most commonly through the use of ornate wrought-iron fencing, bricks, or wood.

Often firing her work numerous times, Alvarado uses traditional ceramic techniques while exploring the possibilities of the material. She models her process to that of relationship-building, welcoming the uncertainty of other factors as a shaping device.

Alvarado's works can be described as quintessentially LA, as they borrow the imagery from the city's hand-painted signs and Santee Alley fashion. She further distinguishes her practice through her use of the spiritual. Her sculptures function as mediums into another world. Alvarado views herself as a creator who must harness the energy of the material and the spirits that live in her work.

— Diana Yesenia Alvarado

◂ *Necio*, 2021
Glazed ceramic, silver, flock
26 x 21.5 x 21 in.

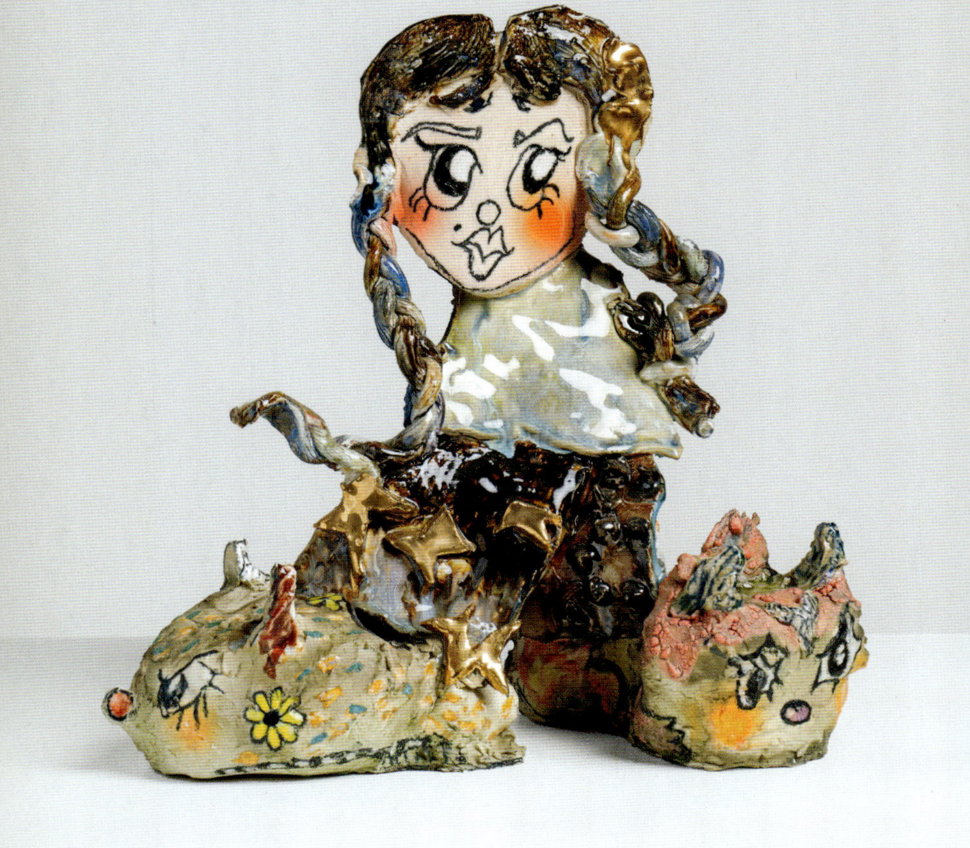

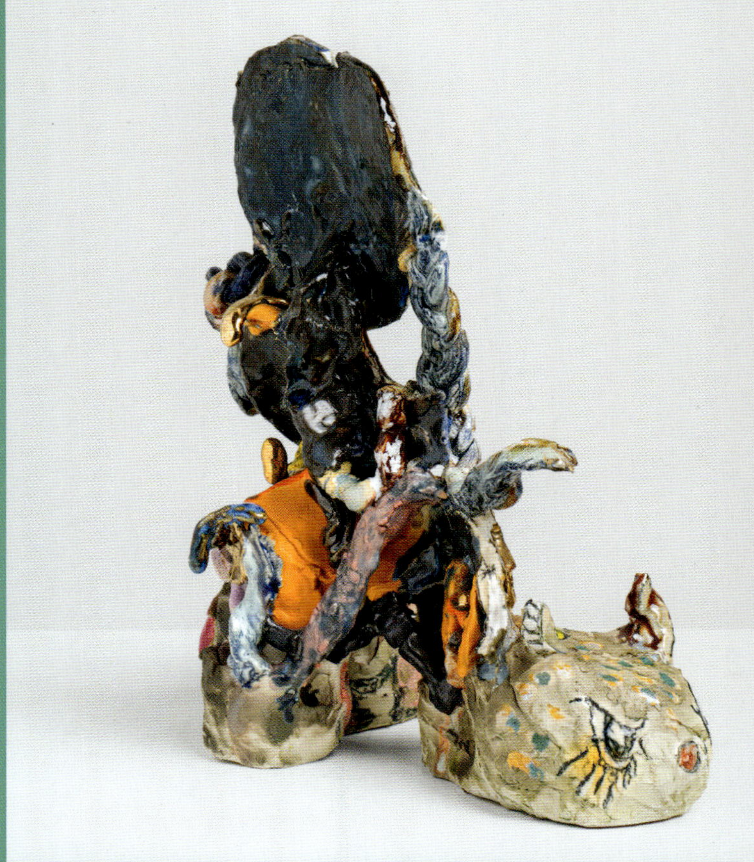

▲ Front and back view of *Estrella*,
2020
Glazed porcelain
11.5 x 12 x 6.5 in.

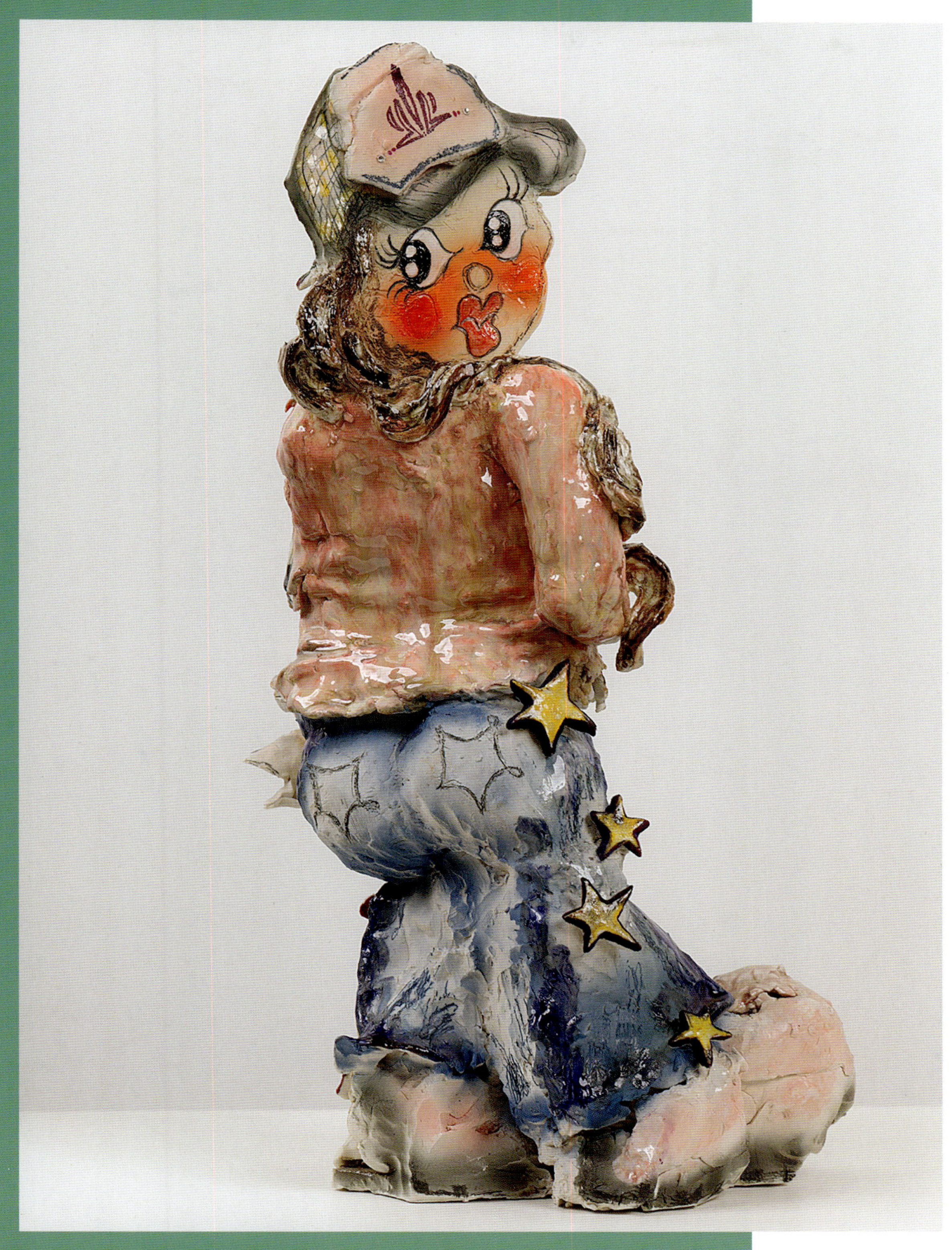

◂ *COQUETA*, 2020
Glazed porcelain
19 x 10 x 10 in.

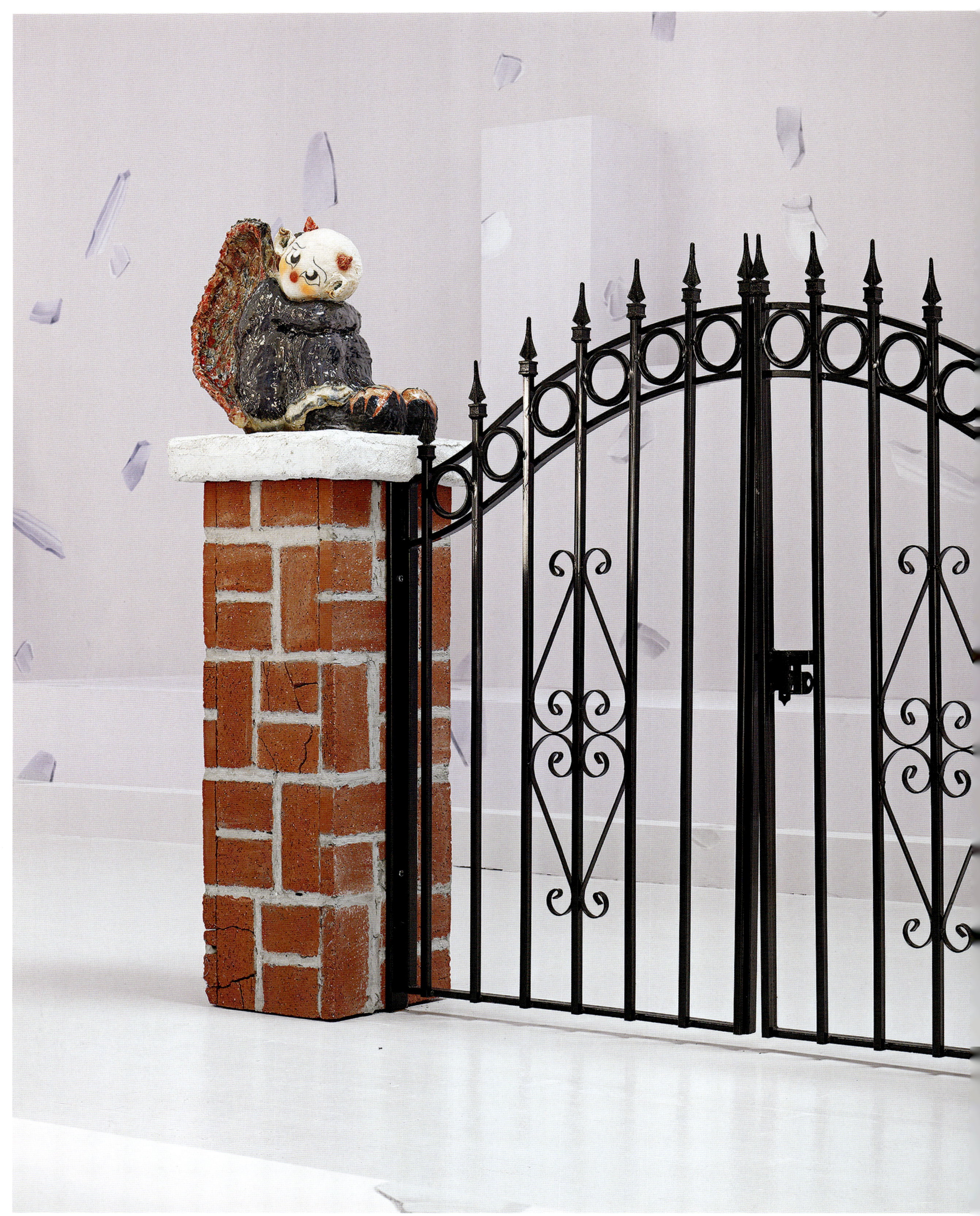

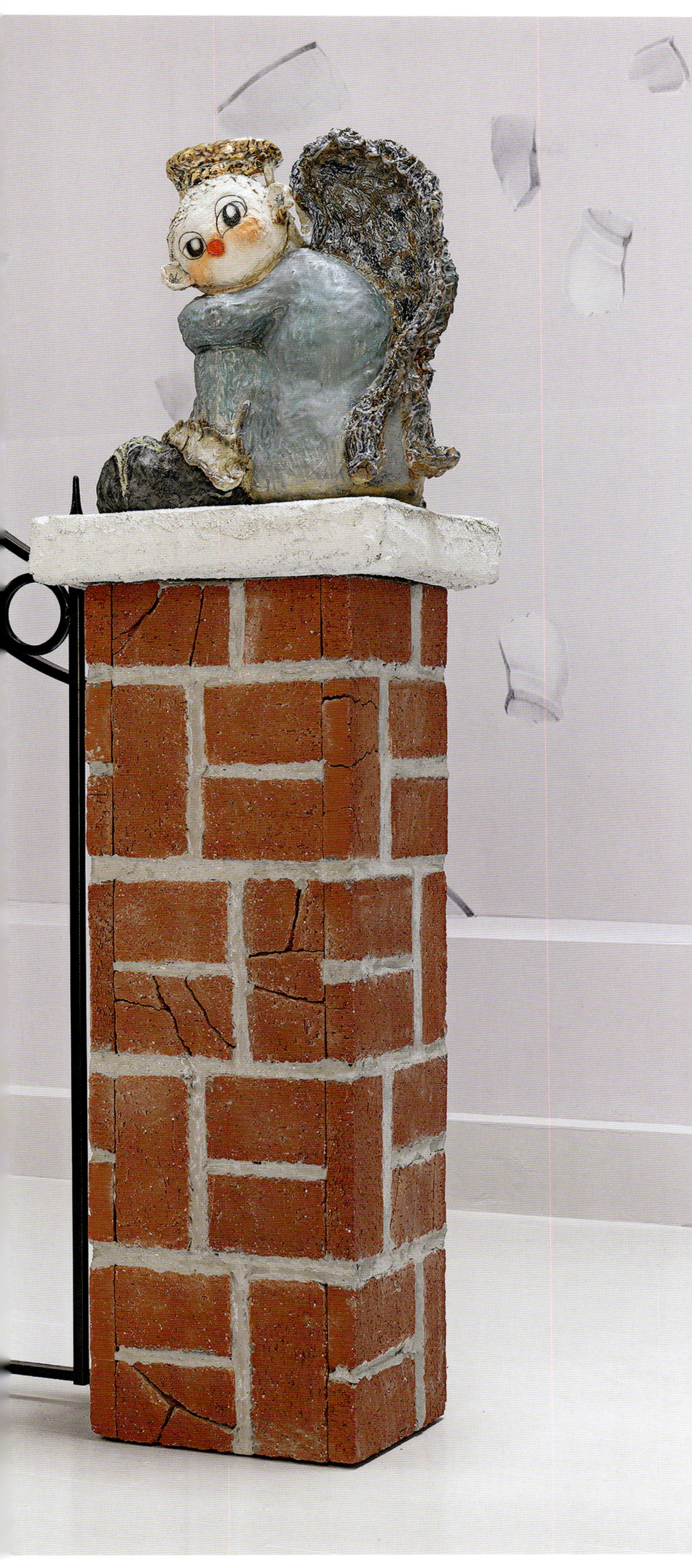

◂ *¿Para dónde?*, 2021
Glazed ceramic, gold, metal,
brick, mortar, wood
Approx. 87 x 28 x 16 in.

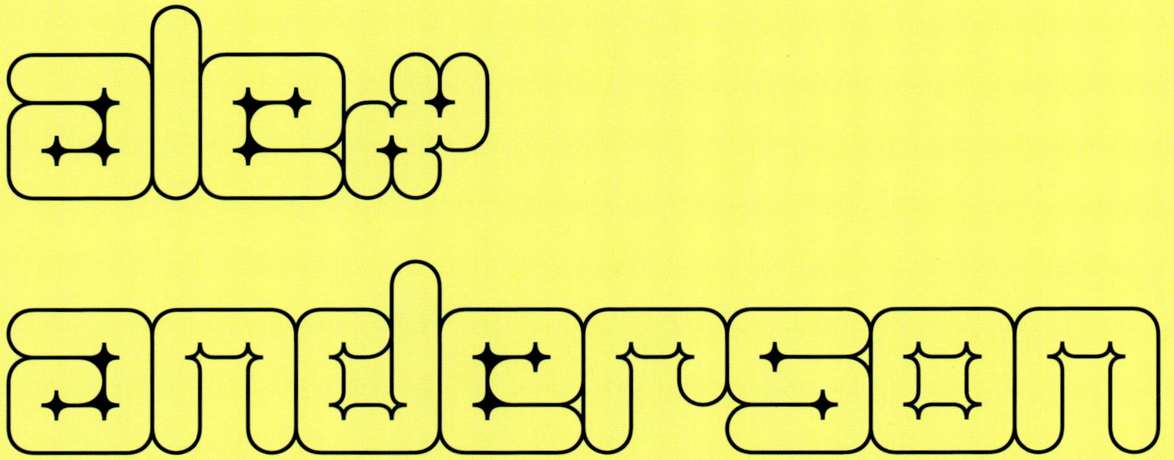
alex
anderson

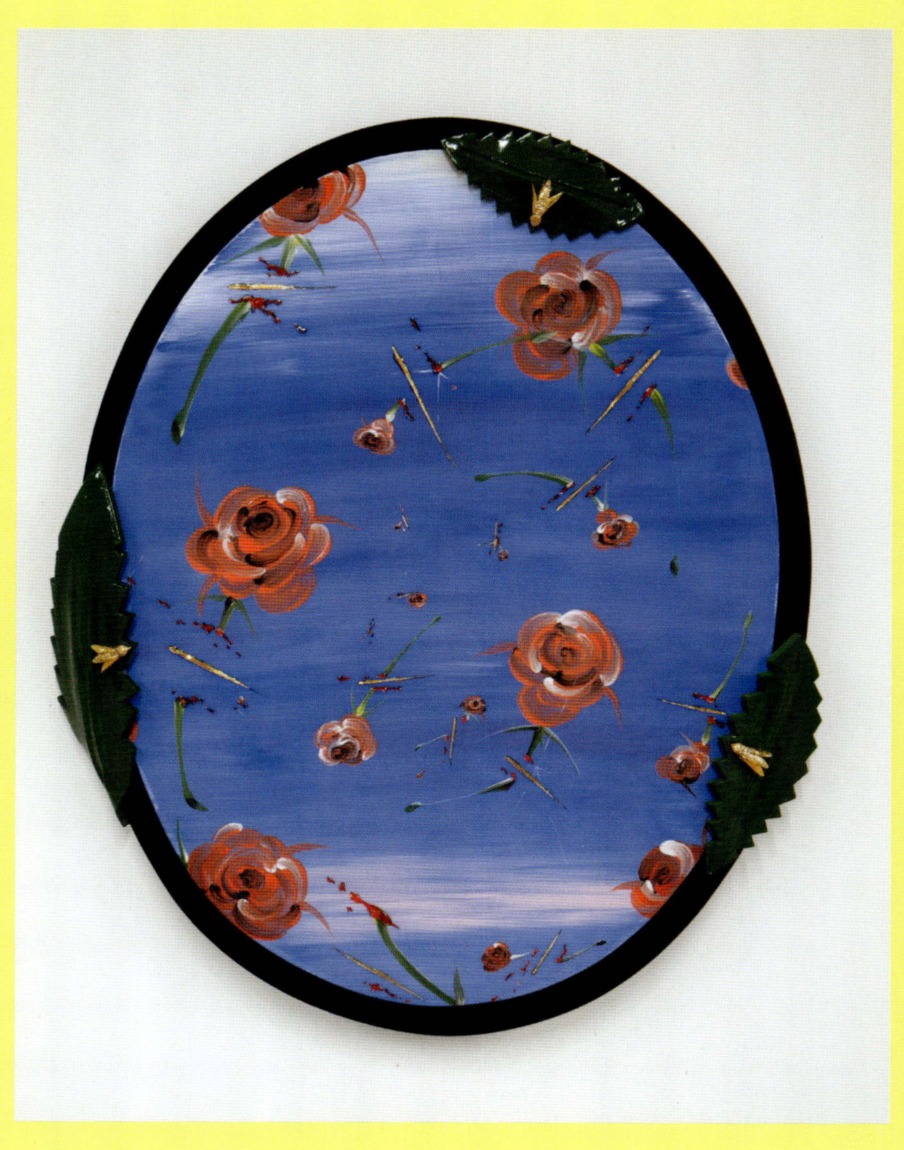

Using millennial twee and pop culture aesthetics, macabre symbolism, and classical art historical references, Alex Anderson (b. 1990, Seattle) creates earthenware works that consider how self-perception is shaped today. By taking up ceramic as his primary material, Anderson considers the multivalence of the medium: its immediate accessibility, its place in Chinese artistic traditions, its associations with narrative on ceramic friezes and the kraters, and the place of porcelain in European imperialist decor. In doing so, he uses the material as a cipher through which to consider his own Black, Japanese, and gay identity, and the weight of what it means for him to be using the medium as a mode of expression.

The artist's recent works take on the forms such as vanity mirrors, serving platters, and hearts. The frames on each of his pieces—some adorned in gold luster—evoke baroque frames on classical artworks in museums, or the gilded decor in European palaces. Glazed and hung on the wall, the works operate between painting and sculpture to upend persistent art world hierarchies around ceramic as a medium.

The facades of Anderson's works are adorned with expressive brushstrokes that reference Japanese and Chinese ink wash painting, with few representative markers other than roses, leaves, and, occasionally, text. The foliage echoes back to memento mori and *vanitas* paintings from northern Europe in the sixteenth and seventeenth centuries, yet Anderson also paints these symbols with a campy sensibility. In these works, he is using pattern and decoration as code: roses and leaves are strategically placed as stand-ins for eyes and lips, with red and blue drops indicating blood and tears to denote passion and pain. The works depict the emotive vulnerability of self-presentation in the age of social media. By not directly representing actual figures in these works, Anderson is using opacity as a mode of protection. One might just as easily see the surfaces on his works as references to filter apps that evade easy subjectivity while also indulging and celebrating the self.

The works consider the contemporary slipperiness between narcissism and self-criticism, and between self-love and self-harm. For *Chaos* (2021), Anderson painted the work's title onto the surface in red, in a style that conveys a deliberate attempt to smudge out or erase the word, perhaps indicating what one might see and want to obliterate within oneself.

Dark Portrait with a Gazing Pool (2022) nods to the myth of Narcissus and the relationship between vanity and the despair of unfulfilled desires. A form that appears like an exaggerated mouth on the work evokes dark histories around minstrelsy. Here, Anderson is commenting on the white gaze—on his own ordinary experience of it, as well as its lingering presence in art history. It is a self-aware nod to possible perceptions that he might encounter in the art world as a "little Black boy [who] makes imperial porcelains."[1] Through the presence of gold bees on *Dark Portrait* (a reference to the *vanitas* symbol for regeneration), the artist stakes his right to self-expression and a perception of self that falls outside of white heteronormative value systems.

— Ambika Trasi

[1] *Little Black Boy Makes Imperial Porcelains* was the title of the artist's solo second exhibition with Gavlak Los Angeles, March 14–July 11, 2020.

◂ *Stratospheric Destruction of Romance*, 2022
Earthenware, glaze, gold luster
21 x 17 x 2 in.

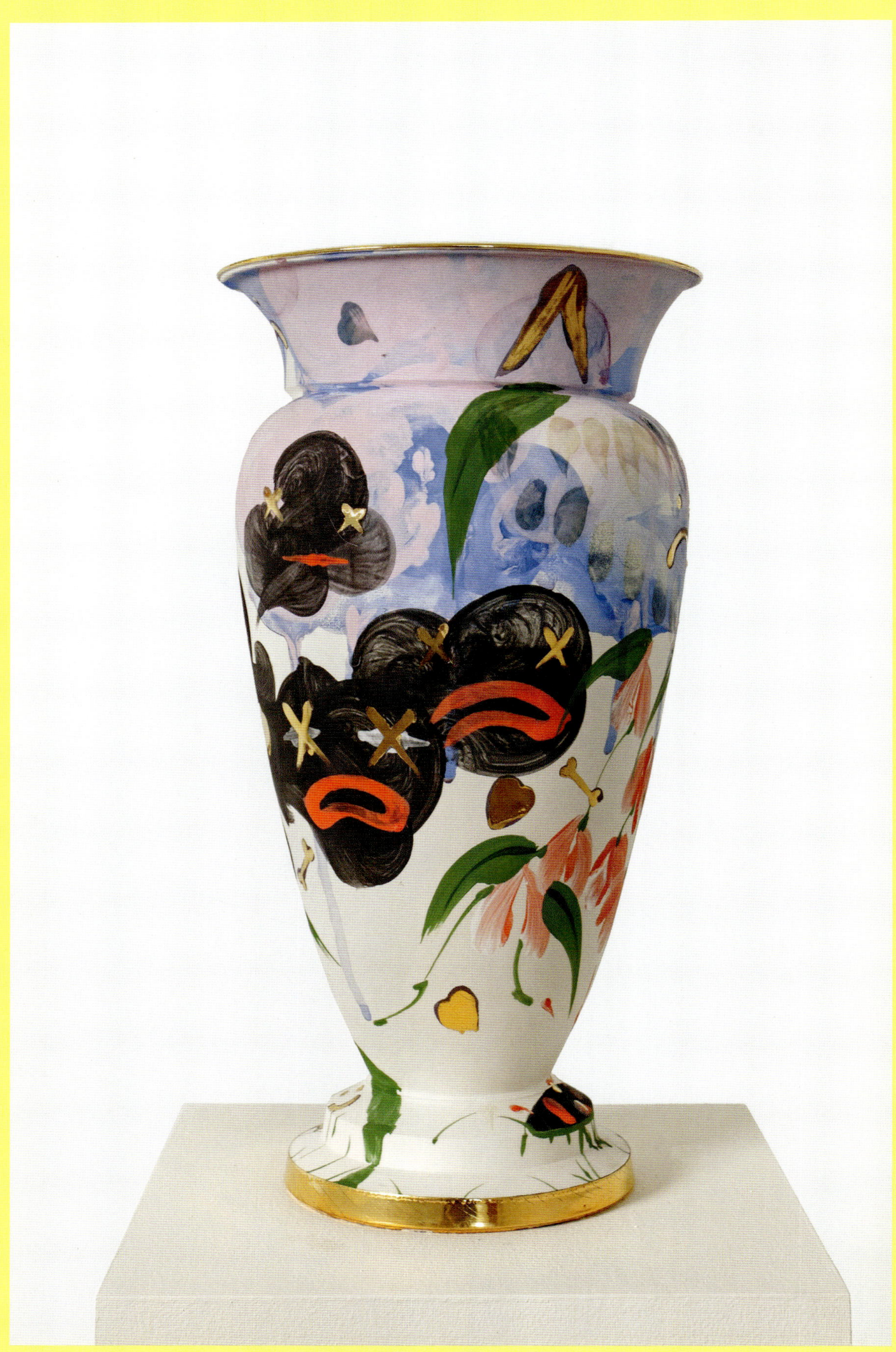

▲ Front and back view of
Dream Vessel I (front), 2019
Earthenware, glaze, gold luster
12.5 x 6.5 x 6.5 in.

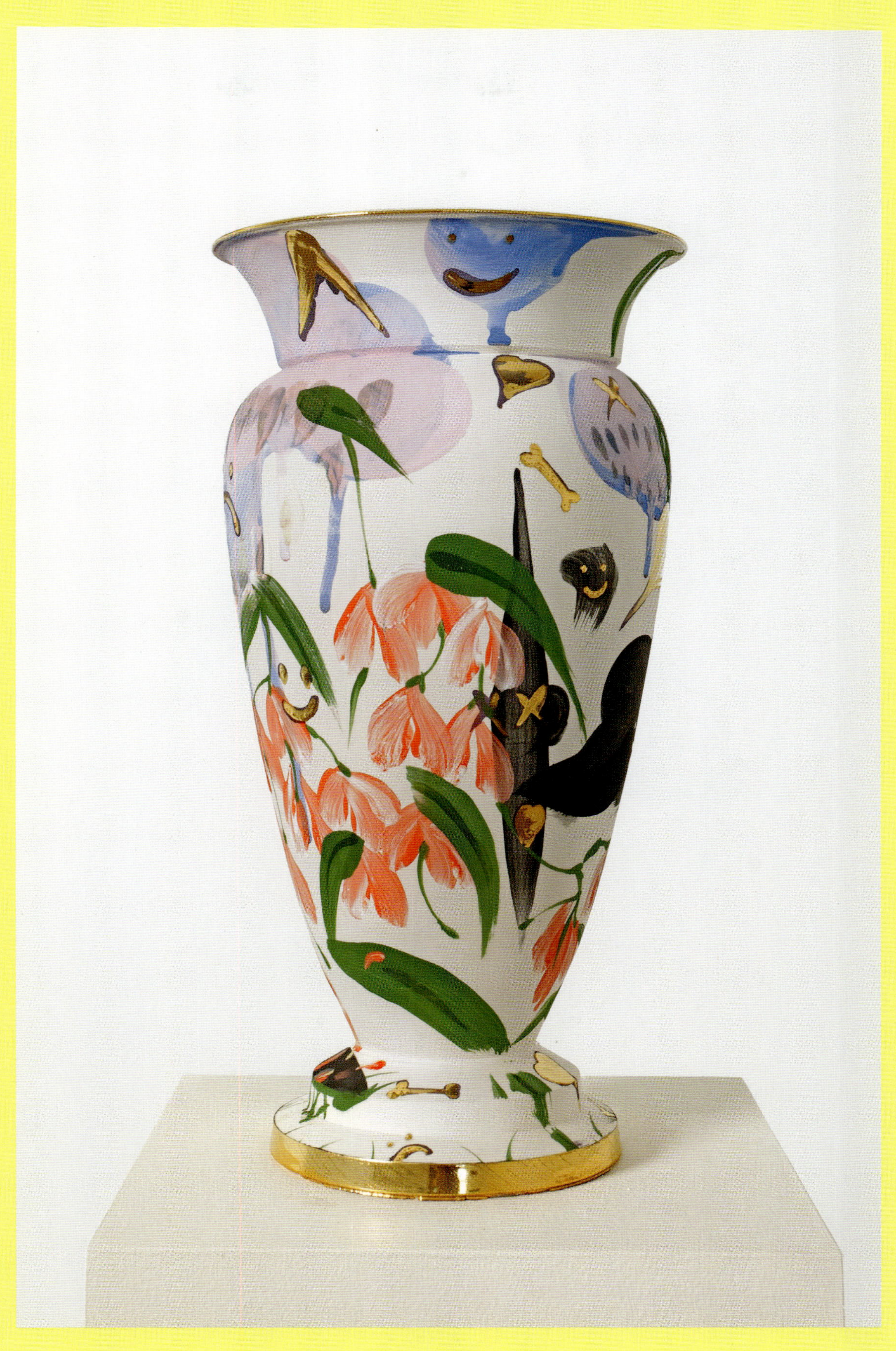

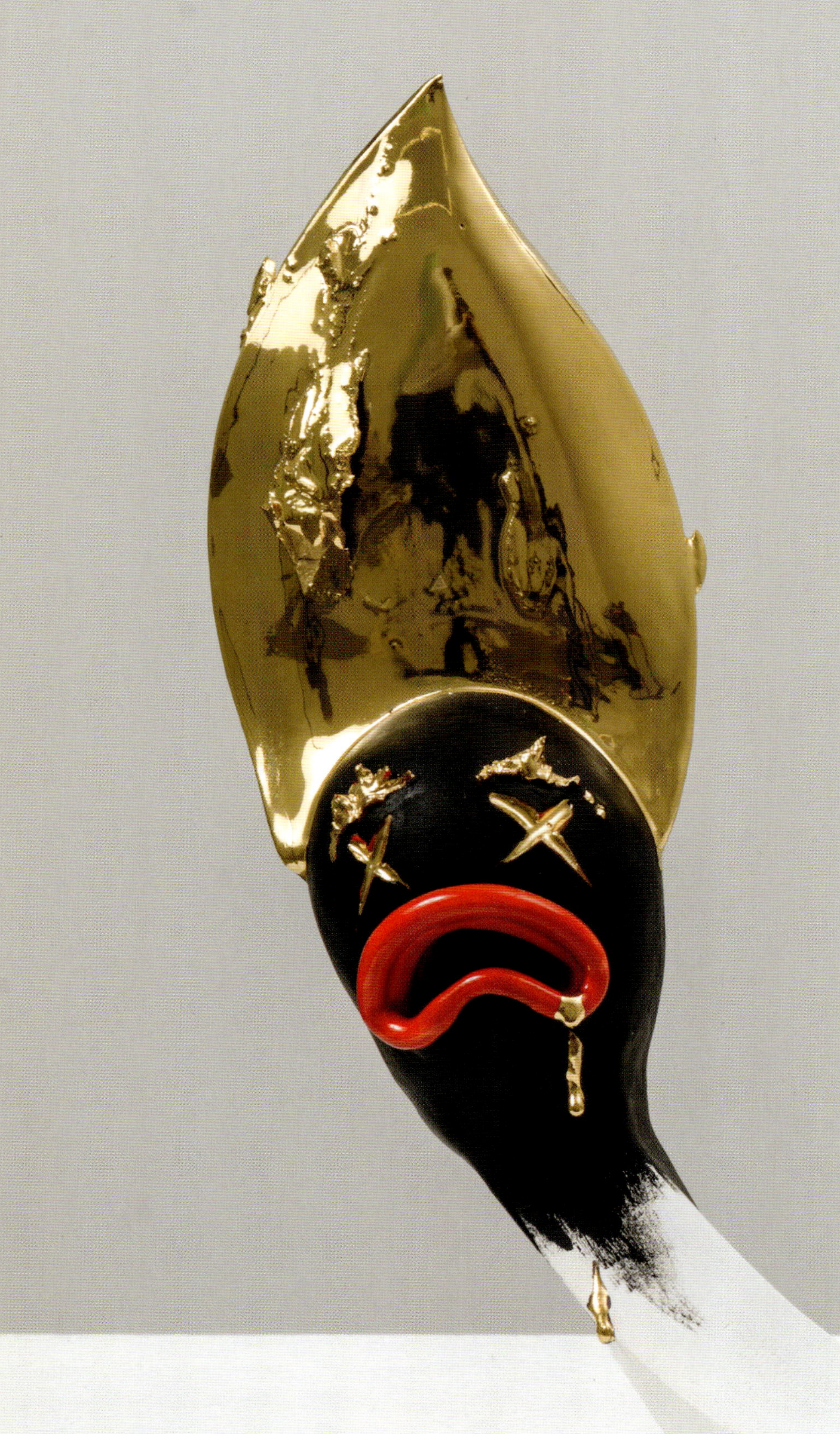

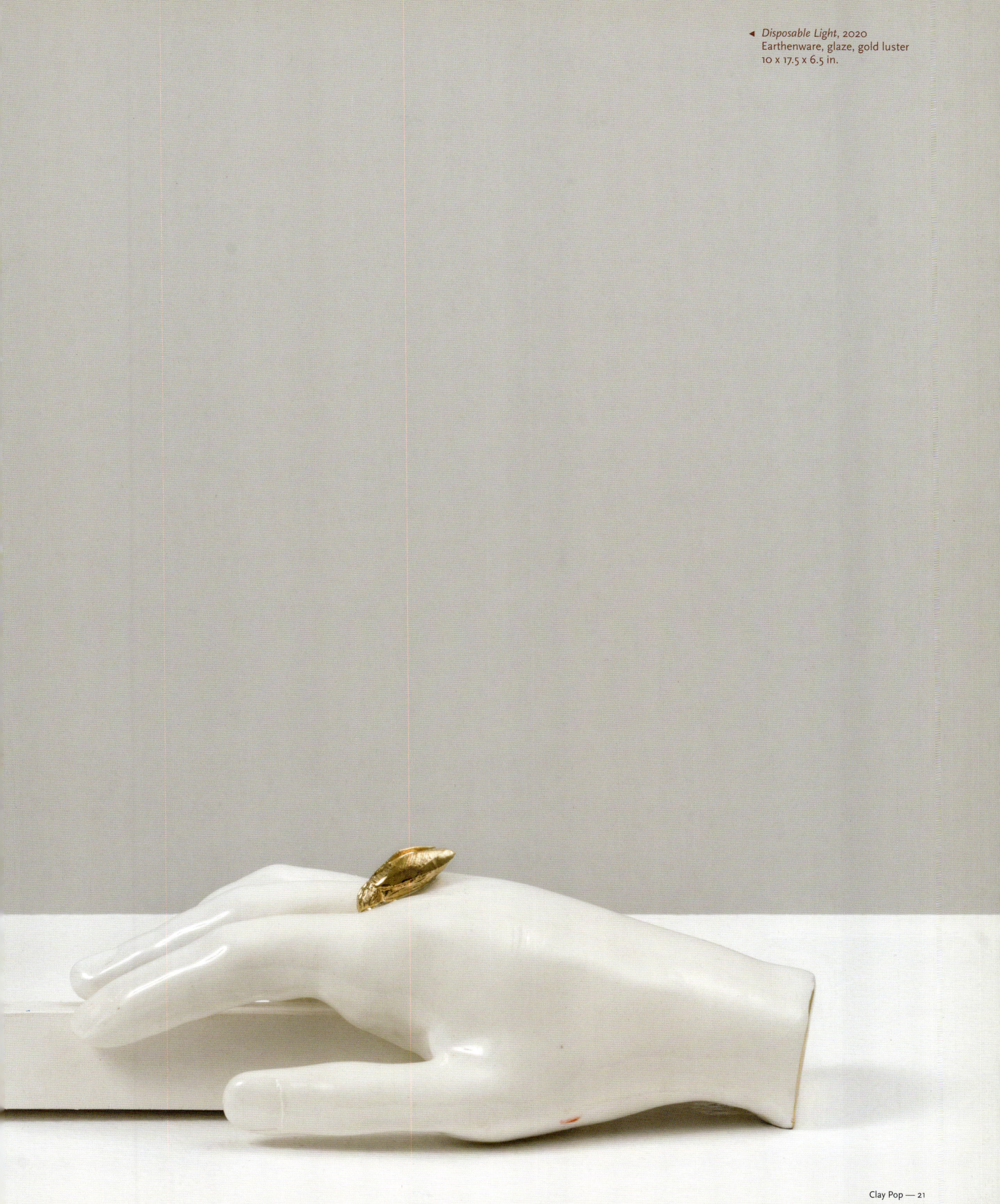

◂ *Disposable Light*, 2020
Earthenware, glaze, gold luster
10 x 17.5 x 6.5 in.

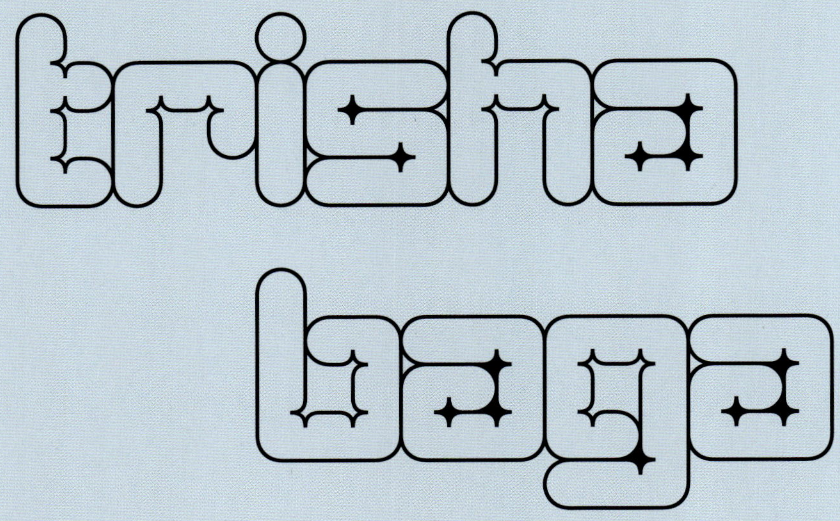
trisha
baga

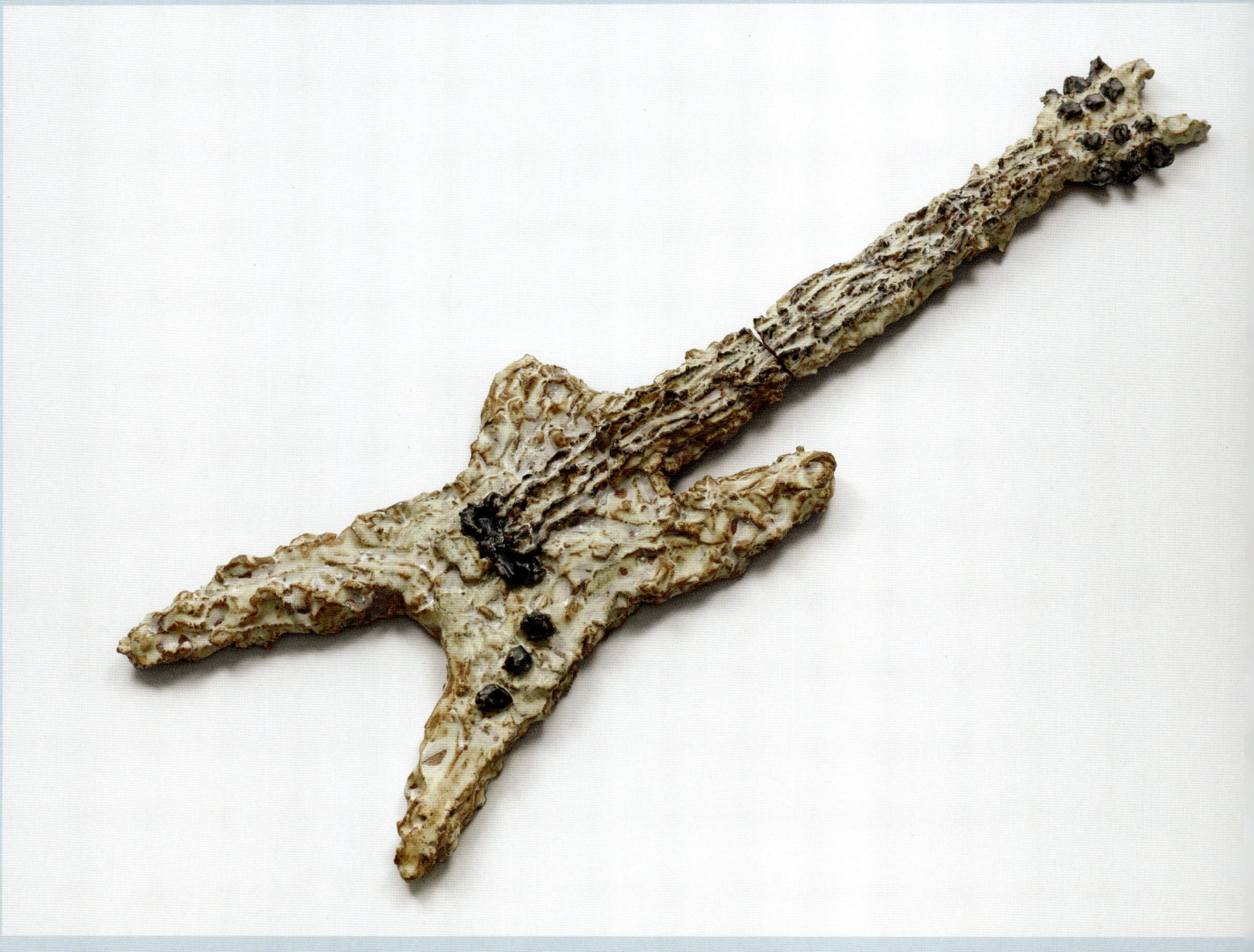

Ceramics are vessels, and the most striking examples by Trisha Baga (b. 1985, Venice, Florida) embrace that containing function with a haptic energy that belies deeper misgivings about technology's colonization of psychic space. The artist's most elaborate works in clay take the form of portrait busts, which Baga enlists to be house-working Amazon Alexas. In one sculpture, a depressed Virginia Woolf (as portrayed by Nicole Kidman in the movie *The Hours*) has an Alexa embedded in the side of her head. In another sculpture, a deftly rendered RuPaul hides her own Alexa in her wig.

Identity in Baga's practice is notoriously leaky and unstable—"a negotiation," describes Pavel Pyś—and the cultural icons that they summon also shape-shift as a matter of course: the trappings of selfhood are worn lightly, there to be assumed and then easily shed.[1]

Baga refers to these brittle, fragmented clay bodies as "calcified casings for virtual assistants."[2] The works' anthropomorphism pokes fun at the confidence that people have placed in these nonhuman helpers. Ever responsive, the sleek devices Baga nestles in handmade exteriors are turned on and speak when spoken to, emitting rings of bluish light that let us know they are listening. Designed to anticipate human needs by converting half-formed desires into online purchases, the figure of Alexa is cast here as a modern-day oracle, ripe for reprogramming.

RuPaul: Calcified Encasing for Virtual Assistant (2018) envelops a piece of technology, whereas other works of Baga's directly depict it. The artist's tabletop sculptures display what one critic calls a "careless virtuosity that self-consciously exceeds their subject matter," turning small appliances into lumpy Pop icons in glazed and fired clay.[3]

A number of the ceramics are "artifacts of technologies that were built for image-making," says Baga.[4] A vintage Canon and an array of framed pictures appear slightly crumpled and blurred, as if succumbing to the downward pull of gravity that softens edges and muddies colors. The camera and the photographs almost seem fossilized, like salvage from Pompeii or a flooded basement. They offer a funny (if somewhat wistful) homage to a bygone era of analogue reproduction. Baga's clay corpus also includes inkjet printers, typewriters, and a slide projector, alongside household items for the basic maintenance of one's space or oneself such as a dust buster or a coffee pot.

Primarily a video artist, Baga views their self-taught pursuit of ceramics as a needed "break from the constraints of the pixel"—a respite from the screen that affords them "a connection to the real world, to physical materials, and to other people."[5] In 2007, Baga cofounded (with their former Cooper Union professor Pam Lins) an ad hoc ceramics club, called Ceramics Club, as a place for artists without formal training in the medium to work with clay as they saw fit. Baga's professional ceramics practice was forged in this lo-fi, communal setting, and the wry spontaneity of their objects retains an amateur's license to riff, "using ceramics as a way to socially interact, make material, collaborate, and see what happens from there."[6]

— Taylor Walsh

[1] Pavel S. Pyś, "Mollusca & The Pelvic Floor," in *Trisha Baga: The Eye, the Eye & the Ear*, eds. Lucia Aspesi and Fiammetta Griccioli (Milan: Pirelli HangarBicocca, 2020), 81, 86.

[2] Interview with Trisha Baga, 2020, Pirelli HangarBicocca.org, https://pirellihangarbicocca.org/en/bubble/interview-trisha-baga/.

[3] Abraham Adams, "Critics' Picks: Trisha Baga," Artforum.com, September 11, 2015, https://www.artforum.com/picks/trisha-baga-54831.

[4] Interview with Trisha Baga, 2020.

[5] Interview with Trisha Baga, 2020.

[6] Press release, "White Room CCCC: Ceramics Club Cash and Carry," White Columns.org, https://whitecolumns.org/exhibitions/cccc-ceramics-club-cash-and-carry/.

◂ *Untitled*, 2018
Glazed ceramic
38.75 x 11.75 x 2 in.

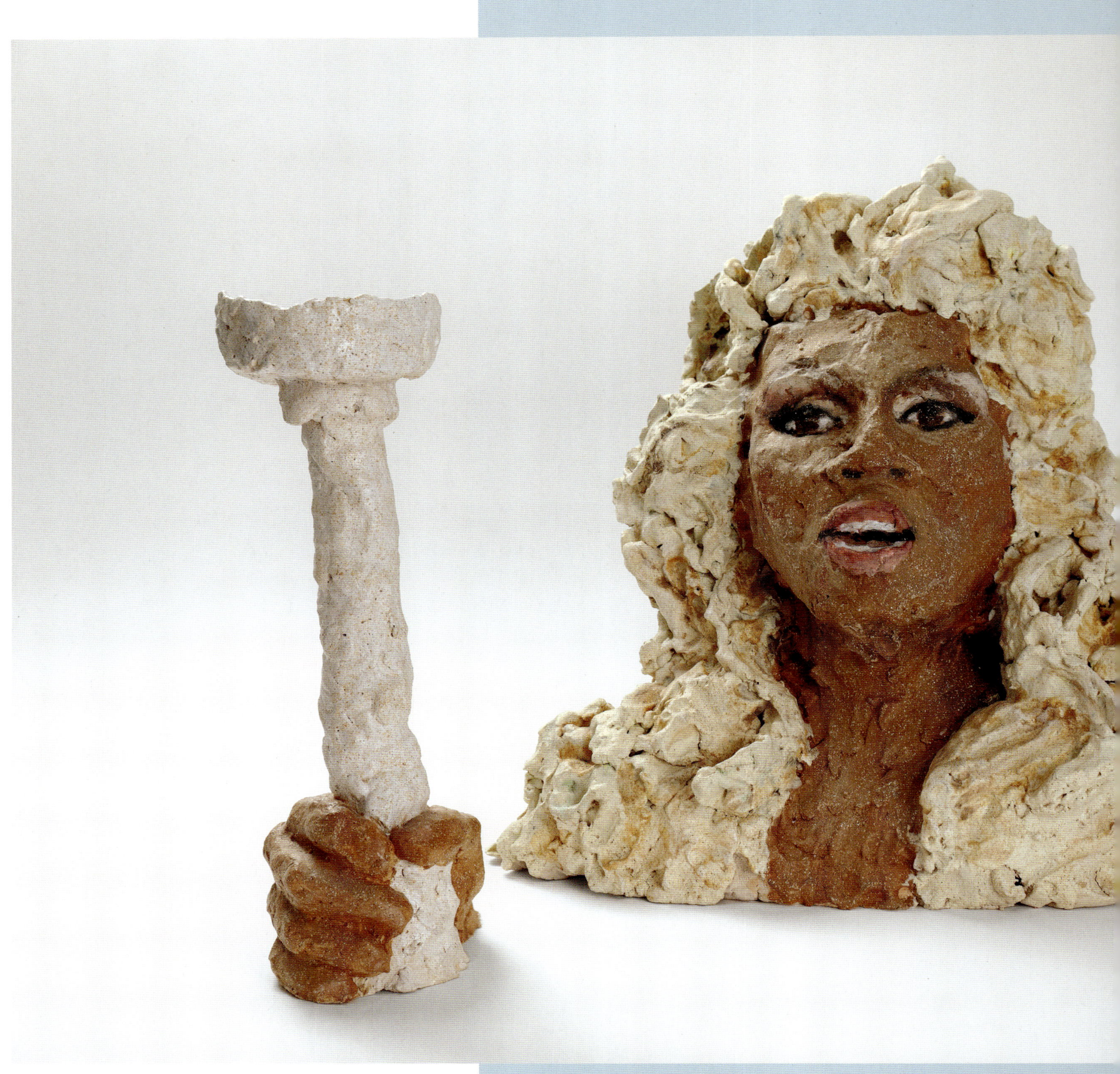

▲ *RuPaul: Calcified Encasing for Virtual Assistant*, 2018
Glazed ceramic, Amazon Alexa device, geode
Overall: 55.5 x 23.6 x 29.3 in.

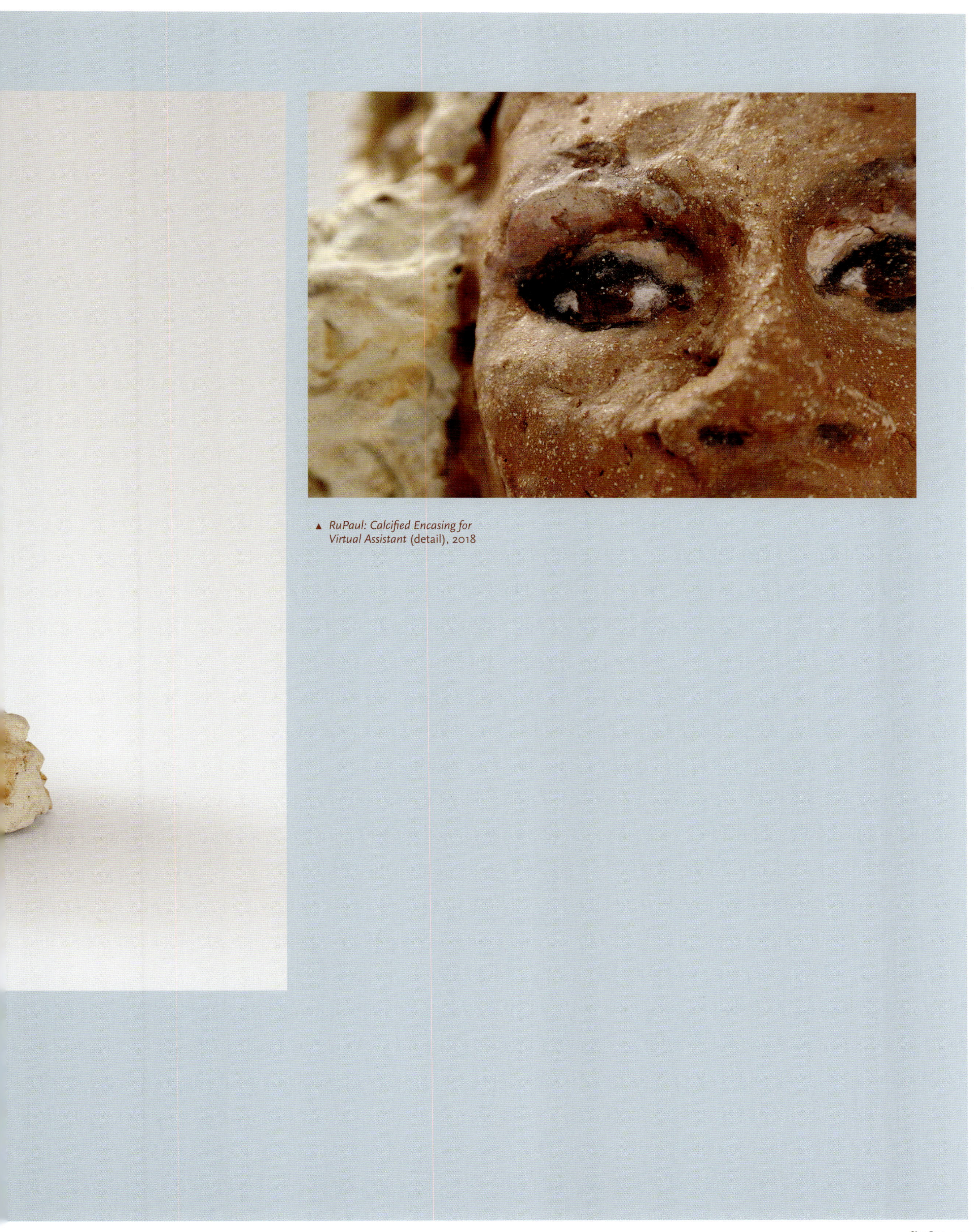

▲ *RuPaul: Calcified Encasing for Virtual Assistant* (detail), 2018

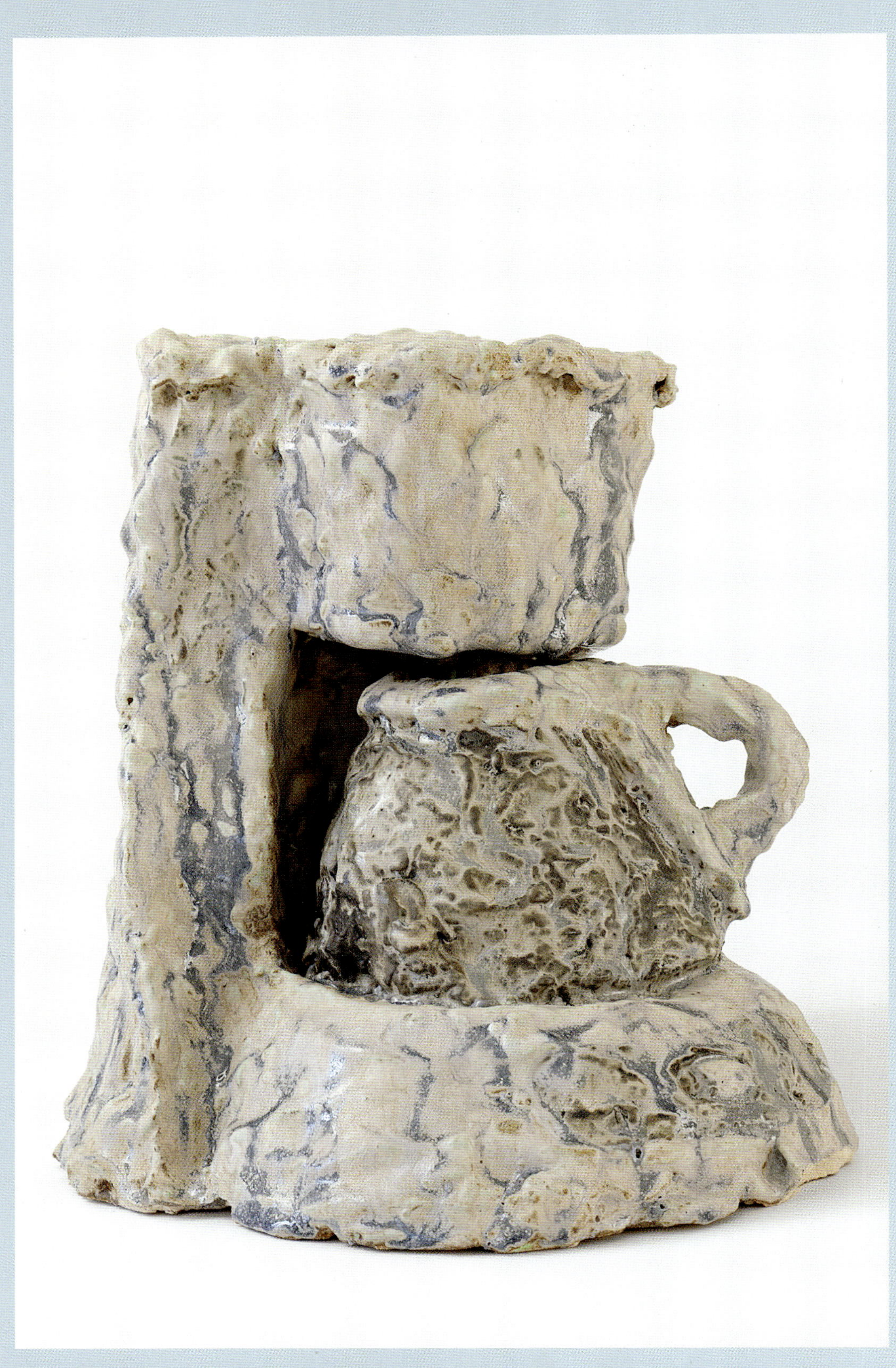

▲ *Coffee Maker*, 2018
Glazed ceramic
12 x 10.5 x 11 in.

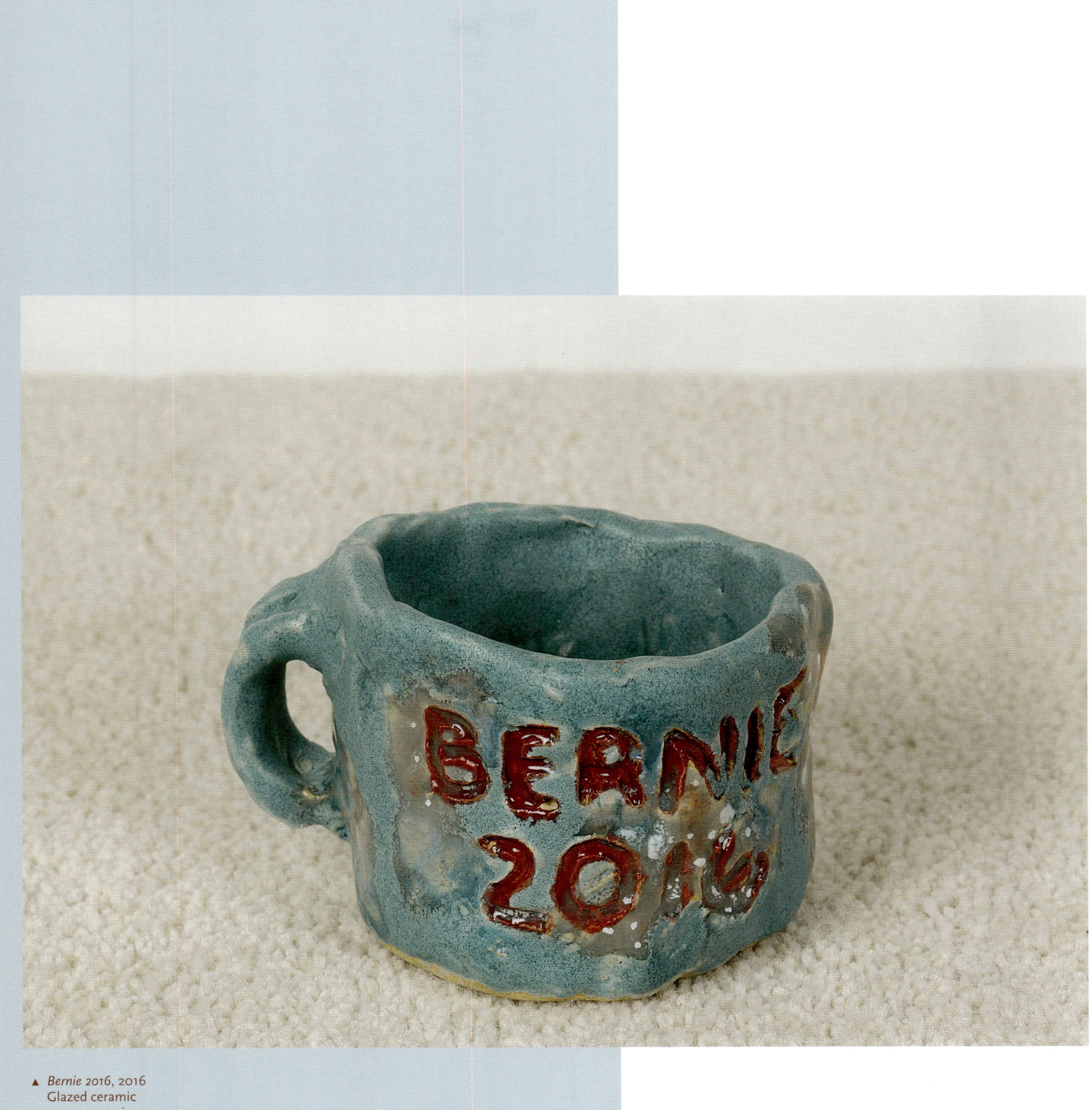

▲ *Bernie 2016*, 2016
Glazed ceramic
2.5 x 4 x 3.25 in.

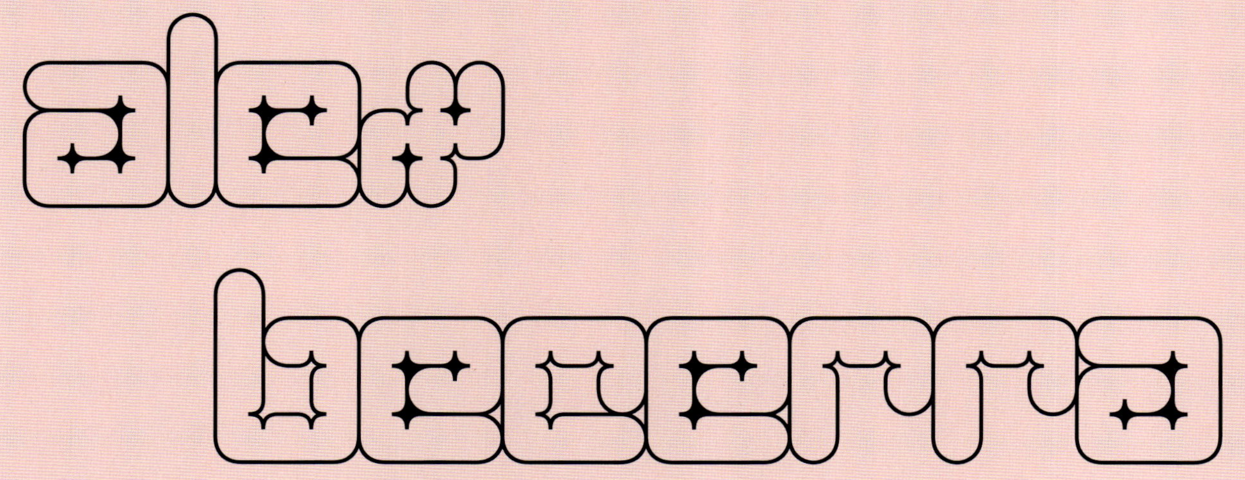
alex
becerra

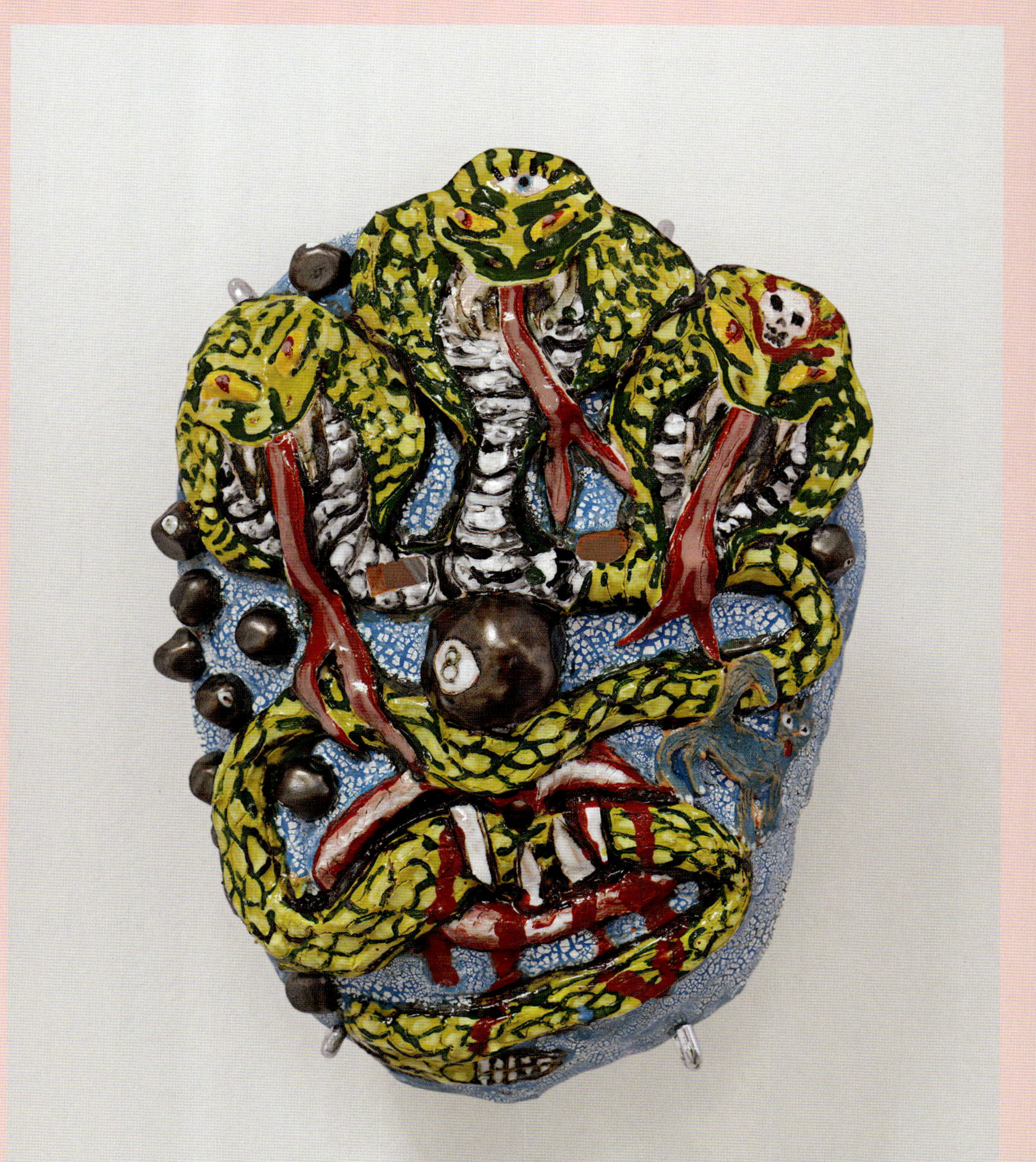

Upcycling, mark making, employing bad glazing techniques, and forever embracing bad ideas, Alex Becerra (b. 1989, Piru, California) uses lived experiences and takes visual cues from his immediate surroundings in his ceramic practice. The creative nature of his works may start from a total rejection of traditional ceramic techniques and unpredicted failures that lead him to find a more resourceful approach to the material itself.

Becerra's new body of ceramic relics is a refreshing match that illuminates a long, dark tunnel. In some works, upcycling studio detritus functions as a new ceramic armature and quite literally becomes a vessel for exploration. For example, Becerra uses every mountable surface on the sculpture *La Nueva Onda* (2021) to create the feeling of a spiritual altar, or as Becerra describes, "the living brain of the studio." Hoarder-like piles of objects inform one another to create what can only be described as a *Gesamtkunstwerk*. One figurative sculpture on the altar serves as a time capsule; it was built from previous glazing failures, kiln explosion fragments, studio trash, and a leftover Subway sandwich.

Viewers of Becerra's work find themselves mesmerized by the awful clutter and leftover items that make up the sculpture. Objects are recontextualized, and they carry a pulse or vibration. Becerra take the failures that are inherent in making artwork and reutilizes them to further push the boundaries of his ceramic practice. Being efficient with materials and breathing new life in previously labeled trash is where he finds his footing. Five-gallon buckets litter the studio closet with old, dried-up clay slabs that he then rehydrates and transforms into a "spiritual mask." It is loosely based on his father's collection of hand-carved wooden masks from Michoacán, Mexico, the region in which he grew up.

Becerra creates exciting movement and color through the process of refiring and reglazing the same object repeatedly until it feels just right, He always strives to create something new and not repeat what he has already done. He wants to be forever inventing and forever cultivating. He strives to find his voice and to avoid mediocrity.

— Michelle Loti Gonzales

◂ *Life's a Bitch (In 3 Phases)*, 2021
Glazed ceramic, mounted on chrome base
17 x 14 x 6 in.

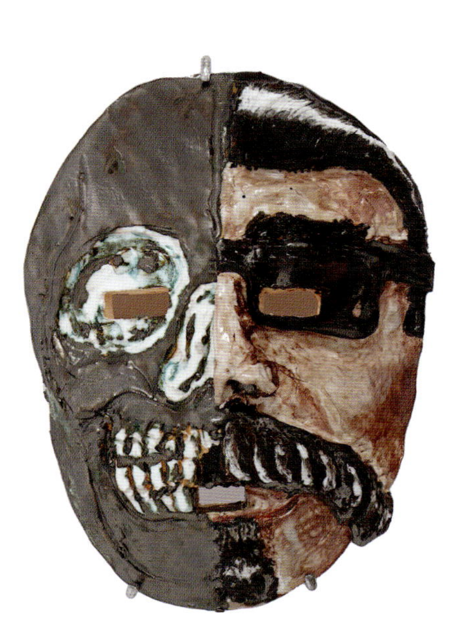

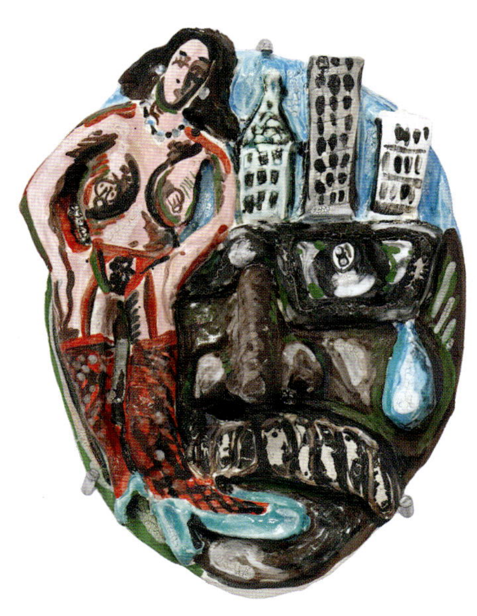

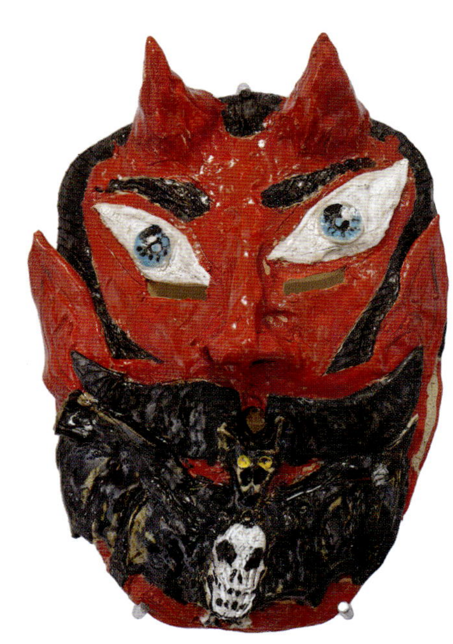

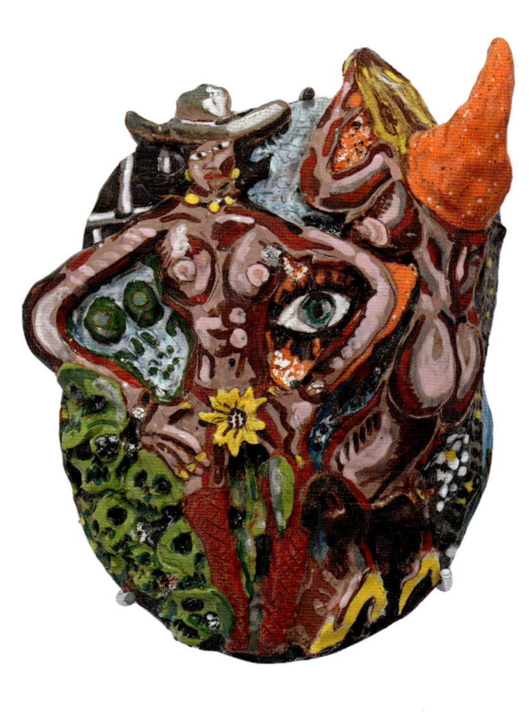

▲ *Smile Now, Cry Later*, 2021
Glazed ceramic, mounted on chrome base
17 x 14 x 6 in.

▲ *Los Angeles City Girl*, 2021
Glazed ceramic, mounted on chrome base
9 x 8 x 6 in.

▲ *El Satanico (Covid19)*, 2021
Glazed ceramic, mounted on chrome base
16 x 13 x 6 in.

▲ *City Girl Hippy*, 2021
Glazed ceramic, mounted on chrome base
13 x 10 x 6 in.

► *La Nueva Onda* (front), 2021
Glazed ceramic and tile, mounted on sawhorse, mixed media
Dimensions variable

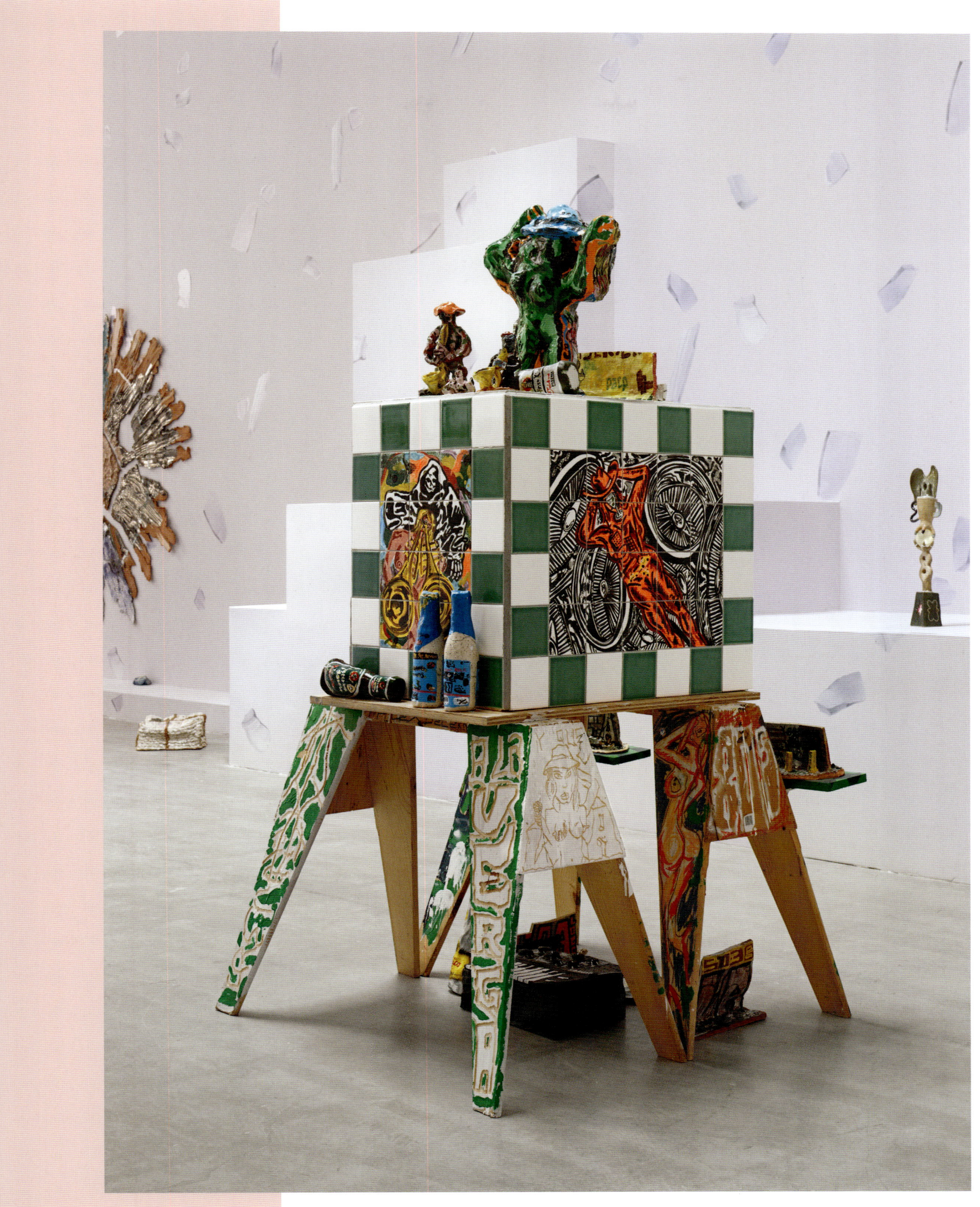

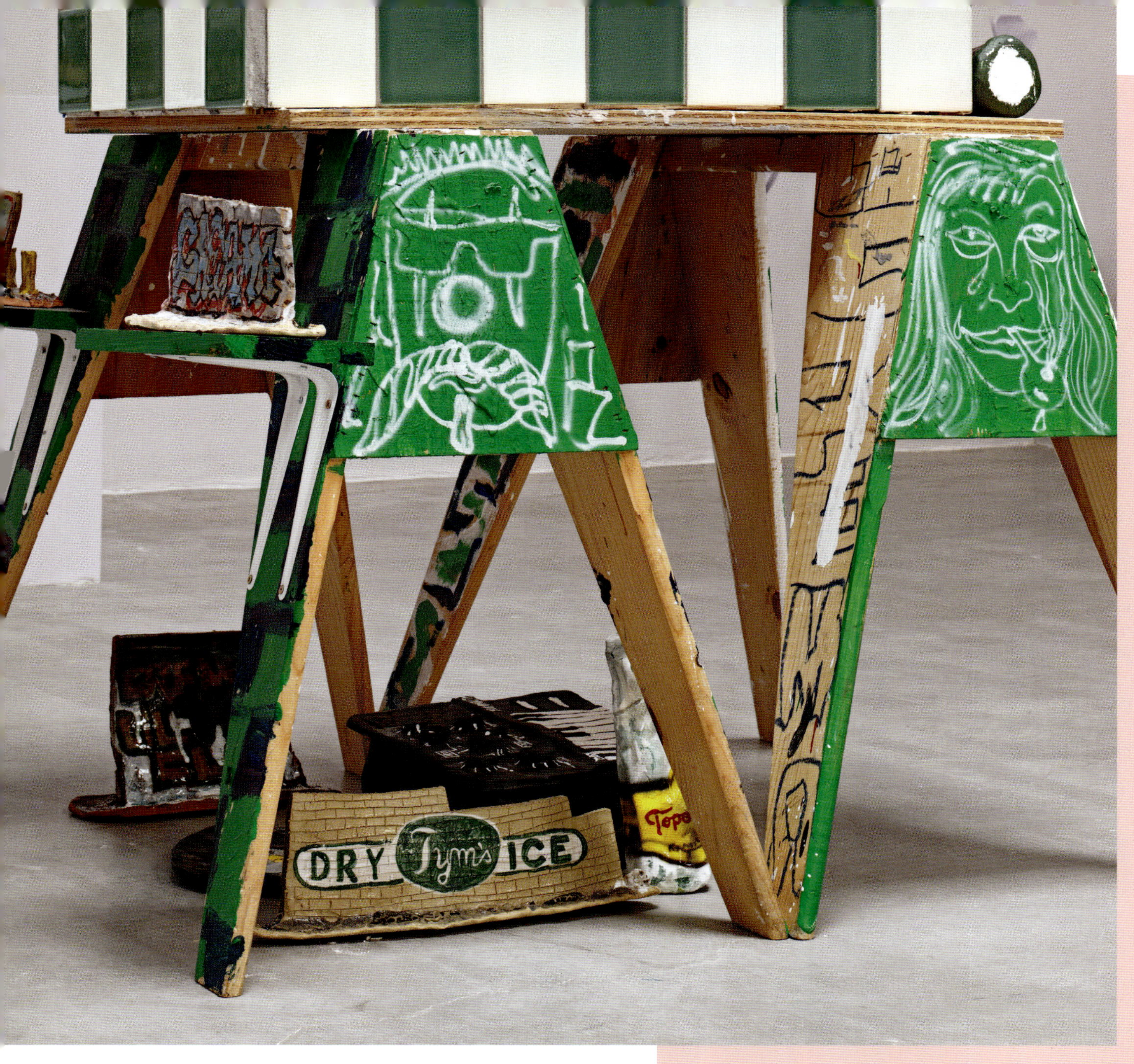

▲ *La Nueva Onda* (back), 2021
Glazed ceramic and tile, mounted on sawhorse, mixed media
Dimensions variable (detail)

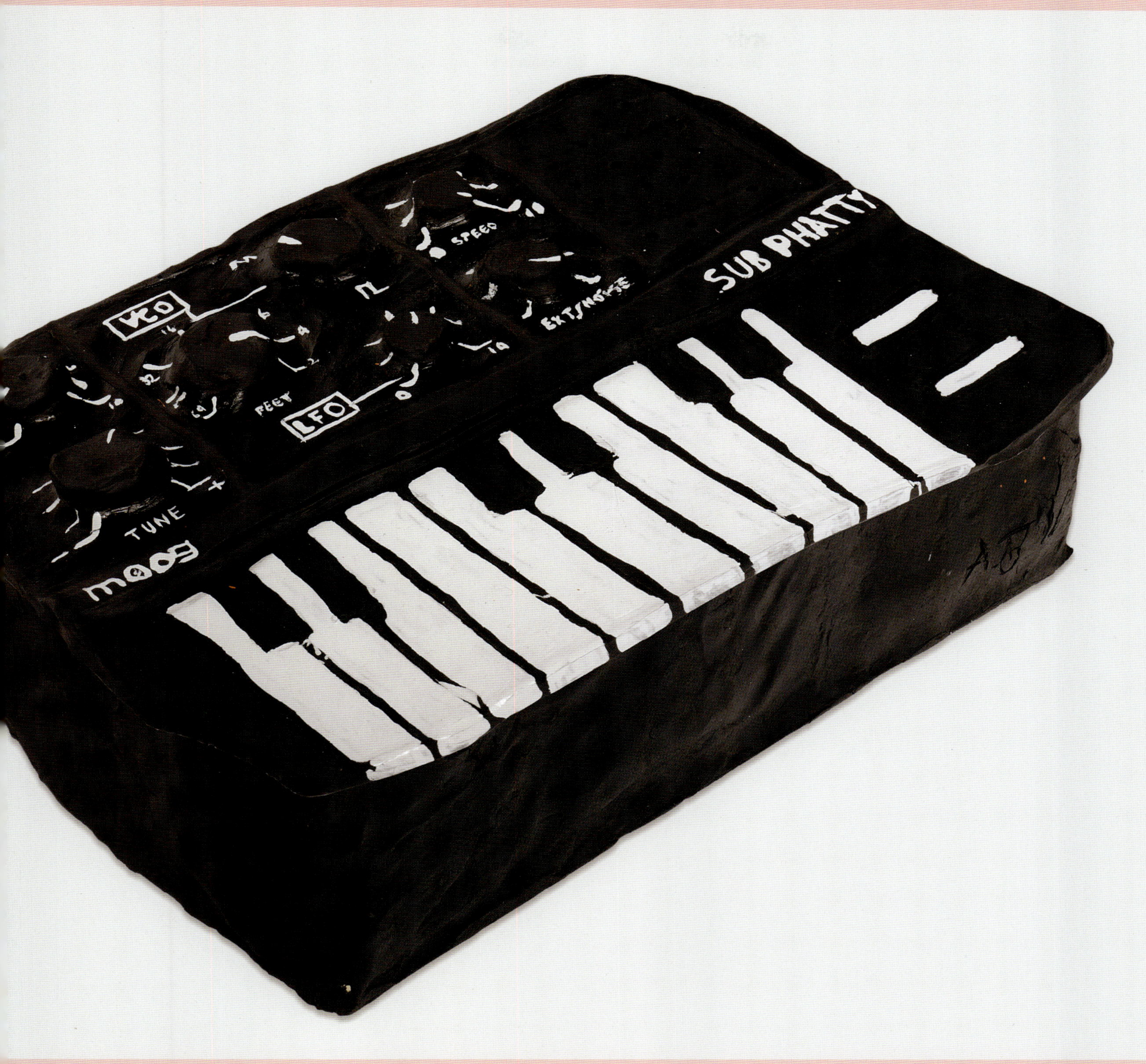

▲ *La Nueva Onda* (detail),
2021

genesis belanger

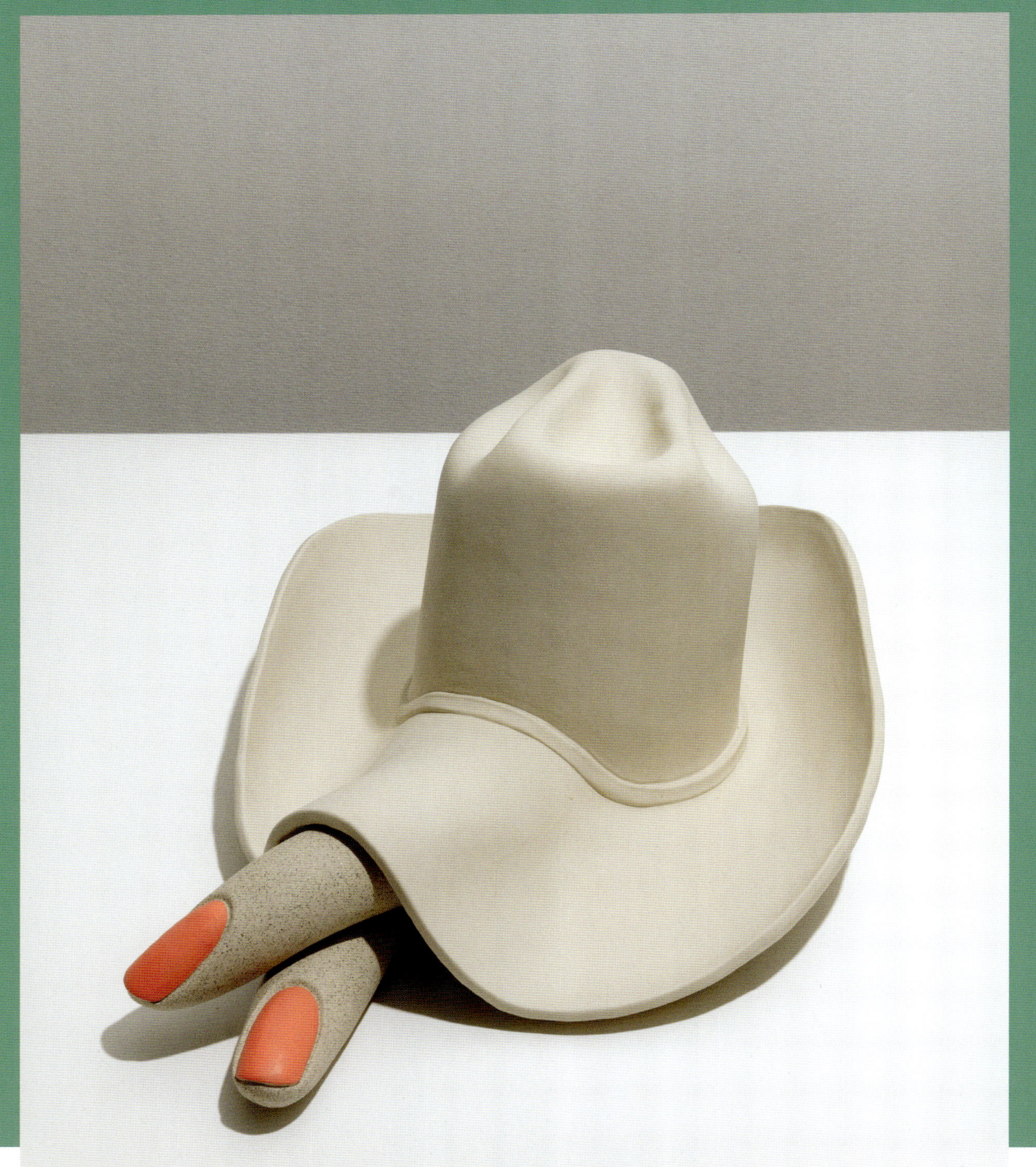

Favoring gendered themes and "multilayered symbols," Genesis Belanger (b. 1978, Massachusetts) creates porcelain and stoneware sculptures and tableaux that perform narratives about systems of power with their polish-perfect fingernails, lipstick-soiled cigarettes, and candy-colored prescription pills.[1] With animated dispositions, at once cheery and melancholic, she endows her sculptures with Pop-facing disguises that traffic in hypercapitalist unease. Striving for an expression that she describes as "odd and lush," Belanger takes her cues from populist and highbrow sources with a penchant for fetishizing and fracturing women's bodies: vintage advertising, contemporary cartoons, and art history.[2] She uses beauty because it is "a powerful tool."[3] Her practice orbits some of the most prominent art movements of the last five centuries—the Baroque, Surrealism, Pop art, and the Chicago Imagists—but her inimitable creations are charged with a self-possessed feminism that undoubtedly appraises this image-saturated moment and surveys social order with dark humor.

Belanger's process is singular and shows the impact of her career in brand marketing on her motives and methods in the studio. She aspires "for the objects to be bodies" and is "particularly attracted to hands and limbs because of the way advertisements sever these parts of women."[4] Selecting porcelains and stoneware for their natural shades, she creates objects that are uniformly matte, with their surfaces masquerading as stone and feigning a patent suppleness. She favors rounds and curves, and forms her shapes from flat patterns pressed into clay sheets rolled out on a slab. The objects, which are hand-shaped, smooth, and hollow, are only fired once. Belanger never uses glazes; instead, she pigments the clay with powdered colors kneaded in with a kitchen mixer. The palette, whose colors Belanger names as "sad" and "nostalgic," is soft and confectionery (creams, beiges, and pastels) and bestows the objects with an air of midcentury wistfulness reminiscent of the warm color scheme of Russel Wright's "American Modern" dinnerware line (released in 1939).[5]

Occupied by objects that relate varying states of being, her choreographed displays air rumors, confessions, feelings, and remembrances. Fraught with personalized incidence, Belanger deploys the absurd to tackle entrenched stereotypes. Humor, she says, is an "an outlet for anger...[it] makes heavy things light enough to tackle."[6] Belanger's installations manifest life's emotional tipping points—hysteria, joy, shame, and dejection—expressions that signify a flawed humanity. Weaponizing splendor and farce, Belanger exposes the entrapments and trickeries lurking inside everyday habits.

This text is excerpted and modified from Amy Smith-Stewart's essay "Genesis Belanger: The Absurdism Behind Everyday Truisms," published in the catalogue that accompanied Belanger's first major solo museum exhibition, Through the Eye of the Needle, *at The Aldrich Contemporary Art Museum in 2020–2021.*

— Amy Smith-Stewart

[1] Katy Donoghue, "Genesis Belanger's Wonderful Nostalgic World in Sad Pastel," Whitewall, August 13, 2018.

[2] Belanger quoted in a video produced by Pioneer Works during her artist residency in Brooklyn, NY, posted February 1, 2018, https://www.youtube.com/watch?v=NjEpBxquFSg.

[3] Taylor Dafoe, "Beauty 'Can Be a Powerful Tool': Artist Genesis Belanger on How Her Surreal Sculptures Address Our Present Moment," *Artnet News*, January 23, 2019.

[4] Christina Nafziger, "Genesis Belanger: Simpsons Episode about the Uncanny," *ArtMaze Mag*, Summer 2018.

[5] Donoghue, "Genesis Belanger's Wonderful Nostalgic World in Sad Pastel."

[6] Stephanie Chan, "Seductive Sculptress," *Renaissance*, May 2019.

◂ *Good Guy*, 2021
Stoneware, oil painted manicure
7.5 x 19 x 12 in.

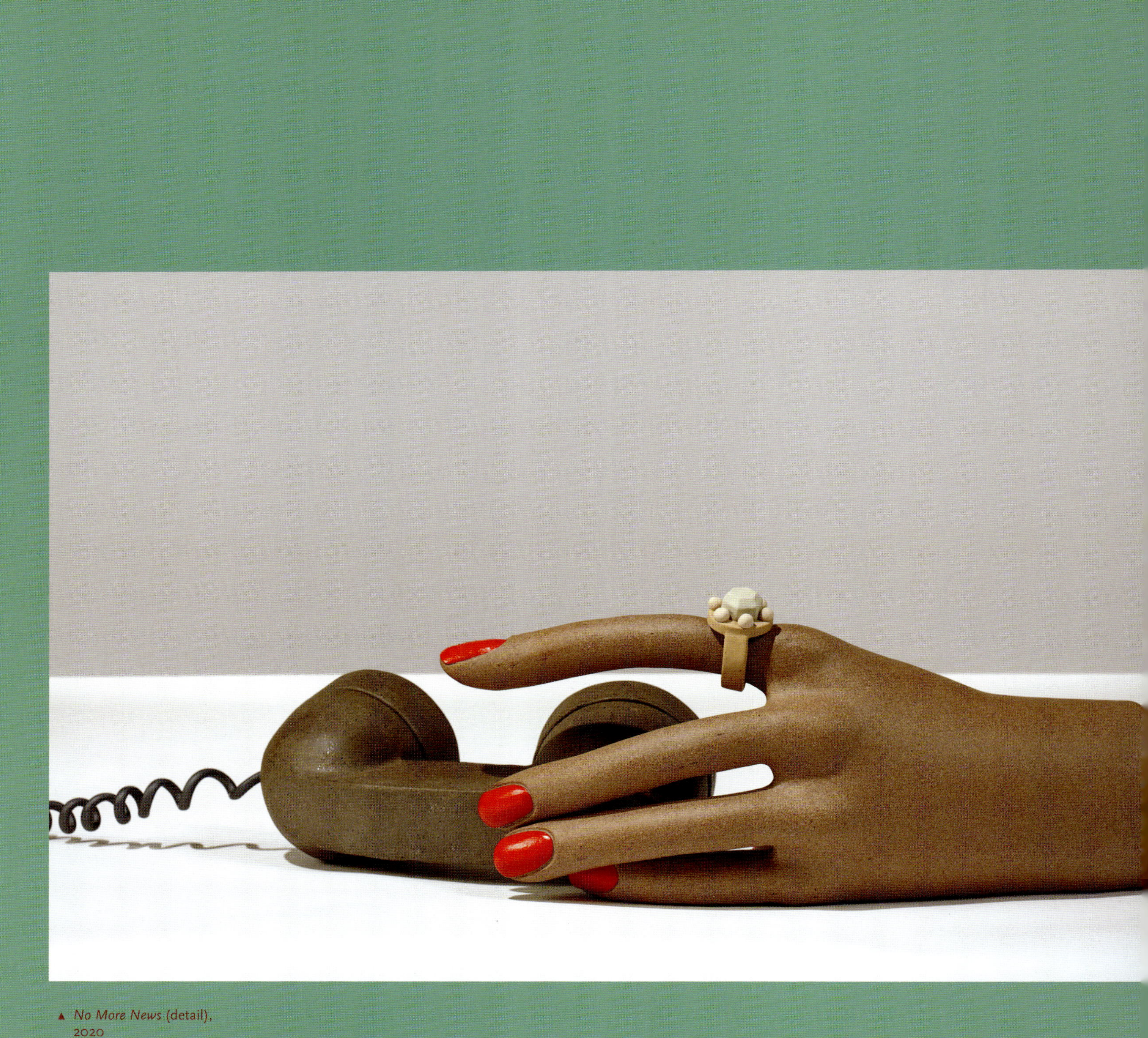

▲ *No More News* (detail),
2020

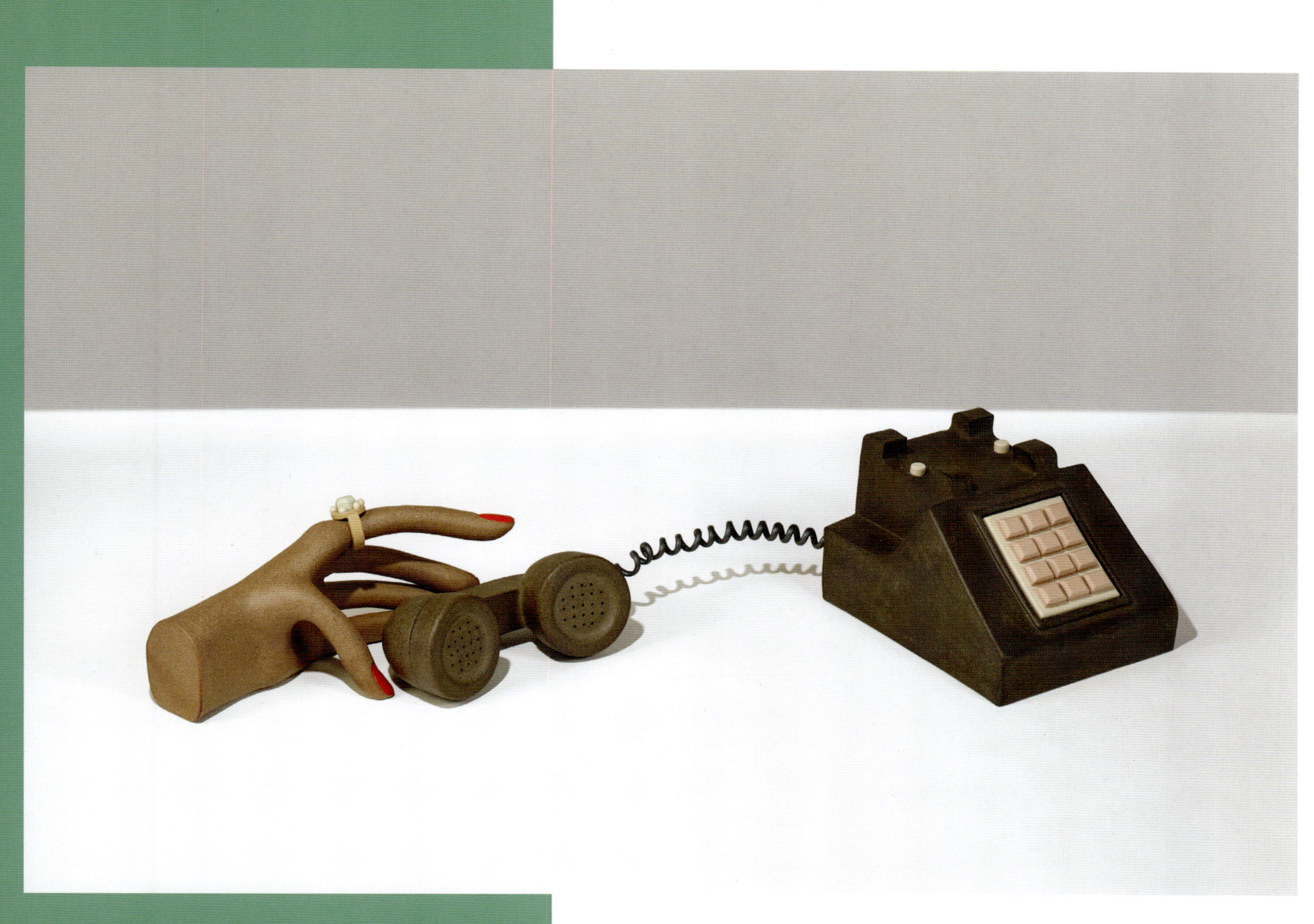

▲ *No More News*, 2020
Stoneware, oil painted manicure, plastic cord, metal, laminated MDF
37.5 x 48.125 x 27.125 in.

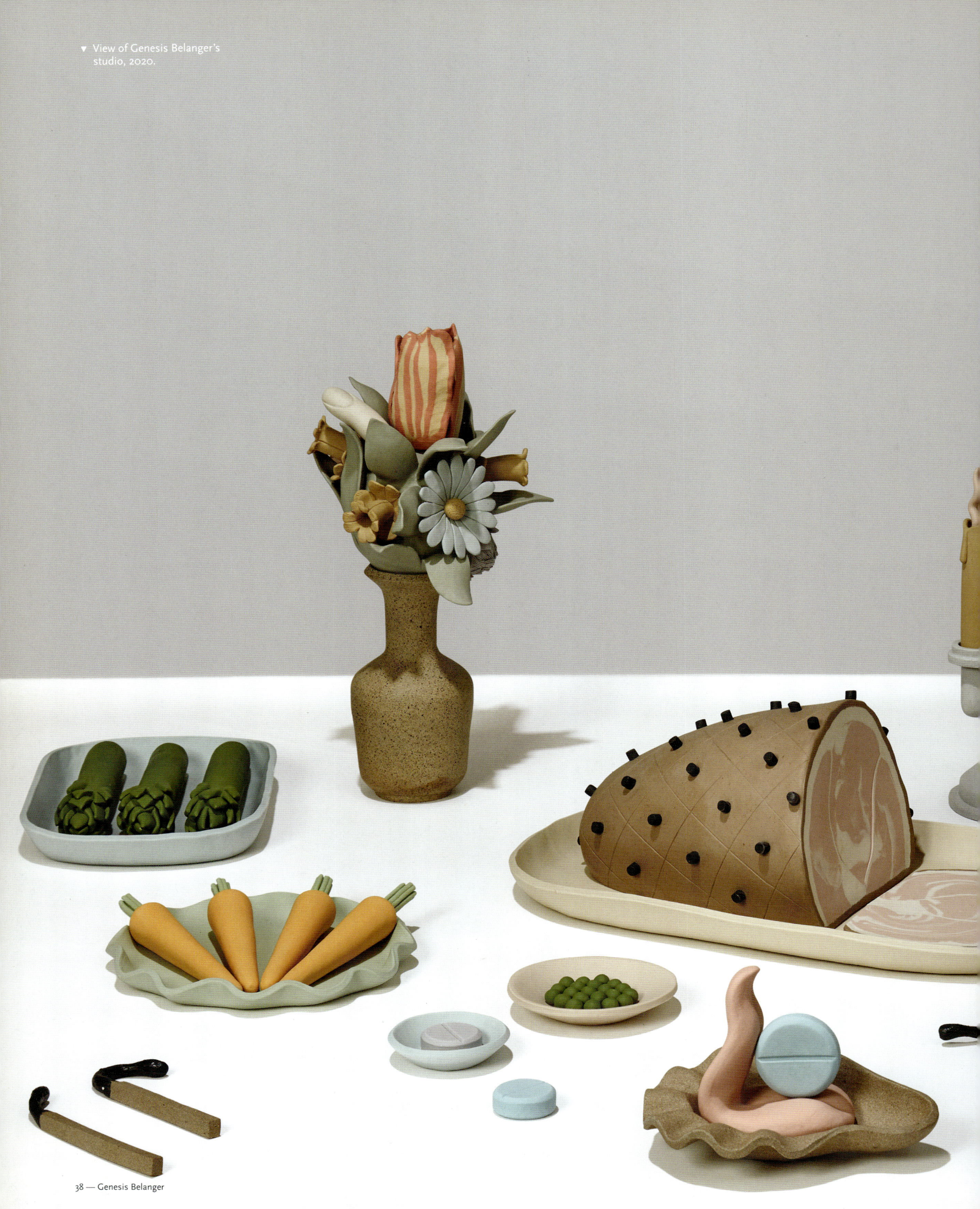

▾ View of Genesis Belanger's studio, 2020.

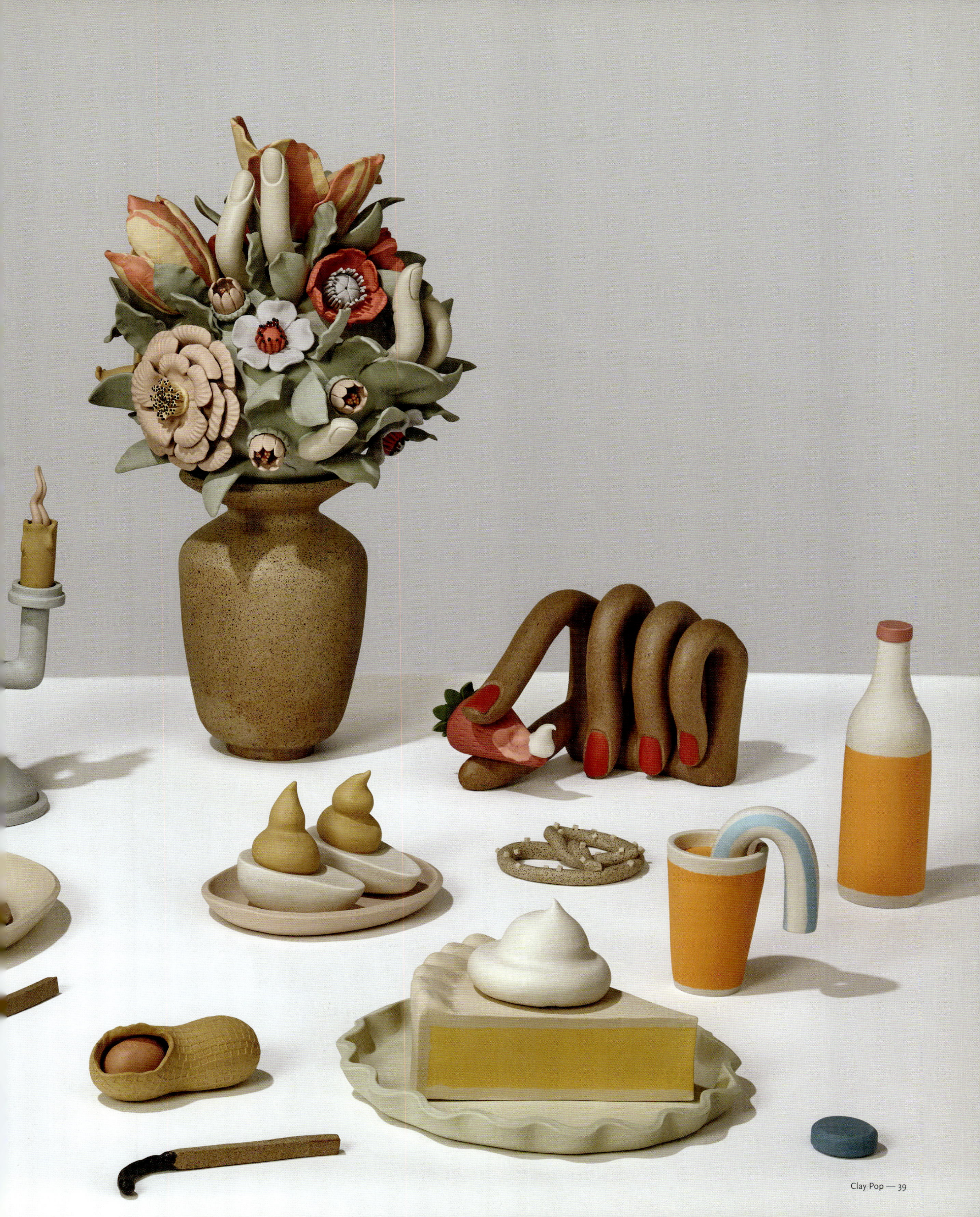

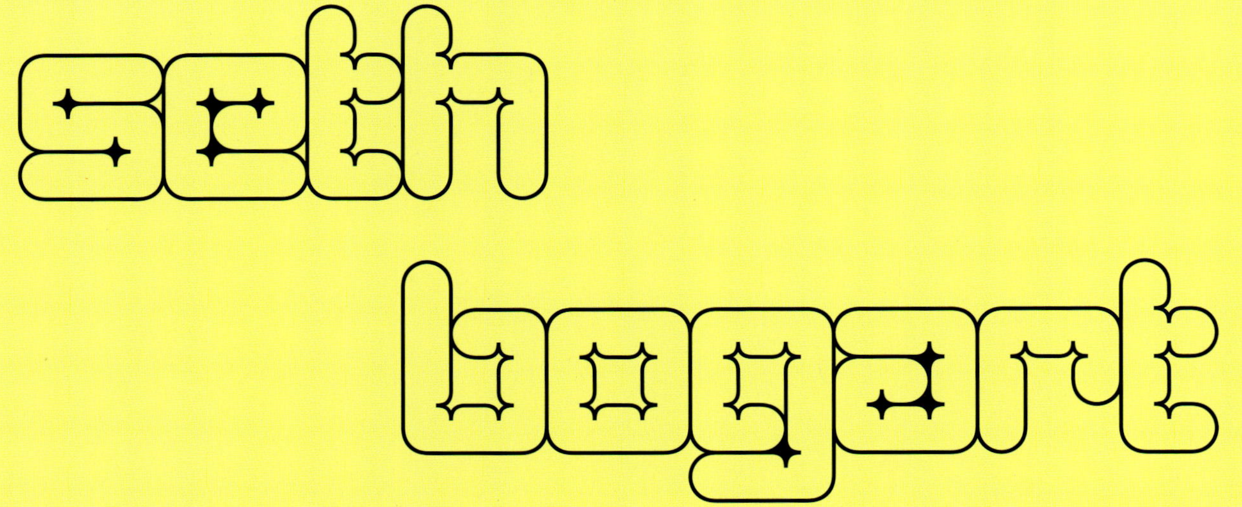
seth
bogart

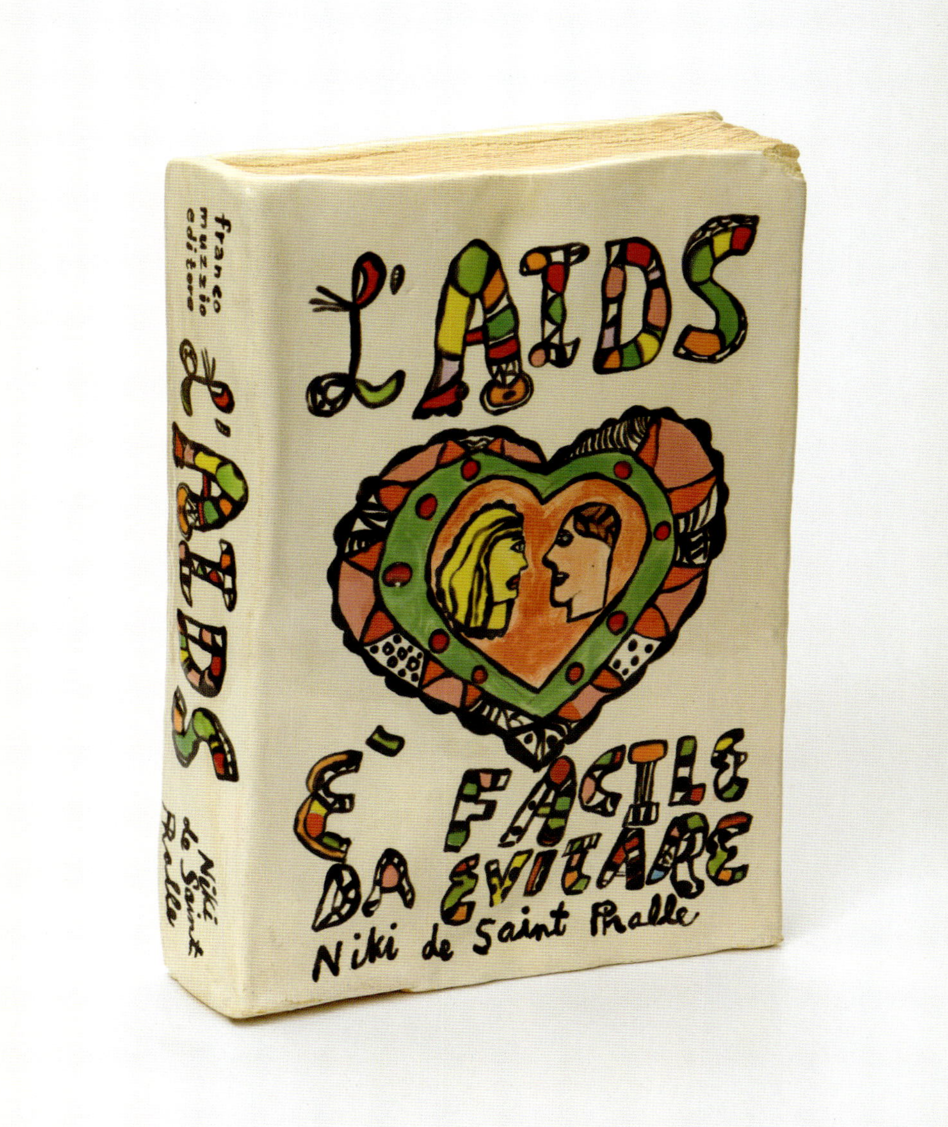
L'AIDS
È FACILE DA EVITARE
Niki de Saint Phalle
franco muzzio editore
L'AIDS
Niki de Saint Phalle

I survey the room from left to right. I read the walls, the pictures, the plants, the furniture, the records, and the books. All of the familiar books stand out to me like I am looking at my own bookshelf. I see another book from an ex's bedside table. I see a book that I read in school. I see a book that I read in one night and a book that I did not finish. We share these memories and the intimacy that connects us to the author's stories, yet we still have our own secret relationship to the covers of these books. "I can't believe you have a copy of *How to Get Rid of Pimples* by Cookie Mueller!"

You cannot read the stories in the book recreations by Seth Bogart (b. 1980, Tucson, Arizona). They are made of clay and glaze. Each has been painted by hand with a sense of care and attention to detail. The typography mimics the font of the original books with a hand-drawn sincerity. The books suggest wear, like they have been thumbed through by many readers. A recreation of a story has been remade in the body of the book. Bogart is building a library that feels connected to a community of friends' favorite books. The library is an archive of his making. This archive then becomes a self-portrait of Bogart in the same way that you enter someone's house and see what is on the shelves.

I am not judging a book by its cover. I know I love the book. Bogart's books cannot be burnt away. They are made in a fire for a story that we want to last. The book covers remind me of when I was a young, queer punk. Symbols of culture are coded in Bogart's works. They invite ways of communicating to each other or being seen by each other—like riding on the bus and seeing a person wearing a Kleenex/Liliput shirt and holding a copy of Jacqueline Susann's *Valley of the Dolls*. This girl seems hot.

— Kate Mosher Hall

◂ *AIDS*, 2022
Ceramic
13 x 10 x 3 in.

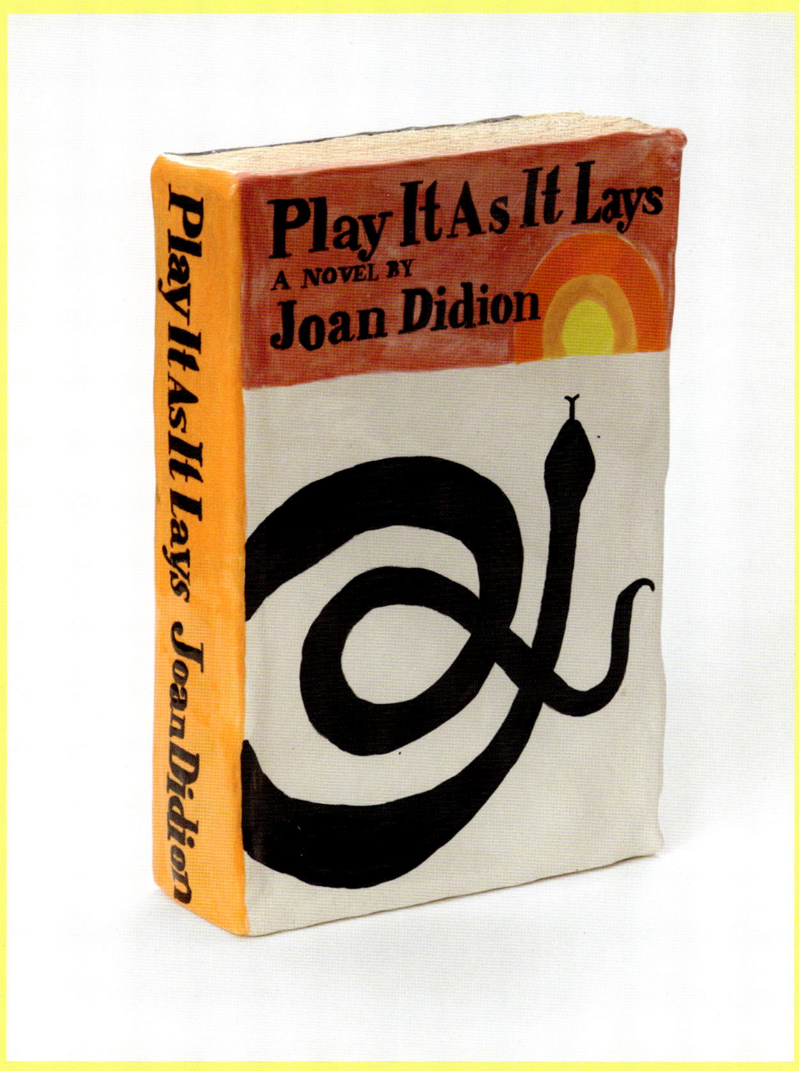

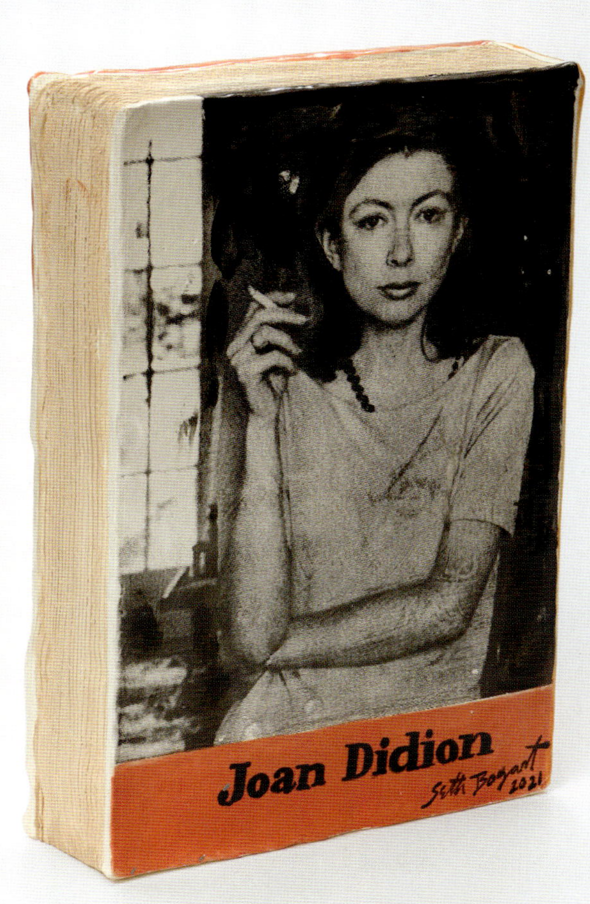

▲ Front and back view of *Play It As It Lays*, 2022
Ceramic
13 x 10 x 3 in.

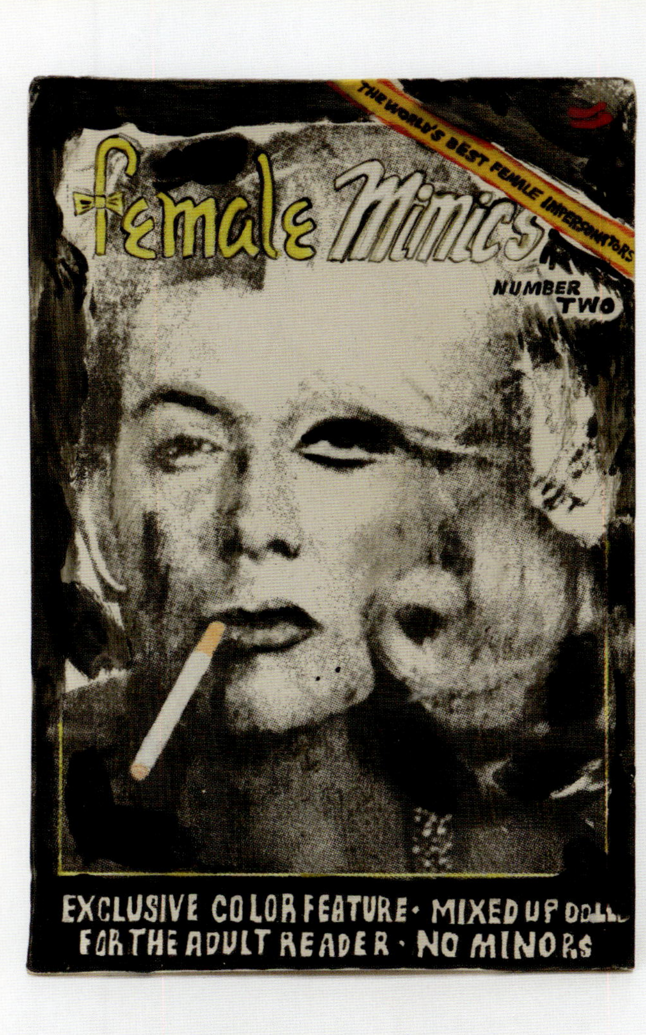

▲ *Female Mimics*, 2022
Ceramic
11 x 9 x 0.5 in.

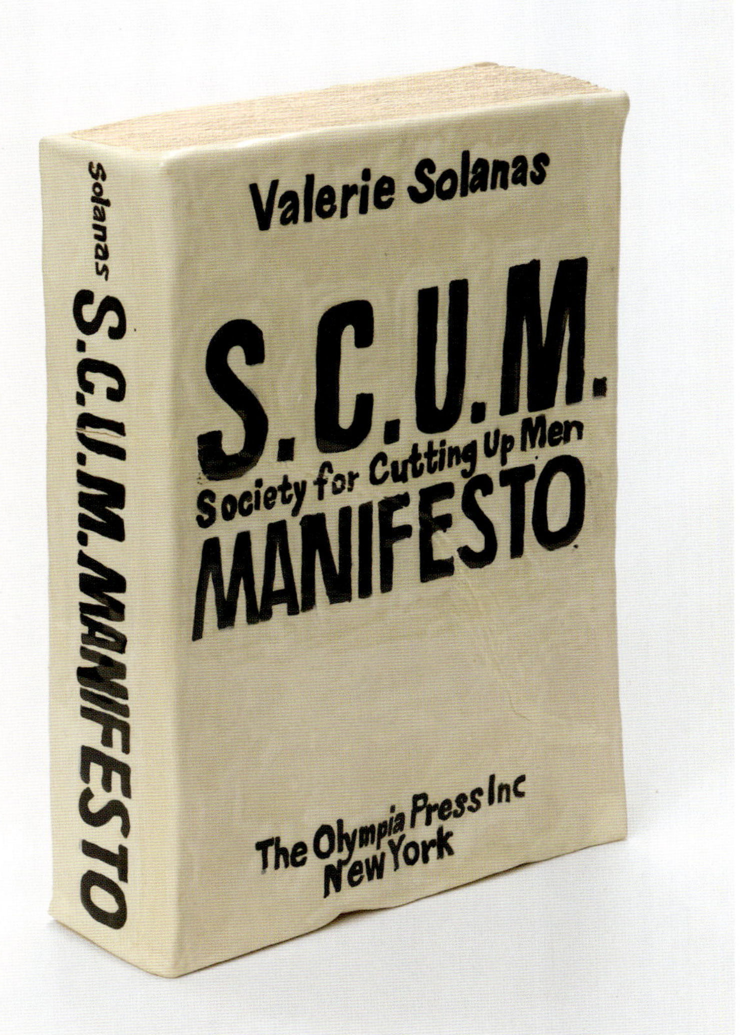

▲ *S.C.U.M. Manifesto*, 2021
Ceramic
15 x 10 x 3 in.

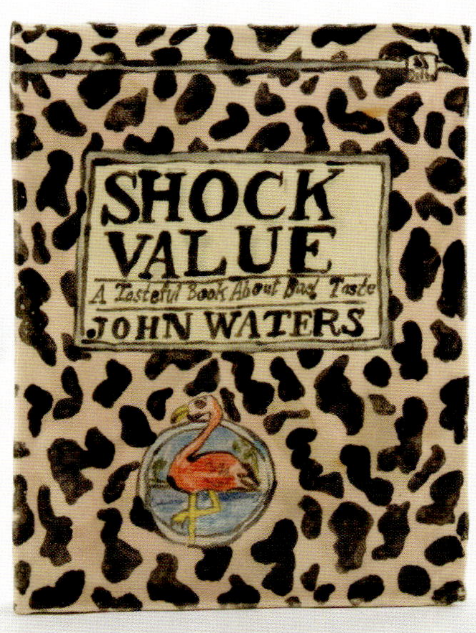

◂ *John Waters Shock Value*, 2020
Ceramic
6.4 x 7.5 x 0.75 in.

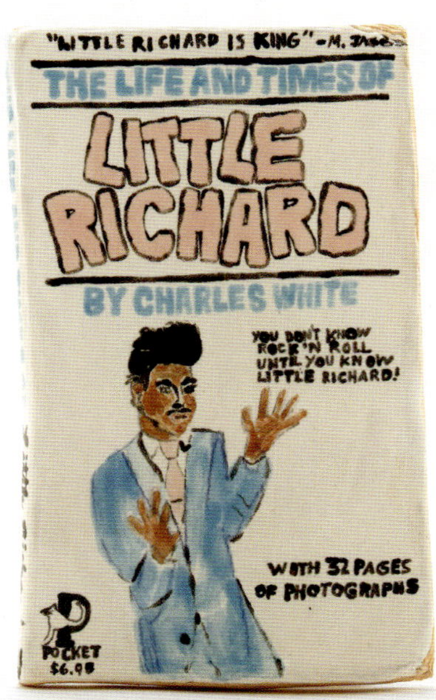

◂ *The Life & Times of Little Richard*, 2020
Ceramic
5 x 8.4 x 0.5 in.

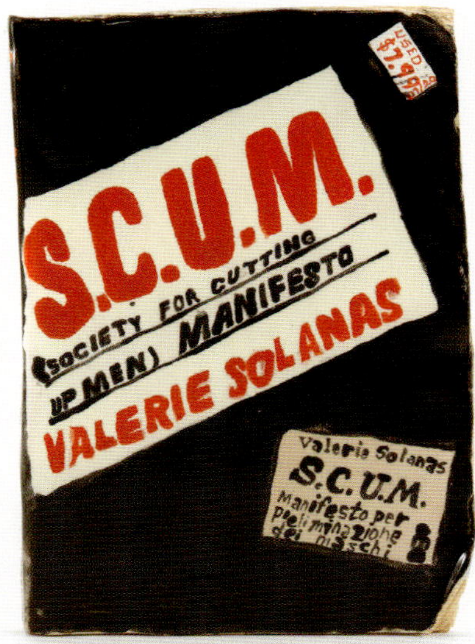

◂ *S.C.U.M. Manifesto*, 2022
Ceramic
15 x 10 x 3 in.

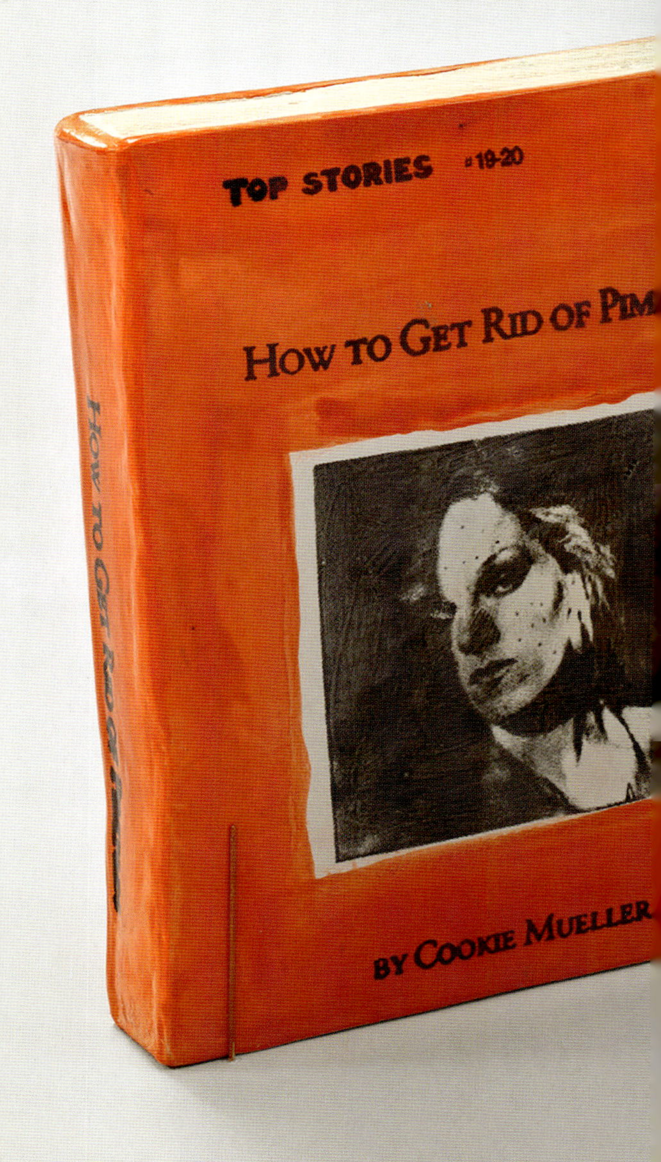

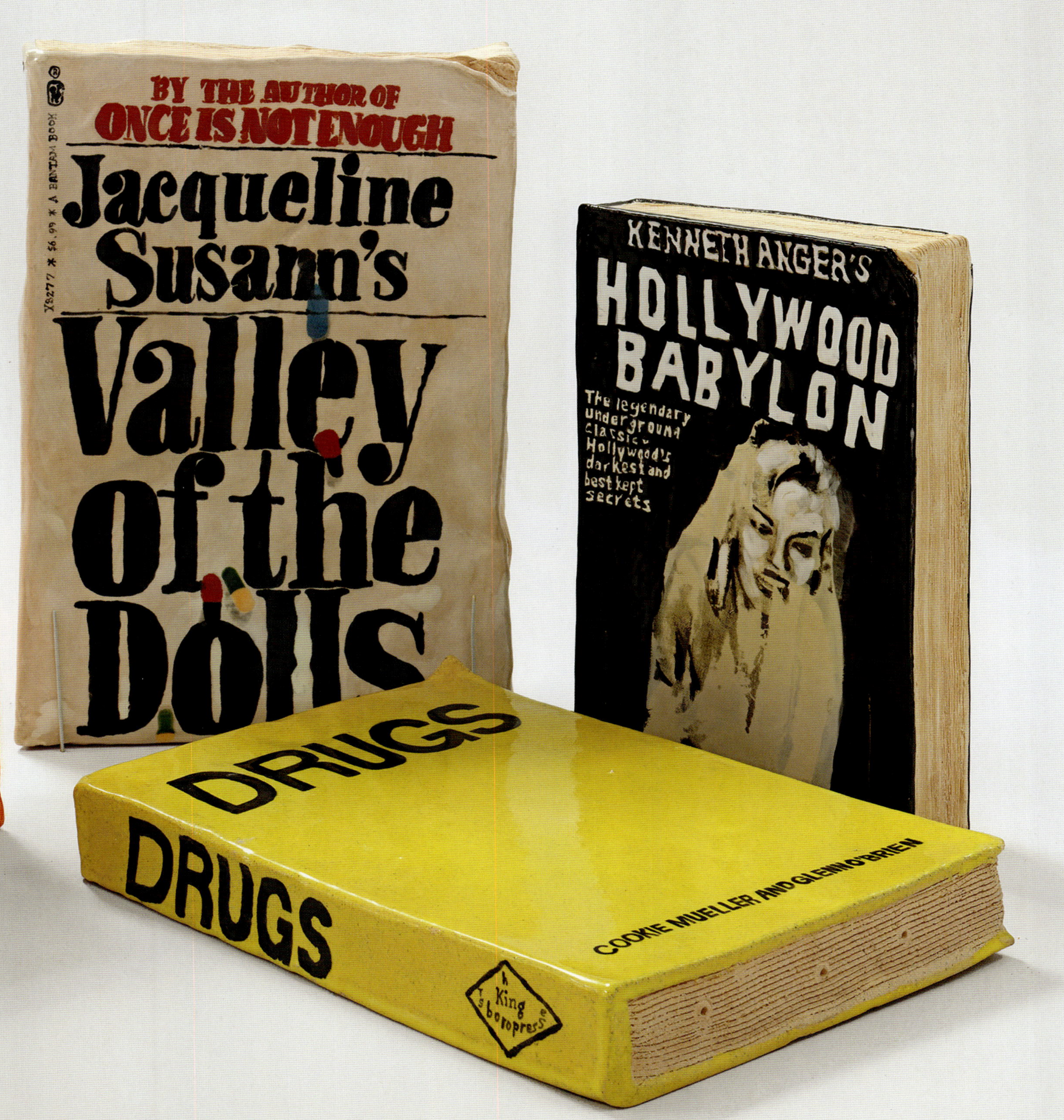

▼ Installation view of Seth Bogart's works in *Clay Pop* at Jeffrey Deitch, New York, 2021.

woody de othello

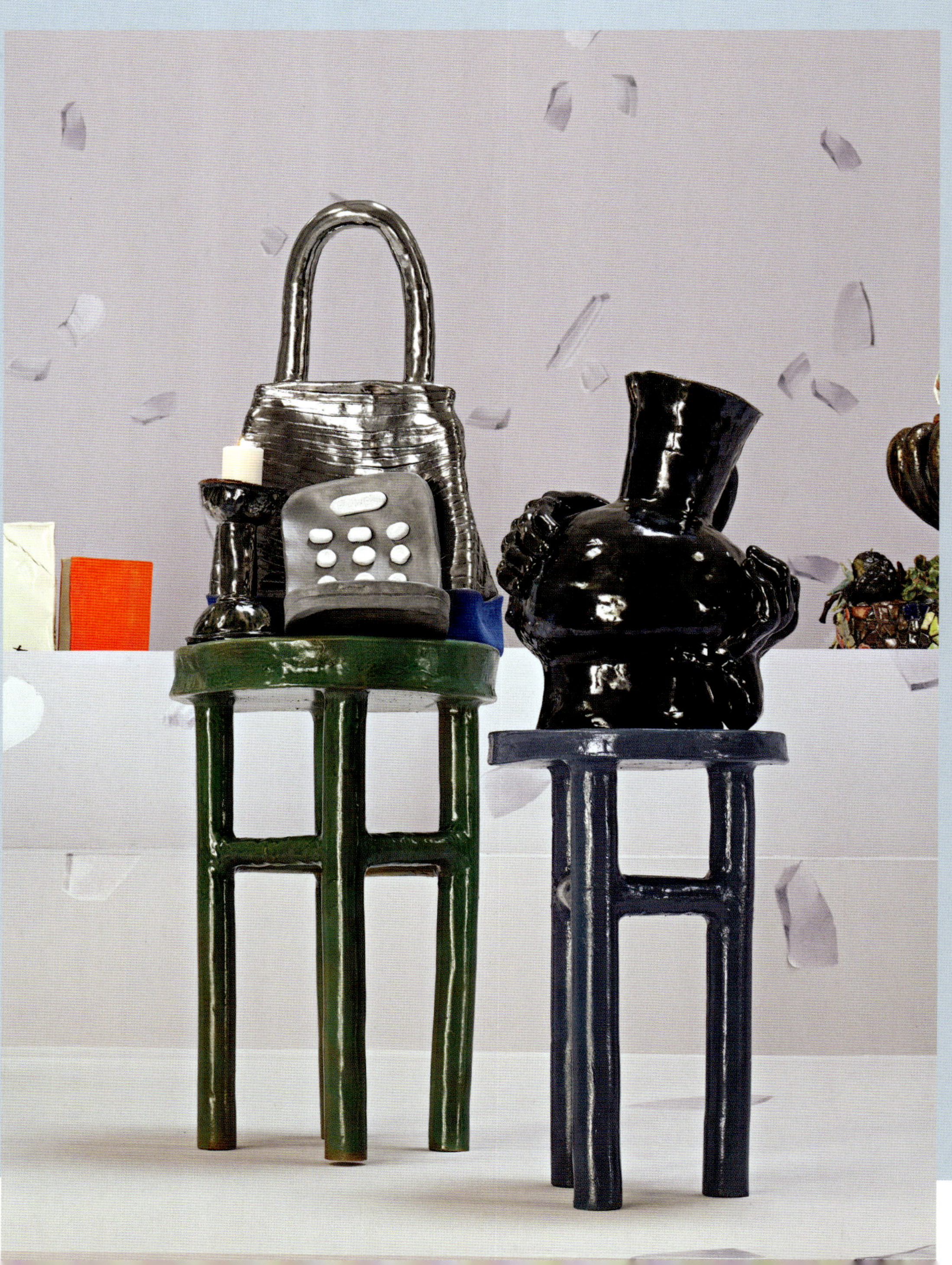

Over the past few years, the ceramic practice of Woody De Othello (b. 1991, Miami) has dwelt on fixtures of domestic space through a particular idiom of unstable household objects—from wobbly air conditioners and houseplants to remote controls and curiously emotive vessels. His boldly colored anthropomorphic forms, which are displayed both alone and gathered in vignettes, posture expressively with gesticulating hands.
A prevalence of large ears, lips, and noses (but not eyes) emerges from large piled forms that droop and sag with corpulent weight. There is an element of humor, but the levity is tempered by the unease engendered by inscrutable forms turned inward.

Othello acknowledges absorbing much from Bay Area legacies of ceramics, yet his connection to clay runs deeper. From first touch, he recalls "an overwhelming feeling that everything I needed to know about my past and future was beholden to clay."[1] Sensitive not only to impression but temperature, humidity, and motion, Othello describes clay as a "humbling" material—a relative sponge that absorbs and holds external pressures. Such receptive physical properties have psychic resonance with African objects known as *nkisi*, referring to an object or container that a spirit inhabits. Used by Othello's ancestral Yoruba people, as well as others throughout the Congo basin, *nkisi* have the power to both contain and release spiritual forces in the physical world.

"Part of me hopes that these objects I make can act as a type of sacrifice, a placeholder for all these negative emotions, so we don't have to live with them,"[2] says the artist. A form of contemporary *nkisi*, Othello's vessels and misshapen objects seem to react to and hold the energies of the space they inhabit, suggesting the power of pressures endured but not seen.

The artist's process involves building up the clay form, slab by slab, until burdened by its own heft, it slumps and folds. The structure is then left to harden before more clay is applied. The substantial mass (some sculptures weigh upwards of 60 pounds) is then perched atop a rickety-looking ceramic stool or leggy end table. These solid, hardened clay objects seem to be on the verge of collapse, a fragility that bestows each piece with a psychological and emotional weight proportional to its physical heft. Glazes are sprayed on rather than brushed to prioritize a smooth finish, maintaining a polished finesse despite the threat of internal fissure, one might say.

Rooted in his own identification with the diasporic search for belonging, Othello's sculptures reflect a fraught notion of home—one shaped and impacted by economic pressures and persistent racism that padlocks and air conditioners cannot keep at bay. Yet, despite the obstacles, the artist keeps making, dreaming, and working to create a space for himself in this world.

— Lauren Schell Dickens

[1] Megan Steinma, "Woody De Othello," The Art Report, October 10, 2019, https://theartreport.org/media/00149.pdf.

[2] Steinma, "Woody De Othello."

◂ *It Is What It Is*, 2021
Glazed ceramic
Overall: 54 x 19 x 19 in.

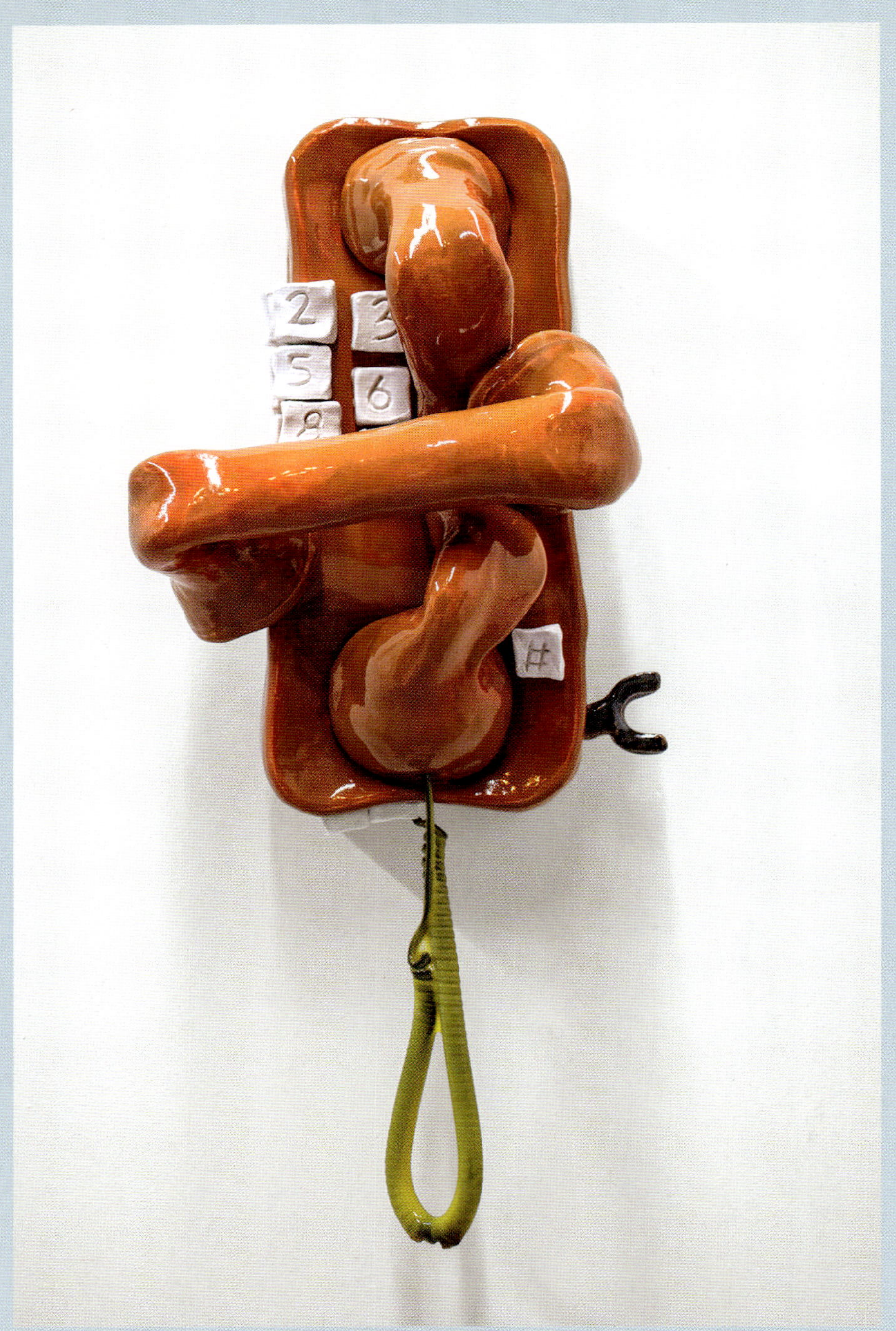

▲ *It Takes Two*, 2019
Ceramic, underglaze, glaze,
VytaFlex (on cord)
16 x 12 x 9 in.

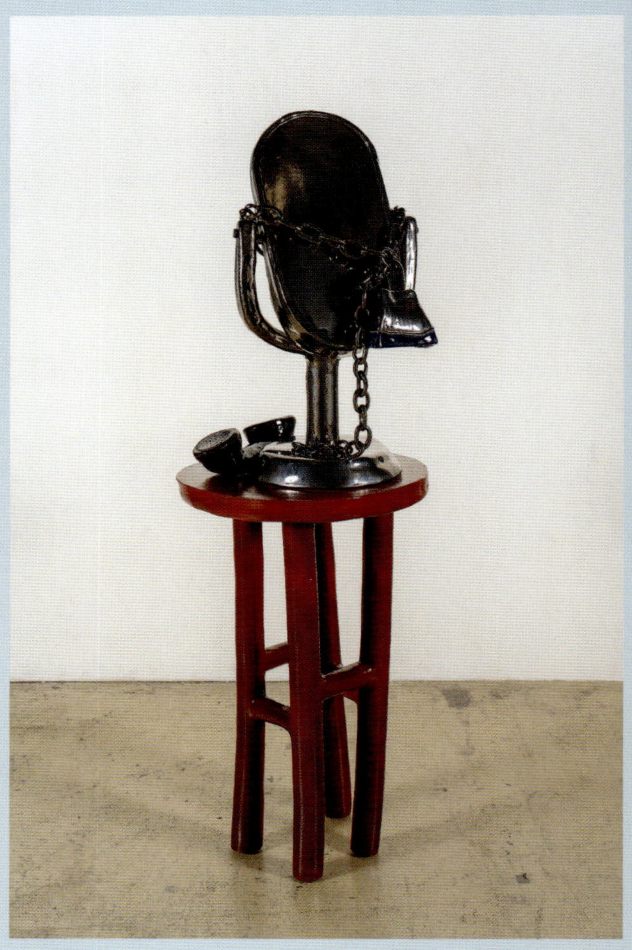

▲ *Still on Hold*, 2021
Glazed ceramic
Overall: 61 x 18 x 18 in.

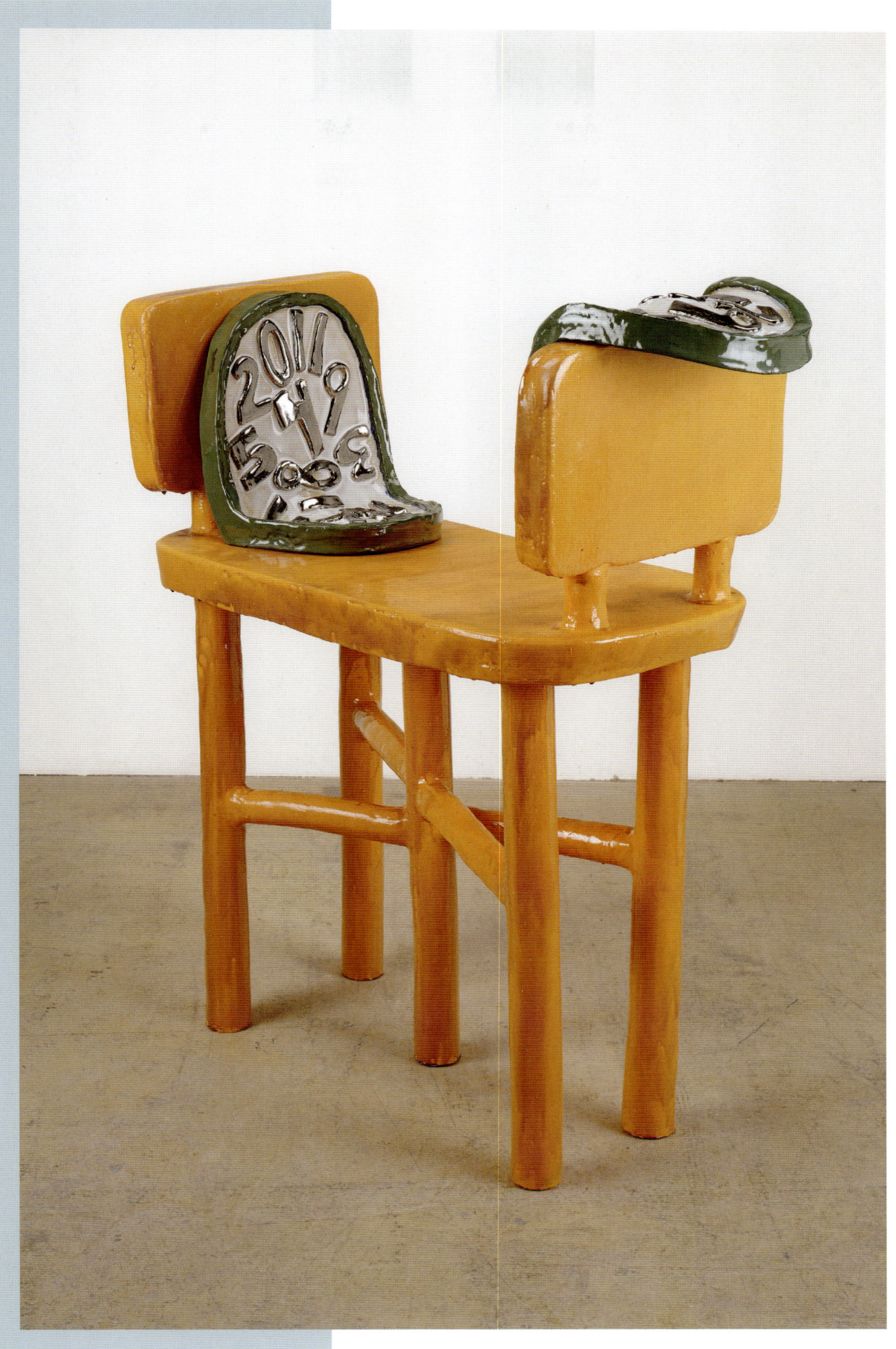

▲ *Face to Face*, 2021
Glazed ceramic, resin, paint
Overall: 41 x 32 x 16.5 in.

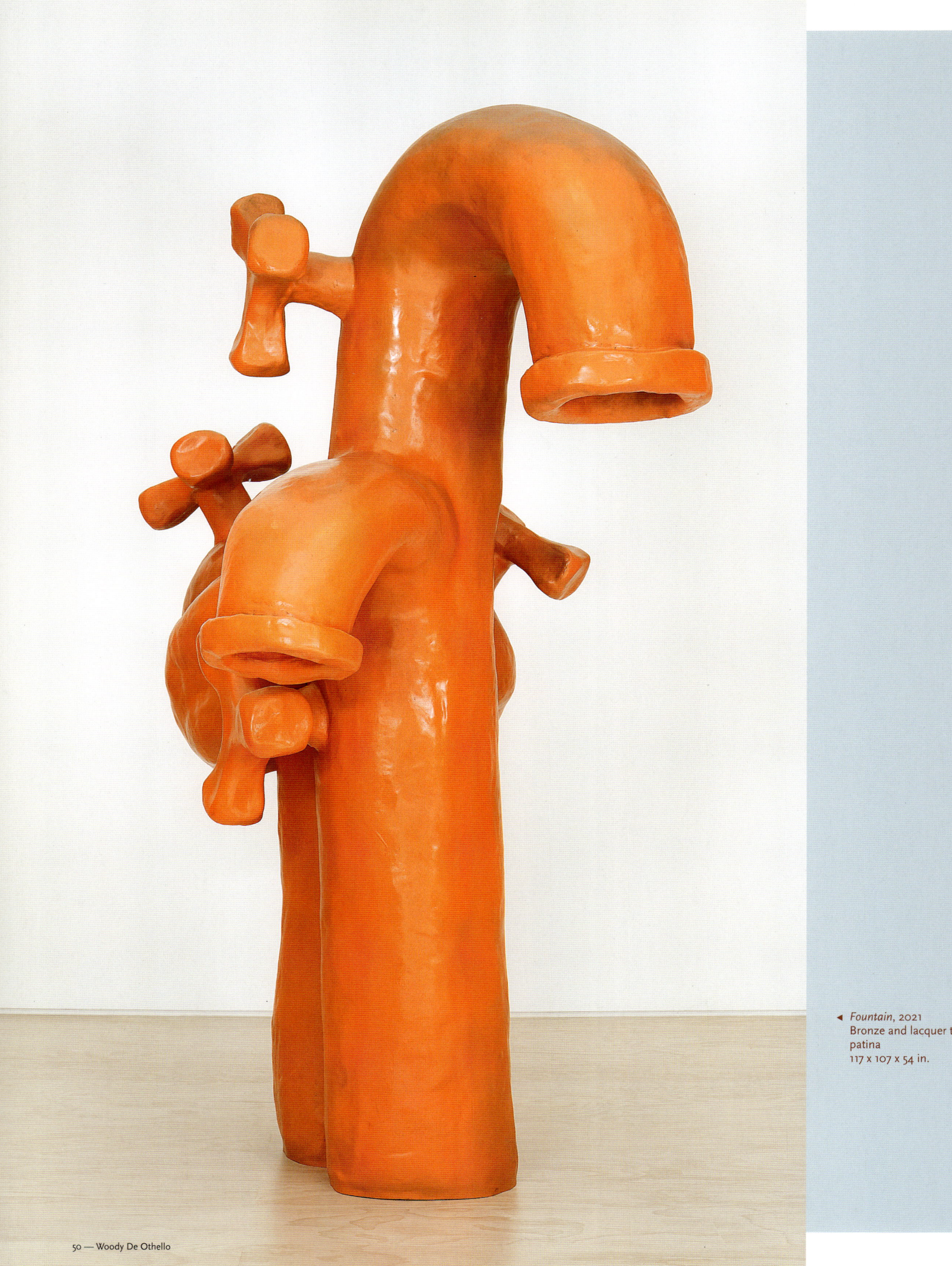

◂ *Fountain*, 2021
Bronze and lacquer topcoat over patina
117 x 107 x 54 in.

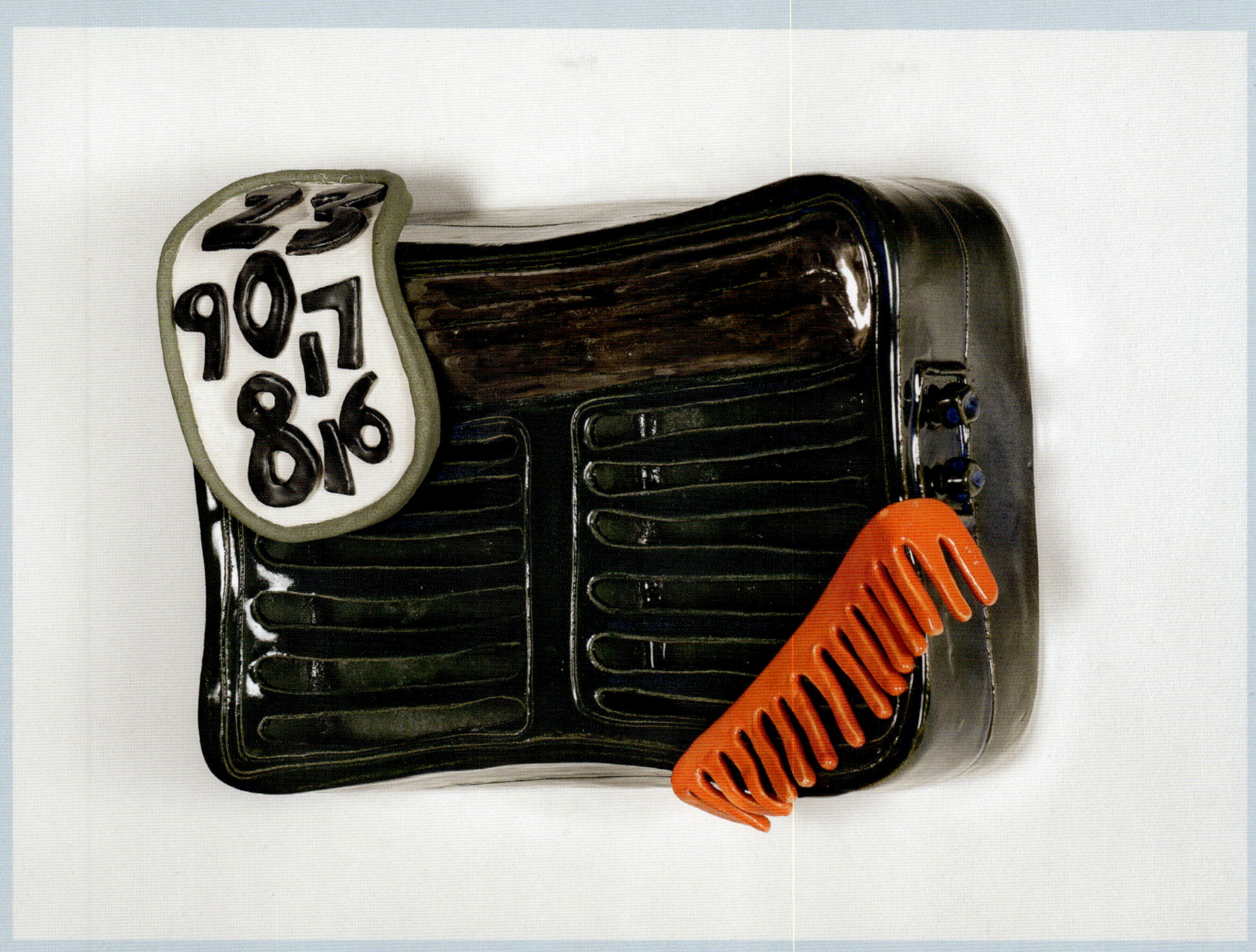

▲ *Clinging On*, 2021
Glazed ceramic
14 x 20 x 5 in.

sharif farrag

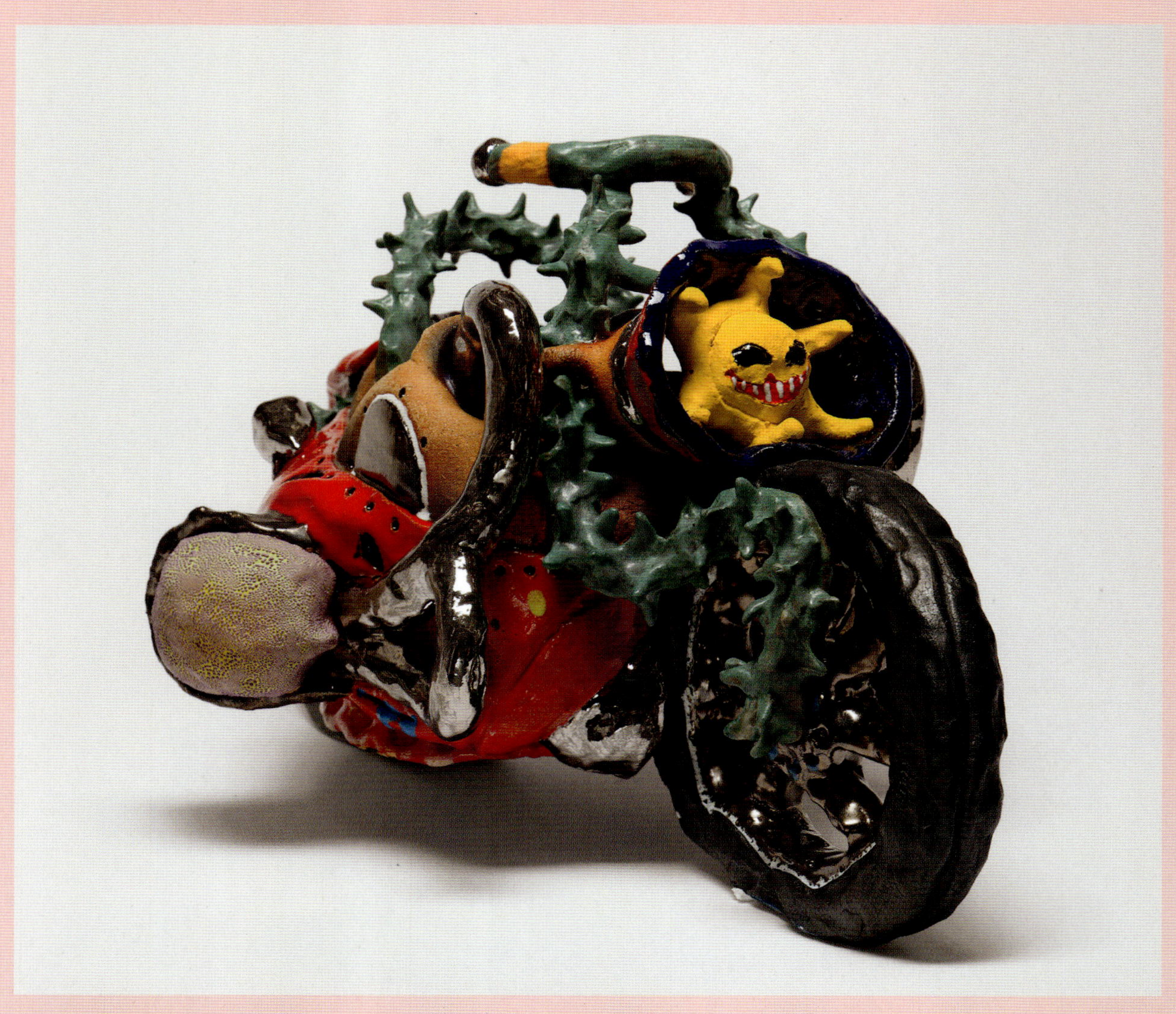

The ancient Egyptian deity Anubis—god of mummification, embalming, and the afterlife—usually takes one of two guises. We might encounter him in full canine form lying atop a tomb, or sporting a snouty, long-eared jackal's head atop a man's body. In the sculpture *Big Dog (Guardian)* (2021) by Sharif Farrag (b. 1993, Reseda, California), Anubis becomes a baggy-jeaned skater replete with BIG DOG brand boxers. The figure is garlanded with freeways and palm trees, as well as floral and spiky anemone-like embellishments that suggest a shoreline at low tide: San Fernando Valley meets the Valley of Kings.

This is an explicitly diasporic sculpture in which each body part seems to thrum on its own cultural frequency. One foot, for example, suggests the SoCal backyard pool of Farrag's American upbringing, whereas the other invokes the transformative process of dealing with your personal demons and coming into your body, with a cowboy boot that morphs into a crocodile. There are also references to the bases common in ancient and classical sculpture in the choice to present the work on the kiln shelf on which it was fired. Farrag notes that it is important for him to remain in conversation with the history of clay functionality, but he is most interested in effectively portraying narrative and drama.

There are all sorts of contortions involved in straddling multiple cultures. In thinking about how to reconnect with his Syrian and Egyptian heritage, Farrag began by twisting and tracing his own body. The result is a chimeric armor-clad guardian angel who cradles a small boy upon one knee like a passed-on ancestor that lovingly watches over the artist and supports him in his journey. ("Big Dog" refers to a common term of endearment the artist calls his various mentors.) The child is trapped yet peaceful, like John Everett Millais's *Ophelia* transposed to a Pacific tide pool.

Implicit here is the loaded dynamic of engaging with ancient Egyptian mythology in the United States today, particularly given its prominence in Afrocentrist movements and Hollywood. Even as he explores these facets of his identity, Farrag grounds the figure in his blue-collar background with the visible boxers. Farrag says, "I have no idea whether I'm Egyptian or whether Egypt was Black or whether *The Mummy* movie was real info."

In its dynamism, *Big Dog* recalls Rodin's description of sculpture as a gesture executed over several seconds, yet it also boasts a calm strength, which Farrag describes as being unashamed and "confident in its own fracturing, in its own disfiguration."

— Rahel Aima

◂ *Sunset Cycle*, 2020
Glazed stoneware
15.5 x 16 x 22.5 in.

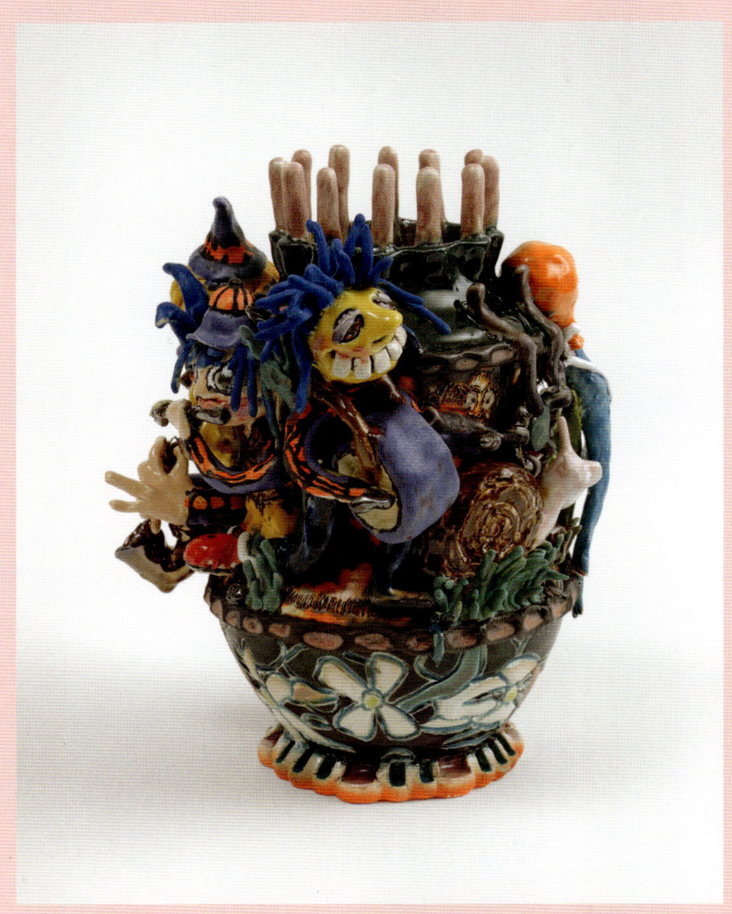

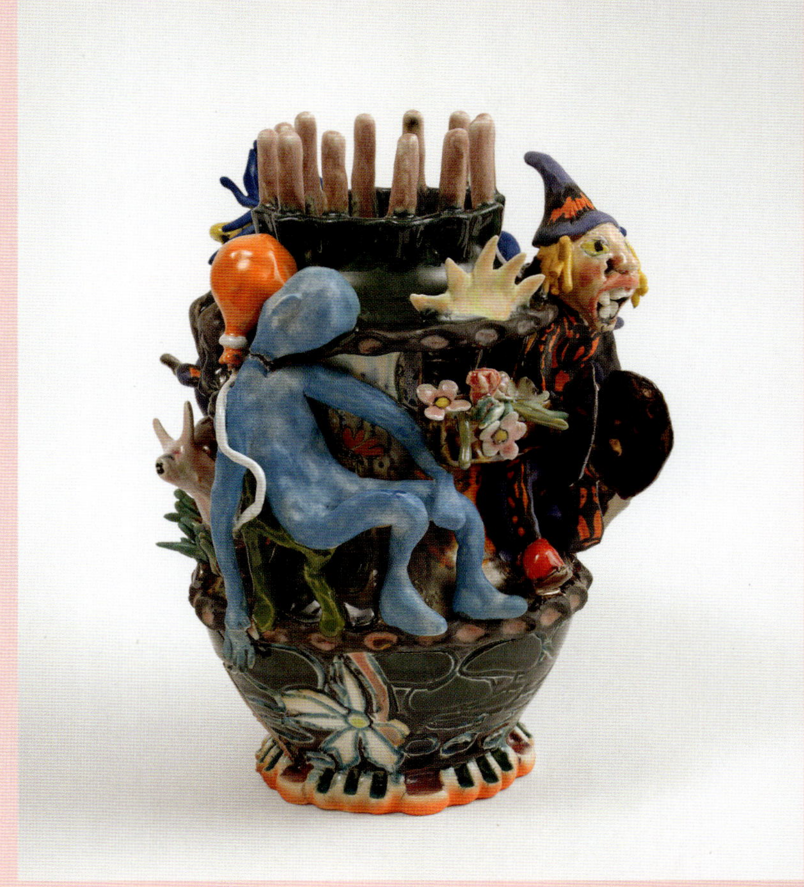

▲ Front and back view of *Floating in a Parade*, 2022
Glazed porcelain
12 x 8.5 x 8 in.

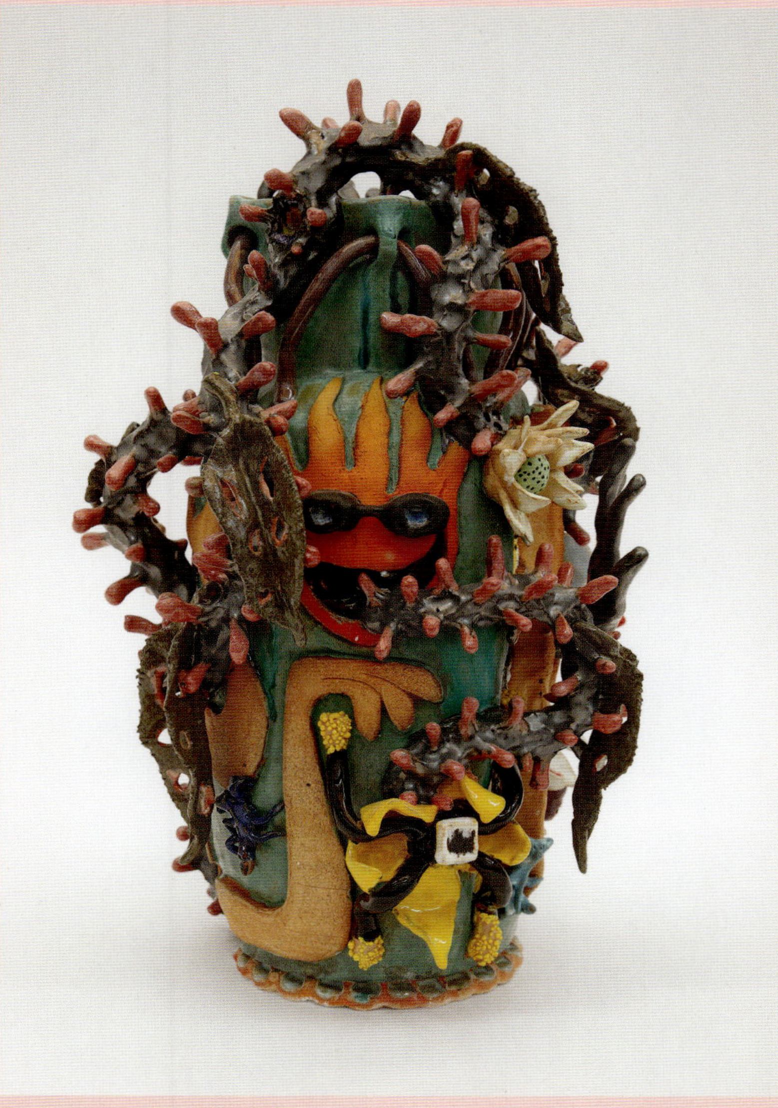

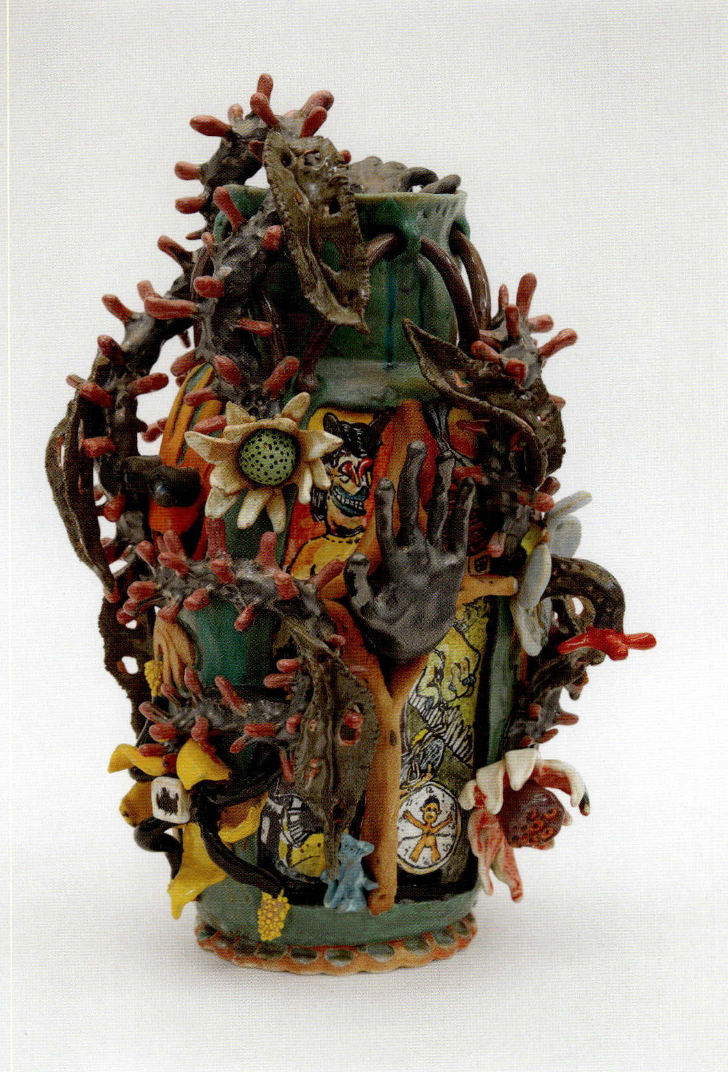

▲ Front and back view of *Trapped in a Pocket Watch Jug*, 2020
Glazed earthenware
19 x 13 x 14 in.

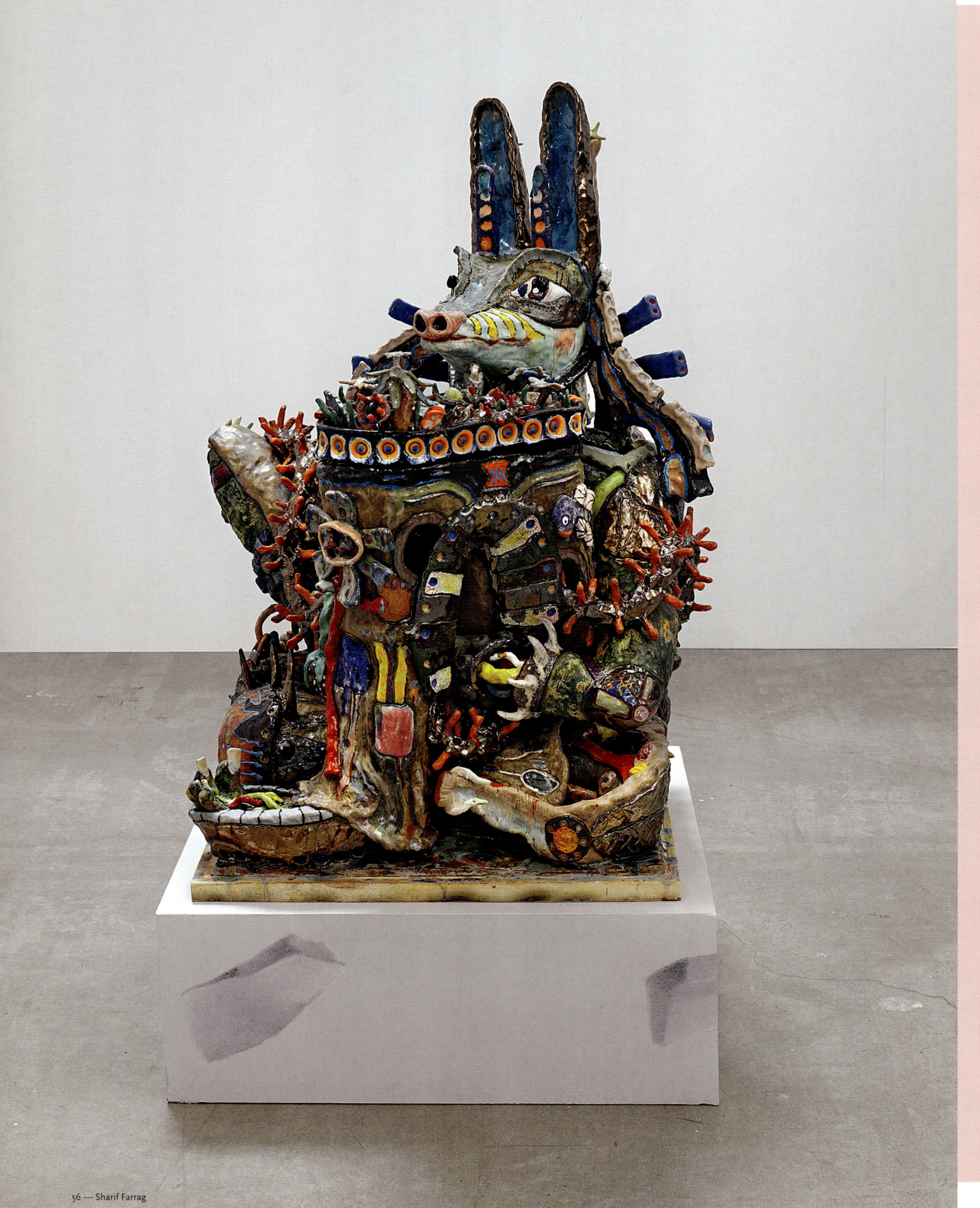

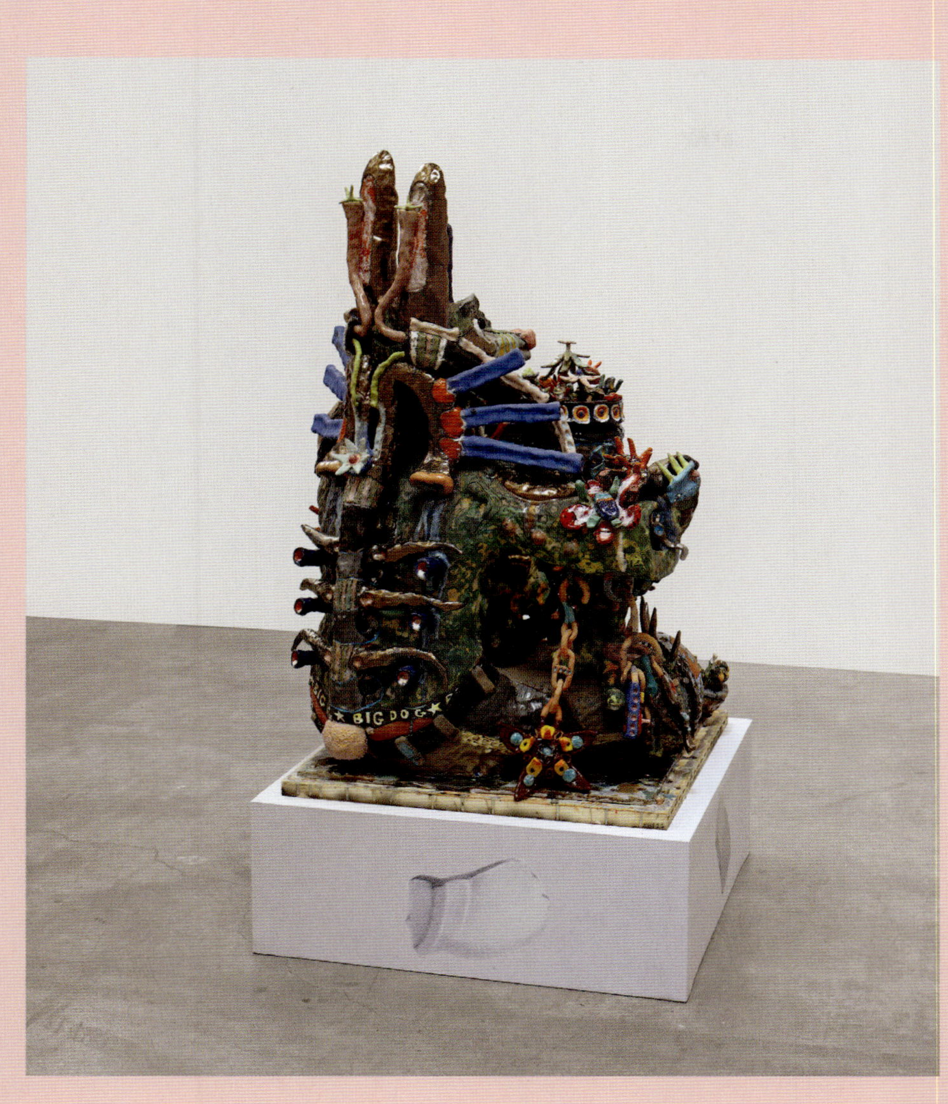

◂ Front and back view of *Big Dog (Guardian)*, 2021
Glazed stoneware
40.5 x 29 x 26 in.

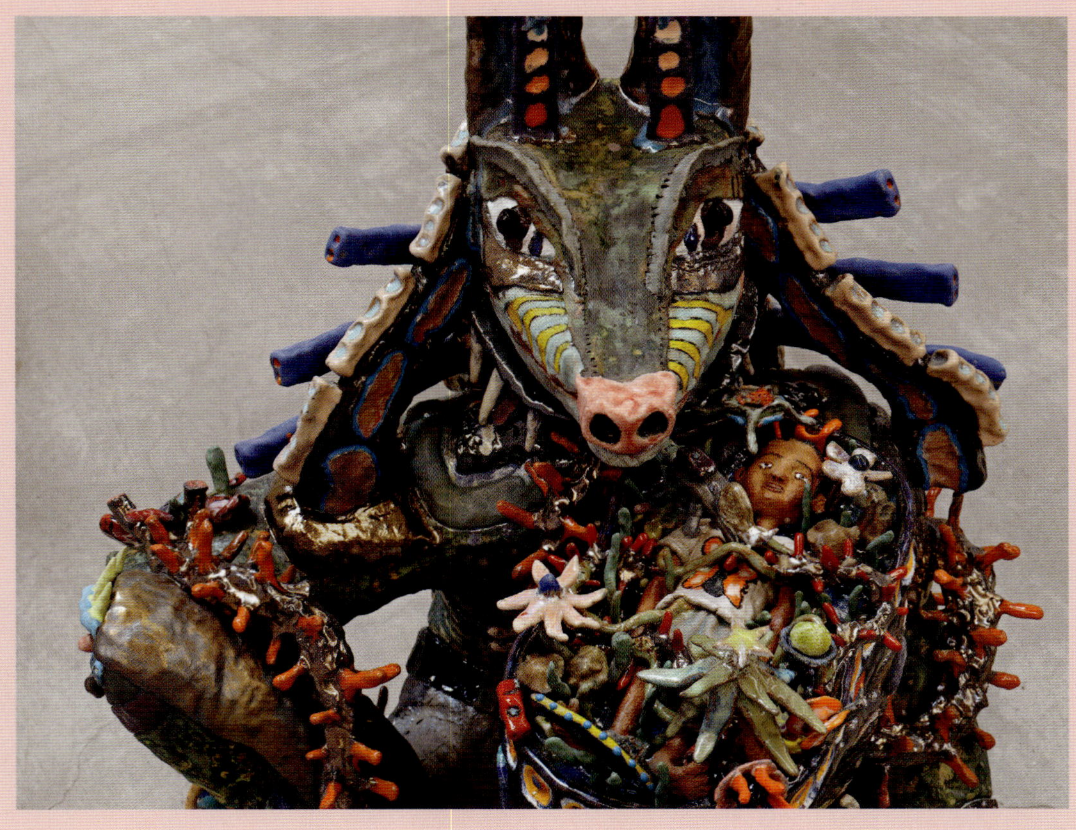

ryan flores

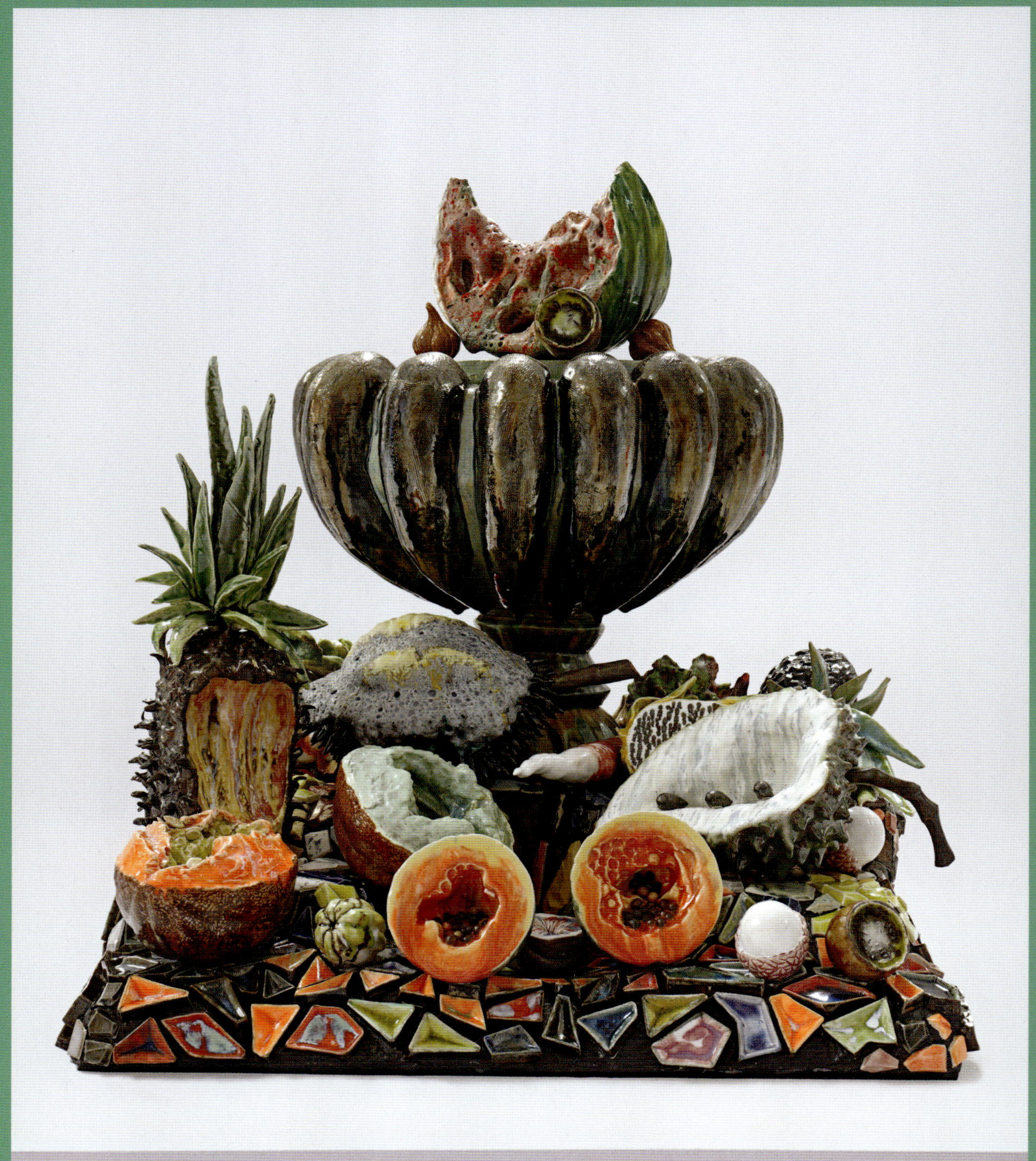

Ryan Flores (b. 1986, Los Angeles) is an artist who works in the medium of ceramics, exploring how colorful, glazed forms draw the eye as they play with expectations. Flores's *Still Life over Stained Glass* (2021) features pineapple, watermelon, honeydew, cantaloupe, soursop, lychee, pitaya, and garlic. The work is a cornucopia of temptation and rot with plenty of decay.

The sculptural arrangement in *Still Life over Stained Glass* references the history of still life painting. Among the earthly delights is a honeydew picked from the baroque painting of Luis Egidio Meléndez and a liquifying watermelon plucked from the surreal harvests of Frida Kahlo. The wet, dripping, and elaborate glazes maximize the sculpture's seductiveness. For the viewer's pleasure, Flores opens the objects' insides. The engorged fruits, which are overly ripe, betray bite marks, rips, ruptures, and cavities. The interiors become formal devices that add to the work's baroque drama, and the gesture also elicits connections between fruit, the body, and sexuality. An absorbed viewer may even experience moments of pareidolia and envision phantom faces in inanimate things.

Arrangement emerges as a critical element to Flores's process. Each fruit is individually sculpted, fired, and glazed. Flores then carefully composes each towering display, like a spoiled centerpiece from last night's palatial banquet. Through the act of arrangement, Flores pantomimes the art of still life composition itself. The use of tropical fruit evokes the role of still life painting as a means of displaying power, wealth, conquest, and colony. "There is an excess or grandiosity around 'low-life' objects," explains Flores. Objects that might suggest everyday use become vestiges of overabundance.

At once Golden Age bodegon (a type of Spanish still life painting that reveals the pantry's victuals) and pandemic-era bodega, Flores's use of seduction and degeneration calls to mind the work of French intellectual Georges Bataille (1897–1962), whose peer, the Surrealist André Breton, once called the "excremental philosopher." Rather than obsessing over ideal forms, Bataille found meaning in the soured and lowly: toes, plant genitalia, viscera, and shit. In doing so, Bataille rejects idealism, expectations, and hierarchies. In *Erotism: Death and Sensuality*, Bataille wrote, "Beauty is desired in order that it may be befouled not for its own sake, but for the joy brought by the certainty of profaning it."

Resting atop a rainbow mosaic of triangles and trapezoids, Flores's sculpture revels in the low life. It profanes and finds beauty through rot. That which we no longer want become objects of desire.

— Owen Duffy

◂ *Still Life over Stained Glass*, 2021
Ceramic, mixed media
35 x 31.5 x 31 in.

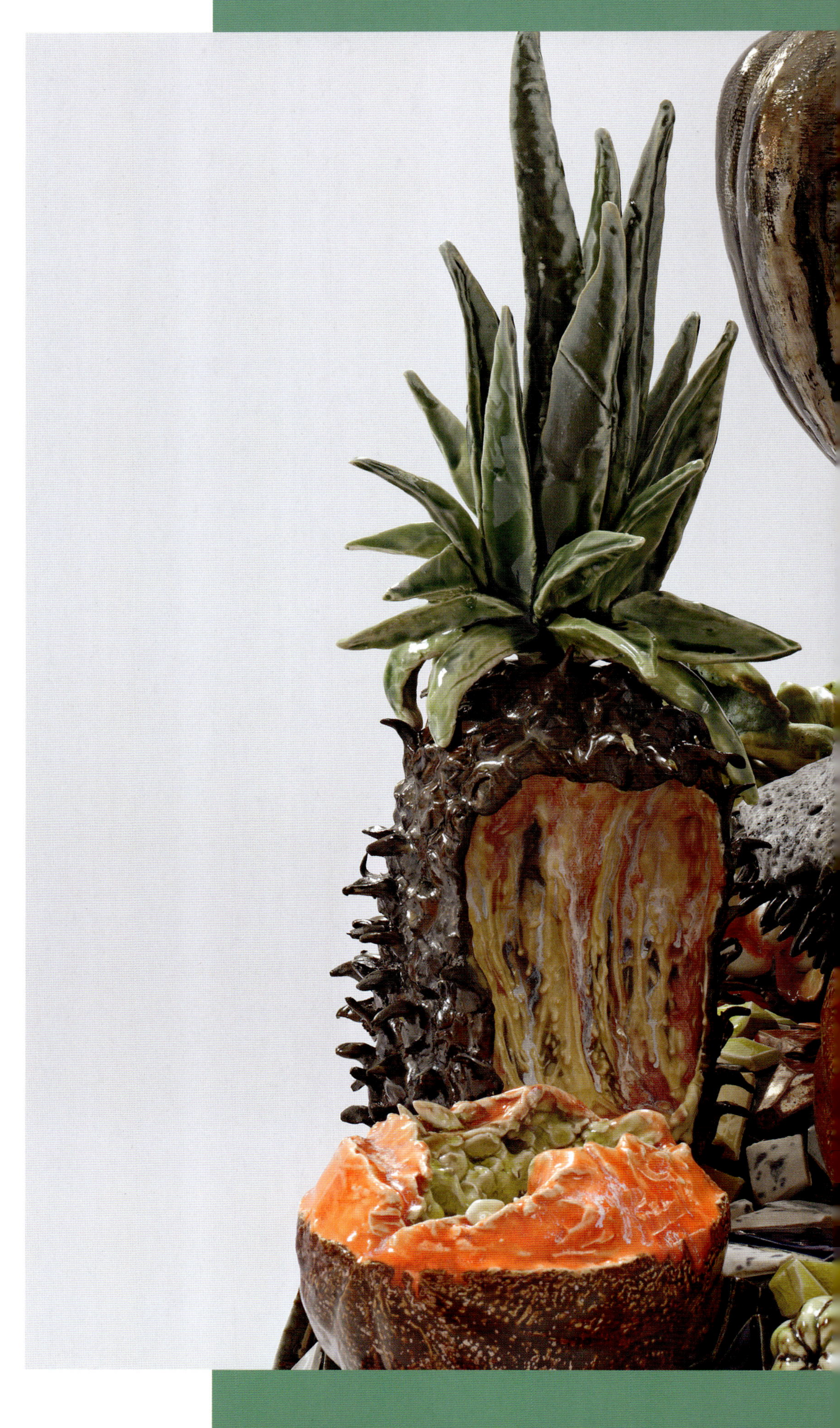

▸ *Still Life over Stained Glass* (detail), 2021

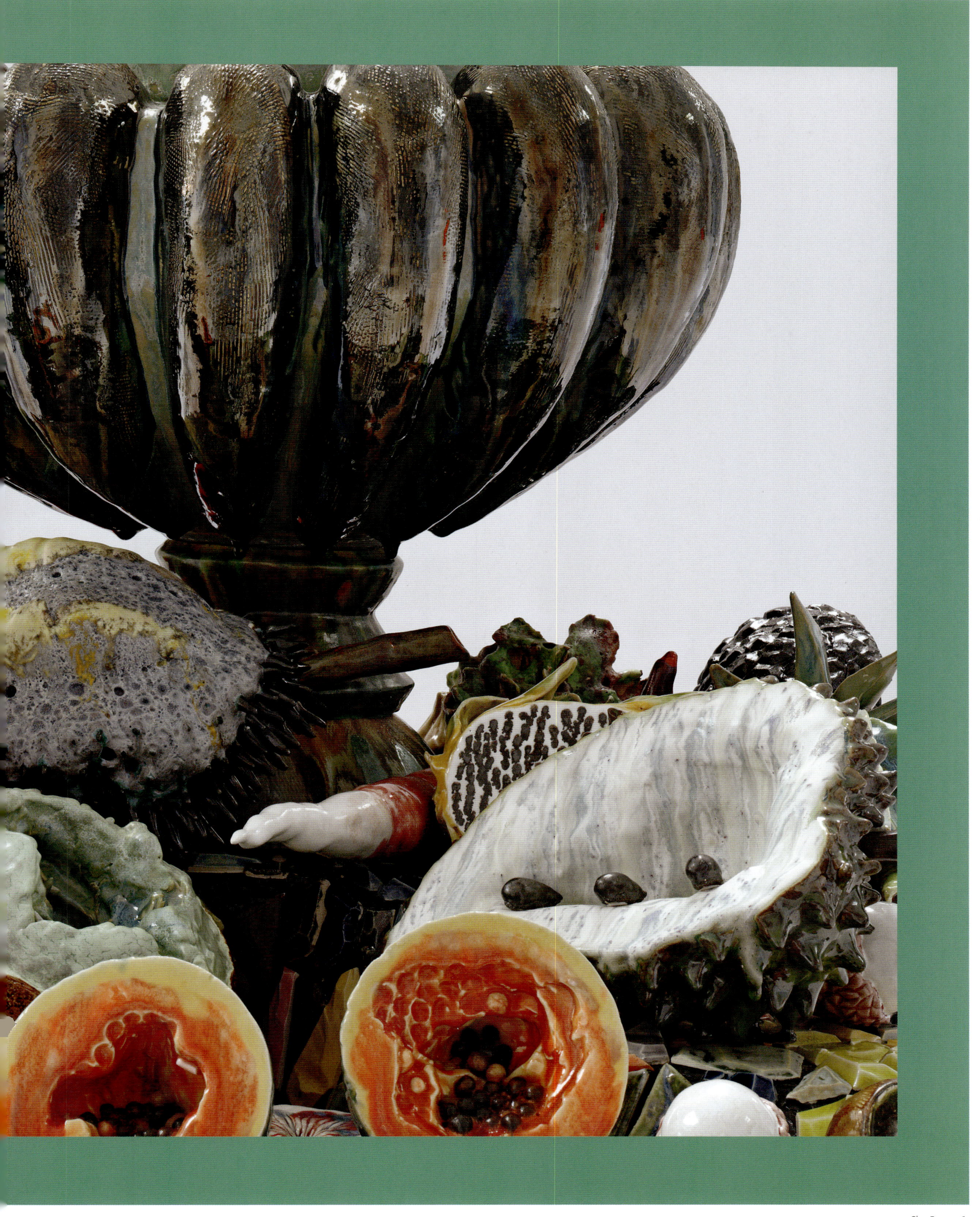

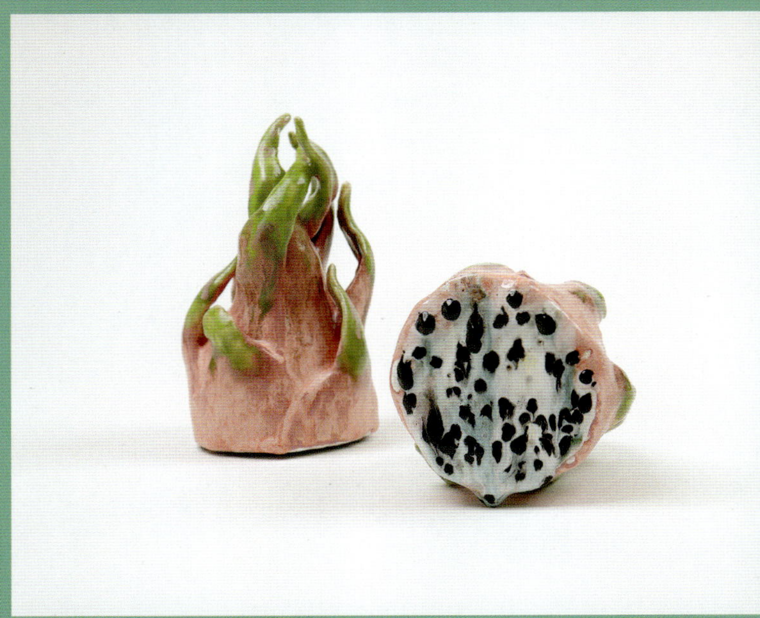

◂ *Pitaya*, 2021
Ceramic
6 x 5 x 5 in. and 7 x 5 x 5 in.

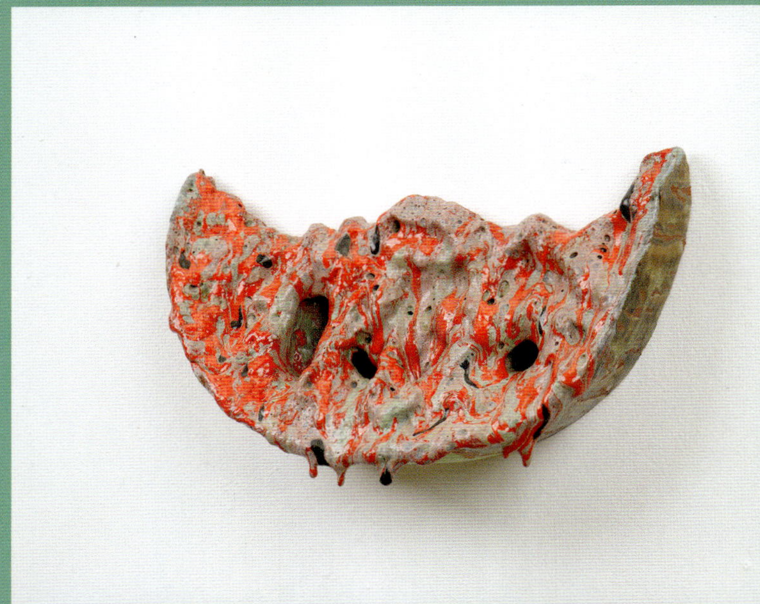

◂ *Watermelon*, 2022
Ceramic
10 x 6 x 22 in.

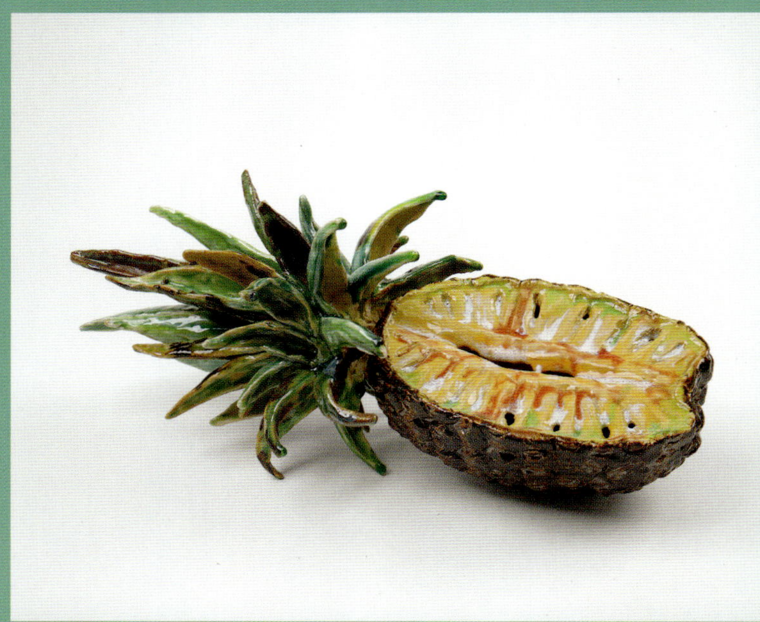

◂ *Split Pineapple*, 2022
Ceramic
8.5 x 10 x 20 in.

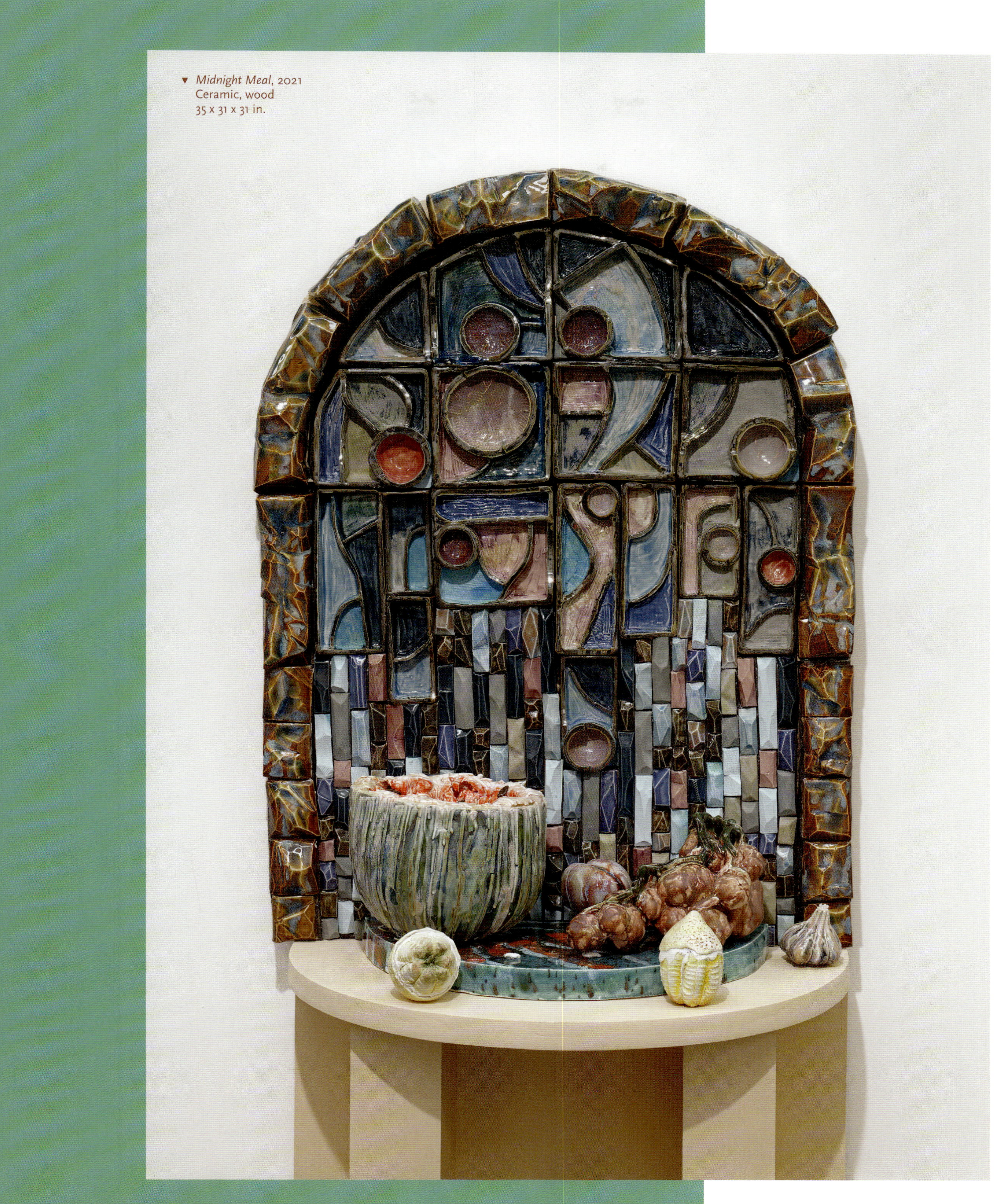

▾ *Midnight Meal*, 2021
Ceramic, wood
35 x 31 x 31 in.

dominique fung

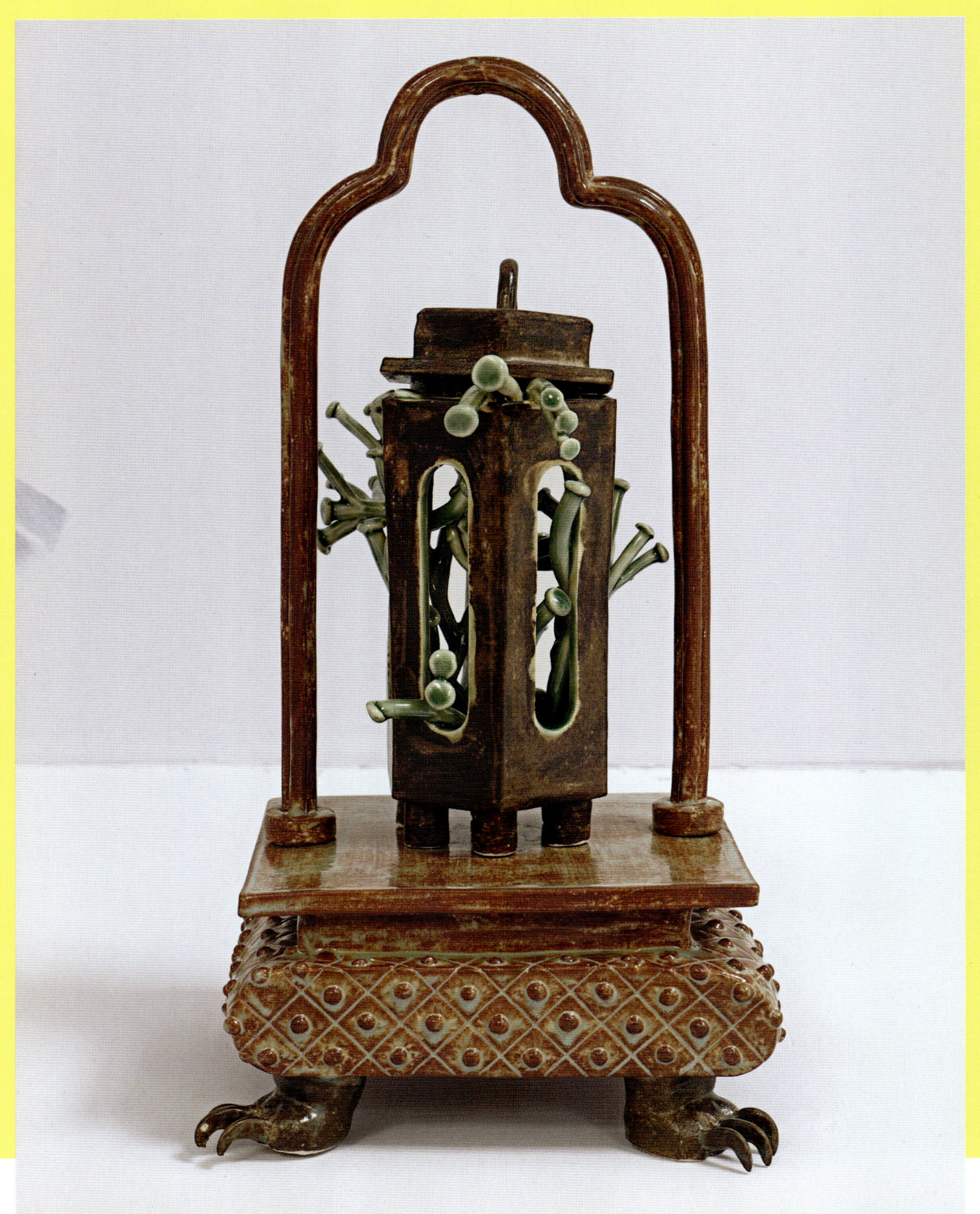

Despite having only started making ceramics about a year ago, Dominique Fung (b. 1987, Ottawa, Canada) has often thought sculpturally throughout her prolific and predominantly painting practice. While creating her oil-on-canvas works that simultaneously transform wares from Chinese antiquity into their own surrealist worlds and confront the Orientalist gaze that renders "the East" as decorative, passive, and feminine, the Brooklyn-based artist considers each painted object as foremost a sculpture. It was thus naturally and aptly that she began to materialize these forms through actual ceramic. Between two recent exhibitions at Jeffrey Deitch Gallery, *Clay Pop* in 2022 and *It's Not Polite to Stare* in 2021, Fung has created a series of new glazed stoneware and porcelain works that further reimagine the embodied potentialities of synthetic objects as human beings.

Fung's work *Synapse* (2021), which was included in the group show *Clay Pop*, is composed of a smaller three-legged vessel perched on a peculiarly textured, four-clawed platform, complete with an arch. What the artist describes as clusters of nerve endings also resemble networks of fungi that emerge from the work's hollowed-out body cavity. Whether in the process of becoming human or decomposing into other forms of matter, life seems to grow from the porous material of the clay and from the alchemical process of ceramic-making itself. In lieu of Fung's paintings, which pay respect to existing objects in auction catalogues and museum collections, this work further creates new in-between forms in three-dimensional reality.

In a series of assemblages for her 2021 solo exhibition *It's Not Polite to Stare*, the artist as collector sourced directly from estate sales across the United States. Six Chinese birdcages, which were speculated to have been handmade in southern China but unknown in origin, become inhabited by personal and ancestral memories through a number of ceramic characters via Fung's surrealist appropriation. These works recall a memory of the artist's—of walking through a park in Hong Kong and speaking to elderly folks who would bring their pet birds out in similar cages so they would not get lonely. Suspended side by side and among several paintings, the objects that replace the animals inside seem to similarly gather in communion yet remain separated by wooden bars. In their anthropomorphizing, these ceramics are a melancholic reflection on lived experiences of loneliness and displacement, as well as Asian diasporic subjectivities.

Fung's practice not only takes a traditional medium such as ceramic and turns it on its head, but also renders arbitrary the very category of "traditional" in relation to "contemporary" art-making. The artist pushes the aesthetics of objectification and dehumanization to rethink the very Western colonial assumptions behind the "object" and "human," and beyond a flattened negation of existing material realities. Indeed, ceramics become bodies in her works, in which such hybrid beings create their own rich life worlds. It is thus through the seductively prosthetic that a new and strange person-objecthood emerges.

— Danni Shen

◂ *Synapse*, 2021
Glazed ceramic
15 x 8 x 7 in.

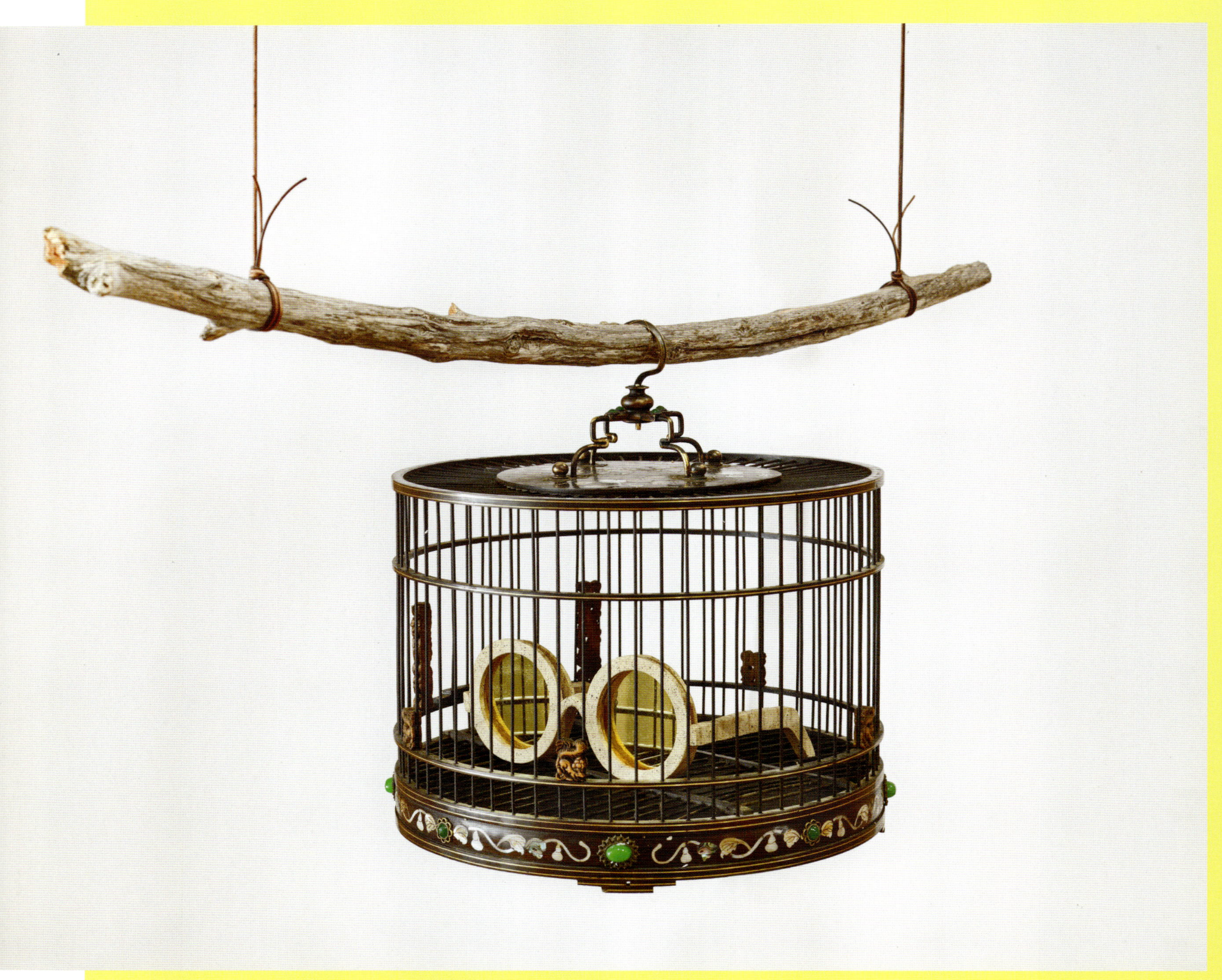

▲ *Eye Contact*, 2021
Found Chinese birdcage, ceramic,
gold mirror plexiglass
12.5 x 12 x 12 in.

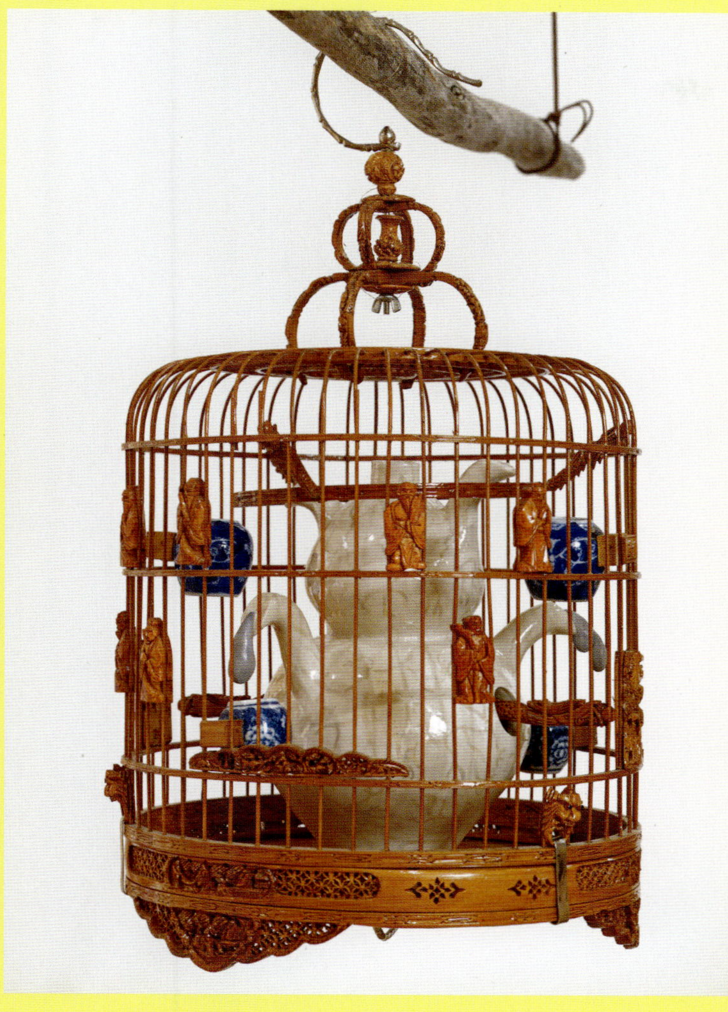

▲ *Vase Transmitting Signals*, 2021
Found Chinese birdcage, ceramic
16 x 9.5 x 9.5 in.

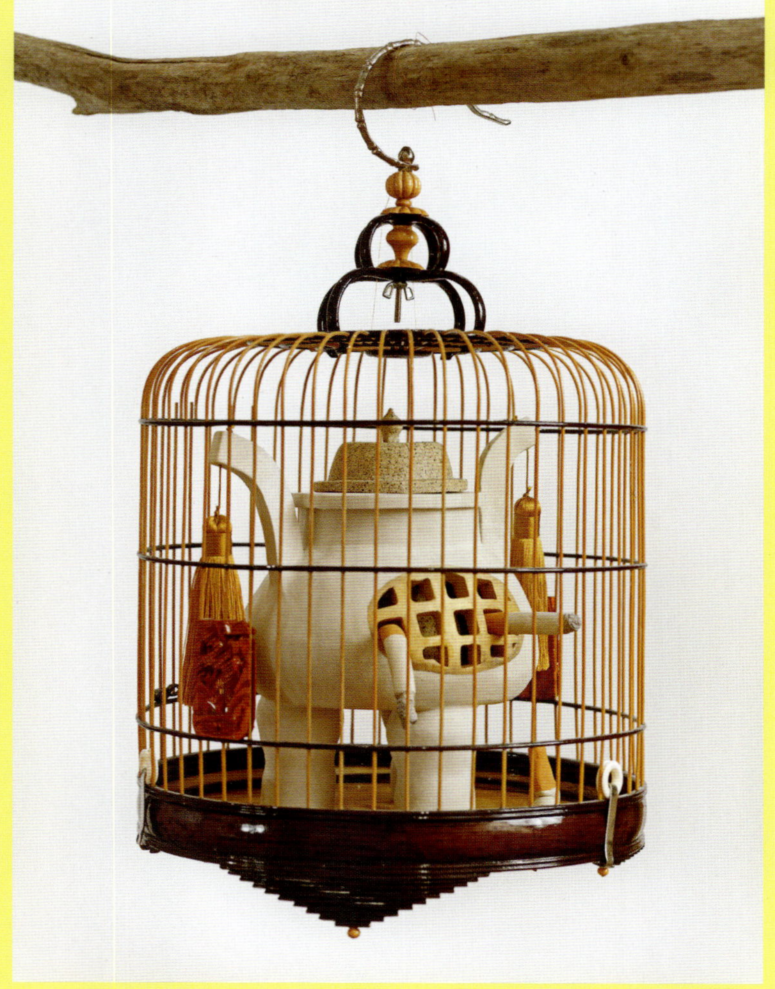

▲ *Tobacco*, 2021
Found Chinese birdcage, ceramic, tassels
15.5 x 9 x 9 in.

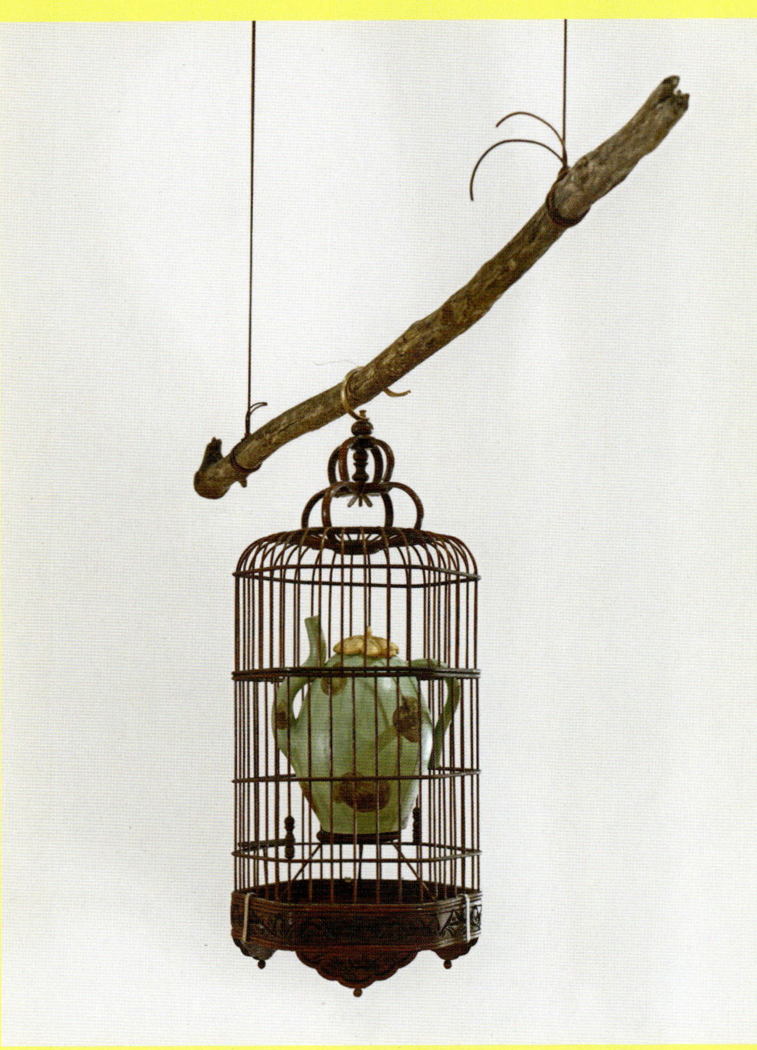

▲ *Egg*, 2021
Found Chinese birdcage, ceramic
15.5 x 7 x 7 in.

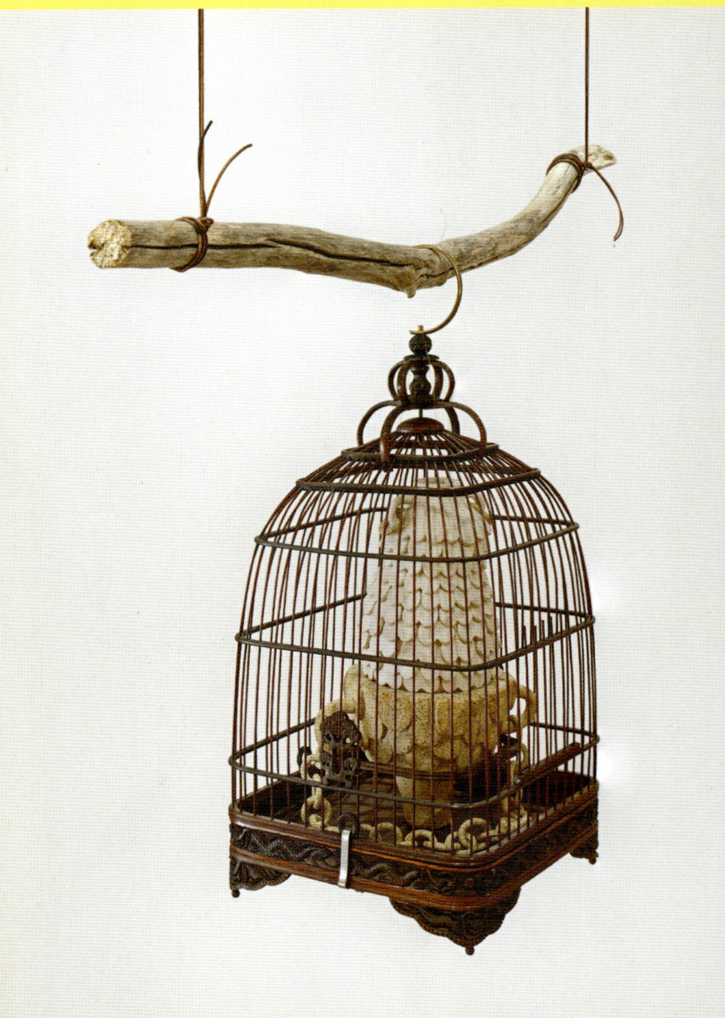

▲ *Protecting the Skin*, 2021
Found Chinese birdcage, ceramic
18 x 8.5 x 8.5 in.

▼ *Lay Your Head on My Pillow*, 2021
Found Chinese birdcage, ceramic, tassels
35 x 28 x 19.5 in.

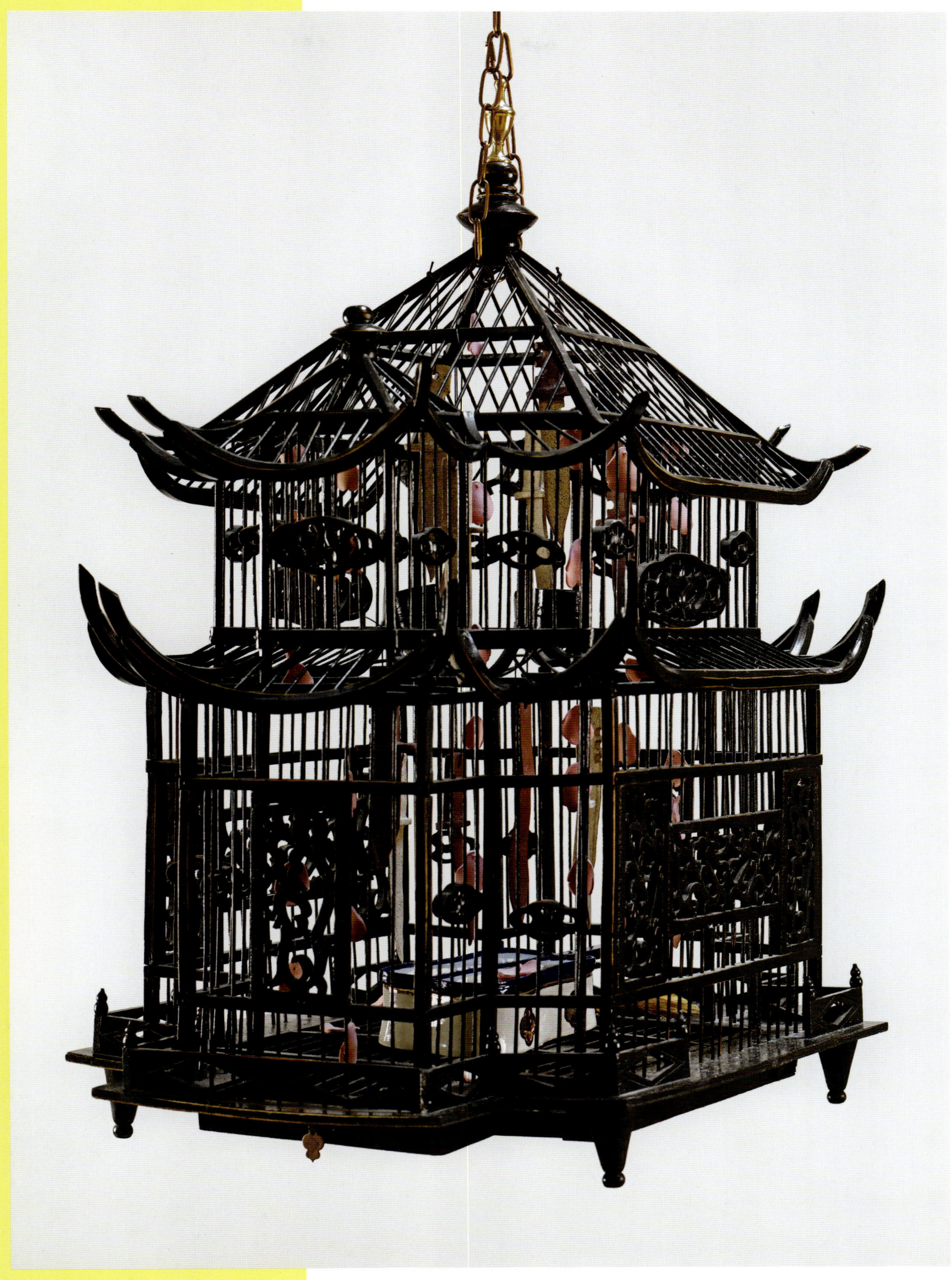

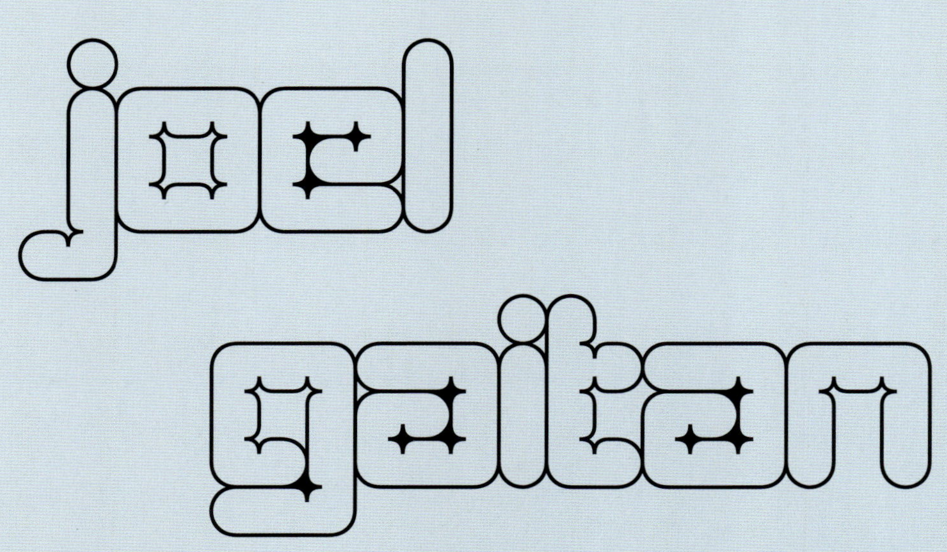
joel
gaitan

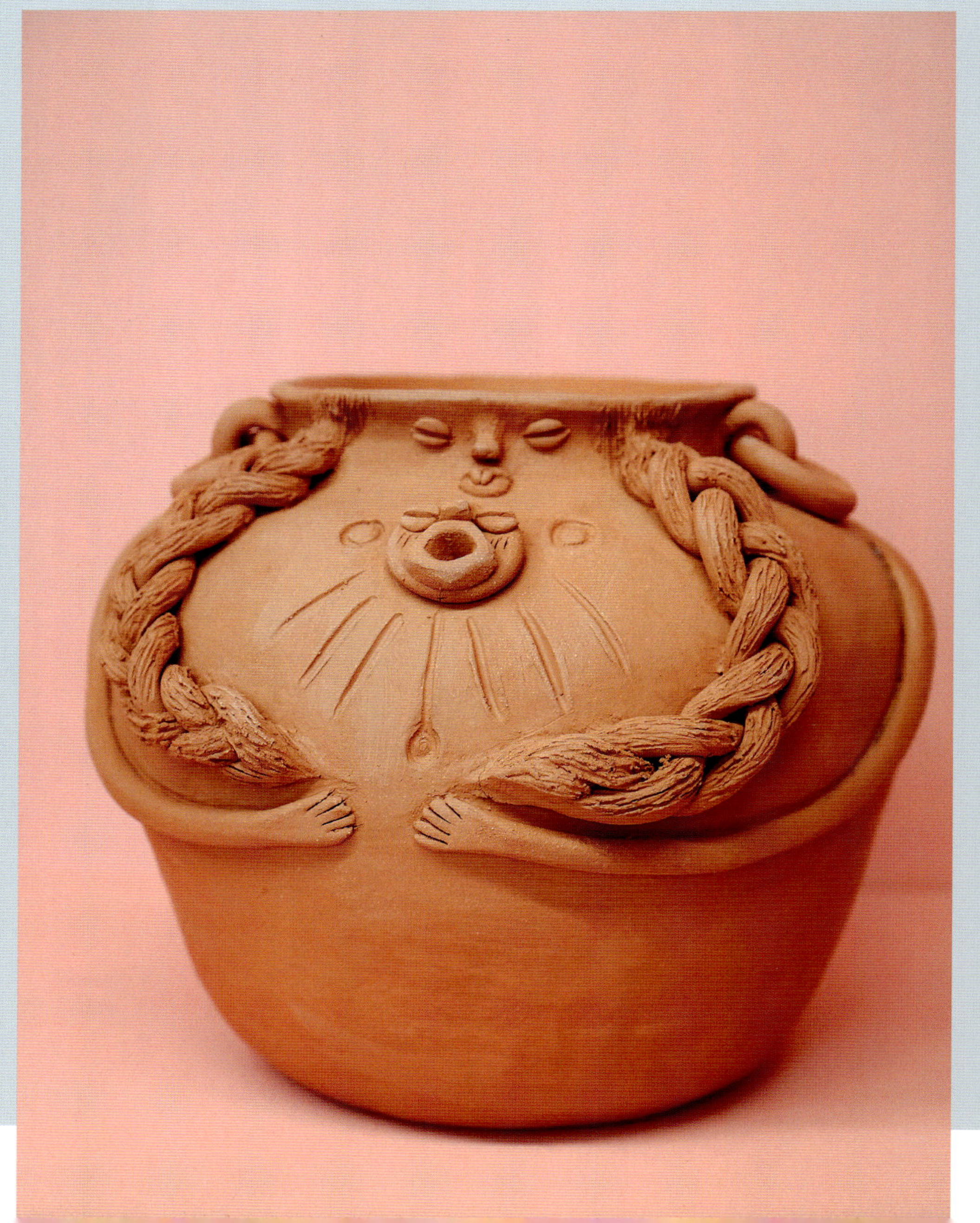

The terra-cotta sculptures of Joel Gaitan (b. 1995, Hialeah, Florida) are mediators between the pre-Columbian civilizations of Central America and our present-day culture. They are rooted in the heritage of Mesoamerican ceramics and are earnest reflections of Gaitan's experiences as a first-generation American-Nicaraguan. Timelines converge in each of his pieces, giving them a distinct resemblance to archaeological artifacts and defiant contemporary art pieces.

Spirituality is central to Gaitan's work. He draws inspiration from his upbringing in the Pentecostal church, as well as from Indigenous spiritual practices. Many of his ceramics bring to mind Aztec or Mayan deity sculptures and religious altarpieces. They tell stories of ritual and ceremony. This aspect of Gaitan's practice is a way for him to reclaim, praise, and give thanks to his ancestors and family, to whom he attributes his interest in art, going back to his grandfather, who was a musician and painter.

Gaitan's first solo exhibition in 2021, *La Pulperia Doña Pina*, was named after his aunt, Doña Pina, a larger-than-life character and master *tortillera* who runs a *pulperia* (a small store that sells food and beverages) in Managua, Nicaragua. His family's influence is evident in the physical shapes of his pots, which resemble the ample bodies of the men and women around which he grew up.

Many of his artworks also actively involve personal themes of identity and his own sexual explorations. They are his research and findings on self-pleasure and intimate experiences with others. Gaitan's ability to do this with humor and playfulness pushes back against any shock two pots engaging in fellatio might bring. The erotic nature of his art additionally carries forward the narrative of Mesoamerican ceramics present in his work. Many pre-Columbian cultures, like the Andean Moche civilization (AD 150–800), created functional clay pots and three-dimensional sculptures that depicted a wide range of sex acts.

Other subject matters in his work are the *mestizaje* of Nicaragua, the mixing of races that occurred after its conquest by Spain, and what it means to be Hispanic or Latinx in a postcolonial world. It is important to note that the terms "Hispanic" and "Latinx" do a disservice to the immense diaspora of cultures that exist in Mexico, Central America, South America, and the Caribbean, including those that existed before its Latin rule. Gaitan pushes to break past any boundaries "Latinidad" can bring and invites viewers to learn what it is really like to be *Nica*. His sculptures and installations revive the ingenuity and aesthetics of seemingly forgotten cultures and elevate them to the highest standard art can be.

— Ivana Cruz

◄ *Para La Chicha Bruja*, 2020
Terra-cotta
10 x 12 x 13 in.

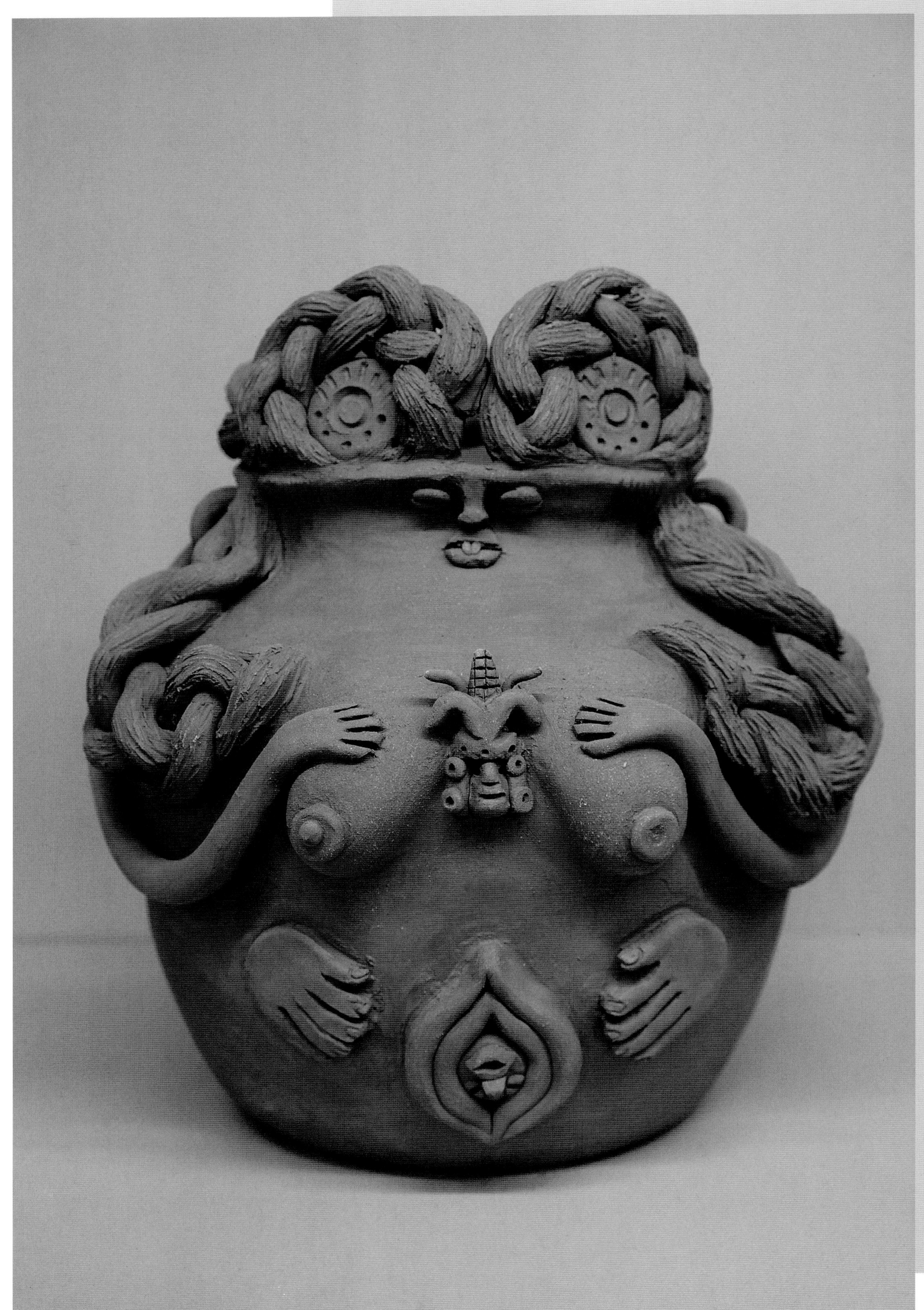

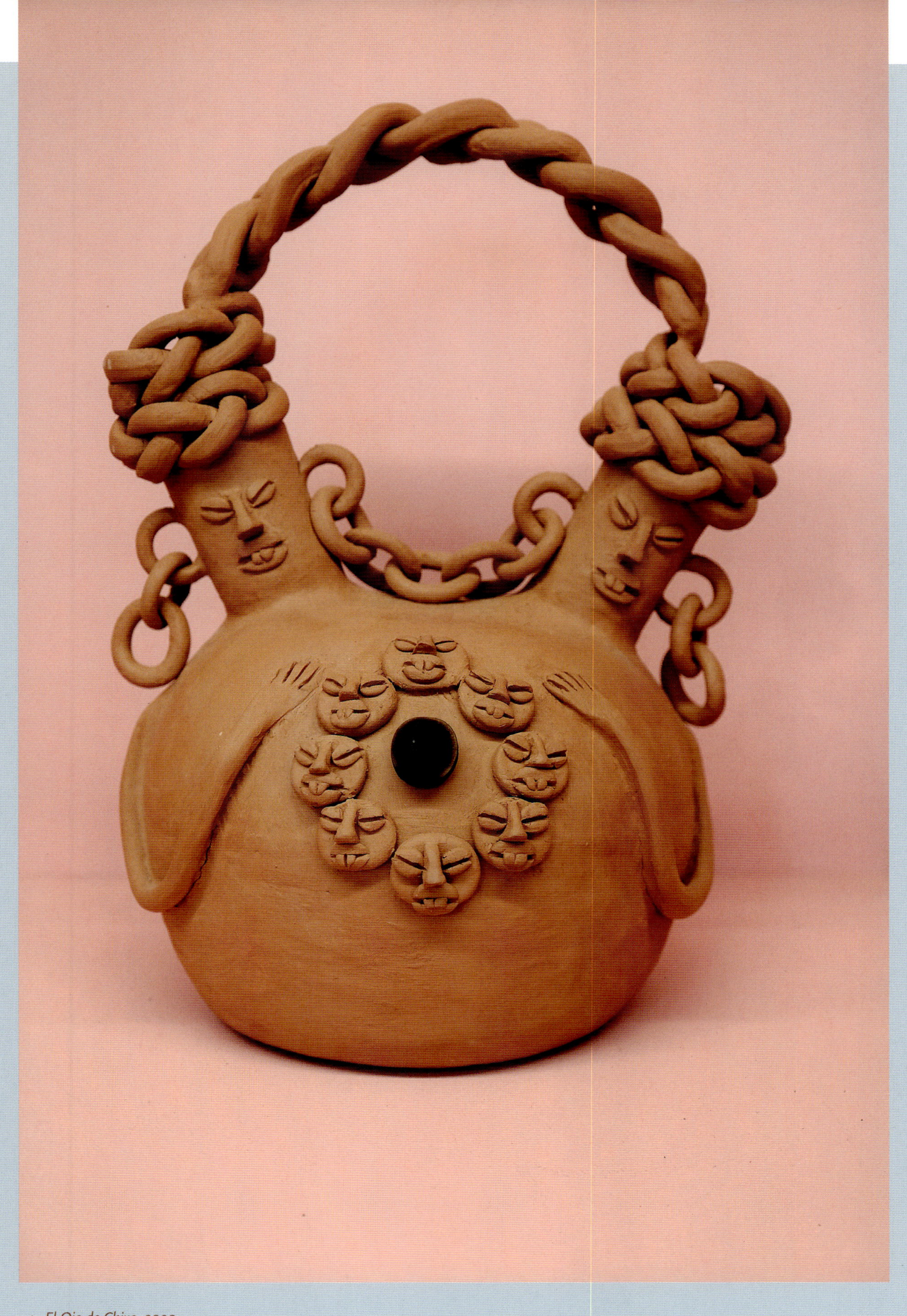

▲ *El Ojo de Chivo*, 2020
Terra-cotta
16 x 11 x 12 in.

◄ *Venus de Managua*, 2020
Terra-cotta
14 x 12 x 14 in.

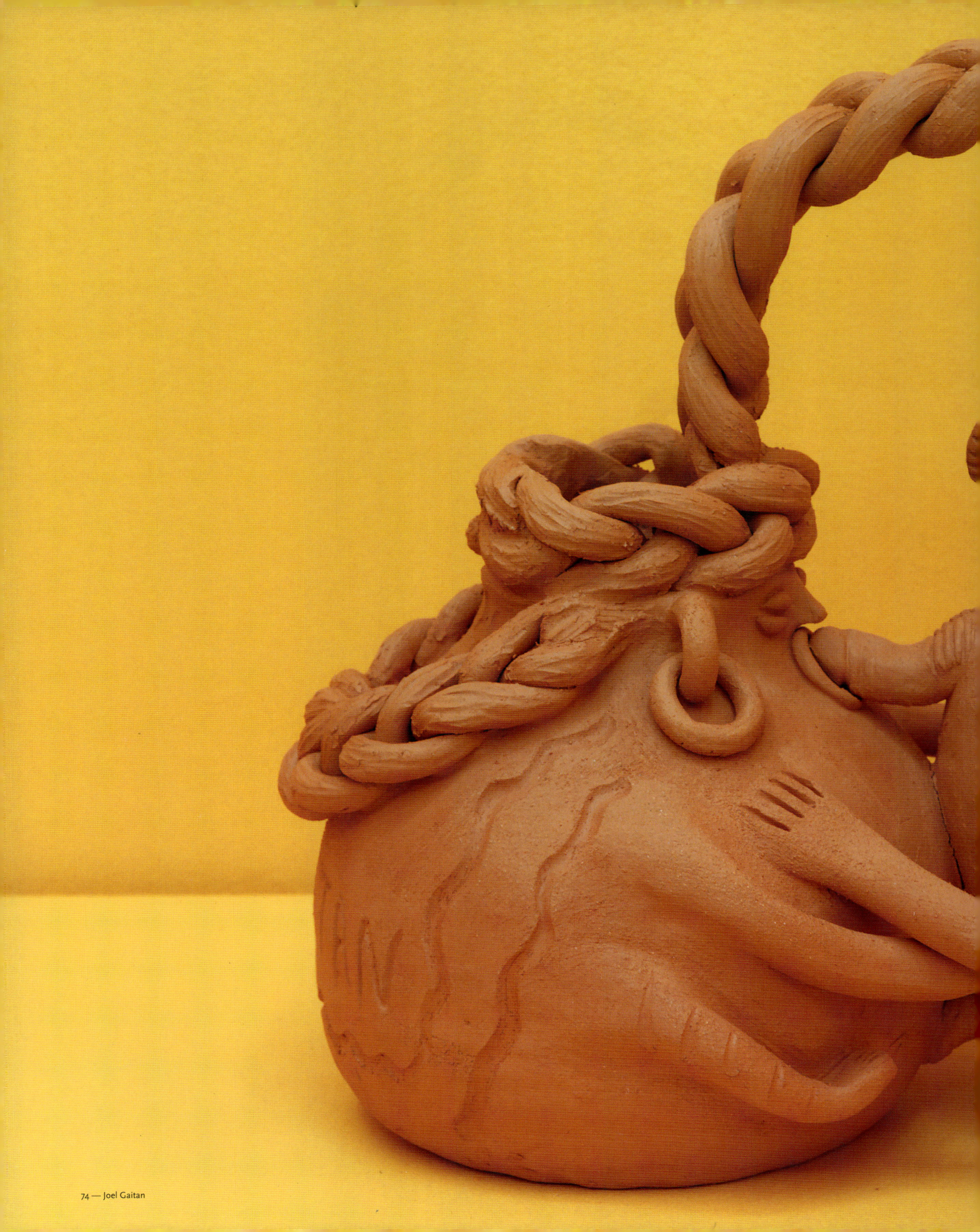

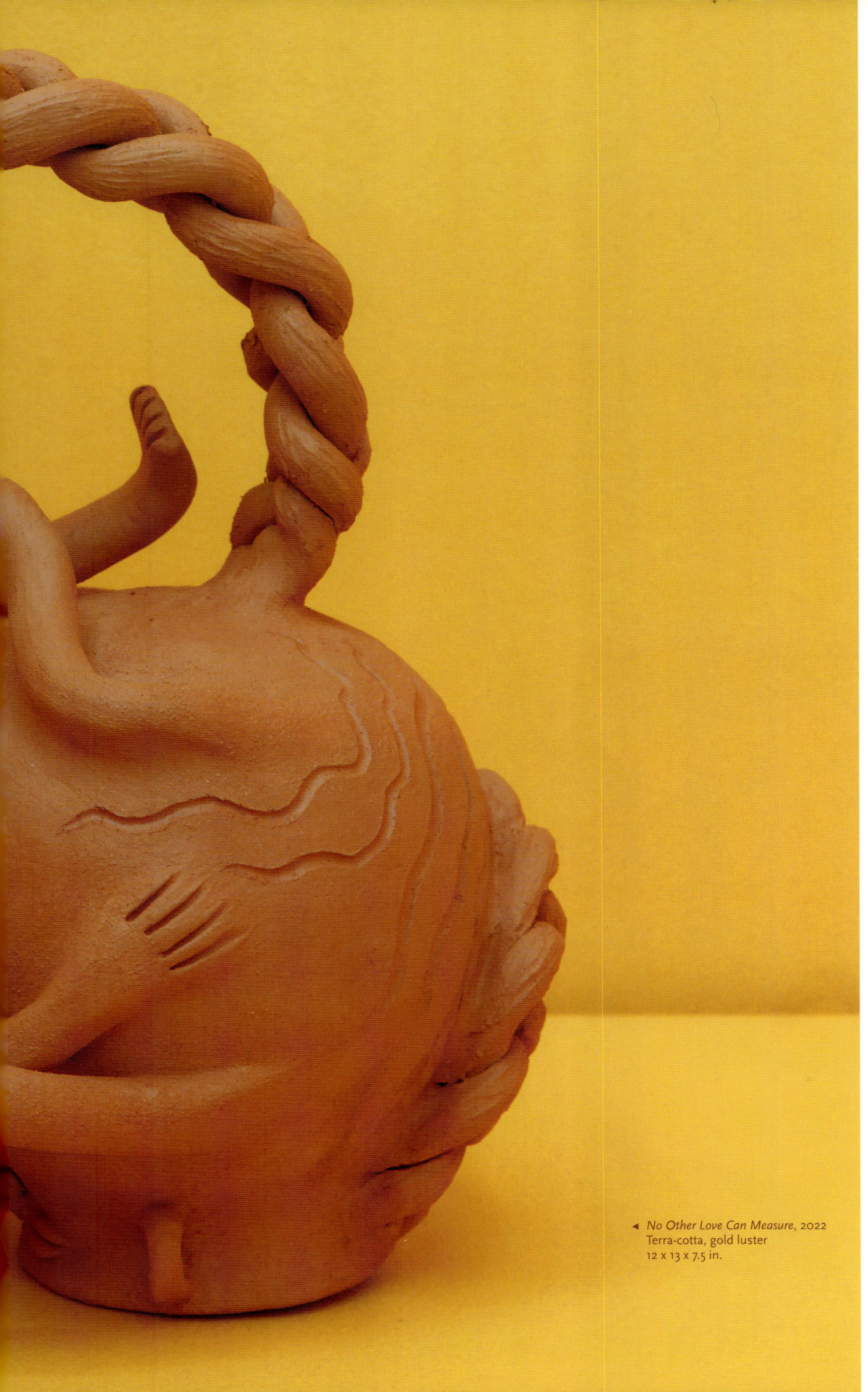

◂ *No Other Love Can Measure*, 2022
Terra-cotta, gold luster
12 x 13 x 7.5 in.

melvino garretti

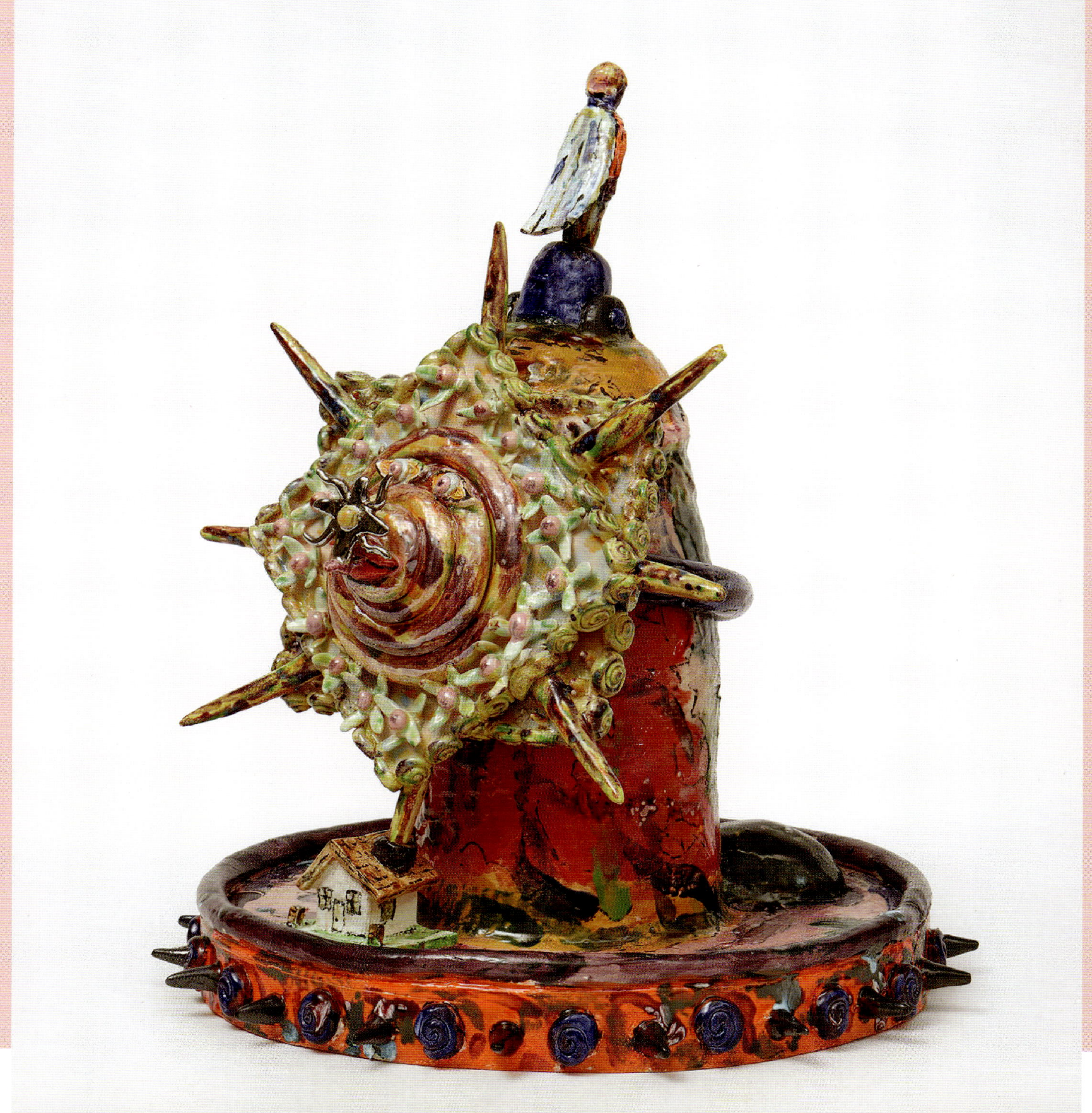

More than an artist, Melvino Garretti (b. 1946, Los Angeles) describes his practice as that of an urban and suburban anthropologist. His work draws on life in the city, his experiences and observations, and history and music. He has always been interested in the ways people reuse and repurpose material.

Garretti grew up in historic South-Central Los Angeles. His first encounters with found art materials came from the fabrics his aunt and grandmother gathered from their laundromat business. They used to make hats for the women at church. Garretti's formal art study began when working with Studio Watts, a pioneering arts-driven collective created to serve the local community in the wake of the Watts Rebellion in 1965. Garretti then went on to focus on ceramics at Great Barrington Pottery in Massachusetts and earned his MFA from the San Francisco Art Institute in 1978.

In the tradition of Garretti's jazz heroes, the experiences of everyday life have served as models for Garretti's ceramic works. Garretti translates the shapes, textures, and idiosyncrasies of found objects into clay. In doing this, narrative scenes emerge and materials take on new meaning and relationships with one another. In *Planet Flowers* (2018), what resembles a ceramic vase with long-stemmed flowers is something other than a functional vessel; the flowers and the vase become one.

Many of Garretti's ceramic works set up a tension between two perspectives: the fact of holding two different things in the same world. The works change as the viewer moves around them. Animals merge with human parts, and appendages extend from the objects as if they were living things continuing to grow. New meaning is revealed as the objects shift with the viewer.

In *Guess There Was Two of You* (2015), two faces are connected through a single column with abstract shapes in their center as a kind of mysterious adhesive. The flatness of the faces resembles masks, conveying abstract emotion. In *A Wonderful Life* (2020), a bear and a human figure fight in a small boxing ring atop the sculpture. The piece is structured as if layers on a cake. The architectural forms become playful and imaginative, at once real and surreal. The circus imagery of abstracted human figures with animals, games, and performance creates a sense of lively chaos tinged with an uneasy feeling conveyed through expressive painterly gestures.

Influenced by his cultural history, Garretti considers the palette and patterns of African masks and textiles. He removes them from a religious context and allows their influence to become more ambient and embedded into the texture of the works themselves. Garretti plays with the tradition of ceramic sculpture, bringing it into a contemporary context and offering breaks in the tradition that might subvert conservative attitudes toward the medium itself. His dynamic glazes give the works a painterly quality. The artist's expressive hand is made visible through his improvised gestures.

About his work in ceramics, Garretti says, "I enjoy being connected with one of the oldest professions on the planet and how the transformation from tribalism to civilization has occurred through this material called clay."[1]

— Gracie Hadland

[1] Melvino Garretti, "Artist Talk: Melvino Garretti," *Art + Practice*, June 15, 2021, https://www.artandpractice.org/public-programs/program/artist-talk-melvino-garretti.

◂ *Mister, The Ring Is Too Big*, 2020
Low-fire ceramic with glazes
16 x 13.5 x 13.5 in.

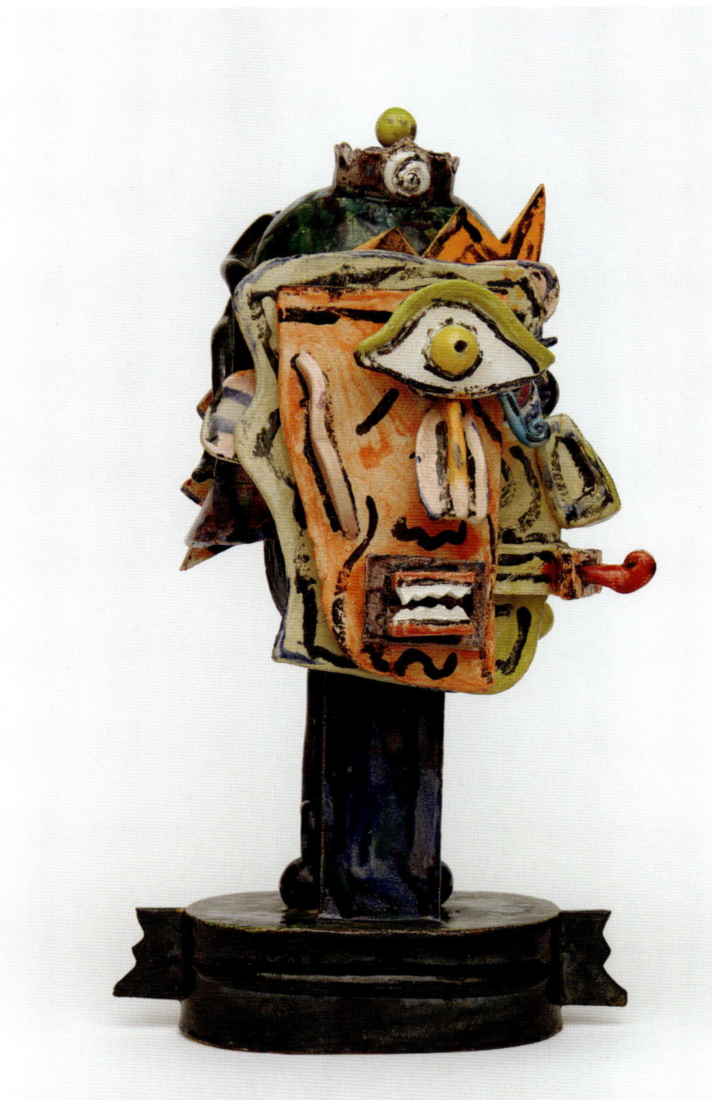

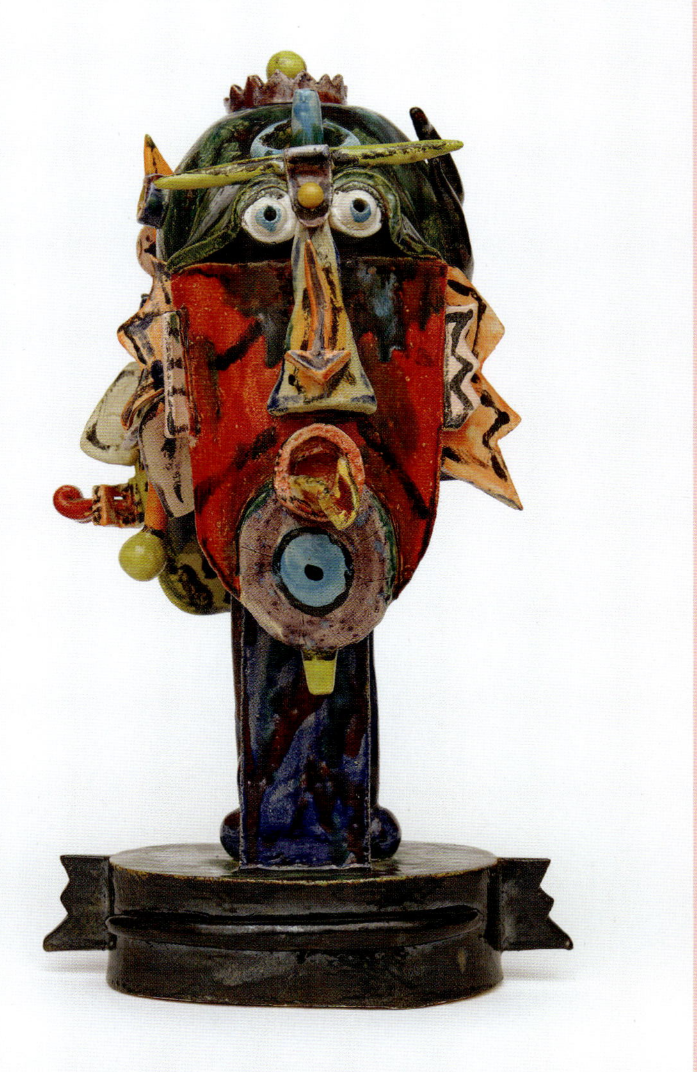

▲ Front and back view of *Guess There Was Two of You*, 2015
Low-fire ceramic with glazes
18.5 x 11 x 12 in.

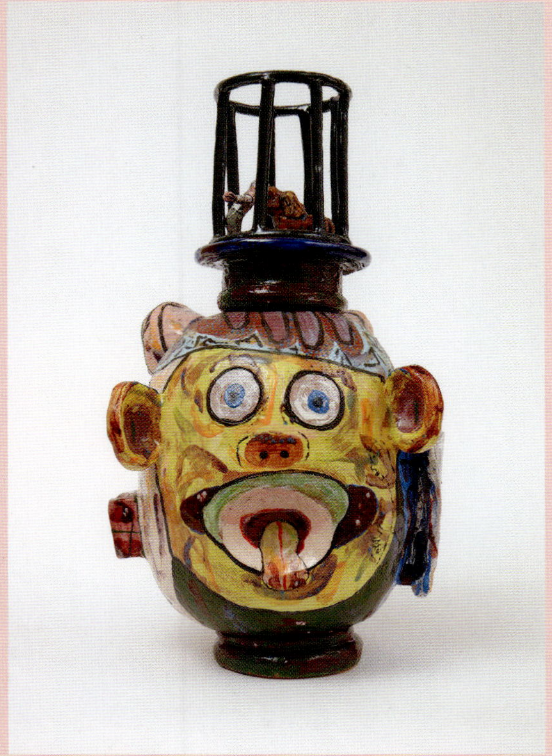

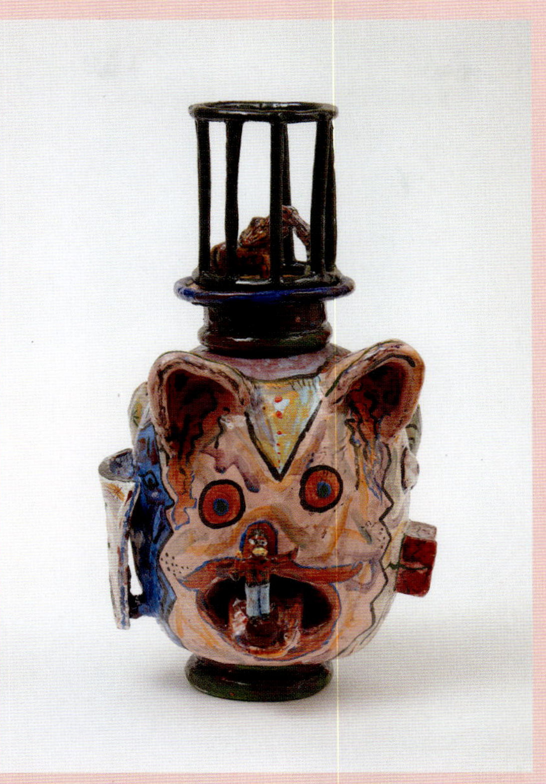

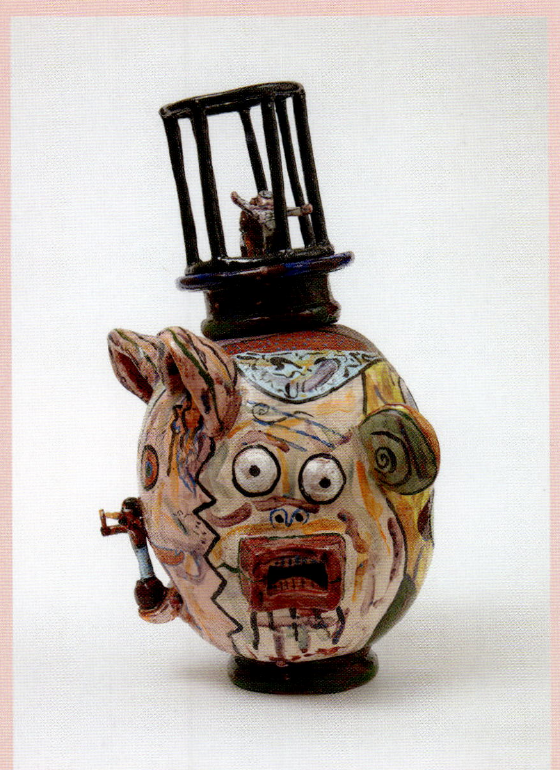

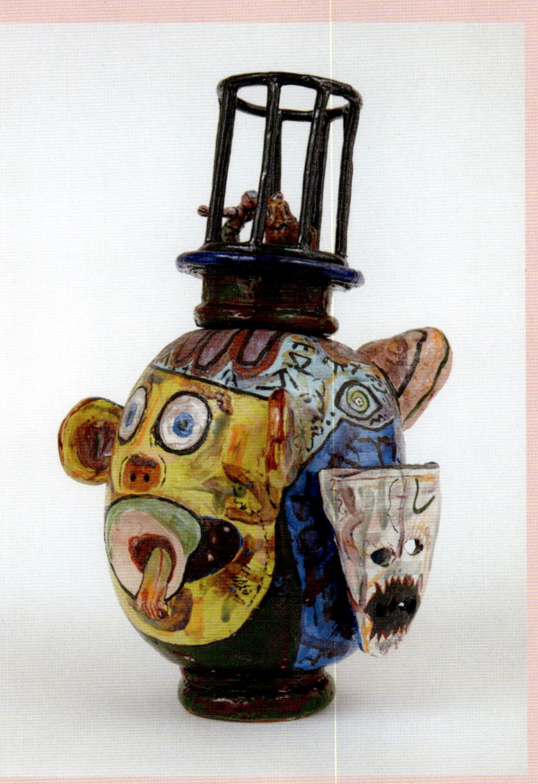

◂ All four sides of *It's Only a Matter of Time...I Haven't Whipped Any Ass Around Here*, 2020
Low-fire ceramic with glazes
17.5 x 10.5 x 10.5 in.

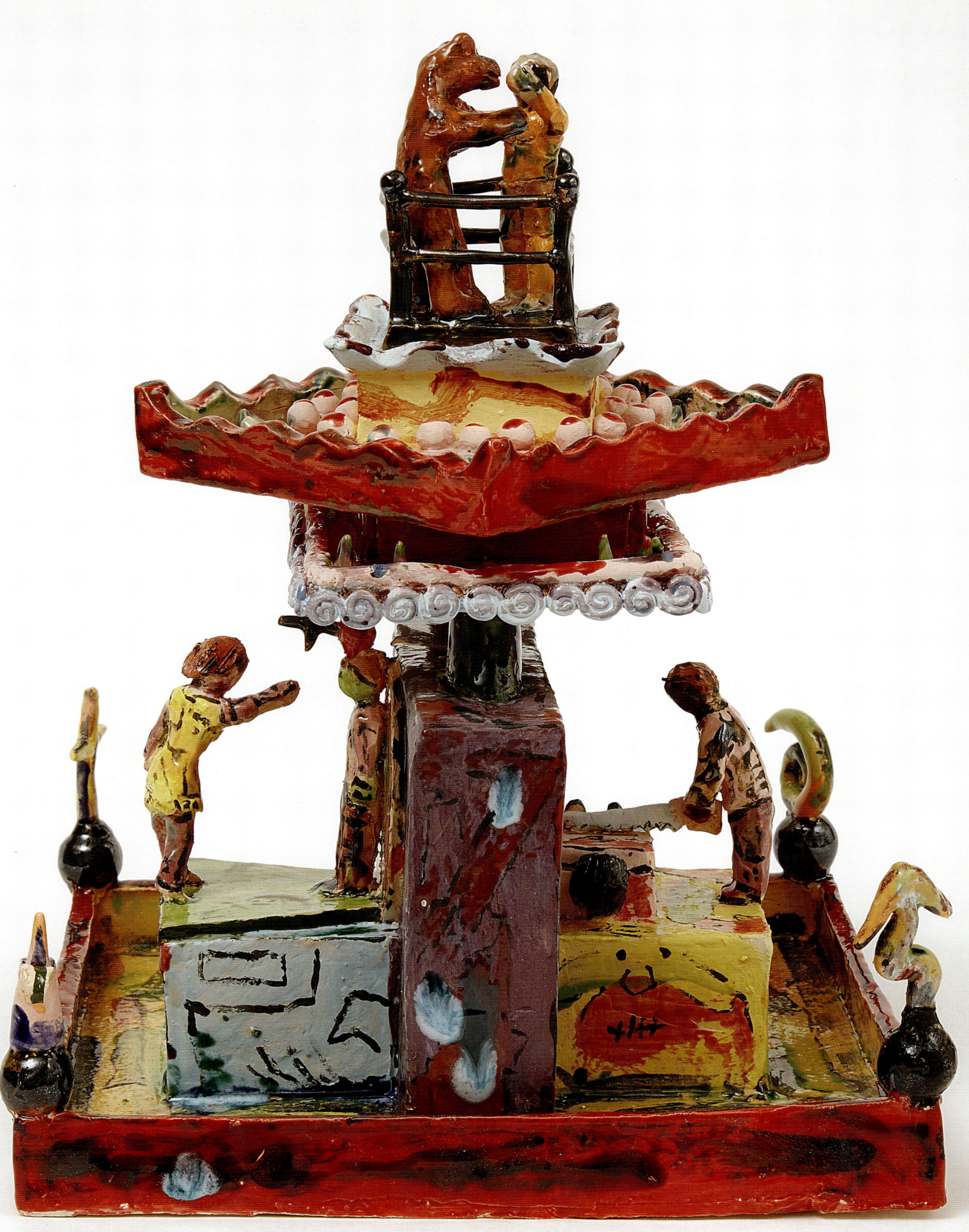

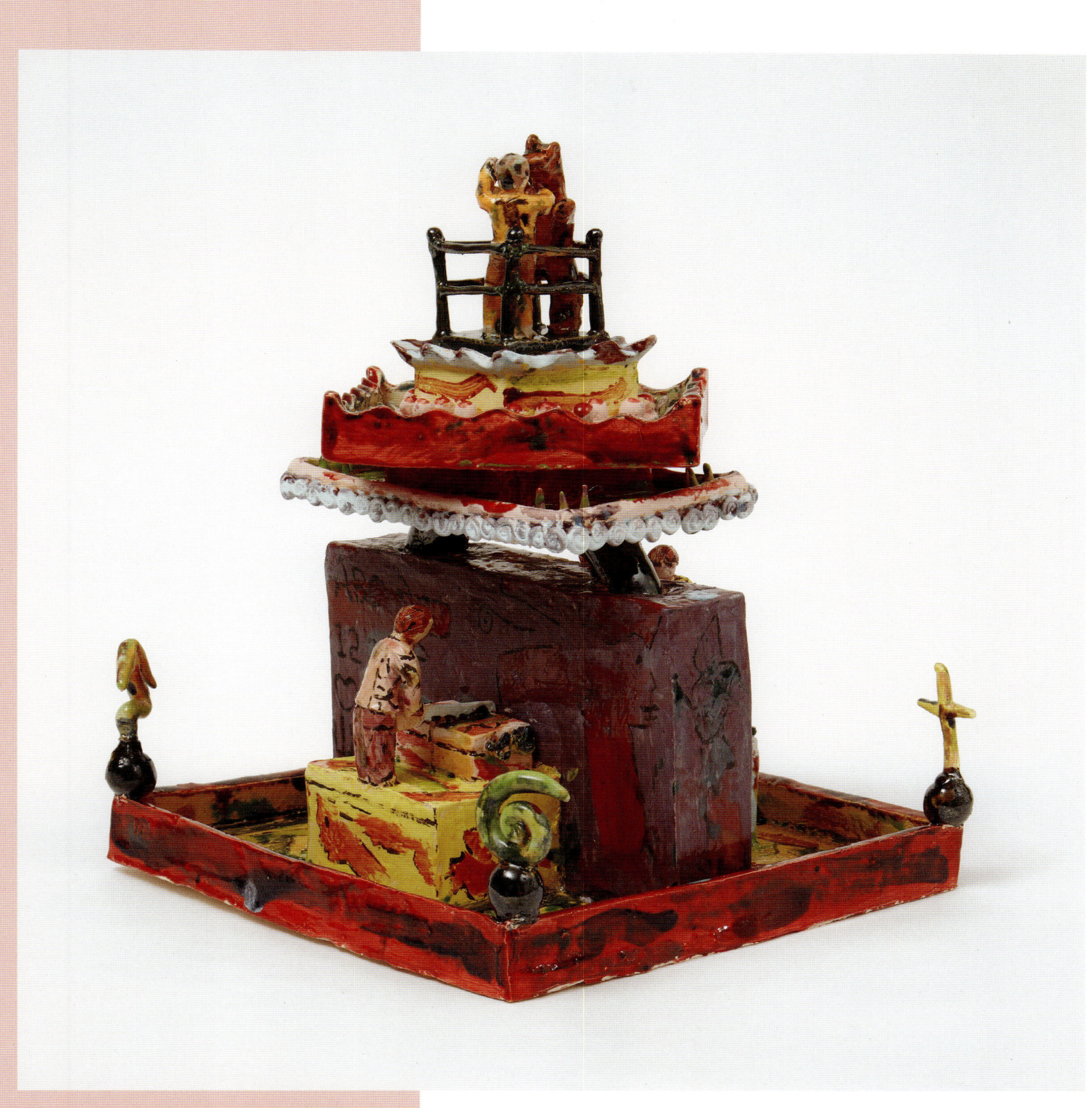

◂ *A Wonderful Life*, 2020
Low-fire ceramic with glazes
11 x 9.5 x 10 in.

raven halfmoon

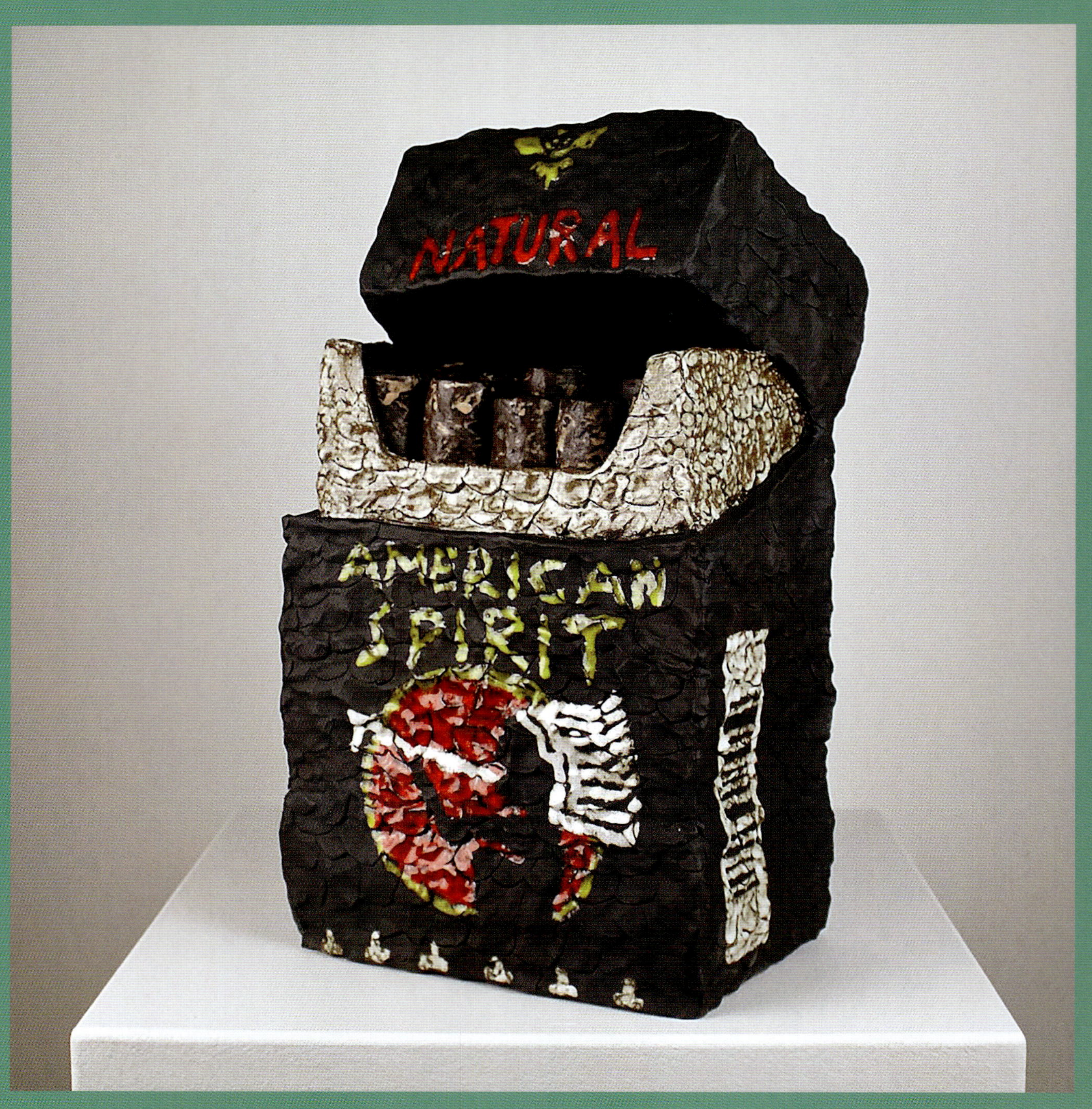

Indigenous artist Raven Halfmoon (b. 1991, Caddo Nation) has had a long love affair with ceramics. She was exposed to the craft when she was a teen living in Norman, Oklahoma.

"My mom took me to see one of our Caddo elders, Jeri Redcorn," Halfmoon says. "She's a phenomenal artist and makes traditional pottery. I remember going to her house, and we made these pots that were just so fun to make. That was my first time handling clay."

Halfmoon later went on to study anthropology, ceramics, and painting, but she found herself increasingly drawn to clay. The material has since become the focus of her work as an artist. Her approach to ceramics pays homage to the traditional work of her ancestors, but it is decidedly more contemporary.

"There's always this entanglement of being a millennial and sharing this history," she explains. "A lot of the figures have a stoic or confrontational face. Being alone in the studio and reading about what happened to our ancestors, it's heavy material."

Halfmoon's most recent work weighs up to 450 pounds and stands almost six feet high. "I've always been drawn to large-scale works," Halfmoon says. "It makes you feel small, and sometimes I think we need moments like that."

Several of Halfmoon's sculptures depict Indigenous women standing side by side. They serve as a representation of the strong Indigenous women in Halfmoon's life. "They represent my grandmother, my mother, and myself," she says. "It represents multiple lineages and generations."

In general, the artist tends to favor creating sculptures of women versus men. "The strongest women I know are Native," she says. "My pieces are very androgynous, though. I don't glaze makeup onto them or give them crazy eyelashes. I'm not worried about making them beautiful. They're meant to be a powerful presence."

Adapted from Christian Allaire, "Indigenous Artist Raven Halfmoon on Interpreting History through Contemporary Sculpture," Vogue, *January 9, 2021, https://www.vogue.com/article/raven-halfmoon-exhibition*

— Christian Allaire

◂ *I Only Smoke When I Drink*, 2017
Glazed stoneware
18 x 14 x 10 in.

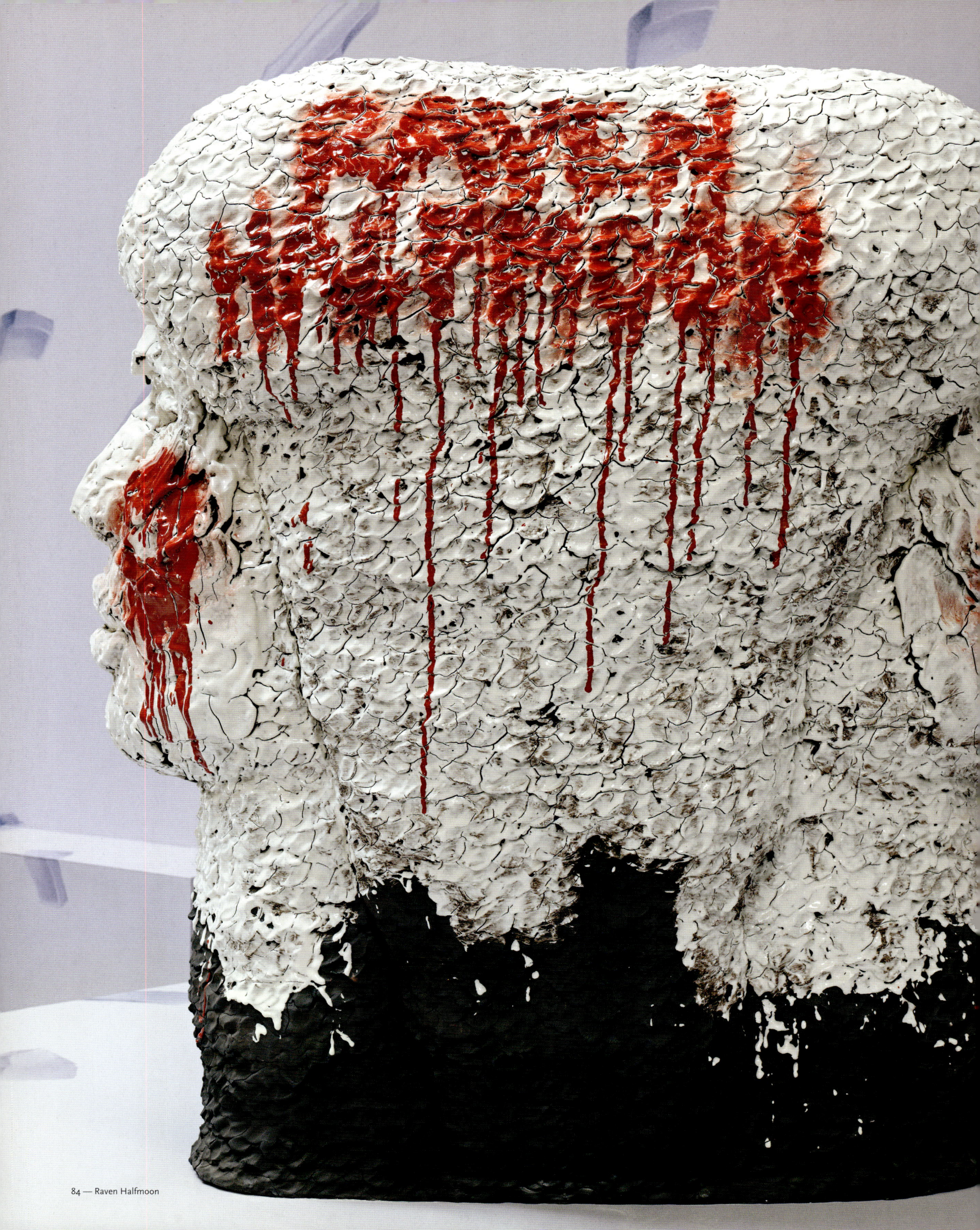

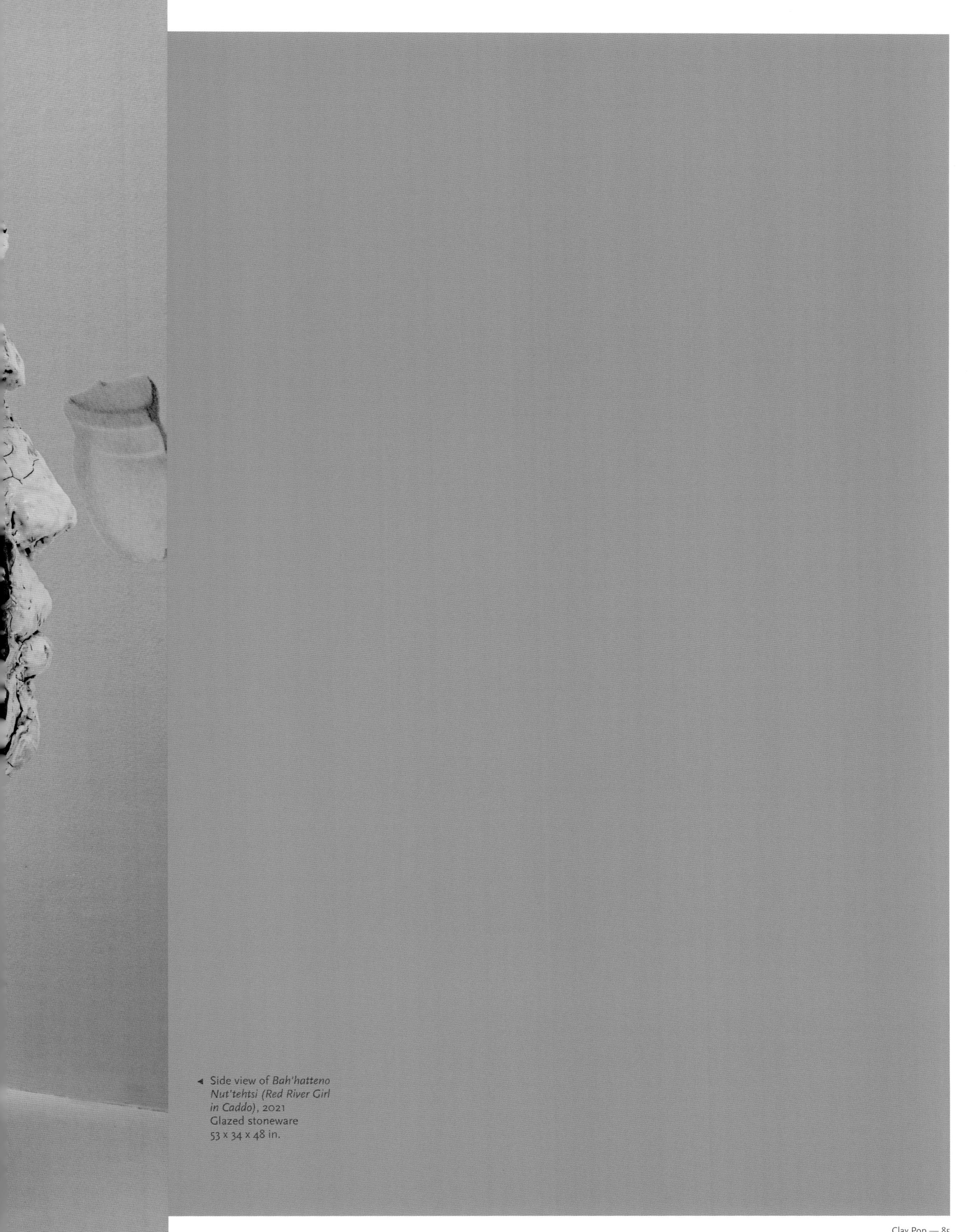

◄ Side view of *Bah'hatteno Nut'tehtsi (Red River Girl in Caddo)*, 2021
Glazed stoneware
53 x 34 x 48 in.

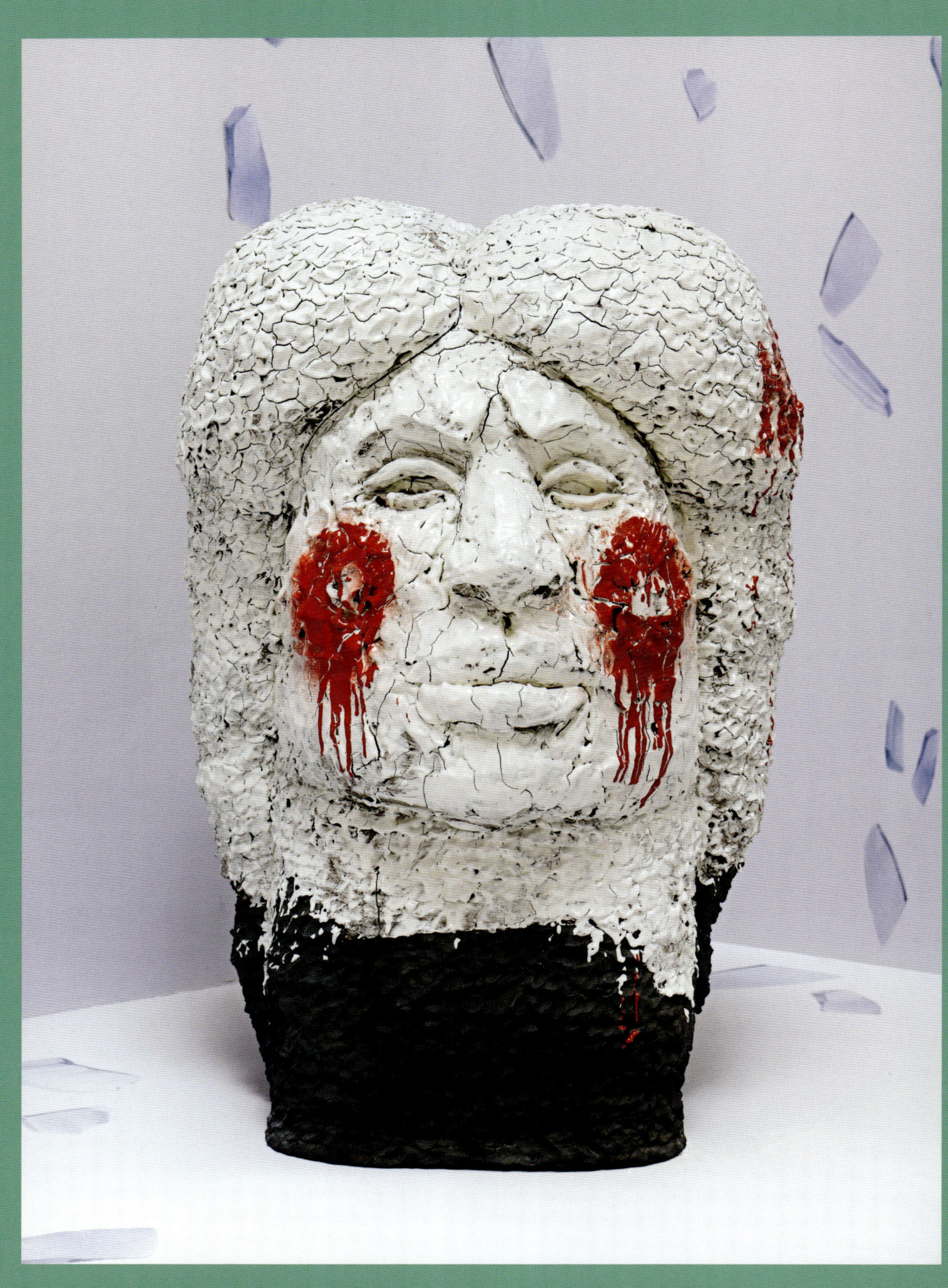

▲ Front view of *Bah'hatteno Nut'tehtsi (Red River Girl in Caddo)*, 2021
Glazed stoneware
53 x 34 x 48 in.

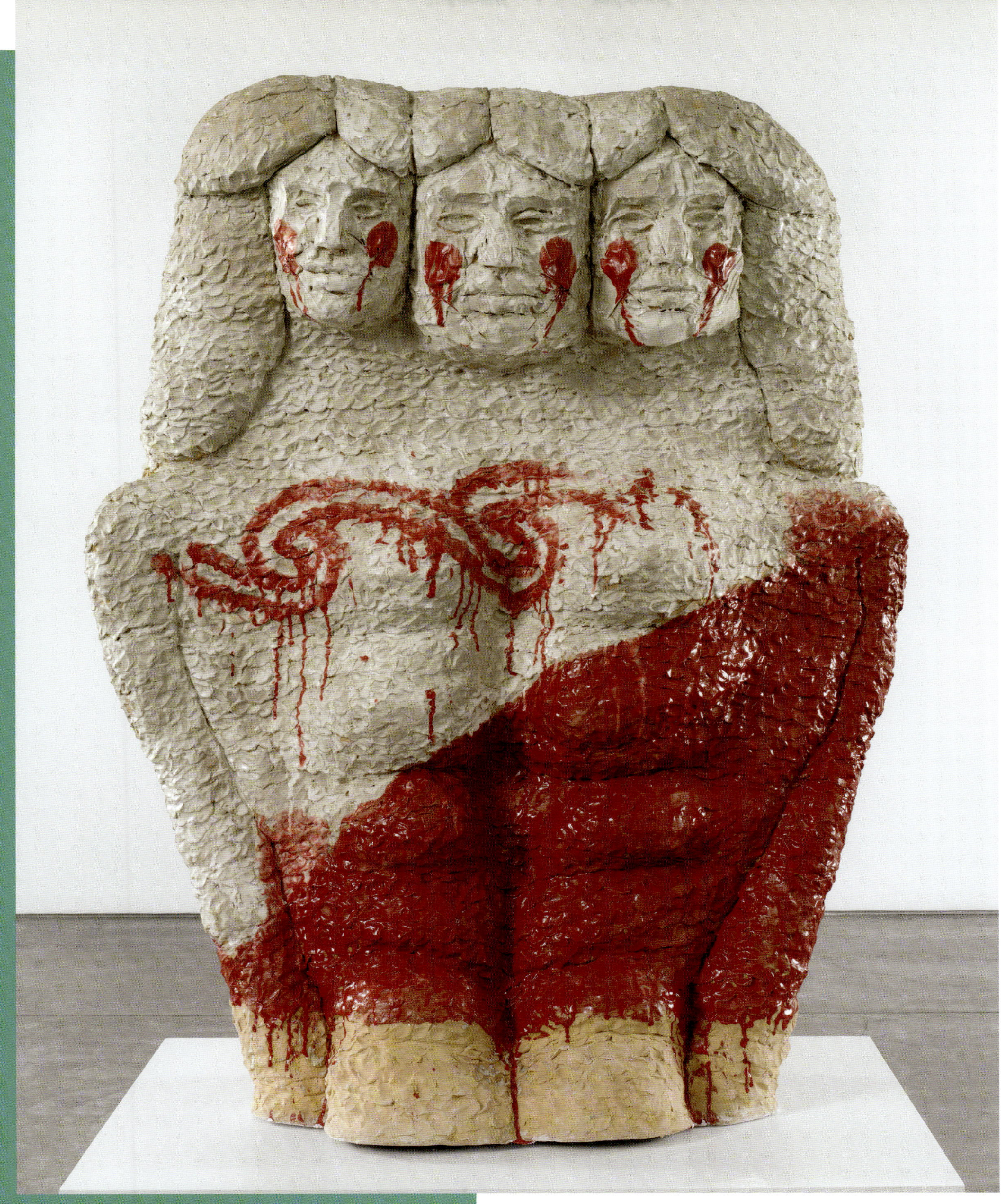

▲ *Hey'-en, Ina, Ika*, 2020
Glazed stoneware
58 x 48.5 x 19 in.

stephanie temmahier

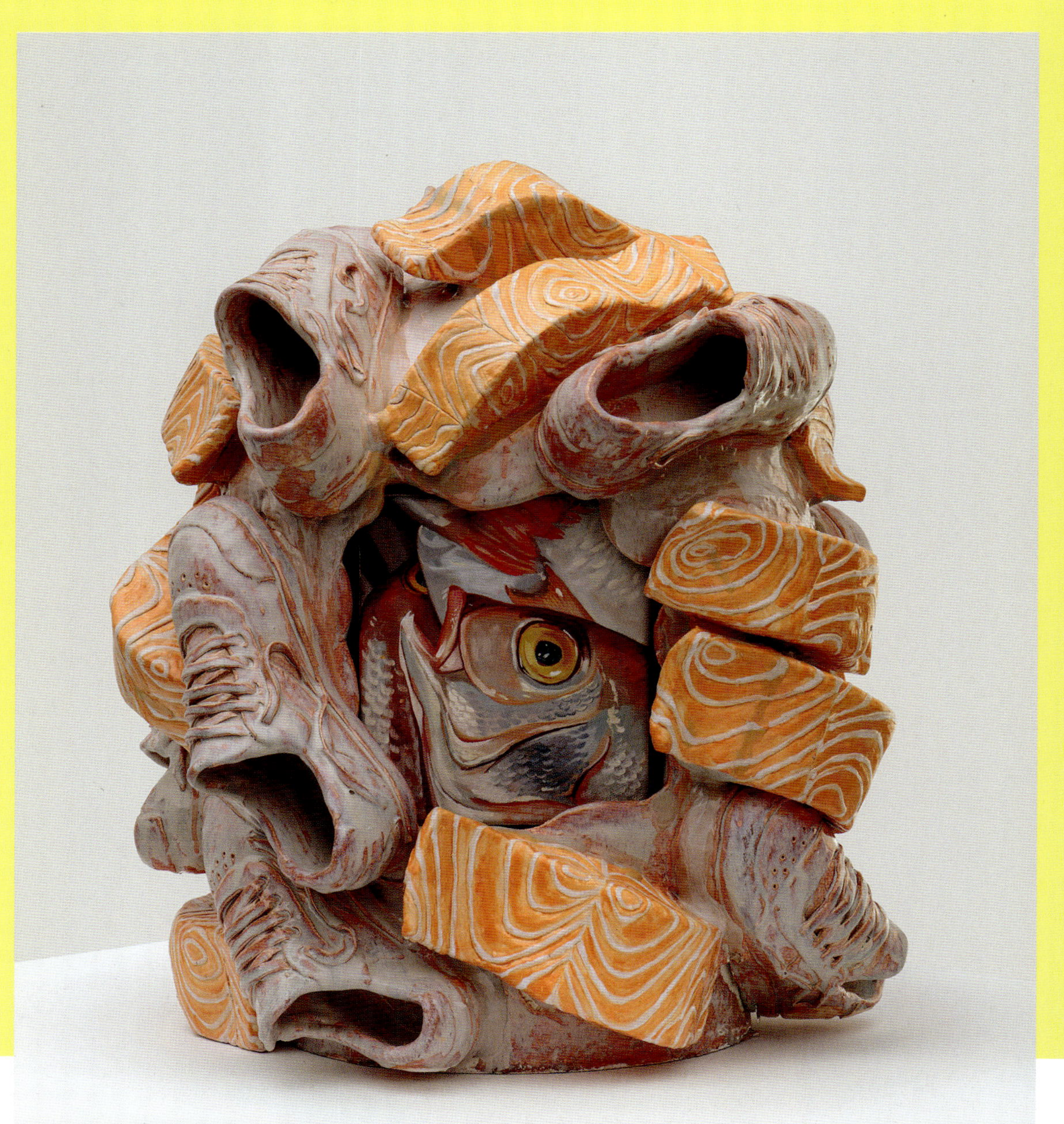

Stephanie Temma Hier (b. 1992, Toronto) is galvanized by working with clay, which is how her artistic process—a composite of painting and sculpture—ordinarily begins. There are innumerable tiny details in her work. Trained from a young age in painted figuration, Hier has developed a strong visual language that includes quirky and unsettling mise-en-scenes of food and wildlife in a style that recalls the Dutch Renaissance. Although her painted canvases are compositionally sophisticated, these elaborate scenes have found their fullest expression with the incorporation of sculptural ceramic into her practice.

Hier crowds her works with the accoutrements of the still life: fruits and vegetables, opulent table settings, assorted meats, and heady blooms. It seems possible to visually gorge oneself on such a toothsome array, although her unusual arrangements are not intended to whet the appetite.

Dismembered body parts, like hands and feet, are also a common motif in her work. Hier is interested in quotidian objects and psychoanalysis, and delights in recontextualizing the detritus of ordinary life to produce a disquieting cognitive dissonance. She welcomes the material that surfaces from the unconscious mind and, in a free associative manner, links seemingly unrelated images to expose veiled meanings or subconscious thoughts: cuts of fish pair with lumpy sneakers; ears sprout in mycelial clusters; hungry fledglings raise their expectant beaks between the unfurling leaves of a cabbage; a wall of asparagus hedges a four-tier cake made of sandwiches on brown bread, topped with a ring of prawns and a courgette rose.

Much of Hier's ceramic work is representational, matching color, form, and texture to a real-life counterpart in uncanny mimesis. Some sport monochrome glazes, further dissociating the objects that she renders from an authentic original to likewise undermine cognitive reason.

For Hier, integrating ceramic into her practice has re-enchanted painting. Her sculptures are capacious, not only because they contain flat canvas within their three dimensions, encircling painted surface with glaze and fired clay—though the stoneware sculptures are neither frames nor secondary to her painted works—but also because the use of ceramic has broadened the conceptual possibilities of her practice. The medium has liberated representational painting from its formalism, permitting Hier a greater degree of technical and conceptual experimentation than figurative painting typically allows. Just as in painting, however, working with ceramic requires scrupulous precision. It is a science that she approaches like a chemist, with careful notes and testing. Ceramics is nevertheless impossible to fully control, and thus possesses an unavoidable element of chance that is fittingly an excellent opportunity for the artist to follow her instinctual drive.

— Sarah Messerschmidt

◄ *Often Seen at Sunset*, 2021
Oil on linen with glazed
stoneware sculpture
27 x 23 x 26 in.

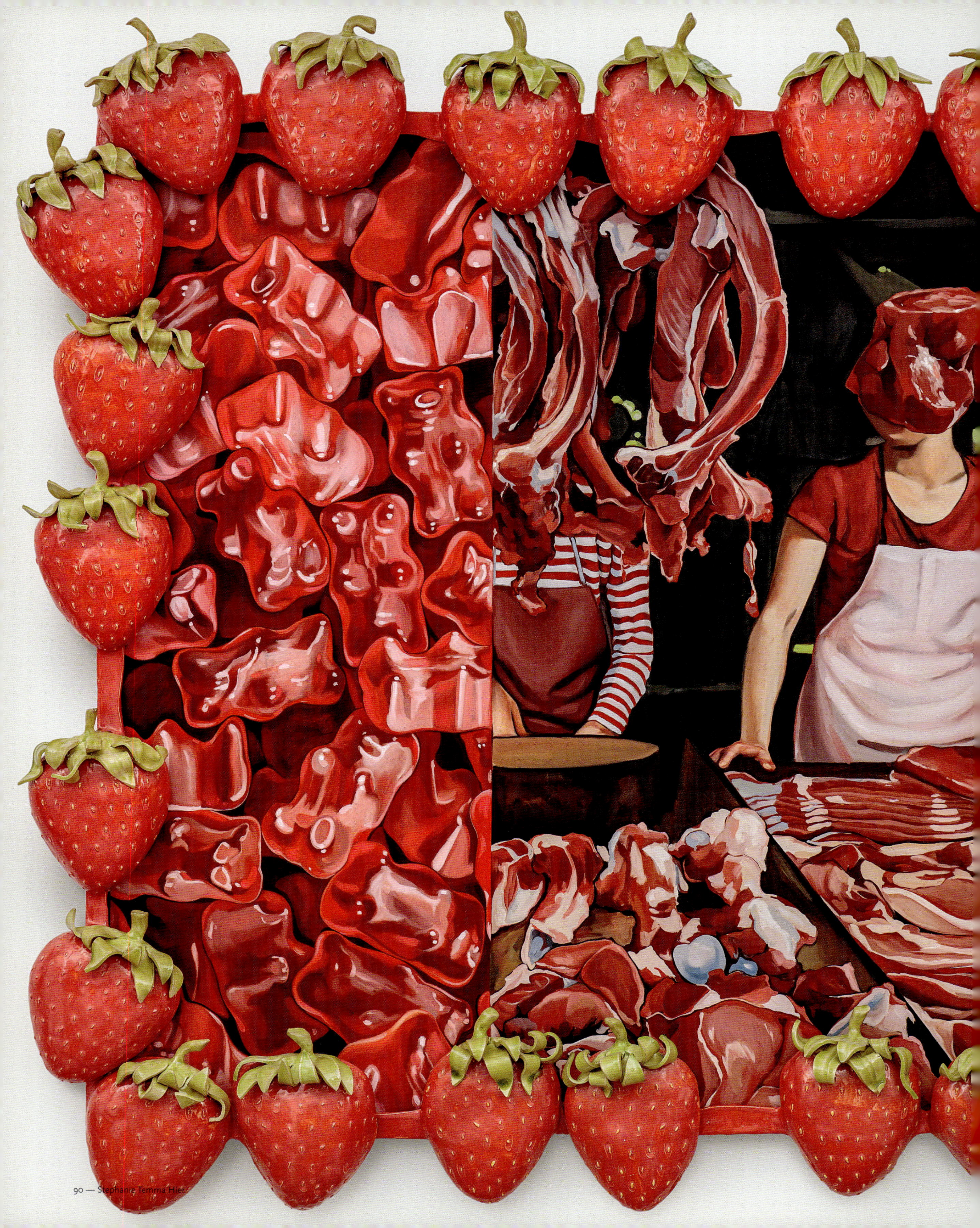

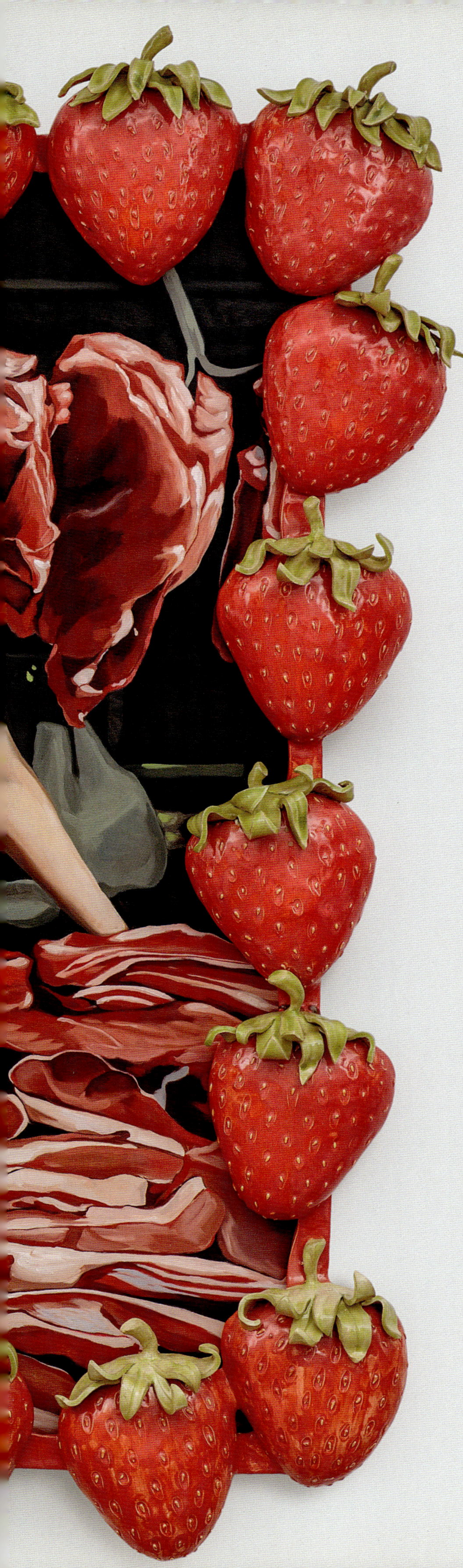

◂ *Sparks and Tremors*, 2021
Oil on linen with glazed
stoneware sculpture
73 x 83 x 7.5 in.

▾ *Take the Butcher's Advice*, 2021
Oil on linen with glazed
stoneware sculpture
41 x 41 x 27 in.

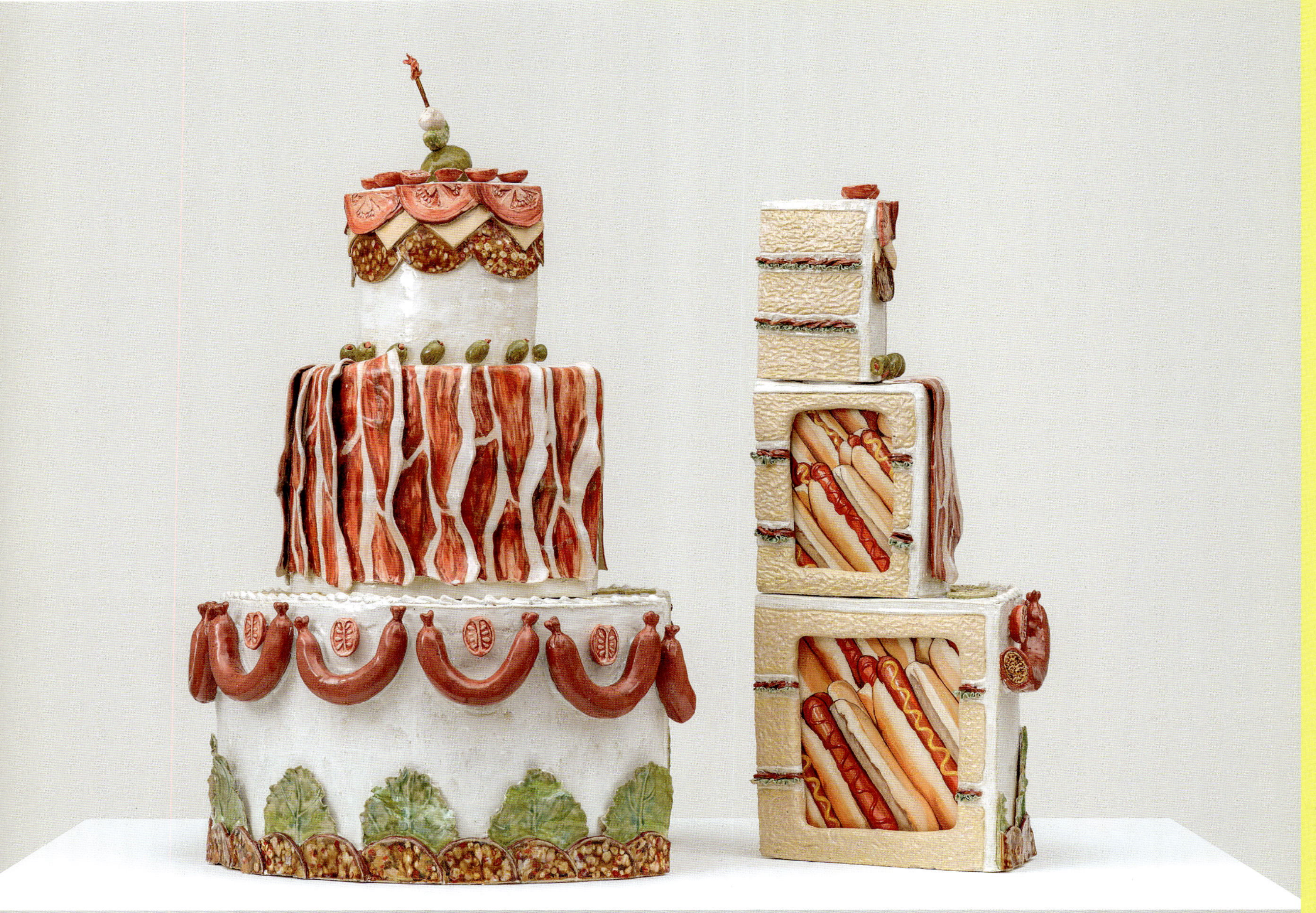

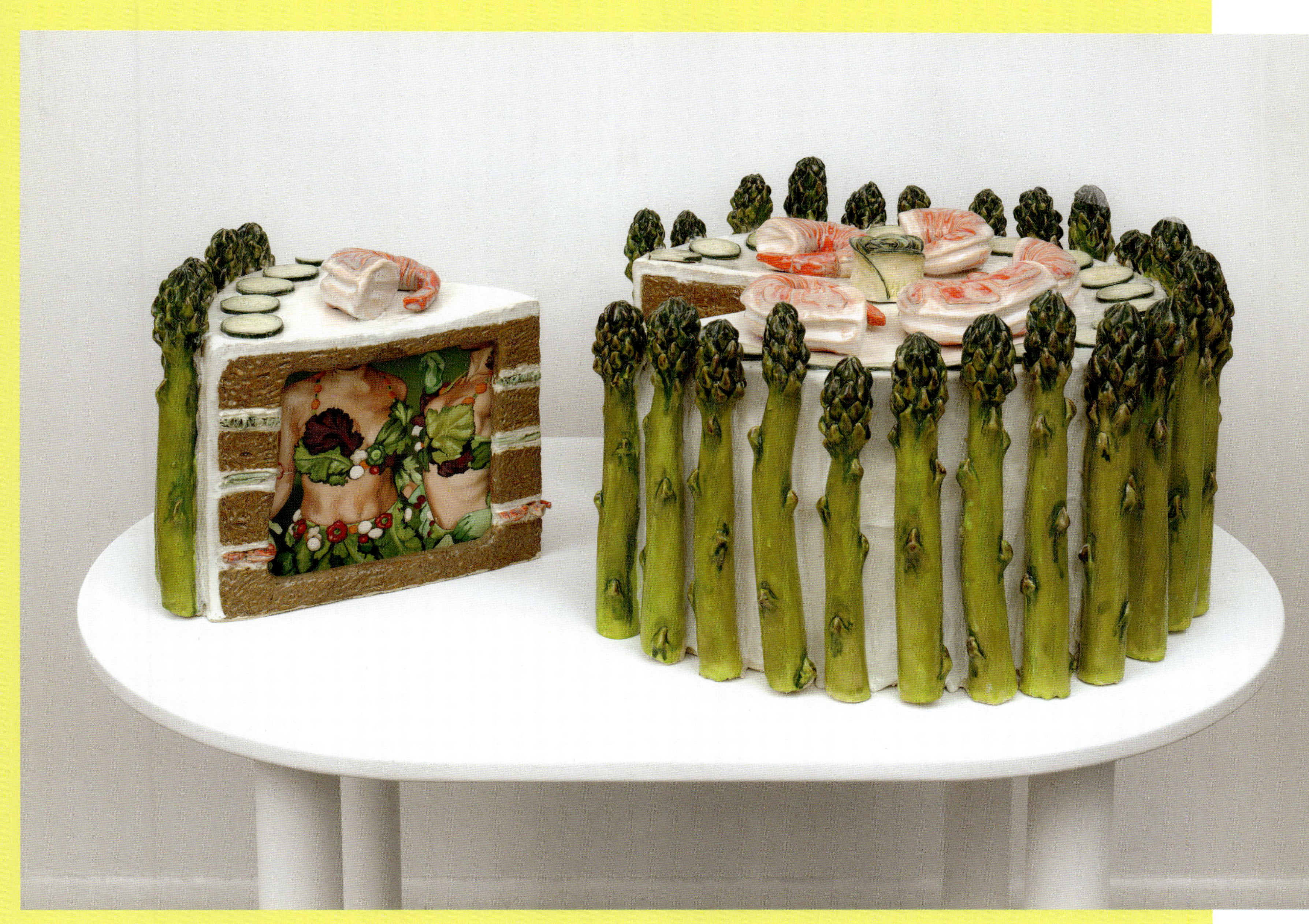

▲ *Real Food for Pretend Chefs*, 2021
Oil on linen with glazed
stoneware sculpture
39 x 36 x 14 in.

kahlil robert irving

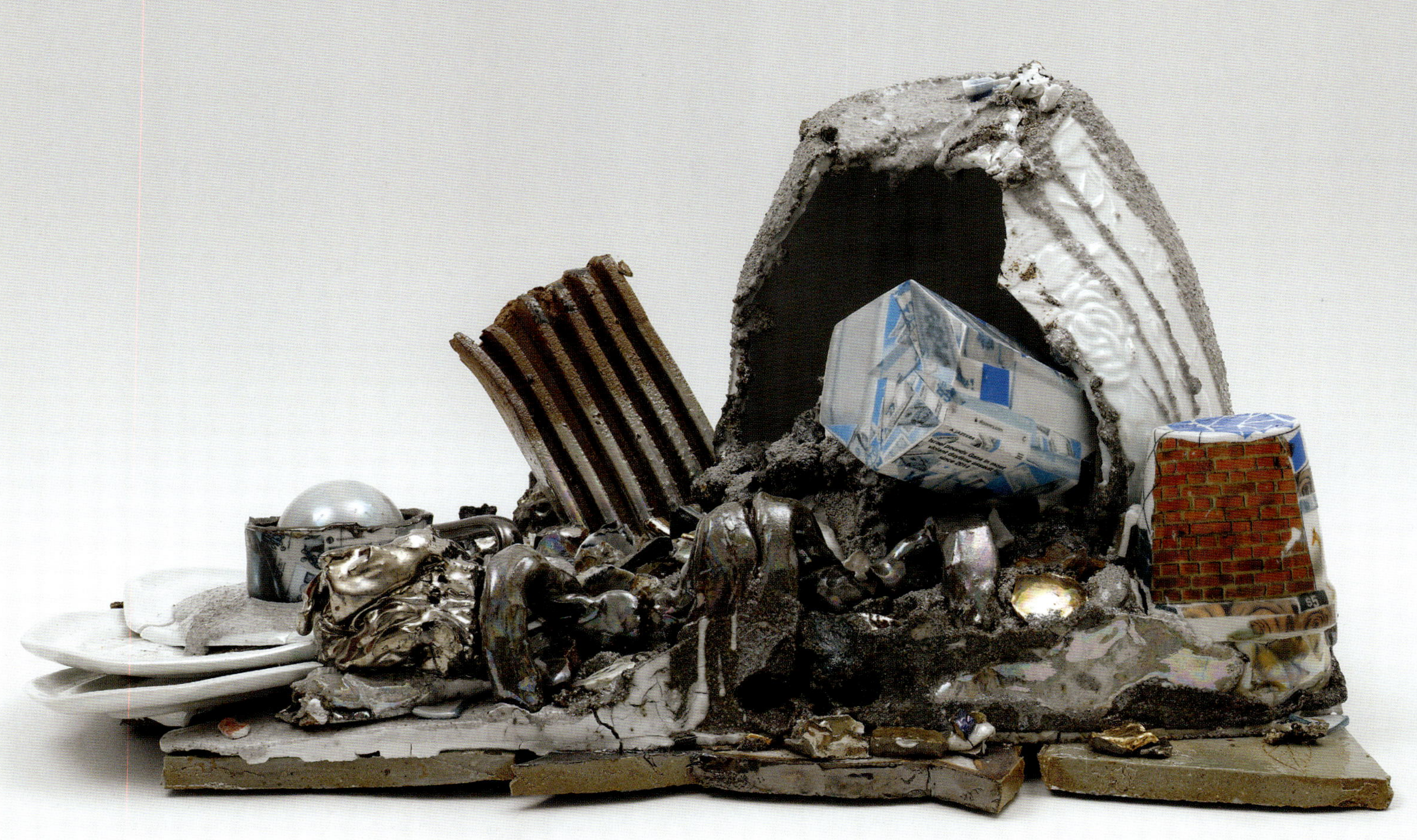

The nontraditional practice of Kahlil Robert Irving (b. 1992, San Diego) mashes collage, painting, pottery, and sculpture together. Irving combines all four to talk about the current moment, the past, and the fleeting future that we see passing between our fingers when using the phone or computer. Irving wants to reference as much as possible that so much can be missed when we are focused on using digital technology.

Irving has a dynamic and ever-evolving relationship to ceramics. Trained as a potter and now working primarily in sculpture, he utilizes clay and its associated techniques to navigate the contested historical terrain of ceramics, architecture, and technology. In each sculptural assemblage, objects are combined to present parts of everyday life and images that are from the digital space of constant motion, rendered still. The goal of the work is not always legible or present and possibly nonexistent. The plausibility of these trompe l'oeil objects demonstrates the mastery of his craft and the impact of manufacturing, labor, and the complicated histories that we inherit living in this life. Like much of Irving's work, the re-presenting of objects is complicating the inherited expectation of material representation by addressing histories of colonialism, cultural appropriation, and their aftermaths. Many sculptures make reference to the inner-city streets by recalling the materiality of the ground as a rich site for materials. Irving also recognizes the function of the street as a place of exchange and commerce and, ultimately, a witness to and catalyst of Black resistance.

The social media posts embedded in Irving's work reference celebratory and complex gatherings of people, the architecture of the internet, and ambiguous screenshots from Irving's social media as a way to present a feedback loop of information that allows for many entry points into the work. However, they do not always tell you the way to decipher the code embedded in the work. This is a way to keep the viewer busy. The focus ranges from historical decorative objects and architectural ornamentation to contemporary meme and technoculture. Irving uses ceramics as a long exposure of materials to capture a collage of contemporary life. Segregation and access demark social privileges, and within Irving's sculptures that information is collapsed and presented equally with gilt and grit.

— Written and edited between the artist and several colleagues

◄ Blue scale | {through the ages up to now/ **memes** ^memories), 2018
Glazed and unglazed stoneware and porcelain, grog, found vintage decals, personally constructed decals (screenshots, memes), black luster, gold luster, silver luster, opal luster, red enamel, gilded pyrometric cones
16 x 24 x 12 in.

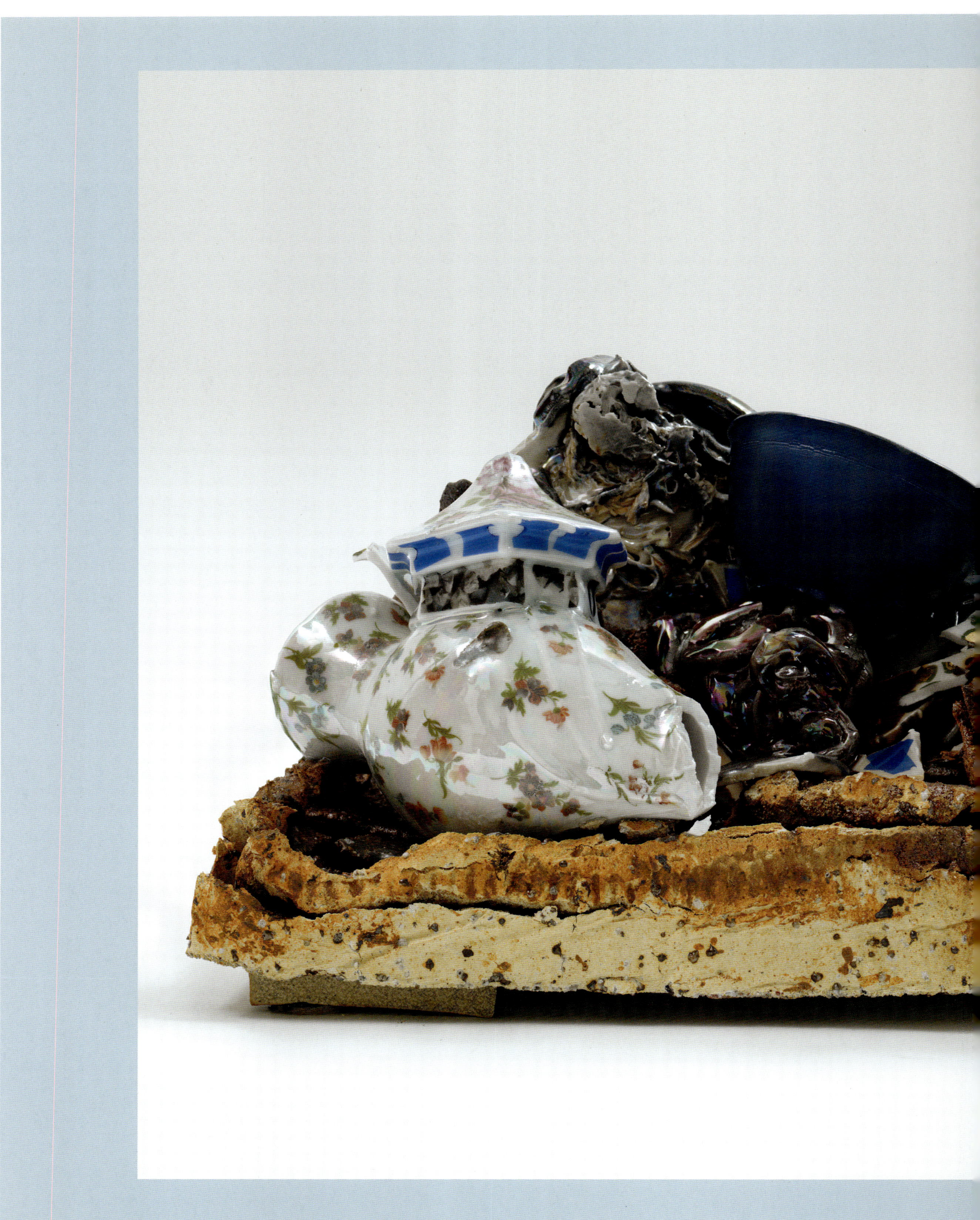

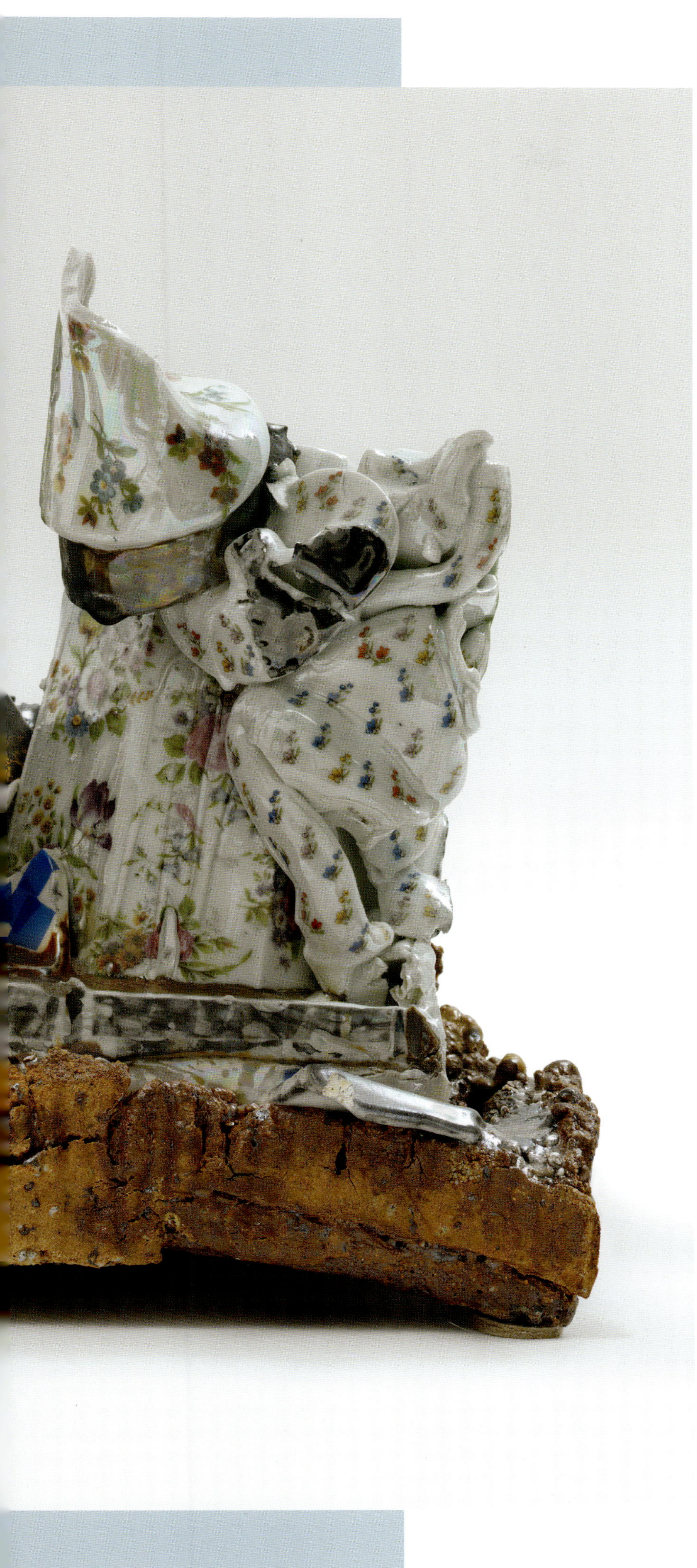

◂ Mix & Match (*PAST (Patterns) MeisseN \ MATTER = collage), 2018
Glazed and unglazed ceramic, found vintage decals, personally constructed decals, luster, gilded pyrometric cones, cone packs
15 x 19 x 12 in.

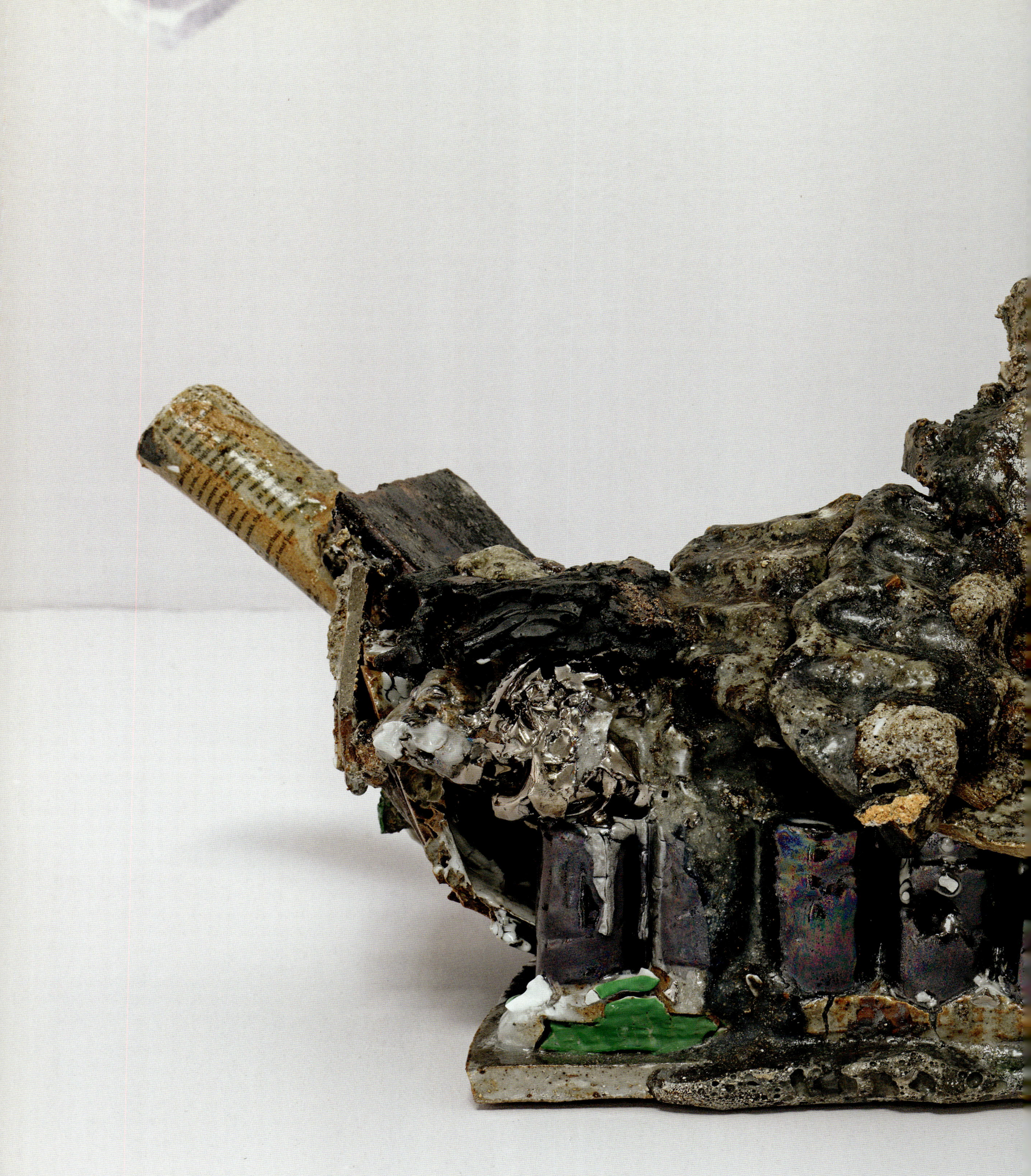

◂ **Rows / Columns:** Daily NEWS of DAILY LAW and LIFE - *(text vase)*, 2018
Glazed and unglazed ceramic, luster, found decals, personally constructed decals
11 x 23 x 11 in.

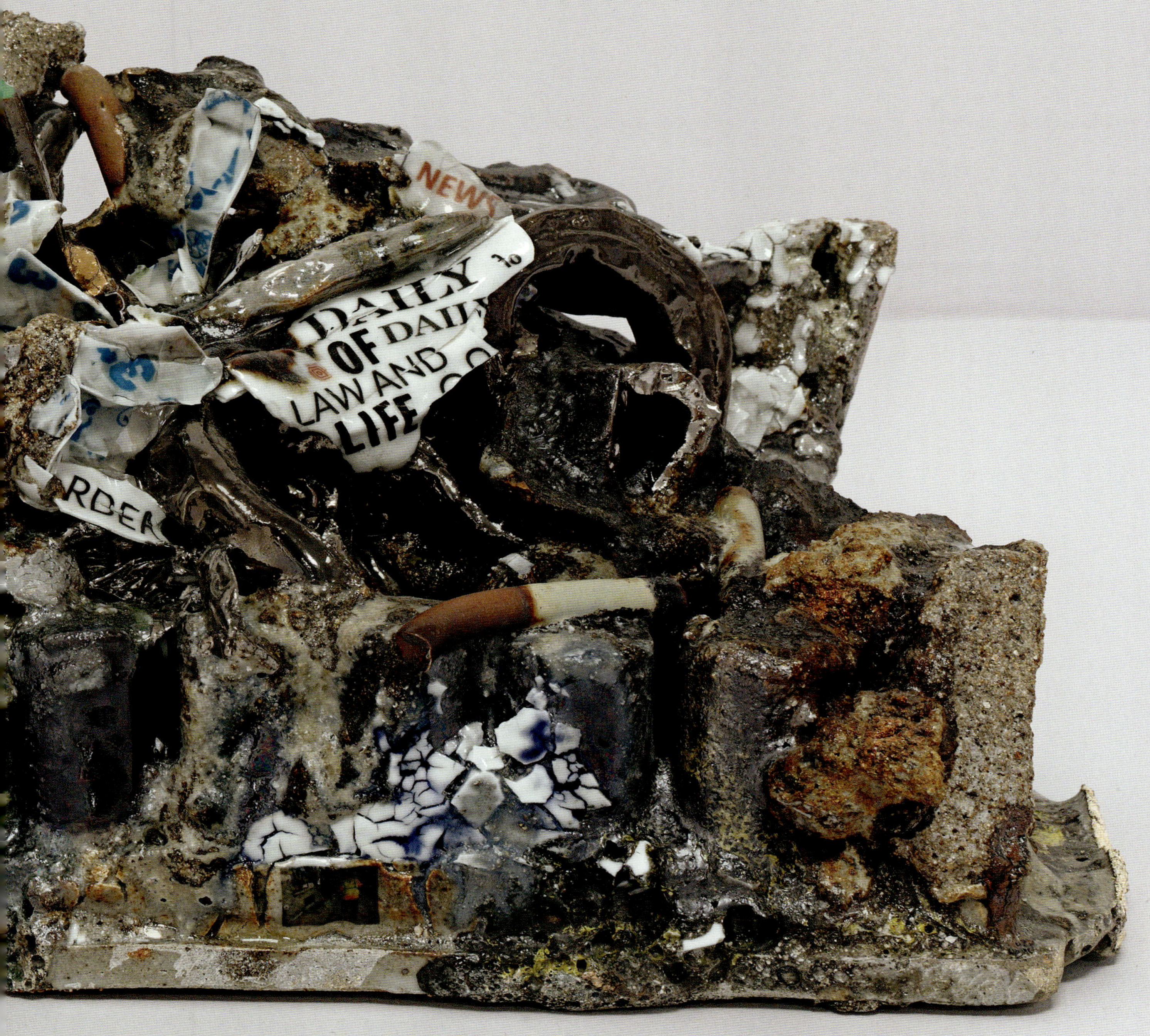

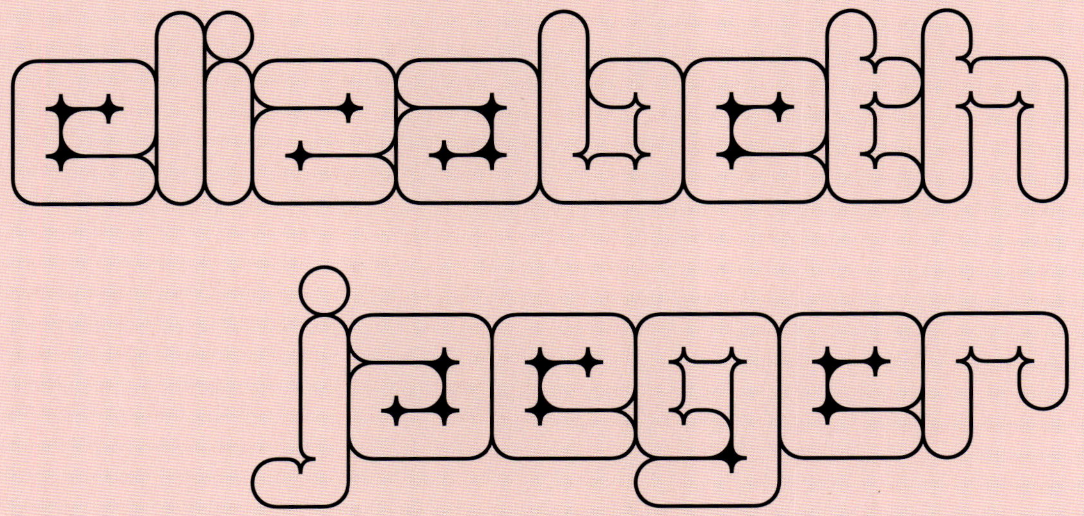
elizabeth
jaeger

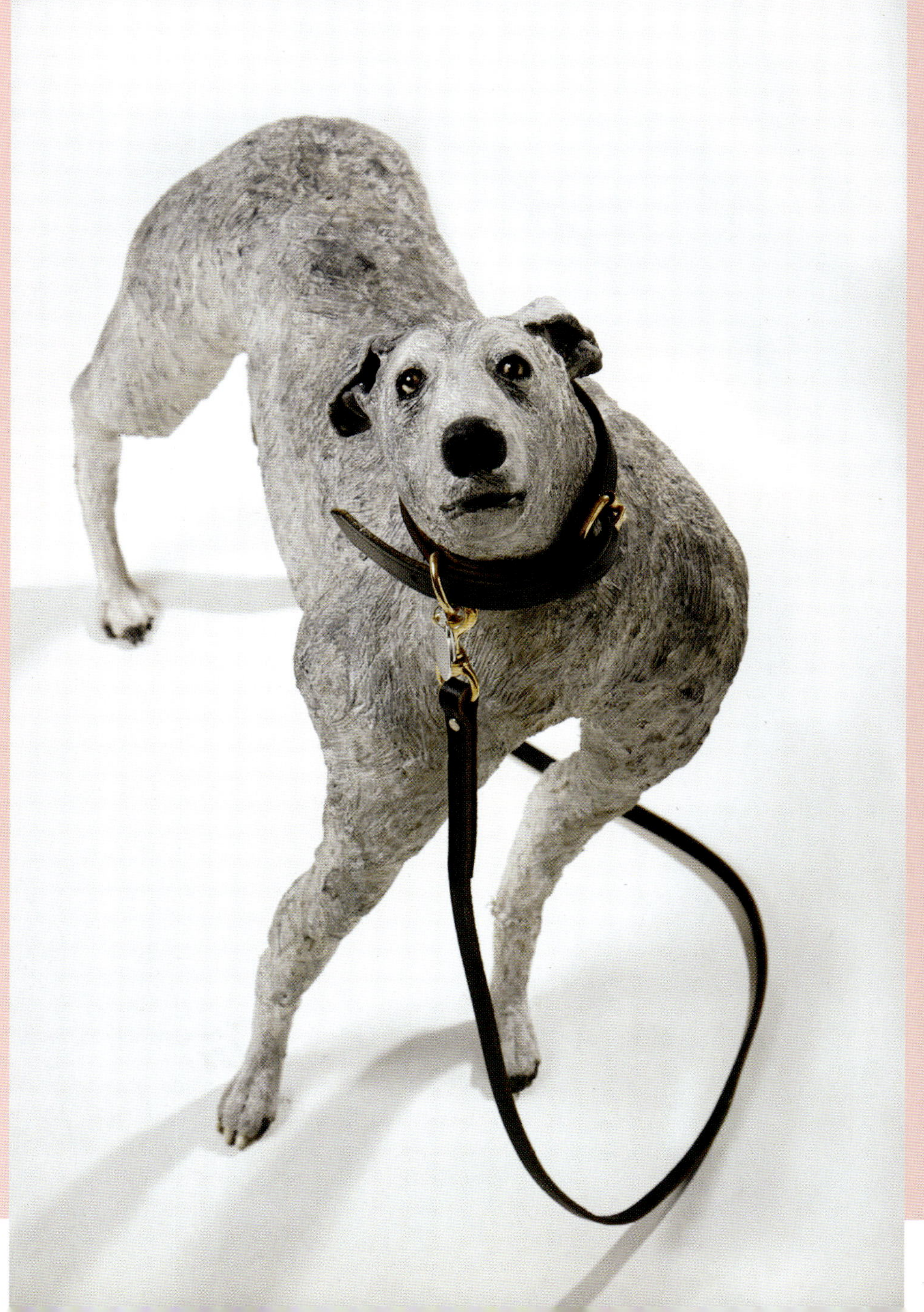

The work of Elizabeth Jaeger (b. 1988, San Francisco) explores the perceptual and psychological implications of sculptural space, engaging the unconscious processes of the imaginary through enigmatic objects whose uncanny presence recalibrates both their surrounding environment and the conditions of their viewing. Jaeger's use of blackened clay renders this transformation in material terms. Each object holds the traces of its transition from wet, like impasto, to firm—pliable and denser—to a hard surface that can be carved and then lightly sanded when bone-dry. The resulting ambiguity of form, shifting between objecthood and flatness, transforms each sculpture into an open dynamic field, creating space for multiple readings.

In *Siren* (2021), a tall bird sits on an elongated, blackened steel perch rising out of a thick spiral of black clay on the floor. In Greek mythology, the siren, which is half bird and half woman, lured sailors to their deaths by enticing ships onto the rocks with her song. The song latent in this silent bird, poised above a watery vortex, invokes not only the male fear and desire inherent in patriarchal readings of the female subject but, more broadly, the looming deathly consequences of ecological collapse.

In Jaeger's most recent body of work, a taxonomy of black clay vessels and bowls of varying sizes hang, float, or rest on thin shelves or steplike forms attached to the surface of seven large, blackened-steel rectangles hung from two walls of the gallery in compositional sequences resembling interior psychic diagrams, or the flow of musical notes across a score. The optical fusion of each vessel with the blackened surface of its steel support sublimates the industrial modernist logic of the rectilinear metal forms into a painterly grisaille that appears as alternately flat and volumetric. This destabilizing of both the painterly and sculptural gestalt is increased by a faint aura of pale-yellow light emanating from behind each rectangle from its yellow-painted back, both diffusing and emphasizing its three-dimensionality in relation to the wall.

In this continual alteration of our perception, each panel generates an image of itself in space almost like a shadow, introducing a temporality that is both corporeal and architectural in its projective cast. The dark silhouettes both flatten and intensify their volumetric forms—the absence of light gradually revealing subtle details that appear as the viewers come close to the sculpture and their eyes adjust. The narrow shape of the first panel appears like a sliver or void out of which a vertical row of metal shelves appears, holding an ascending sequence of black clay vessels, whose size and shape determine the height of, and intervals between, each shelf. The language of industrial modernity—serial production, repetition, standardization, the mechanized cut—is internalized and transformed into a symbolic space that also holds the quietly assertive presence of larger anthropomorphic vessels that evoke the body.

These corporeal forms—elongated amphorae with absurdly extended handles, necks, rims, bellies, and sloping shoulders whose surface holds the trace of the artist's fingers—introduce a sensual tactility that has five aspects: archaeological, anthropomorphic, musical, filmic, and domestic. A group of three, rendered in black clay soaked in black ink and placed one above the other on the second narrow panel—one suspended from its neck by a cut-out gap in an open box—read as archaeological specimens doubly decontextualized, first by Jaeger's extension of their handles into curved shapes that drape across and loop into each vessel's mouth, and then by the sublimation of that erotic gesture into a larger composition whose rectilinear framing and grisaille flatten the vessels

◂ *Jimmy (Dog 1)*, 2014
Ceramic, Hydrocal, loose graphite, paint, leather, brass printed tag with dog name from owner
31 x 34 x 12 in.

[1] Edward Olszewski, "Distortions, Shadows and Conventions in Sixteenth Century Italian Art," *Artibus et Historiae* 6, no. 11 (1986): 101.

[2] Briony Fer, "Eva Hesse and Color," *October* 119 (Winter 2007): 33.

into an almost cinematic representation. Each loop appears to represent the same curved handle at three different moments, raised, falling, and fallen, softening the clay's rigidity into an implied corporeal pliability, and freezing that temporality into a still sequence, like frames in a film.

In the final three of the seven panels, the narrow slivers widen to become planes, shifting the dynamic field from a score to a portal. The rise of the domestic interior in the nineteenth century paralleled the appearance of window and museum displays, manufactured furniture, photography, film, archaeology, and the modern artist's studio. Traces of them all are present in this installation, and the three portals loosely contextualize them within the psychological frame of gendered domestic space, staging it as a site of both projected anxiety and subversion.

The patriarchal distancing of art from domesticity, home, and values associated with a private, familial space is dismantled in Jaeger's collapsing of the boundaries between private, creative, domestic, industrial, and public space. The uncanny presence of domestic objects also evokes author Edward Olszewski's description of the sixteenth-century studio practice of drawing the cast shadows of clay table models in changing angles of artificial light, reinscribing the studio and the home as intertwined, non-hierarchal spaces.[1]

The ambiguity of scale and form in these enigmatic compositions signals an unfixed meaning, articulated in the subtle monochromatic tones of grisaille which, as Briony Fer argues, "stands as a kind of shorthand for the blurring of binary oppositions and the undoing of prevailing systems of thought"; in Jaeger's haptic, relational forms, sculpture proposes a new model of itself as else.[2]

— Chrissie Iles

▸ *Siren*, 2021
Copper, ceramic, wood
Overall: 68 x 36 x 16.5 in.

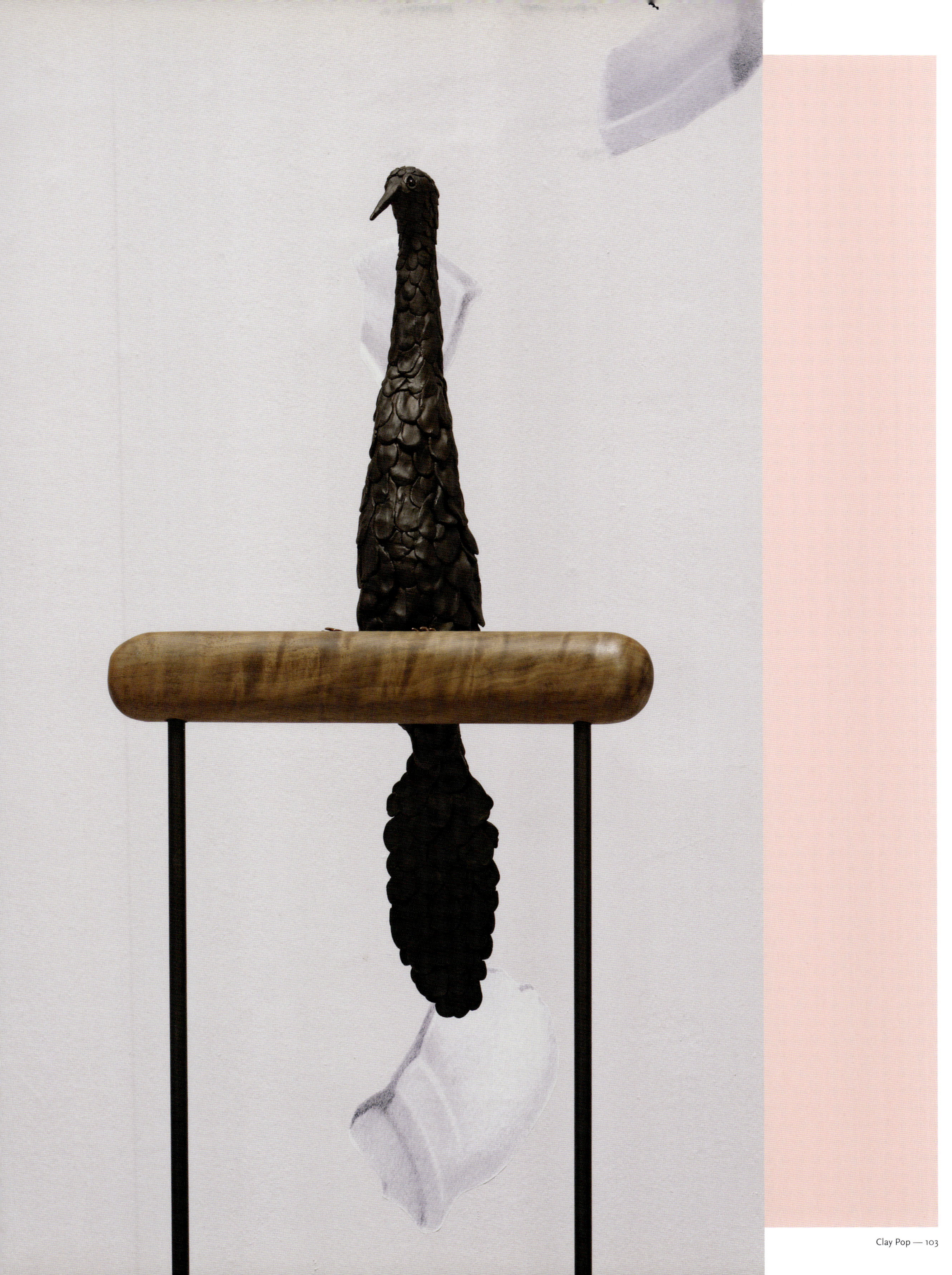

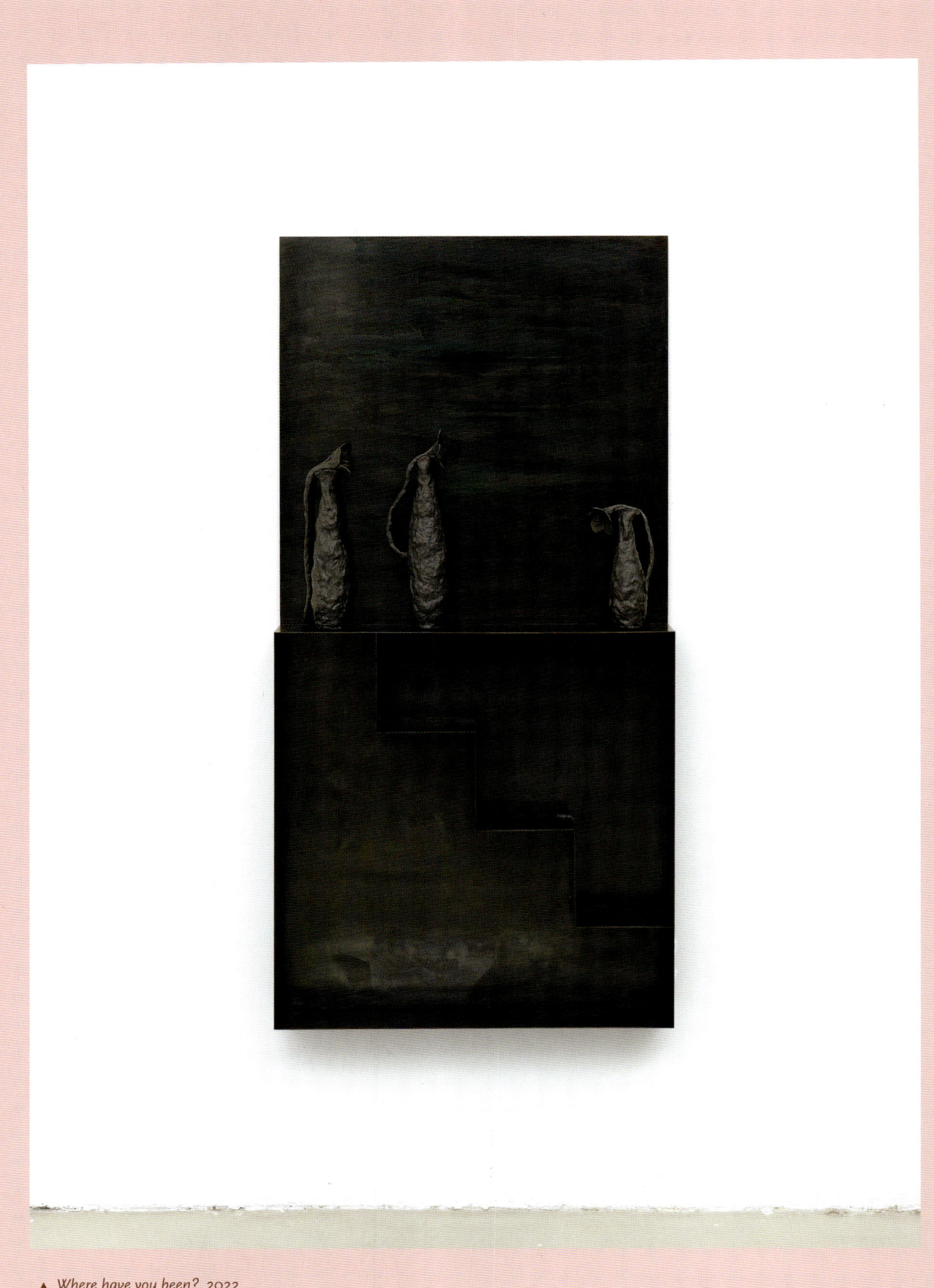

▲ *Where have you been?*, 2022
Ceramic, blackened steel
Each work 63 in. tall

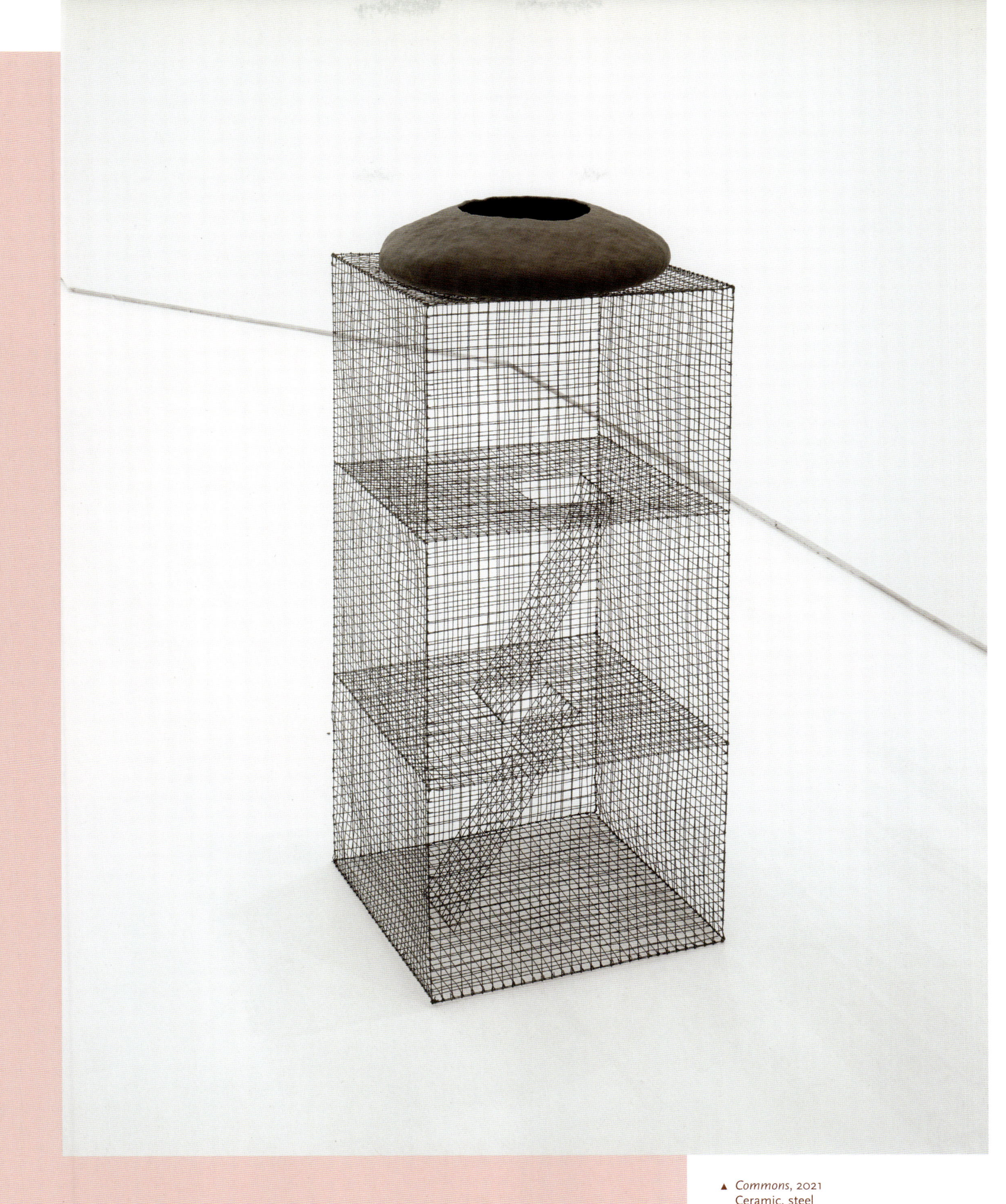

▲ *Commons*, 2021
Ceramic, steel
Ceramic: 14 x 15 x 4 in.
Pedestal: 15 x 15 x 32.5 in.

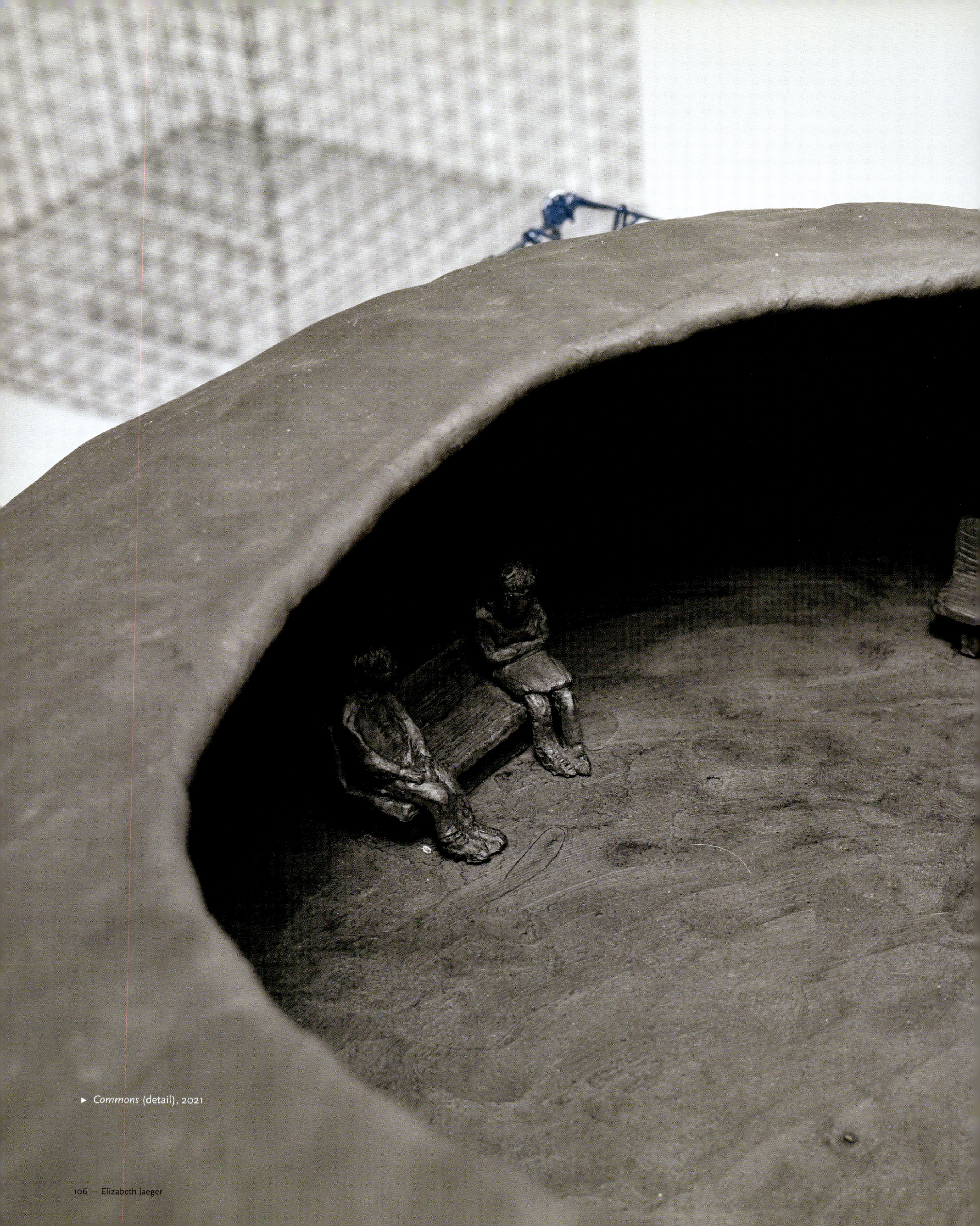

► *Commons* (detail), 2021

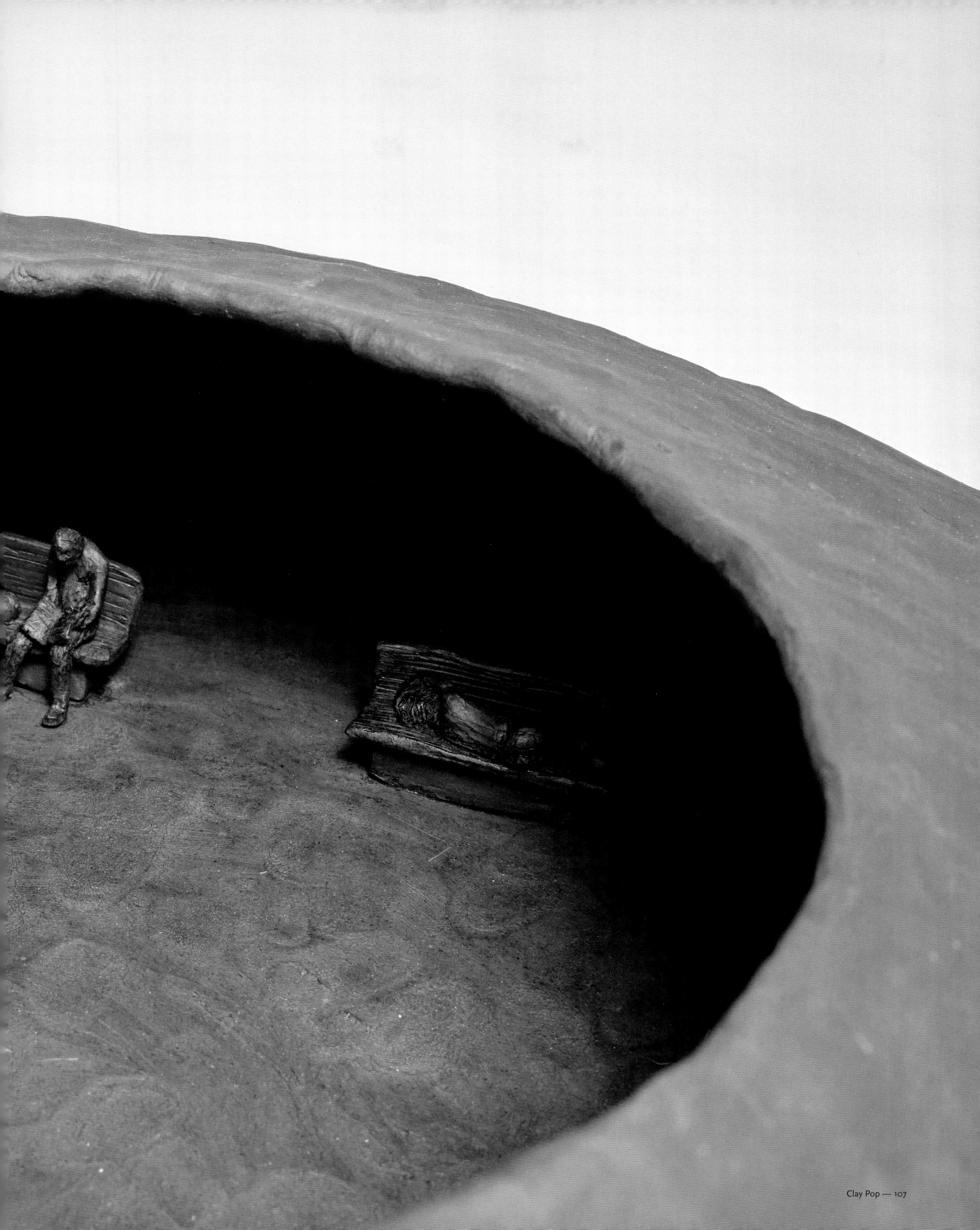

heidi lau

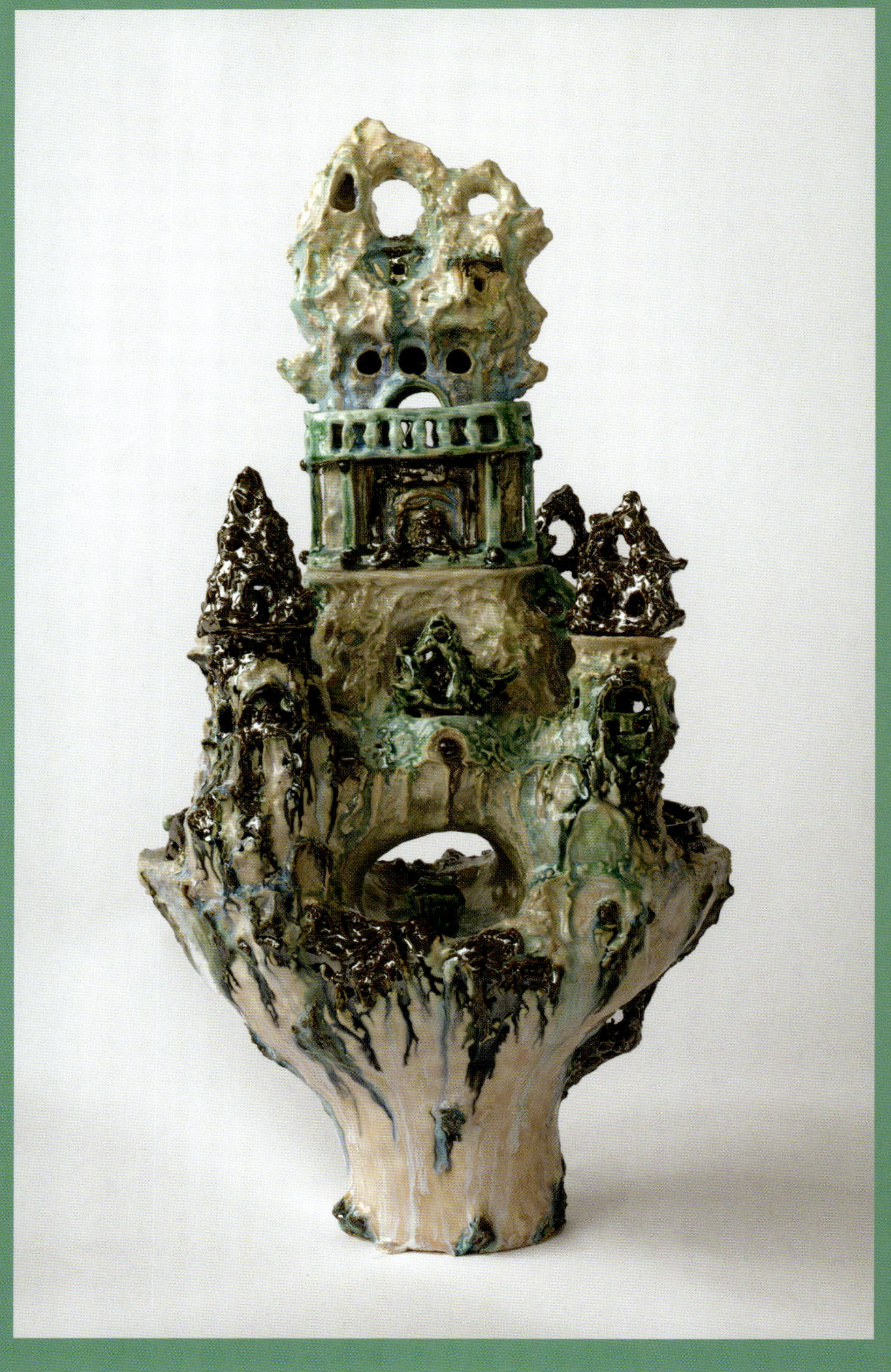

Something more than loss haunts the ceramic works of New York–based artist Heidi Lau (b. 1987, Macau, China), who has been transforming Taoist ritual tokens of death, mourning, and remembrance into oblique monuments for an impossible ancestry. They are impossible because of loss and ruination, and a sense of homelessness produced by the histories of colonization, displacement, gentrification, and the continued invisiblization of Macau in cultural and political configurations of global Chineseness. They are impossible also because of pain, ambivalence, and rage against the home—a feeling of homesickness that must contend with the cruelty and violence of one's own origin, perhaps of all origins. The conditions of the diasporic artist are such that she has managed to make this impossibility generative.

"I feel like if I have to be othered, I would rather be an evil monster and not this soft, mythical creature," explains Lau.[1] Resentment, an emotion alternately maligned and celebrated for its political potentiality, finds new expression in Lau's pursuit of alternative origin stories through the matrilineal genesis myth of Nüwa, the Chinese goddess who created humans by molding mud. Lau's intensive work process channels the self-cultivation practices of women Taoist practitioners from the eleventh and twelfth centuries (during the Song and Yuan Dynasties) as a mode of world-making—this time with difference. Laboring alongside rather than manipulating the medium of clay, the artist uses her body and hands to serve as a mediating device between fantasy and tradition, nostalgia and amnesia, reclamation and destruction, and the dead and the living. Animating her glazed and fired ceramic objects, which have passed a threshold of transformation with no return, are unearthly morphologies of life and undead beings born out of the subterranean rancor of the native place.

Hand-building each piece from miniature chain mail to large-scale skeletal installations with cosmological ambition, Lau has crafted a distinct iconography composed of ritual and funerary objects, traditional and colonial architectural fragments, fossilized primordial creatures, and dismembered body parts, looking archaic and science fiction-ish at the same time. All will not be legible to all, but no matter. Ultimately, these luminous and voluminous sculptures are not portals to the otherworld or the underworld, but necessarily opaque and rugged testaments to how some have struggled to live in an uninhabitable present.

— Kang Kang

◄ *Mercury Six-spouted Vessel*, 2020
Ceramic with crystalline glaze
25.5 x 8.5 x 13.5 in.

[1] Jack Radley, "Decolonial Reincarnation: An Interview with Heidi Lau," Berlin Art Link, March 2, 2021, https://www.berlinartlink.com/2021/03/02/heidi-lau-greenwood-cemetery-studio-interview-death-ritual/.

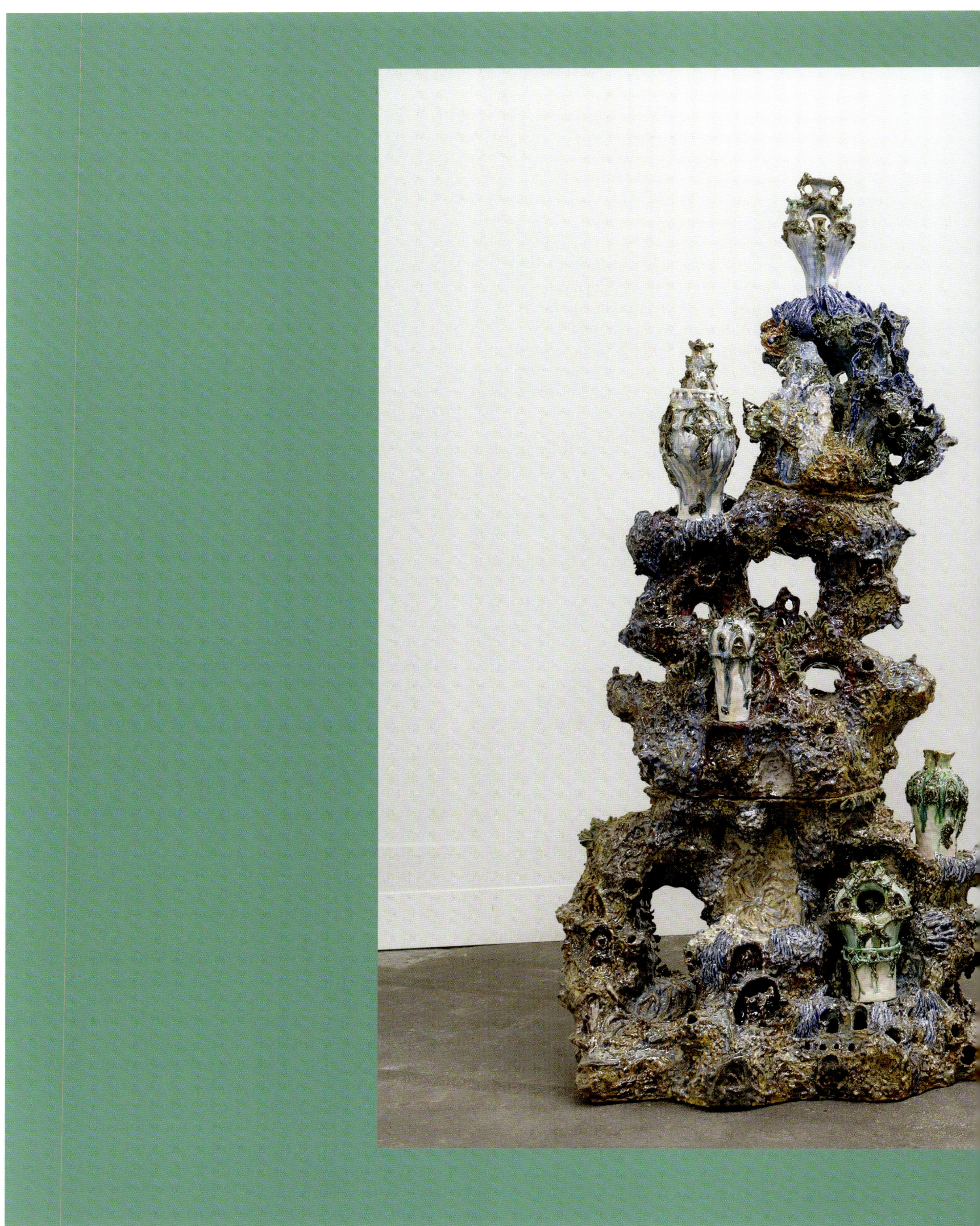

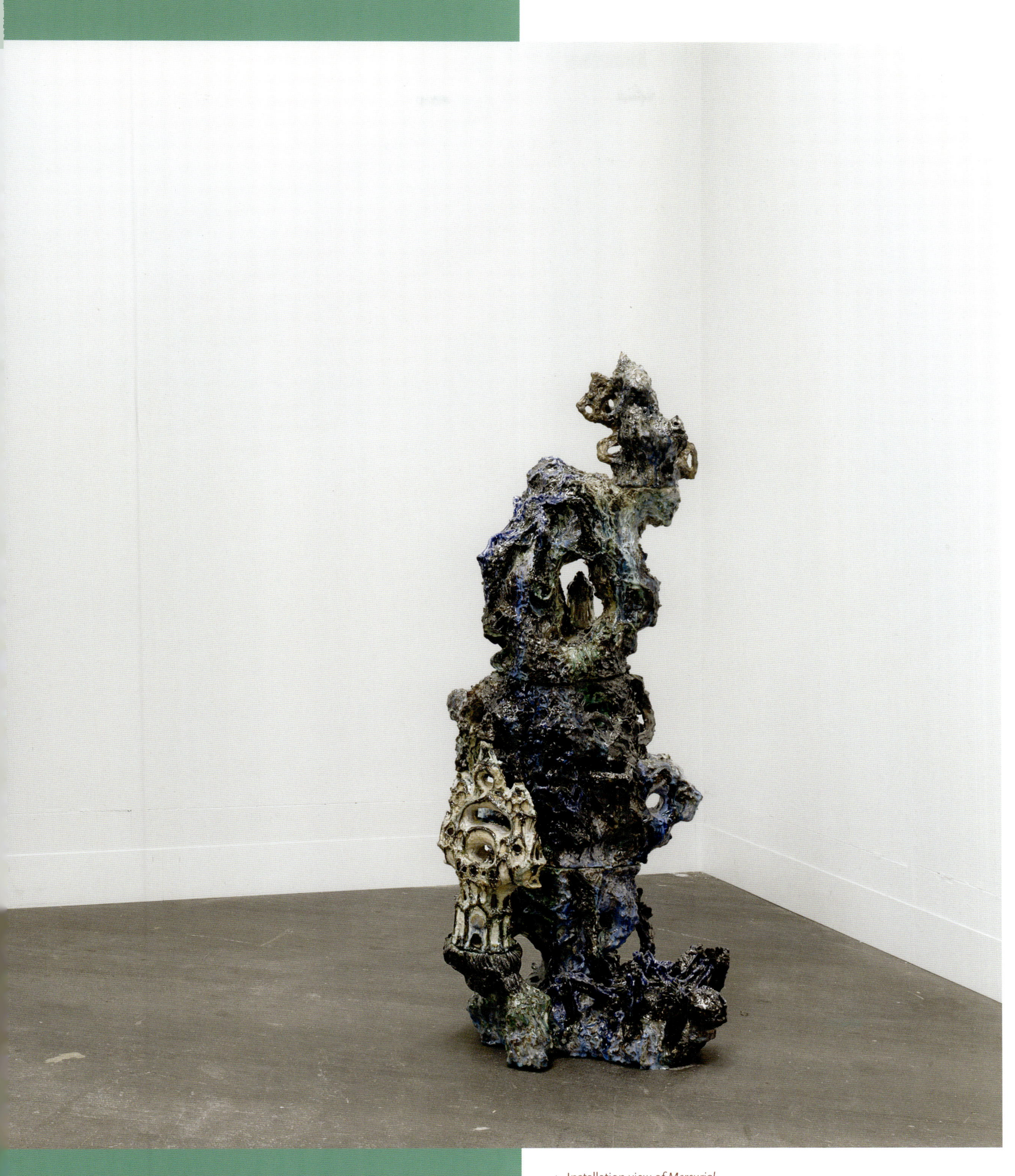

▲ Installation view of *Mercurial Grounds* at Liste, Basel, 2021.

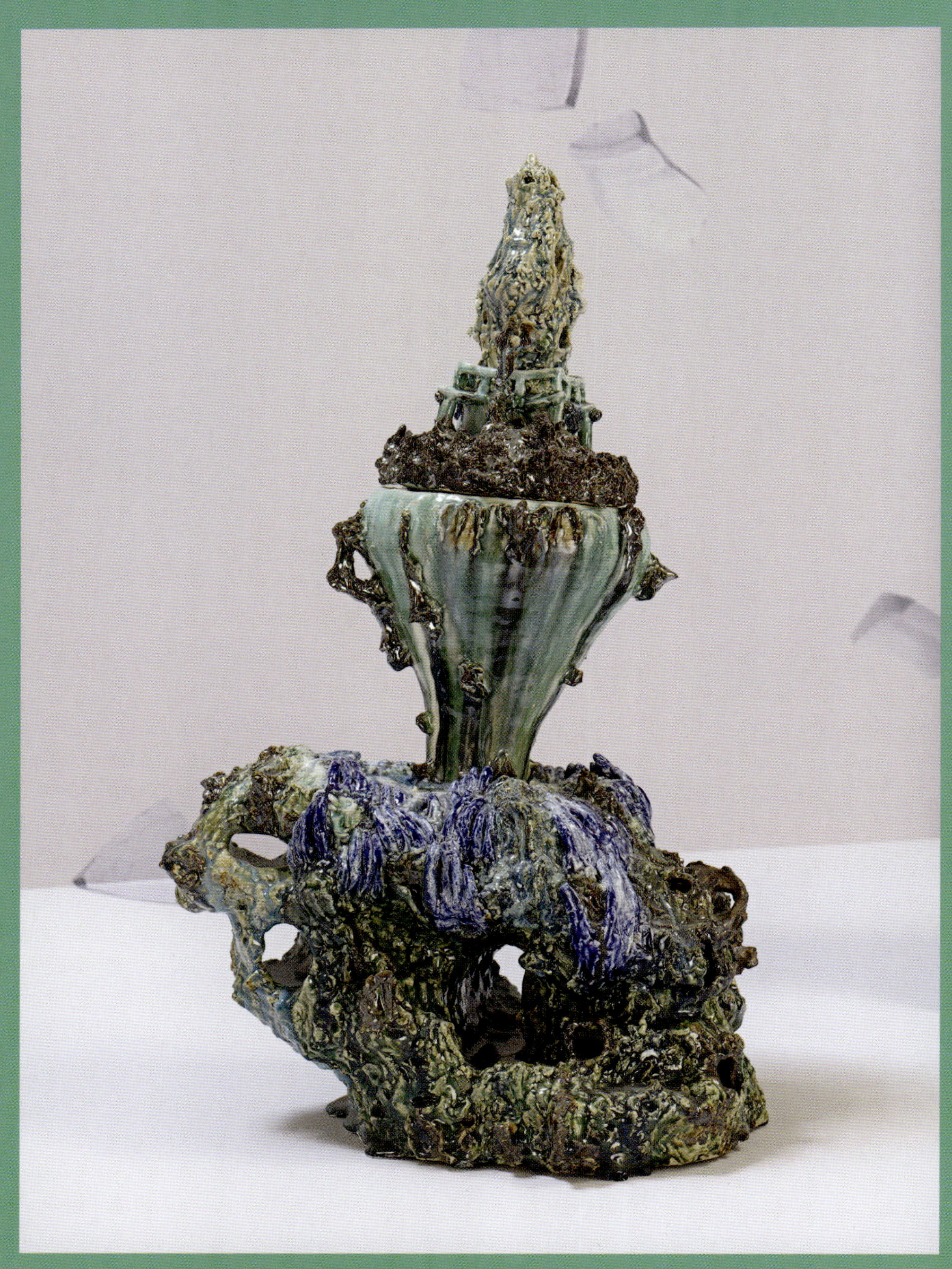

▲ *Play II*, 2021
Ceramic
32.5 x 17.5 x 14.5 in.

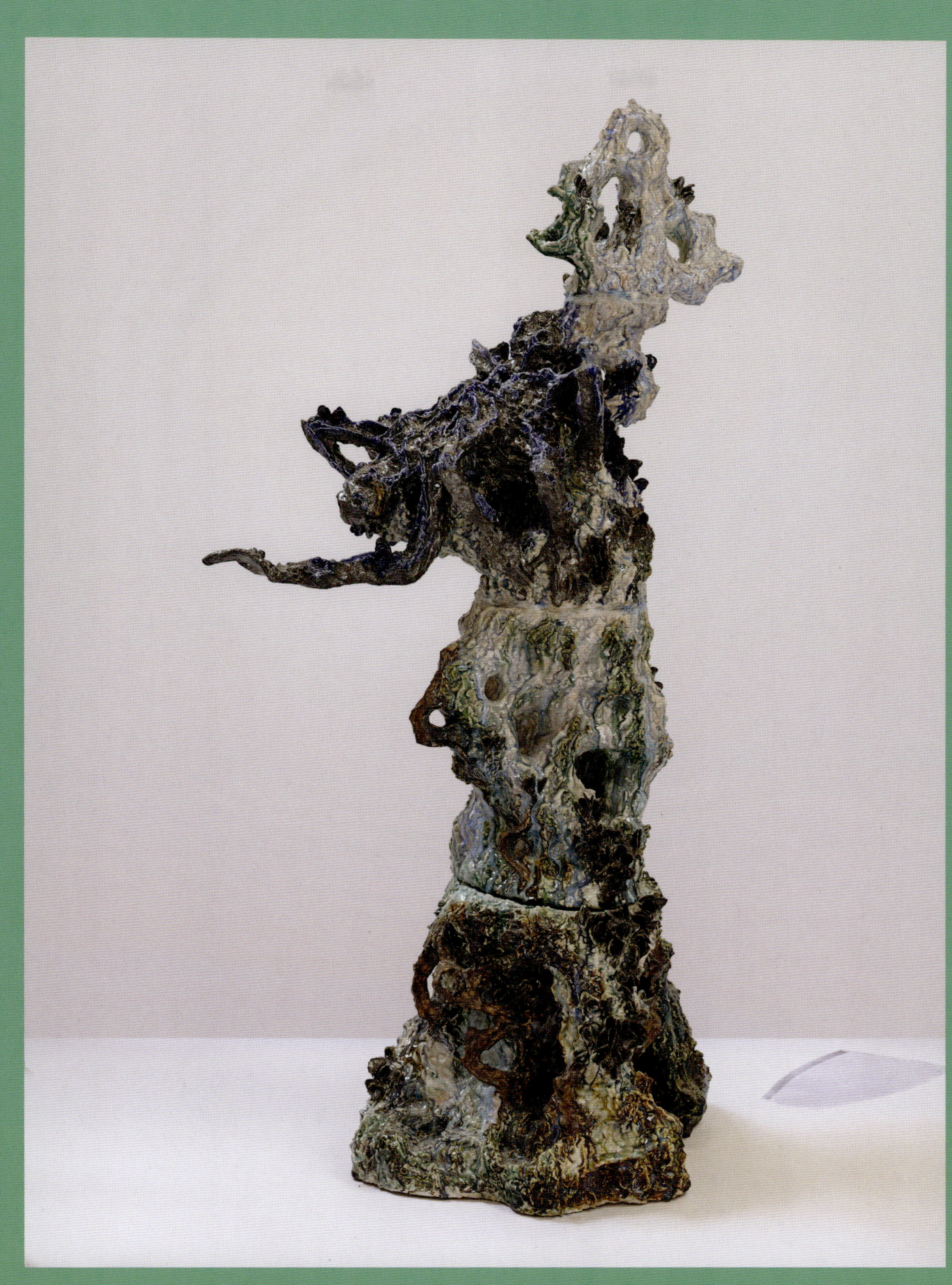

▲ *Play I*, 2021
Ceramic
54 x 32 x 18 in.

grant levy-lucero

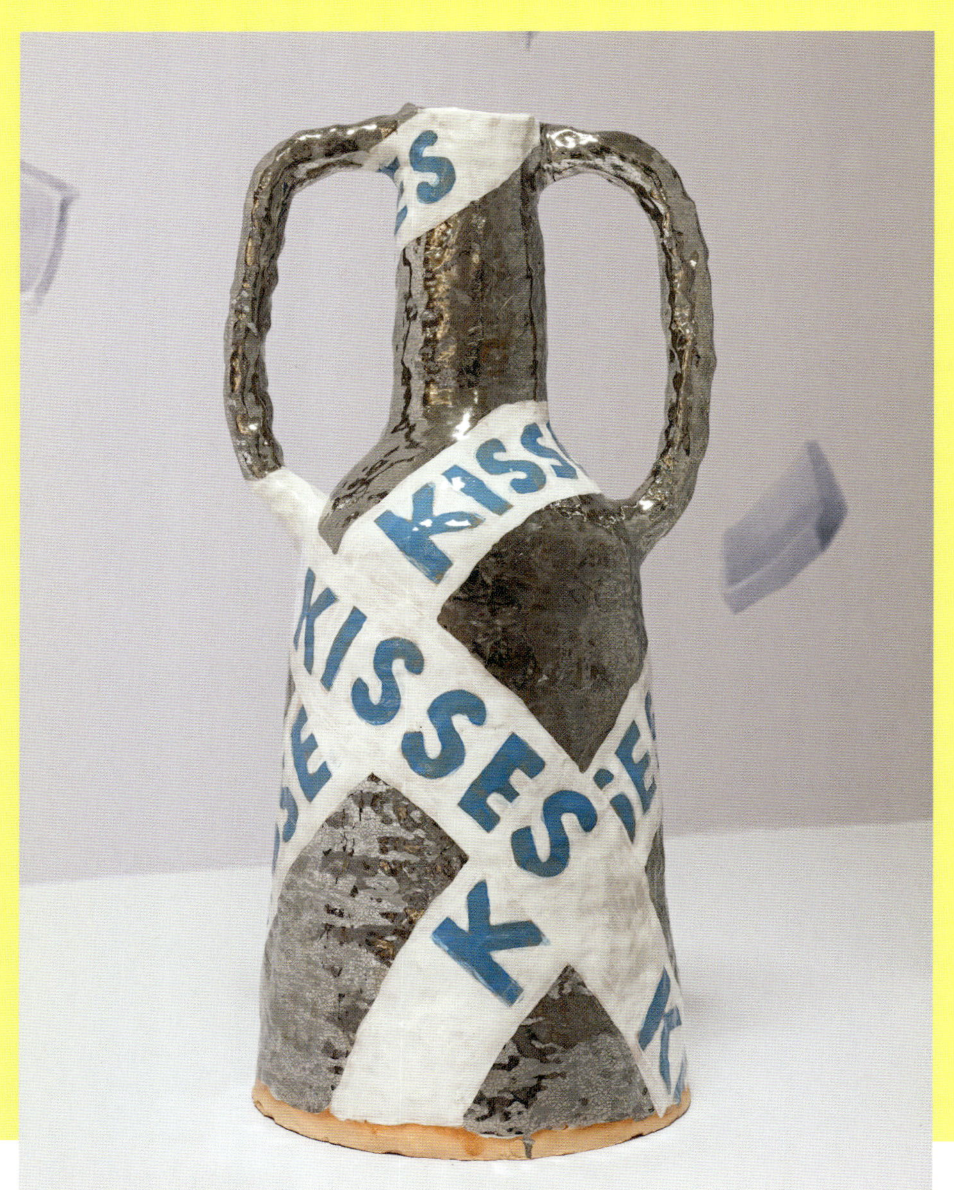

Grant Levy-Lucero (b. 1981, Los Angeles) is known for fusing classical antiquity with the vernacular of the everyday, playfully placing the grammar of American consumer culture in dialogue with the recollective power of the senses. Across his practice, Levy-Lucero finds continuous inspiration in the hand-painted signage that he sees while walking through Los Angeles—DIY advertisements for convenience store offerings. His works also embrace more impressionistic imagery, making visual references ranging from the Musée de l'Orangerie to Venice Boulevard. Working with the traditional Greco-Roman amphora, Levy-Lucero has developed a unique aesthetic vision that is centered on lived experience and an irreverence for the distinctions between high and low culture.

Levy-Lucero borrows the decorative and narrative capabilities of the vessel from the Archaic and Classical periods, but his final hand-built pots are not exact reproductions so much as allusions to the established ceramic shape. The brand logo, reimagined upon the distinctively art historical form, is abstracted from its conventional associations. In turn, Levy-Lucero's imagery opens itself to the possibility of a new relation with the collective consciousness, one rooted in sensory activation rather than easy recognition. The works seem to almost rhyme with a cold soda, an adolescent memory, or a familiar neighborhood, but ultimately, they take on a unique identity: our perception untethered from commercialism.

— Jayne Pugh

◄ *Wouldn't You Like Somebody to Love*, 2021
Glazed ceramic
26 x 12.5 x 11 in.

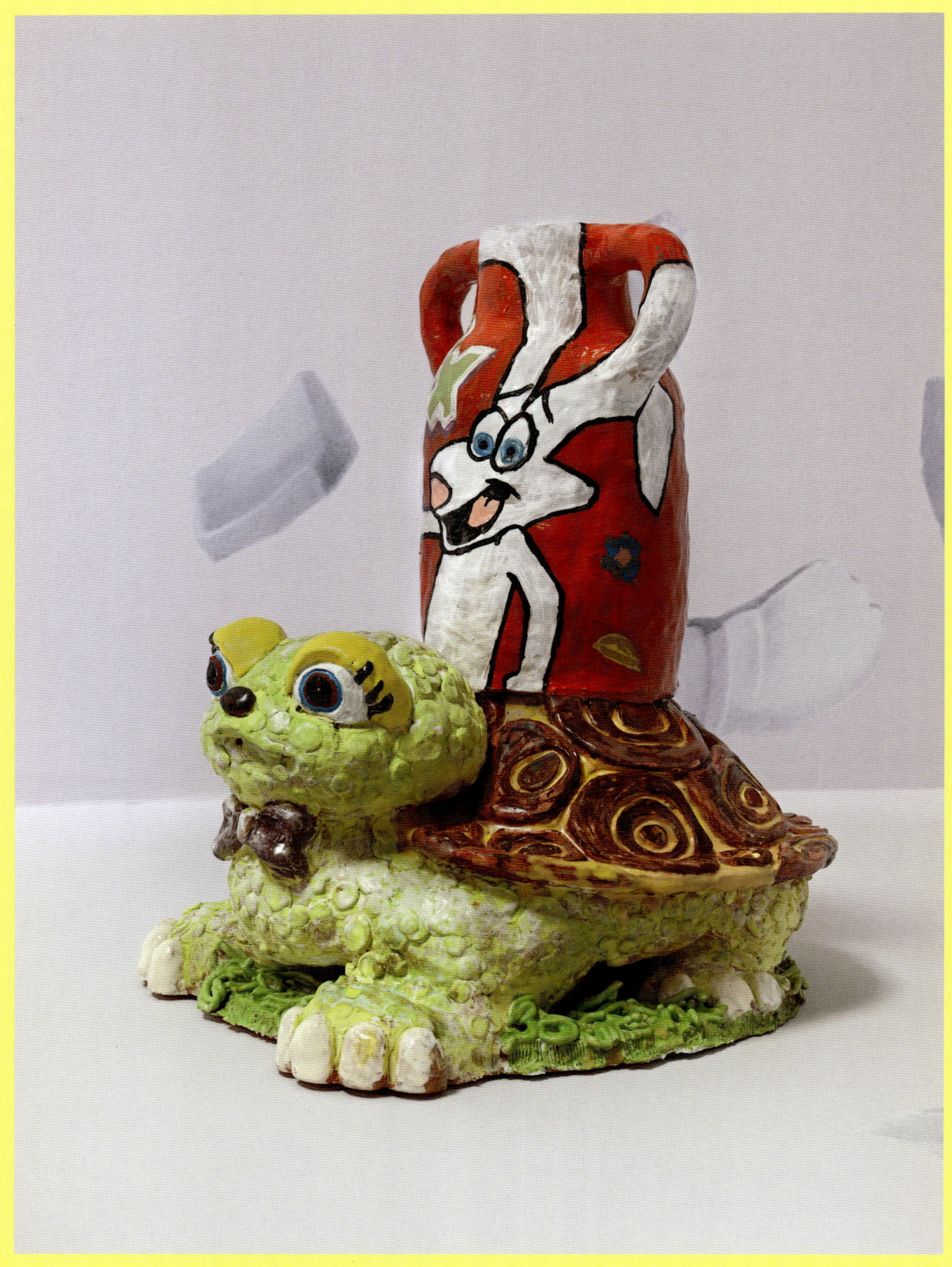

▲ *Trix the Rabbit and Shelly the Tortoise*, 2021
Glazed ceramic
21 x 19 x 16 in.
Collaborative sculpture between the artist and Alake Shilling

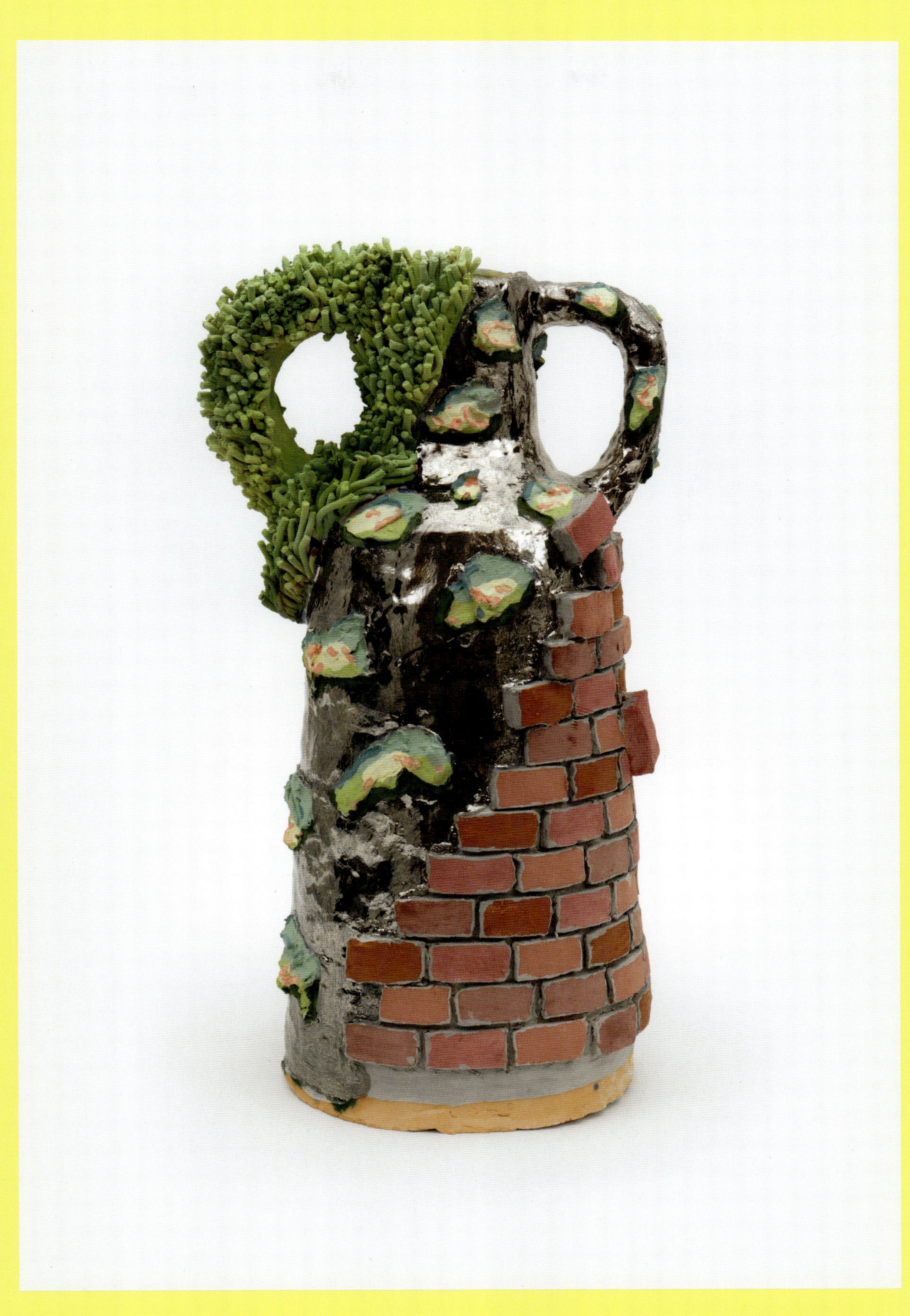

▲ *Reflection Lilies on Wilshire*, 2021
Glazed ceramic
22.5 x 14 x 11 in.

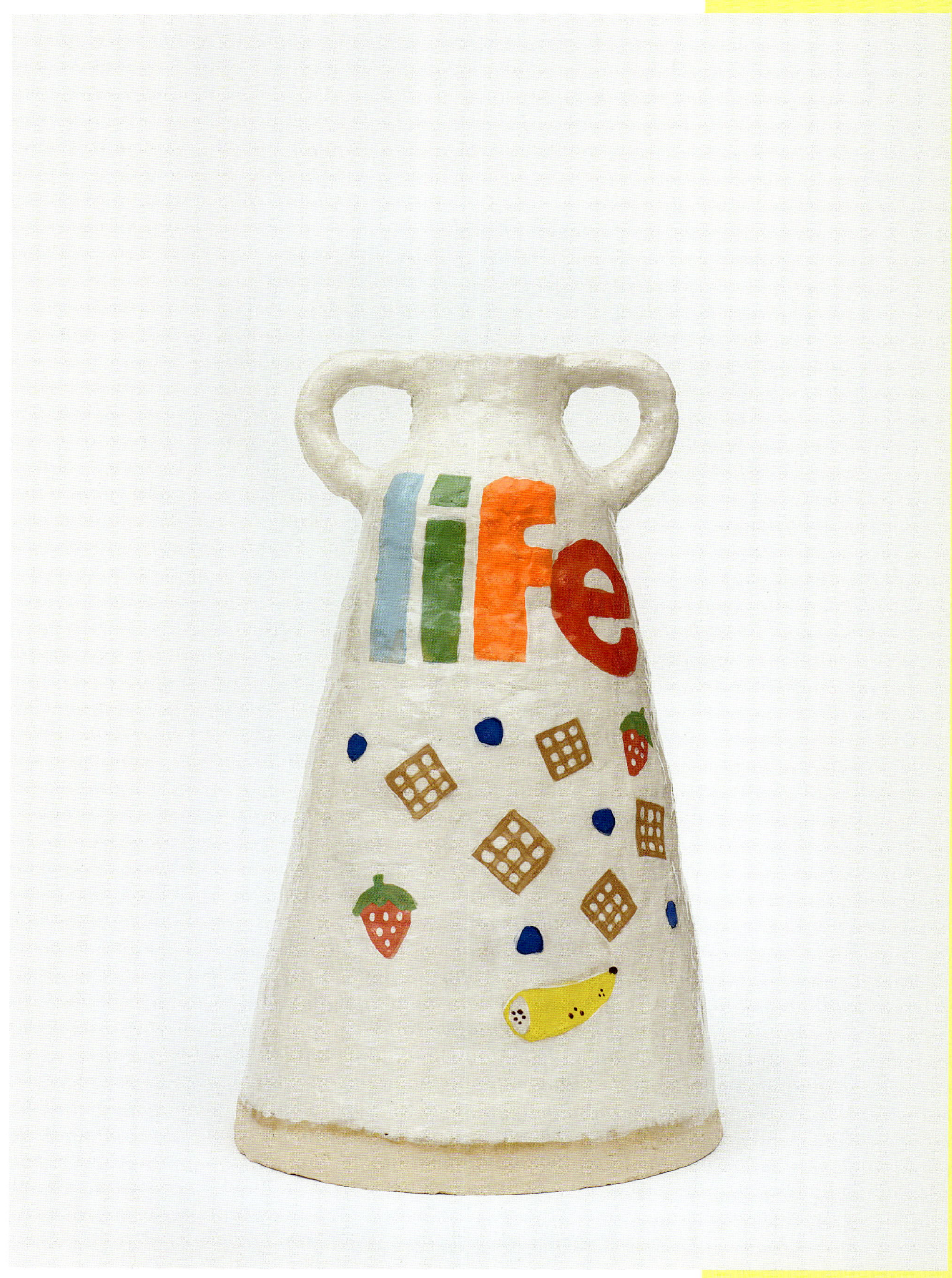

▲ *Smart & Final Life*, 2019
Glazed ceramics
24 x 14.5 x 15 in.

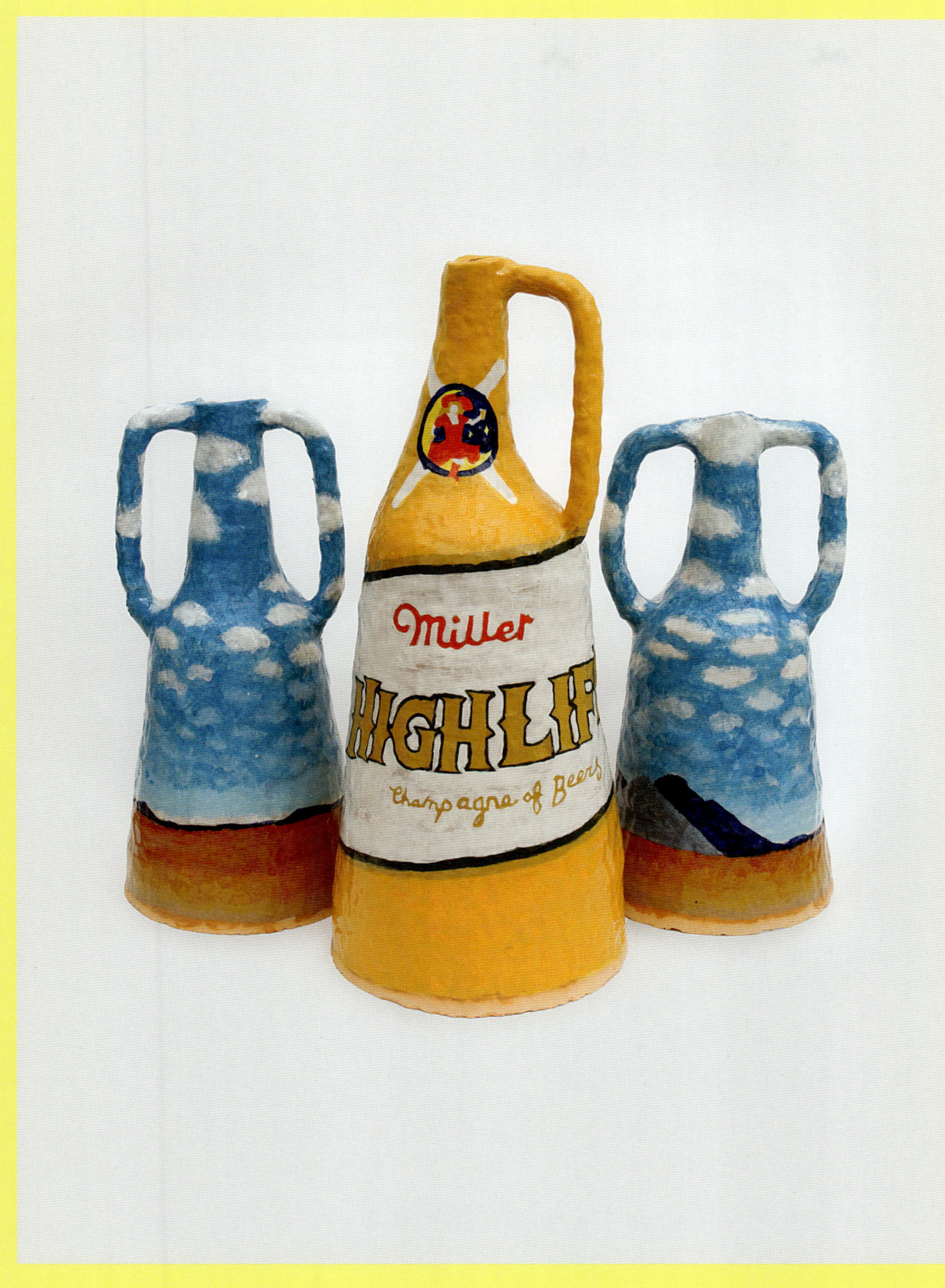

◂ *High in the Sky*, 2021
Glazed ceramic
From left: 23 x 11 x 11 in.;
29 x 14 x 13 in.; 23 x 11 x 11 in.
Overall dimensions variable

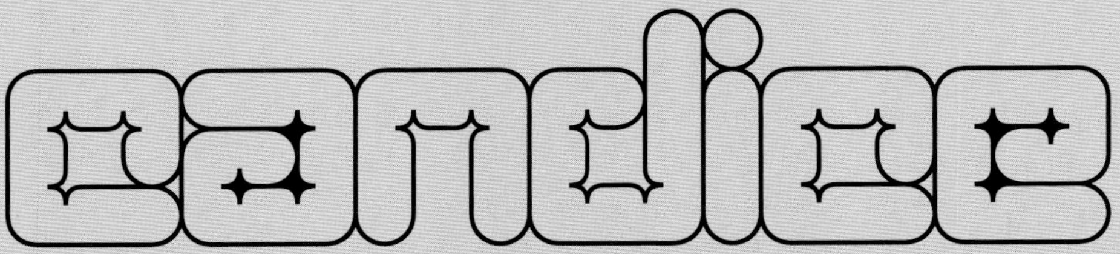

lin

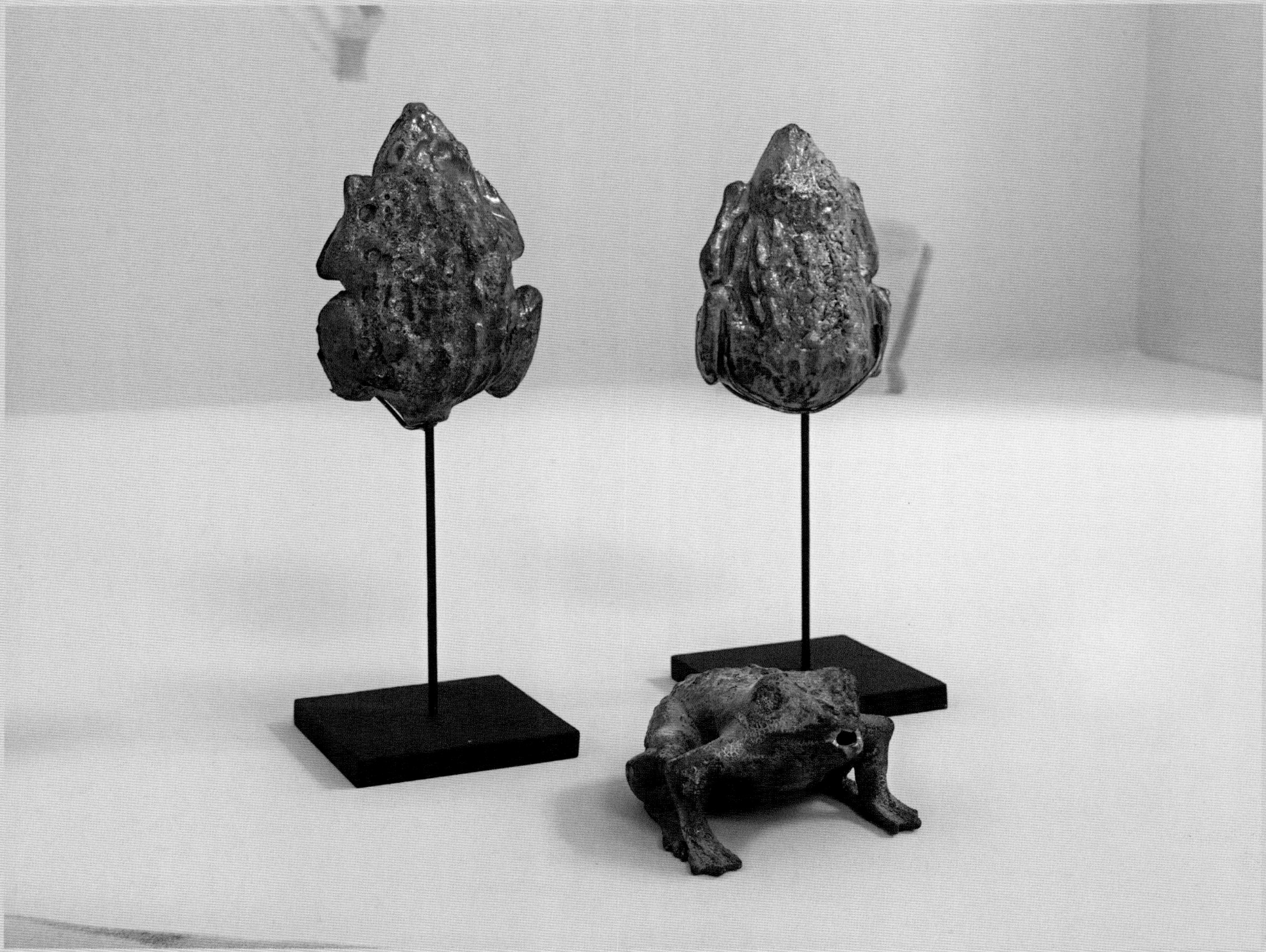

Candice Lin (b. 1979, Concord, Massachusetts) is an interdisciplinary artist who works in installation, sculpture, drawing, ceramics, and video. In her sculpture *Untitled* (2021), the bodies of frogs are pockmarked, mottled, irregular, and lustrous. The frogs either squat like watchful sentinels or are penetrated from behind and mounted into upright kabobs—mouths open to the sky. Like all living things, they are irredeemably the product of their environment, subject to its capricious rule.

Heat and oxidization have colluded to produce the glittering opalescent glazes that ripple across the frogs' surfaces, offering occasional shocks of blue, through a Japanese technique known as *raku*. Other histories intrude: the clay from which their batrachian physiques are formed hails from the bayous and swamps of the Saint Malo region, a coastal community at the eastern tip of the boot of a state today known as Louisiana. Often identified as the first Asian American settlement, Saint Malo's history is more unwieldy than that. Filipino indentured workers who deserted Spanish ships (the Manila galleons) settled there, as did a maroon community led by Juan San Malo—peoples of African descent who both escaped and actively resisted the domination of slavery.

Lin's sculpture *Witness (Gray Version)* (2021) is likewise impaled. A lithe metallic stand suggests ribs, topped by a *raku* mask also made of Saint Malo clay. Long hair covers the open lapels of a jacquard jacket, partially obscuring its lining of handmade fabric resist-dyed in indigo by the artist, printed with, among other things, a motif of feline paws. Lin's long-standing interest in indigo also operates within a wider practice based in researching the archives of colonial commodities and working with living organisms, as in the process of indigo-dye fermentation.

Nestled uneasily within the folds of the human and not, the toxic and enchanting, and the historical and speculative, Lin is an artist for whom the past runs rivulets of ugly gold. Materials are synaptic; they are catalysts for an associative logic that sunders received narratives and strict cultural logics in favor of weirder confluences. Craft traditions and other forms of feminized work—making and dyeing fabric, concocting botany and herbal medicine, and working with clay—are potent sites for such investigations. These objects are not only hand-formed—a product of Lin's own artistic labor, fingers manipulating their wet plasticity—but also the indelible result of a fine-grained soil that registers histories of unfree labor and its political contestation.

— Catherine Quan Damman

◂ *Untitled*, 2021
Raku-fired ceramics
4.5 x 5.5 x 3 in.

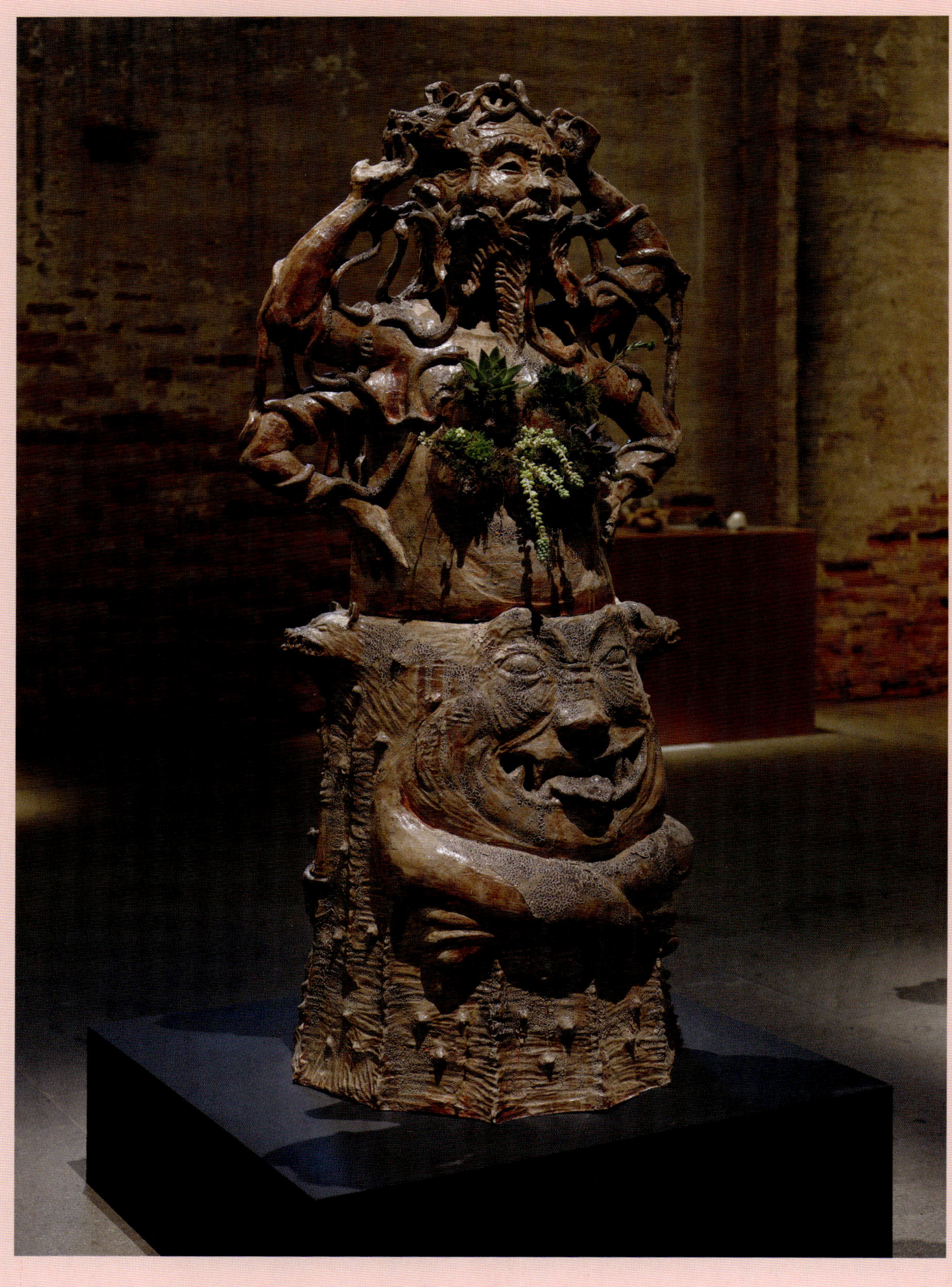

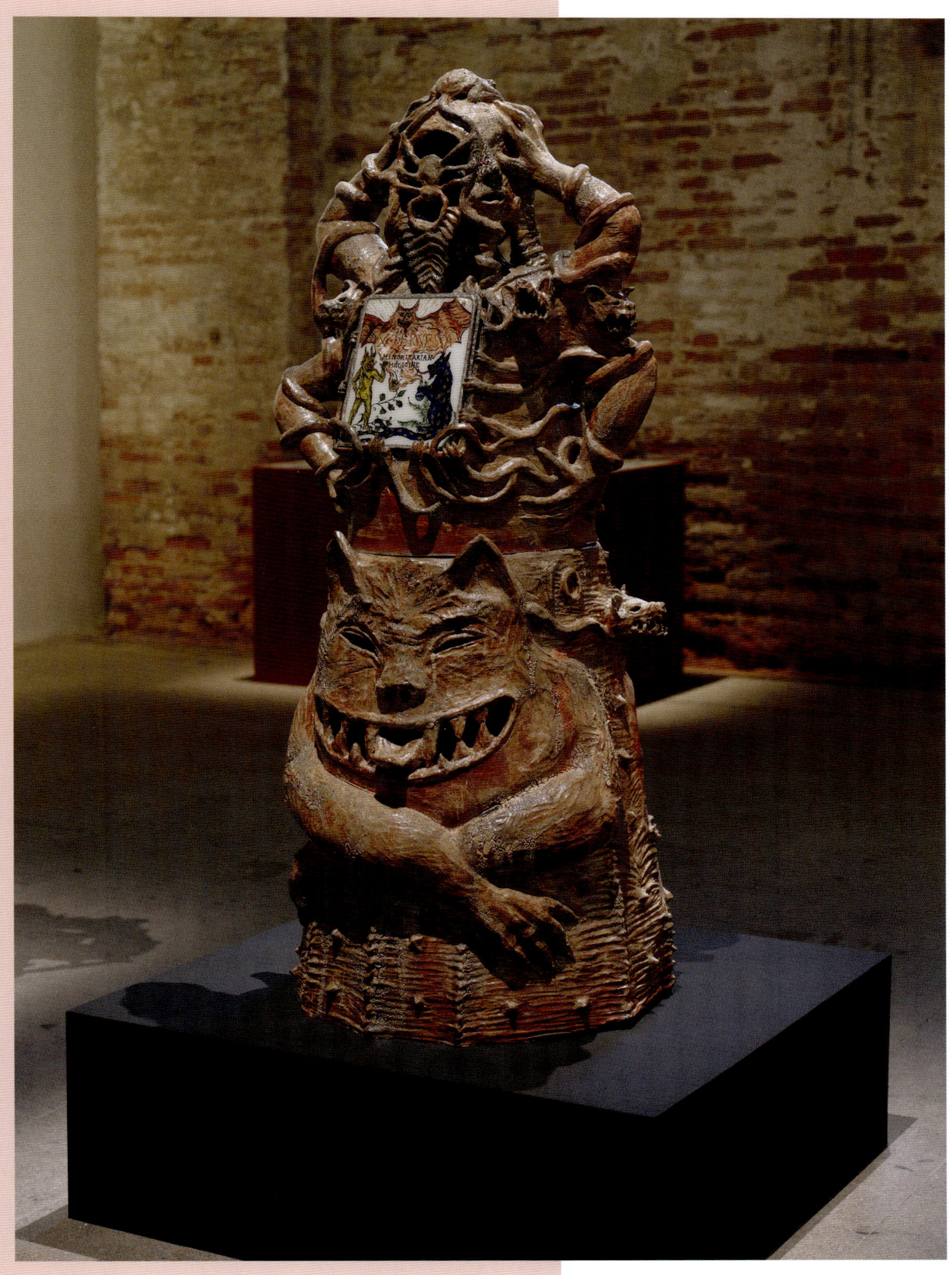

▲ Front and back view of *Xternesta*, 2022
Glazed ceramic, reverse painted bound artist's recipe book, reverse glass painted tabletops with collaged paper elements, ceramic and porcelain objects, cast bronze, aluminum, and pewter, glass jars and bottles with pewter solder, silver talismans, and paper collage, various tinctures including abortifacients, indigo leaf, milky oat tops, and Clairvoyant Testosterone, subitism incense burner with ume, spice, and resin incense, copper sulfate crystallizer, taxidermied iguana with chromium(III) potassium sulfate crystals, crystallized copper sulfate, blown glass terrarium, dead silkworms, scented lard, papier mâché, dried, resin-coated, and wax-sculpted plant material, copper electroplated Chinese herbs and mushrooms, kudzu bioplastic, kudzu root, dried reishi, alcohol, white urushi lacquer, fermented rice liquid, kombucha (black tea, sugar, yeast), Saint Malo mud, fermenting hardware, rocks, minerals, herbs, oak gall, poison
Dimensions variable within installation

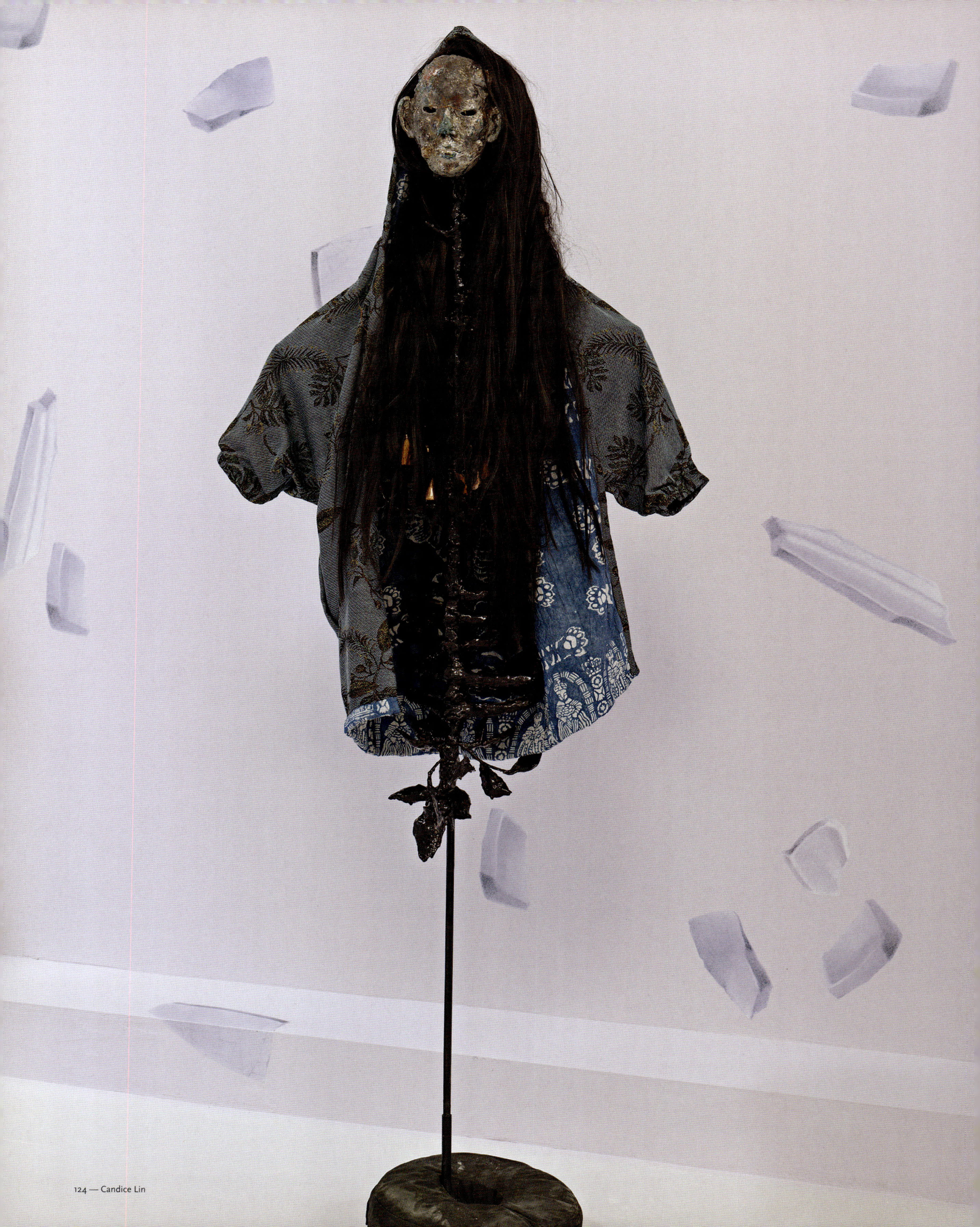

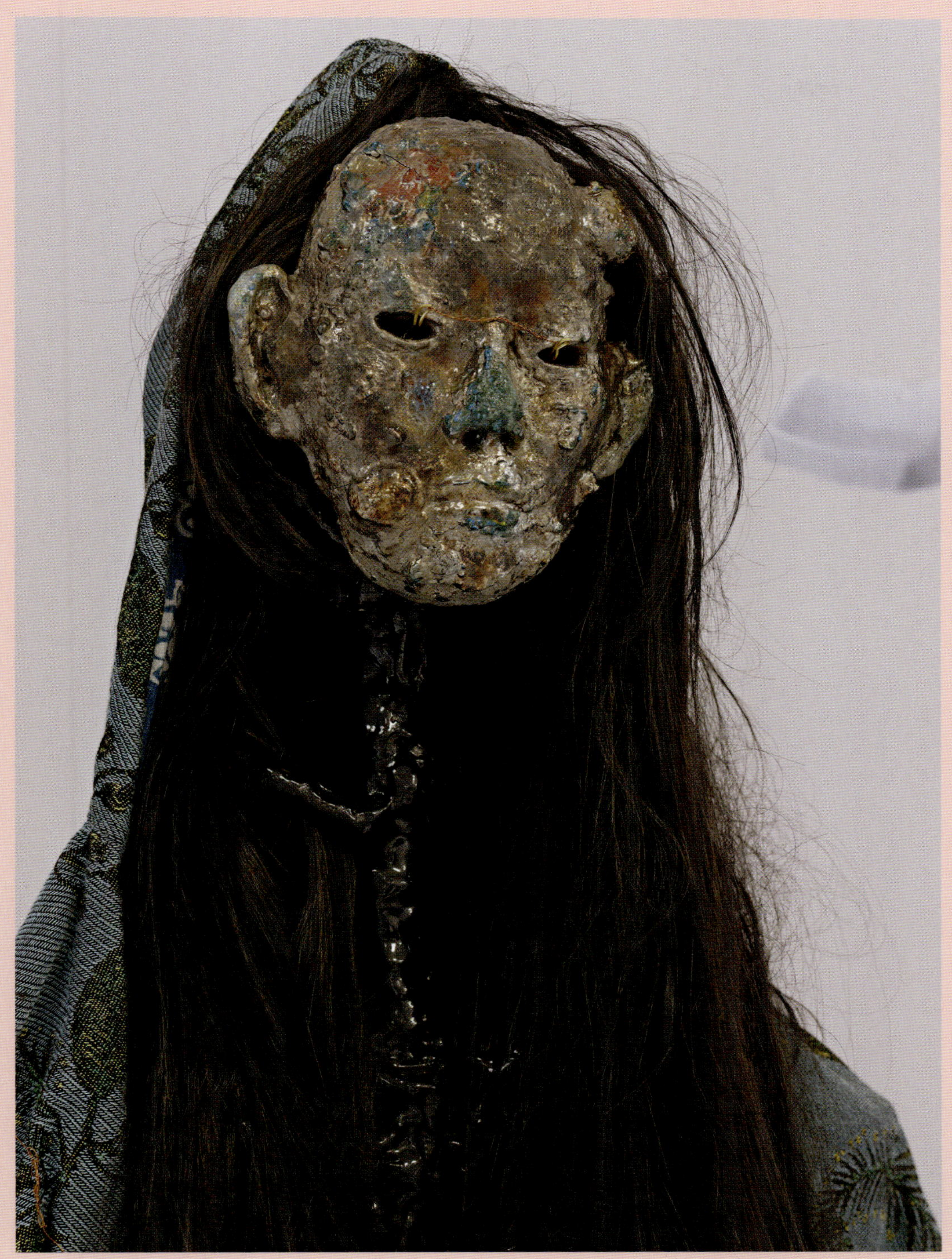

▲ *Witness (Gray Version)* (detail), 2021

◂ *Witness (Gray Version)*, 2021
Raku-fired ceramic mask, epoxy resin, jacquard-woven garment lined with handmade batik, wig, metal stand
76.5 x 31 x 13.5 in.

jasmine little

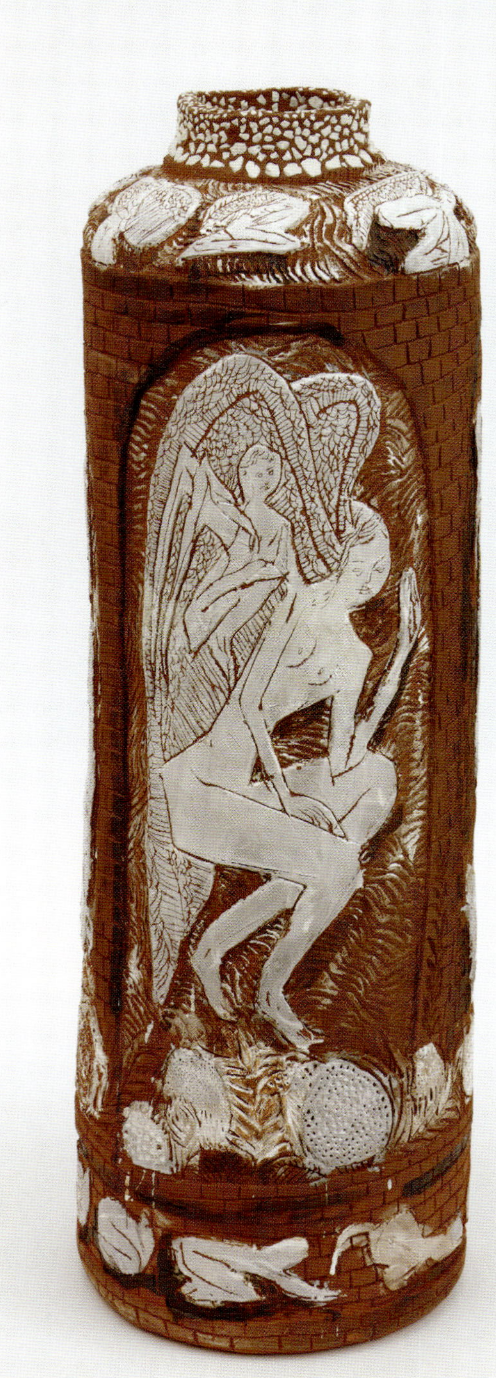

Jasmine Little (b. 1984, (Portsmouth, Virginia) creates ceramic sculptures that take a variety of forms, drawing influence from both utilitarian and decorative pottery. Her work is composed of large, cylindrical stoneware vessels with figurative iconography carved into their exterior surfaces. The numerous and varied influences in Little's work span the entirety of the human experience. Flemish and Renaissance painting, medieval illuminated manuscripts, Safavid period carpets, Greek black-figure and red-figure pottery, and Japanese woodblock prints are among the sources referenced in her work. The imagery oscillates between the extremes of elation and abjection while insisting on the perennial power of the object.

The decorative carvings of these surfaces are dictated in part by the material itself and the firing technique. Little has used a unique formula of clay hand-mixed in California, which incorporates foreign substances that create a distinctive surface. She carves directly into this clay while it is still wet, then inlays additional materials including porcelain, common gravel, and, most notably, clinker bricks salvaged from a local Arts and Crafts–era house in Pasadena, California. Clinker bricks, which were famously utilized by Greene & Greene Architects, are misshapen and discolored bricks that are created by hotspots within the kiln. These excavated bricks resonate with Little's work on a technical and material level because they carry a lineage of Californian craftspeople.

Little's work foregrounds a communal aspect of ceramics that breeds cross-pollination and slippage between artists working in physical proximity to each other. By utilizing materials specific to a single location while employing imagery that is universal to us all, Little creates objects that are overwhelmingly human.

— Jasmine Little

◂ *Multi-Booting*, 2021
Stoneware, porcelain, glaze
46 x 14 x 14 in.

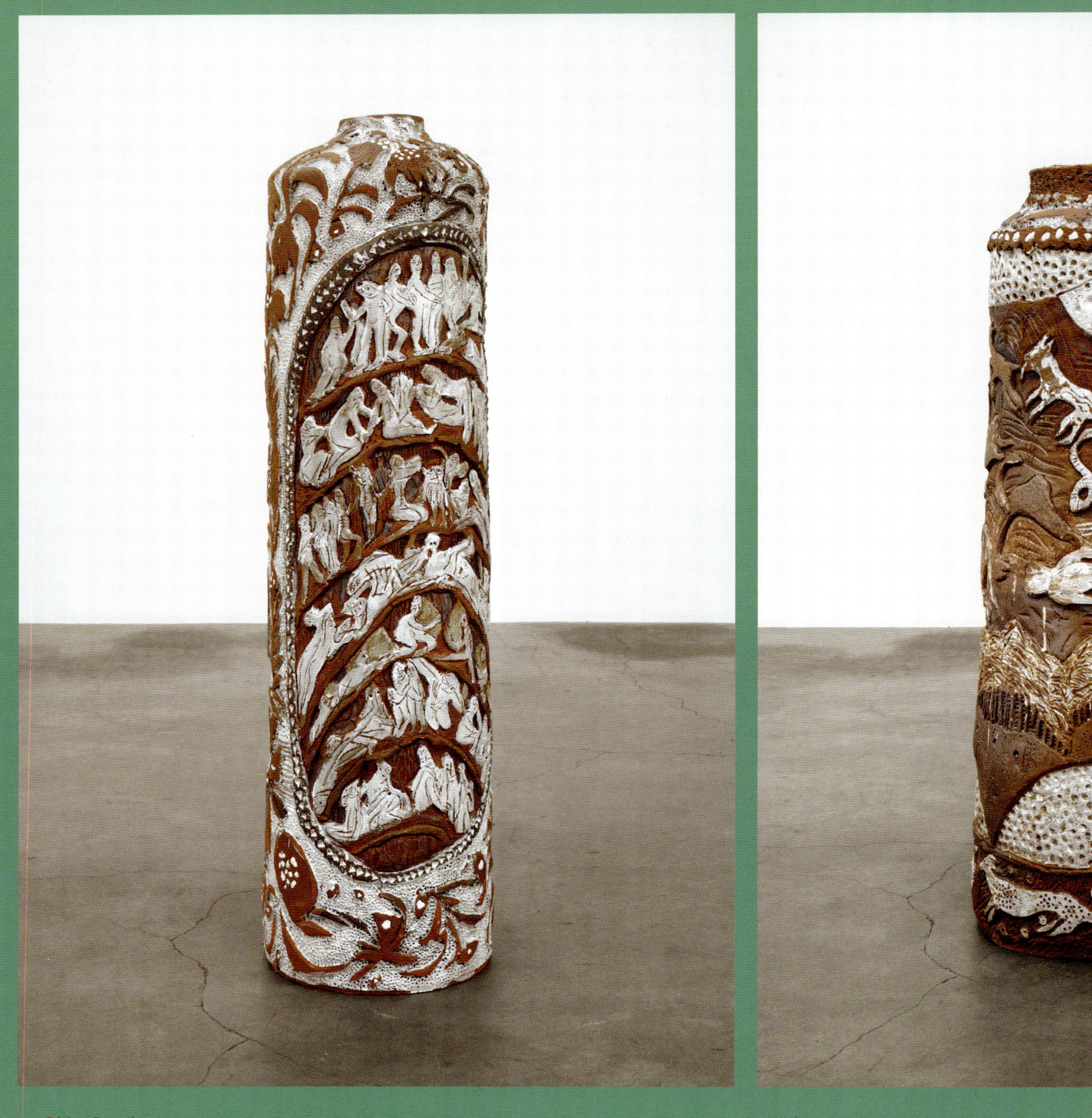

▲ *Divine Comedy*, 2019
Stoneware, porcelain, glaze
50 x 15 x 14.5 in.

▲ *Chase*, 2019
Stoneware, porcelain, brick, gravel, glaze
51 x 20 x 20 in.

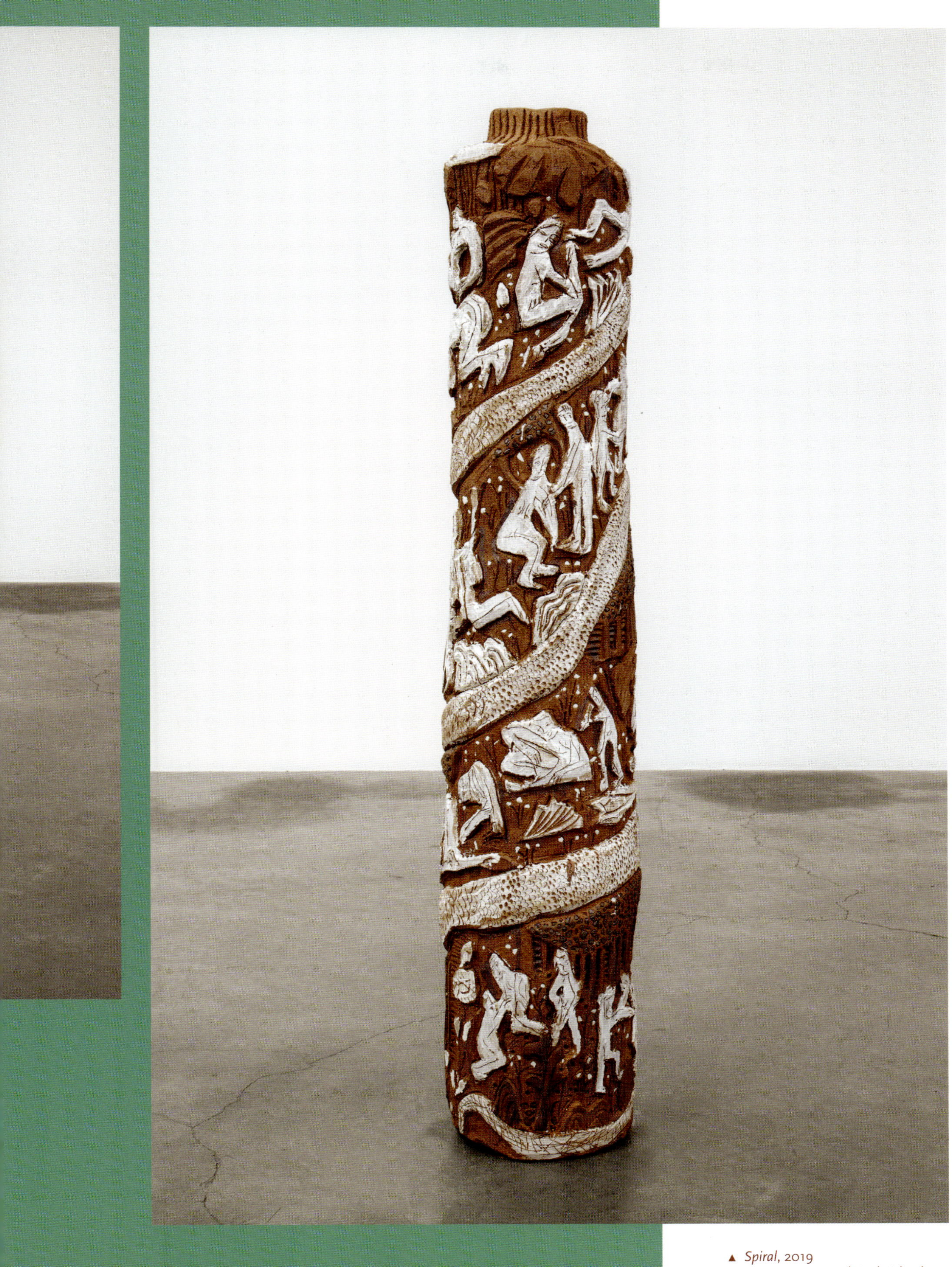

▲ *Spiral*, 2019
Stoneware, porcelain, brick, glaze
59 x 10.5 x 10.5 in.

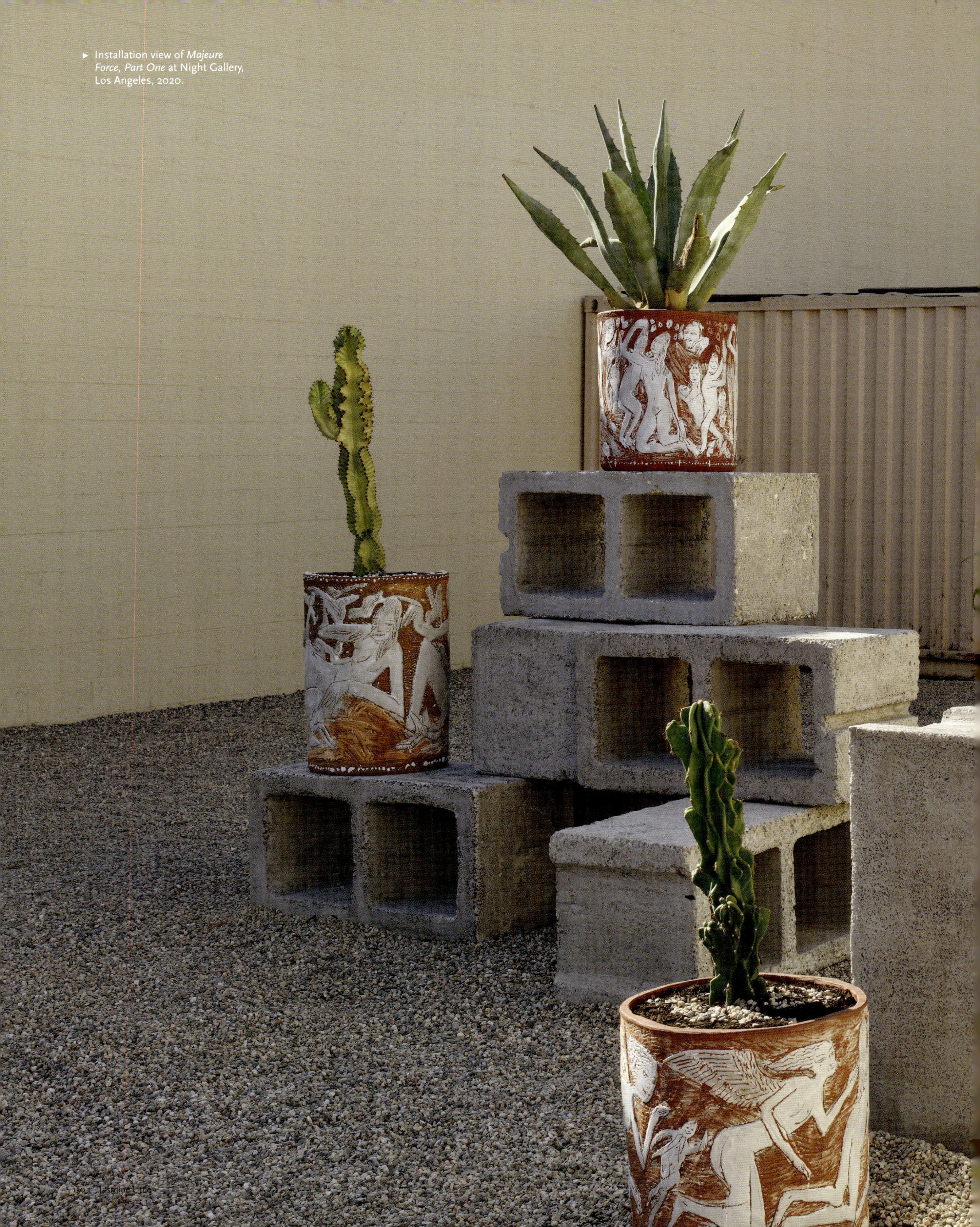

► Installation view of *Majeure Force, Part One* at Night Gallery, Los Angeles, 2020.

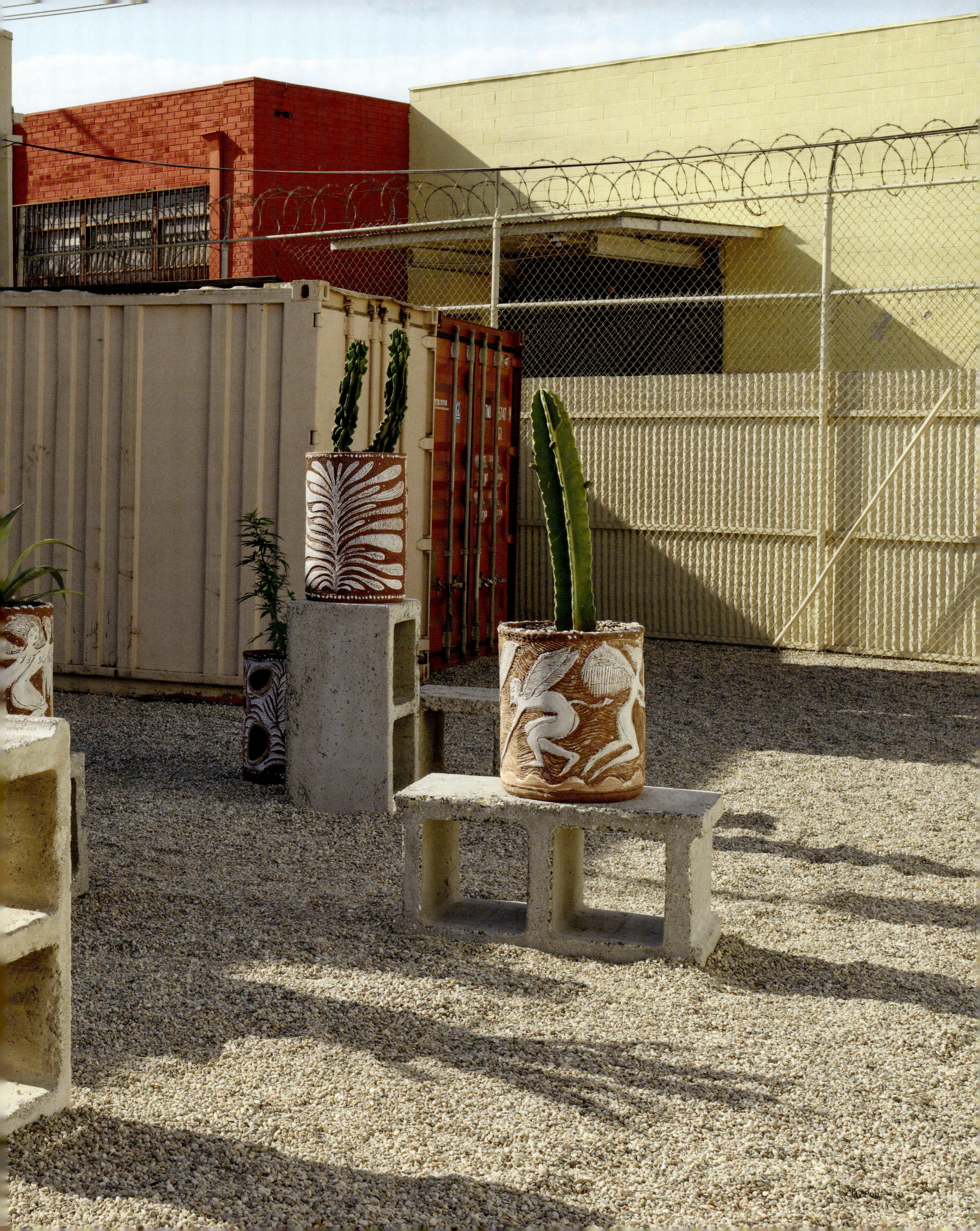

lindsey mendick

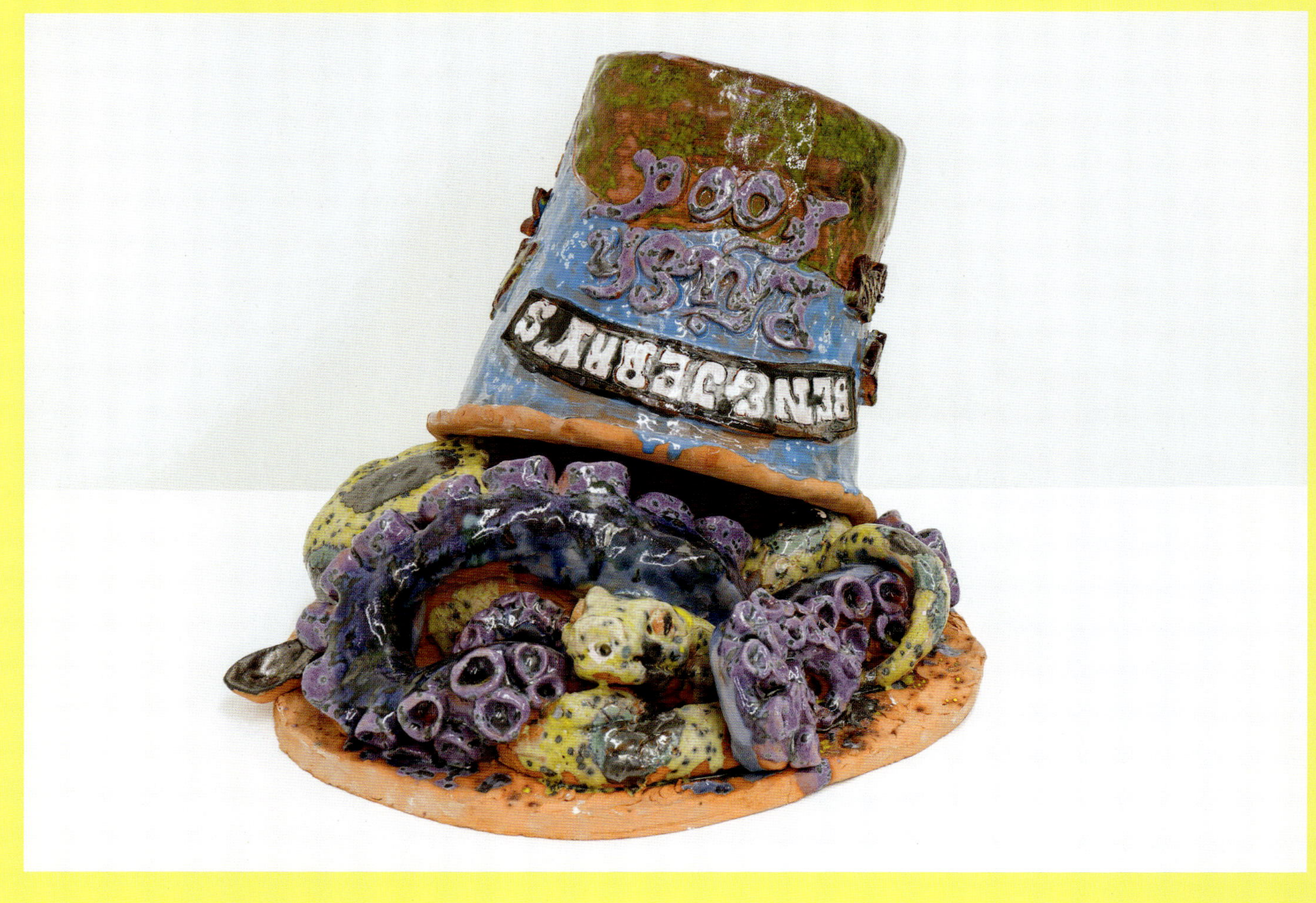

An octopus arm snakes its way suggestively out of an orifice in a glazed ceramic vase. A penis pops up between some soggy chips in a golden polystyrene takeaway box displayed within a traditional glass vitrine. The concept of care was far from my mind the first time I saw the work of Lindsey Mendick (b. 1987, London).

The concept of care was far from my mind the first time I saw Lindsey Mendick's work. Initially, I was struck by her humor, which fuses the grotesque and the everyday within deliciously glossy glazes. But there is also something deeply cathartic about her work. She has said that a desire to connect with others is what drives her to create. Although her work is often autobiographical, it is not just about her; it is about the viewer. It is *for* the viewer.

Mendick told me that she sees opening up about her darkest thoughts and memories as an act of care. In the UK, where the artist lives and works, the British are known for their "stiff upper lip," the expectation that people will suppress their emotions in public, especially the uncomfortable ones. By outing her most intimate experiences and inner conflicts, Mendick lets us know that we are not alone—that our deepest, darkest thoughts, well . . . we are probably not the only one who has had them.

Mendick's work gathers threads from seemingly disparate places and weaves them together, creating dysfunctional installations that fit together so harmoniously that I have questioned whether the connections have always coexisted—as if she has uncovered something so obvious, so intrinsic, that I must have always been aware of it.

Her 2021 show *Hairy on the Inside* at Cooke Latham Gallery in London wove together myths about werewolves and her experience with polycystic ovary syndrome (PCOS) by way of the lunar cycle and a fertility clinic. In the installation, werewolves in hospital gowns sit around on functional chairs in the clinic's waiting room. Their huge ceramic toes poke out of ceramic Crocs and Birkenstocks, while children's toys rot away on a play mat. Aspirational paintings of Wolfie, a model werewolf mother living an idealized family life, hang on the wall. In one scene, Wolfie grins a toothy smile, kneeling beside a bathtub where her children are playing. It is all a bit grotesque, a bit unsavory, and stamped with Mendick's trademark humor.

Although one of the most commonly discussed effects of PCOS is difficulty conceiving, Mendick is most bothered by the excessive hair growth. She grew out her facial hair for the highlight of the show: a film created with her partner, artist Guy Oliver. While sipping a large glass of red wine, she recounts her experiences of having an "unacceptably" hairy body. The film was cut with footage of nightmarish werewolves from the movies—their backs rippling, claws erupting, as hidden identities are forced into sight.

As much as Mendick was revealing intimate details of her own life, as someone who struggles with PCOS, I also felt incredibly exposed by visiting the exhibition and by just knowing the work existed at all. So many of us keep aspects of our own lives hidden away. We are taught to be ashamed of our bodies, our thoughts, and our backgrounds. Although *Hairy on the Inside* felt like it was made just for me, it also revealed something that many

◂ *Phish Food*, 2018
Glazed ceramic (two parts)
10.6 x 12.6 x 13 in.

women experience, albeit often in secret. It is estimated one in ten women in the UK have PCOS and, considering the way it is reviled by society, female facial hair is a surprisingly common symptom.

While something tangible - hair - is erupting out of the female body in the guise of a wolf in the artwork, there are also other far more slippery things that are slinking out from the shadows. Mendick has described her works as "leaky," or unable to contain all that is objectionable to polite society. To me, it feels like Mendick is done with being palatable in both her art and life. She gushes about artist Tracey Emin, an early and continuing inspiration. It was an encounter with Emin's famous tent, *Everyone I Have Ever Slept With, 1963–1995* (1995), that first got her excited about making art that was fun and did not play by the rules. The tent, which contained the names of 102 people with whom Emin had slept in both a sexual and a platonic sense, appealed to Mendick with its rudeness and naughtiness.

There are anxieties and sometimes contradictions that come with creating this kind of work. You might think that Mendick is fearless and brazen. She (emotionally) bares all on Instagram. In her work *Are You Going to Destroy Me?* (2020), she paints her partner as a vampire, lustily baring his teeth as she lies below him, boobs out. She talks candidly about her difficult relationship with her father and the challenges she has faced with obsessive-thought disorder. But, I do not think she is fearless. There is both bravery and fragility in her work. Creating art—let alone art that is so deeply personal—can be both a joyful and an anxiety-provoking experience.

Part of this anxiety is down to expectations of how women should think and behave. Women, Mendick explained, are expected to occupy a shifting middle ground—not too fat or thin, too loud or quiet, too sloppy, too strait-laced. She mused over whether her current popularity relates to people's interest in an acceptable, middle-class, Fleabag level of mess. What would happen if she was revealed to be a good deal messier and more chaotic than believed, or if tastes changed?

In 2022, Mendick made *Off With Her Head*, an installation that looked at morality as a way of controlling women and how women, from Anne Boleyn to Monica Lewinsky, have been suppressed throughout history. Her work continues to perform a "spilling out" of herself and her thoughts, and it also explores the violent constraints that try to contain us. As women, we are continually forced to police ourselves. Each choice that we make is seen as a political statement—whether it is lasering off facial hair or wanting to lose weight. I know I feel it about how I wear my Afro hair. When each personal choice is scrutinized as an expression of a wider political belief, it can become overwhelming and leave us stagnating in a place of indecision. And art, Mendick feels, is sadly becoming one of the worst places for this policing.

Mendick is not giving the middle finger to fitting in. She is not a cool, quirky outsider. All of her "unapologetically me" stuff does not mean not wanting or needing the things that society tells us we should want and need: a fancy holiday, a hair-free face, or a gushingly romantic Valentine's day. Gone are the days when it was cool to be mysterious and reserved. Now, it is cool to care and be emotional and to shout about it all.

— Debbie Meniru

▸ *First Come, First Served*, 2020
Glazed ceramic
17 x 12.2 in.

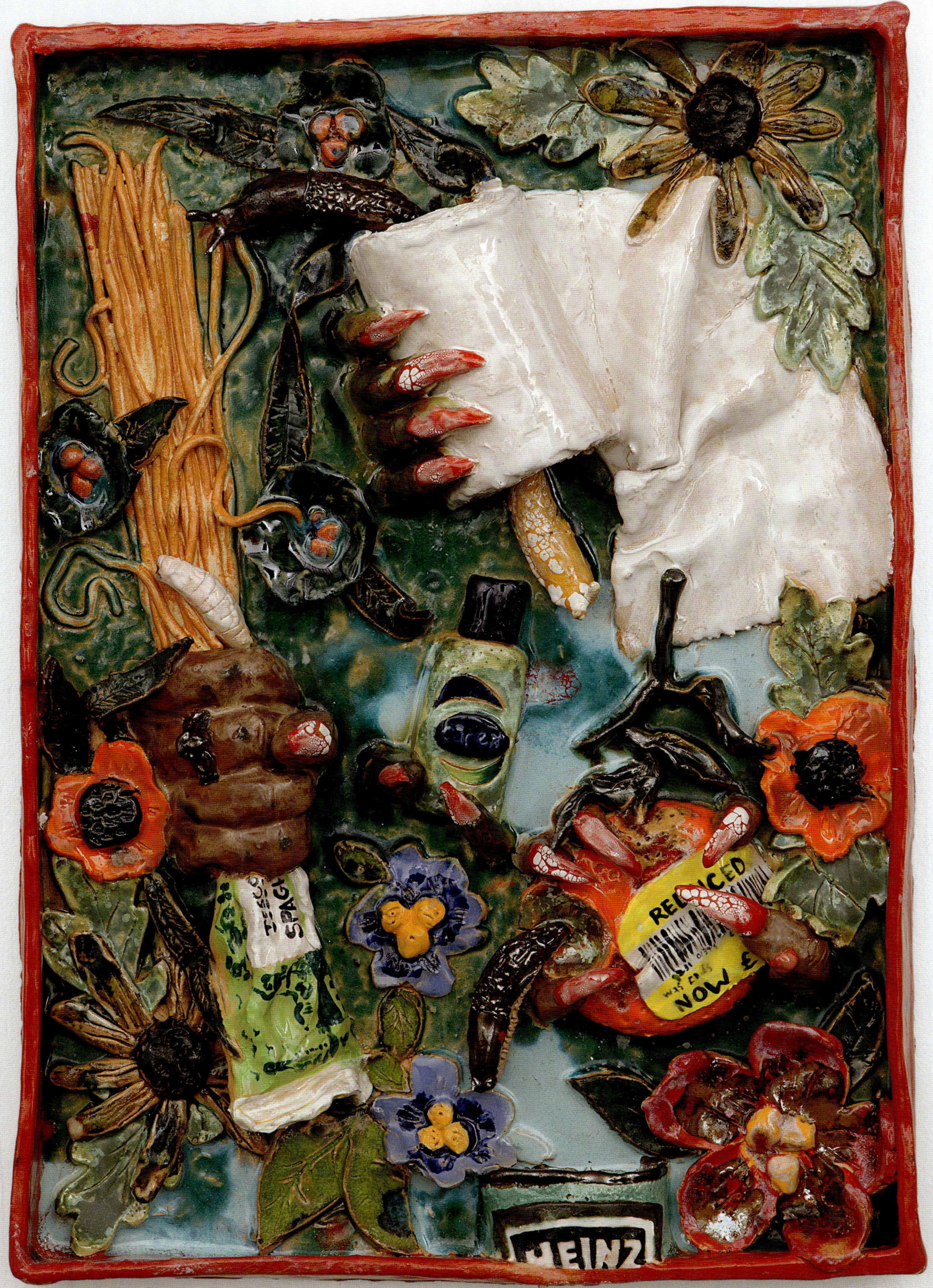
NOW £
HEINZ

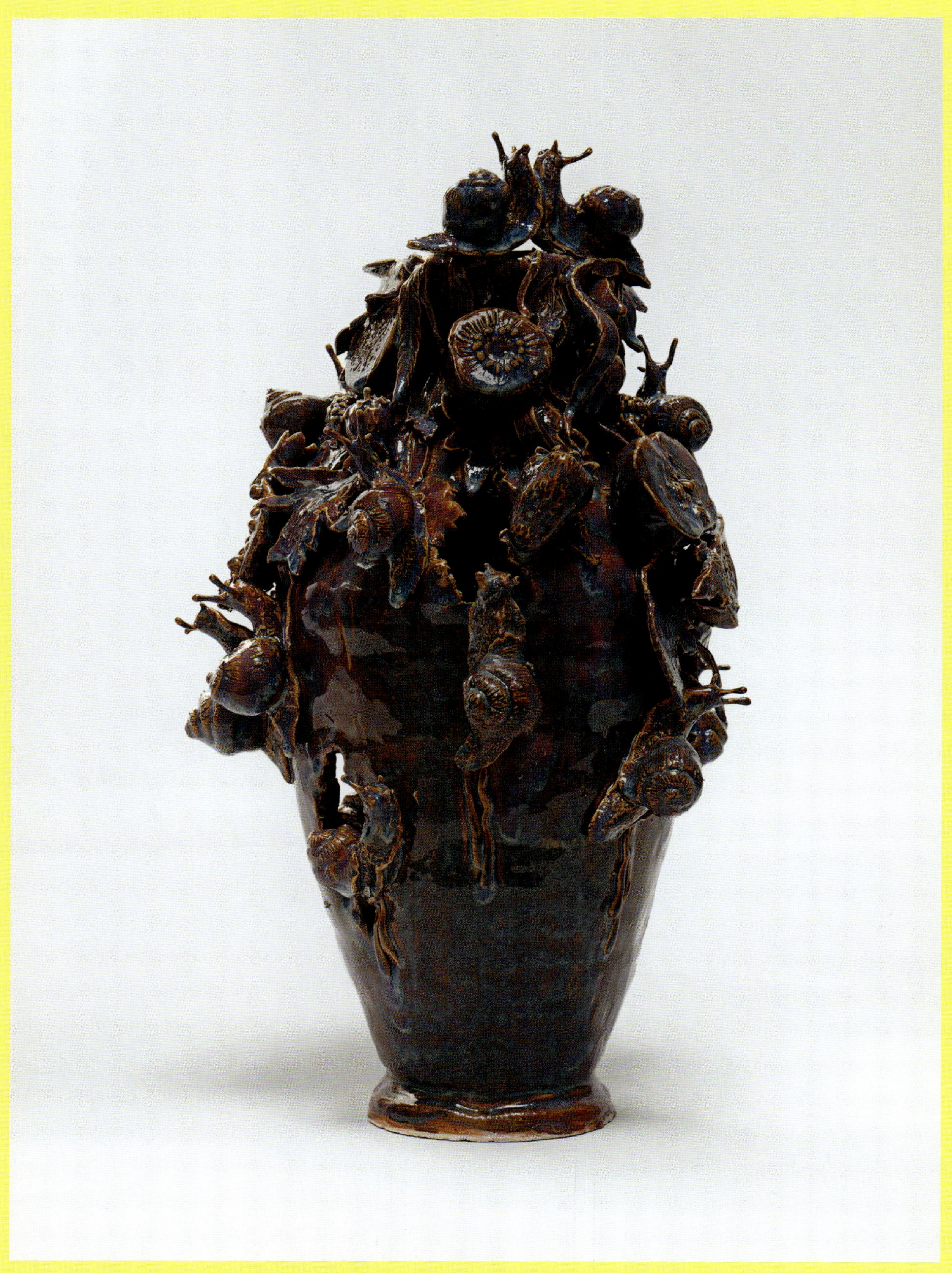

▲ *Shaggers*, 2021
Ceramic
20 x 11 x 11 in.

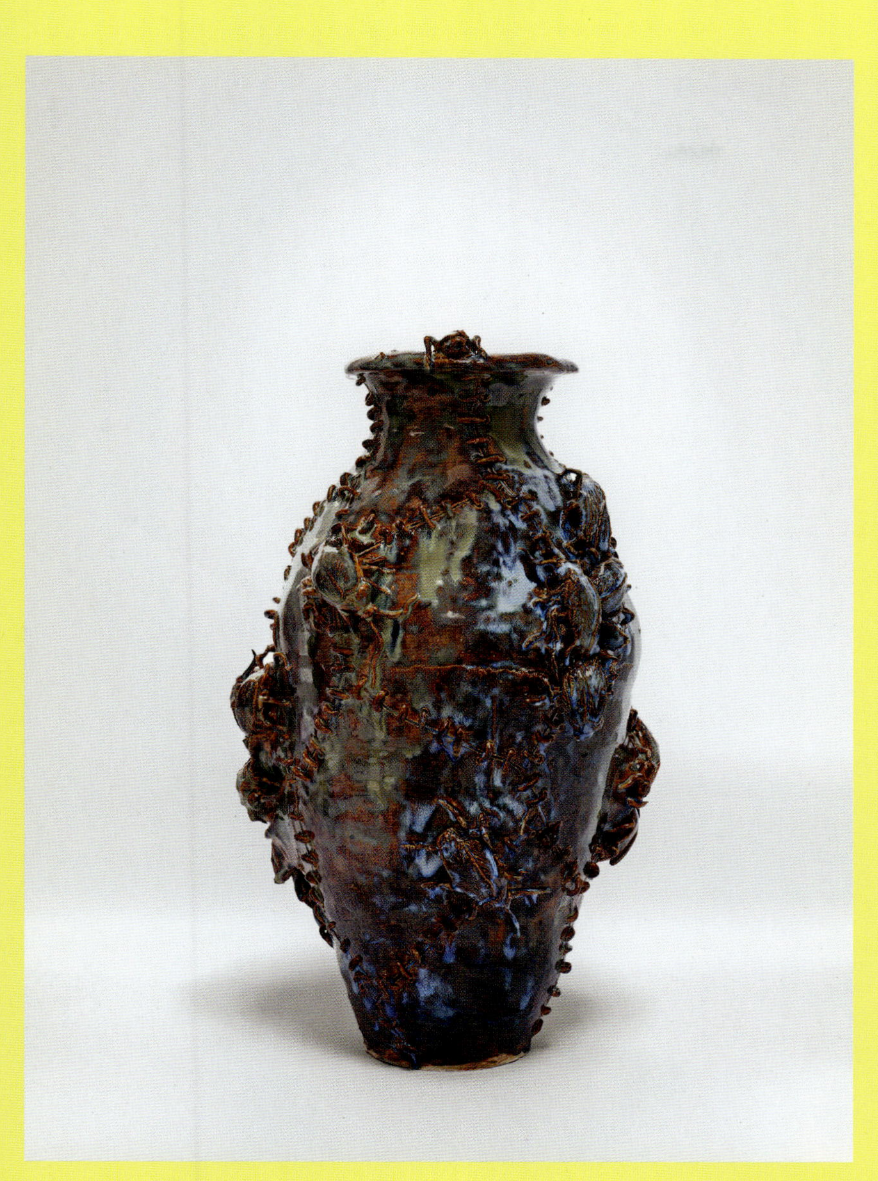

▲ *Skin Suit*, 2021
Ceramic
16.9. x 2 x 2 in.

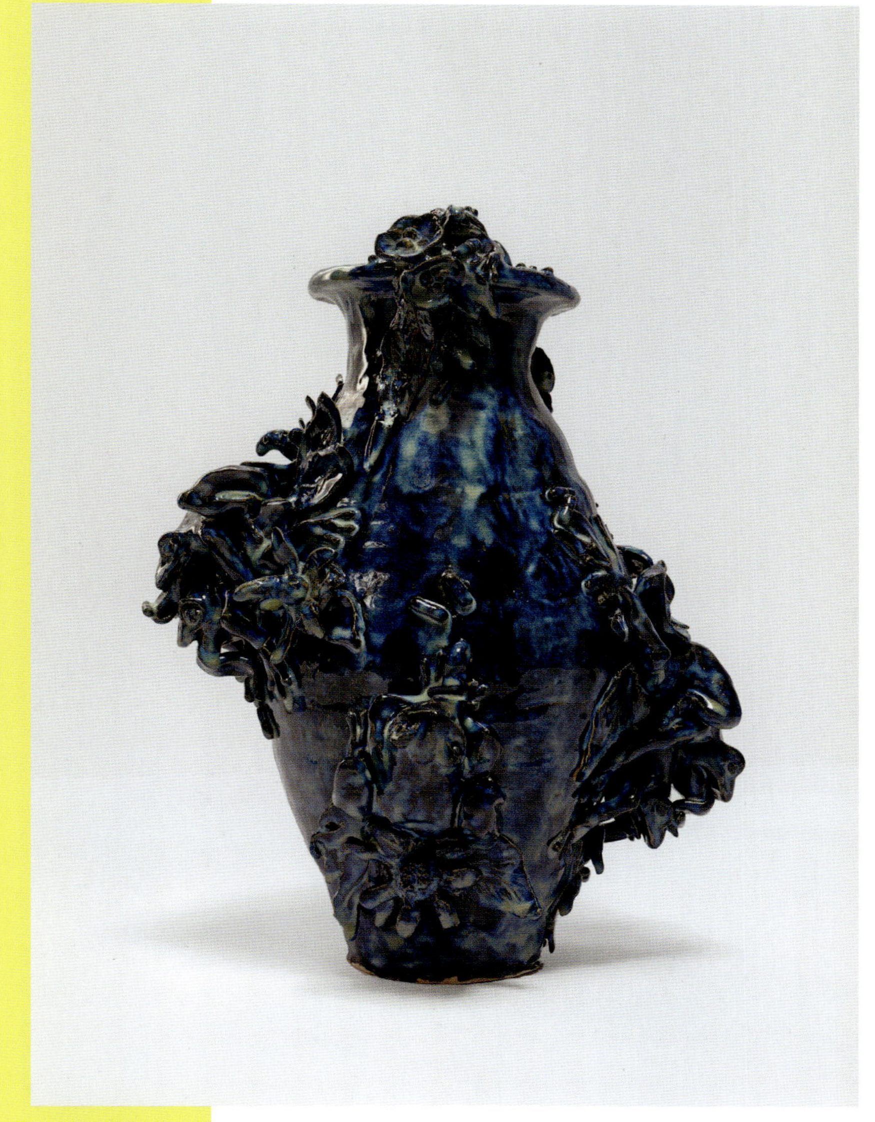

▲ *Sex and Drugs*, 2021
Ceramic
18 x 11 x 11 in.

keegan monaghan

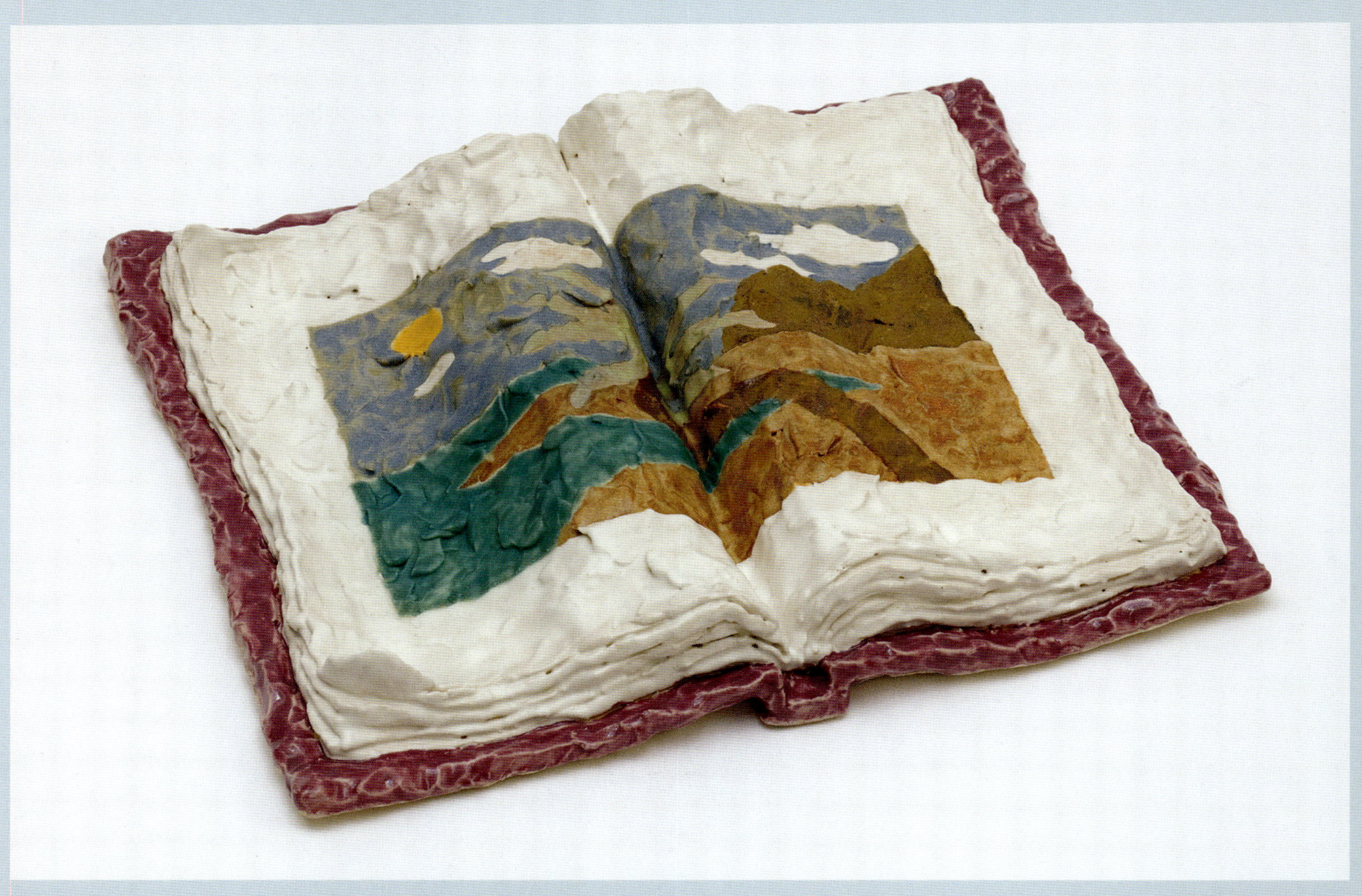

Known primarily for his scumble-layered, densely worked paintings, which frame uncanny depictions of everyday life, Keegan Monaghan (b. 1986, Evanston, Illinois) has also been a devoted ceramicist. Although it is tempting to read Monaghan's approach as treating ceramics as a bridge between sculpture and painting, the artist regards ceramics as a resoundingly painterly medium—though one that sidesteps some of the trappings of traditional oil painting.

In contrast to painting's slow-accruing, open-ended process, the modeled clay object invites speed and closure, a hard-out that comes with the firing (and once again with the one-shot of the glazes). Resisting painting's preoccupation with the long meditative process, this incitement for speed and closure invites litheness, experimentation, and brevity. Monaghan leverages this enforced tenuousness into gambits of legibility, where the object is suggested with fewer and fewer moves—an ongoing push toward the abstract. If Monaghan's paintings invoke a surface pregnant with the mystery of latent color, worked-over drafts, and fugitive marks, these ceramic works trade in economy (an albeit goopy one) with the artist asking, "What is the least amount of moves that will still read?"

As objects, these ceramic works exist in the world and thus rent from the psycho-spatial dimension present in all of Monaghan's painted works. The point of view is through a keyhole into a window located across an alley. These ceramic works are painted objects freed from painted space. The affective associations of painterly rendering can exist solely for the formal benefit of the object. Monaghan refers to these articulating marks, with their specific thumbed-into-being quality, as "impressions." He links them to nineteenth-century painting with its iconic daubes, pokes, and flicks of paint, which are haphazard up close but producing a gestalt of unity from a distance. Monaghan's "impressions" are the site of the work's most essential tensions: legibility vs. abstraction, improvisation vs. contemplation, and control vs. happenstance. It is a mark that forms one of the fundamental pieces of Monaghan's artistic syntax—the poignancy of a thing barely, but surely, come into being.

— James English Leary

◂ *Book*, 2020
Ceramic
9 x 10 x 1.375 in.

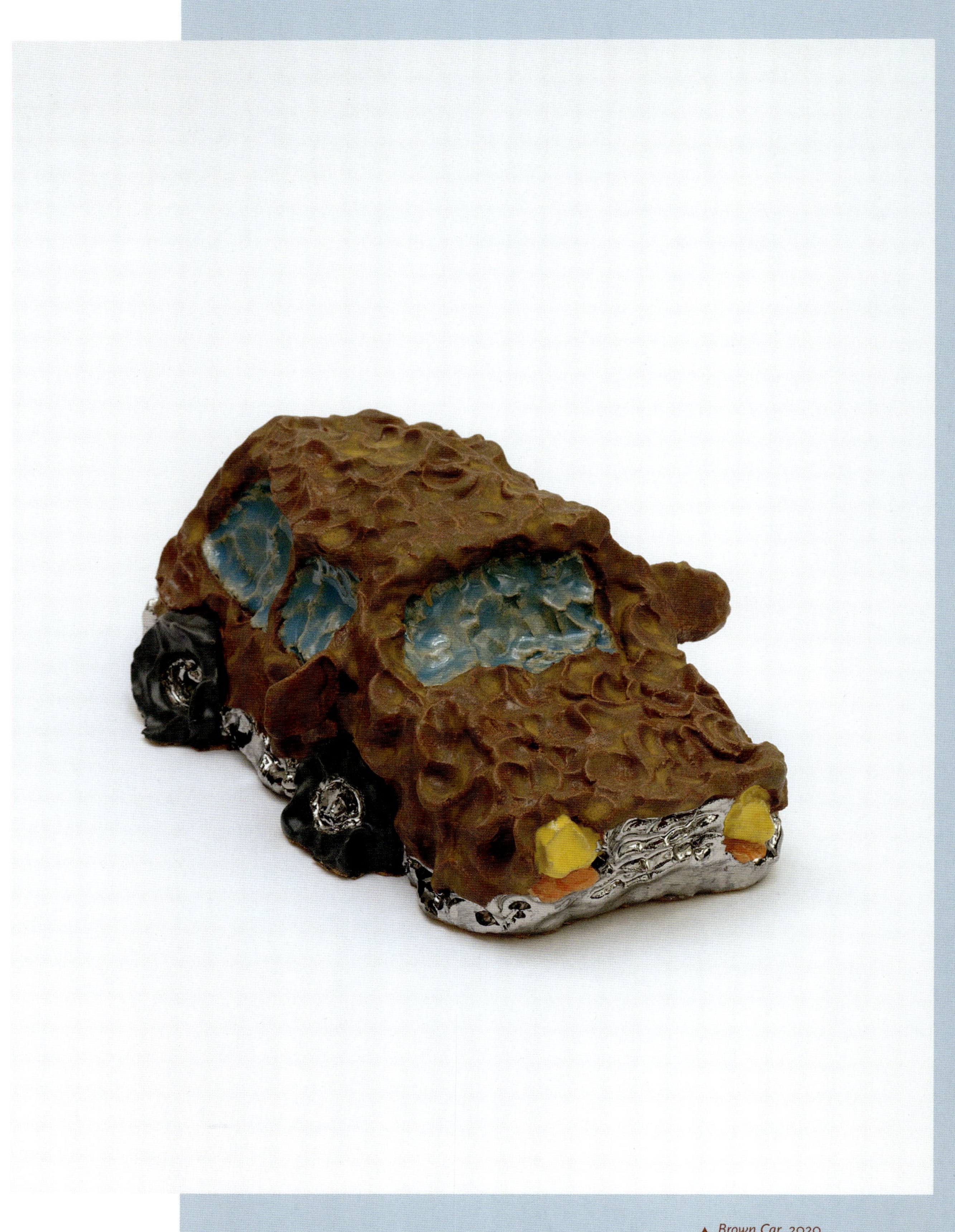

▲ *Brown Car*, 2020
Ceramic
10 x 6.5 x 4 in.

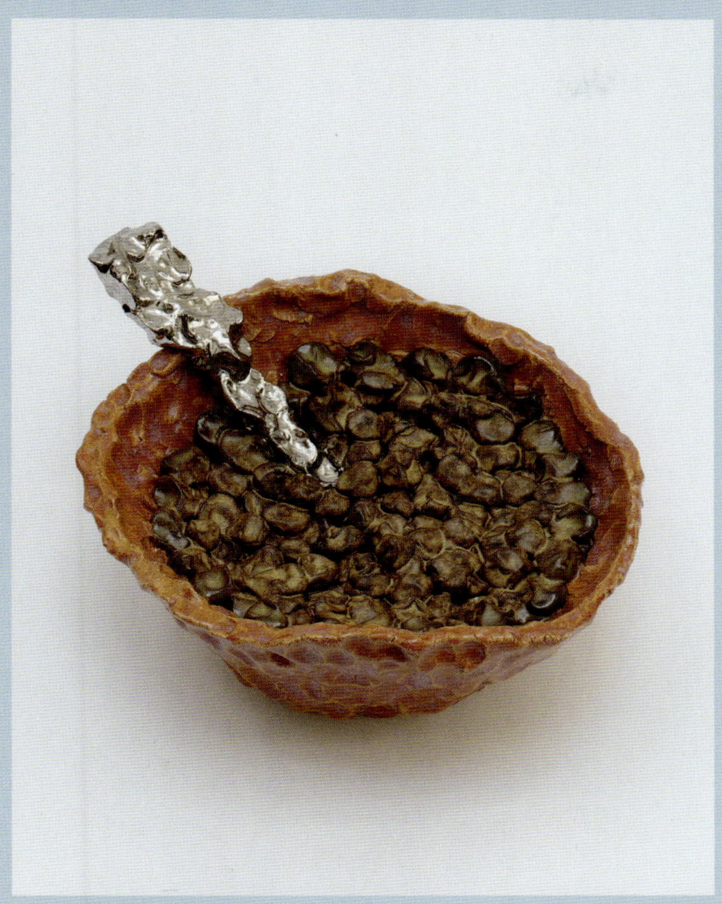

▲ *Bowl of Food*, 2020
Ceramic
9 x 7 x 4.5 in.

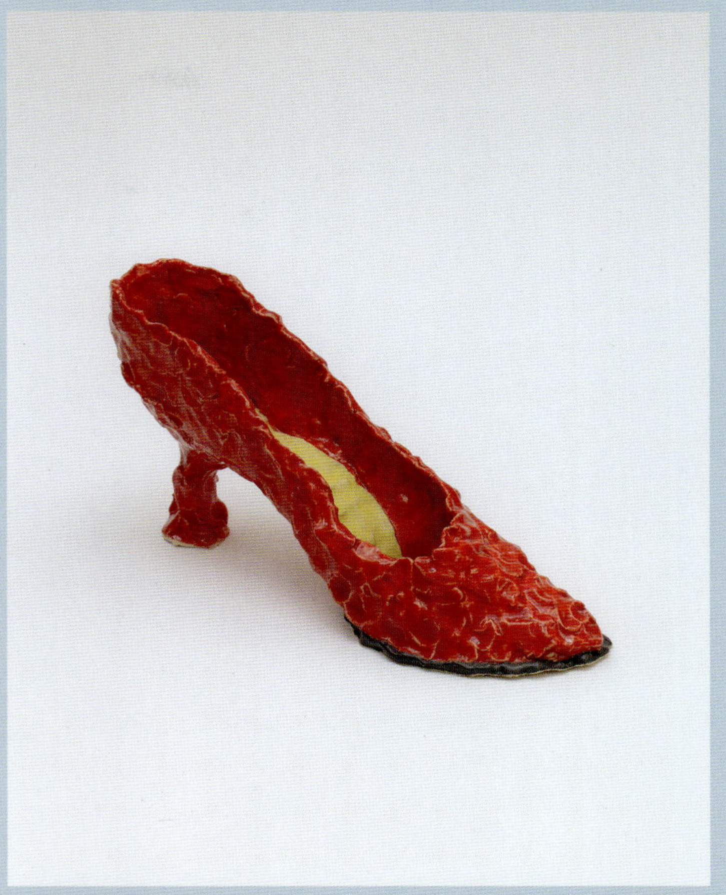

▲ *High Heel*, 2020
Ceramic
12 x 3.5 x 5.5 in.

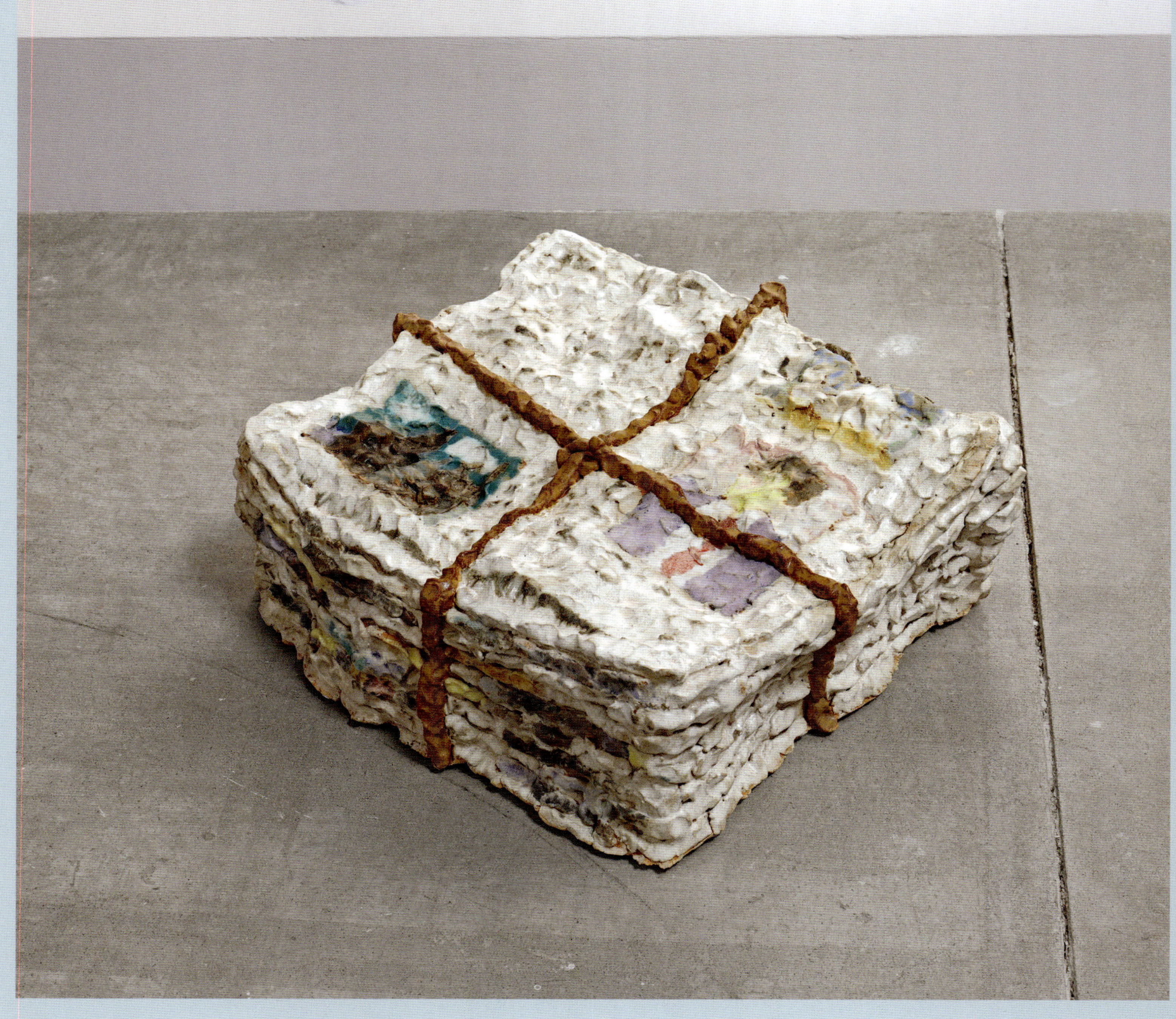

▲ *Newspapers*, 2021
Glazed ceramic
6 x 16.6 x 14 in.

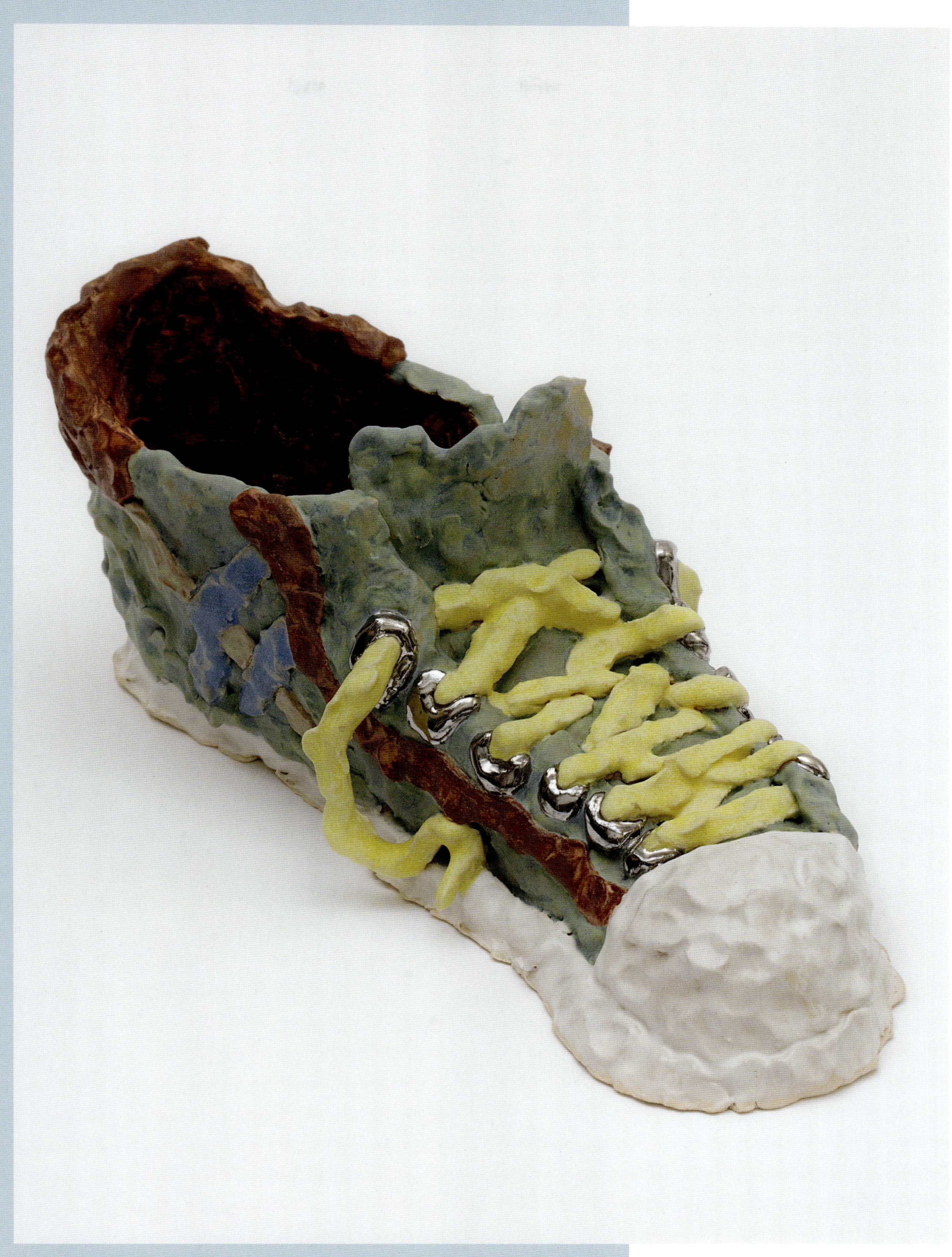

▲ *Sneaker*, 2020
Ceramic
11.5 x 3.5 x 4.5 in.

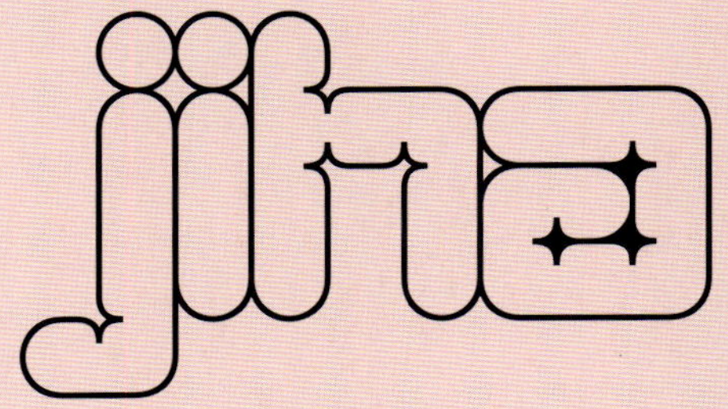

moon

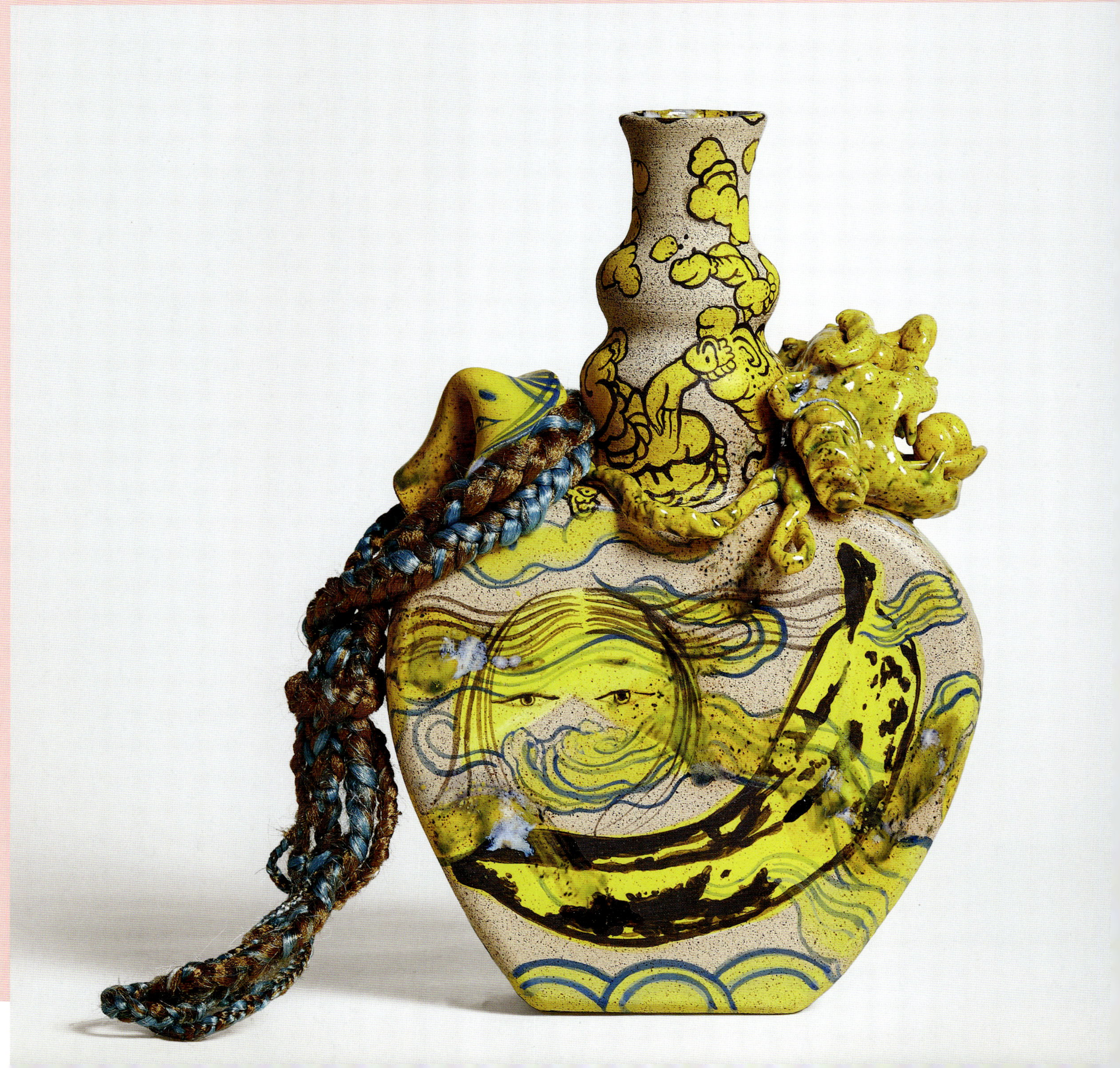

Jiha Moon (b. 1973, Daegu, South Korea) is a contemporary artist who focuses on painting, printmaking, and sculptural ceramic objects. After getting a BFA and MFA in Korea, Moon immigrated to the United States in the late 1990s. As an immigrant in her late twenties and already a practicing artist, Moon decided to get an MFA at the University of Iowa to underscore her willingness to start anew. In 2012, Moon, who had gained wide acclaim for her paintings and prints, was awarded a grant from the Museum of Contemporary Art of Georgia. She used the award to sign up at a local clay studio in Atlanta, where she has lived for many years.

In her ceramics, Moon has merged the vessel with a creature. Sometimes, the creature has a head, torso, and feet; other times, it is just a head, signified by a large, garish mouth full of menacing teeth. Her sources include teapots, incense burners, sake bottles, and face jugs that first appeared in the American South in the mid-1800s and are attributed to Black slaves working in South Carolina. Her amalgamation of Eastern and Western sources, which cannot be easily taken apart, reminds us that one's identity is made up of multiple sources.

Moon uses a number of sources in her ceramics. They range from high art to folk art, and from Pop culture to kitsch. She glazes and paints the vessel's entire surface, both inside and outside, and attaches various objects such as ceramic fortune cookies, banana peels, pinkish round forms topped by red nipples, and synthetic hair. Along with these objects, her images include eyes, stylized yellow waves that can be read as blond hair and a commentary on America's ideas of beauty, cartoony figures and symbols derived from Mexican Milagros, and various fruits and animals. Often humorous, Moon might place ceramic fortune cookies to suggest a creature's ears or as the pot's handles.

Moon's ceramics can be understood as household gods, mythic creatures, animal spirits, dolls, and idols, whose exact motivations remain unknown to us. Are they benign or sinister presences? Do they protect us? Or are they tricksters waiting to pull the rug out from under our feet? Complex and resistant to any reductive reading that we might try to apply to them, Moon's figures are endearing and outlandish, comical and provocative, and challenging and unsettling.

— John Yau

◂ *Lucky Face*, 2021
Earthenware, underglaze, glaze, synthetic hair
12.75 x 9.5 x 4.5 in.

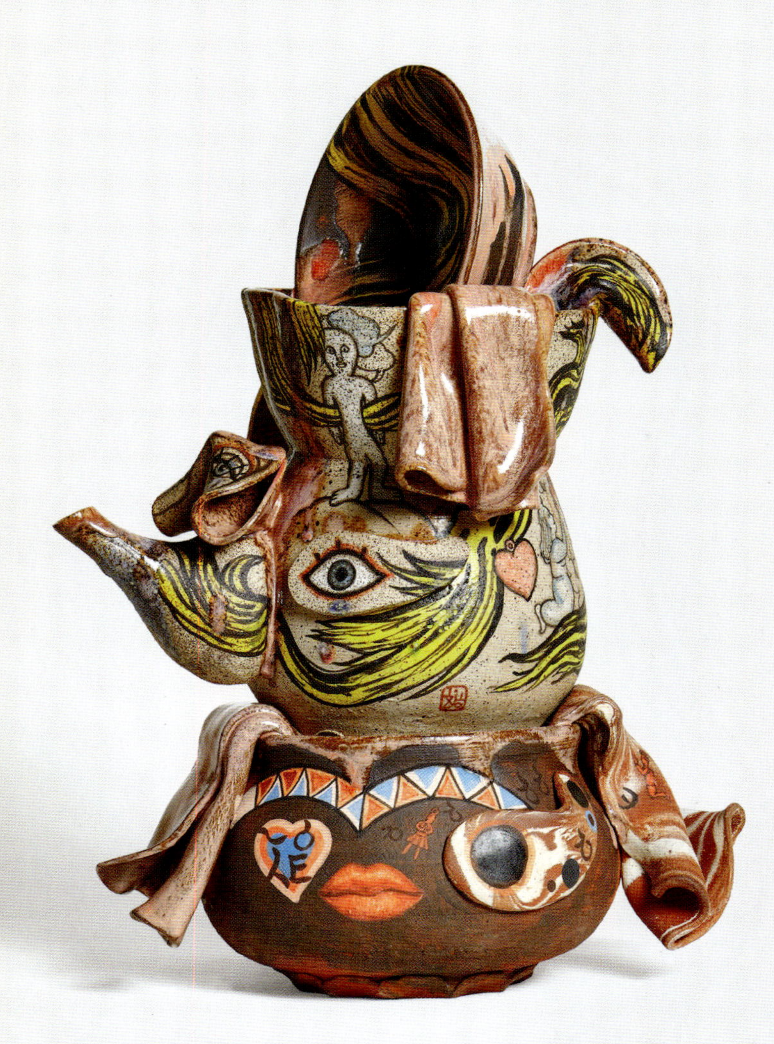

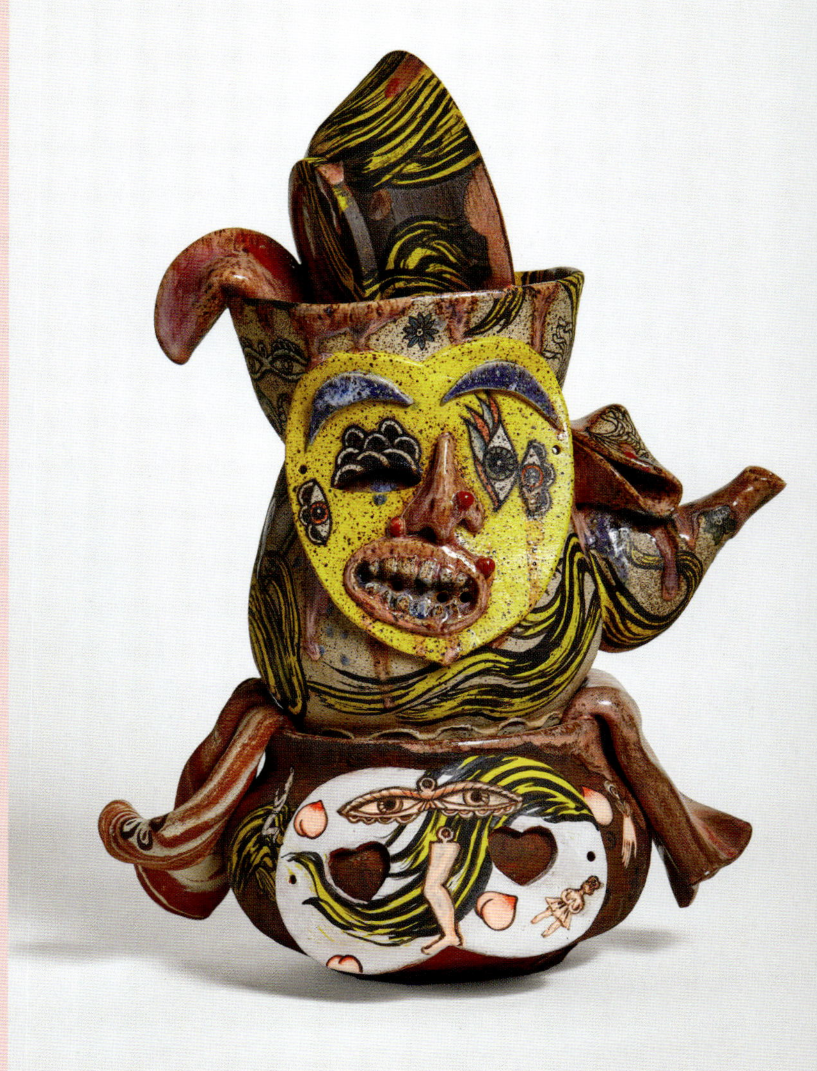

▲ Front and back view of *Full Moon Face Jug*, 2021
Stoneware, earthenware, porcelain slip, underglaze, glaze
17.5 x 13.5 x 8 in.

▾ *Yellowave Genie*, 2021
Stoneware, underglaze, glaze
11.5 x 10 x 6.5 in.

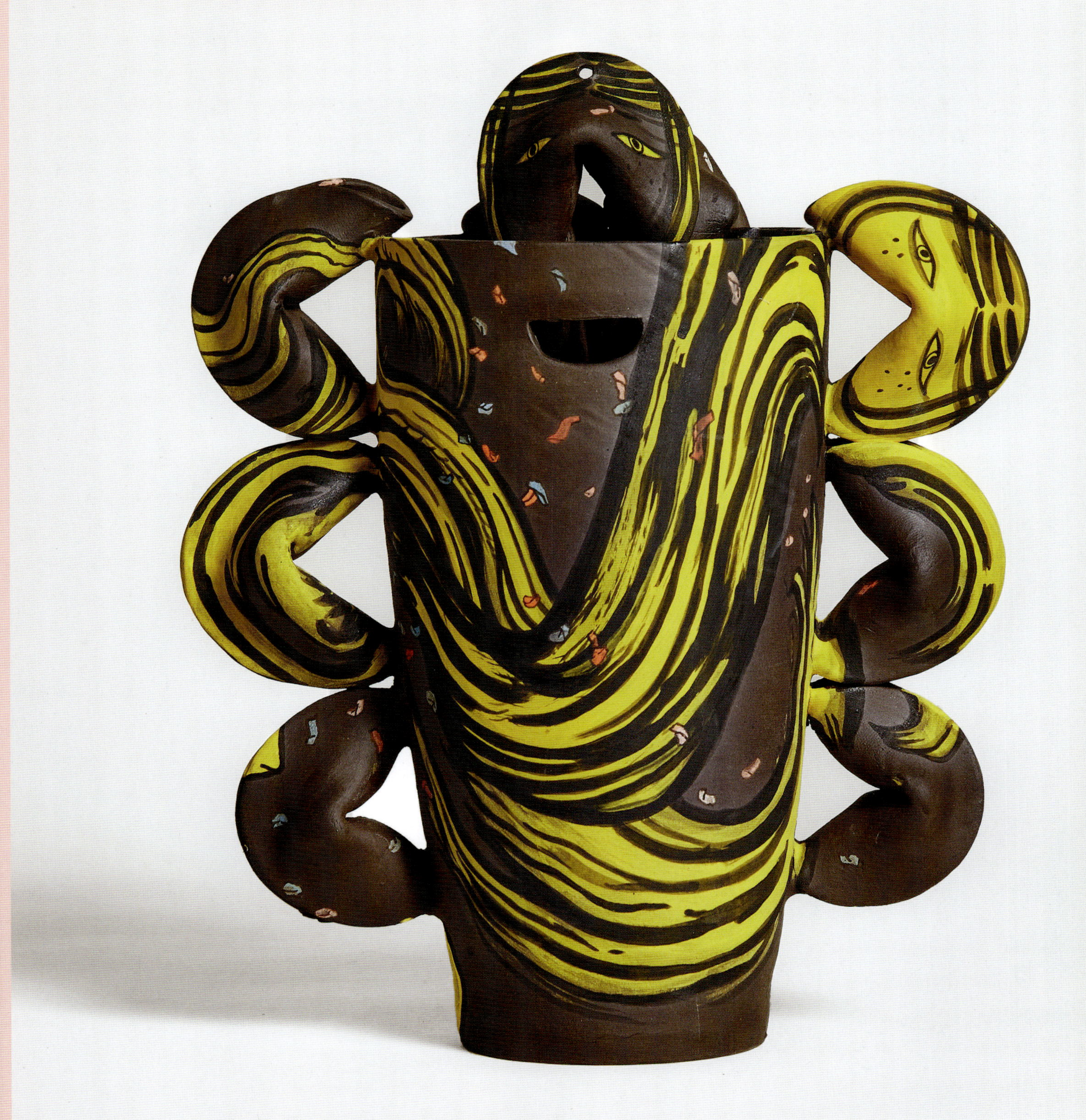

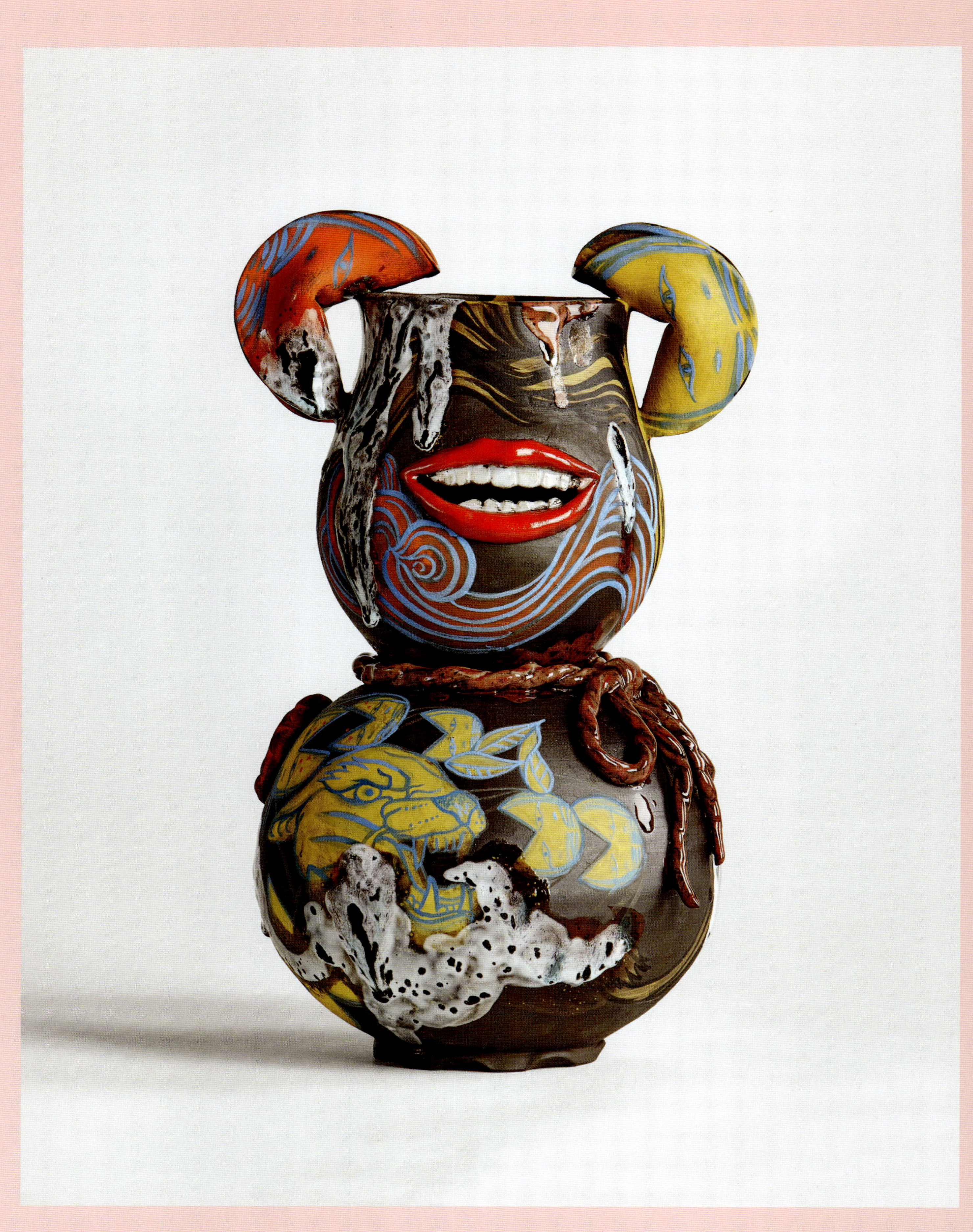

▲ *Yellowave Simcheong*, 2021
Stoneware, underglaze, glaze
12.75 x 8 x 8 in.

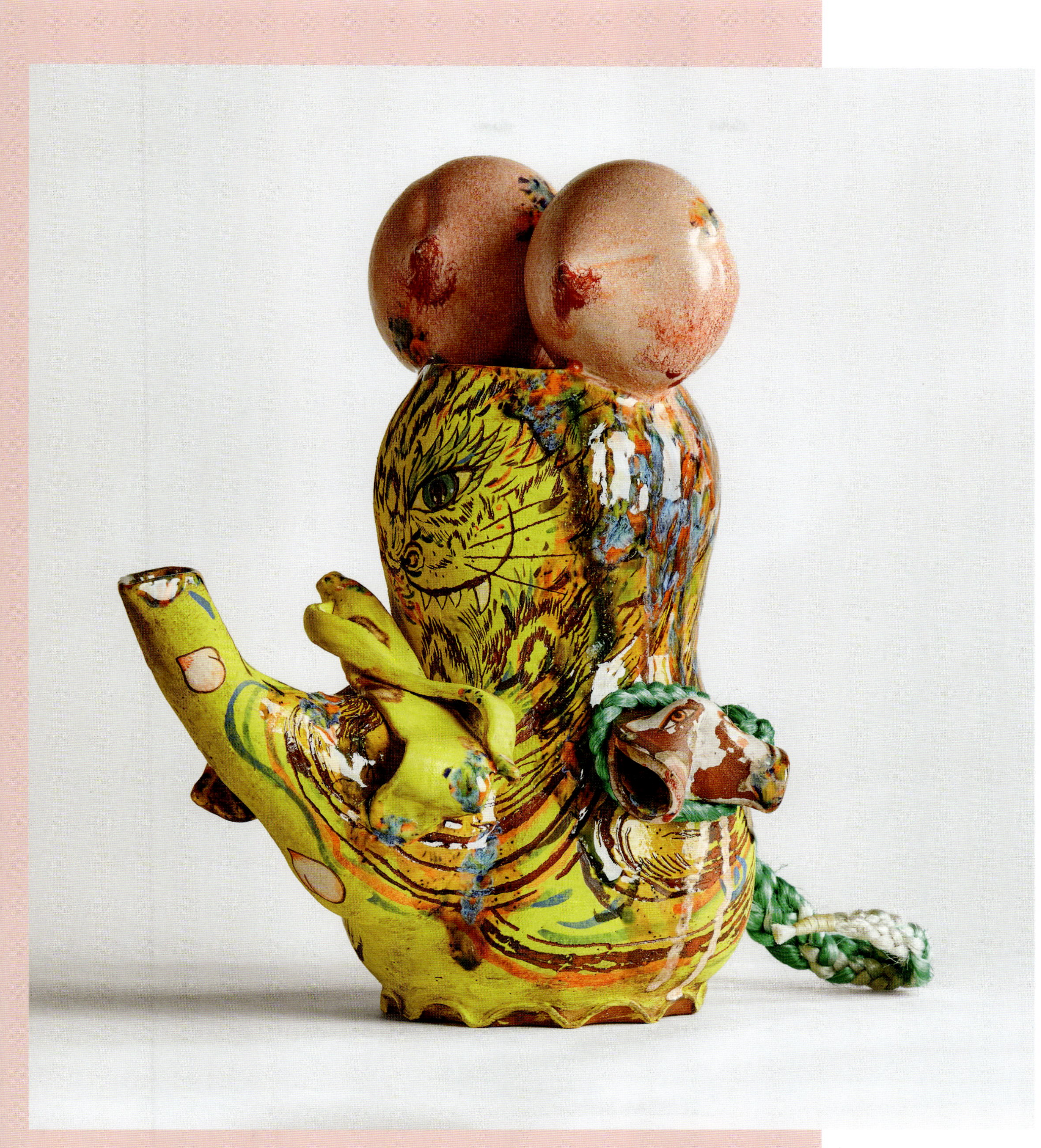

▲ *Tiger Mama*, 2021
Earthenware, underglaze, glaze,
synthetic hair
12.75 x 8.5 x 12 in.

masato mori

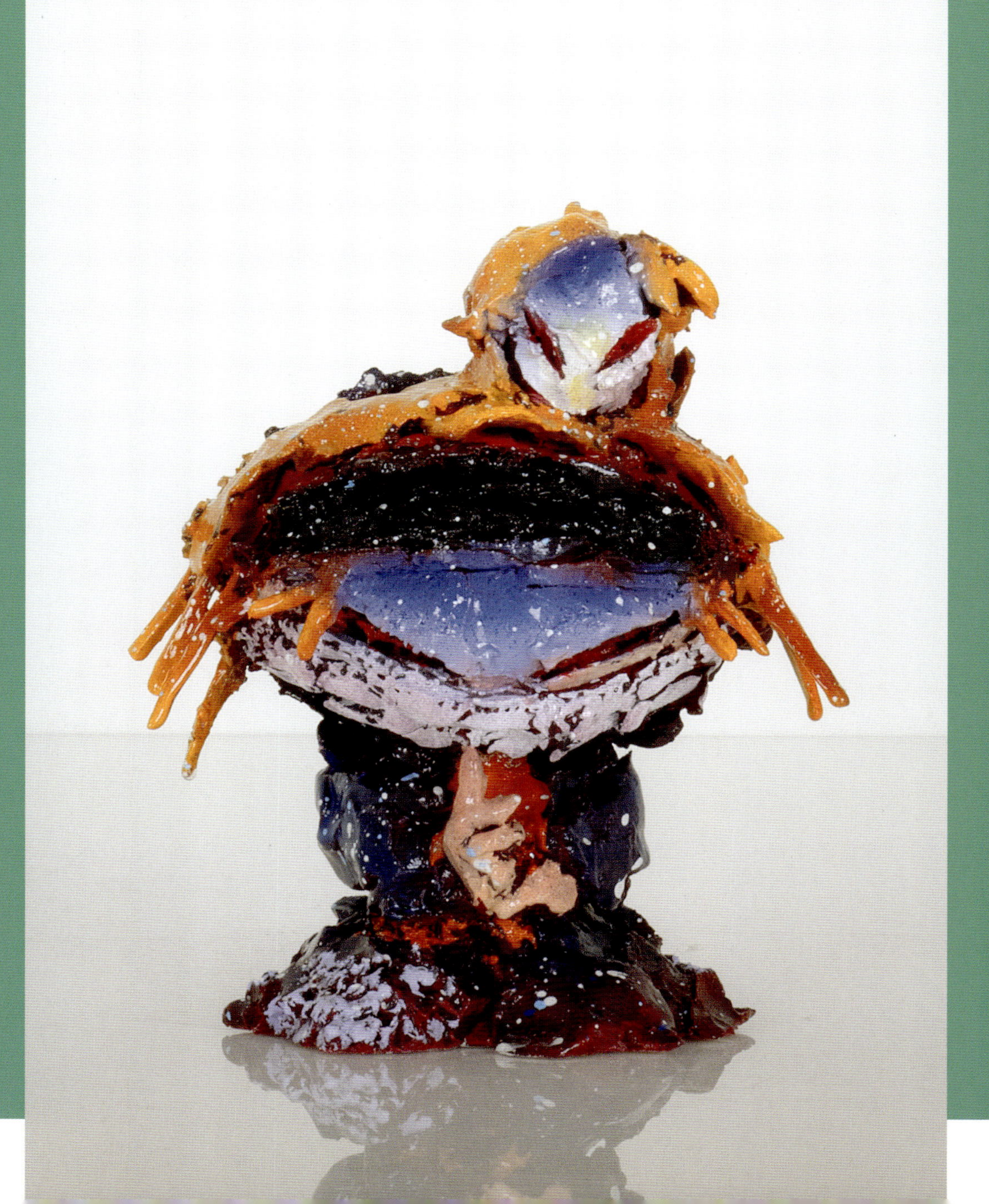

Masato Mori (b. 1976, Tokushima Prefecture, Japan) is a Japanese modern and contemporary artist. Mori's paintings are characterized by their vivid colors and complex texture. They simultaneously present a somewhat comical and light impression. In the process leading to this style, Mori repeatedly analyzed the various influential relationships that serve as the root of his creative activities—in particular, seeking out points of correspondence between his own aesthetic perspective and that of comics, video games, and animation.

In Mori's recent works, it is possible to discover a certain affinity with artists like Jean Dubuffet, Paul Klee, Pablo Picasso, and Wassily Kandinsky, who had studied children's paintings and art produced by those with disabilities. Here, viewers are able to capture glimpses of the clues that lead to unraveling Mori's artistic practice, such as innocence and purity that, in essence, are considered as fundamental themes within art. For Mori, who had learned the joys of drawing through copying popular comic book characters, the manifestation of such correlations within his work had perhaps been a natural course of progression.

What should particularly be noted with regards to Mori's process of creation is the correlation between three-dimensional and two-dimensional works. Mori likes to use graphics that he has drawn with a pen tab tool as preliminary sketches for his paintings. The act of expressing different textures to his graphics through the process of applying paint to the canvas is an important part of his artistic practice. Three-dimensional works, such as ceramics and bronzes, that Mori produces are based on colored pencil drawings that have been sketched from his finished paintings.

The process of creating different media such as graphics, painting, drawing, and 3D works as if to facilitate interactions between the three-dimensional and two-dimensional realms is a technique that Mori naturally arrived at through repeated experimentation.

— Shinji Nanzuka

◂ *Bamboo Dance* (detail), 2021

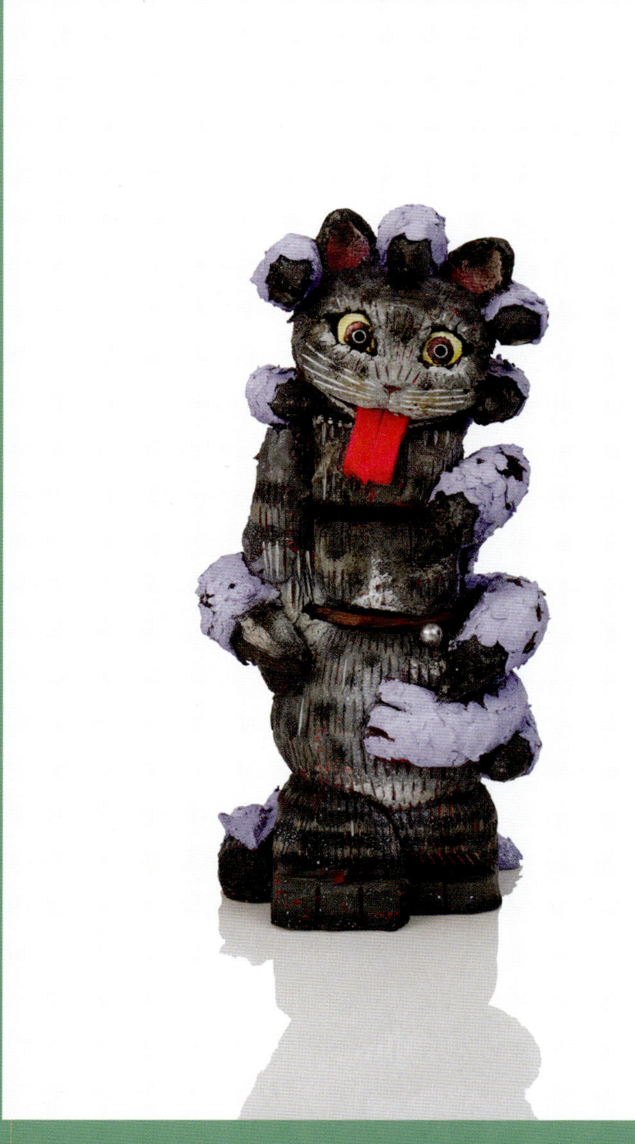

▲ *The Cat Is Mine*, 2019
Acrylic paint, acrylic spray, oil chalk, oil paint on ceramic
12.6 x 7 x 7 in.

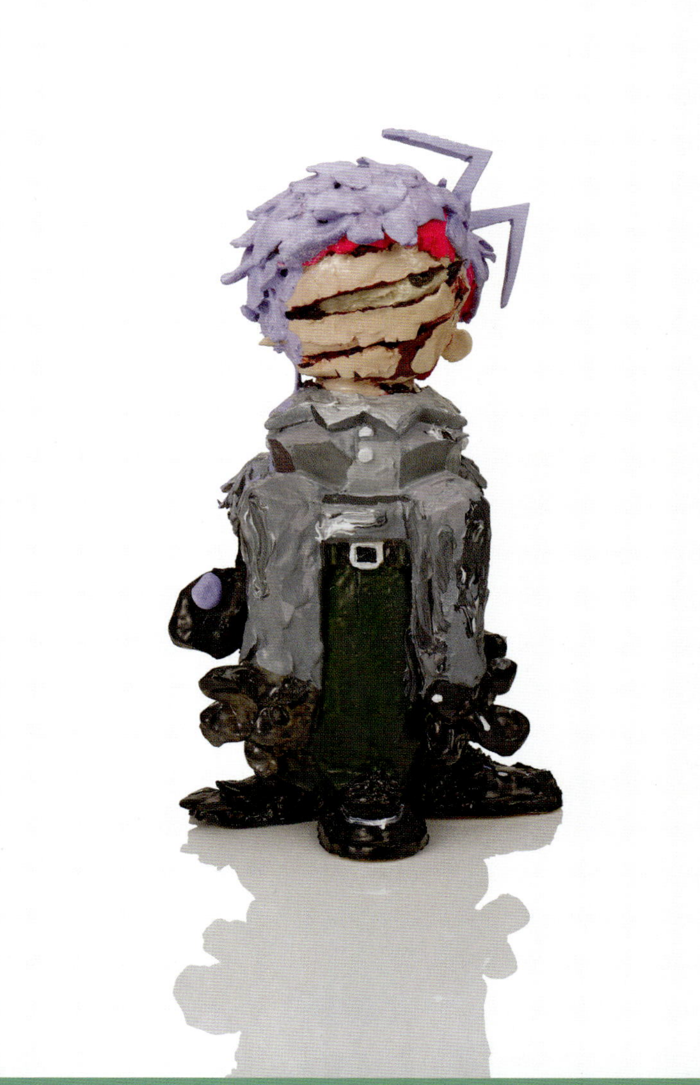

▲ *Profile*, 2019
Acrylic paint, acrylic spray, oil chalk, oil paint on ceramic
9.8 x 5.5 x 5 in.

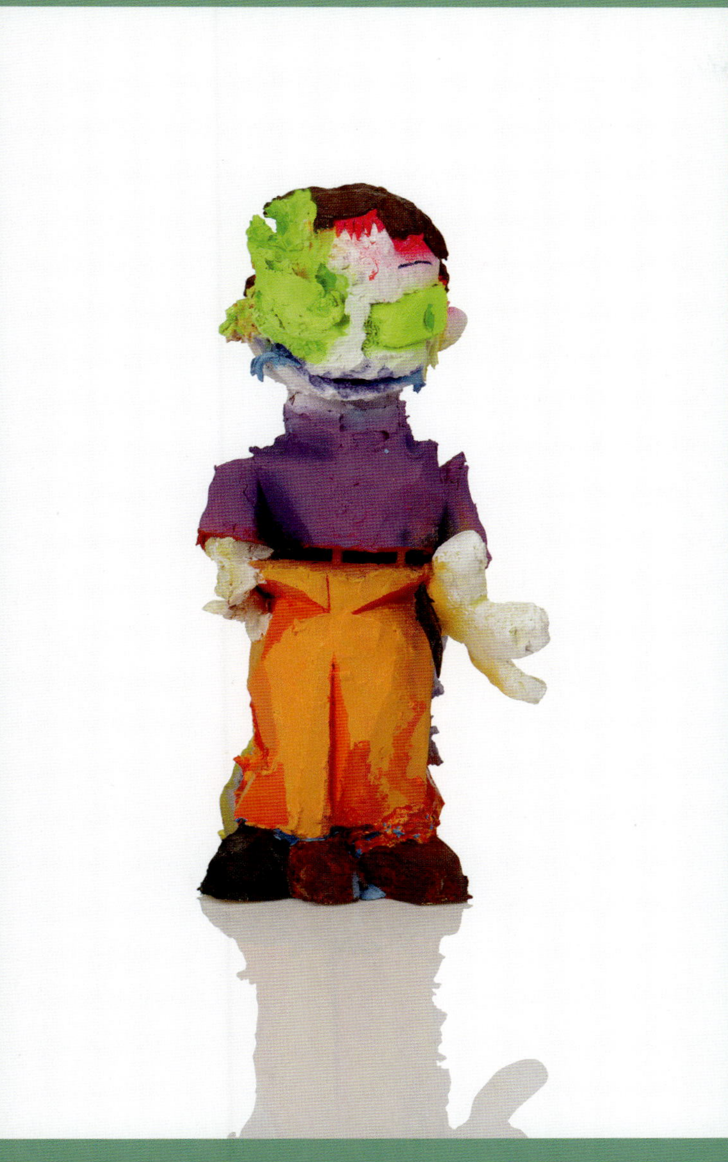

▲ *Sunshower* ①, 2019
Acrylic paint, acrylic spray, oil chalk, oil paint on ceramic
9.4 x 4.7 x 5.5 in.

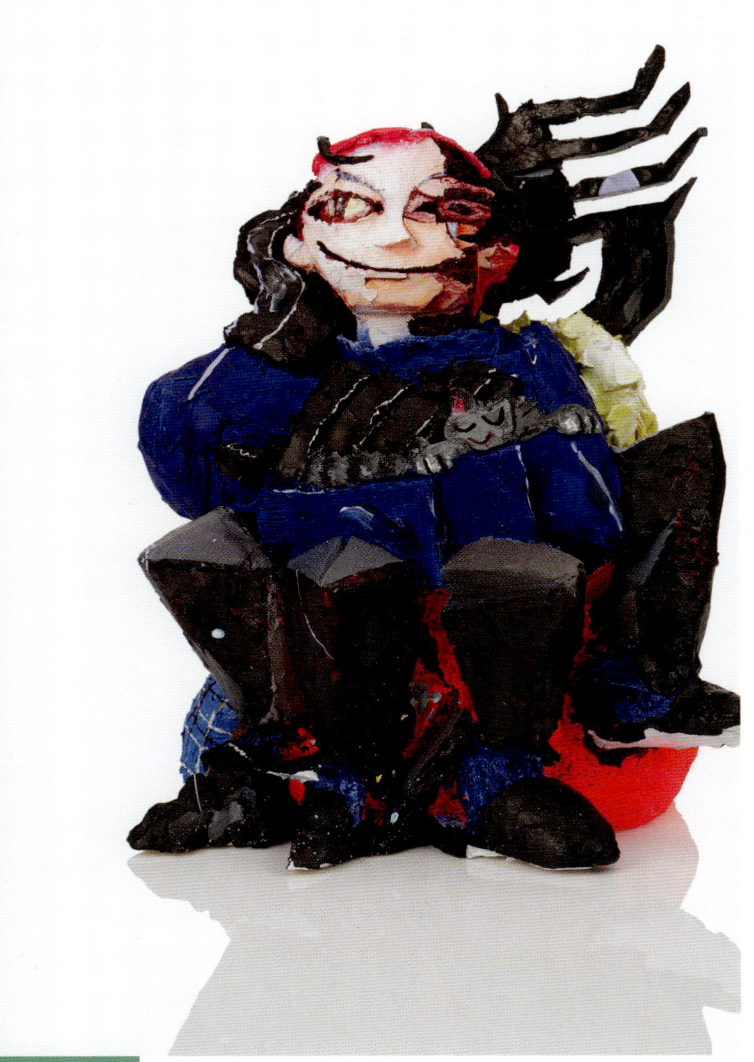

▲ *Sunshower* ②, 2019
Acrylic paint, acrylic spray, oil chalk, oil paint on ceramic
8.2 x 7 x 6.6 in.

▸ *Bamboo Dance*, 2021
Glazed ceramic
Set of nine ceramics: variable dimensions

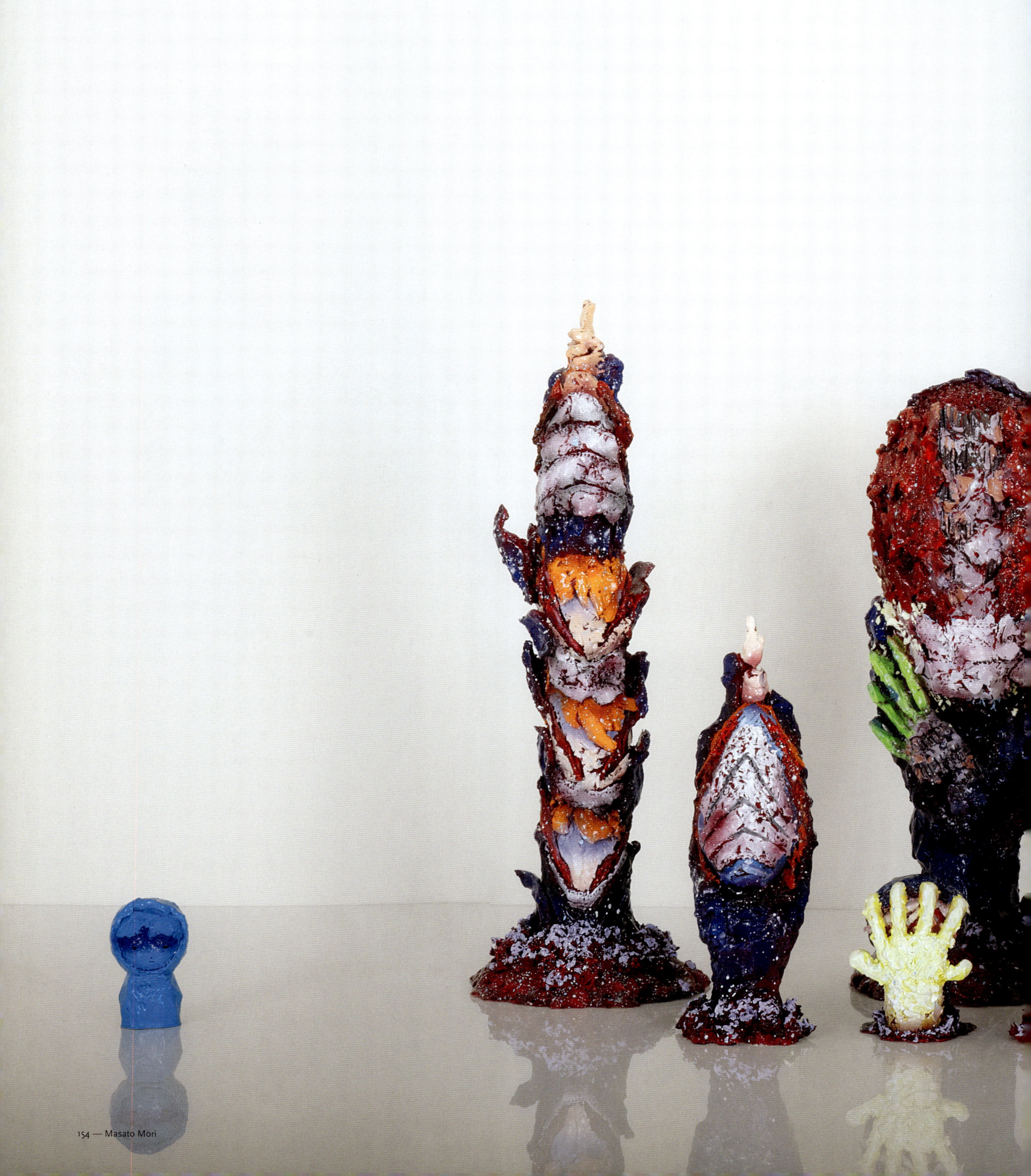

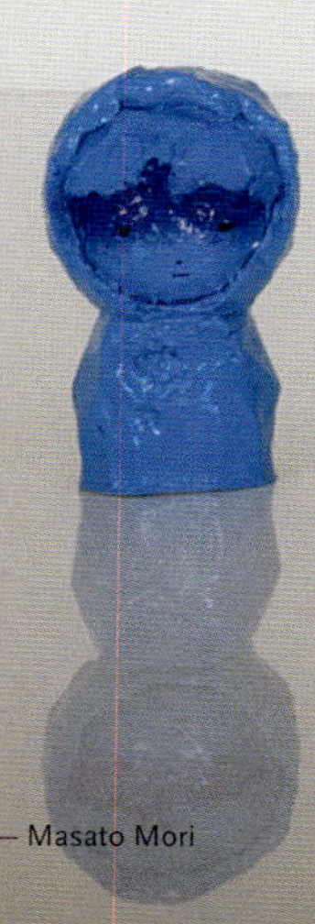

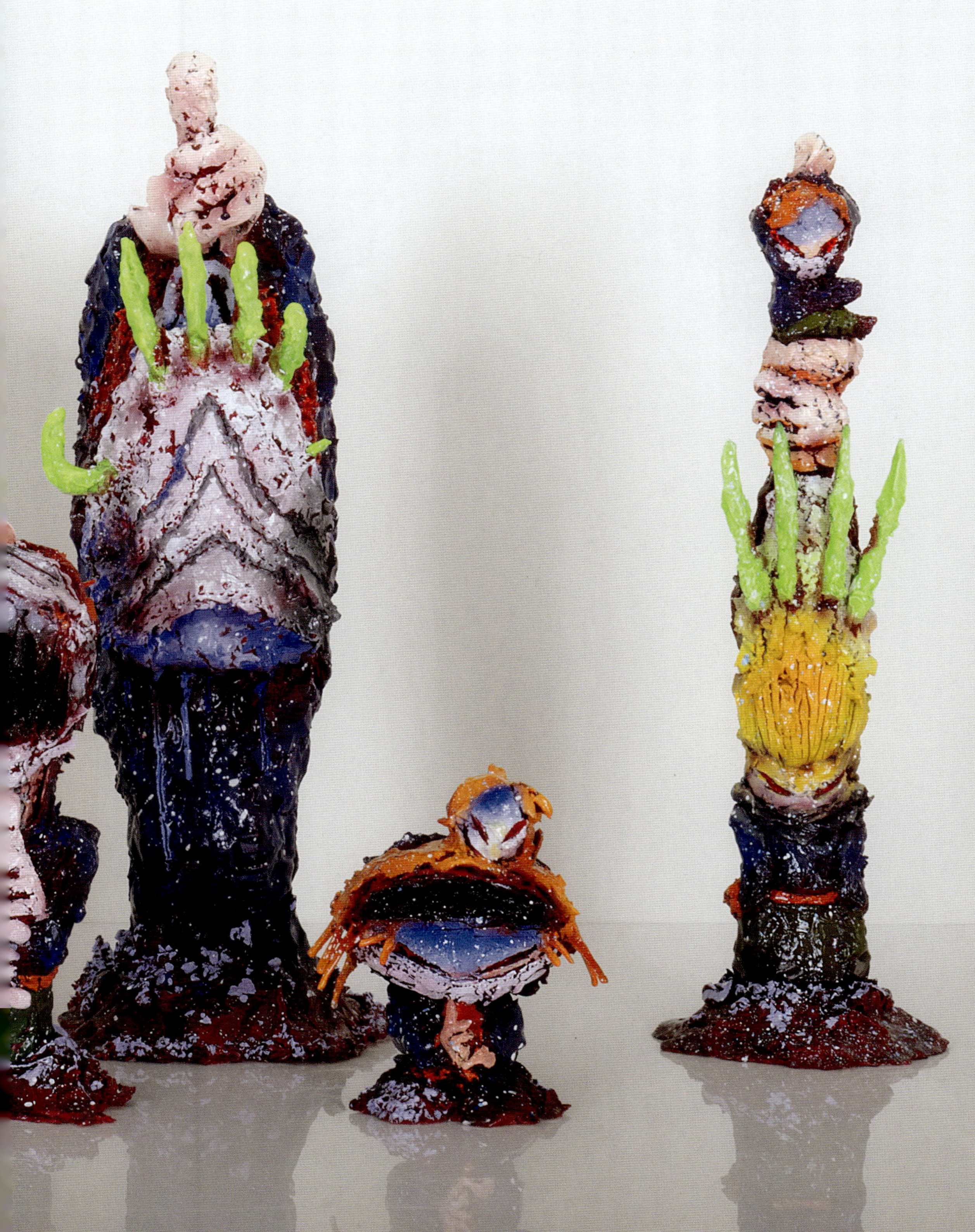

narumi nakanekapan

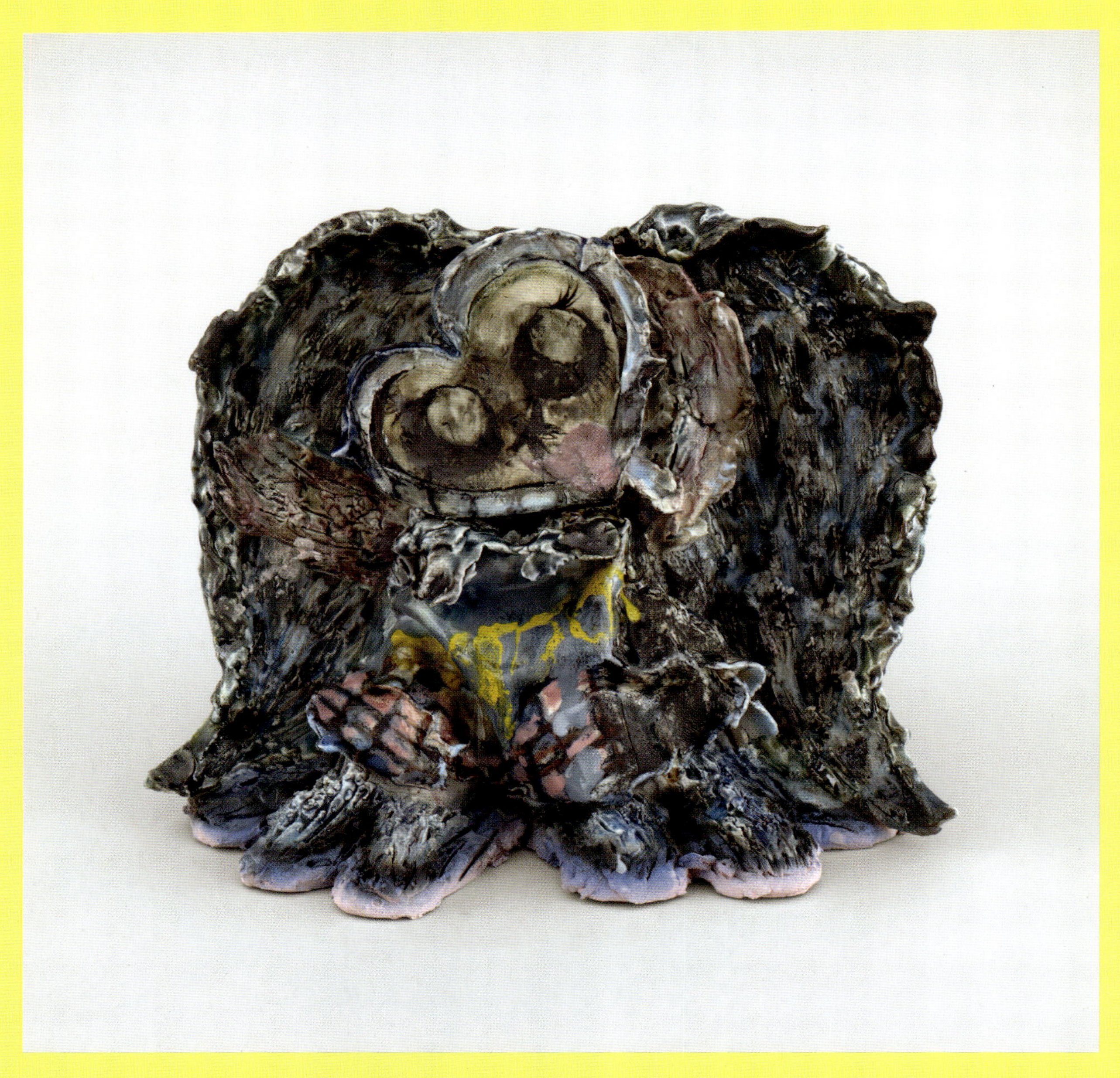

Narumi Nekpenekpen (b. 1998, Kashiwa, Japan)

Scrolling through Narumi Nekpenekpen's Instagram page (@narublu), I come across an assortment of selfies, old family photos of the artist as a child with her Japanese mother and Nigerian father, and various screen grabs—mostly from films and music videos. In addition to these and most prominent within her feed are images of Nekpenekpen's hands. Adorned with chunky silver jewelry, the artist's hands appear either on their own or together with one of her in-progress clay sculptures. Self-captured in the process of shaping, painting, or simply caressing one of her works, these images of Narumi's hands feel important.

I have never met Narumi in person but, from this collection of photos, I understand her hands to be special. Large and with long elegant fingers that taper always to a great manicure, I imagine Narumi's hands to be nurturing and assured. Placing the artist into a tactile relationship with the world around her, Narumi's hands transmit the language of her rich internal world into the soft clay that awaits.

Nekpenekpen's hands conjure spells that awaken a small but fierce army of lovers. Glazed in vivid hues of cobalt blue, tangerine, and powder pink, her clay figures are tiny in comparison to the human form, but immense relative to the flecks of earthen elements that constitute the clay from which they have been made. With big doe eyes, heart-shaped pouty lips, and cobby bodies, they gesture with a strength and urgency that far outweigh their size.

Nekpenekpen's work traverses questions surrounding identity and belonging. With titles such as *bitterness; it thaws in yellow* (2022) and *it tasted so good, how would I have known?* (2021), the artist's clay figures act as a form of personal introspection, connecting interior processes to the world around her. Channeling the unbounded language of dreams, and exploring color and texture, Nekpenekpen's pieces are the result of moments of intense emotion—the purging of feelings of sadness, frustration, and, at times, rage.

In her process, slab porcelain clay is pushed and pulled into a central foundation onto which the artist affixes a head, chunky limbs, and, like armor, highly textured garments, chains, and other accessories. Nekpenekpen is interested in what clay wants to do on its own as well as what can emerge from their immanent relation. With her process of hand-building informed by both incongruity and imperfection, Nekpenekpen's characters come to life where mistranslation begins. In their playfulness, her clay figures protest the binary of high and low art, resisting the Western commodification of culturally different aesthetic forms. Untethered from preexisting ways of seeing and making, Narumi's hands create a family: a community of others where dependency is essential to existence, and in which love reigns supreme.

— Kate Wong

◂ *bitterness; it thaws in yellows,*
2022
Glazed porcelain
8 x 10.5 x 5.5 in.

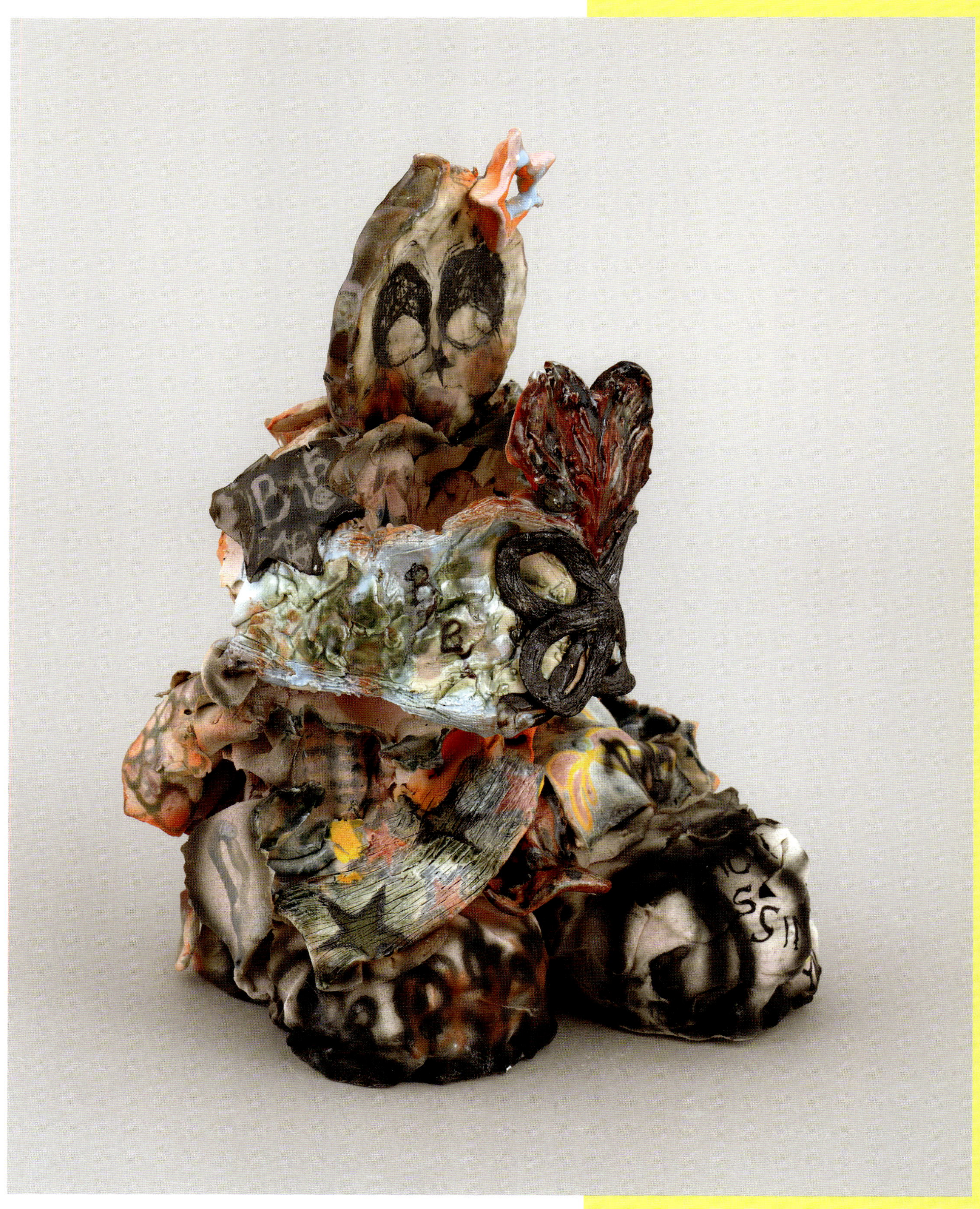

▲ *my chipped tooth oozing*, 2021
Glazed porcelain
12 x 9 x 6 in.

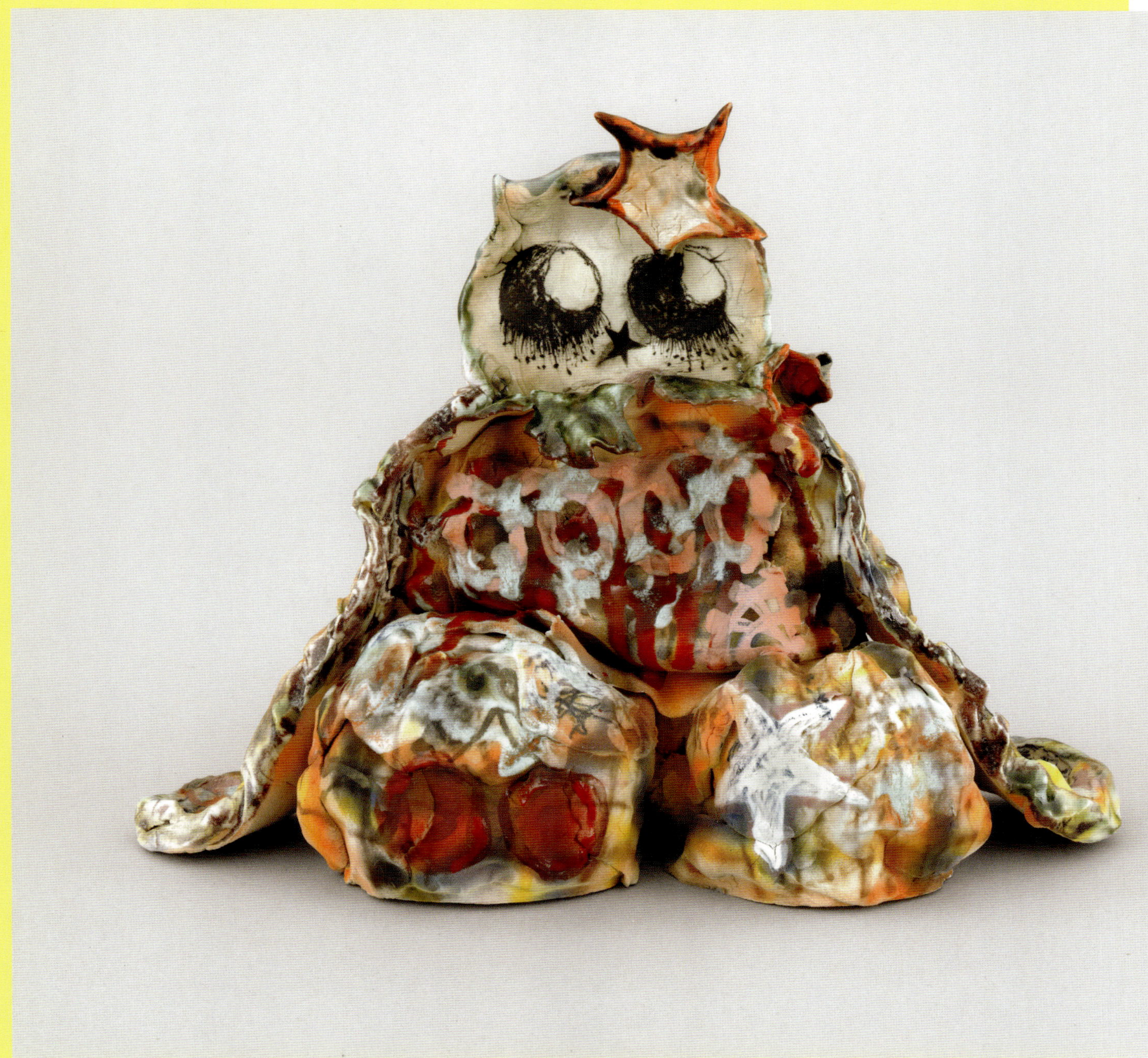

▲ *biting into the sky, sands in greeting,*
2021
Glazed porcelain
9 x 11 x 5 in.

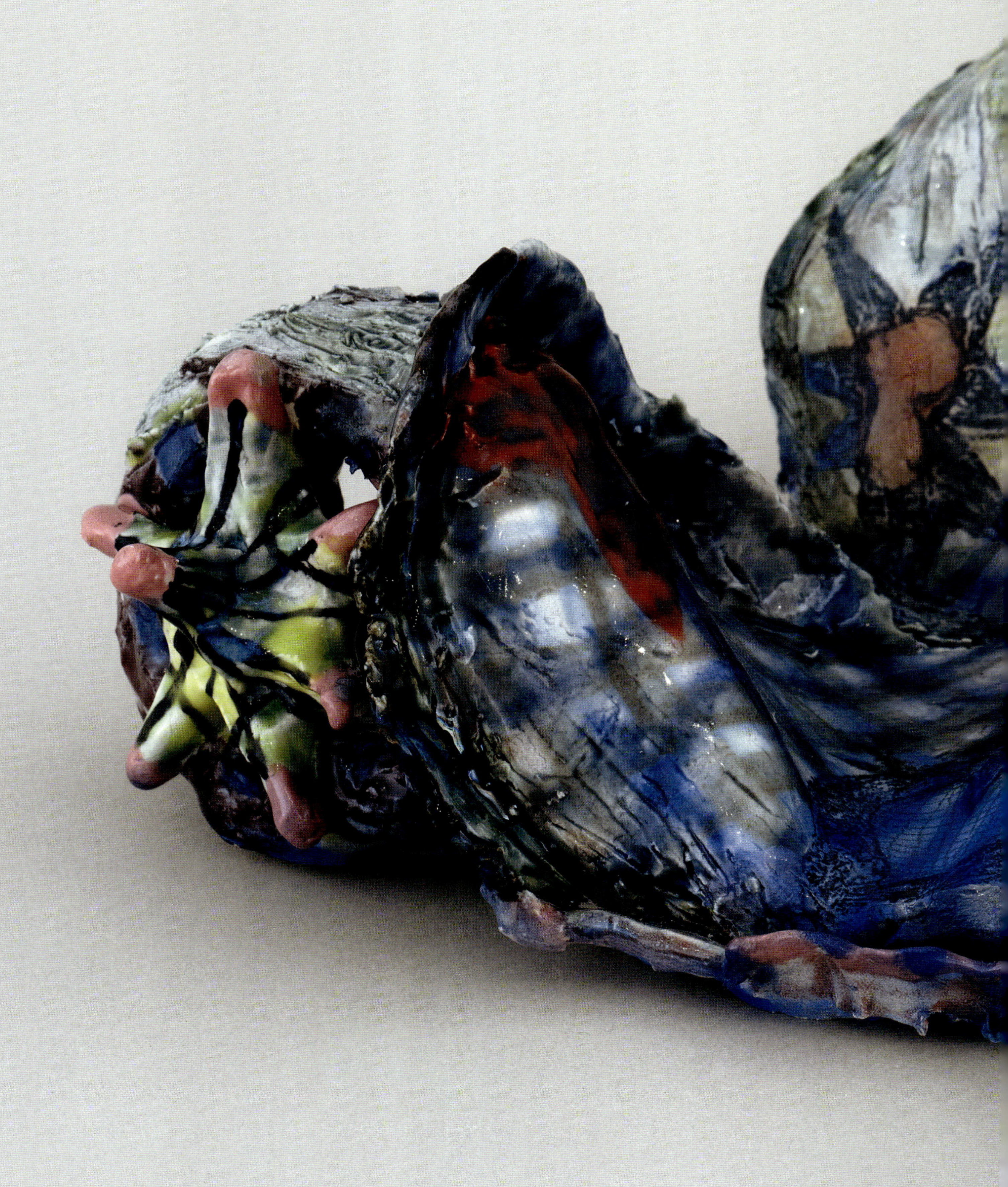

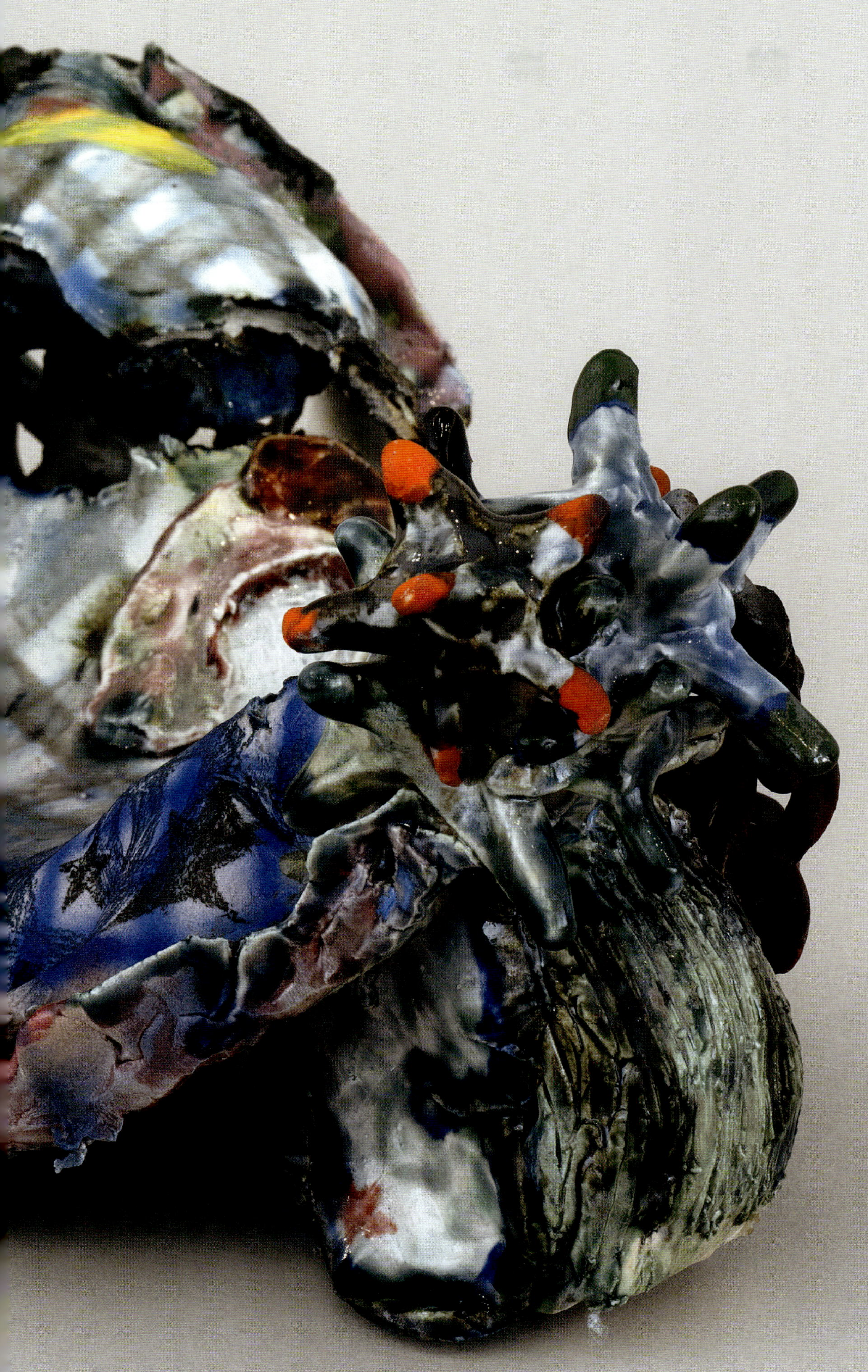

◂ *sugar water (remix)*, 2021
Glazed porcelain
5.5 x 10 x 12 in.

ruby

neri

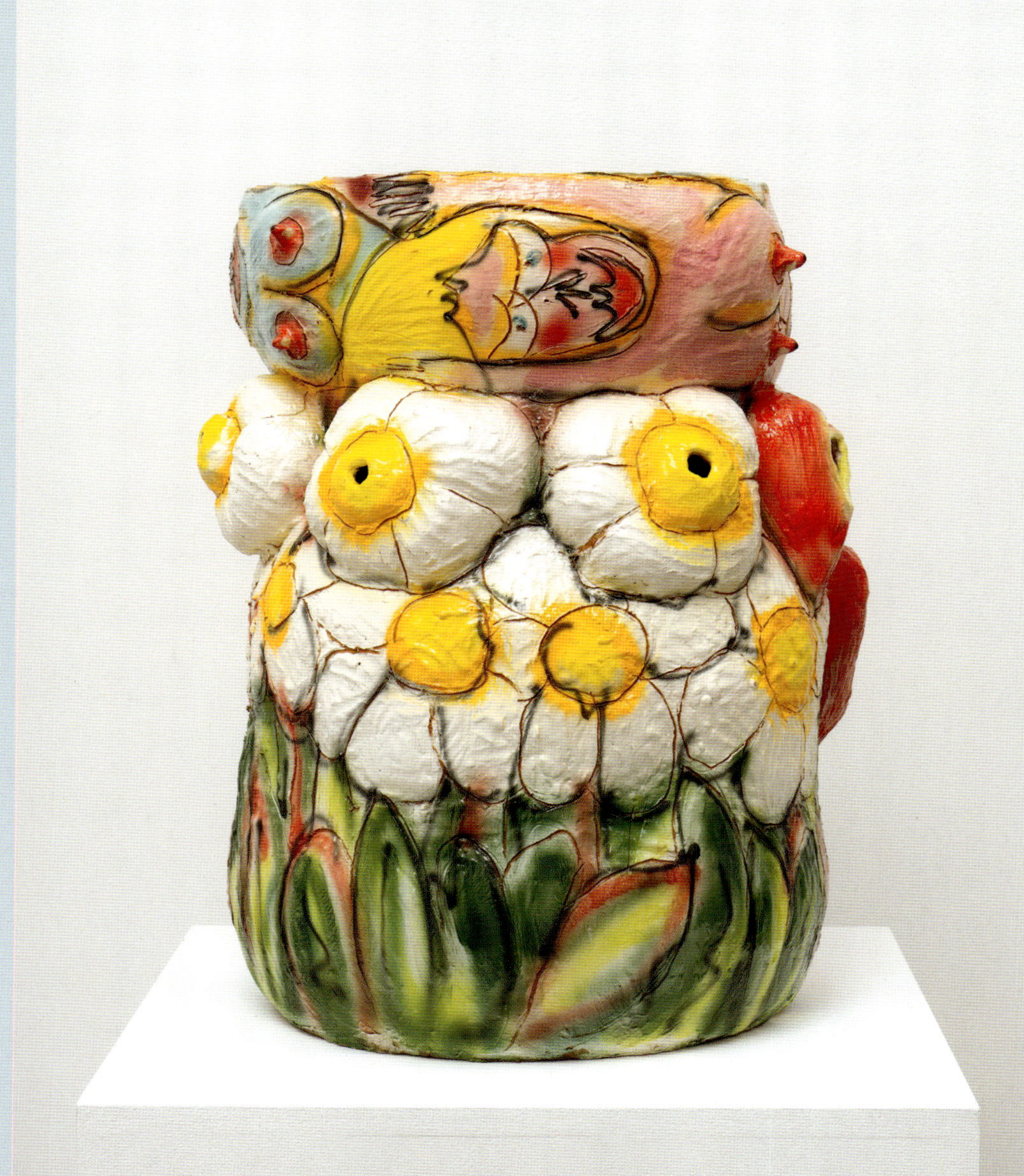

In pottery parlance, the parts of the vessel are named for the human body: foot, belly, waist, shoulder, neck, mouth, lip. Ruby Neri (b. 1970, San Francisco) doubles clay's distinctive descriptors by shaping and glazing her sculptures in ways that reinscribe correspondences between body and object: foot for foot, belly for belly. This equivalence between object and subject illustrates her impulse to mine the fundamental qualities of her materials. Her clay sculptures look squeezed and pressed into shape. Surfaces are rough and lumpy; shapes are awkward, off kilter, or oddly scaled. Both exterior and interior surfaces are marked by the deeply grooved channels of finger-pulled clay. Female bodies—her primary subject—are sprayed into shape with fleshy hues and delineated with black lines. Details like eyes and fingernails are incised. The resulting surfaces pulsate with vitality.

Neri tags her pots with large signatures, a gutsy embellishment at once signature and nameplate: *I made this, this is me*. The authority that a signature carries, as a kind of claiming and identification, offers a way in which to consider Neri's particular approach to art-making and how she renders a dimensional female body.

I submit that I have more questions than conclusions about her work, especially when confronted by the ways it simultaneously embraces and dodges caricature. Her sculptures seem to ask me if I like (or dislike) looking at these lady pots with their bright and shiny colors, stylized pudenda, yellow-haired handles, tits and ass, high kicks, puffing cigarettes, and daisies.

In clay, Neri forces compositions of contorted and differently sized women in teeming tableaux so peculiar as to betray the artist's sense of humor and play as well as her button-pushing instincts. When invited to include a sculpture in the exhibition *Clay Pop*, she placed the titular words in bubble-letter relief into the hands of two figures. She claimed the exhibition title twice!

For Neri, the body is a supple framework. Her sculptures complicate and neutralize the cliché of woman as vessel—a concept fundamental not only to ceramic history but to human history. Though her work exists within and continues a story of art by women that moved the needle on an objectified subject, Neri does not consider her body of work overtly feminist. Indeed, her imagery complicates easy conclusions. We're talking about naked ladies here. What is clear is her devotion to the unswerving directives of her own desire around the materiality of clay, its sensuousness, and its bodily yielding to the pressure of the hand.

Excerpted and modified from "The Ladies, The Ladies," in Ruby Neri *(Los Angeles: David Kordansky Gallery, 2016).*

— Jenelle Porter

◂ *Untitled*, 2020
Glazed ceramic
23 x 17 x 17 in.

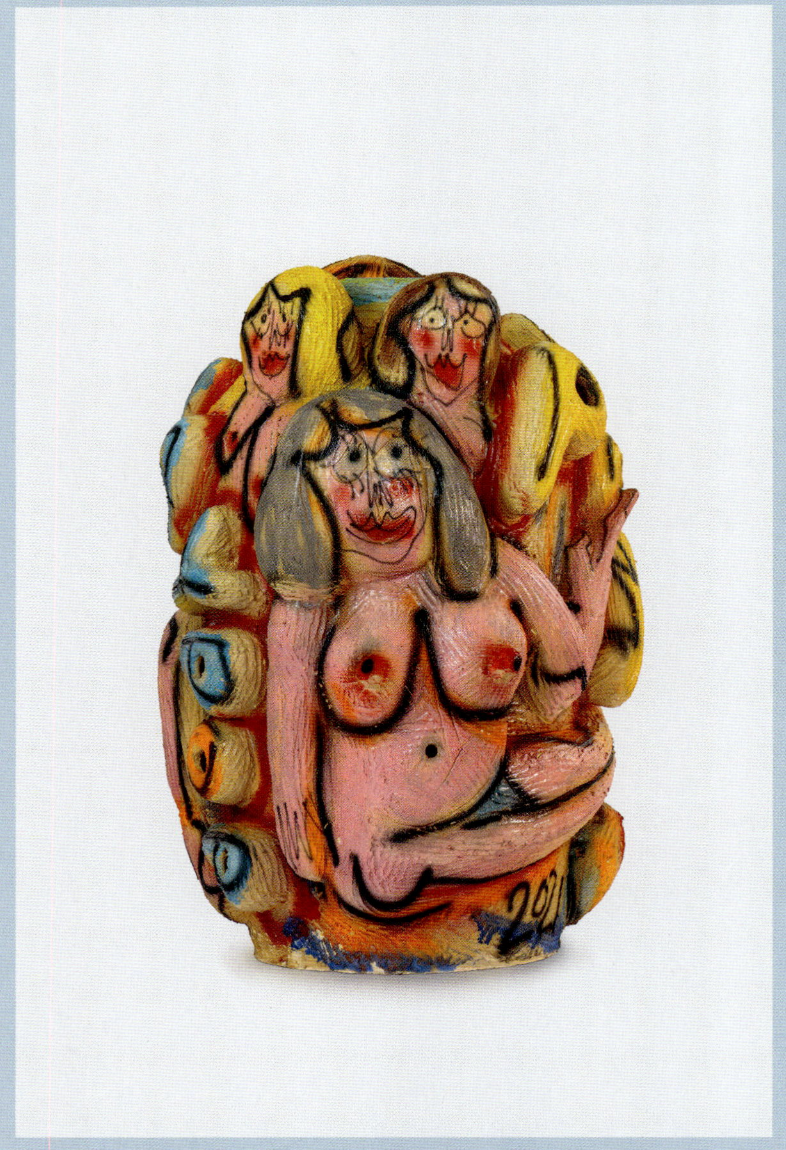

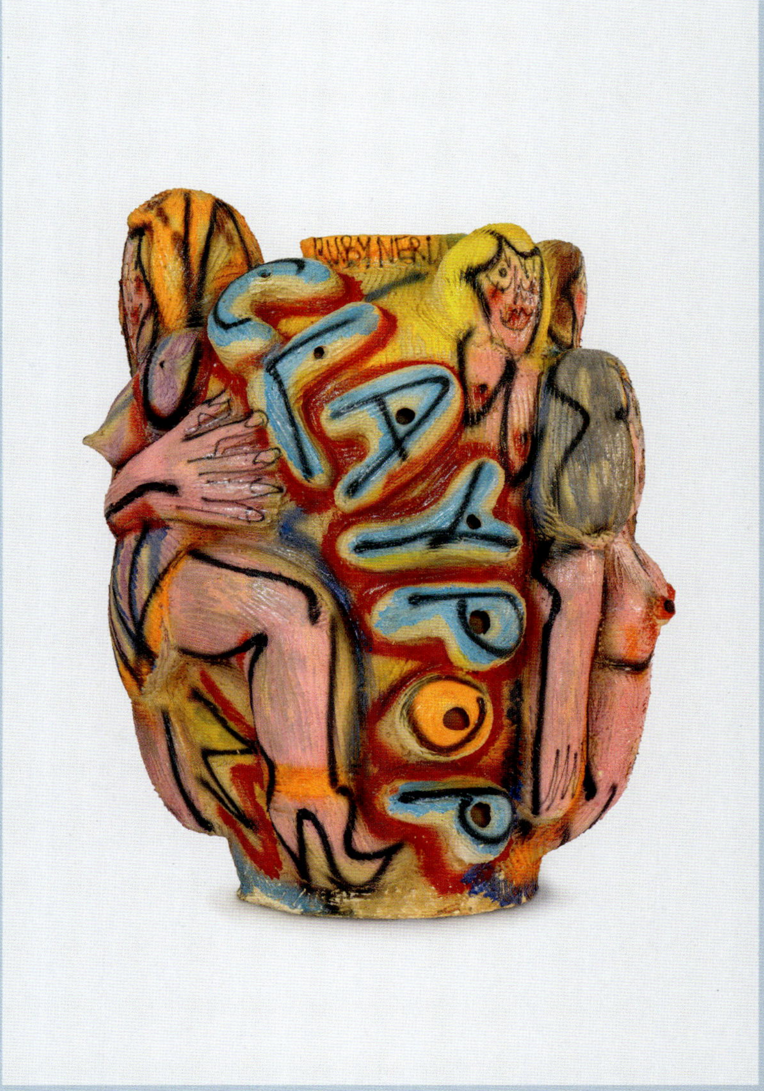

▲ All four sides of *Clay Pop*, 2021
Glazed ceramic
46 x 36 x 31 in.

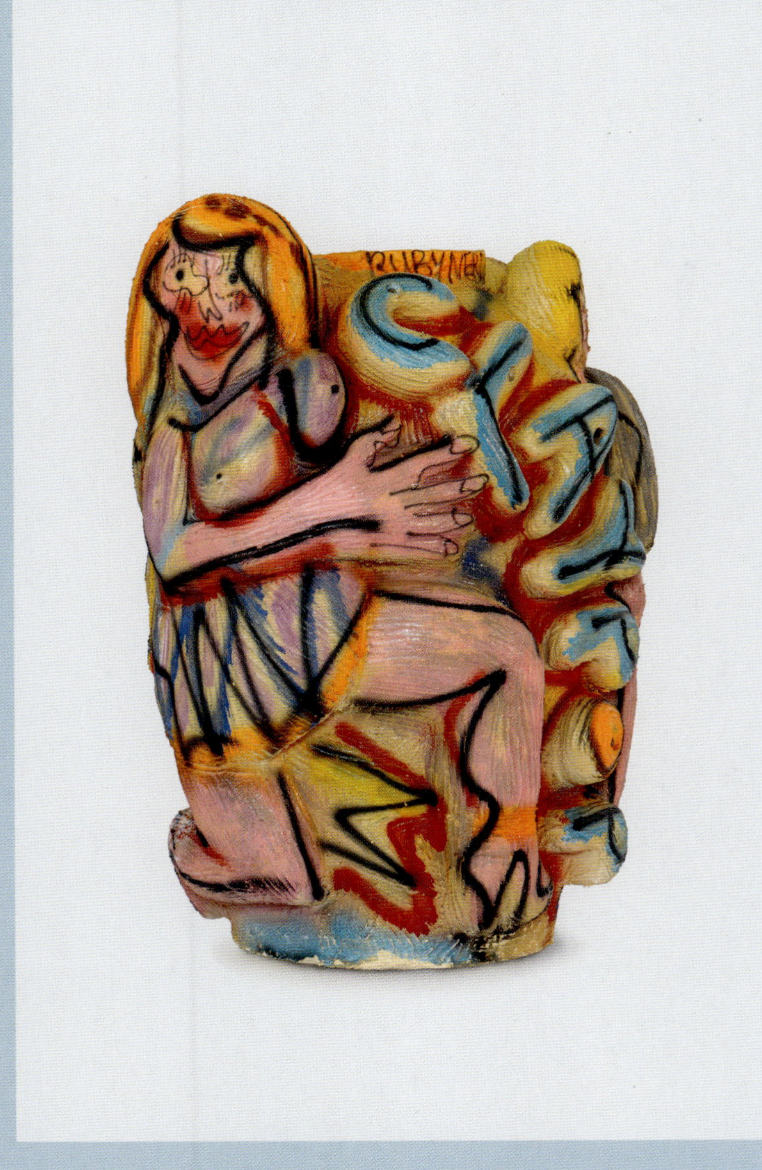

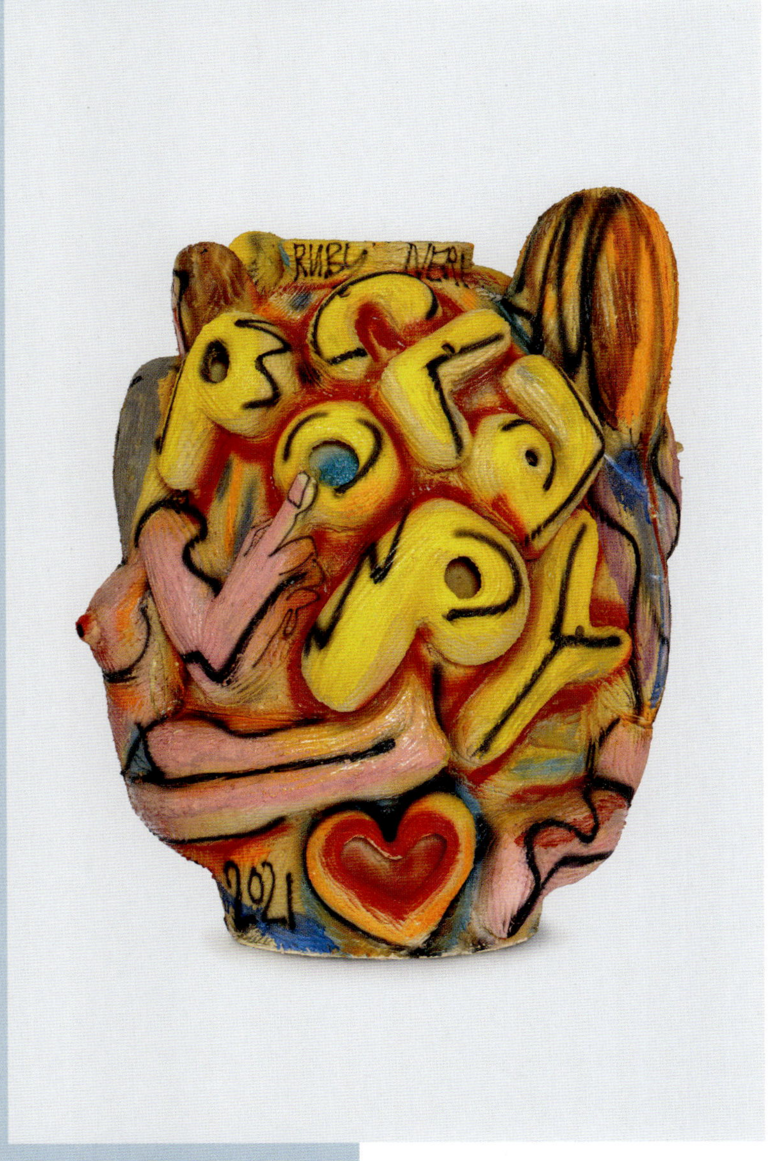
RUBY NERI
2021

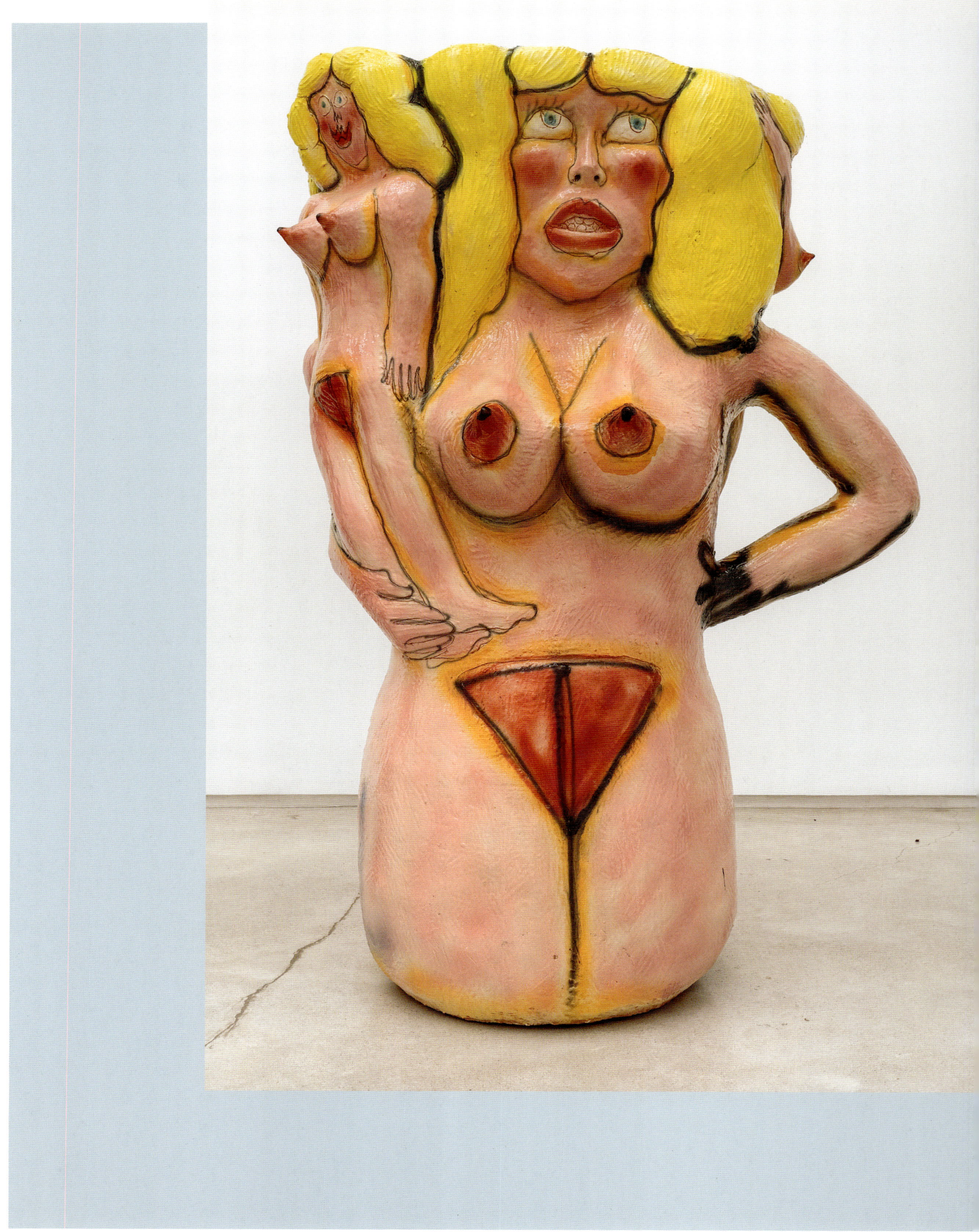

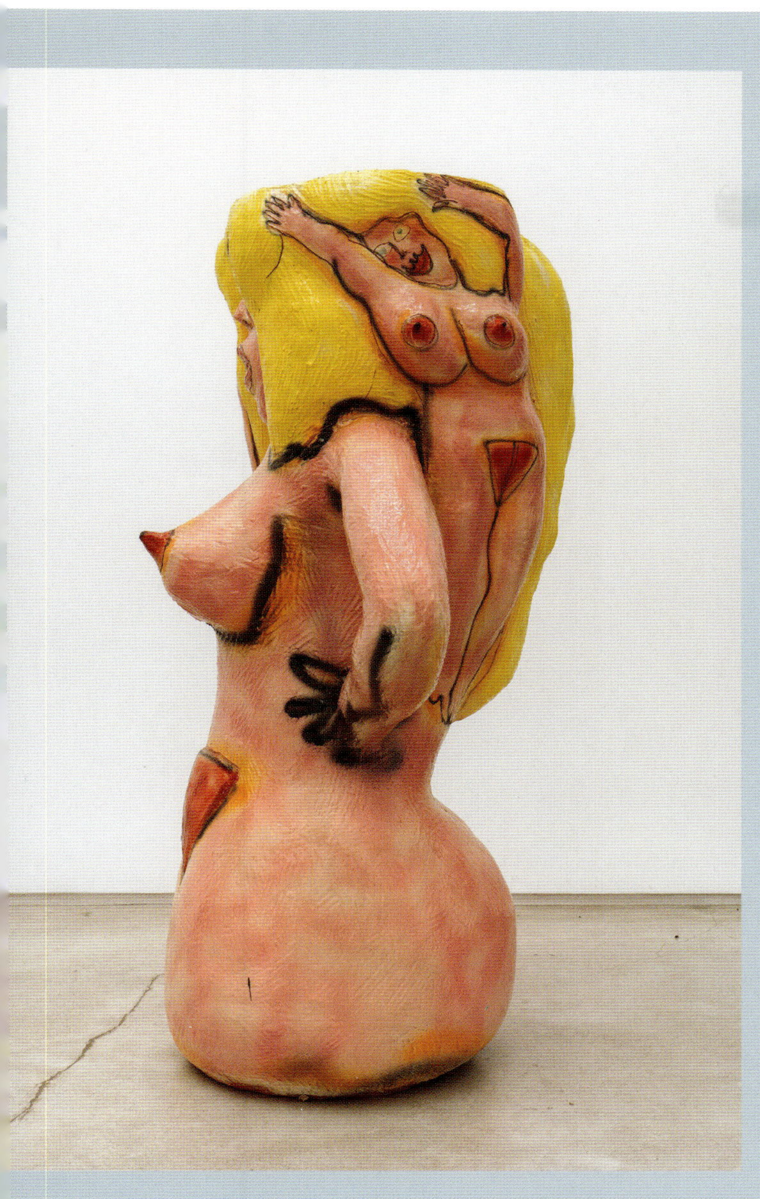

◂ Front and side view of *Untitled (Woman with Doll)*, 2019
Glazed ceramic
59.75 x 43 x 29.5 in.

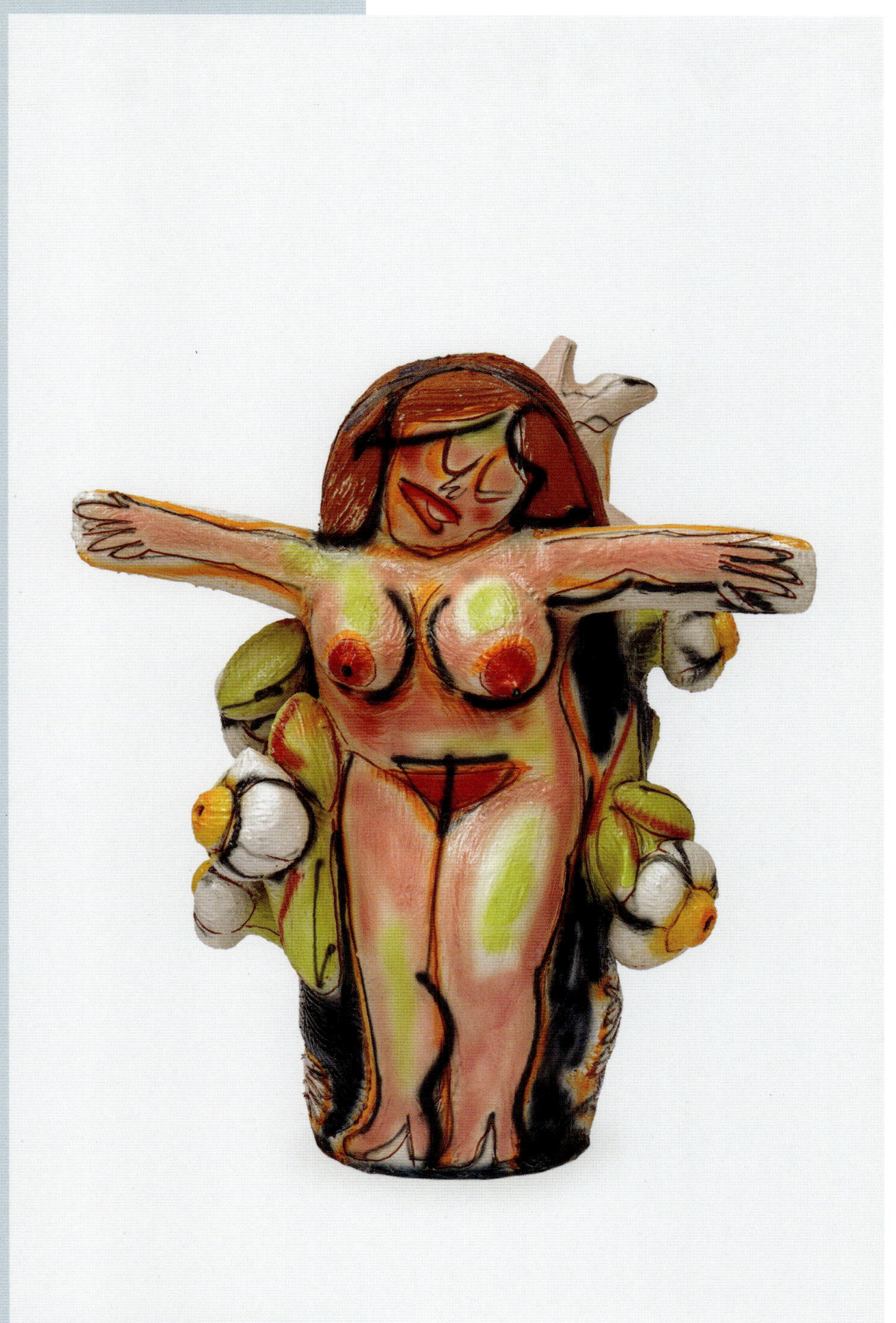

▴ *Disarray*, 2021
Glazed ceramic
42.5 x 37 x 27 in.

brian rochefort

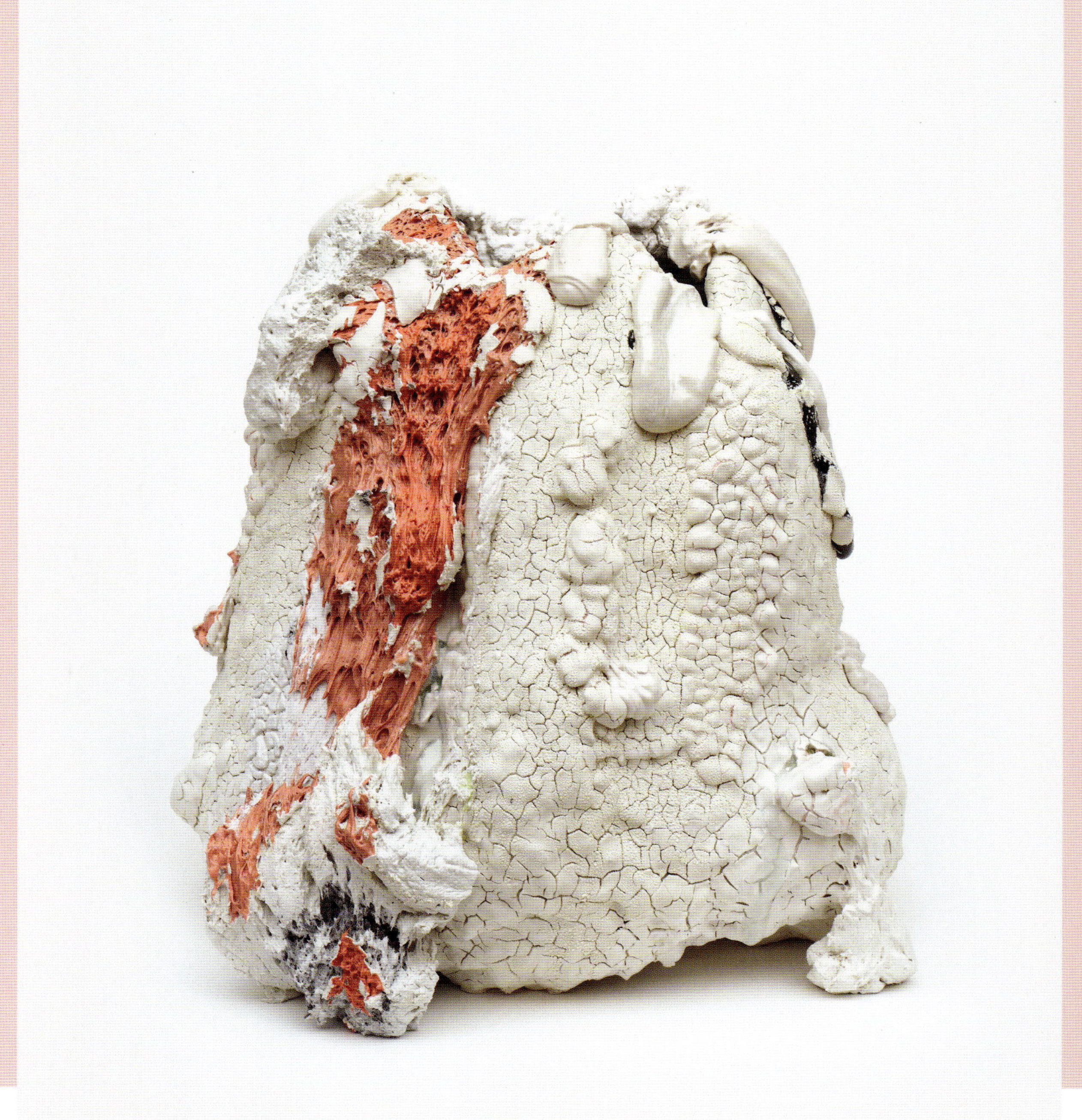

Brian Rochefort (b. 1985, Lincoln, Rhode Island) masters the art of glazed and layered ceramic works with vibrant encrusted surfaces. His iconic sculptures resemble craters—large vessel-like sculptures made of glazed stoneware and earthenware, oozing with vibrant colors that mimic the explosiveness of natural surroundings. At first glance, the sculptures seem to range across the entire color spectrum, but upon close inspection, each ceramic sculpture reveals a world in itself—a rupturing microcosm with its own story to tell.

Rochefort breaks apart unfired clay objects, builds upon them with more material, and then fires each layer of glaze to produce volcanic masses that overflow with color and character. The surfaces of the sculptures are a blend of rough, uneven clumps and smooth, bubbly drips, all suspended in place by the kiln firing. Solid vibrant chunks flow over previously laid gradients, while cracked exteriors and painted glass fragments peek from beneath translucent splatters. Sitting at the base of each sculpture are pooled glazes and melted glass, mimicking the natural beauty of a cave structure among other natural phenomena.

"At first glance, the artworks may appear accidental or experimental, but they are carefully thought out and meticulously airbrushed and glazed," explains the artist. "I work with twenty to thirty different glazes and colors that I have developed over the years to react in certain ways at different temperatures. This does not mean there is no chance involved with my work. It just means there is more control of the material than expected."[1]

Faced with the artworks by Rochefort, the viewer is capable of experiencing the extraordinary, be it from the future or from the past. The artist is able to create sculptures that look chaotic and broken yet controlled and beautiful with vibrant colors and textures that nod to artists like Franz West and Willem de Kooning.

Through rigorous investigations into process and material, Rochefort's work manifests a level of expertise in ceramic-making. It exudes a confident sense of color while resisting the formal and technical confines of the medium of tradition-bound ceramics, exploring new territories of freedom, invention, and play.

— Brian Rochefort

[1] A. T. Wilkinson, "Interview with Brian Rochefort," Visual Atelier 8, September 2, 2020, https://visualatelier8.com/2020-8-brian-rochefort.

◂ *White Dwarf*, 2020
Glazed ceramic, glass fragments
22 x 21 x 20 in.

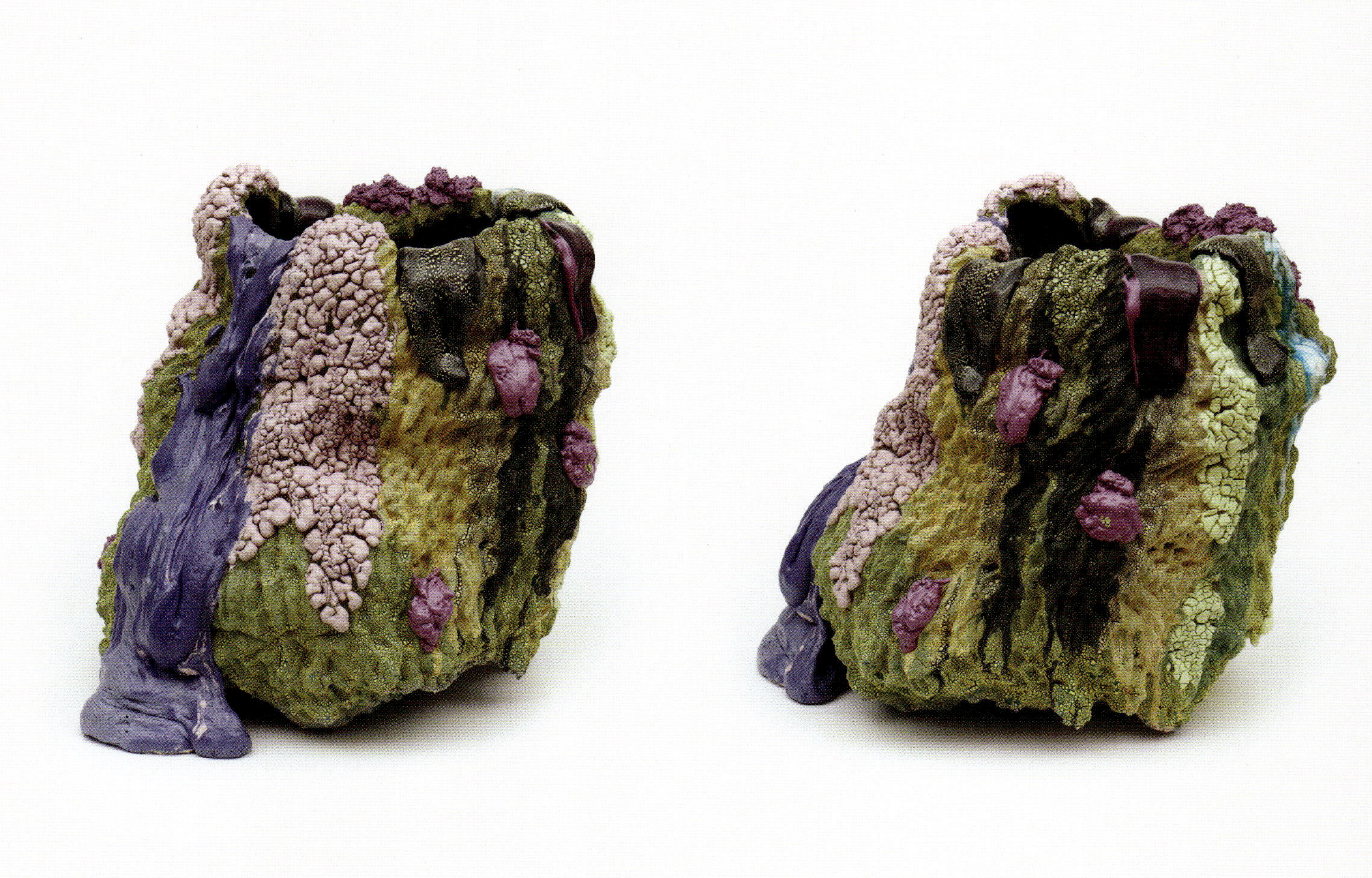

▲ *Captain Planet*, 2020
Glazed ceramic, glass fragments
24 x 22 x 20 in.

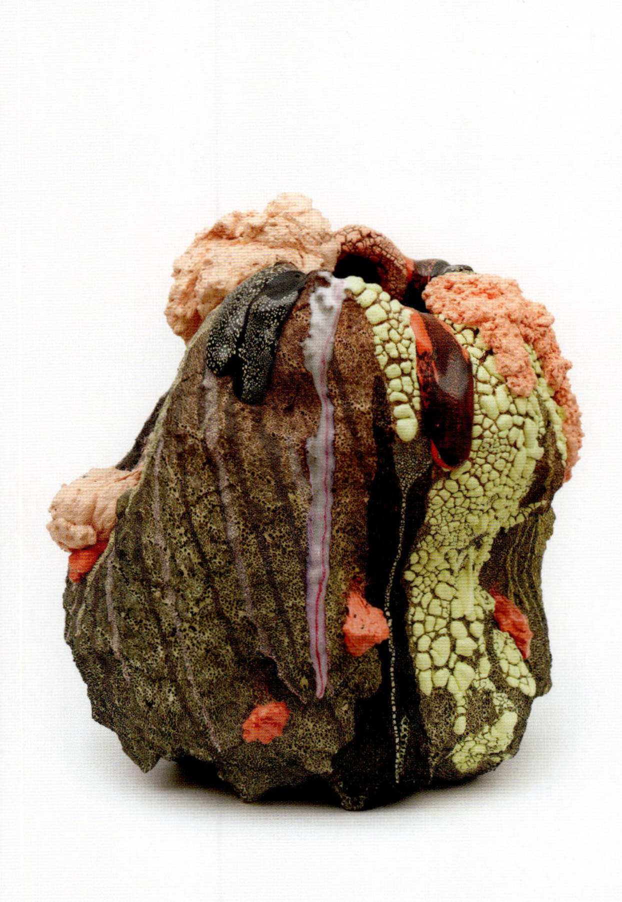
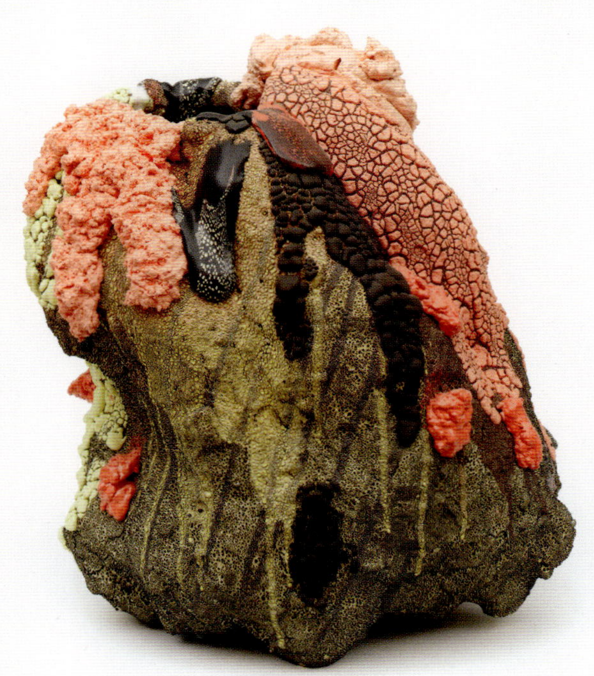

▲ *Leopard*, 2021
Ceramic, glaze, glass fragments
24 x 22 x 23 in.

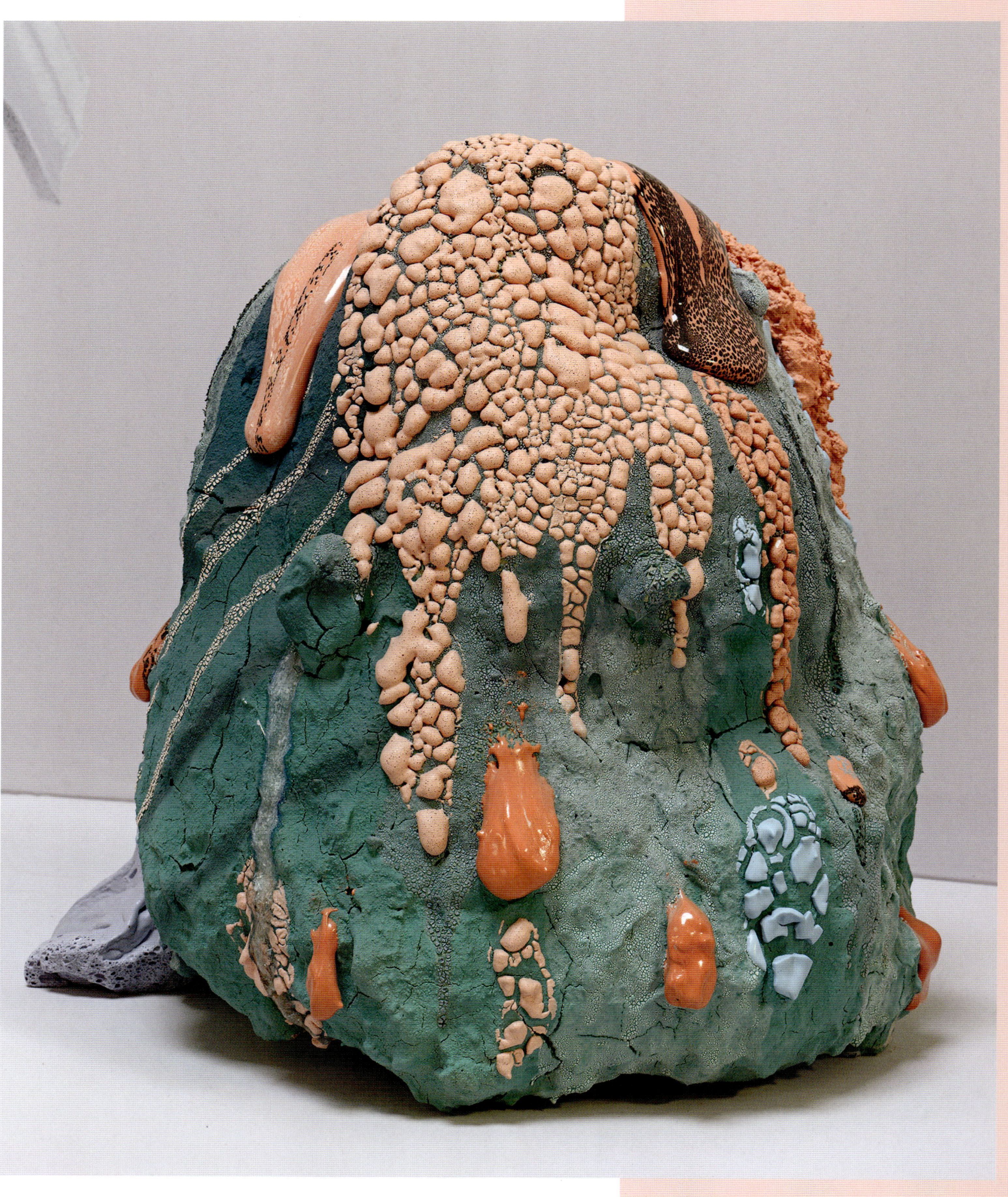

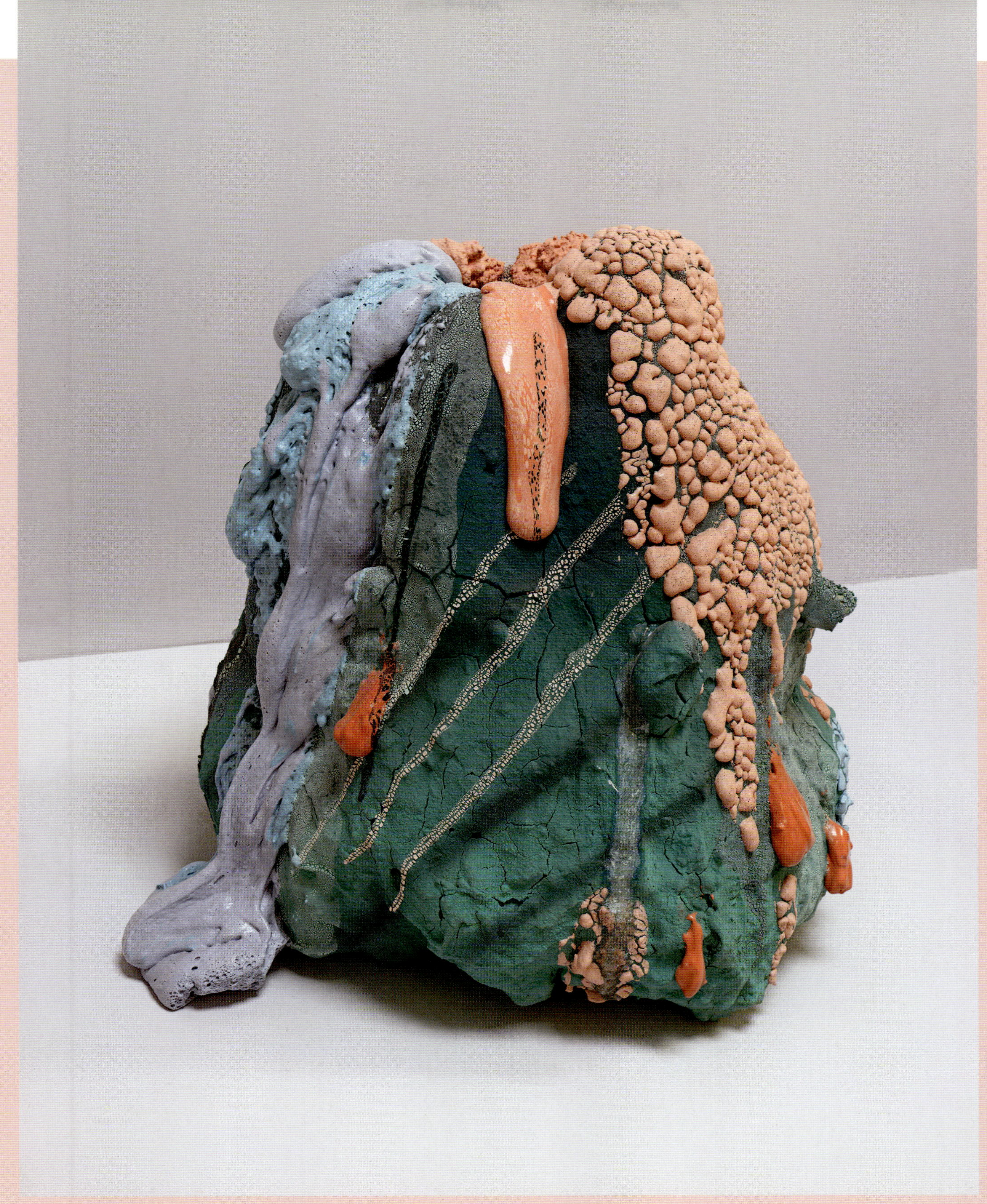

▲ Side and front view of
Predator, 2021
Glazed ceramic, glass fragments
17 x 16 x 18 in.

jennifer rochlin

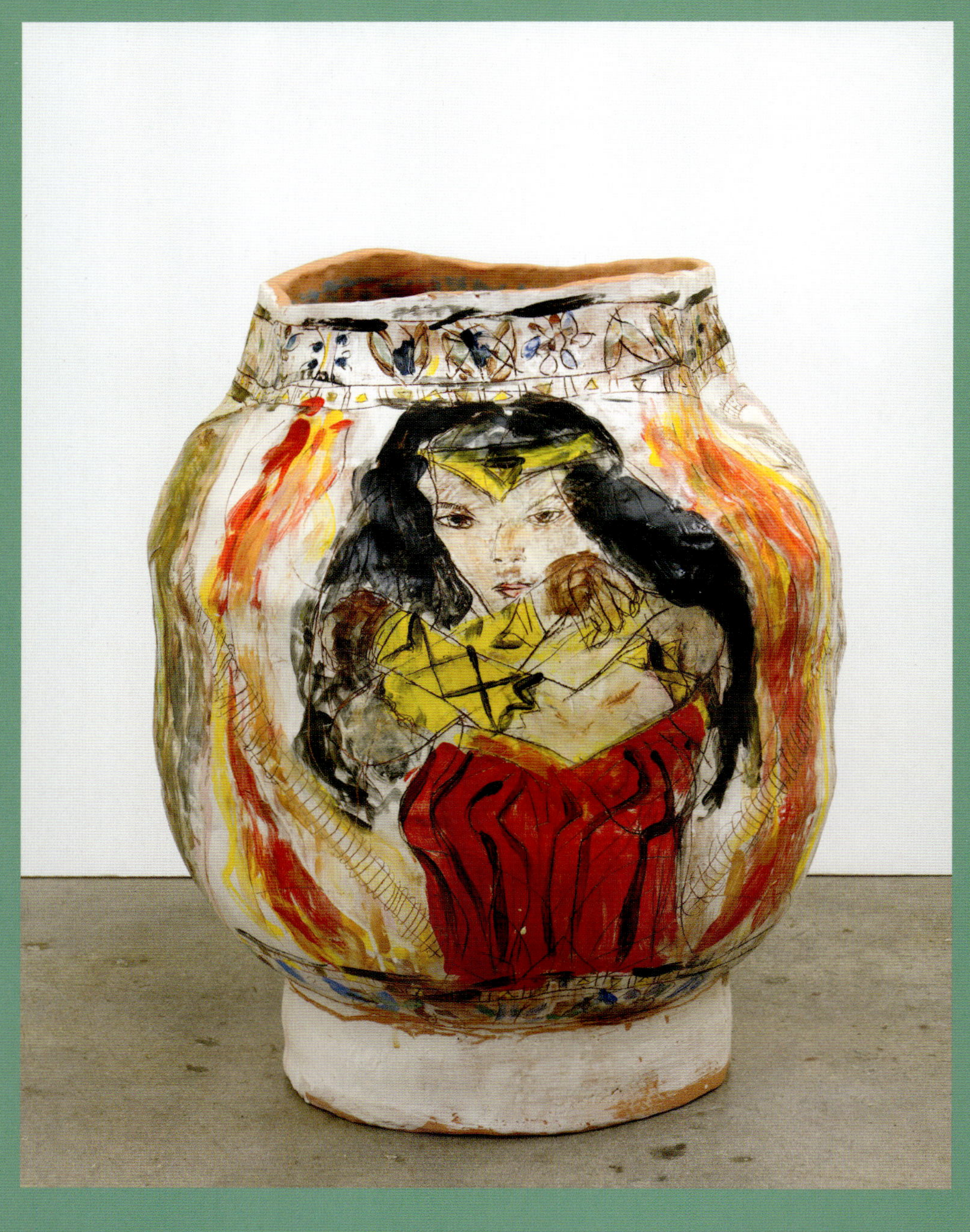

Topography, specifically that of Southern California, has frequently been highlighted as either subject or setting in the ceramic sculptures of Jennifer Rochlin (b. 1968, Baltimore, Maryland). Hand-built vessels with patches of dense color stand proxy for the wrinkled valleys and swollen foothills of the Los Angeles basin. The "vessels" (function implied only) become sculptural stewards of a woven narrative, densely scored and populated on the imperfectly delicate volumes.

Rochlin's vessels are glazed in a painterly manner with color that is then pierced and scratched through. The lacerations of red clay on the surfaces of these canopic jars loosely resemble the burn scars and fire roads of the most recent blazing tree line. Rendered in the expressive and dissolving manner of a sudden Pacific coast shore break on wet sand, the marks mingle and conspire to create patterns and outlines hemming the fragile imagery of the day.

Similar to the sprawling web of Los Angeles neighborhoods, these demarcated zones of imagery are like edits and fades in a nonlinear film experiment, containing memories of personal and collective significance. Evident in the wandering picture plane of each circumference is the promise of possibility in the evolving new day, and the sensorial drift and bleed of life in Southern California, where the infinite drone of the freeway sounds like the oceans double, concrete vectors become waves for wheeled riders, and a local mountain lion (known as P22) becomes a celebrity, stalked by paparazzi and surreptitiously fed by neighbors, like some stray cat Robin Hood. It is with these spliced links of narrative flow and punctuation that Rochlin delights the viewer with images of sunlight reverie and quiet contemplation.

— Jason Meadows

◂ *Wonder Woman, Rocks, Sea, Shields / Rope Pattern*, 2018
Glazed ceramic
25 x 33 x 24 in.

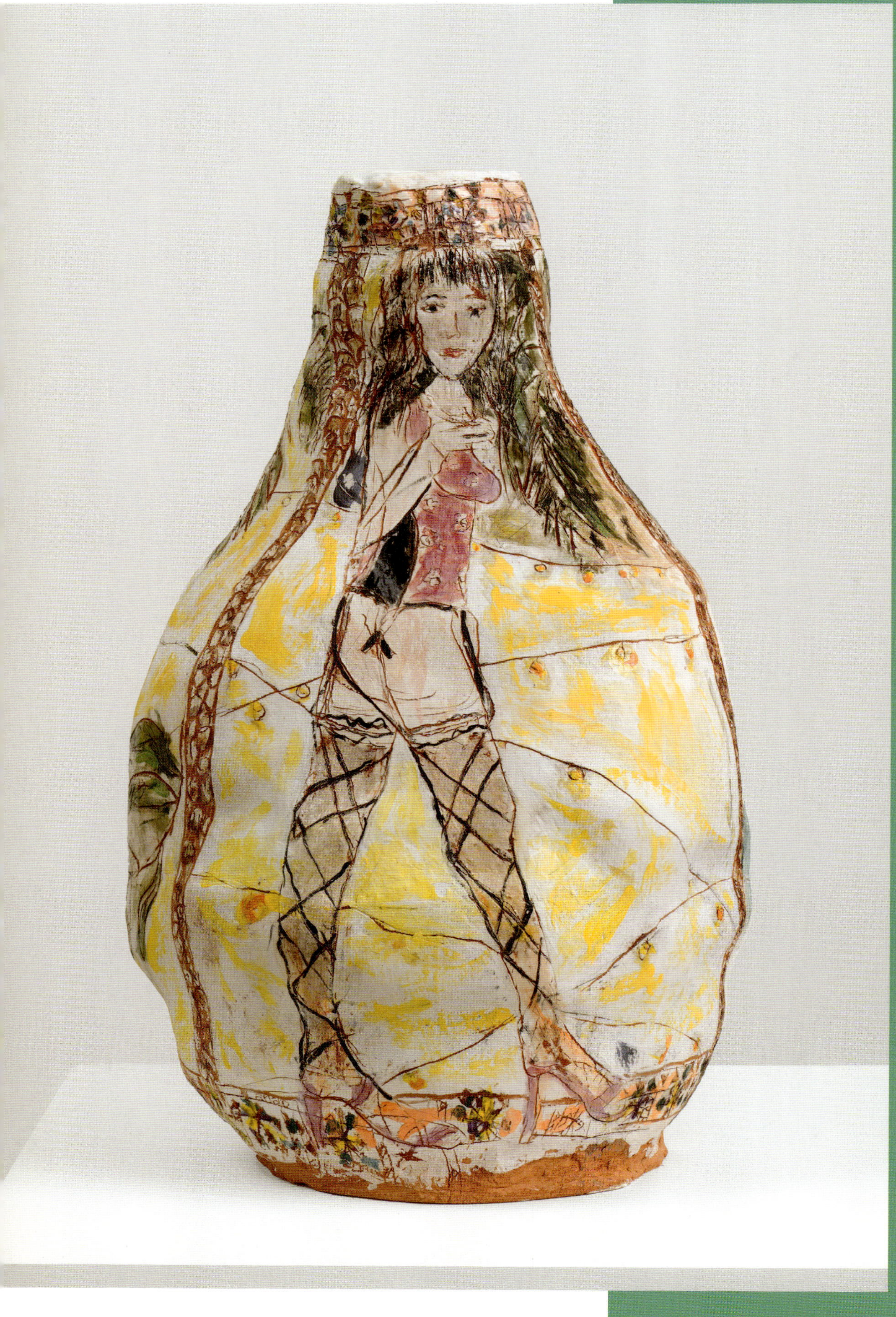

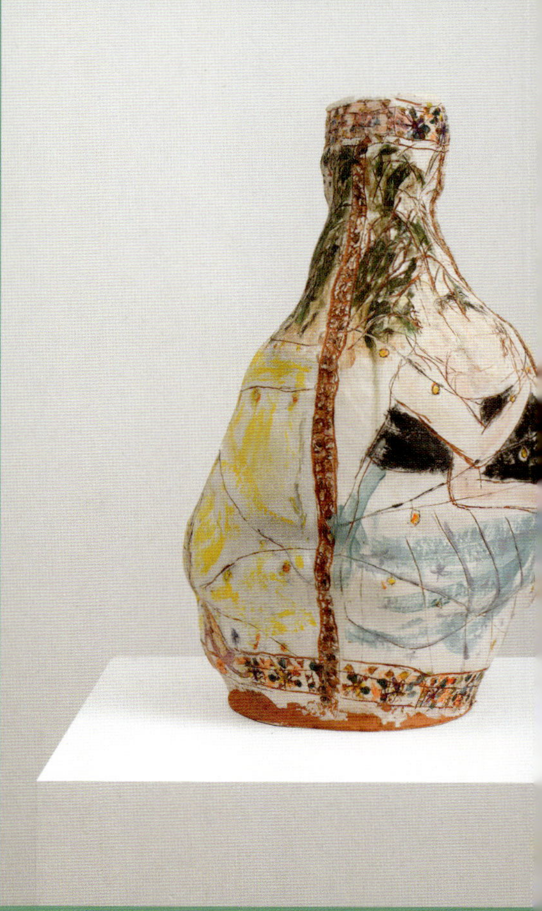

◂ All four sides of *Four O'Clocks*, 2020
Glazed ceramic
33 x 19 x 16 in.

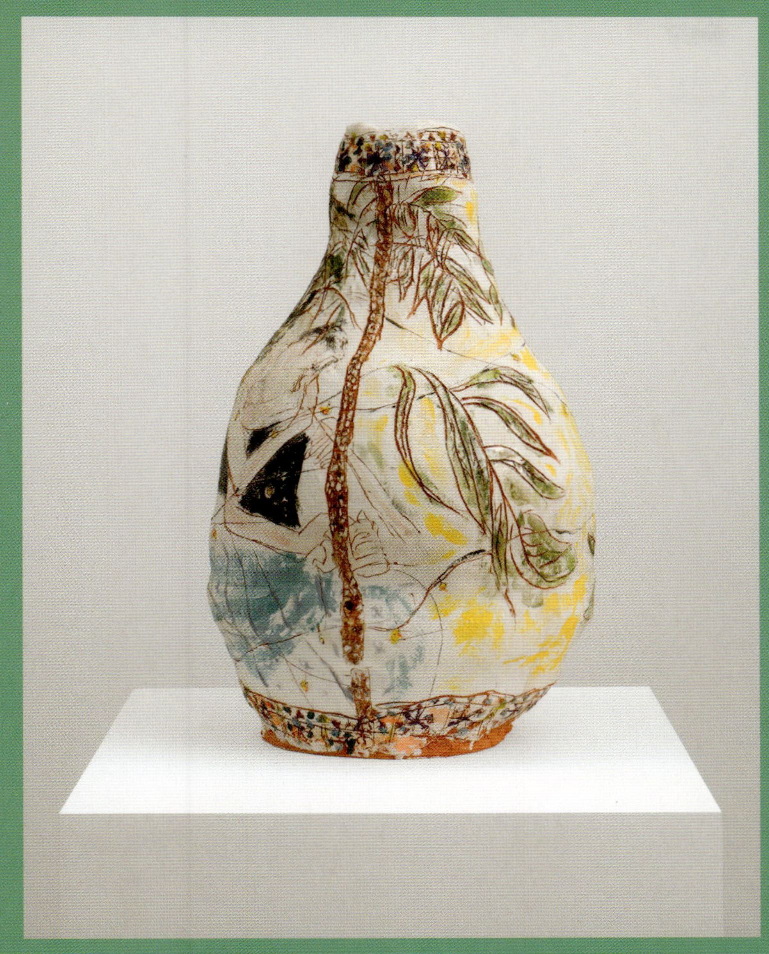
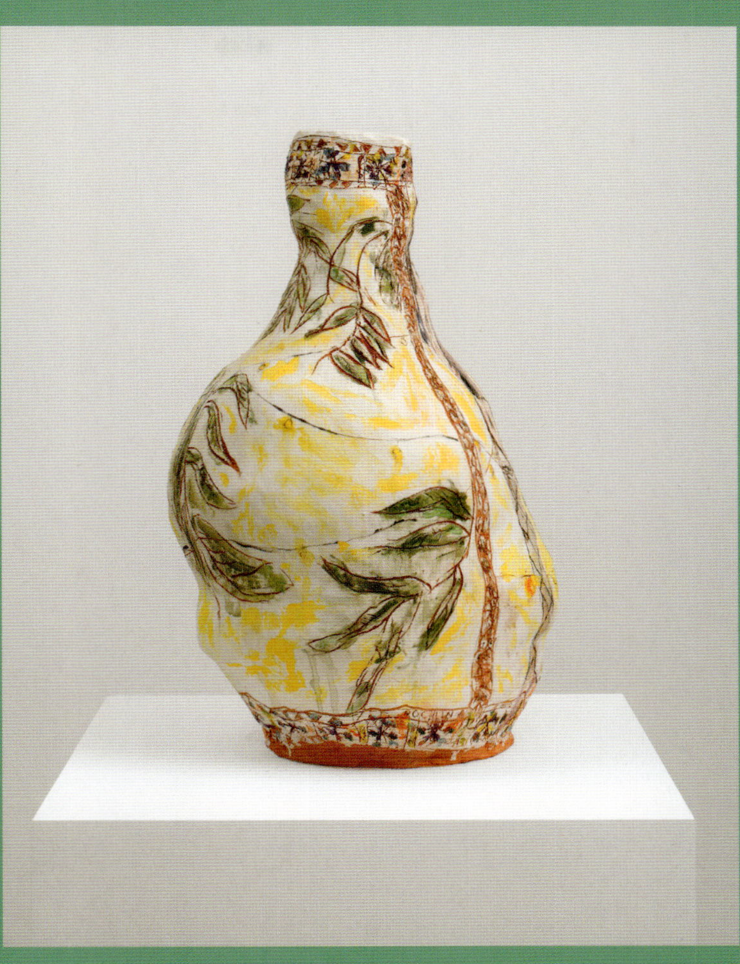

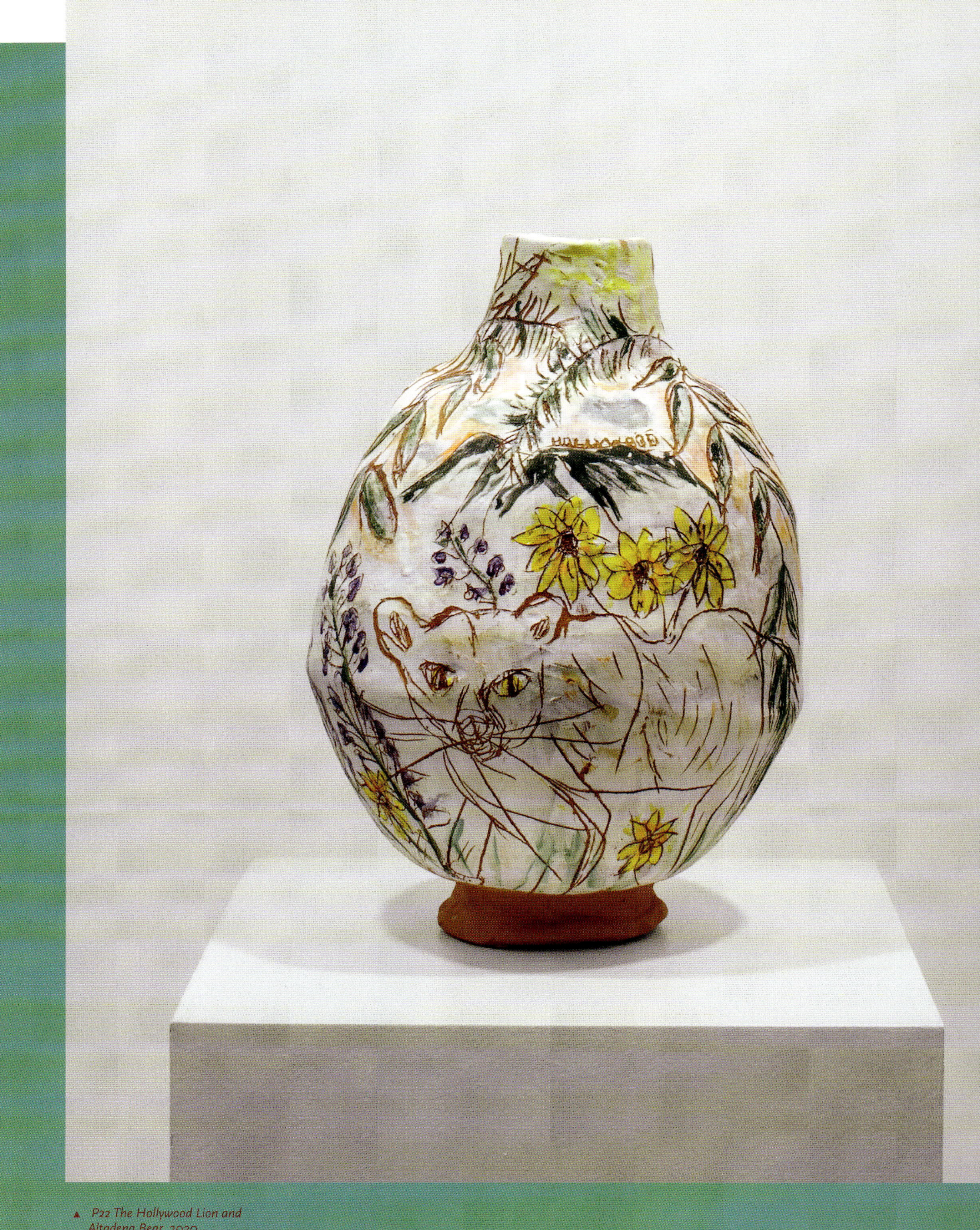

▲ *P22 The Hollywood Lion and Altadena Bear*, 2020
Glazed ceramic
16 x 11 x 11 in.

▼ *Quiet Splendor*, 2021
Glazed ceramic
20 x 13 x 12 in.

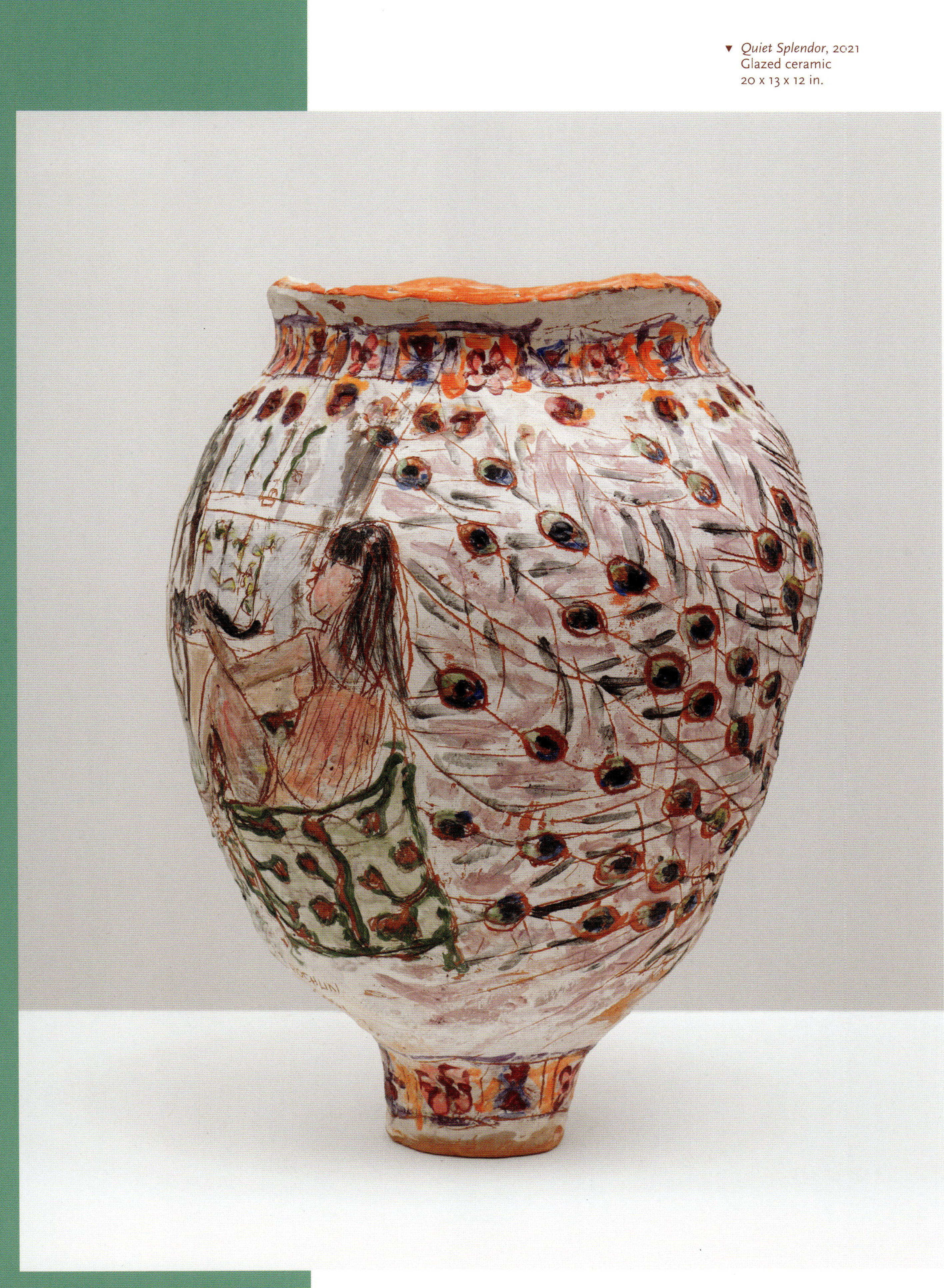

brie

ruais

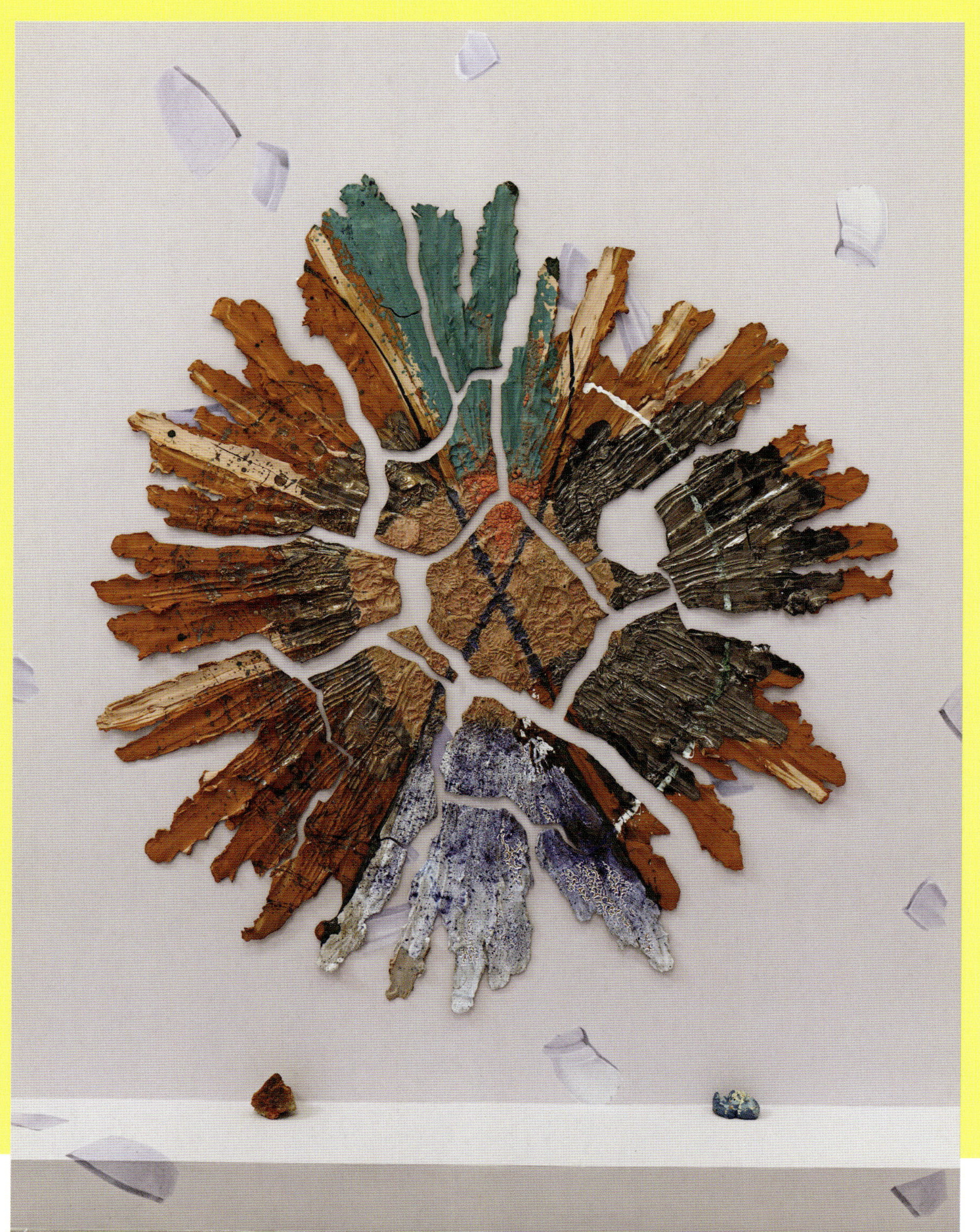

Brie Ruais (b. 1982, Southern California) presses, prods, folds, flattens, wrestles, smears, kneads, and cinches her work into being. She stands, kneels, or crouches on a mass of clay equivalent to her bodyweight, and spreads and skids the raw matter into swirls, bursts, and thrusting or twining lines. Each work chronicles the vigorous process of its own making. Furrows from the trails of her fingers give the surfaces dynamism and direction. Toe prints and indentations from heels, knees, and elbows create ridges, clefts, mounds, and fissures. Ruais separates the rugged forms that she has enacted into irregular tiles, cutting the leathery clay with a knife, tearing it by hand, or allowing it to dry and crack into sections on its own, like soil's parched, crusty skin. She glazes the pieces in painterly swipes of umber, glossy pewter, wine, jade, milk, and more; fires them; and then reassembles the parts, mounting the entirety on the wall or floor. Her sculptures are earthworks on the scale of the individual body—landscapes of singular energy.

For all of the geological implications at play in these re-imaginings of basic matter, Ruais's process is also a striking analogue to the shaping of the raw clay of the self. There is the oscillation between fragment and whole, fragile and sturdy—integrity as not only a product of physical force and cohesion but also an echo of interior conditions. And there is the declaration of bodyweight as a defining parameter. It is a feminist reclamation of a metric traditionally used to objectify the female body and delimit its beauty and desirability. Ruais recasts bodyweight as a source of strength, agency, and power. Her body is a wise, primal tool, at once above and one with the malleable matter that she sculpts.

Ruais's work resonates with a range of process-oriented, performative precedents of the sixties and seventies, from those sited in the landscape to those grounded in the home. She merges the vocabulary of conventionally feminine and textile-based pursuits with the scale and muscularity that the generation of Peter Voulkos and John Mason introduced to ceramics. Her works nod to Lynda Benglis's pleated sculptures and obliquely and wryly to Eleanor Antin, who centered her own bodyweight in the wry, landmark photo series of 1972, "Carving: A Traditional Sculpture."

Fired and fixed in place, Ruais's work remains ever in motion, both visually and intellectually. The sculptures are as dense with metaphorical implication as the surfaces are rich, agitated, and alive. Even while asserting a palpable, here-now immediacy, the work assumes a kind of conceptualizing distance—a meta-perch over the essentials of time, place, raw matter, motion, and the body. Ultimately, what Ruais sculpts are the pulsing energies and vital forces, and the rhythms and tides animating it all.

— Leah Ollman

◂ *Spreading Out from Center, Anchoring in Place*, 2021
Glazed stoneware, hardware
Approx. 89 x 85 x 2.5 in.

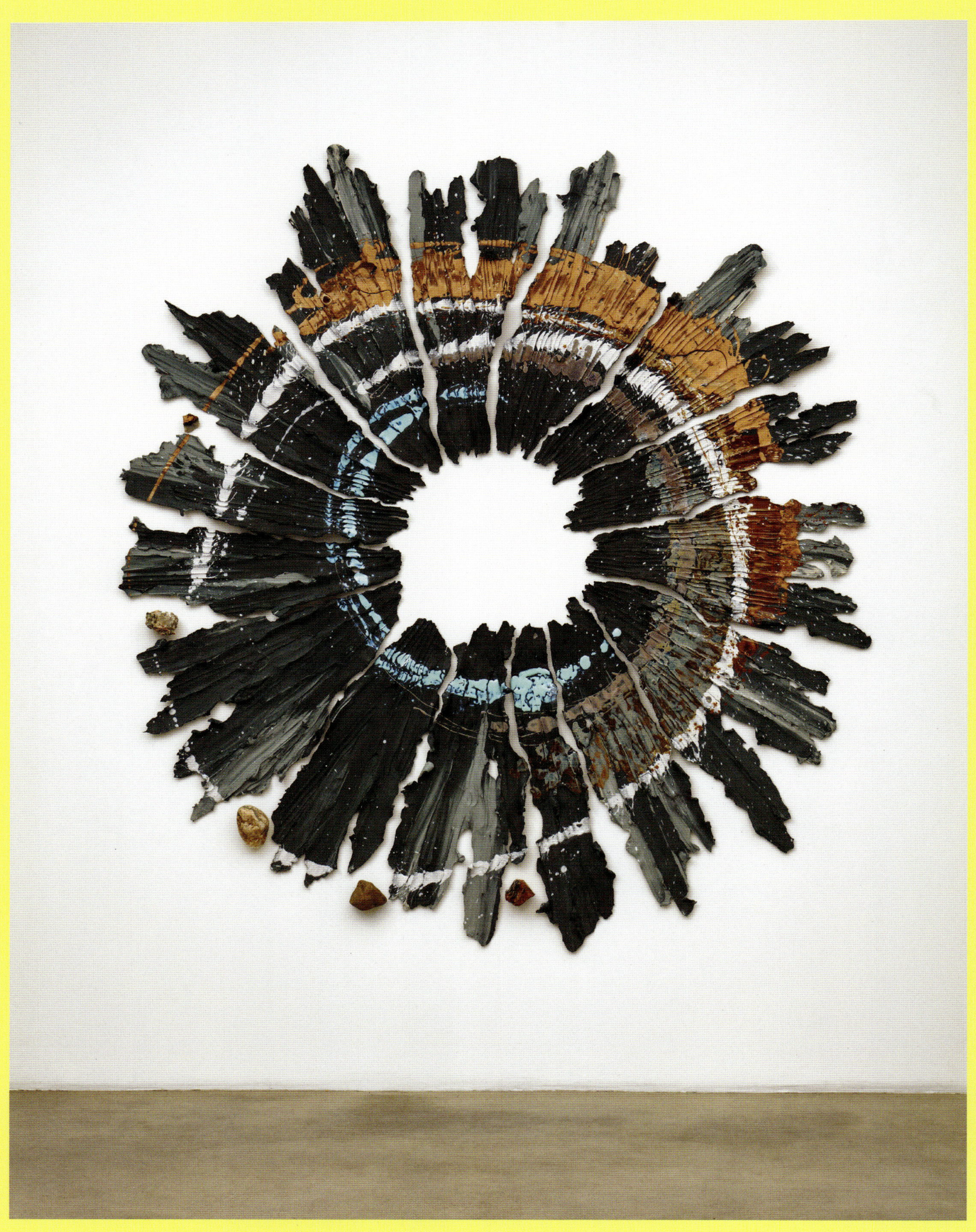

▲ *Circling Inward and Outward, 128lbs*, 2020
Glazed and pigmented stoneware, rocks, hardware
96 x 92 x 3 in.

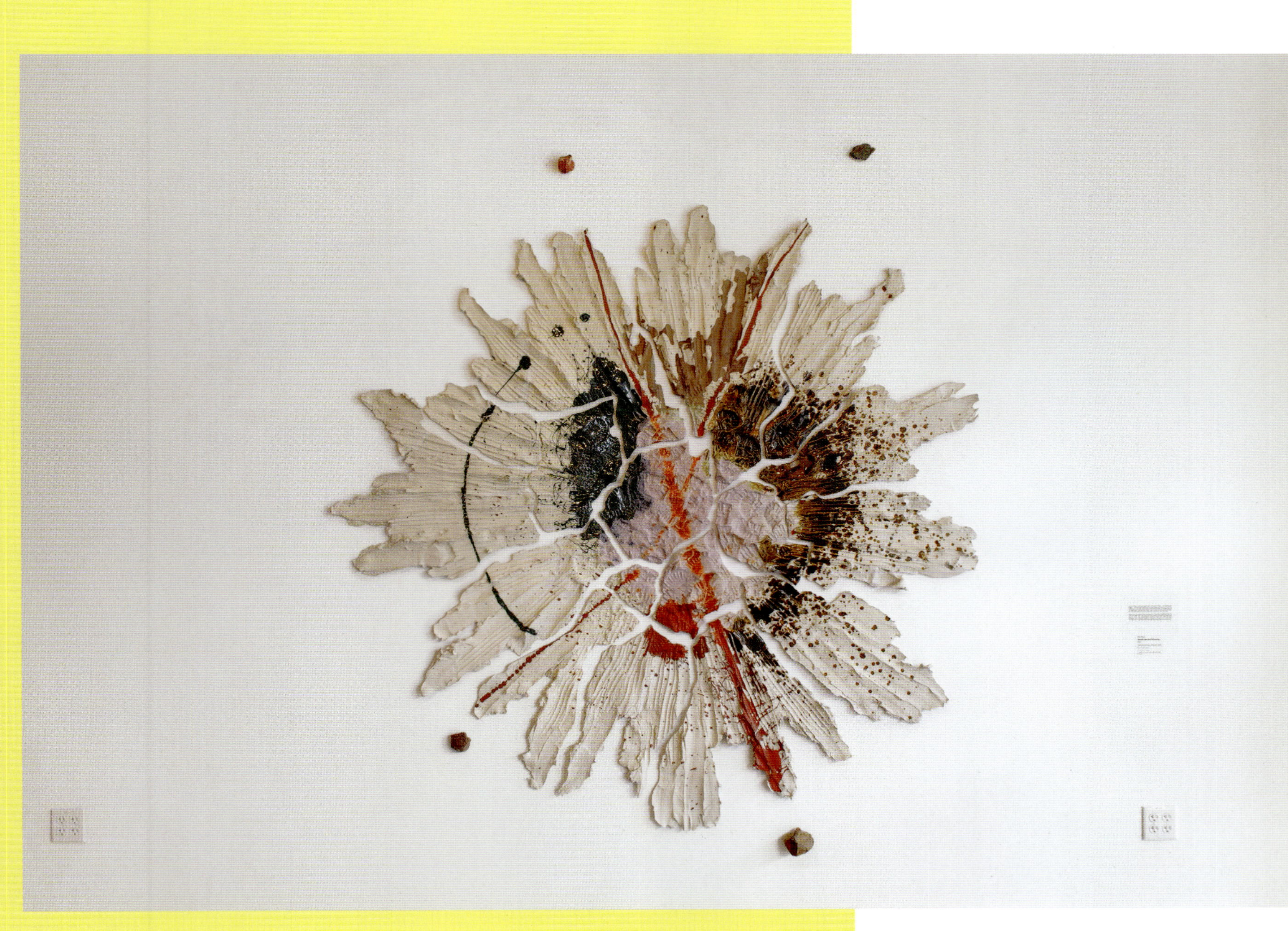

▲ *Destruction and Discovery, 130lbs*, 2021
Glazed stoneware, hardware, rocks
97 x 87.5 x 3 in.

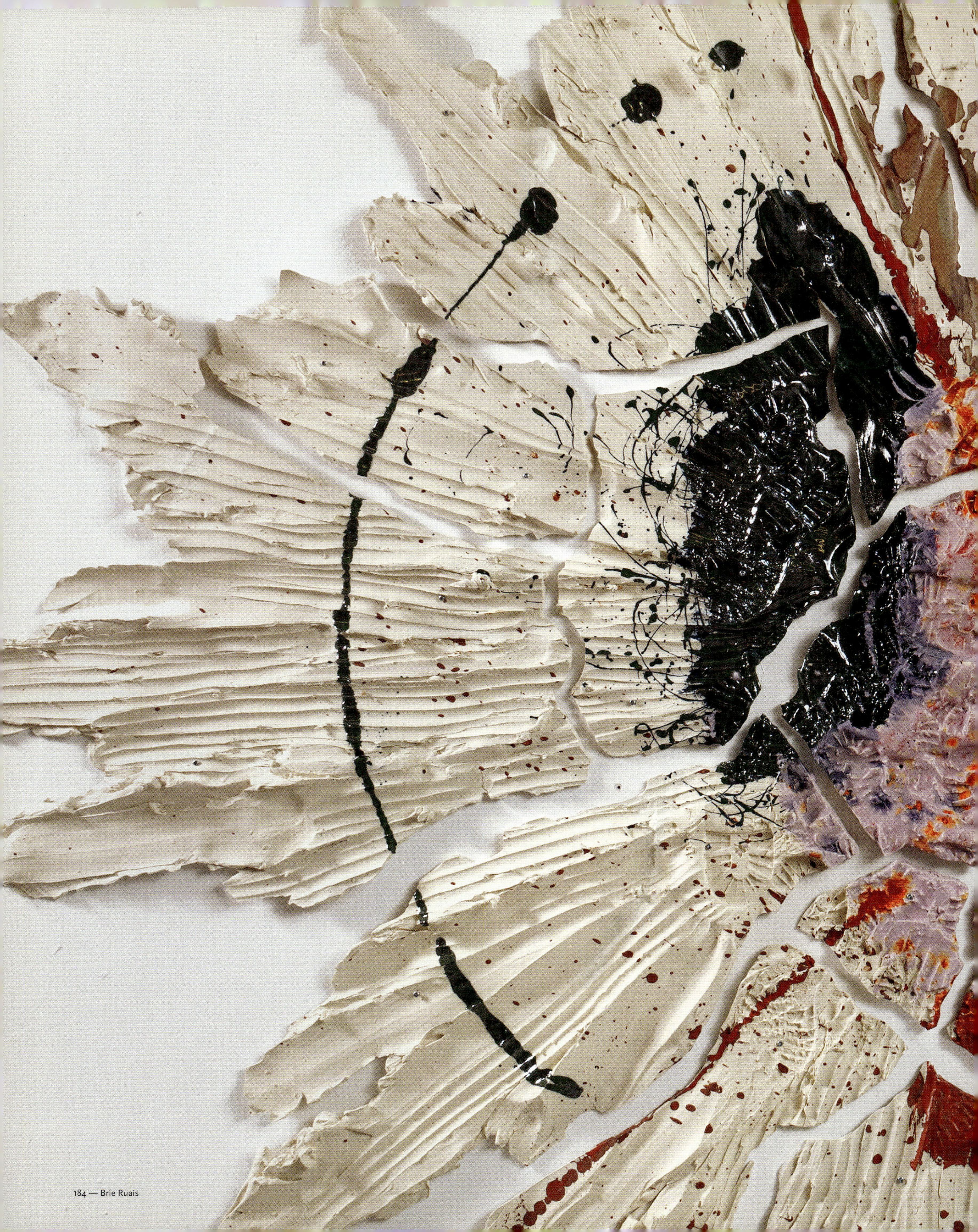

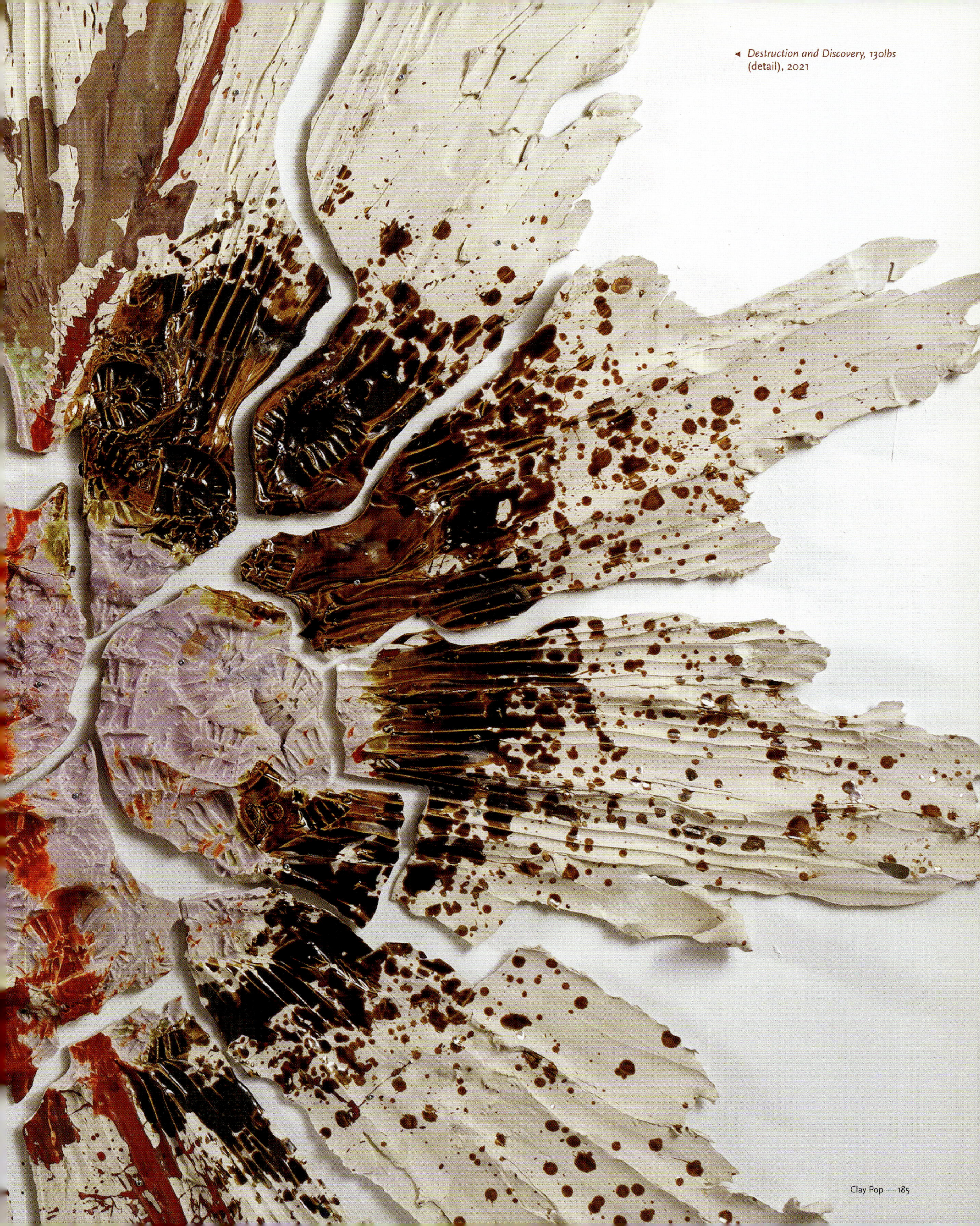

◂ *Destruction and Discovery*, 130lbs (detail), 2021

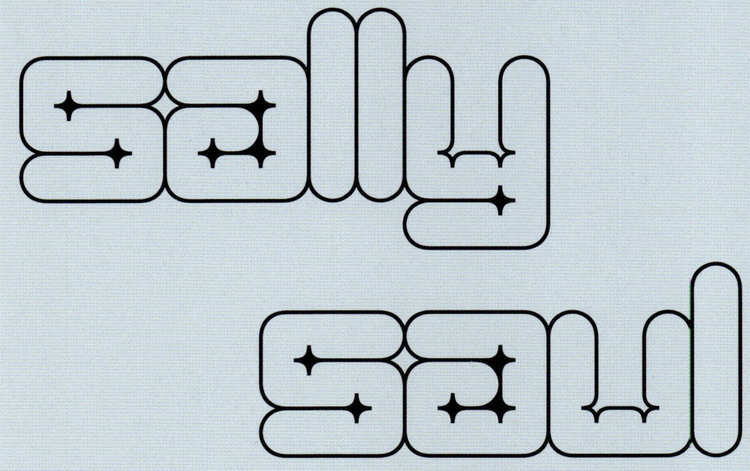
sally
saul

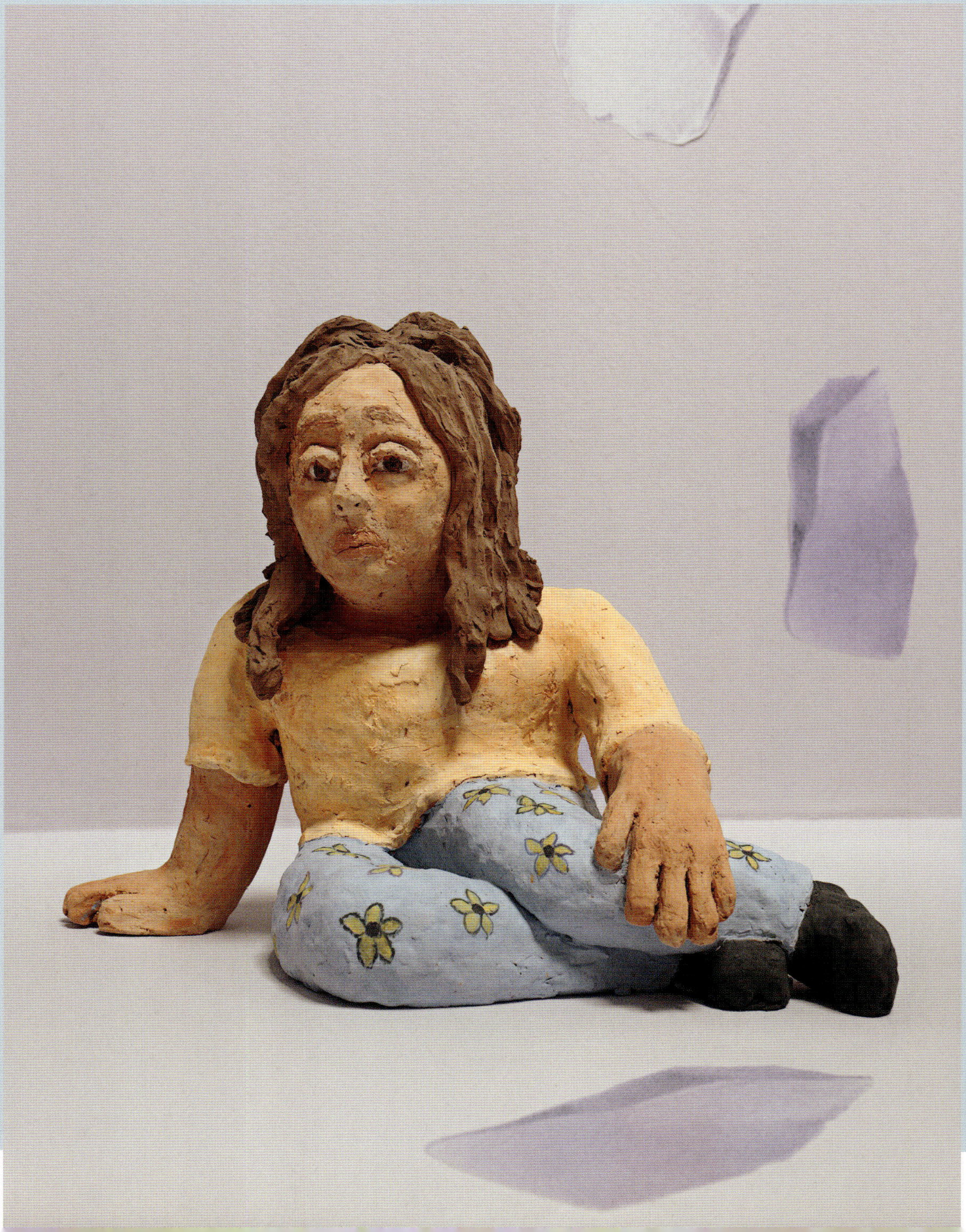

Clay is an art medium that I first took note of while I was living in the California Bay Area, where ceramic artists were enthusiastically opening up the field to new possibilities. Their work was my first inspiration to try my hand at clay. However, it was not until the early 1980s when I was living in Austin, Texas, that I could become seriously involved with clay. I signed up to take classes at the University of Texas, which had an excellent ceramics department. It was a place where I could learn and have a place to work. Now, my husband and I live in upstate New York in the mid-Hudson region, surrounded by greenery. Our sage green studio blends in nicely.

My influences have been numerous. One was the medieval bosses in Norwich Cathedral in England. They are painted carvings—mainly, biblical scenes looking down at you—placed where the ceiling supports the join. The carvings are lively, portrayed with humor, humanity, and imagination. There are pre-Columbian influences, the Tang Dynasty, English and Italian, and many American artists.

I think there are more directions one could take in the clay world than any other art medium. As for me, my work is primarily figurative, often with some reference to nature. I think of my figures as having something to say, perhaps privately. Sometimes, I make some reference to the past—what is gone, what is still here, how much time has passed—and occasionally have a grouping of a figure or two with objects that extend the meaning.

— Sally Saul

◂ *Thinking Things Over*, 2021
Clay, glaze
13 x 14 x 13.4 in.

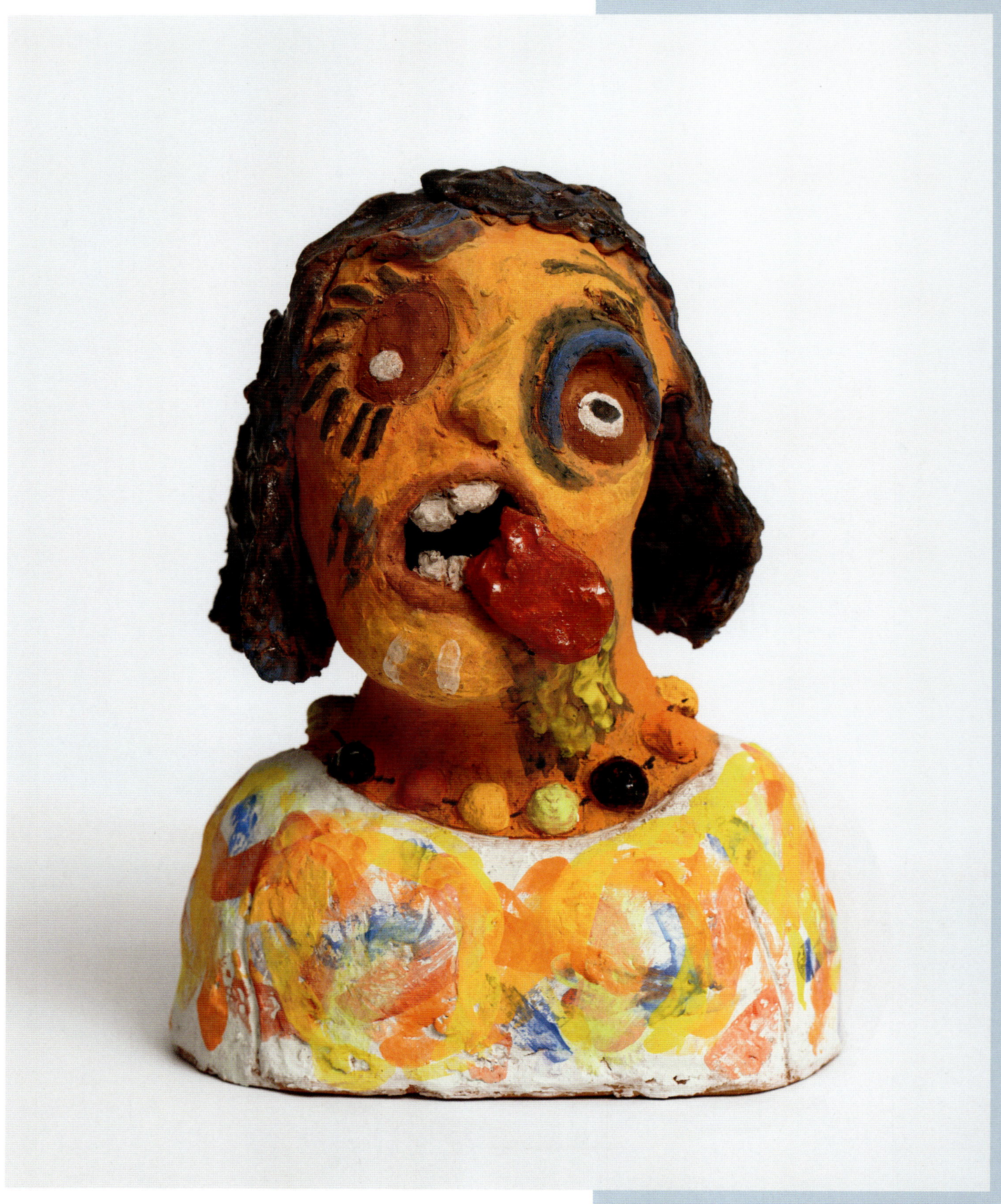

▲ *Transformed*, 2020
Clay, glaze
11 x 8.5 x 6.5 in.

▸ *Meditation Tree*, 2020
Clay, glaze
34.5 x 12 x 11 in.

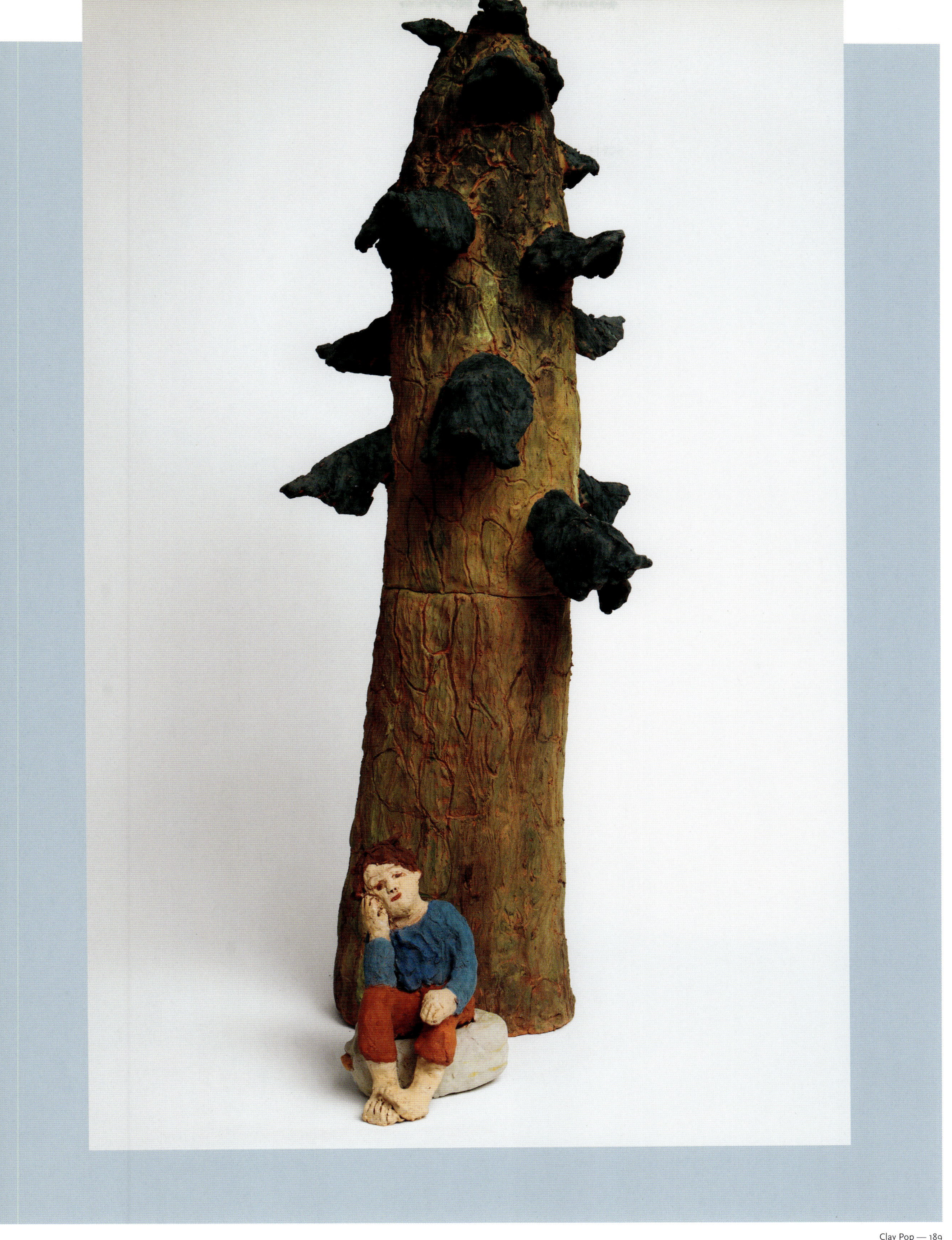

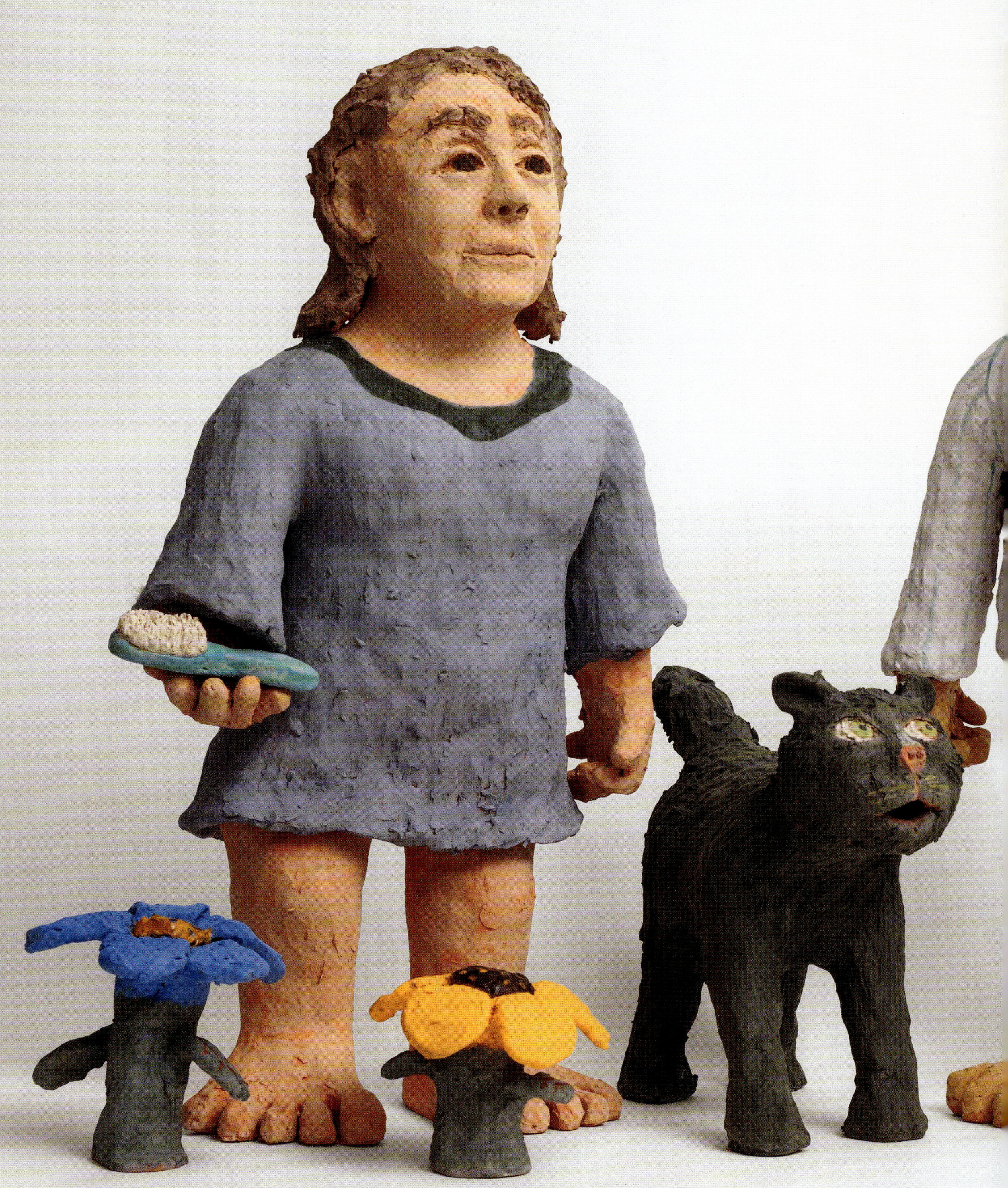

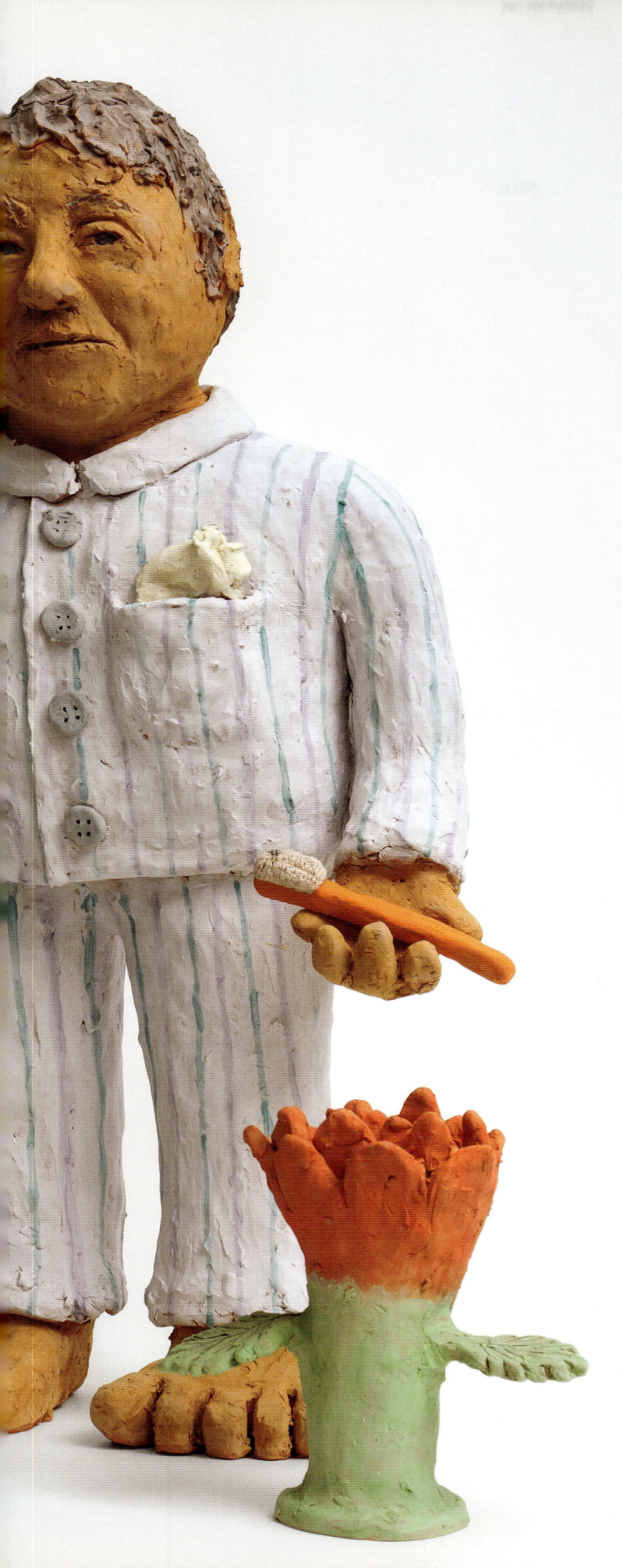

◂ *Back and Forth*, 2019
Clay, glaze
25.5 x 27 x 22 in.

stephanie h. shih

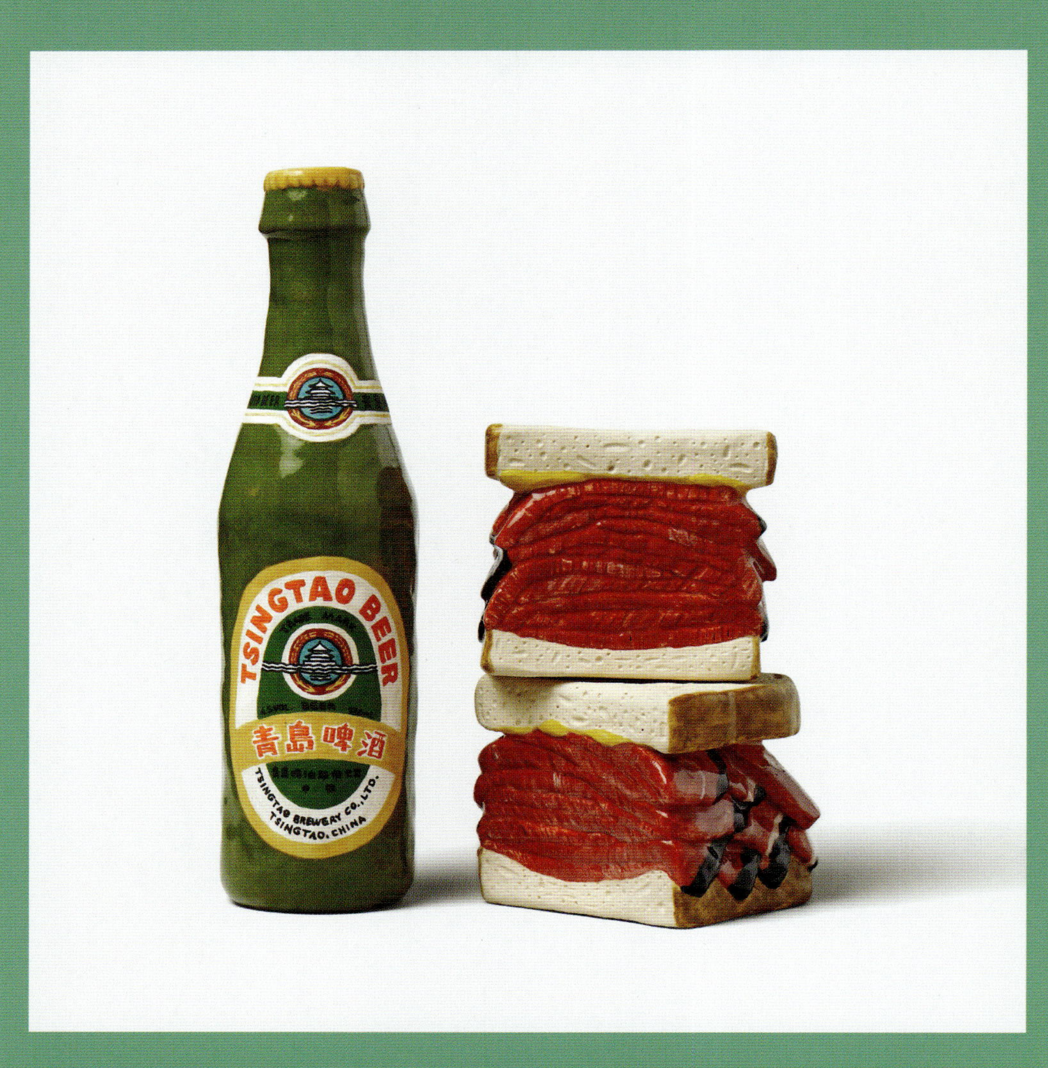

A daughter of Taiwanese immigrants, Stephanie H. Shih (b. 1986, Philadelphia) never formally trained in the arts. At college, she studied journalism, working both front- and back-of-house restaurant positions throughout school, before starting a decade-long copywriting career that included brief stints in food writing and food marketing. In her twenties, art was a personal pursuit rather than a professional one, which she practiced at different community studios in Brooklyn. When she was 32 years old, she folded a few porcelain dumplings by hand, and did so again the next day, and the day after, until she had made nearly a thousand.

In these early works, Shih connected different parts of her life from the "muscle memory of folding them with all my *ayis* [aunts] around the table" to her experience with food preparation and writing about it.[1] Making them got Shih thinking about all the different roles that food played in her life. It was akin to a Proustian moment—the vivid linking of taste and memory—that triggers different associations and feelings. Isn't eating a certain food a way to connect to one's culture, continue a tradition, remember a world that no longer exists, and be transported to a moment tinged with nostalgia and filled with melancholia, while living in a country that regards you as an outsider?

In an interview, Shih explained her choice of subject:

> I [...] wasn't trying to make realistic food—I was making a sculptural object. I wanted to do something that was a nod to other Chinese [...] who would know that the most important dipping sauce was not soy sauce at all. The first grocery I ever made was black vinegar. I wanted to choose an ingredient I felt would be very familiar to the community, while probably being fairly foreign to another.[2]

Recognizing that the term "Asian American" refers to people from different countries, cultures, and ethnicities, she has made food products that reflect those differences: detailed bags of Botan rice, containers of chili oil, squeeze bottles of Japanese Kewpie mayonnaise, and cans of Spam, which is popular in Hawaii and South Korea. The attention Shih pays to the labels and decorative designs that characterize each of these products is unparalleled.

— John Yau

[1] "This Asian-American Artist Creates Community with a Porcelain Pantry," *Edible Brooklyn*, November 28, 2018, https://www.ediblebrooklyn.com/2018/stephanie-shih-porcelain-ceramics.

[2] Jory Shareff, "Ceramic Artist Stephanie H. Shih on the Meaning of Memory and Clay," *Cultured*, June 26, 2020, https://www.culturedmag.com/article/2020/06/26/ceramic-artist-stephanie-h-shih-on-the-meaning-of-memory-and-clay.

◀ *Open Sundays*, 2022
Ceramic
8.5 x 3.5 x 3.5 in.

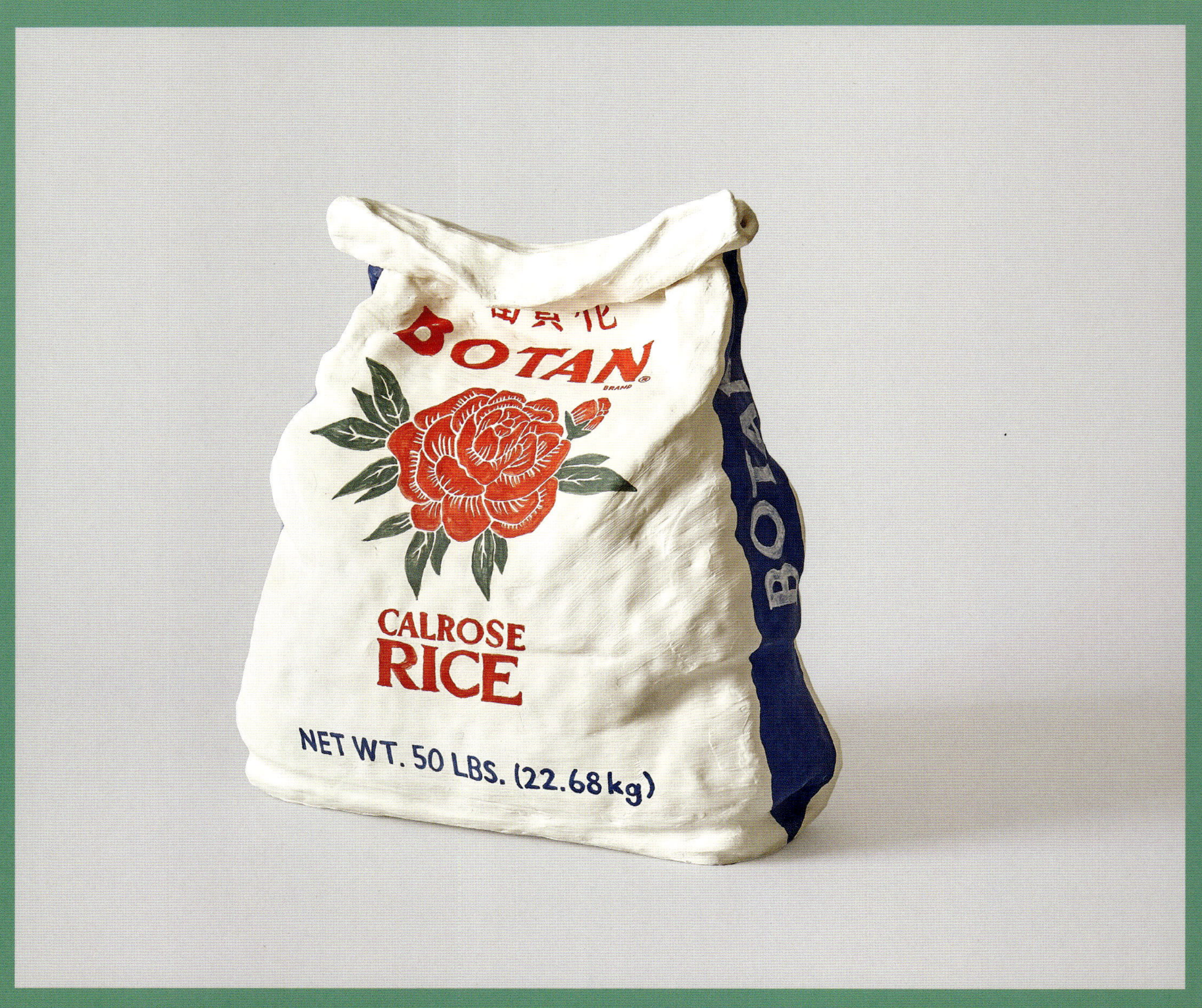

▲ *Botan Calrose Rice*, 2019
Ceramic
14 x 12 x 5 in.

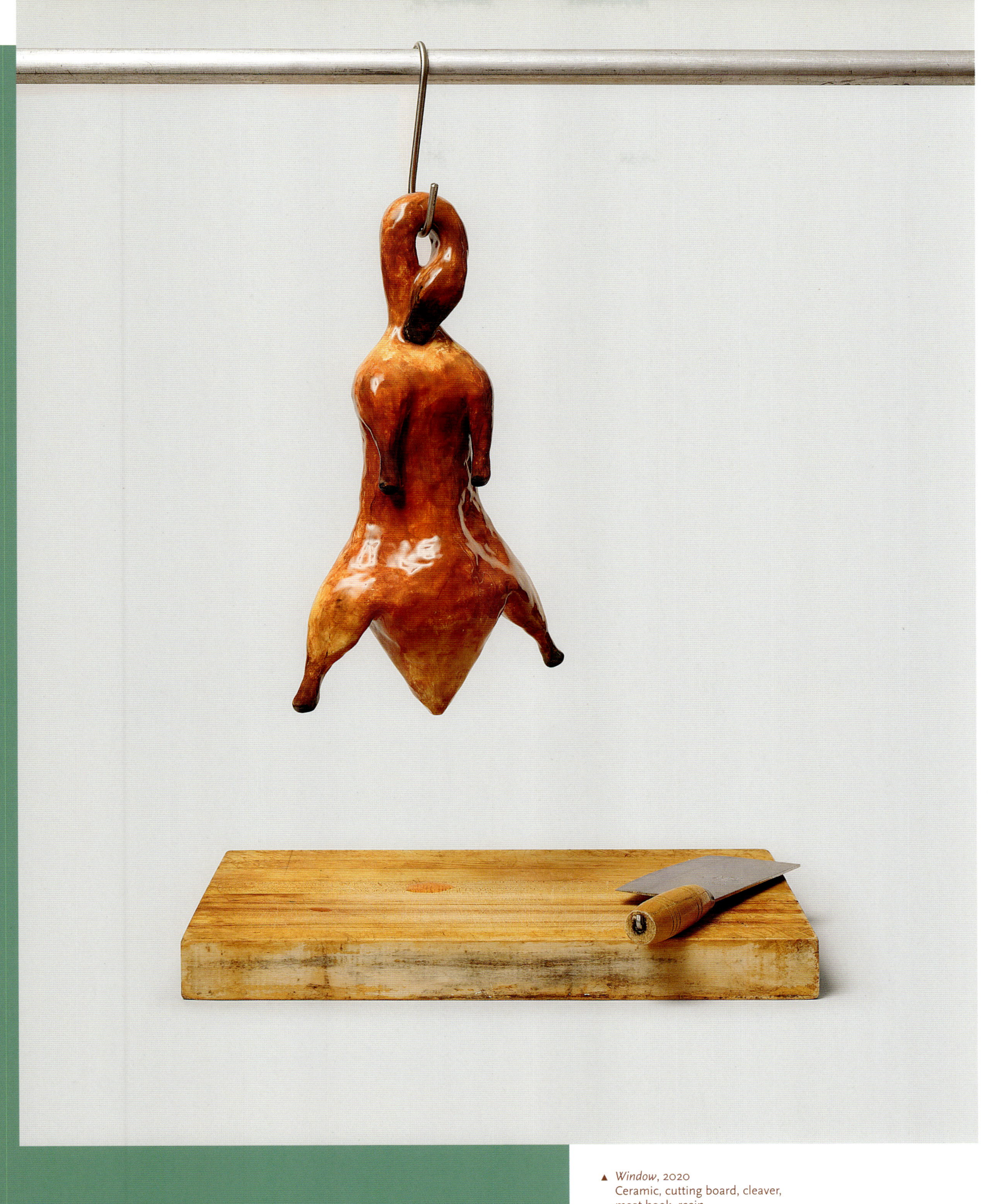

▲ *Window*, 2020
Ceramic, cutting board, cleaver,
meat hook, resin
28 x 19.5 x 13.5 in.

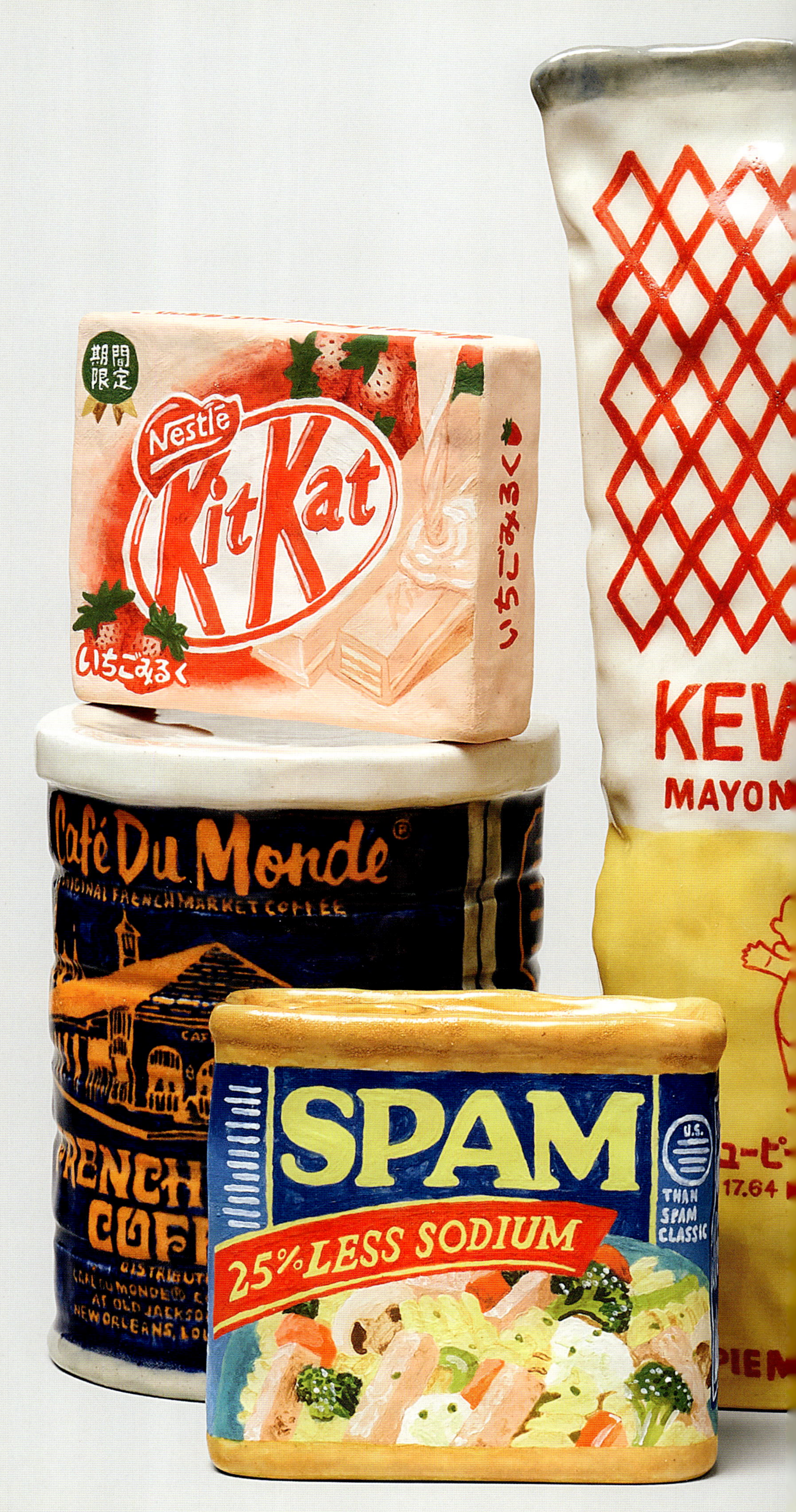
期間限定
Nestlé
KitKat
いちごみるく
いちごみるく
Café Du Monde
FRENCH MARKET COFFEE
SPAM
25% LESS SODIUM
U.S.
THAN SPAM CLASSIC
17.64

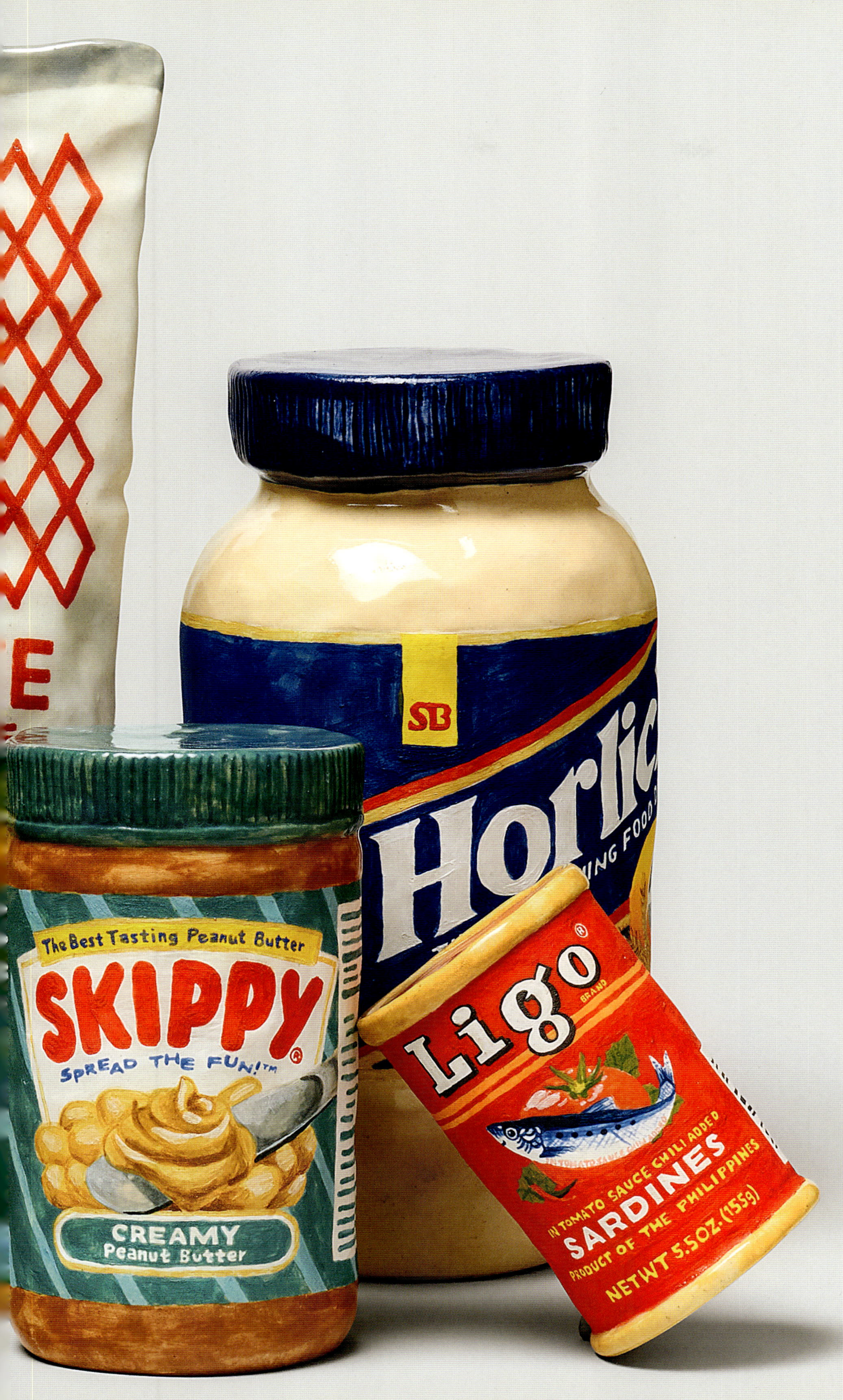

◂ *New World Mall*, 2021
Ceramic
11 x 14 x 7 in.

alake shilling

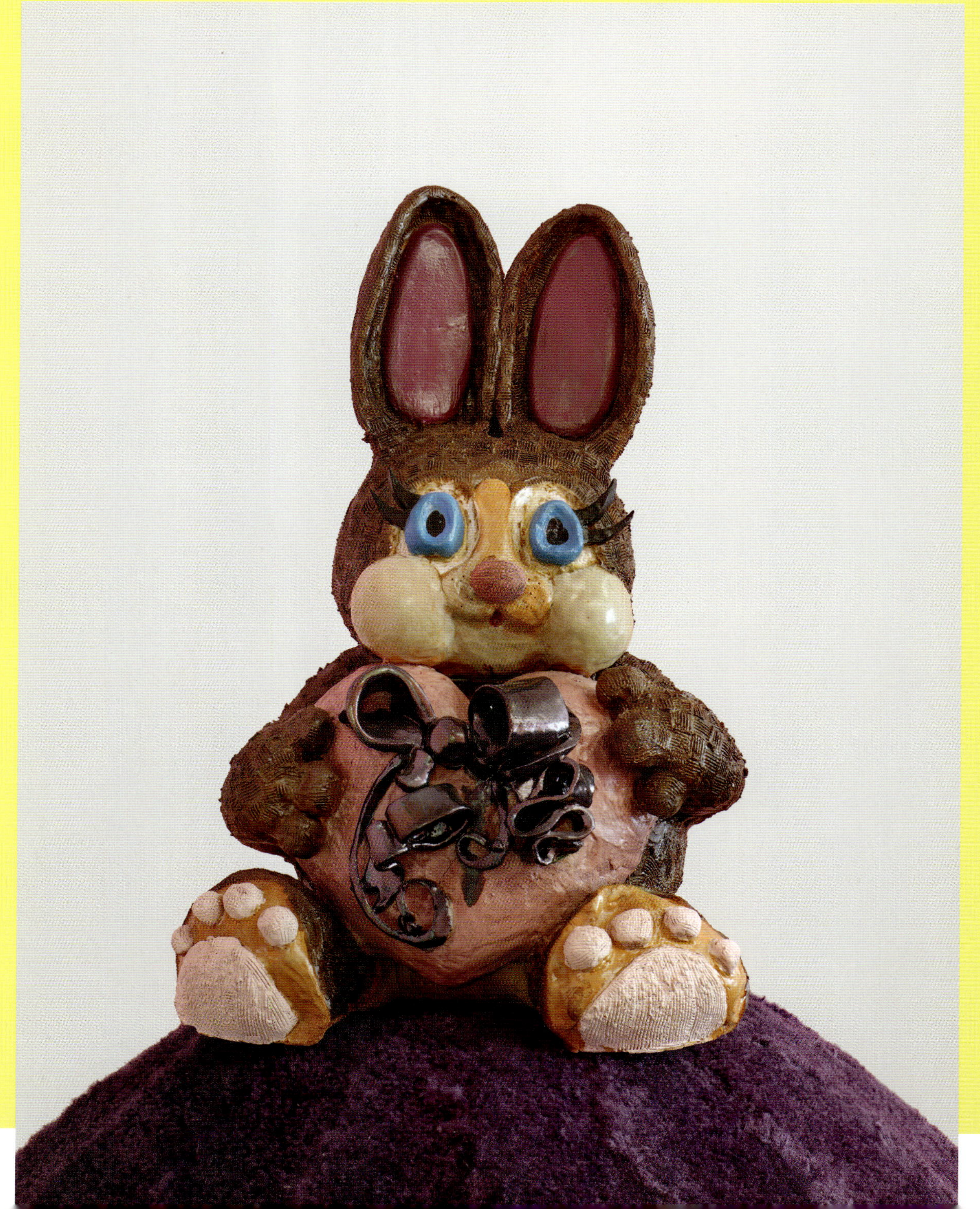

Alake Shilling (b. 1993, Los Angeles) claims, rightfully so, that artists and athletes have a lot in common with each other. They each rely on a blend of innate talent, unwavering commitment, and a constant drive for progress. Watching sports documentaries, Shilling has seen how athletes can hone their talents through determination and repetition—setting goals and then willing themselves to practice until they excel. In this same vein, the ceramicist builds and rebuilds many of the same characters until she is confident in their refinement. Her lovely ceramic garden kits are evidence of this.

Shilling notes that ceramics have long been second nature for her. The whimsical characters for which she is known are evidence of the intuitive approach that she has taken during the five years that she has focused on hand-building—a process in which she feels the material works with her, to the extent that her low- and high-fire clays become unique spirits rather than inanimate objects. The relationship between artist and material brings each piece to fruition in a unique way. Shilling finds this romantic: the ability to work on something until she is pleased with the outcome, simply by sourcing her preferred materials and using her hands.

The artist hopes to continually learn and evolve. She is intent on creating large-scale works that fit seamlessly, and perhaps even strikingly, in an outdoor setting. Although today she keeps her glazes and underglazes simple, Shilling would like to study the chemistry of glaze in more detail and eventually include more glass and rock in her pieces—as long as her material remains forgiving enough to allow reworking if she wishes to make adjustments. Today, the majority of her ceramics, including frogs, bears, and ladybugs, are medium-sized. They are rife with vibrant colors and textures so compelling that the figures seem to come alive. Shilling explains that her art is both innate and the product of physical and mental labor. It is strenuous, but the results are worth it.

Today, Shilling works with remarkable patience and care in her new temporary studio, a space that she will be sharing with friend and fellow artist Darren Romanelli for the next year. She is committed to refining her cast of ethereal characters, and she will continue to focus on exactly that: working toward the perfect ladybug, remaking each creature until she achieves a near-perfect formula.

Shilling's work has become less abstract in recent years, though she has expertly maintained the cartoonish, playful nature for which she is celebrated. Perhaps this is because, in the artist's words, "the material has a mind of its own." Shilling's hand-built works are designed to resemble garden tree kits with pastel colors and subtle physical details—the blushing cheeks of a rabbit, endless lashes adorning a turtle—that make the works come alive.

— Charles Moore

◂ *Chocolate Bunny Loves Everyone*, 2021
Glazed ceramic
22.5 x 15 x 15 in.

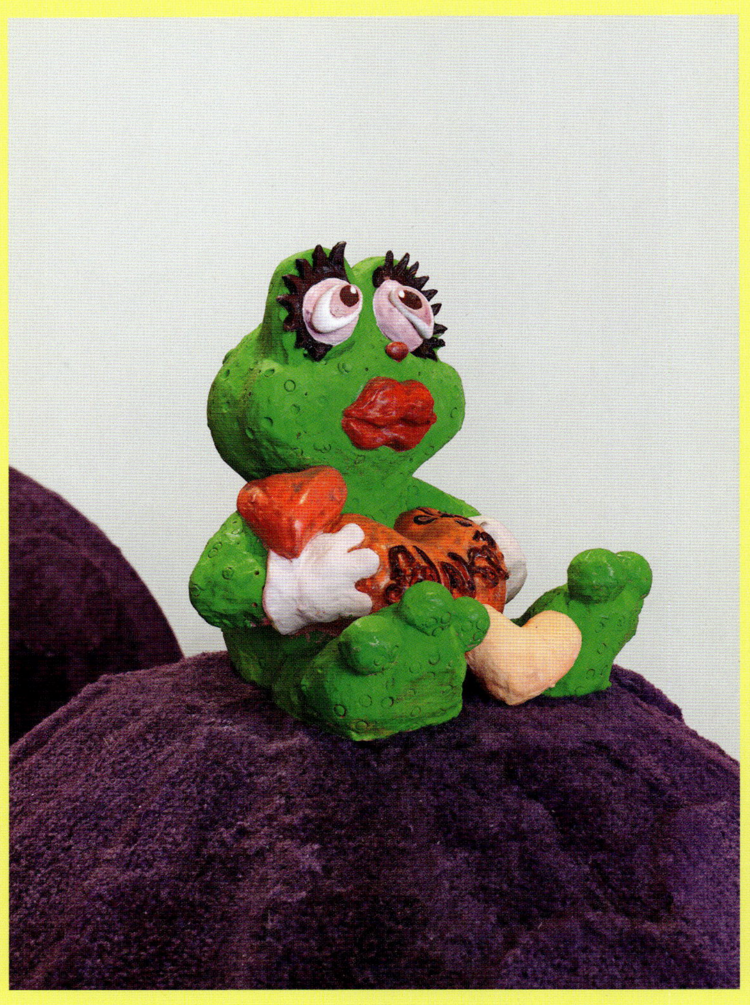

▲ *Little Frog Loves Alake*, 2021
Glazed ceramic, enamel paint
12 x 12 x 12.5 in.

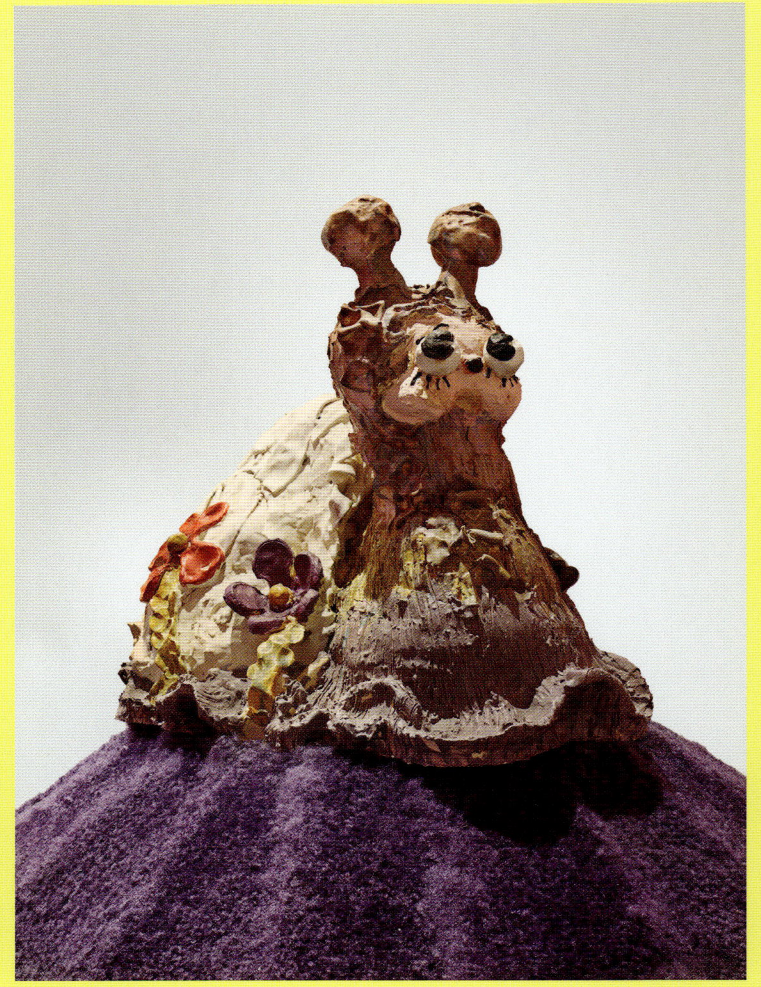

▲ *Snaily Boop*, 2021
Glazed ceramic
15 x 13 x 18.5 in.

► *Baby Chick*, 2021
Glazed ceramic, Flashe paint
18 x 13 x 13 in.

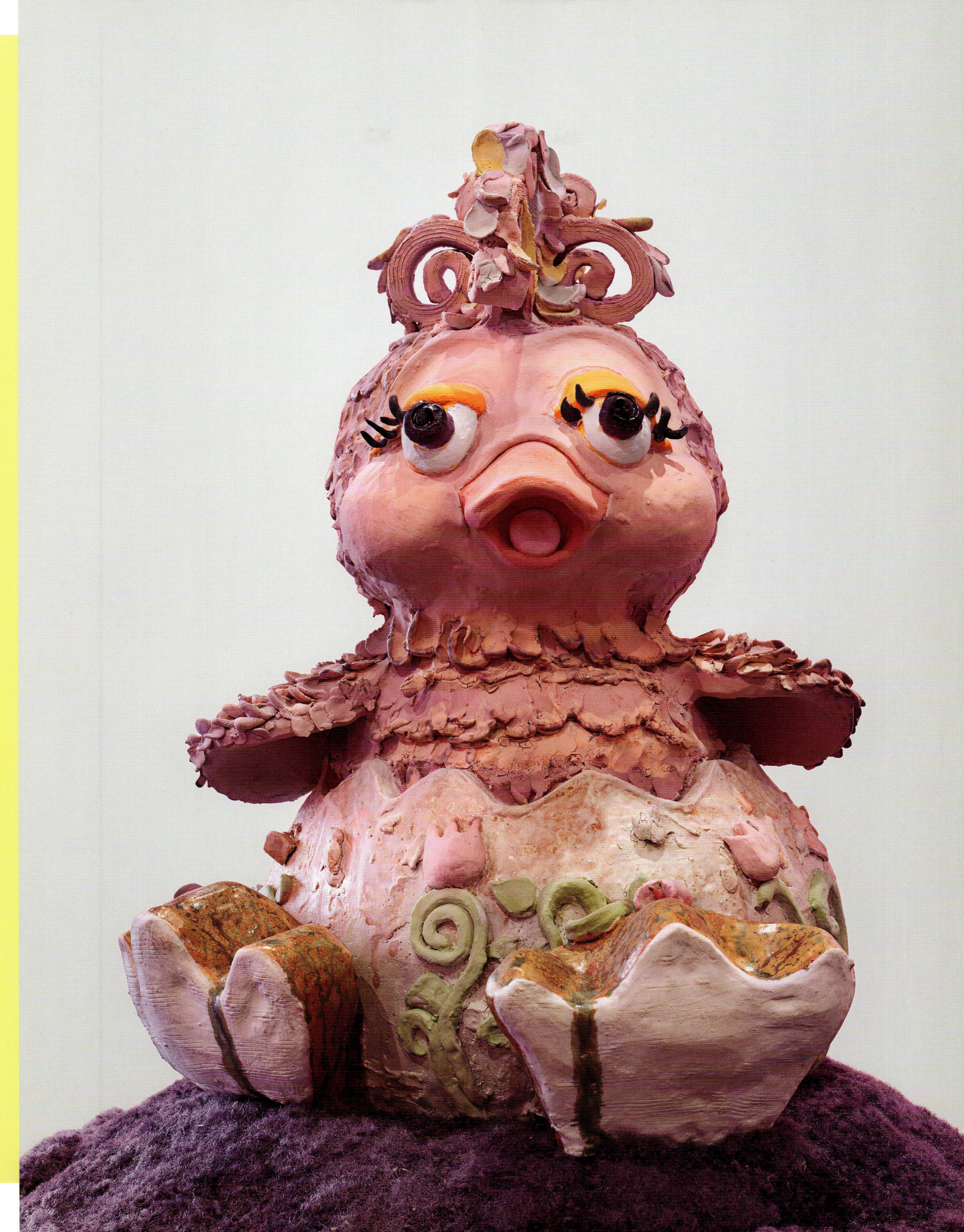

▼ *Best Buddies*, 2021
Glazed ceramic and enamel paint
14 x 25 x 16 in.

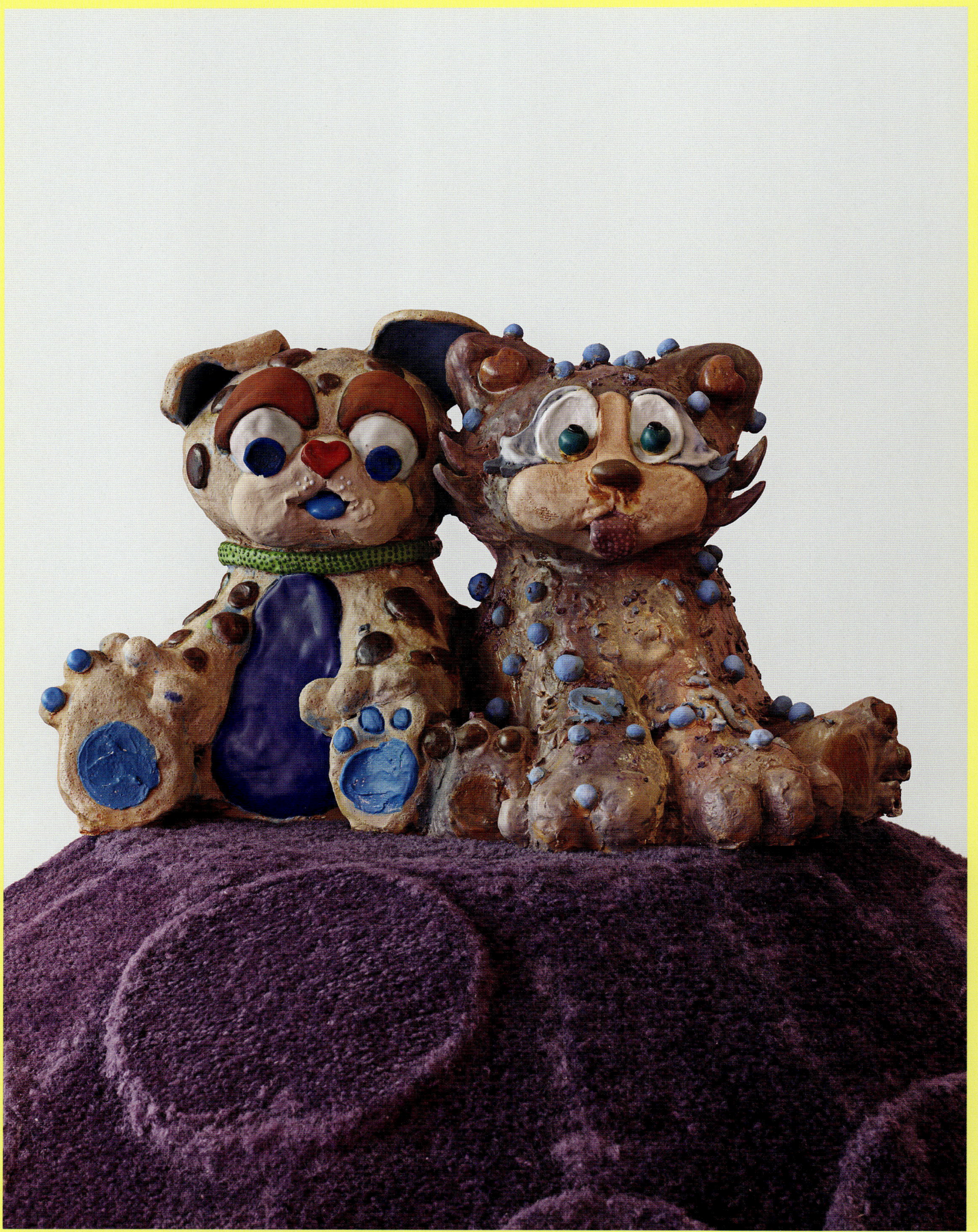

▾ *Mister Spitz*, 2021
Glazed ceramic, enamel paint
18 x 24 x 25 in.

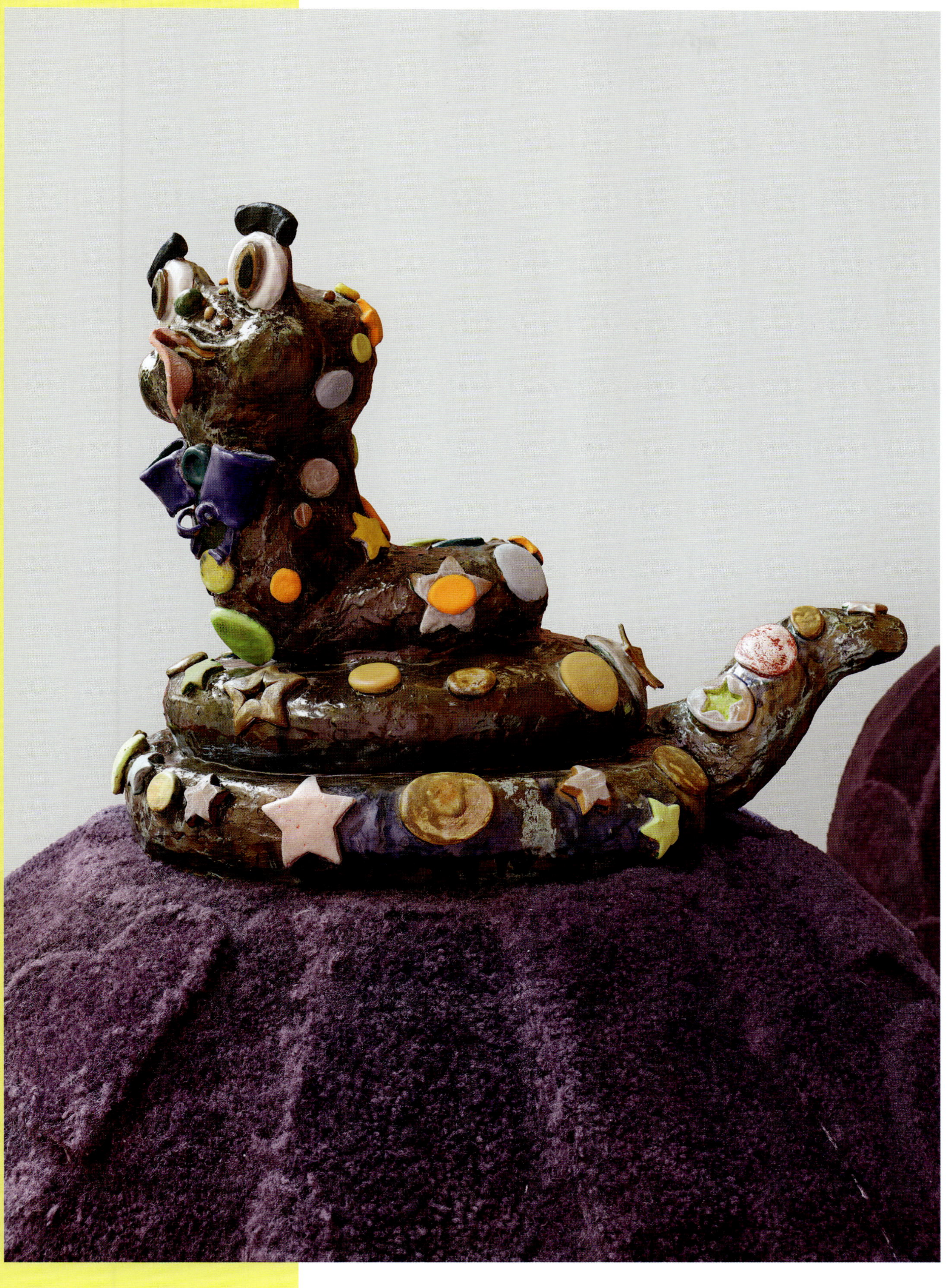

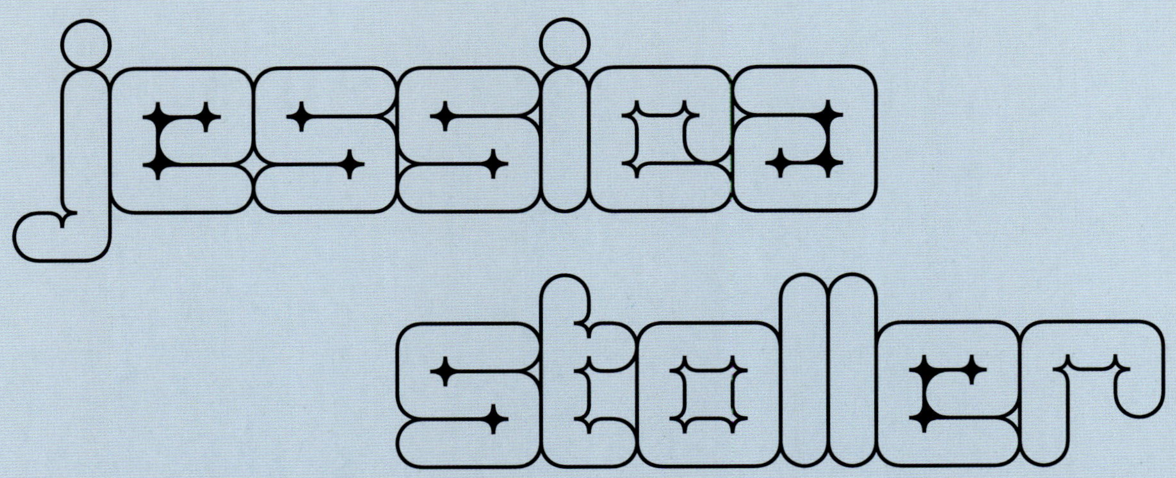
jessica
stoller

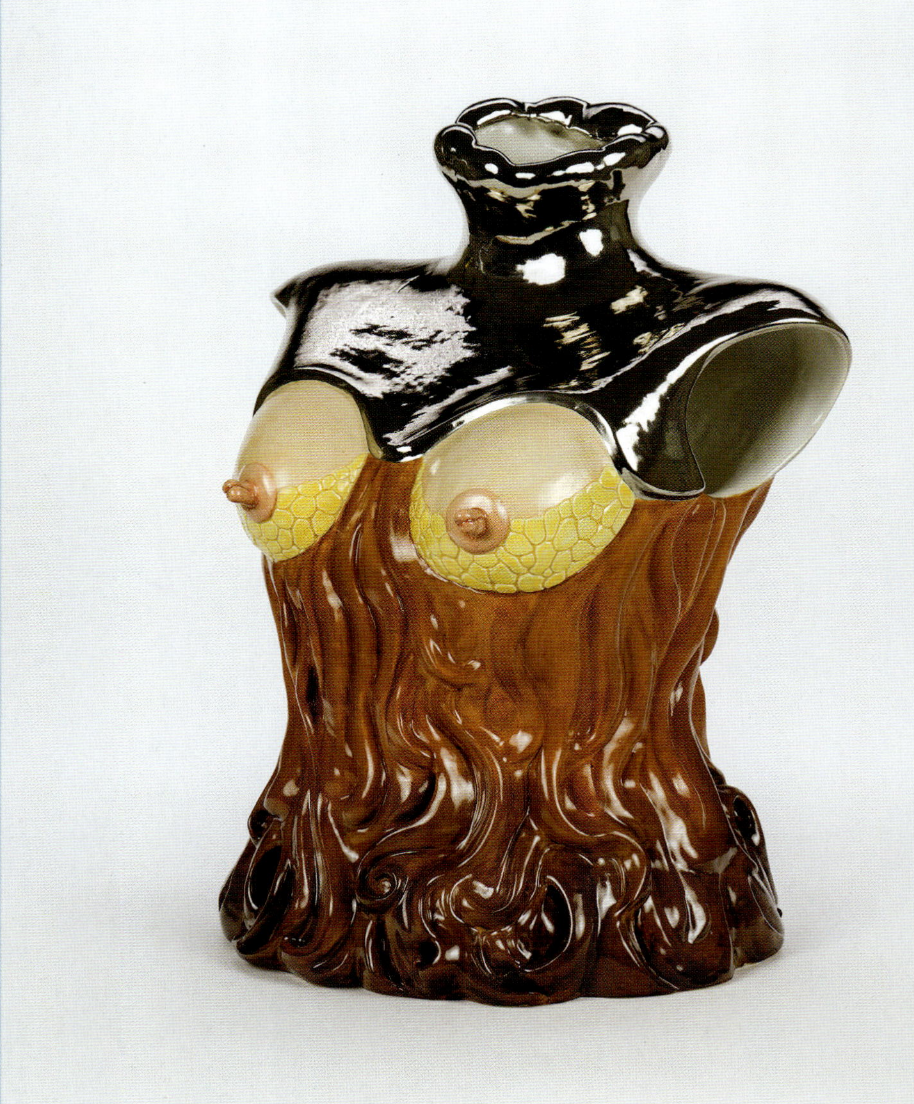

André Breton once described Frida Kahlo's work as "a ribbon around a bomb." His words could also apply to the witty and subversive sculptures of Jessica Stoller (b. 1981, Detroit, Michigan). Stoller's sculptures first seduce and then explode into contrary objection. Each work, fashioned out of porcelain—a medium with a rich history linked to luxury and desire—and glazed in soft pastels, with lusters and delicately detailed flourishes, deploys tactile sensuosity to veil shrewd critique.

Spread, Stoller's solo exhibition at P·P·O·W in 2020, was introduced by a group of sculptures with profiles resembling ordinary vases or urns. The bodies of these vessels, however, morph into tasseled breasts or buttocks surrounded by delicate lace. Their forms were further embellished by such incongruous features as a base with four gilded feet ending in long, painted nails; lids ornamented with butterflies and writhing snakes; and handles that doubled as ears with large, dangling earrings. In addition to slyly reworking the traditional vase, Stoller's often grotesque revisions upend the patronizing view of women as decorative accessories; instead, they celebrate the allure of the noncanonical, extravagant female body.

A number of Stoller's works explore the analogy between porcelain and skin. In a series of skillfully crafted, wall-mounted mirrors, Stoller replaces the glass with ceramic renderings of dimpled, pimpled, wrinkled, and sagging flesh. Set within gold frames adorned with elaborate profusions of colorful porcelain flowers, these mirrors offer a fragmented reflection on beauty and vanity.

Other pieces invite appreciation of the breast. In one wall-mounted series, singular forms and groups in a range of skin tones and sizes—some with piercings—explore the breast as an expressive form rather than an object of erotic fascination. Stoller's freestanding *Breastplate* (2019) with bared, milk-filled breasts set against silver flesh above and flowing brown hair below suggests armor and a corset, coupling nurture and sustenance with power and perseverance. *Bloom* (2019) focuses on fecundity and growth through exaggerated, almost Bosch-like fantasy. Set on a low table that offers views from above and all around, a reclining, fragmented female body with opened legs is surrounded by strange flowers and surreal biomorphic forms that promise an erotic banquet of profuse life and orgasmic pleasure.

Stoller's small female figurines and busts, most between 10 and 12 inches high, comment on the often-erased aging body. Inspired by observations of her own body and those of her mother and grandmother, these figures—some covered in hair, others raising a sagging arm or posed as skeletal busts with grinning faces and flamboyantly exposed, incongruously fleshy breasts—disrupt ideals of beauty and the social prerogatives of youth culture to emphasize intimate encounter with, and fanciful delight in, the physicality of the mature female body.

Stoller's skillful technique is evident throughout her work, reinforcing and subverting her subject matter. Her engaging sculptures honor women's work, even as they destabilize distinctions between high and low, art and craft, and decoration and function.

An earlier version of this piece was published as "Jessica Stoller," Sculpture *magazine, November 18, 2020, https://sculpturemagazine.art/jessica-stoller/.*

— Susan Canning

◂ *Breastplate*, 2019
Porcelain, glaze, China paint, luster
17.25 x 13 x 9 in.

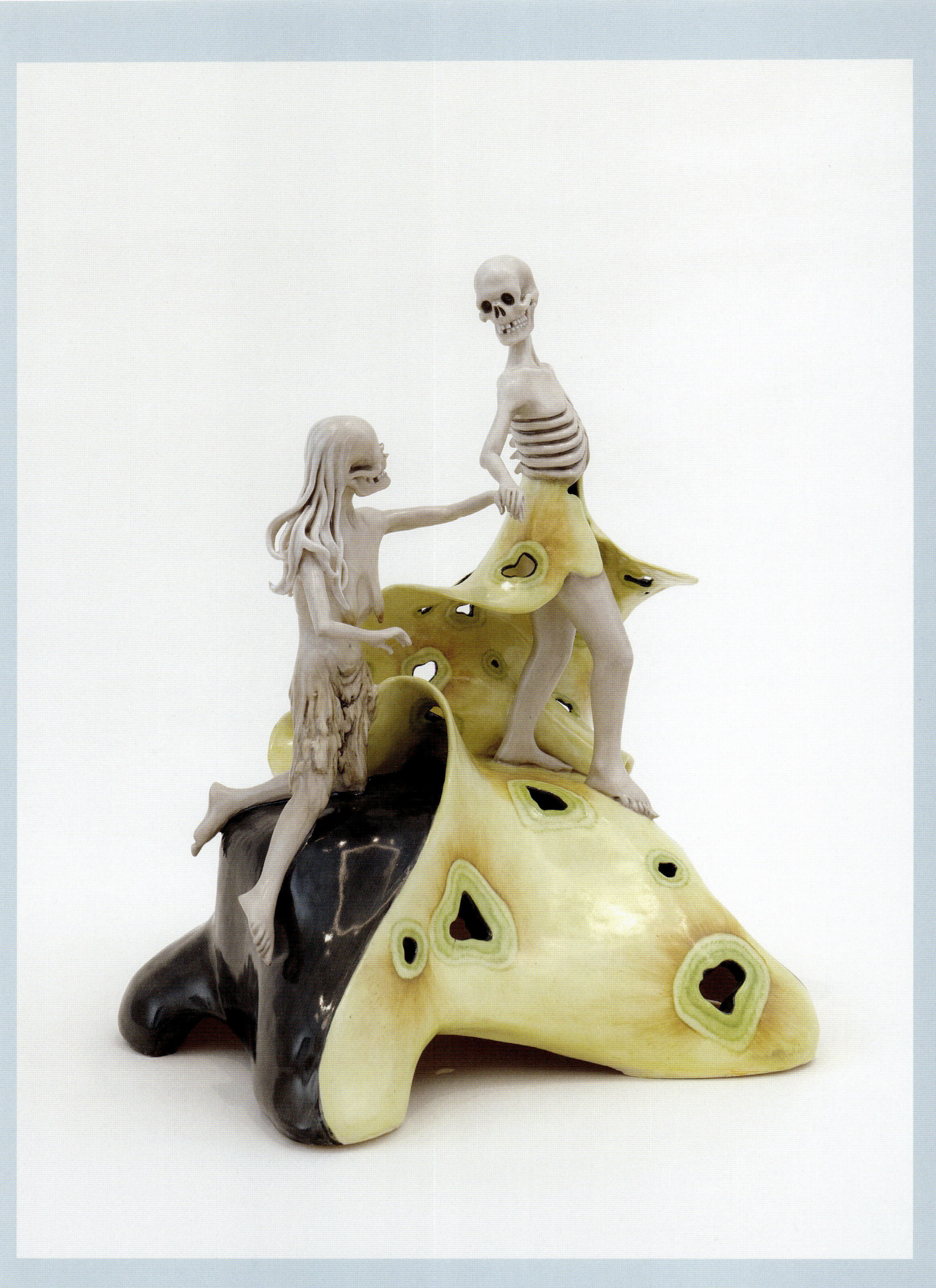

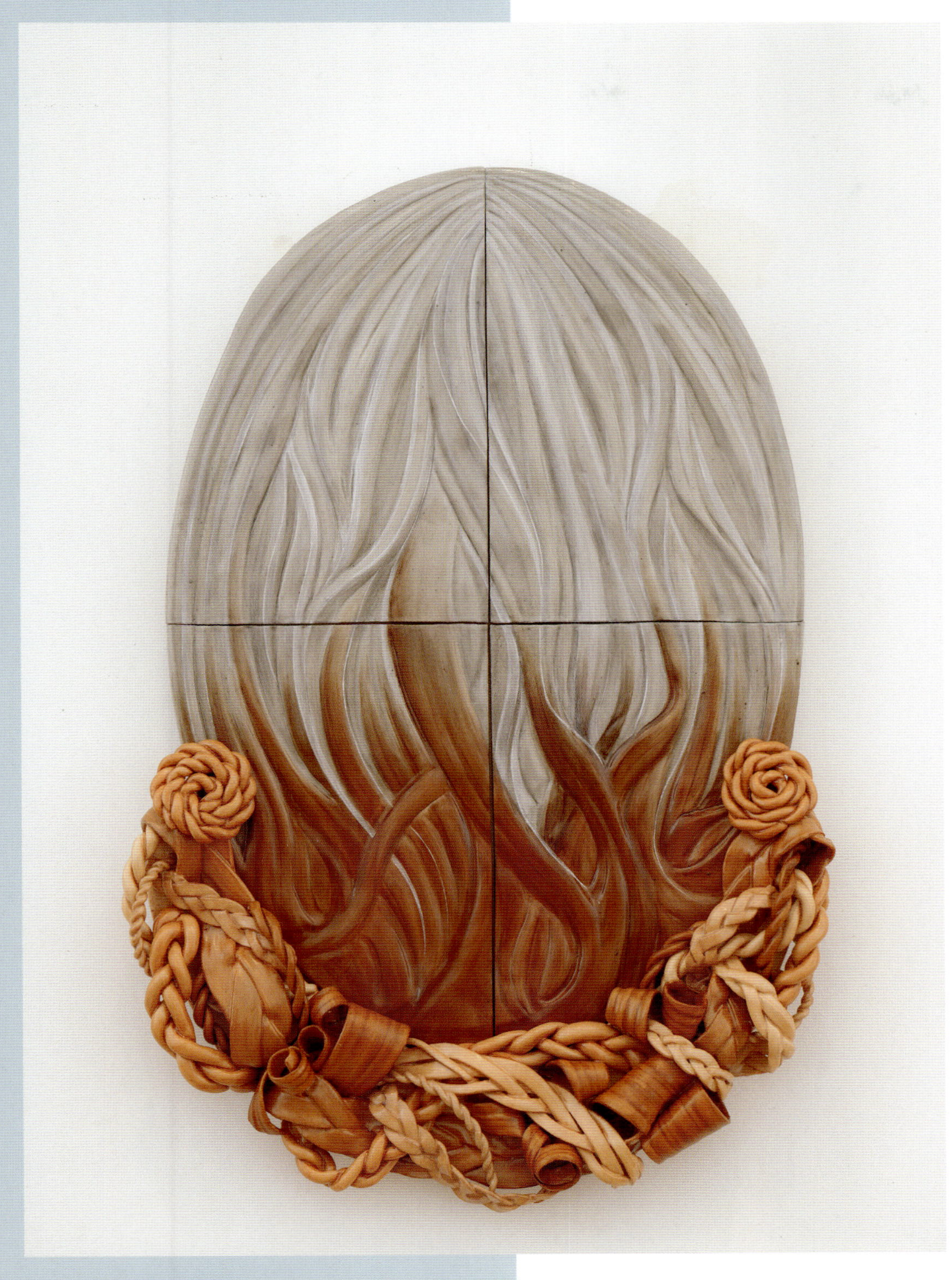

◂ *Untitled (Crown)*, 2021
Porcelain, glaze, China paint, wood
24 x 16 x 2 in.

◂ *Untitled (Embrace)*, 2021
Porcelain, glaze, China paint, luster
11 x 9 x 14 in.

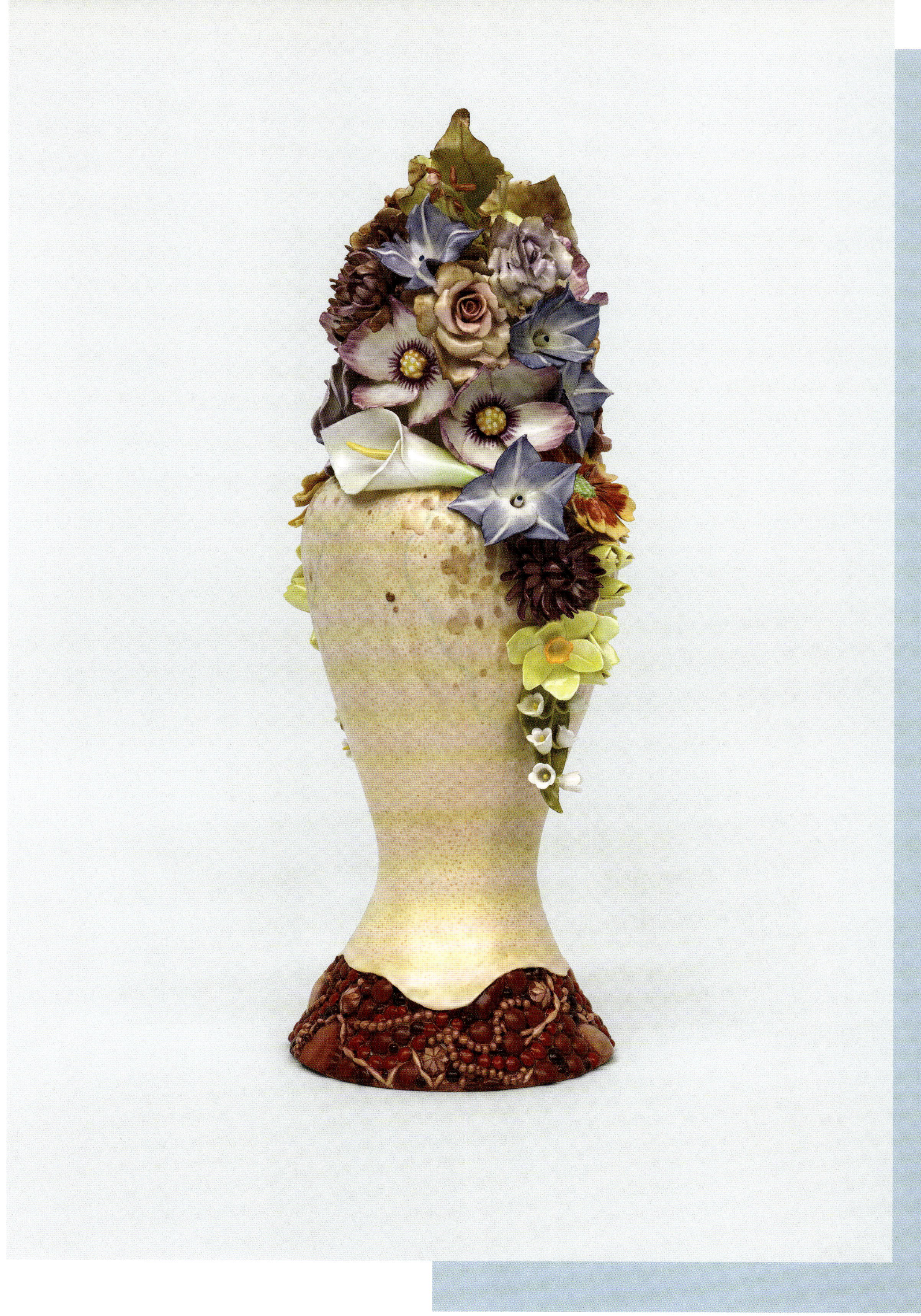

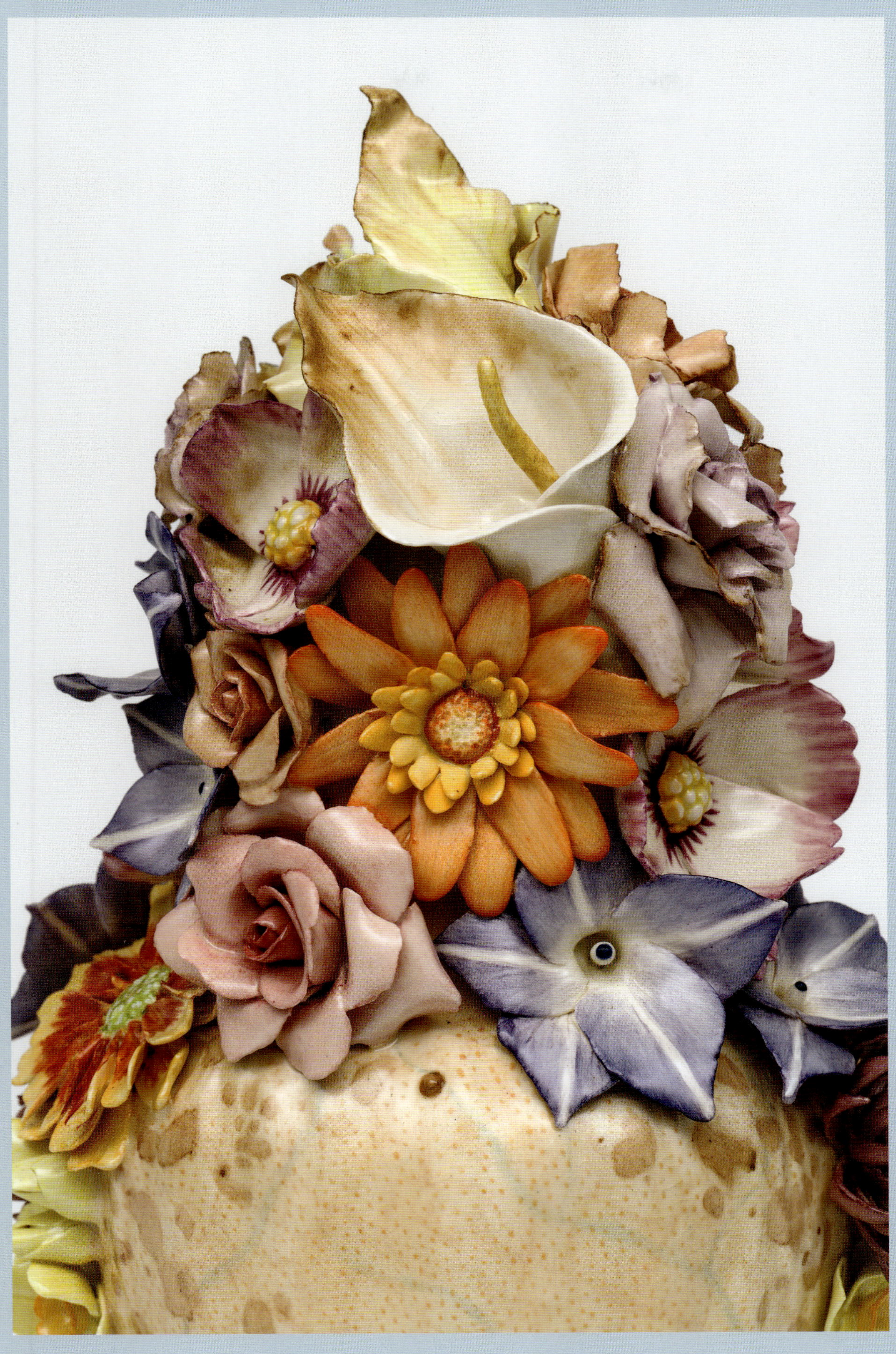

◂ *Untitled (Fade)*, 2022
Porcelain, glaze, China paint, luster
16 x 9 x 5 in.

▴ *Untitled (Fade)* (detail), 2022

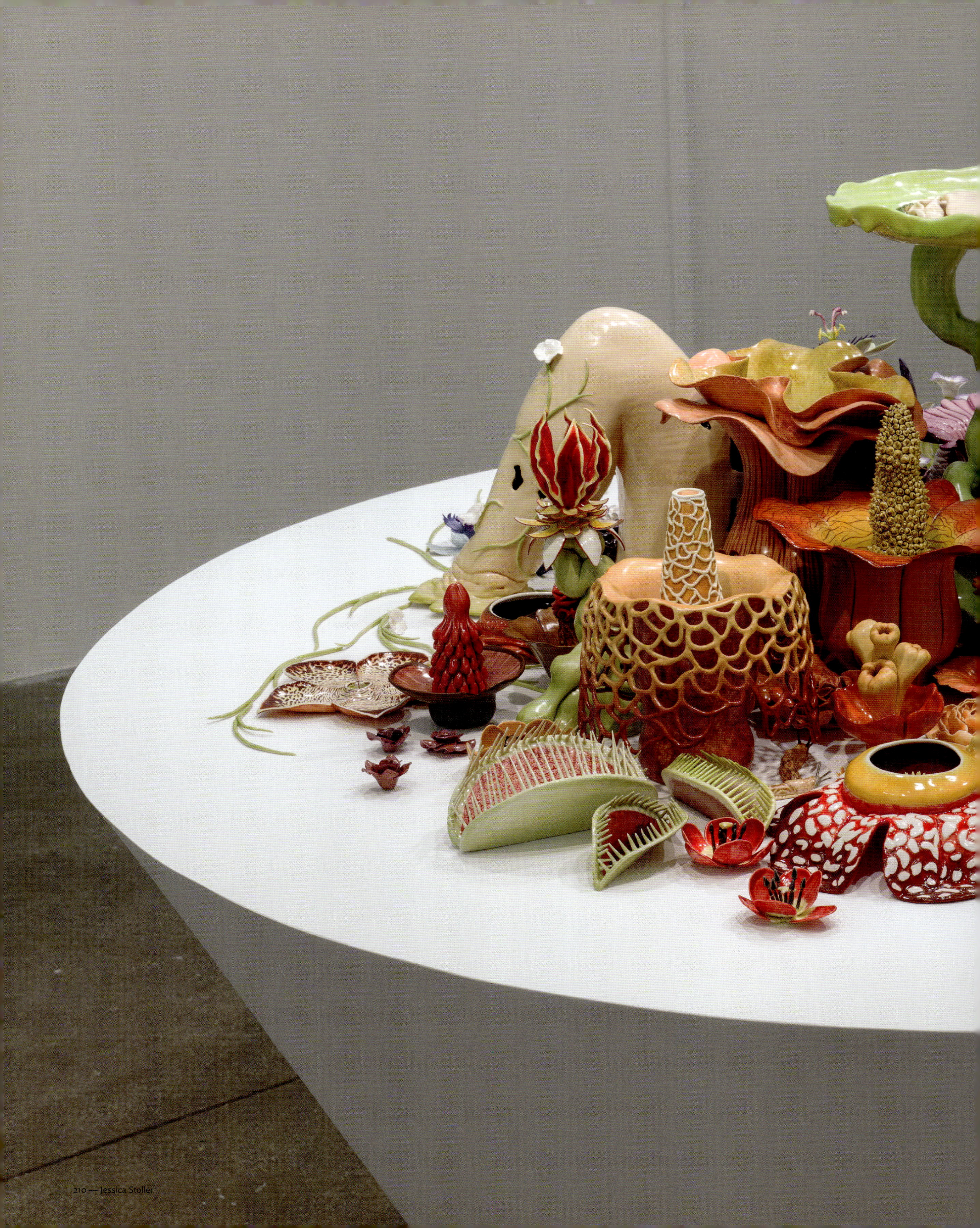

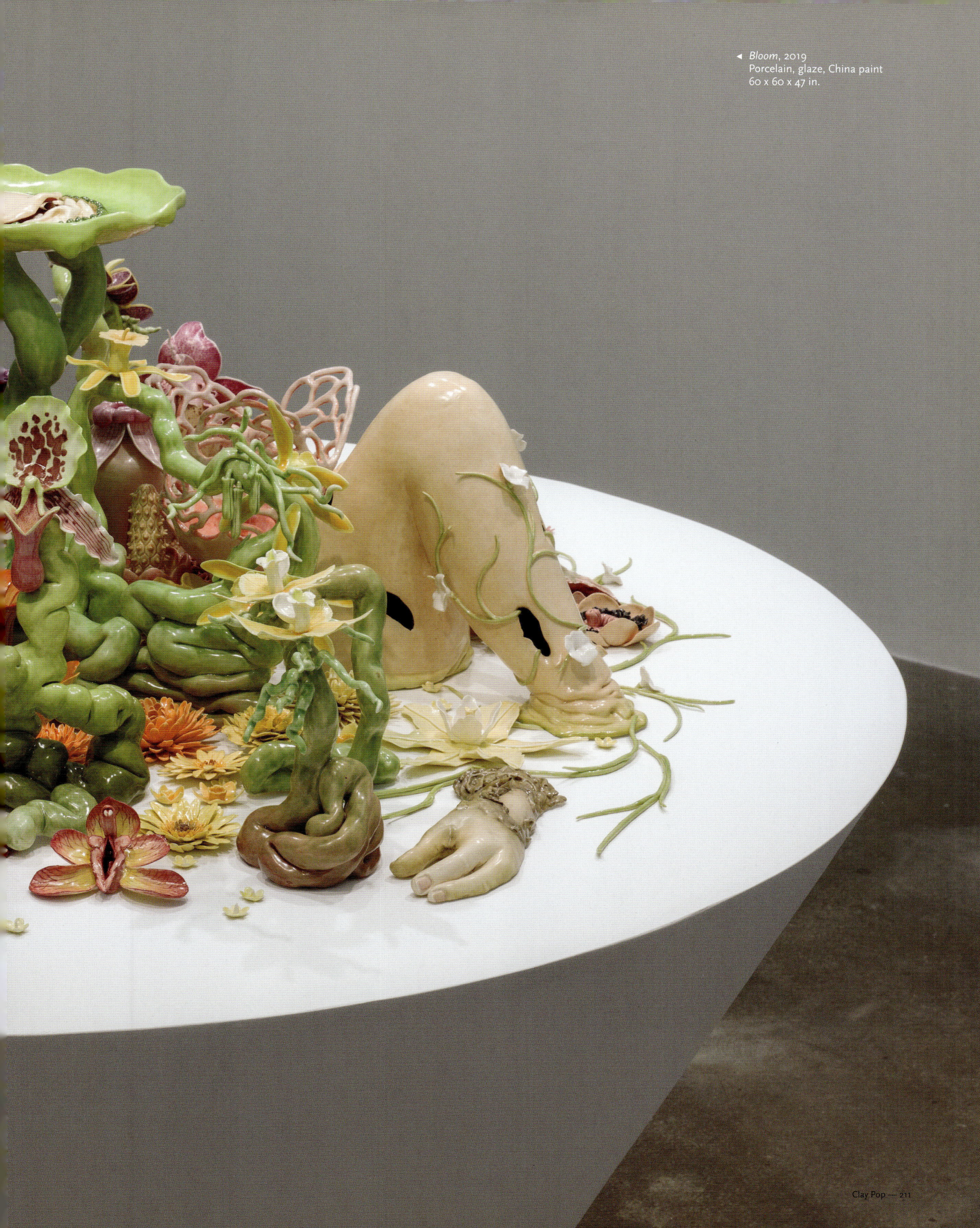

◂ *Bloom*, 2019
Porcelain, glaze, China paint
60 x 60 x 47 in.

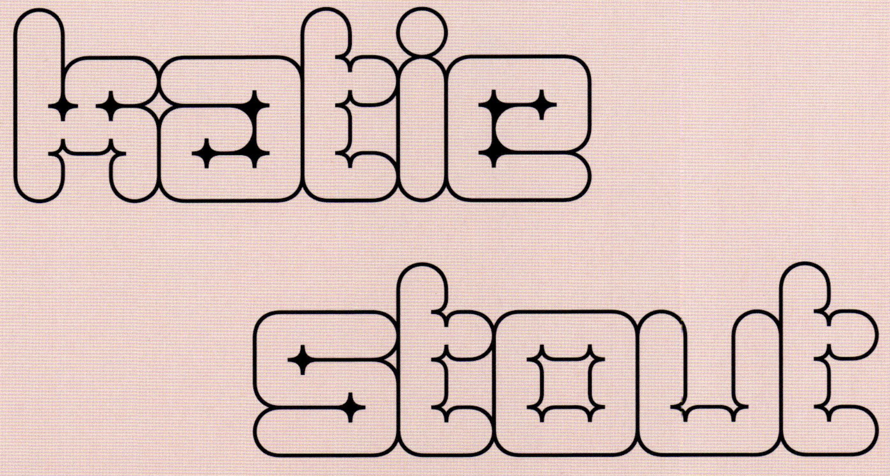
katie
stout

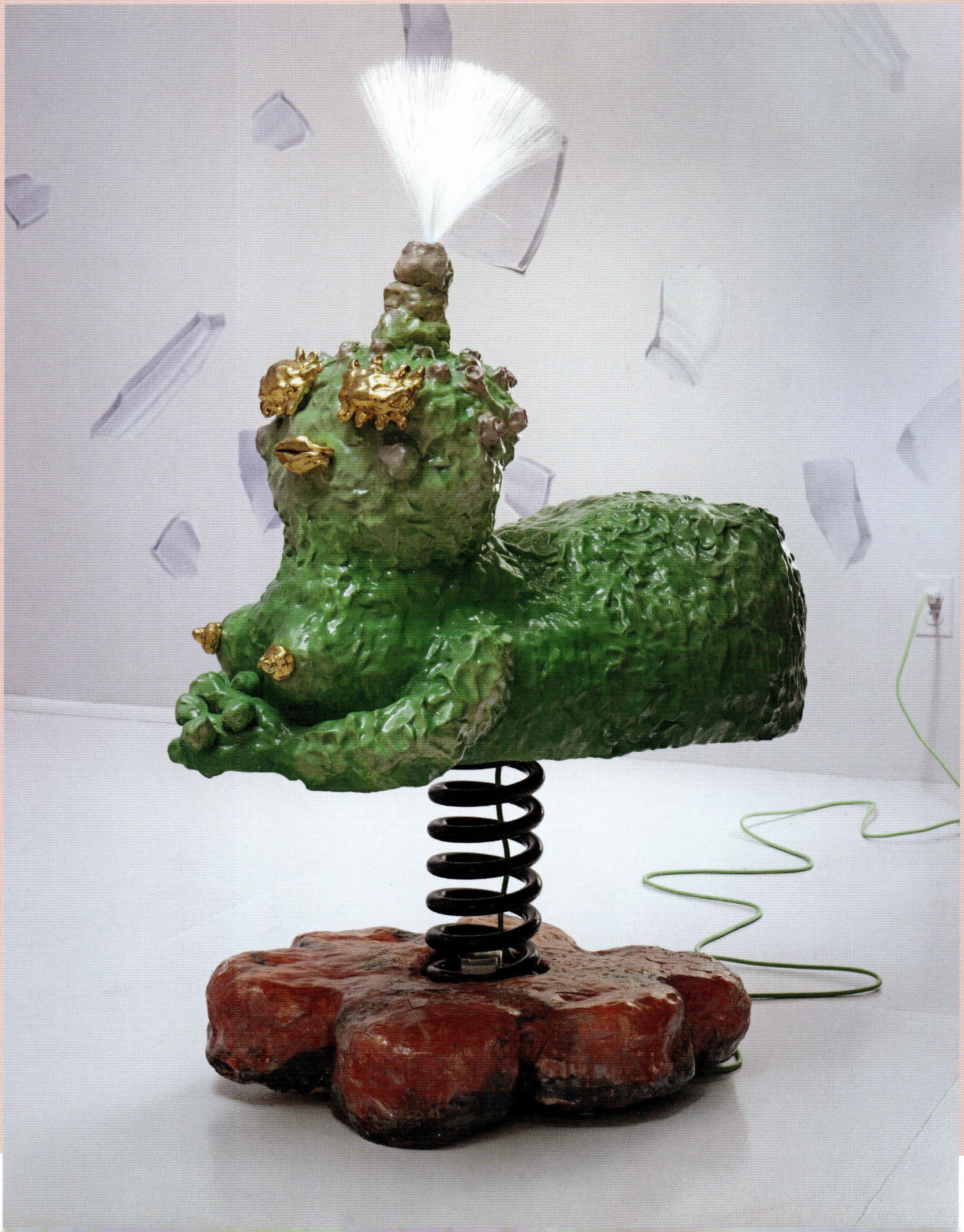

Where You Land Will Not Be a Resting Place

Underneath the lamplight, a perversion
   of stars. An hour passes, there was never
much in it anyway. Understand here there are no

windows, there is a cave with many mouths
   misshapen and hollow. There is the suffering
that has been carefully coiled and pinched

and hardened bright—orange warning, pink like
   the underside of a wrist. And what is a room
if not an effort at containment—each object a reminder

of all the ways a day can embarrass you. Don't take it
   so personally. Your surroundings melt like hard
candy into a molten puddle, and the sugar

in all its infinite sweetness, how it burns. This, you accept,
   is the treachery of play. How else to account for such
unmitigated splendor? Above you, the poor facsimiles

of nature—gold and green and blue radiating
   their own manufactured squeal, strung like
planets broken from their orbit: fixed. You stay

too. You've slept in worse. From the coiled creature
   in the corner comes a little laughter, springs a little
levity, and why not? This room is a place in place of peace.

— Cherry Pickman

◂ *Frog Rider*, 2021
Hand-painted and glazed
ceramic, illuminated fibers
and metal
48 x 21 x 30 in.

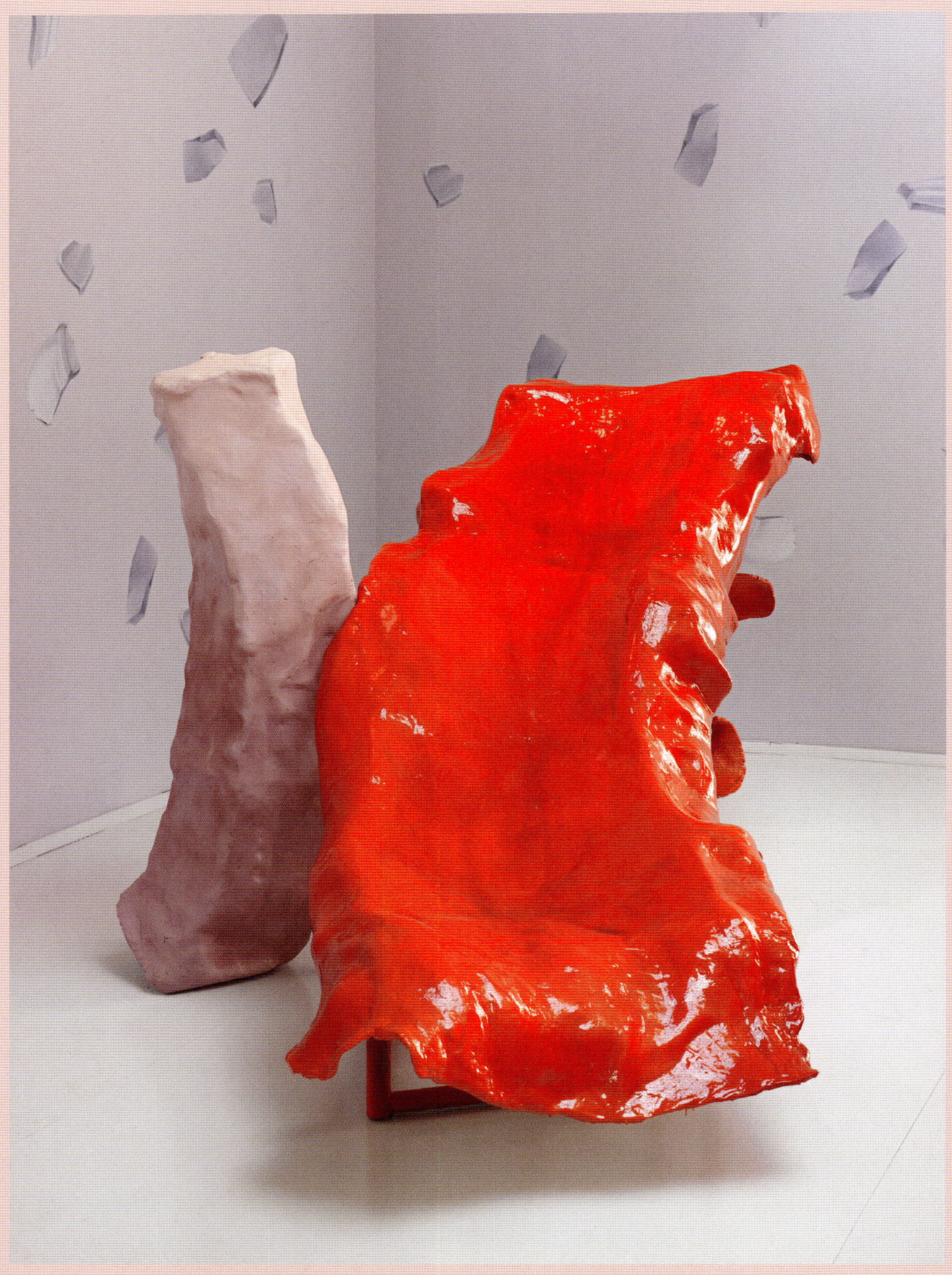

▲ *Slide*, 2021
Hand-painted and glazed ceramic and metal
45 x 60 x 86 in.

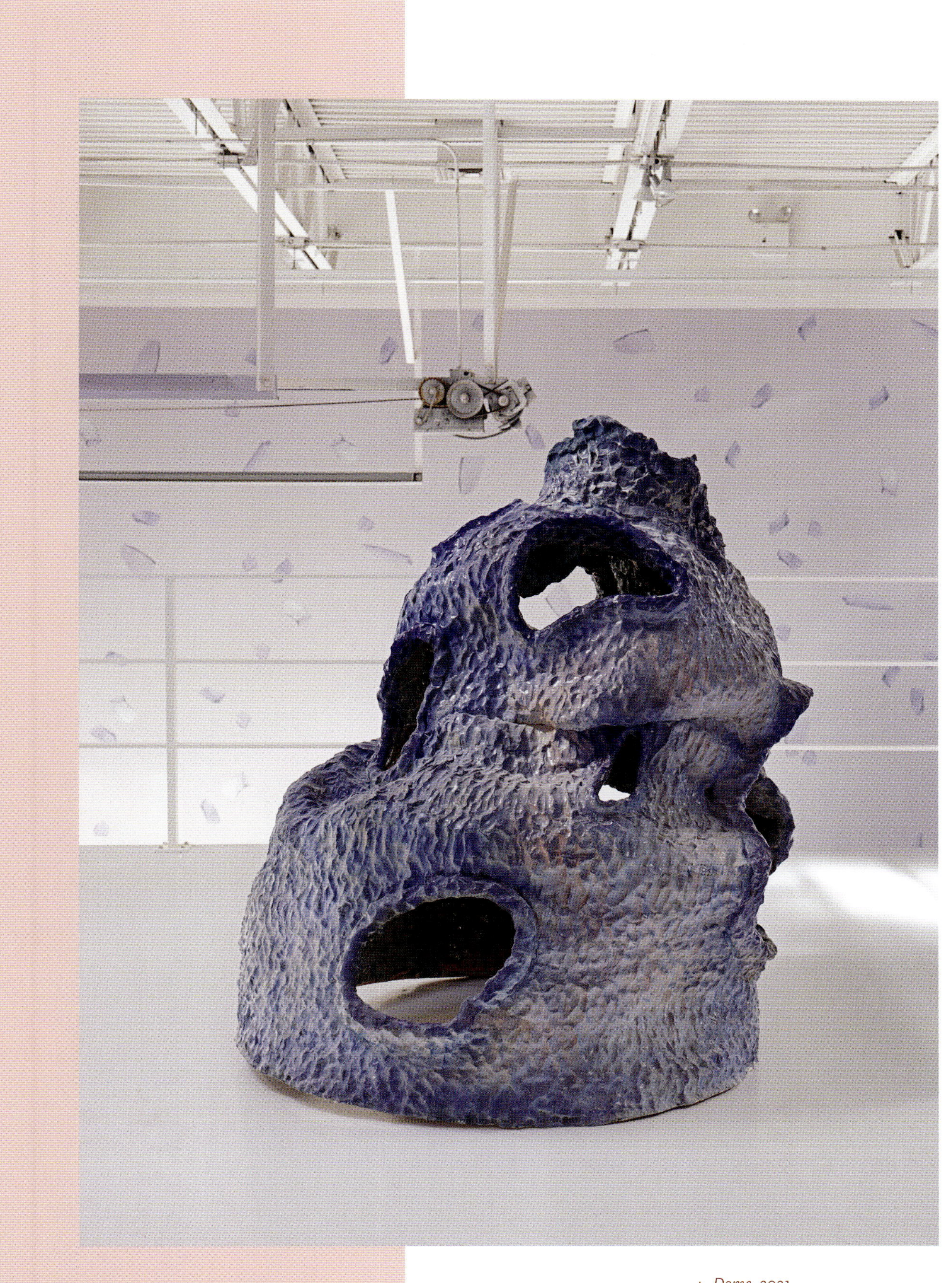

▲ *Dome*, 2021
Hand-painted and glazed ceramic
51 x 42 x 47 in.

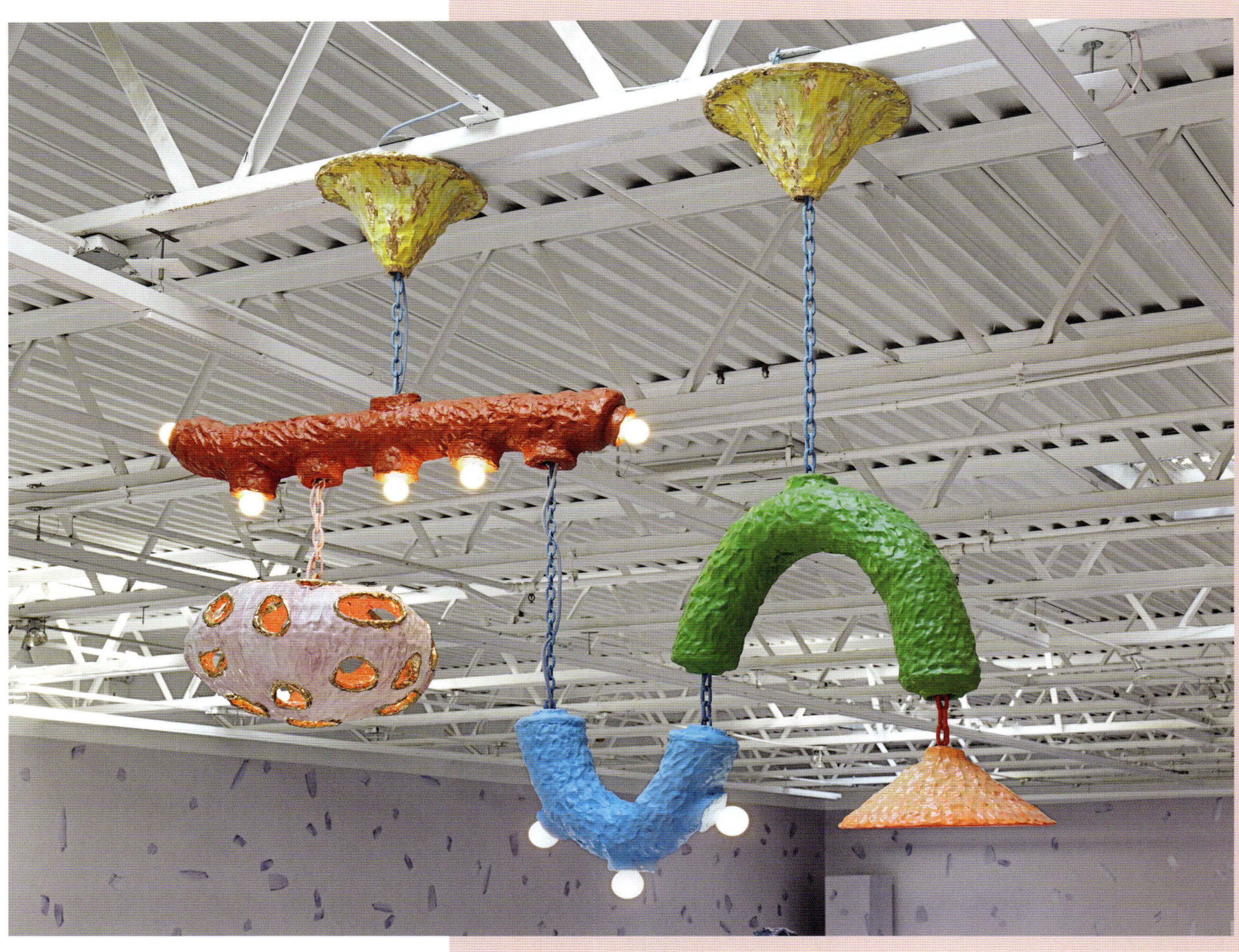

▲ *Untitled*, 2021
Hand-painted and glazed ceramic
63 x 20 x 68 in.

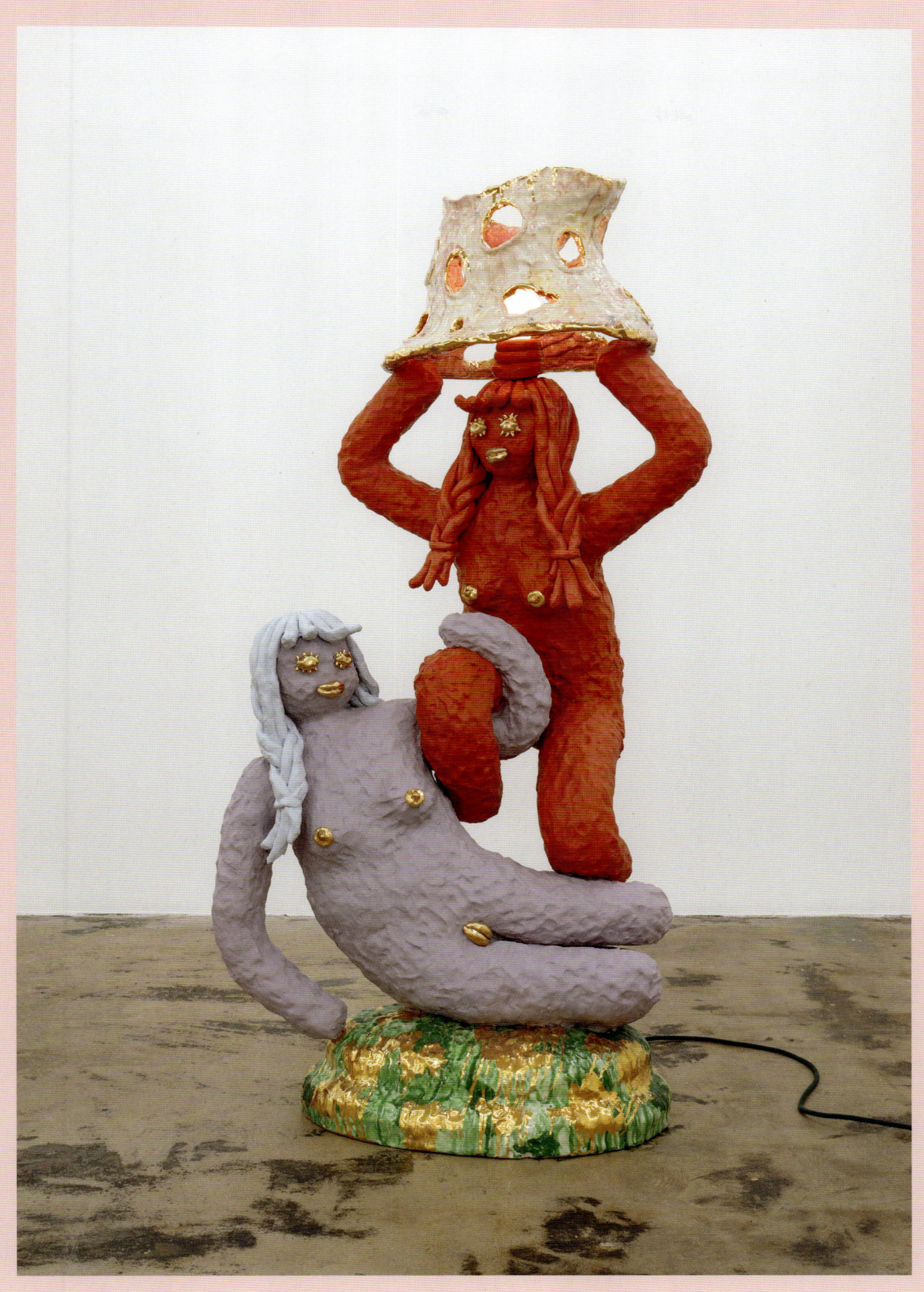

▲ *Double Lady (Roman Embrace)*, 2020
Ceramic, paint, glaze, gold luster
57.5 x 30 x 22.5 in.

magdalena suarez frimkess

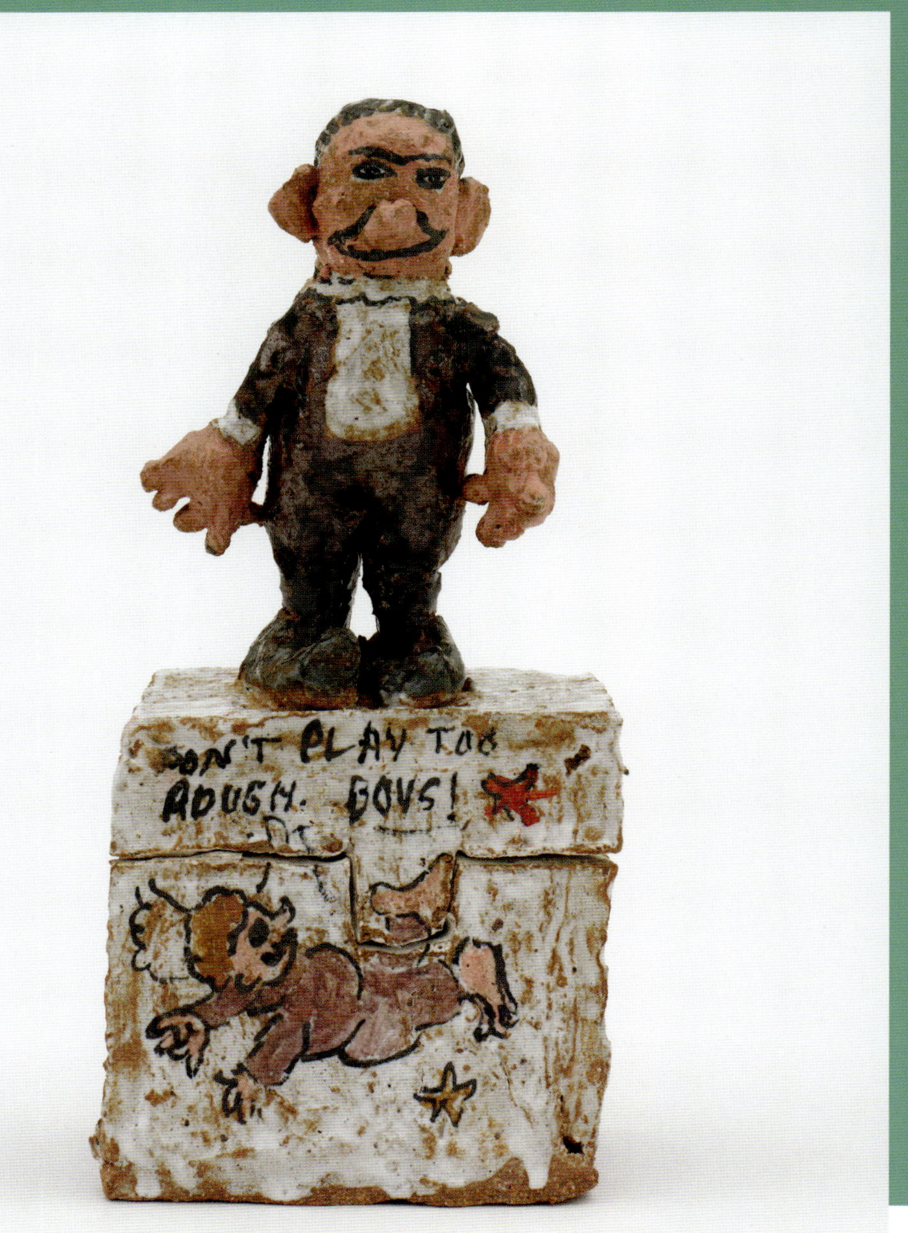

For nearly six decades, Magdalena Suarez Frimkess (b. 1929, Caracas, Venezuela) has maintained a daily practice of creating an autobiography without words. Rather than telling her story by weaving together anecdotes of the rather dramatic turns her life has taken as she moved from Venezuela to Chile and finally the United States, she has instead chosen to sculpt in clay, over and over again, a personal pantheon of cartoon deities, demigods, and mortals who have acted as her very own Greek chorus.

A painter and sculptor by training, Suarez Frimkess has invoked a cast of characters from the animated world of cartoons: Minnie and Mickey Mouse, Popeye and Olive Oyl, Felix the Cat, Betty Boop, and Condorito, among others. The artist manifests these denizens of cartoon-land as intimately scaled, hand-built, and painted ceramic figures that stand as autonomous icons of the characters that they represent while also sometimes taking the form of fragments of illustrated comic book cells that she paints with glaze directly on the surface of roughly formed functional vessels (cups, vases, and the like) or tiles that can be fixed into a floor or wall.

Her Minnie Mouses stand as sentinels worthy of the goddess Athena, while Felix the Cat plays the role of the clever trickster. Olive Oyl and Popeye play out the eternal return of the traditional gender narrative of the damsel in distress, while Betty Boop stands in contrast as a solitary representative of strong, self-possessed womanhood. And, finally, Condorito, the anthropomorphic Chilean comic strip bird known for his absurdist slapstick humor, plays the role of sage or oracle. As Suarez Frimkess says, "Condorito is my philosopher."[1]

Although Suarez Frimkess is an admirer of Andy Warhol, her serial channeling of these characters from pop culture has never been about creating a machinelike sameness that was the elder artist's dream. Whereas Warhol wanted to become a machine through his appropriation of pop culture, Suarez Frimkess instead embraces the comforting and almost meditative qualities of repetition along with the surprising "newness" that comes with each subsequent iteration of a character as she mindfully works the clay in her hands. For her, every repetition of a form or a figure produces something new. In her words, repetition "breaks the monotony. It's never, never the same. It is not possible that you can do the same thing like you're a machine, then it will be a factory. It's always something new, and you always learn something. Isn't that what the musicians do? They're playing one thing over and over and over."[2]

Emphasizing the paradoxically immense and profound philosophical depth of her comic pantheon's ethos while insisting on keeping her work at an intimate and nonheroic scale, Suarez Frimkess has quietly used her hands to channel her own voice through those of her muses. This has become a necessary daily practice for the artist through which she has been able to tell us her own life story through other means. Regardless of the pop origins of her iconography, Suarez Frimkess's work is derived directly from her life. "Nothing is invented," says Suarez Frimkess. "It's all reality. Nothing is made up. That's the only thing I can do. My art is my life. I think it's an autobiography."[3]

— Hanneke Skerath

[1] "A Conversation with Magdalena Suarez Frimkess," Kaufmann Repetto, accessed September 29, 2022, https://kaufmann-repetto.viewingrooms.com/viewing-room/5-a-conversation-with-magdalena-suarez-frimkess.

[2] "A Conversation with Magdalena Suarez Frimkess," 2022.

[3] "A Conversation with Magdalena Suarez Frimkess," 2022.

◂ *Untitled*, 2020
Glazed ceramic
8.5 x 3.75 x 3 in.

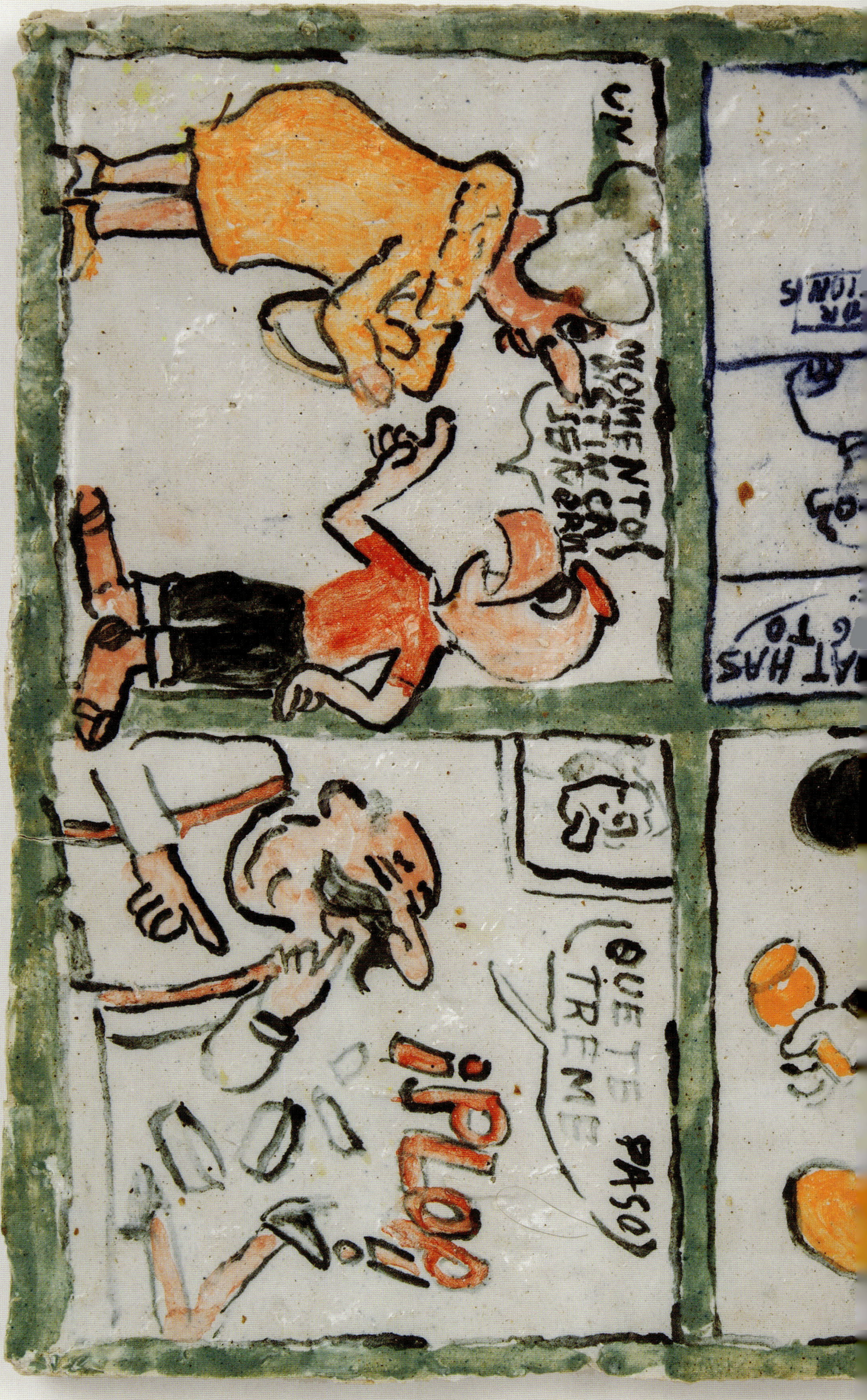

▸ *Untitled*, 2020
Glazed ceramic
11.625 x 9 in.

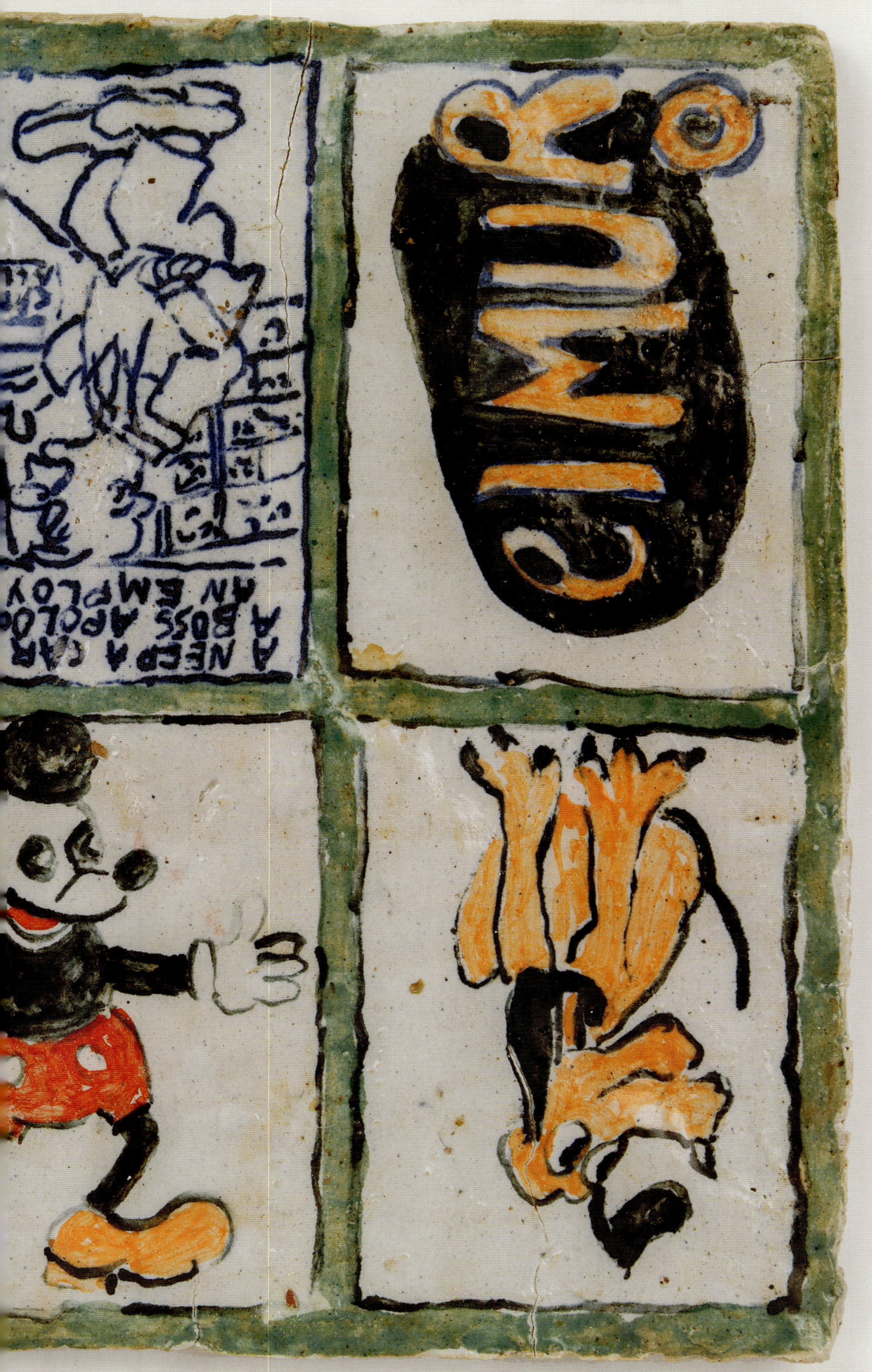
A NEED A CAR
A BOSS APOLO
AN EMPLOY

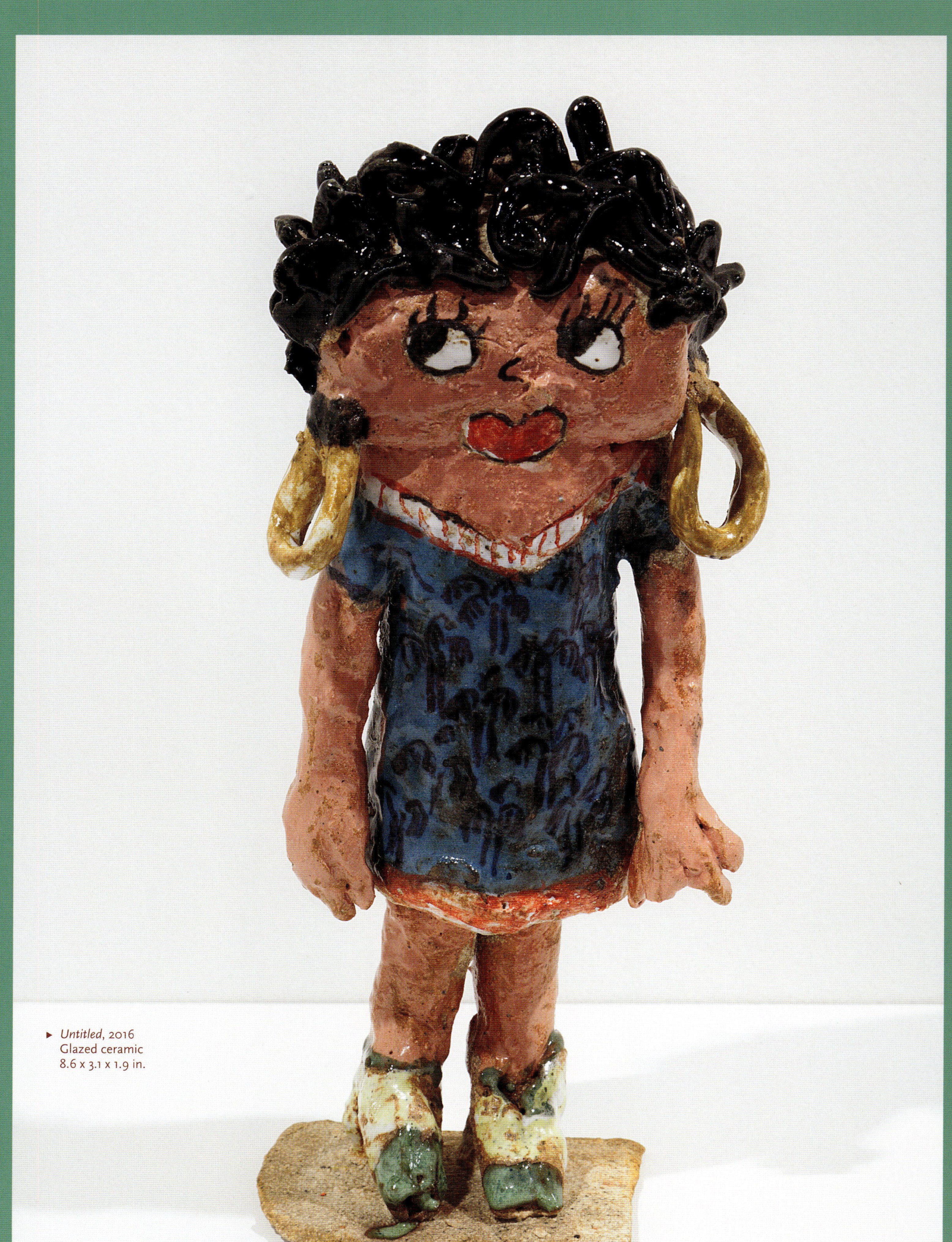

▸ *Untitled*, 2016
Glazed ceramic
8.6 x 3.1 x 1.9 in.

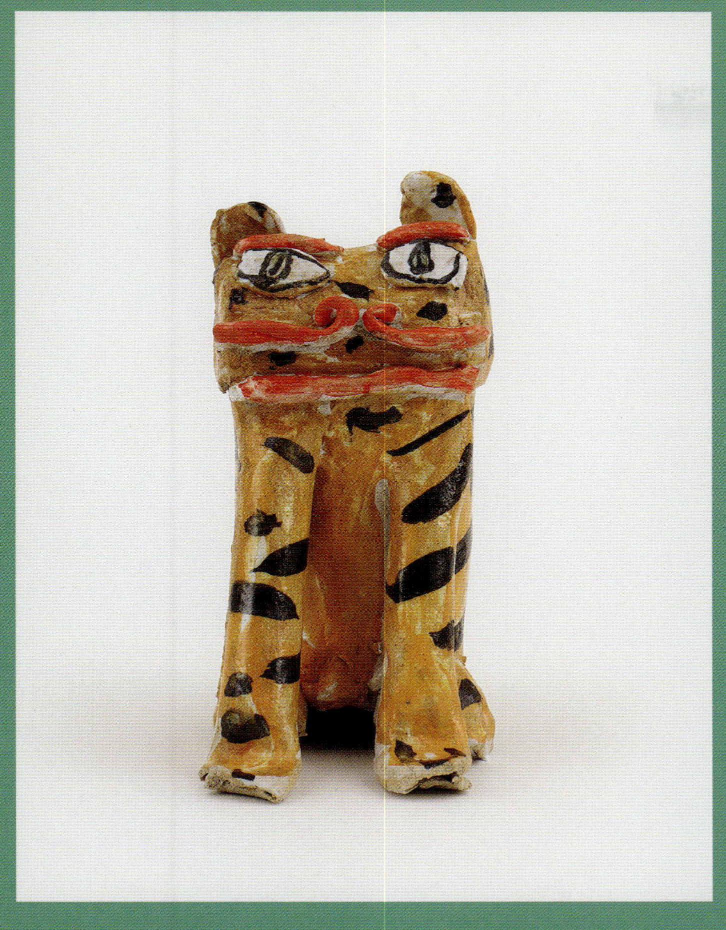

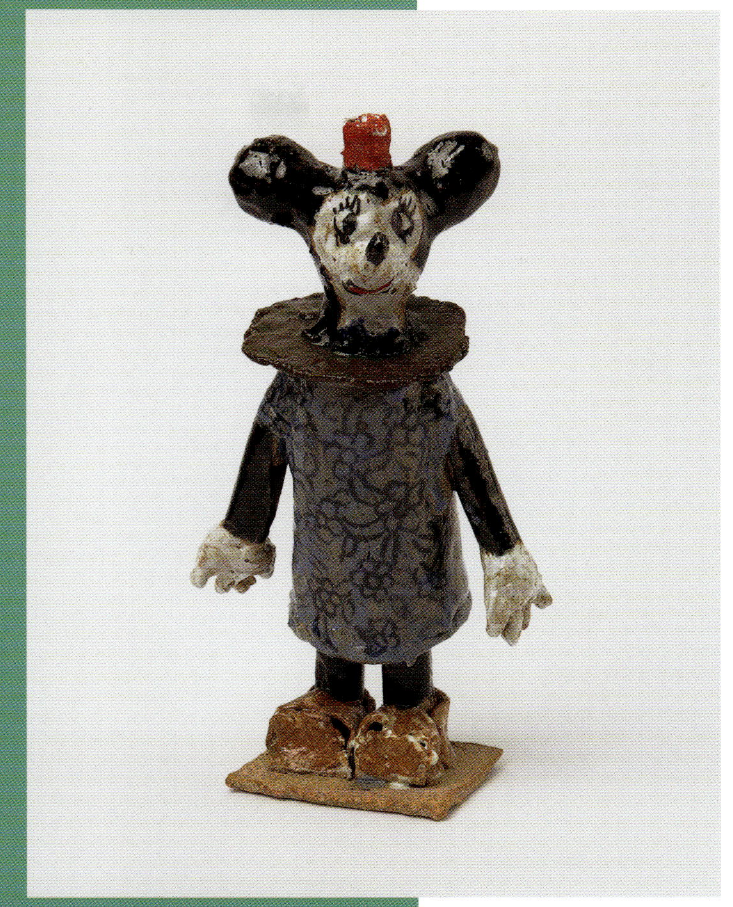

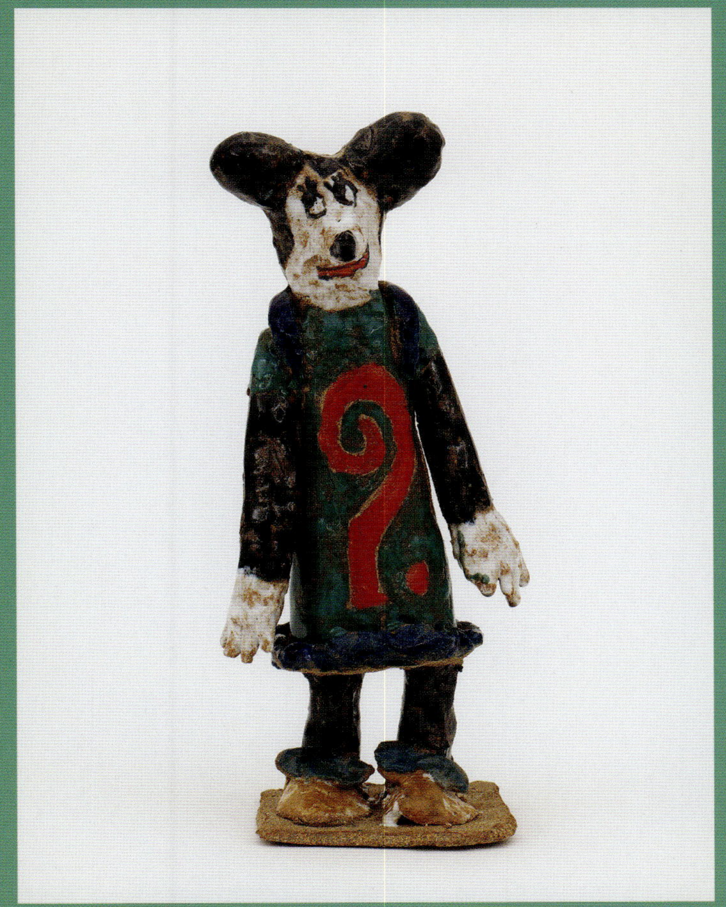

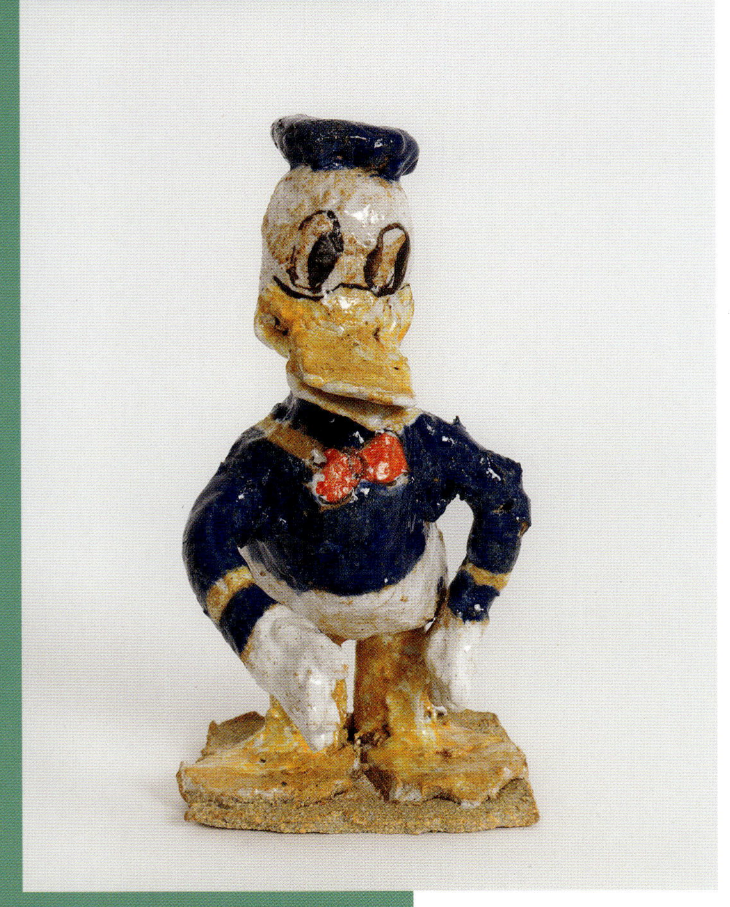

▲ *Untitled*, 2020
Glazed ceramic
6 x 4.5 x 3.25 in.

▲ *Untitled*, 2021
Glazed ceramic
9.75 x 4.75 x 3.75 in.

▲ *Untitled*, 2020
Glazed ceramic
8.5 x 3.5 x 4 in.

▲ *Untitled*, 2018
Glazed ceramic
6.4 x 3.4 x 5.4 in.

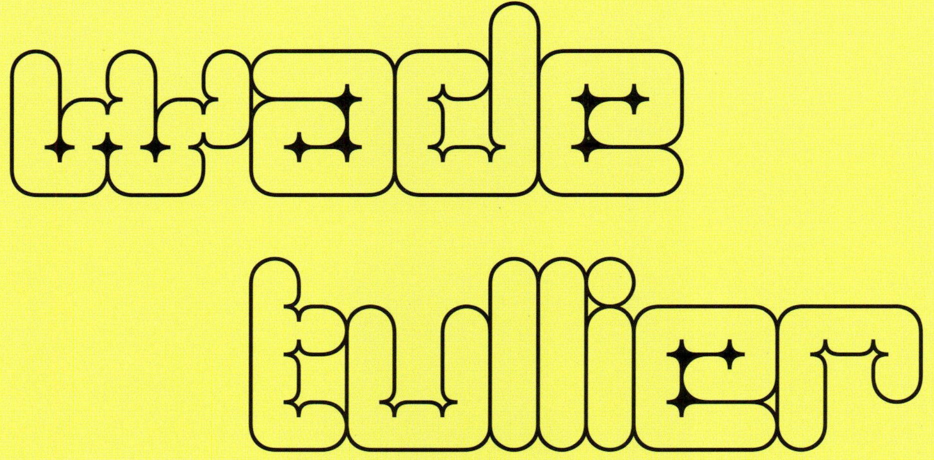
wade
tullier

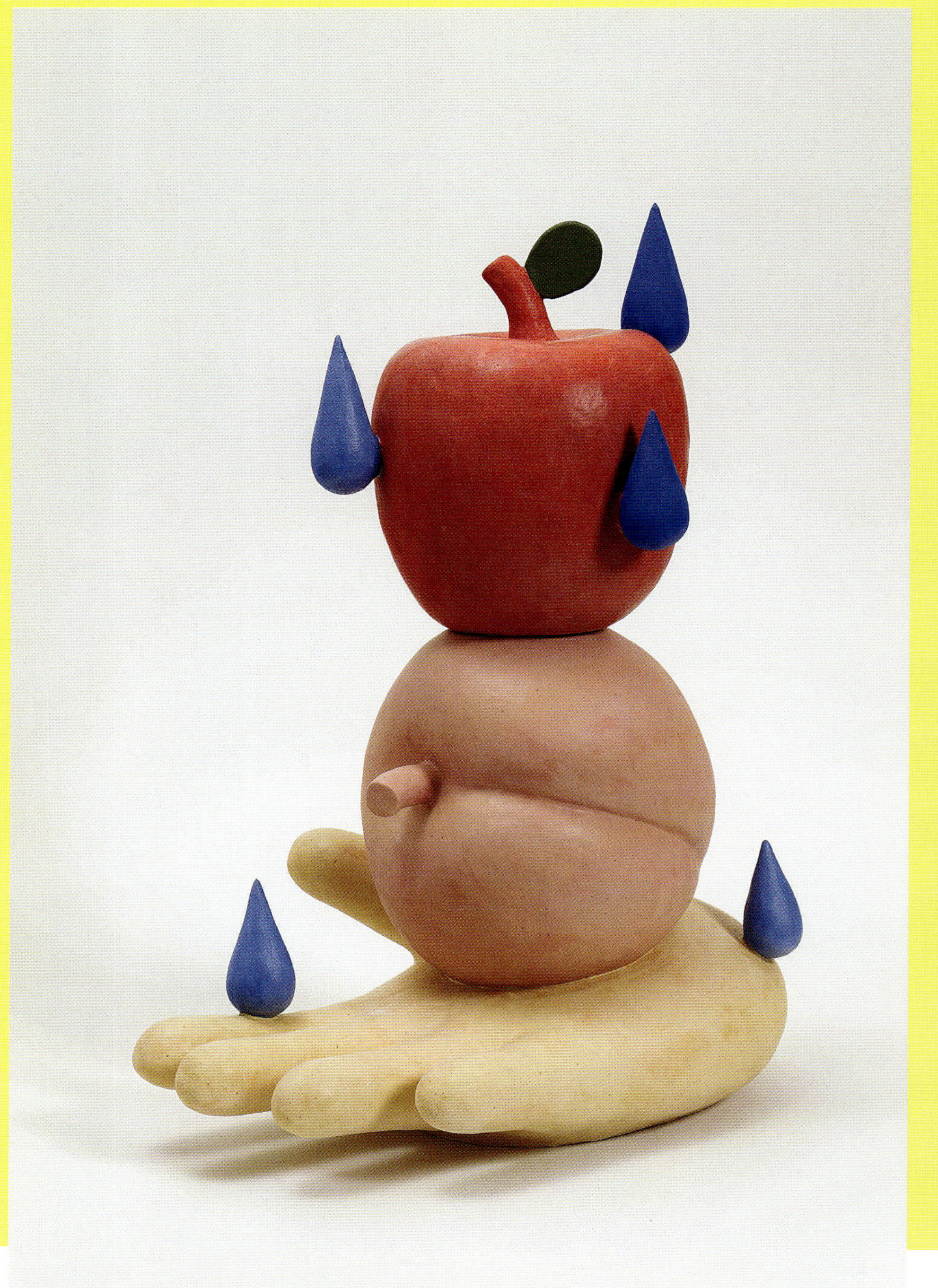

One's first impression of the recent sculptures from Detroit artist Wade Tullier (b. 1988, Baton Rouge, Louisiana) is their utter charm. Friendly, cool, and eccentric—like terrifically unthreatening alien visitors—they seem to fit right in. These characters and their accoutrement are sheathed in beautifully glazed finishes reminiscent of a well-used 24-count box of Crayola crayons. Primary and secondary hues—and black, white, and gray—the spirited palette fulfills a promise of friendliness and delight. We know this chromatic universe; we were raised with the buoyancy of cheerful color.

The subjects brought to life in these uncanny sculptures are culled from a world of mythical archetypes that share an implicit awareness of all the bedtime stories heard by children for generations. Born of Tullier's imagination with skilled hands that shape their soft contours, these figures can, at times, expose some of the deeper recesses of our psyche. Whatever intimacy the work might elicit, a veiled, troubling subtext is also felt: one moment innocent and likable, the next secretive and creepy. What exactly we take away from these encounters rests squarely within the heart and mind of the viewer.

This motley cast of players and the props that they fashion play key roles in an abstruse narrative formed in Tullier's mind. Brought to life through exquisitely rendered, fired, and glazed clay sculptures, they evoke a shady netherworld. When we begin to inspect the work closely, it becomes clear precisely what is depicted. Disembodied heads and limbs, empty shoes and boots, animal skulls, suspicious fruit, and sinister-looking owls are the set pieces Tullier directs from the deeper recesses of his darker dreams. If we choose not to see them as actors and props in some eerie play, we might read them as talismanic, symbolic of deeply primal subconscious forces. Either way, there is a fomenting apprehension that builds the longer we remain close by.

One of the most satisfying spells that Tullier conjures occurs when he begins "ganging" and stacking his "toys" into totems. In this case, the work becomes a poetic stanza, or a mantra spoken over and over to rid us of our demons. Maybe they are rhymes, interrupted by an off-color phrase or a word twist that starts to form a new language. Regardless, these moves only add to the diabolical pleasure of his work.

There are many ways to reflect on Wade Tullier's practice; what we should avoid is any search for "meaning." Instead, we can recognize a luminous and haunting nature that is also melancholic and wistful. It is built from the emotions of a life experienced as a human being who spends a lifetime in the company of other human beings. The joy we take away from the work comes with equal amounts of suspicion. This is exactly where we often find ourselves, struggling to find harmony with emotions often in conflict. Wade Tullier senses that precarious balance and offers a safe place to land.

— Dan Devening

◂ *Hand with Peach, Apple and Drops,*
2022
Glazed ceramic
21 x 14 x 28 in.

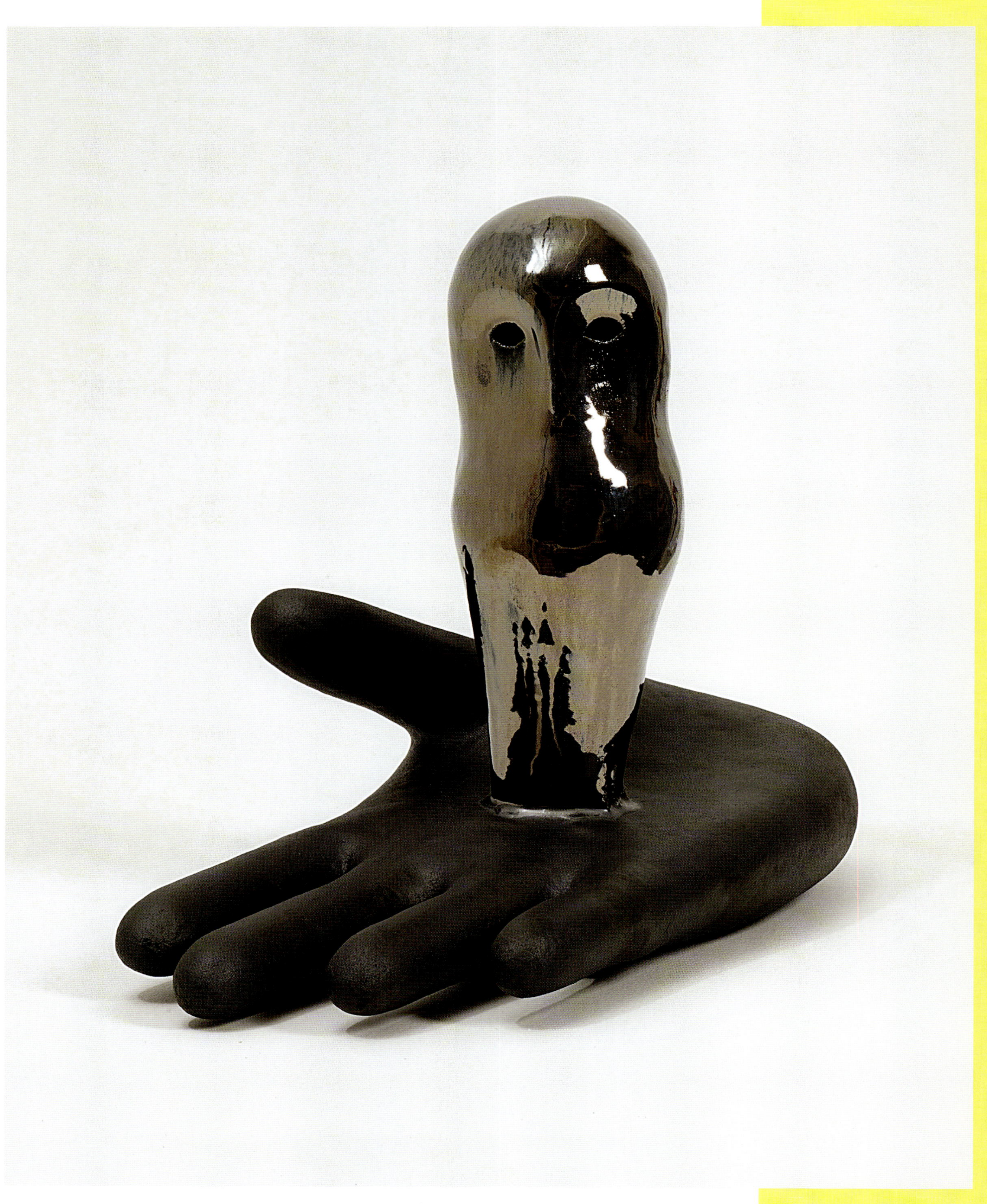

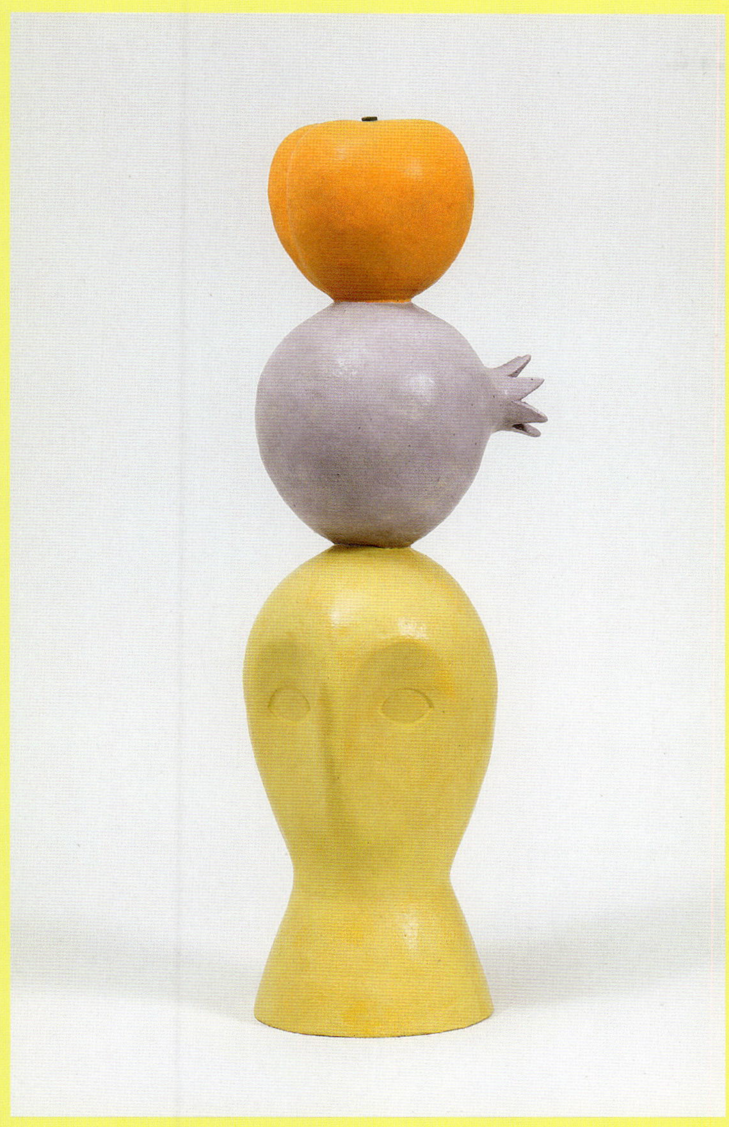

▲ *Owl Figure with Pomegranate and Apricot*, 2021
Glazed ceramic
26.5 x 9 x 7.5 in.

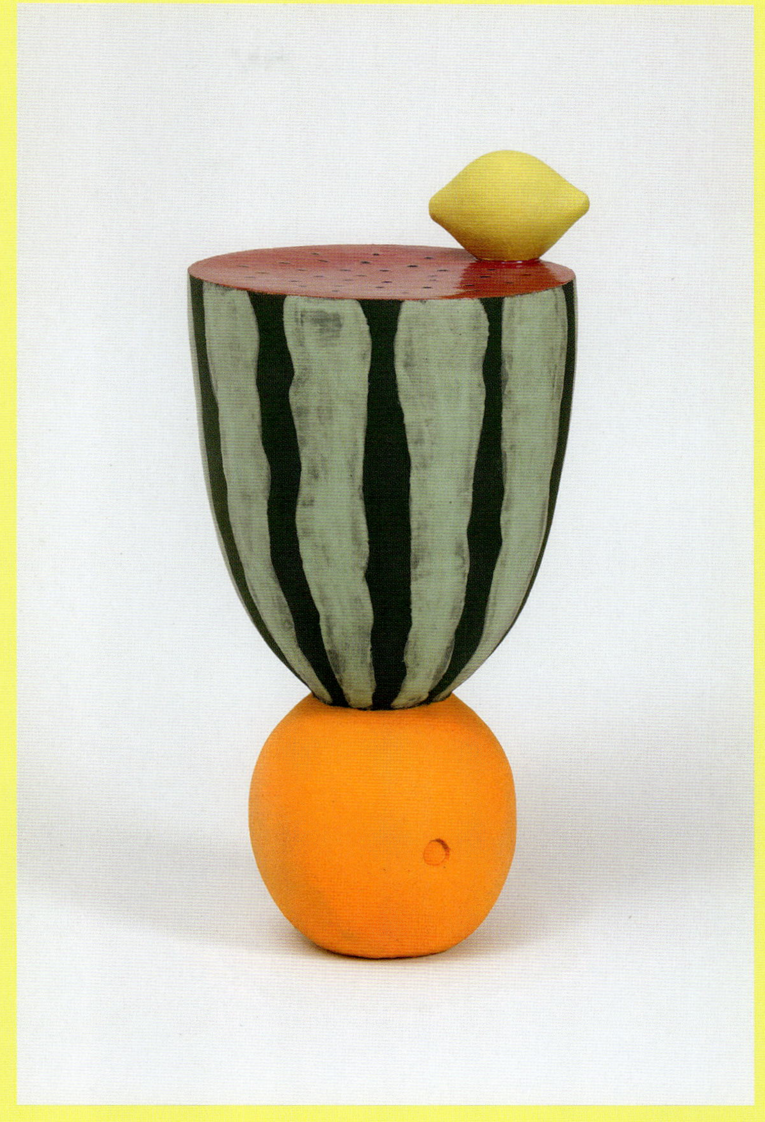

▲ *Watermelon with Lemon and Orange*, 2021
Glazed ceramic
9.5 x 9.5 x 19 in.

◄ *Hand with Owl*, 2021
Glazed ceramic
17 x 22 x 13 in.

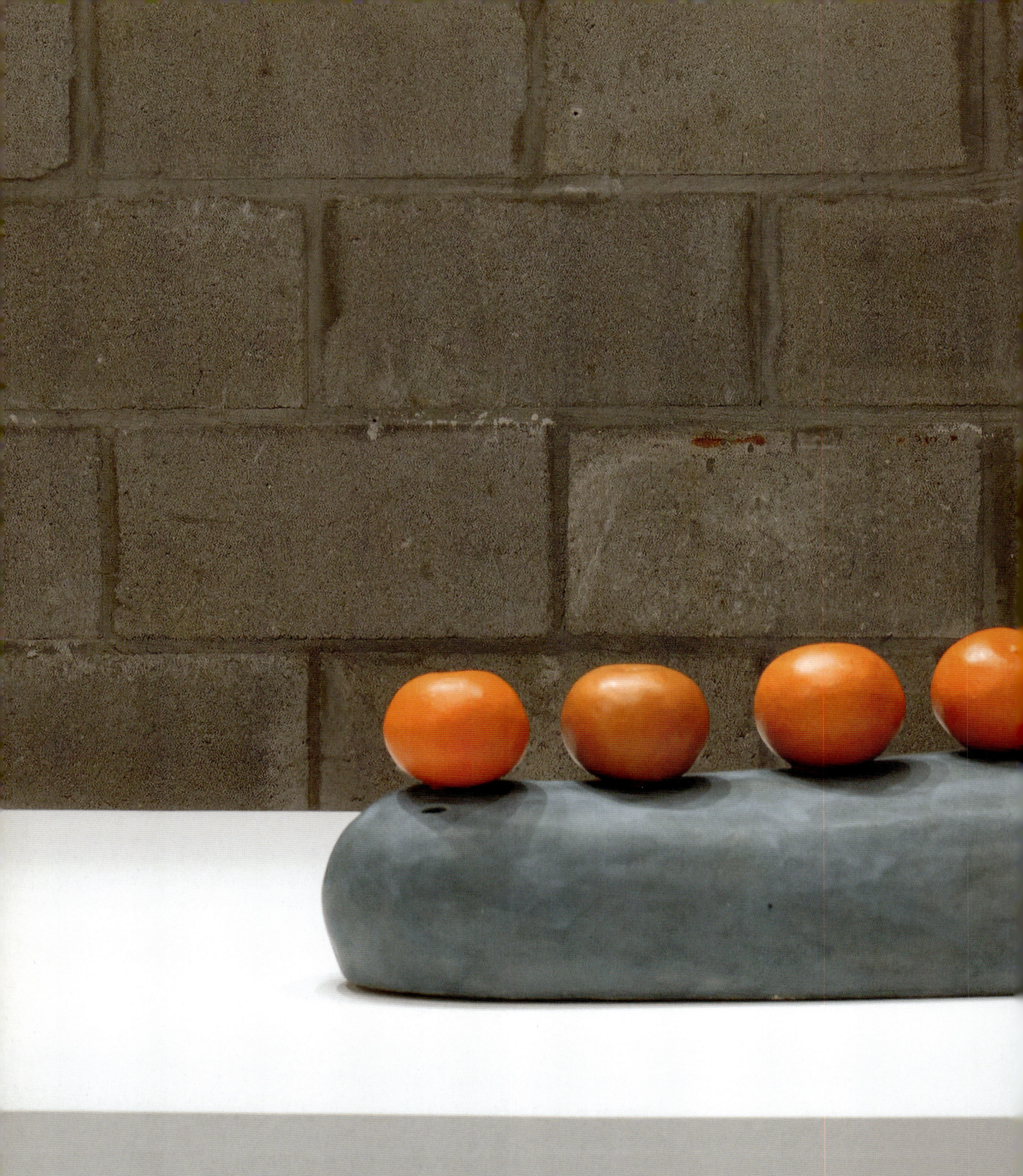

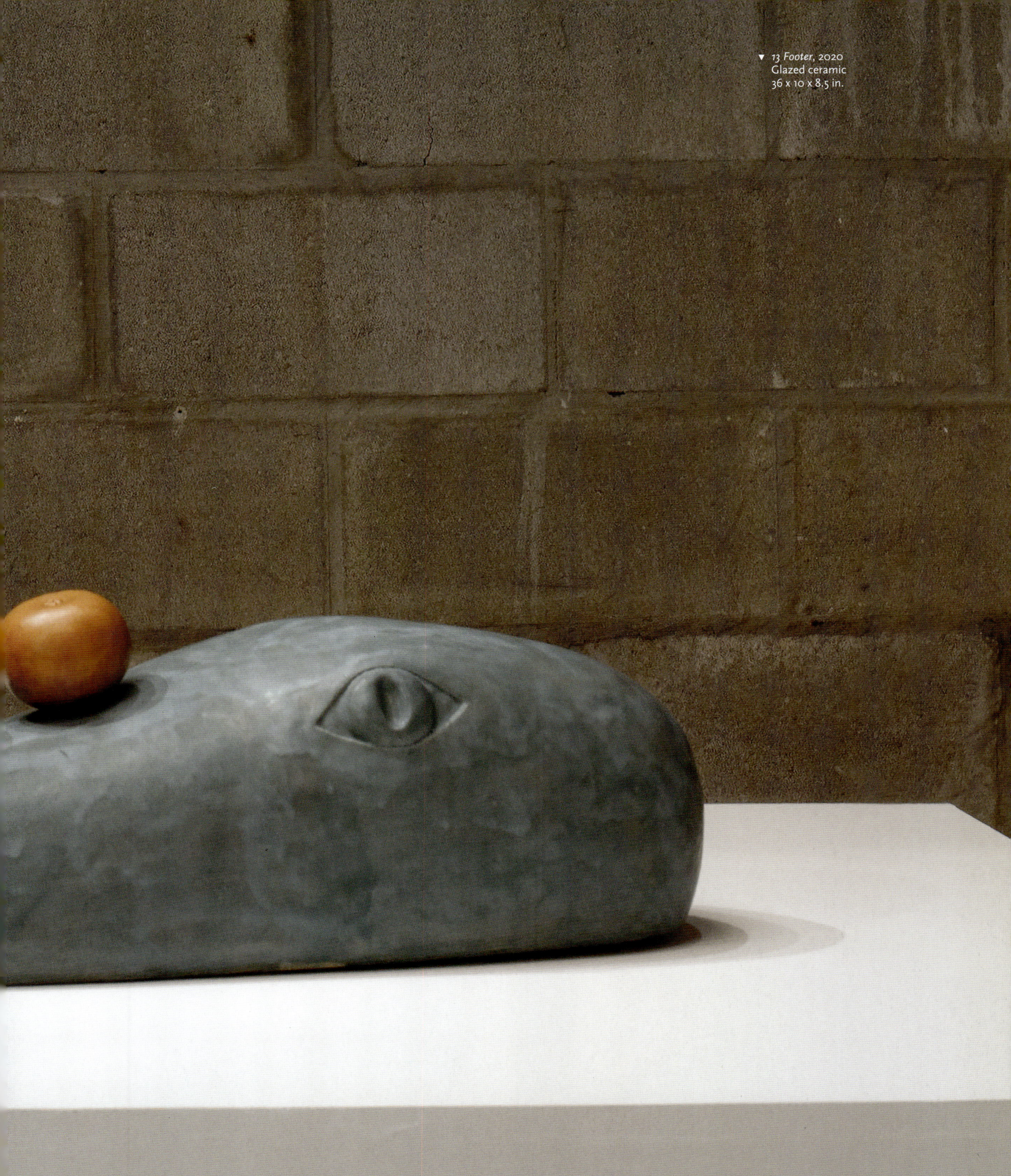

▼ 13 *Footer*, 2020
Glazed ceramic
36 x 10 x 8.5 in.

amia yokoyama

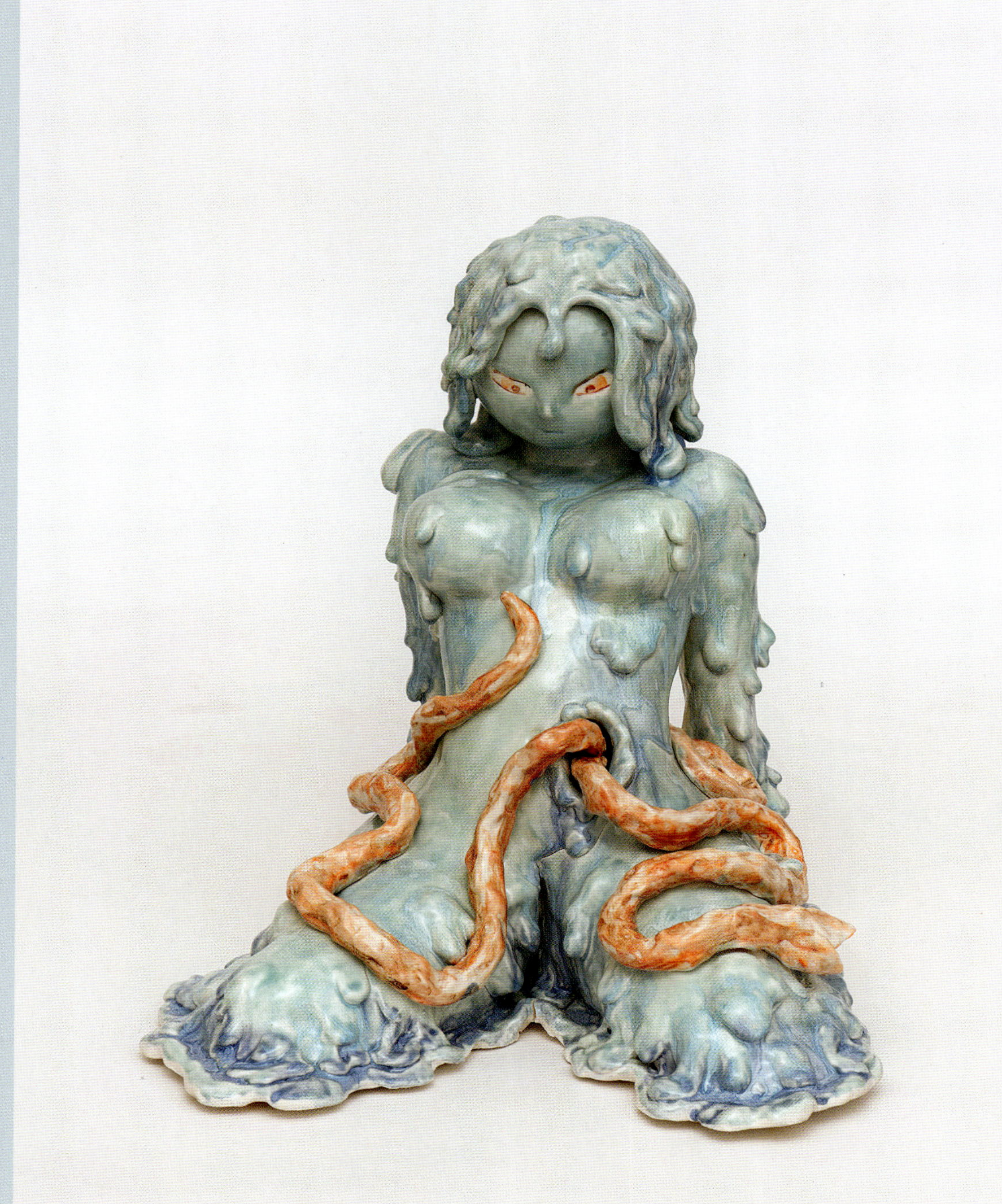

Amia Yokoyama (b. 1988) is a multimedia artist who works with experimental animation, video, sculpture, and installation. In Yokoyama's porcelain sculptures, the body of a girl melts. She melts but never dissolves; she is baked into the eternal process of her own undoing. She evokes the glutinous squish of her original material (wet clay) in a coil of associations. Hard, soft, hard, soft. Girl, thing, girl, thing. The curves of her body are cartoonishly globular and almost pornographic. She connotes anime characters, video game heroines, and worlds of sketched and rendered fantasy. Her surfaces are mottled blues—the color of a pool at night—and her limbs glow. It is unclear if she is covered in slime or if she is slime brought to life, soggy with the effort of transmutation. Myth chimes in, disrupting all our digital allusions. Yokoyama never lets a category settle or entrap. Her objects belong to a sci-fi future and an ancient past—the wave and the cliffside, the pregnant and the newborn, the wound and the bliss.

We tell ourselves lies about the limits of our bodies—that we are the tips of our fingers but not what they touch, that our skin encloses instead of leaks, that our holes must be protected and hidden at all costs, except the ones from which we breathe, speak, eat, hear, and see. Yokoyama's ceramics puncture the viscous seal of those dishonesties, letting other truths and possibilities rush out. In her work, edges are unreliable. The self can double and disperse, and the places our bodies open up to in the world are not breaches but portals. Here, fetish flickers between its two meanings, which are really the same meaning: lust and faith. It is a touchless orgasm—an unforeseen miracle.

Sometimes, in Yokoyama's sculptures, two melting figures collide, merge, and kiss. Sometimes, they wrestle, ride each other, or slither around like eels, vines, or babies. Wild animals—the rusty wings of an eagle or the amber licks of a snake—live among the melting girls. Yokoyama's ceramics make a utopic proposition, surely, but without the need to justify how and why it will feel good. Maybe goodness needs to be left behind to enter these new ways of making. Yokoyama's utopic bodies promise something beyond good or evil, and beyond pleasure or pain. Feeling was always more than enough.

— Audrey Wollen

◂ *Of All the World Passing Through*,
2021
Ceramic
17.375 x 16.875 x 17.375 in.

▾ *Harbinger (Tengu)*, 2022
Porcelain and glaze
11 x 9 x 10 in.

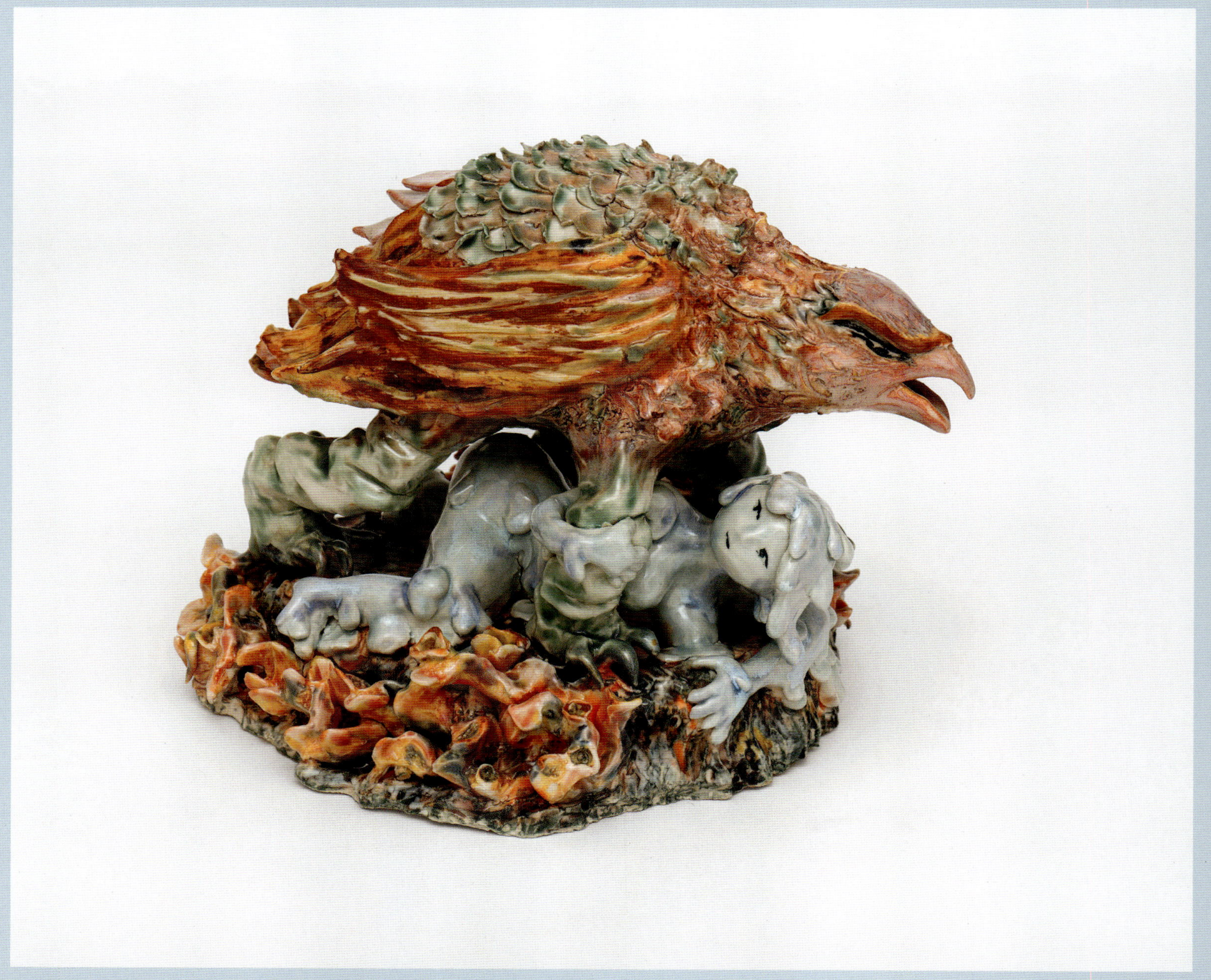

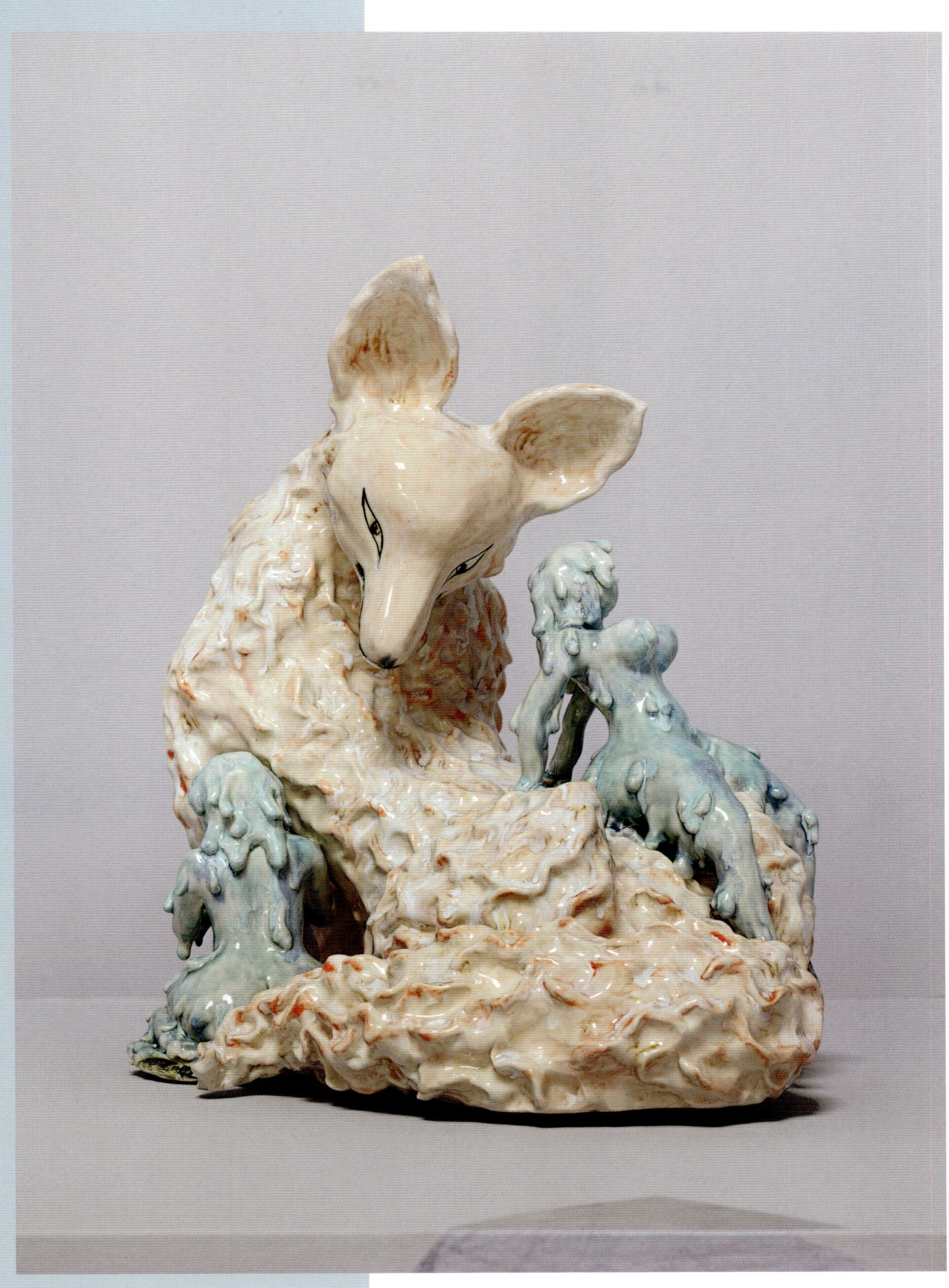

▲ *Waiting between the Celestial*, 2021
Glazed porcelain
12 x 18 x 17 in.

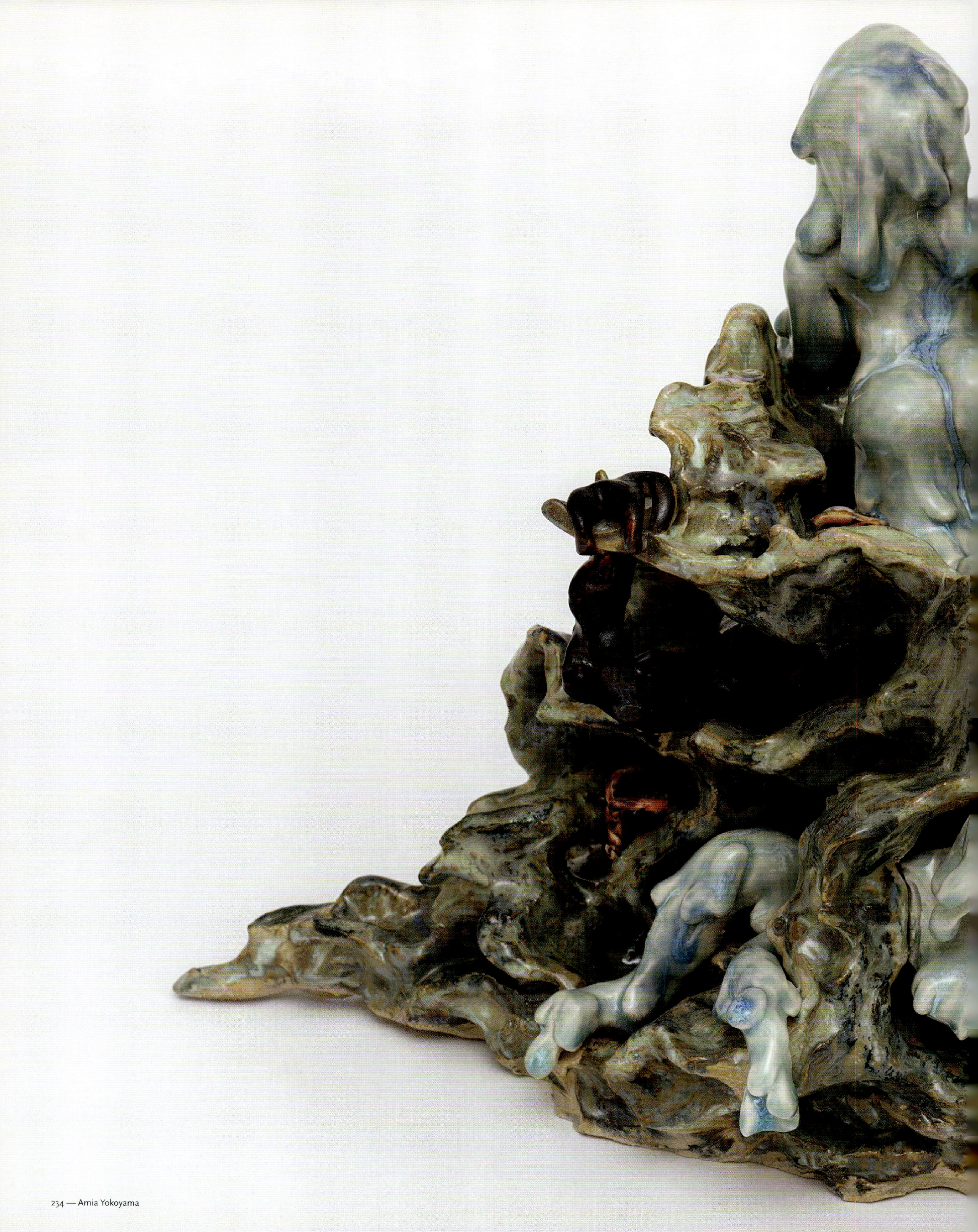

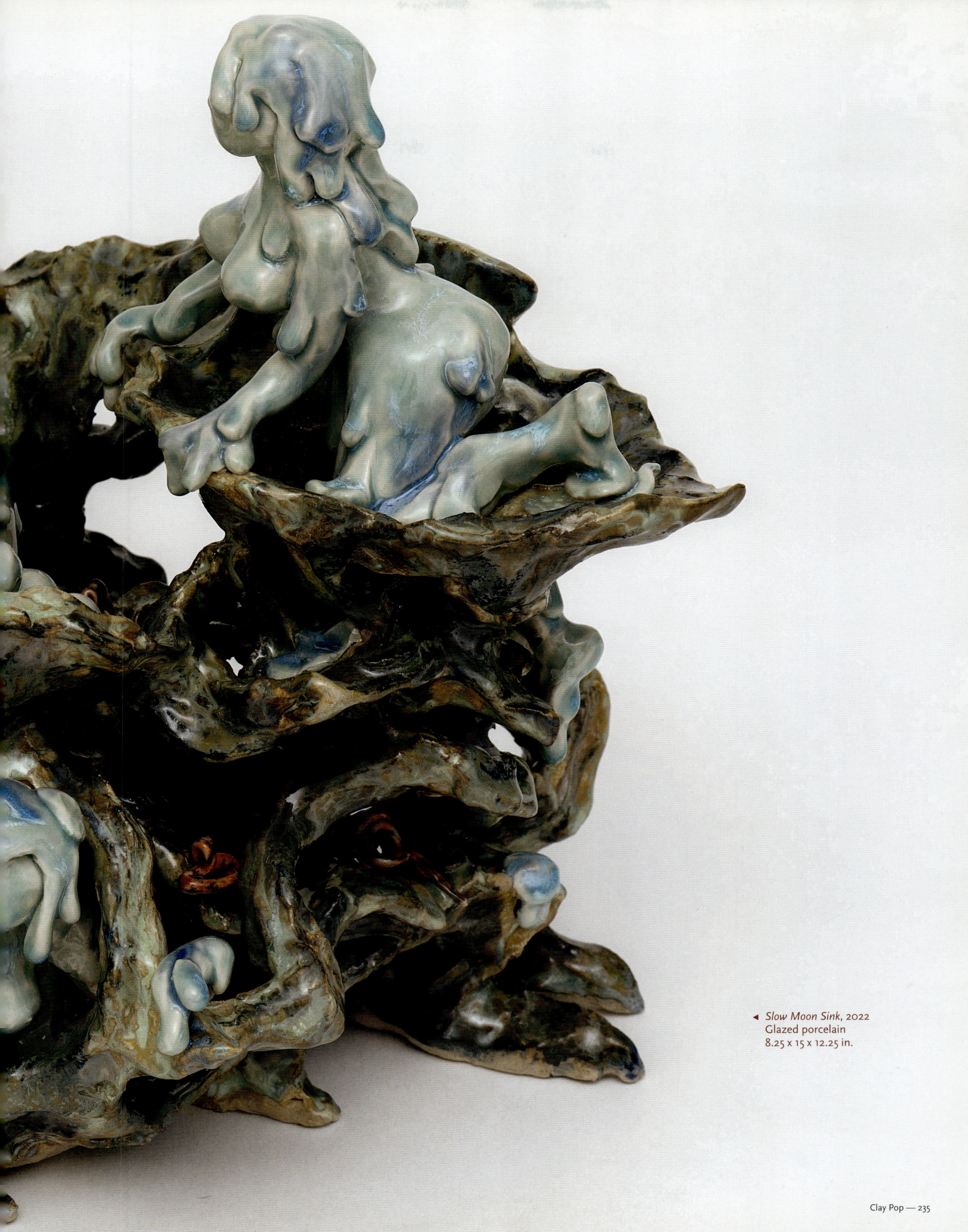

◂ *Slow Moon Sink*, 2022
Glazed porcelain
8.25 x 15 x 12.25 in.

bari ziperstein

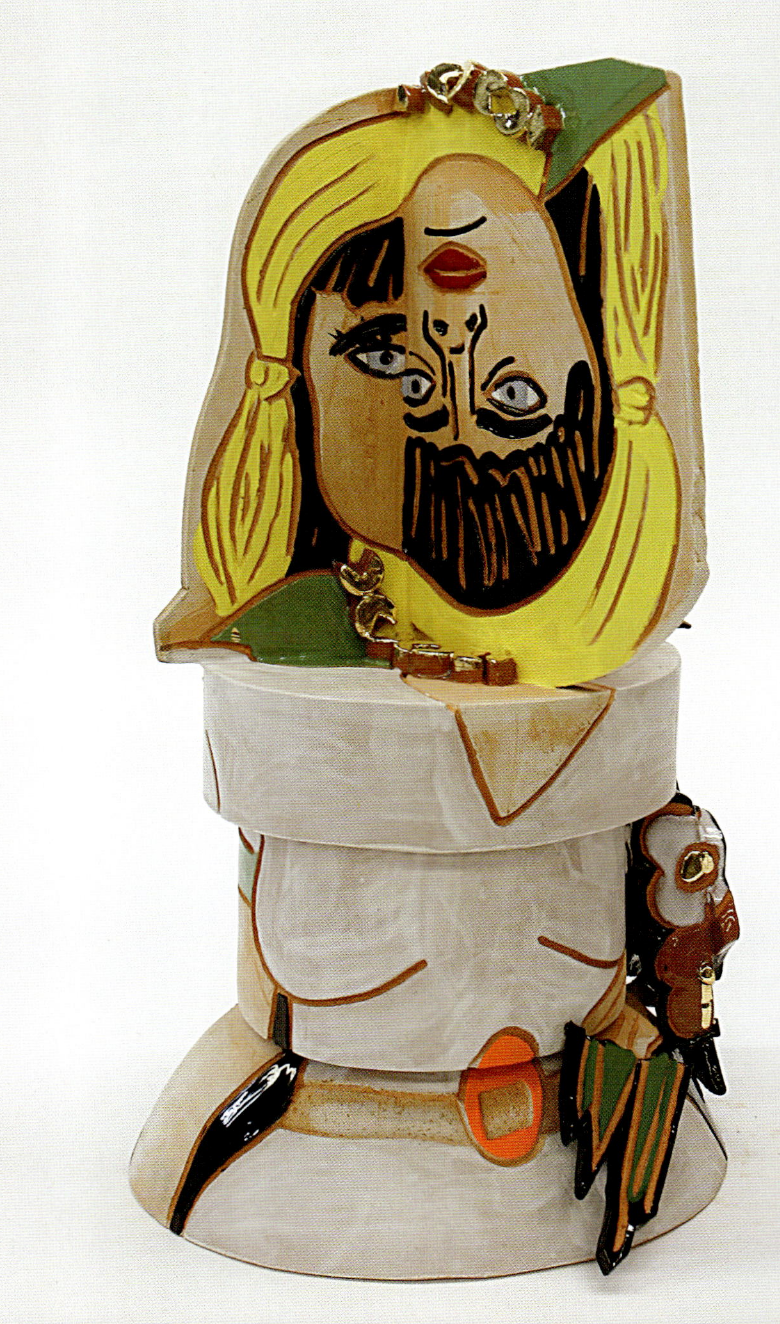

Over the past twenty years, Bari Ziperstein (b. 1978, Chicago) has made a variety of ceramic sculptures, ranging from intimate tabletop objects to architecturally scaled public sculpture. Her work foregrounds materiality and pushes the limits of scale, while bringing considerable imagination to her use of color and finish. Her inventiveness is especially evident in her use of form and composition. Using terra-cotta and stoneware, Ziperstein celebrates the material and formal history of her medium as both utilitarian and narrative. The slab construction method she uses requires flattening clay into pliable sheets that can be curved, rolled, cut into shapes, layered, and incised to create drawings on the clay's surface in a technique known as sgraffito.

Ziperstein's process often starts with archival materials to explore the ways that visual culture and the built environment signal repressive social and political ideologies. Her recent work combines research in archives of propaganda from the former USSR with her interests in industrial design and Brutalist architecture. The surfaces of Ziperstein's vessels are covered in sgraffito drawings based on archival Soviet-era textile designs and "public service" posters and other print materials. The forms are inspired by industrial design, urban infrastructure, and Brutalist buildings and monuments in the United States and abroad, including countries such as Russia and Poland, to which Ziperstein traces her own familial origins. Her juxtapositions of patterns and forms raise questions about narrative, decoration, and the political messages that are embedded in our aesthetic choices. With present-day nationalism rising around the globe and Russia's unjust war in Ukraine beginning in February of 2022, her visual reference points are newly prescient. As the world stands at the precipice of a third World War, the connections between our present sociopolitical moment and Cold War-era Europe that Ziperstein draws on are urgent reminders of a not so distant past.

Working with two-dimensional source material overlaid onto three-dimensional forms, Ziperstein creates dynamic visual and referential contrasts, animating flat patterns and images across shapes and volumes. This intentional clashing of forms, patterns, concepts, and time periods heightens the criticality of the work. Why were these forms and patterns made in the first place? What do they communicate, and to whom?

Ziperstein follows her research back to the original hand-drawn designs made by working artists who are largely lost to history, many of whom were female. Her gesture of remixing patterns, images, and forms that were never intended to harmonize proposes a rejection of totalitarian alienation and social organization, trading in authoritarianism for a politics that is more egalitarian and allowing something new and beautiful to emerge.

— Corrina Peipon

◂ *A Girl in a Football Jersey with a Bunch of Flowers*, 2019
Terra-cotta, glaze, underglaze, luster
19 x 11 x 11 in.

▾ *Dandelions and Squiggles*, 2021
Glazed stoneware
19 x 21.5 x 21.5 in.

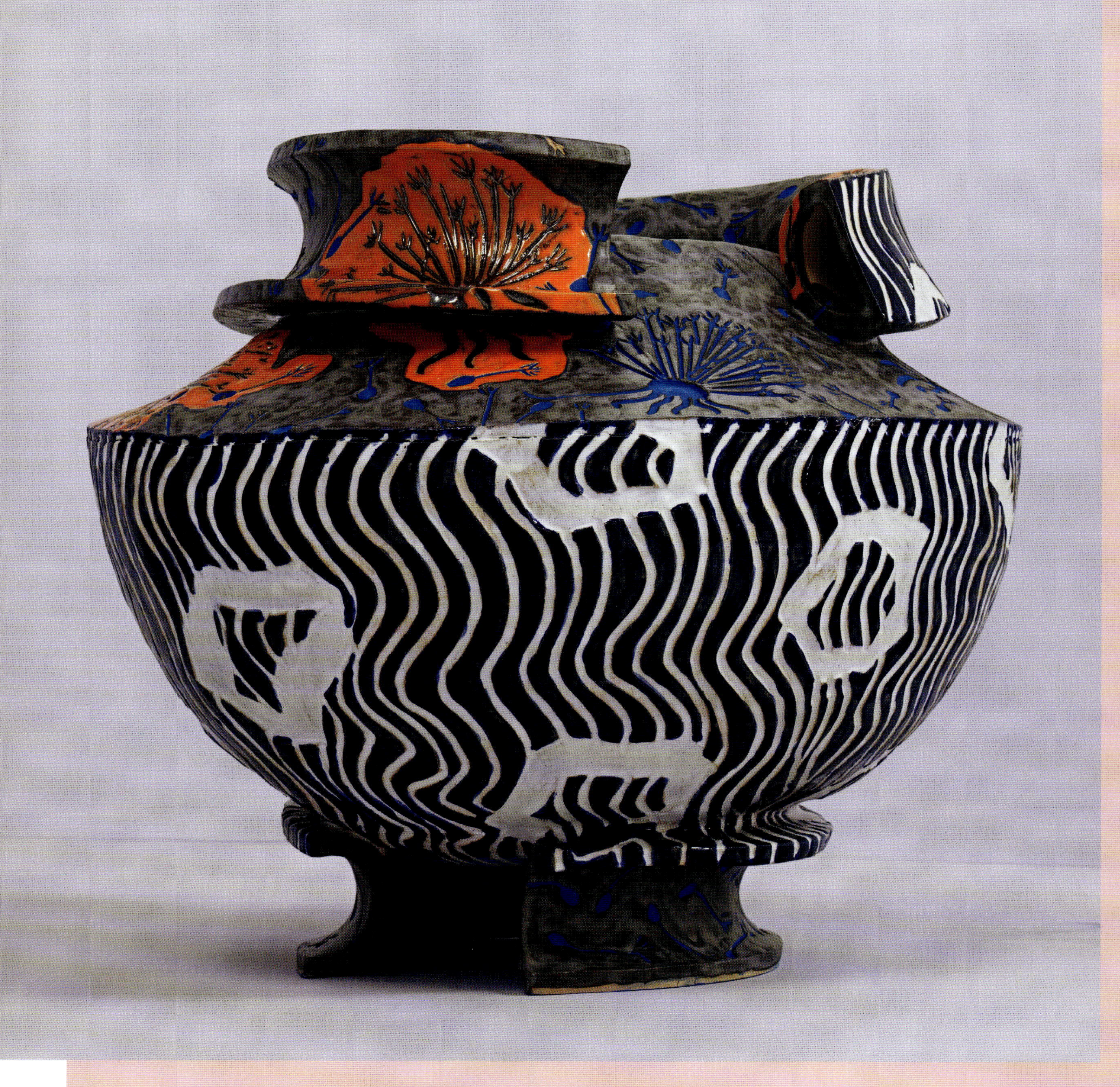

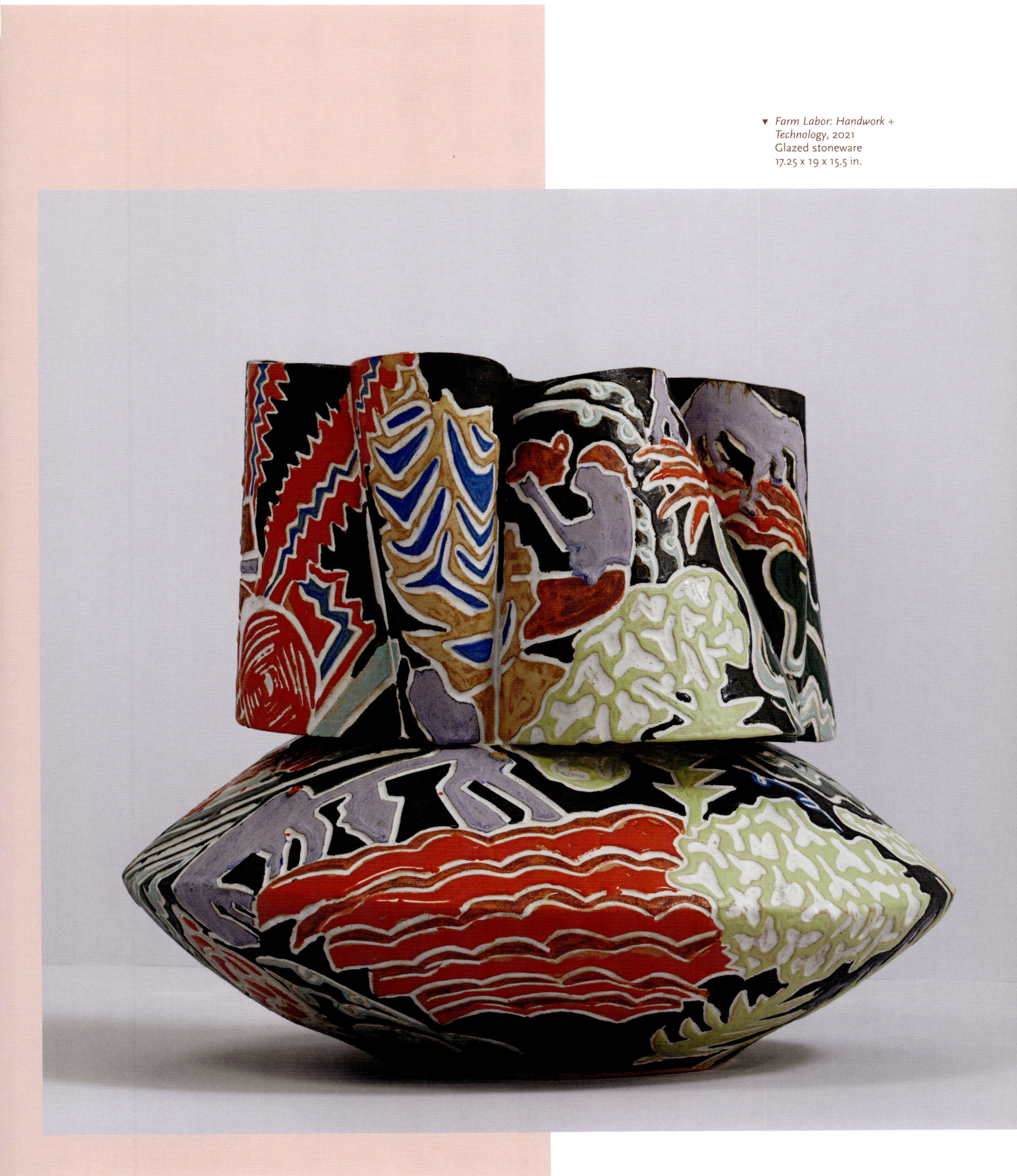

▾ *Farm Labor: Handwork + Technology*, 2021
Glazed stoneware
17.25 x 19 x 15.5 in.

◂ *SO LONG AS WOMEN ARE NOT FREE THE PEOPLE ARE NOT FREE*, 2018
Stoneware, glaze, underglaze, mounted on walnut
25 x 9.5 x 9.5 in.

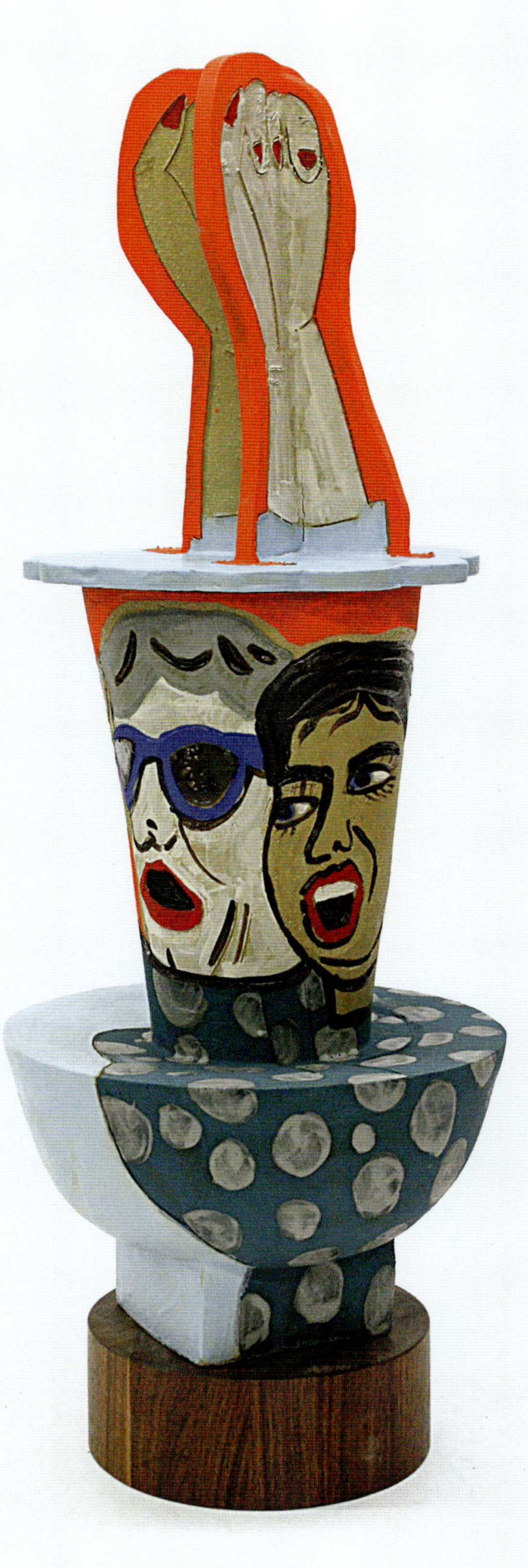

▸ *Gathering Cotton*, 2019
Terra-cotta, glaze, underglaze, luster
14 x 8 x 8 in.

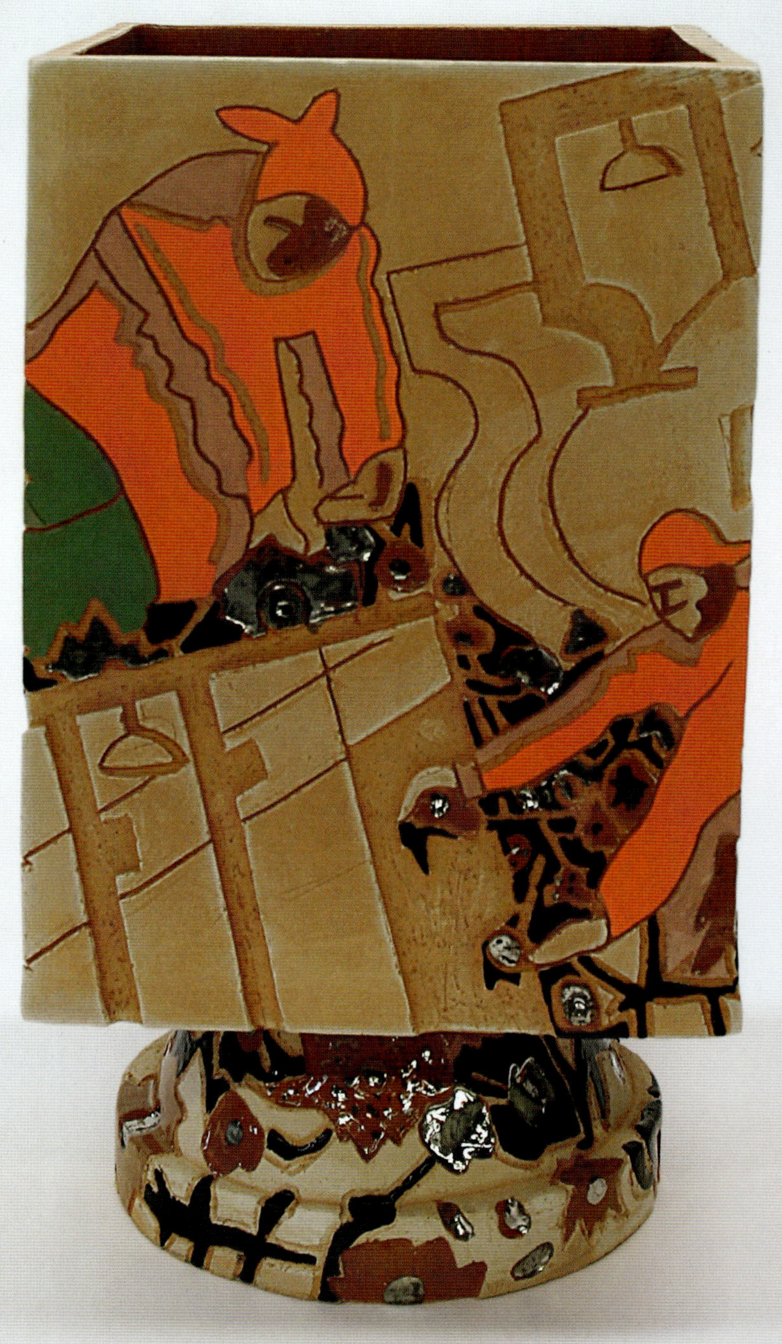

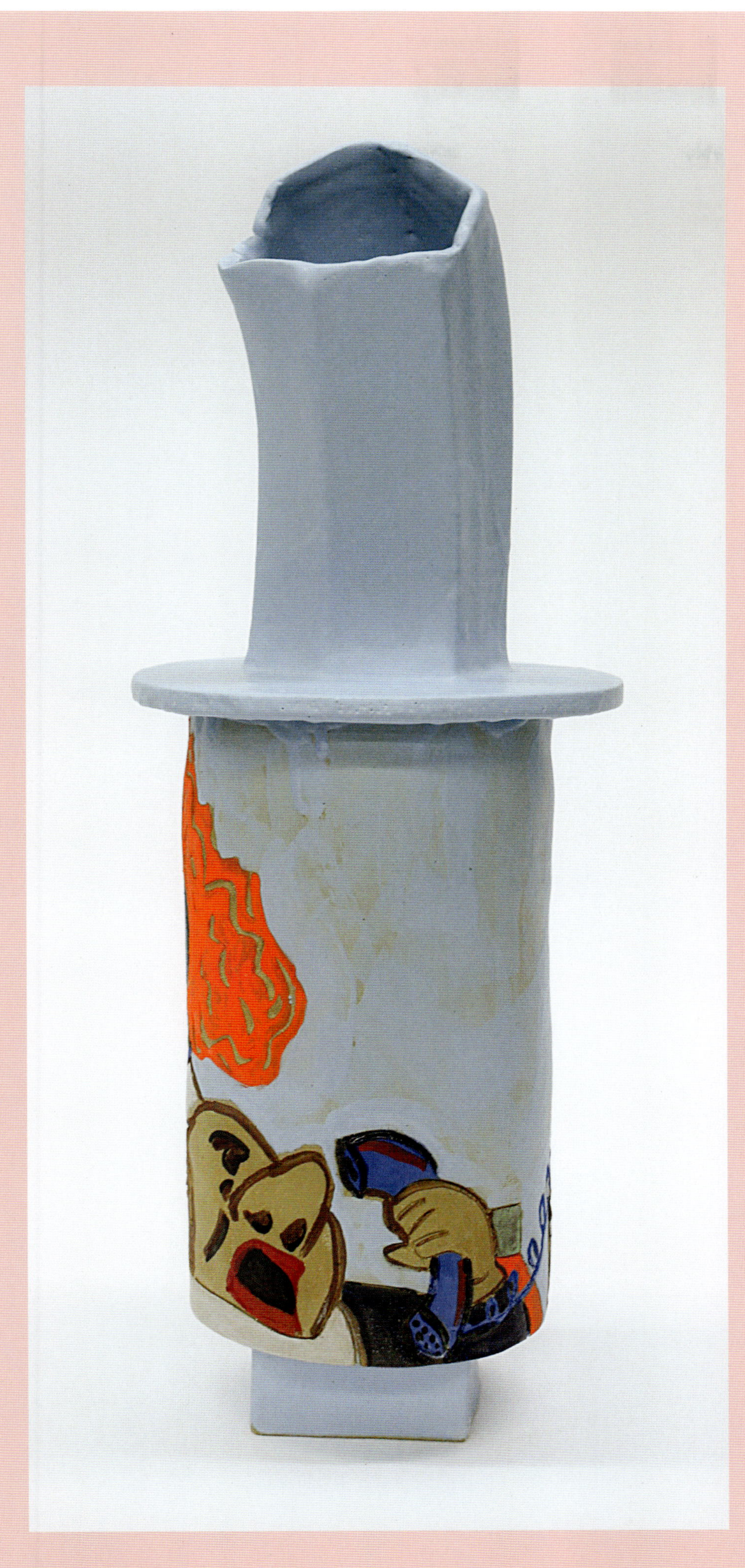

◂ *Will apply "skill" hunt for business, lie and stretch out the business trip*, 2018
Stoneware, glaze, underglaze
23 x 8.5 x 8.5 in.

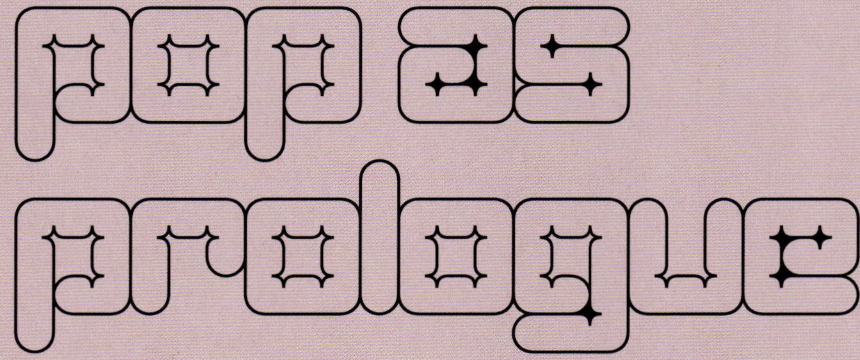

MICHAEL LOBEL

What is Pop Art? This question was first posed in print in a notable series of interviews with artists, including Andy Warhol, Jasper Johns, and Roy Lichtenstein, that appeared in *Art News* magazine in the early 1960s.[1] The artists each had their own take on that question and, more than half a century later, any definitive answer to it is still difficult to pin down for a variety of reasons. For one, the term *Pop Art* had a relatively wide geographic spread even at the beginning, having first been floated in discussions among members of the Independent Group in London in the 1950s, before it crossed the Atlantic to identify what American artists like Warhol, Lichtenstein, James Rosenquist, and Claes Oldenburg were doing in their work. From that point on, Pop exploded into a global phenomenon, finding a marked presence in the practices of artists in Latin America, Asia, and elsewhere. More broadly, modern artists had regularly drawn on the products of popular culture long before the emergence of Pop in the middle of the twentieth century, as evidenced by the investigations of such figures as Gustave Courbet, Vincent van Gogh, Hannah Höch, Yasuo Kuniyoshi, and Stuart Davis, among many others.

One helpful set of parameters for navigating these questions was articulated by art historian and critic Robert Rosenblum just a few years after Pop's initial emergence in the United States. Rosenblum, trying to suss out a way to define the movement, described a singular coincidence of form and subject matter as the key distinguishing feature of this new artistic sensibility:

> If Pop art is to mean anything at all, it must have something to do not only with *what* is painted, but also with the *way* it is painted; otherwise, Manet's ale bottles, Van Gogh's flags, and Balla's automobiles would qualify as Pop art. The authentic Pop artist offers a coincidence of style and subject, that is, he represents mass-produced images and objects by using a style which is also based upon the visual vocabulary of mass production.[2]

Rosenblum provides a concise and particularly useful description that helps us understand what made the work of artists in the postwar period different from earlier instances in which modern practitioners used popular subject matter. In his formulation, the Pop artist not only treated commercial subjects but also depicted them using techniques drawn from, as he put it, "the visual vocabulary of mass production." In this respect, the figures associated with Pop in the United States had a leg up on things because many of them had extensive prior experience in commercial fields: Warhol in advertising and window display, Ed Ruscha in graphic design, and Rosenquist as a billboard painter. The latter's involvement in that context was particularly dramatic because, in the years before he became a Pop artist, Rosenquist had earned his living clambering up scaffolds high above Times Square and other New York City locales to paint large-scale advertising signs for products like Hebrew National Salami and Schenley Whiskey.

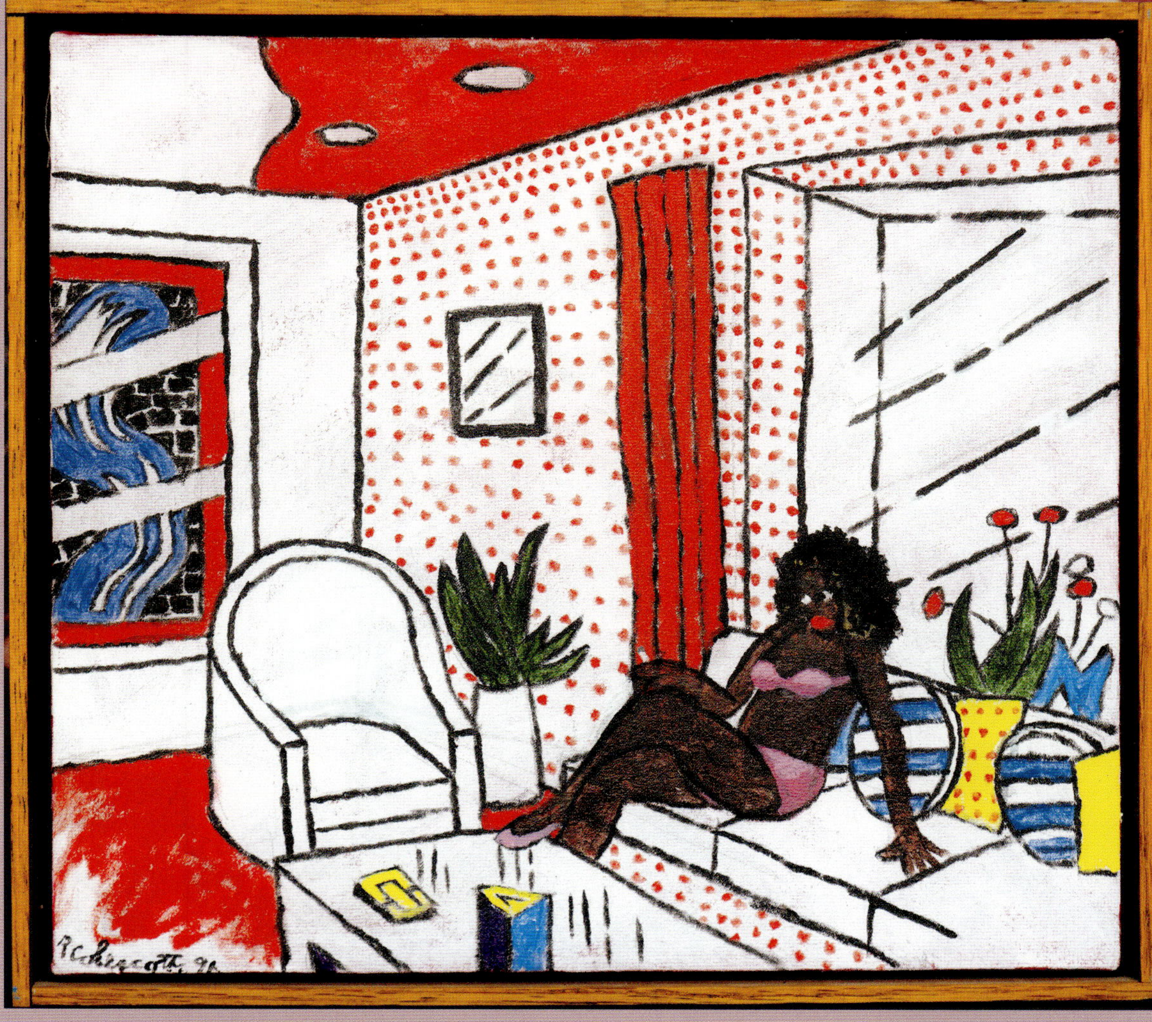

Robert Colescott
Interior II - Homage to Roy Lichtenstein, 1991
Acrylic on canvas
16 x 18 in.

We could amplify Rosenblum's observations by pointing out that most of the artists associated with the first wave of Pop in the United States had made their way through periods of more expressive touch and paint-handling. This had been true of Lichtenstein's embedding of images of Mickey Mouse and Donald Duck within fields of gestural brushstrokes just prior to his breakthrough Pop painting *Look Mickey* (1961), and of Oldenburg's *The Store* (1961), for which he filled a Lower East Side storefront with sculptural facsimiles of common objects. Their surfaces were not shiny and new but encrusted with dripped and gloopy paint. In this way, *The Store* looked back to the painterly language of Abstract Expressionism while heralding a new artistic engagement with the everyday products of consumer culture. The move to the aesthetic described by Rosenblum involved a kind of formal tidying up. As the work of the first generation of American Pop practitioners evolved over the course of the 1960s, it tended overall to become cleaner, tighter, and more streamlined, as evidenced in Oldenburg's abandonment of the paint-encrusted surfaces of *The Store* for shiny vinyl and vacuum-formed plastic, or Lichtenstein's similar embrace of slick, modern materials such as Mylar, Rowlux, and Plexiglas. This aspect of Pop, echoing the surfaces of glossy magazine pages and movie and television screens, came to emblematize the cool sensibility of the 1960s, a quality it shared with the roughly contemporaneous Minimalist movement. And, for the most part, it is this version of Pop that is most readily visible in the present day in art history textbooks, auction catalogues, and museum displays.

With this background in mind, the contemporary artists whose works in clay are assembled in this book do not appear to borrow, at least not exclusively, from 1960s American Pop. As a group, they are less interested in the characteristics most often associated with the canonical version of the movement—cool, hard-edged, streamlined, impersonal—than in an array of divergent values, ones more aligned with such qualities as the cartoonish, the erotic, and the unabashedly handmade and subjective. If Pop offers a backdrop for these contemporary practices, then one might look not so much to its initial emergence but rather at the creative possibilities that were unleashed, Pandora's boxlike, in its wake. These were manifested in the growing sense, within the artistic realm, that myriad niches and corners and cubbyholes of the culture could be mined for inspiration—not just Hollywood and Madison Avenue but also the subcultural and subaltern.

For historical insights into the approaches represented here, we might look instead to the later 1960s and 1970s, for what one might categorize as a post-Pop moment or generation. The latter category would include

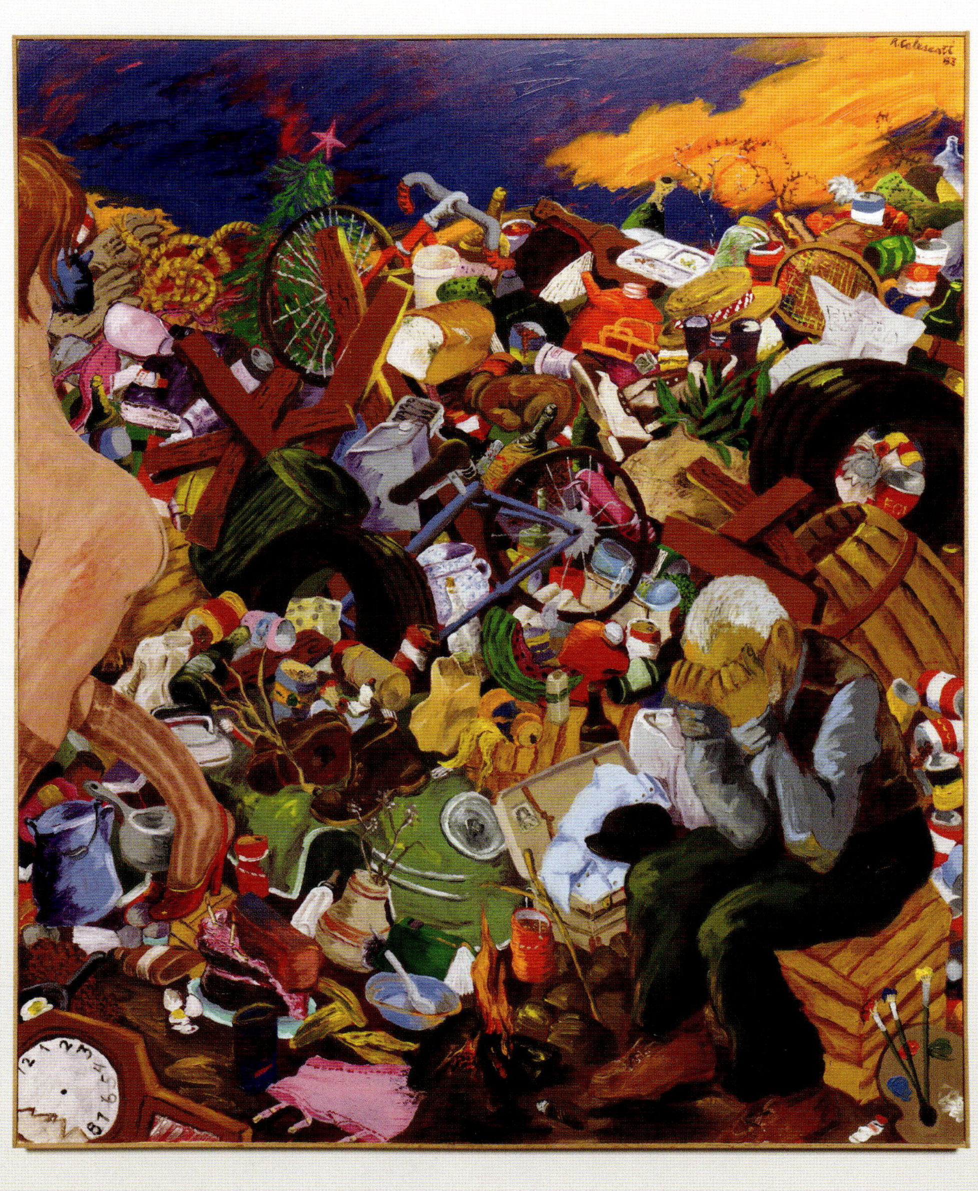

a swath of artists who, in the wake of the movement's initial wave, took up popular subjects with a different eye and a divergent range of experiences, often critiquing first-round Pop in the process.

If we were looking for an apt historical precursor for the approaches to Pop subjects assembled in the present volume, the work of an artist like Robert Colescott would be a good place to start. Colescott was, at least in part, engaged with confronting, critiquing, and working through some of mainstream Pop's central assumptions. His work draws no less on popular imagery than that of artists like Lichtenstein and Rosenquist, but it refuses any claims to a putatively generic or mainstream (read: white) vision of mass culture. In some of his earliest engagements with such subject matter, which date to the late 1960s and early 1970s, Colescott gravitated to characters like Aunt Jemima and Colonel Sanders, advertising icons that put the intertwining of American consumer culture with the nation's legacy of racism on full view. Such investigations spanned nearly the entirety of Colescott's career. Later, in the 1990s, he would appropriate the image of a sleek, modern living room by Lichtenstein in order to rework and transform it, forcing a reckoning with the Pop artist's signature aesthetic. Colescott's reworkings of Lichtenstein's dot screens are not utterly standardized but irregular and haphazard; his painted surfaces are not slick and hard-edged but unapologetically scuffed and blotchy, revealing the presence of the artist's hand; and the protagonists he inserts into Lichtenstein's otherwise sterile interiors are borrowed from the lexicon of American racial caricature. Another aspect of Colescott's vision, on view in a series of 1980s canvases, is his general inclination not to pare down but to pile up, slathering on both pigment and pictorial elements—figures, objects, settings, historical references—in equal measure. In *Down in the Dumps: So Long Sweetheart* (1983), Colescott's erotic preoccupations are on full view, as he portrays himself with head held in hands, a reference to a sorrowing figure by Van Gogh, while a nude woman in stockings and heels exits stage left, evidently spurning her admirer. The action is set against a towering trash heap, its assembled refuse filling nearly the entirety of the composition.

The sense conveyed by Colescott's picture of a world filled to overflowing with everyday objects echoes the critic Walter Benjamin's famed invocation of the angel of history who, blown backward into the future, watches the wreckage of the past piling inexorably behind him. And, to my eye, it is this vision, not of stylized detachment but of excess and overload, that is more consonant with our current era and a wide swath of contemporary artistic practices. So many aspects of Colescott's approach continue to resonate today: his focus on the toxic legacies of American racial disenfranchisement, his exultation in formal excess, his intertwining of sexual and artistic identities. Not to mention that his presentation of himself as a sorrowing artist, one plunged into a melancholic reverie, seems particularly consonant with our current, quasi-apocalyptic moment. Colescott's vision resonates because he responded to Pop with an outré, explosive maximalism. In his work, more is more is more is more—an attitude in keeping with a general artistic inclination toward the additive, layered, and accumulated, rather than the subtractive and all-on-the-surface.

◂ Robert Colescott
Down in the Dumps: So Long Sweetheart, 1983
Acrylic on canvas
84 x 72 in.

Of course, Colescott was not working in isolation. If Pop might serve as one historical touchstone for the artworks assembled in this volume, then equally relevant is California Funk, which followed hot on Pop's heels, in the mid- to late 1960s, and to which Colescott had significant connections (he was born in the Bay Area and lived and worked for long periods in various West Coast locales). In the catalogue essay for a 1967 exhibition that strove to categorize the Funk sensibility as it manifested in the visual arts, curator Peter Selz observed:

> Funk art is hot rather than cool; it is committed rather than disengaged; it is bizarre rather than formal; it is sensuous; and frequently it is quite ugly and ungainly. Although usually three-dimensional, it is nonsculptural in any traditional way, and irreverent in attitude. It is symbolic in content and evocative in feeling....Funk art looks at things which traditionally were not meant to be looked at.[3]

Now we're getting somewhere. Selz's description resonates strongly with the spirit, sensibility, and formal approaches evident in the present volume's collection of practitioners. We can trace a direct connection as well, in that Sally Saul, one of the artists featured in this book, has been married for nearly five decades to Peter Saul, a leading figure associated with California Funk (works by Saul were included in Selz's 1967 show). But perhaps an even more significant and telling connection is to be found in the fact that the Funk cohort included a goodly number of artists working in clay, Robert Arneson and David Gilhooly among them.

In a similar vein as Colescott's painterly sullying of Lichtenstein's modern interiors, Arneson's 1965 clay work *Crisco* puts Funk's undoing of Pop on full display. Reviewing a later exhibition of ceramic art from the West Coast, which included Arneson's piece, critic Peter Schjeldahl described *Crisco* as "a shiny, bright-colored reproduction of a lard can sprouting rotten vegetables and some repellent stuff that in turn sprouts human fingers."[4] Like the artist Paul Thek, who in the very same year as *Crisco*'s creation turned one of Warhol's iconic *Brillo Boxes* (1964) on its side and filled it with a repellently veristic hunk of raw meat sculpted in wax, Arneson bursts open the packaged foodstuff so widely celebrated in twentieth-century American consumer culture, undoing it—and, by extension, Pop—from within. Arneson's predominant valence is the force of bodily excess, the scatological, and the scabrous. (A deeper historical dive would be needed to determine if, at the time Arneson made the piece, *Crisco* had already taken on its later disco-era associations with gay sex.) Arneson's use of clay is fitting, in that *Crisco* ossifies an ephemeral item, giving greater permanence to an object ordinarily viewed as readily disposable.

One thing many of these post-Pop practitioners were grappling with was that the cool, detached sensibility associated with the first wave of American Pop tended to undercut a direct, full-throated delivery of social and political critique. Artists like Warhol, Lichtenstein, and

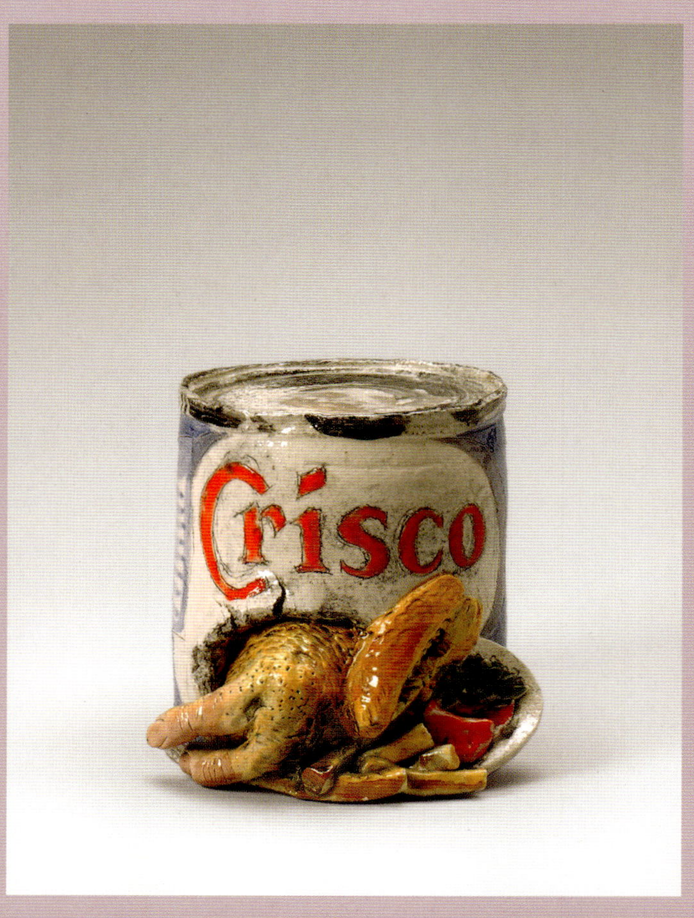

◂ Robert Arneson
Crisco, 1965
Polychromed glazed ceramic
6.125 x 6.375 x 6.375 in.
Bequest of James H. Stubblebine, 1987
Hirshhorn Museum and Sculpture Garden

Rosenquist did take on political subjects, but their messages were often muddled, challenged, or stymied by the consumerist sheen of their imagery. No such issue with Colescott, Saul, and Arneson, all of whom delivered vigorous social and political messaging in their work. Such was the case as well with noted Chicano artist Mel Casas. In 1965, the same year Arneson produced *Crisco*, Casas began his *Humanscape* paintings, a series on which he continued to work over the course of several decades. The earliest pictures in that group focused on motifs common to Pop, including automobiles and movie screens. As the series developed, and as Casas's engagement with Pop subjects expanded, the critical valence of his paintings became more pointed. As with Colescott's imaging of Aunt Jemima, Casas made use of such figures as the Frito Bandito, a cartoon advertising mascot for Fritos brand corn chips that drew on popular, denigrating stereotypes of Mexicans. Casas's intention to launch a simultaneous critique of such tendencies in both mass media forms and Pop artworks alike is evident in his 1973 painting *Humanscape 70 (Comic Whitewash)*. The work's references to Pop are abundant: in its vibrant color scheme, its thought-balloon text, the superheroes frozen in action, and the prominent Lichtenstein-esque brushstroke positioned near the very center of the composition. Amplified by the title, which Casas has included captionlike below, the work's message is clear. According to comic book lore, these heroic figures have dizzyingly varied back stories—from wealthy Gotham City playboy to Norse god to exiled alien from another planet. Yet they all display the same bland, pinkish skin tone, attesting to the general racial homogeneity of the comic books. In turn, Casas contrasts the heroes' monotone complexions with the slightly darker cast of the young protagonist in the picture's foreground. The artist directs his challenge at the unbearable whiteness of the conventional comic book genre and also, by extension, at Pop art's reiteration of the same.

In that landmark series of interviews that posed the question "What is Pop Art?" and which supplied the world with such iconic quotes as "I want to be a machine," Warhol talked extensively with the interviewer, critic Gene Swenson, about Pop Art and queerness. This aspect of the interview has remained generally unknown, as the queer content of Warhol's comments was excised from the original, published version of the interview and was only recently restored by a scholar committed to writing art history from an LGBT perspective—a scholar who, one notes, belongs to the same millennial generation as a good number of the contemporary clay artists featured here.[5]

Given that queer content was often obscured or submerged during Pop's first wave—as when curator Lawrence Alloway chose not to include a monumental male nude in a pivotal 1963 exhibition at the Guggenheim Museum in New York City—we can look to a slightly later moment for more emphatic artistic formulations of queer identity, as in the work of artist Thomas Lanigan-Schmidt. A piece like *Twinky as a Prima Ballerina (Self-Portrait)* (1967–69) displays the youthful exuberance and insouciance one might expect from an artist then still in his teens. With a photo of the artist's face collaged onto the figure of a ballerina doll, the ensemble surrounded by decorative edging and healthy dollops of glitter, the piece uses fragments of consumer

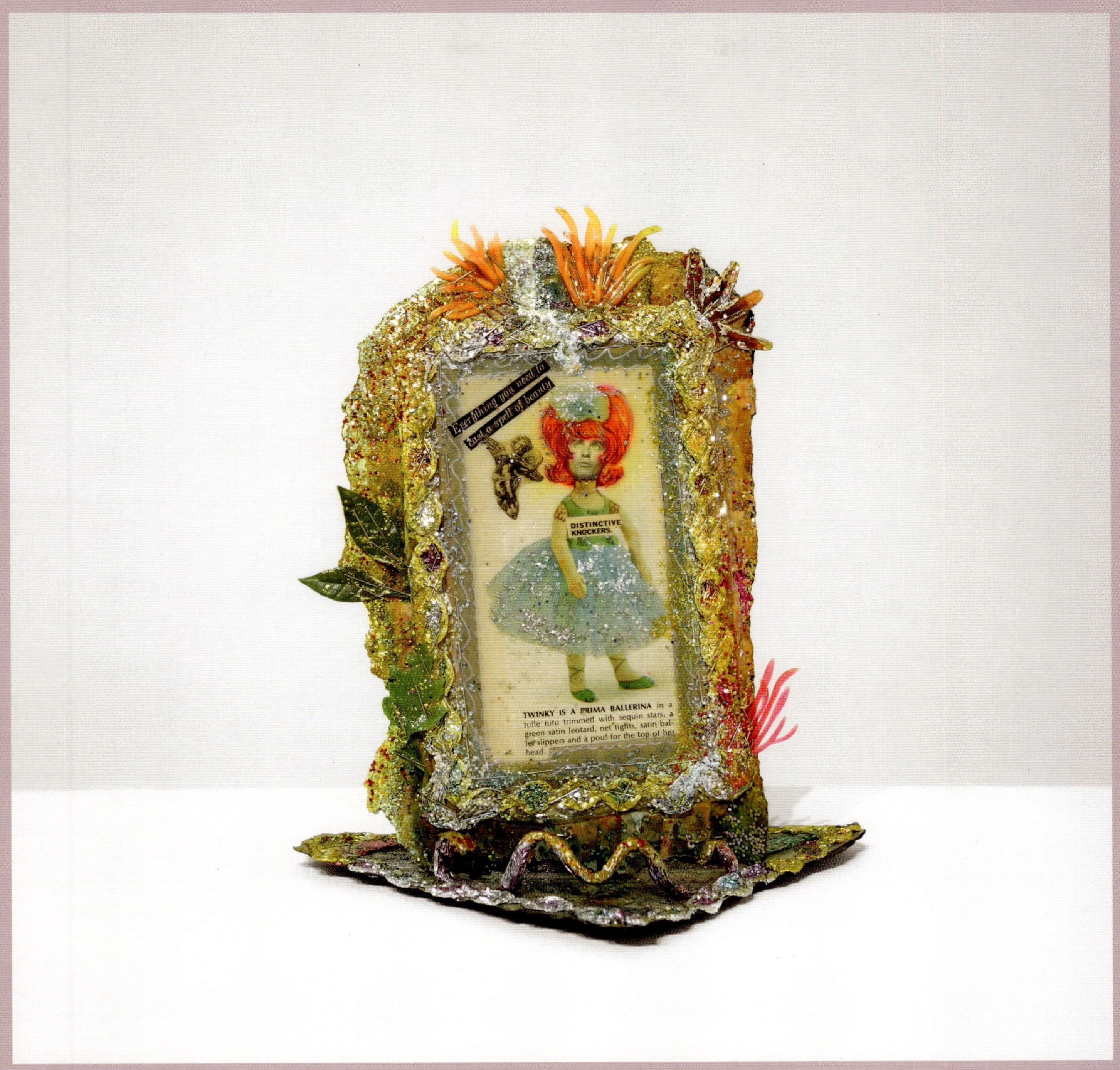

▲ Thomas Lanigan-Schmidt
Twinky as a Prima Ballerina (Self-portrait), 1967–69
Foil, printed material, linoleum, glitter, cellophane, staples, acrylic paint, found objects, and other media
9.75 x 7 x 3.5 in.

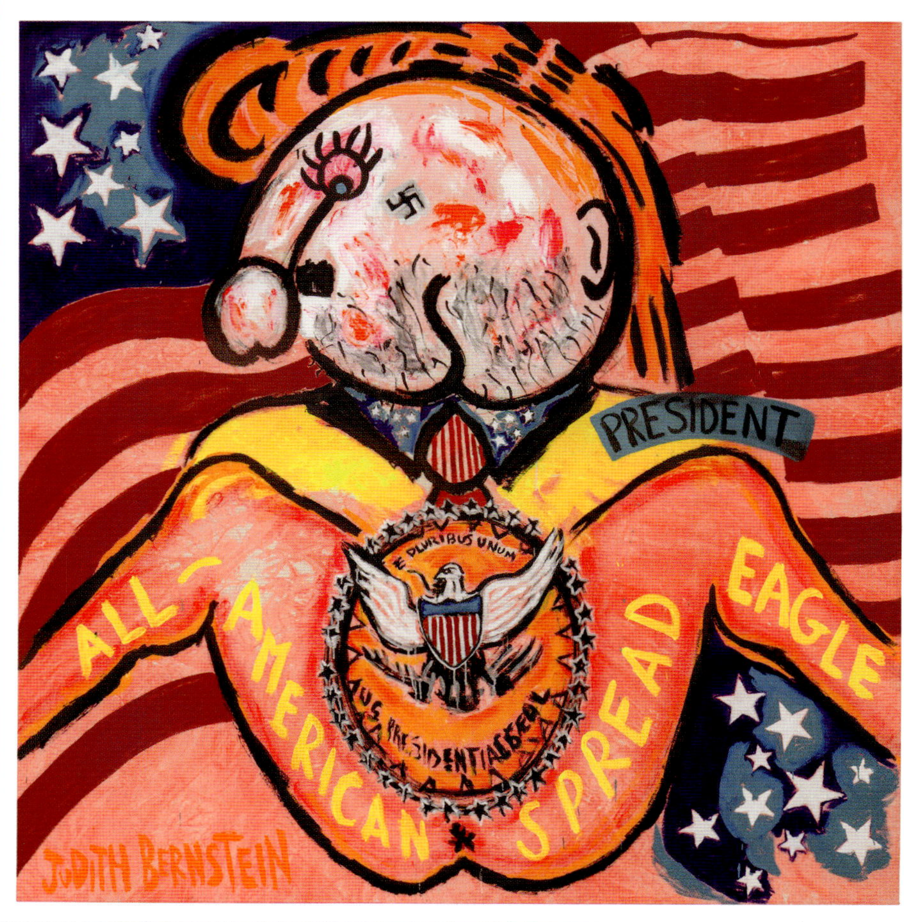

◂ Judith Bernstein
President, 2017
Acrylic and oil on canvas
90 x 89.5 in.

culture to deliver a campy yet touchingly sweet—and unrepentantly queer—take on the genre of the artist's self-portrait. Given that it was completed the same year as the watershed Stonewall Riots, in which Lanigan-Schmidt participated (he was one of those present in the Stonewall Inn when a police raid sparked that epochal event), the work is fittingly a visual riot of textures and colors conveyed through foil, linoleum, and glitter.[6] As such, if Lichtenstein's Rowlux and Oldenburg's vinyl had paved the way, Lanigan-Schmidt's use of materials ordinarily associated with the less rarefied domain of arts and crafts highlights how Pop and other movements (including Fluxus and Minimalism) had broadened the scope of available artistic media in the 1960s.

The historical moment we have been surveying also witnessed the profound impact of second-wave feminism, which made itself felt in the visual arts as in many other domains. During her graduate studies at Yale in the mid-1960s, Judith Bernstein began to build an artistic response to a particular aspect of popular culture. While the latter term, within discussions of Pop Art, tends to evoke the products of the modern mass media and consumer culture, it can also, in a broader register, connote myriad forms of popular expression, ones that have persisted throughout long periods of human history. For her part, Bernstein found inspiration in the graffiti scrawled on the walls of men's bathrooms, a crude and coarse form of communication ordinarily unseen by women. Before long, she began to produce paintings and drawings that, energized by the era's flowering of feminist consciousness, confronted themes of male aggression and sexual license. More recent works by Bernstein, created during the Trump presidency, explore related imagery, with figures sporting dicks as noses, assholes as mouths, and other polymorphously perverse appendages. The high-keyed color, intentional hamfistedness, and unabashed vulgarity of Bernstein's imagery fit the tenor of our times, given that the bluster, bravado, and sheer shamelessness of political figures like Trump, and the wrenchingly divisive politics he has sown, call for something other than an artistic pose of restraint and composure. Bernstein's art is unapologetically and strategically loud, raucous, and boisterous.

In recent years, advertisements for the iPhone have touted the inclusion of ceramic components in the device's display to produce a tougher, more high-tech material. One could thus readily conceive of a contemporary sculptural practice in clay that wholeheartedly embraced the sleekness of the many designed objects of our digital age, all those smartphones and touchscreens and the like. Yet the artists whose work has been assembled here mostly reject the sheen, gleam, and streamlining so often proffered as the predominant aesthetic of the modern. If their Pop aesthetic engages with our digital moment, it is not so much in its sleekness and putative efficiency but rather in its equally evident aspects of excess and overload: in the obnoxiously pleading exhortations of spam emails; the mocking irreverence of memes; and the unrelenting visual overload of gifs, animations, and

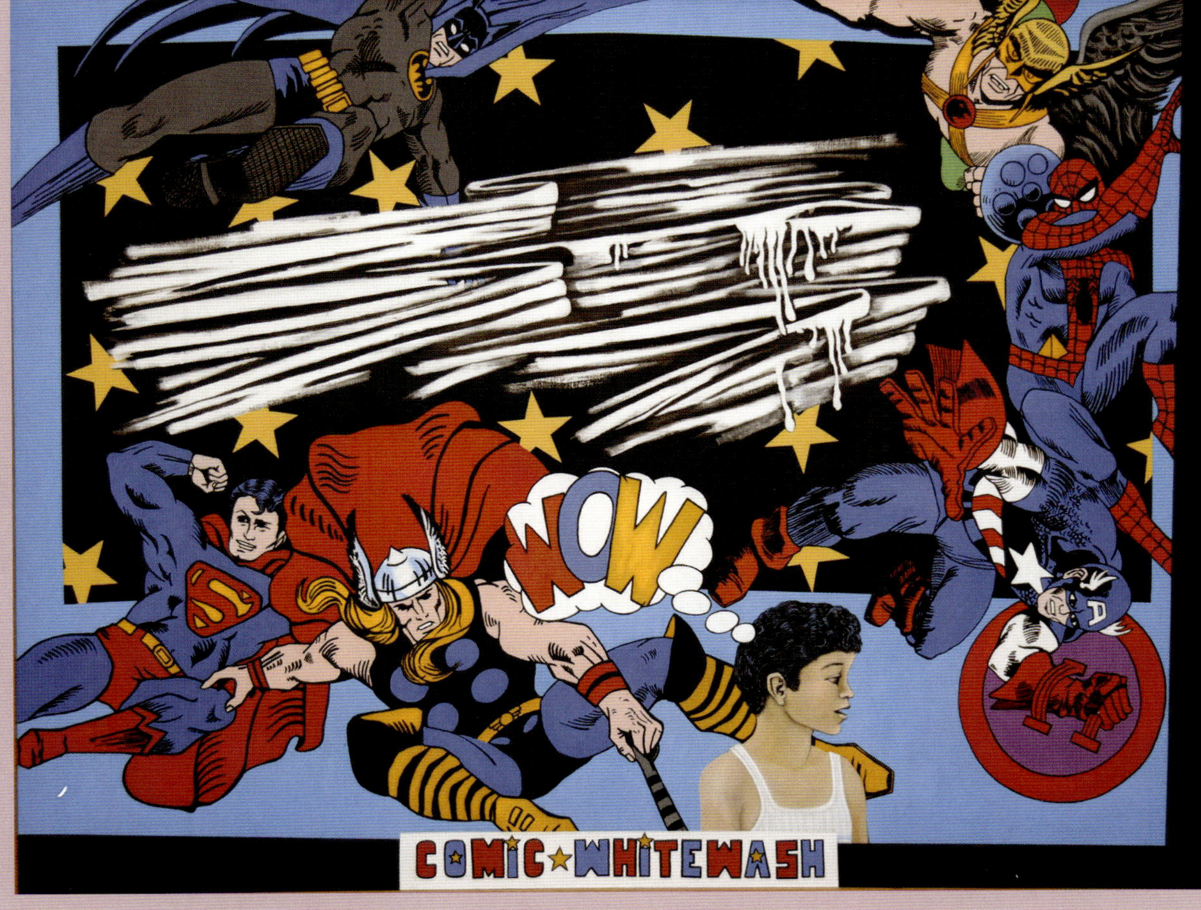

◂ Mel Casas
Humanscape 70 (Comic Whitewash), 1973
Acrylic on canvas
72 x 96 in.

pop-up ads. In this way, for all its evident cheer and buoyancy, Pop might become a fitting vehicle for scrutinizing some of the less salutary aspects of contemporary experience, ones that call out for further artistic intervention and critique.

Notes

1. Gene R. Swenson, "What Is Pop Art? Answers from 8 Painters, Part I," *Art News* 62, no. 7 (November 1963): 24–27, 60–64; and "What Is Pop Art? Part II," *Art News* 62, no. 10 (February 1964): 40–43, 62–67.

2. Robert Rosenblum, "Pop Art and Non-Pop Art," *Art and Literature* (Summer 1965): 80–93; reprinted in *Pop Art: A Critical History*, ed. Steven Henry Madoff (Berkeley: University of California Press, 1997), 131.

3. Peter Selz, "Notes on Funk," in *Funk*, exh. cat. (Berkeley: University Art Museum, University of California, Berkeley, 1967), 3.

4. Peter Schjeldahl, "The Playful Improvisation of West Coast Ceramic Art," *New York Times*, June 9, 1974, 19.

5. Jennifer Sichel, "'Do You Think Pop Art's Queer?' Gene Swenson and Andy Warhol," *Oxford Art Journal*, 41, no. 1 (March 2018): 59–83.

6. "Maximalist Art: An Interview with Thomas Lanigan-Schmidt by Jonathan Weinberg," in *Thomas Lanigan-Schmidt: Tenemental (With Sighs Too Deep for Words)* (New York: Howl Arts, Inc., 2018), 18–27.

artist bios

Diana Yesenia Alvarado
Diana Yesenia Alvarado's clay sculptures present a sense of childhood with an innate twist of Los Angeles. The distinct and quintessential symbolism that is depicted through Alvarado's gestures may visually depict the sounds, smells, people, and colors of her neighborhood in Southern California, but her work touches people outside the confines of her city.

Alex Anderson
At the core of Alex Anderson's current body of work is a philosophical, existential examination of identity politics. Based in Los Angeles, the 30-year-old gay, Asian–African American sculptor is an artist working against stereotypes and racialism prevalent in today's society. By working in an unexpected medium and channeling methodologies that surround artistic production in ceramic arts, Anderson creates fantastic, multifaceted sculptures that are both subversive and whimsical. Anderson uses the classical aesthetics of Western power, which ironically share space with the aesthetics of queer camp cultural production, to translate the structures that govern his lived experience in society and others' social perceptions of his identities into form. While his work engages with the ceramic canon and draws from the Western art historical canon at large, it primarily operates at the core of post-blackness.

Trisha Baga
In recent years, Trisha Baga has increasingly incorporated ceramics into their practice, working on a scale unconventional to the medium and often reproducing functional objects, articulating yet emptying their operational details. Her ceramics often seem to express a hypothetical primordial rendering of the reality that surrounds us (printers, microscopes, cameras, telephones), while her paintings of desertlike landscapes composed of sesame seeds on wooden surfaces depict material versions of the pixelated images of the videos.

Alex Becerra
Working in painting, drawing, sculpture, and ceramic, Alex Becerra explores the way we view modernity, often chopped up into bits and sliced together. Developing a reputation as a provocateur, Becerra has earned comparisons to both Philip Guston and Mike Kelley for his animated brushwork and dark imagery.

Genesis Belanger
Genesis Belanger's work is characterized by the treatment of objects as surrogates for the body. Sculpted in porcelain and concrete and tinted in fondant hues, everyday objects take on human features as they begin to resemble us. Belanger's still life sculptures—compositions of furniture, fruit, and flowers loaded with signs and symbols—are increasingly contextualized by their surroundings, which are psychologically charged spaces created by the artist. The effect is uncanny, toeing the line between comfort and disquiet, and the beautiful and strange.

Seth Bogart
After nearly two decades on the campier, glammier edges of the rock underground with bands like Hunx and His Punx, Seth Bogart has become known in recent years as a polymath painter, illustrator, ceramicist, clothing designer, and proprietor of the online shop Wacky Wacko, but even more so for curating a world of queer fantasy. His color-bursting installations have included a faux sex shop (2018's *Lick*). Among Bogart's most beloved pieces are his sculptures of gay-bar matchbooks and delightfully subversive toothbrushes, and his brash "Grrrls Do Everything Better" shirts, depicting an illustrated history of women inventing punk.

Woody De Othello
For the past few years, Woody De Othello has been constructing semianthropomorphized sculptures of everyday household objects. De Othello's glossy, bright sculptures are full of whimsy, which belies their more serious messaging about accessibility, politics, and history.

Sharif Farrag
Sharif Farrag's fantastical, autobiographical ceramic universe is populated with wildly overgrown forms teeming with dripping flowers, shadowy insects, gasping maws, and a riot of colors, textures, and sheens. Farrag has been a resident artist at the Ceramics Department of California State University, Long Beach, since 2018.

Ryan Flores
Ryan Flores explores material seduction and its connection to the viewer through the use of ceramic objects.

Dominique Fung
Second generation Chinese Canadian painter Dominique Fung refigures art history to give her subjects real agency. Fung's early artistic passions were informed by Vermeer, Manet, Rembrandt, and Goya, but her sense of Chinese heritage was largely informed by vessels and objects that she saw at home and on display at the Metropolitan Museum in New York. "[These objects] made me question my place in the world and how I felt in terms of my displacement from my origins," explains Fung. Delicately rendered, these objects populate dreamlike scenes that continue the legacy of Surrealism in their play with scale, time, and gravity. In Fung's paintings, the decorative language on which Orientalism relies is more than just ornamental; these ancient vessels and sculptures are animate protagonists in their own right.

Joel Gaitan
While celebrating life, death, and the afterlife, Joel Gaitan's work studies the matters of self-identity, sexuality, and ancestral lineage. From forgotten tongues to erased cultures, Gaitan immerses into traditional hand-building clay techniques, keeping a sacred tradition from Nicaragua and Central America alive in a colonized world. Gaitan highlights Nicaragüense lifestyle and aesthetics with oil paints in portraits that use elements of poetry, colors, and storytelling. With pottery and painting, Gaitan pays homage to the ancestors, both those who have been encountered and those who have not.

Melvino Garretti
As an original member of the Studio Watts Workshop, Melvino Garretti has stood as a pillar in the West Coast ceramic community for more than fifty years. His works helped to inspire a lush period of experimentation within the Los Angeles Black artistic community. Garretti's energetic ceramics are easily recognizable through his abstract, colorful, jazzlike formations.

Raven Halfmoon
Raven Halfmoon, Caddo Nation, channels generations of ancestors in her totemic sculptures. Considering herself a cultural preservationist, she is realizing Native American art's relevancy now more than ever. In this larger conversation about identity and heritage, Halfmoon appropriately uses these themes in her work to connect with elders and peers.

Stephanie Temma Hier
Stephanie Temma Hier combines ceramics and oil painting to create wall works that contrast material and subject matter. She often focuses on photorealistic still lifes and surrounds each canvas with custom frames composed of intricate sculptures. Hier is often drawn to motifs related to food and consumption, and her busy arrangements further evoke our ingestion of an overflow of visual culture in the digital age.

Kahlil Robert Irving
Kahlil Robert Irving has recently garnered critical acclaim for his pioneering work with ceramic assemblage. His sculptures carefully recreate the everyday detritus of littered sidewalks with resplendent shards of porcelain, punctuated by decals from his social media engagement. Irving's ceramics practice exposes the underlying material and cultural histories of the medium.

Elizabeth Jaeger
Elizabeth Jaeger's sculptures embed common figural elements in existential concepts of reality and perception. Sculptures like elongated human bodies with masklike faces, truncated torsos, greyhound dogs, empty furniture, and vases typically start with a personal experience or event. From there, they unfold a larger picture of phenomenological concerns. Despite a seeming familiarity with the objects' figurativeness, there is a sense of disquiet and subtle uncanniness inherent in Jaeger's work that challenges the viewer's relationship to their own physicality, their surrounding, and their consciousness.

Heidi Lau
Reconfiguring fragmented personal and collective memories, Heidi Lau makes collections of symbolic artifacts and zoomorphic ruins as materializations of the archaic and the invisible, taking inspiration from colonial architecture and tenement houses in Macau that have mostly been demolished or gentrified beyond recognition. In the process, Lau continuously reenacts the nonlinearity and materiality of the past, molding a tactile connection to the disappearing, impossible identity of home.

Grant Levy-Lucero
Grant Levy-Lucero borrows the decorative, narrative capabilities of the vessel from the Archaic and Classical periods of the Greco-Roman world—when they carried etchings on the exterior that depicted scenes from life, Homeric tales, and the world of the gods. In this inexact appropriation, Levy-Lucero asserts that mythology is not an enshrined concept of the past but something that grows and changes with the zeitgeist.

Candice Lin
For the past decade, Los Angeles–based artist Candice Lin has investigated the cultures and histories embedded in objects and materials related to colonial trade, alternative healing practices, and bodily functions. These include things that carry stranger textures, more pungent scents, and heavier burdens than typical art materials, such as tobacco, urine, and tea as well as live insects and dead animals. Lin is a skilled and endlessly curious craftsperson who transforms these things and the stories they tell into artworks that mobilize critical issues such as race, gender, and trauma in unconventional ways.

Jasmine Little
The numerous and varied influences in Jasmine Little's work span the entirety of the human experience. Flemish and Renaissance painting, medieval illuminated manuscripts, Safavid period carpets, Greek black-figure and red-figure pottery, and Japanese woodblock prints are among the sources referenced in her work. Little's work foregrounds a communal aspect of ceramics that breeds cross-pollination and slippage between artists working in physical proximity to each other. By utilizing materials specific to a single location while employing imagery that is universal to us all, Little creates objects that are overwhelmingly human.

Lindsey Mendick
Lindsey Mendick's work is a riotous exploration of femininity, taste, and identity. Mendick's practice is hinged to her skilled work in ceramics, which she describes being drawn to for its tactile nature and its desire to be manipulated by the maker. By playfully combining low culture iconography and high culture methods of construction, Mendick creates humorously decadent and elaborate installations that enable the viewer to explore their personal history in a cathartic fashion. In addition to her solo sculptural practice, Mendick is a cofounder of the Proudick platform, which is at once an artists' collective, a project space, and a place for exchanging ideas and learning about ceramics.

Keegan Monaghan
There are two equally powerful forces running perpendicular to each other in Keegan Monaghan's paintings and ceramics. One is image, the other is material. In his ceramics, texture is so hand-wrought, the artist's fingerprints are preserved in the clay.

Jiha Moon
Jiha Moon is a contemporary artist who focuses on painting, printmaking, and sculptural ceramic objects. Born in Daegu, South Korea, Moon is currently based in Atlanta, Georgia. Moon's gestural

paintings, mixed media, and ceramic sculpture explore fluid identities and the global movement of people and their cultures. "I am a cartographer of cultures and an icon maker in my lucid worlds," says Moon. She takes cues from wide ranges of history of Eastern and Western art, colors and designs from popular culture, Korean temple paintings and folk art, internet emoticons and icons, and fruit stickers and labels of products from all over the world. She often teases and changes these lexicons so that they are hard to identify yet stay in a familiar zone.

Masato Mori
Masato Mori's paintings have both a heaviness and a comical quality. Mori analyzes the various influential relationships between his own aesthetic perspective and that of comics, video games, and animation, which are sources he has continued to explore over the years. In recent years, he has explored themes such as innocence and mindless absorption in art.

Narumi Nekpenekpen
Narumi Nekpenekpen was born in 1998 to a Japanese mother and a Nigerian father. She was raised in both Kashiwa, Japan, and Los Angeles. In Nekpenekpen's work, slab porcelain clay is pushed and pulled by hand into an assembled tableaux of personal allegory. Patchworks of woven clay and clunky hand-modeled chains evoke and negotiate complexities of human history, the ontology of trauma, and of self-introspection.

Ruby Neri
Ruby Neri's use of sprayed glazes links her ceramics to the street art she produced in the late 1990s as a member of what would become the San Francisco–based Mission School, connecting a contemporary urban art form with the archaic power of prehistoric wall-painting and object-making. The ceramic vessels that have dominated Neri's production recently evoke both earthy tactility and psychological intimacy. She depicts the human body as a porous instrument of pleasure, terror, and everything in between. This places her within a lineage of recent Los Angeles–based artists that include Mike Kelley, Paul McCarthy, and Charles Ray, while her penchant for hand-driven craft connects her to the Bay Area Figurative and Funk movements.

Brian Rochefort
As an avid explorer of the earth's natural beauty, Brian Rochefort is often inspired by volcanic landscapes, remote tropical rain forests, and protected barrier reefs. Unfired clay objects are broken apart, built upon with more material, and then fired between each layer of glaze to produce volcanic masses or craters, overflowing with color and character.

Jennifer Rochlin
Trained as a painter, Jennifer Rochlin took up ceramics as a way to expand her painting practice into three dimensions. Rochlin uses terra-cotta clay to hand-build vessels in coil and slab methods, creating familiar forms that echo the long history of ceramics. Undulating with dents and bulges, Rochlin's vessels reject direct homage in favor of suggesting the unpredictable, beautiful variance of human bodies. Her works are not production pots but are something apart, individual and free.

Brie Ruais
Brie Ruais's work pulls the viewer in relation to the Earth. It is a conduit for emotional and physical connection—a channel for listening, healing, rejoicing, grieving, nurturing, and transforming. Her pieces are abstract results of a language of movement that she has developed through intuition and metaphor. Over the years, Ruais's work has evolved in meaning through various relationships: her physical relationship to the material, her relationship to the environment, the clay's relationship to the earth, and the work's relationship to mapping.

Sally Saul
Throughout her long ceramics practice, Sally Saul has combined both playful and subversive visions. Her background in literature gives her a deep and original feel for a very wide range of subjects—from flora and fauna to more conceptual subjects such as confinement and gender. "Memory, or an editing of memory, informs several of my pieces. Material in a quilt, a pattern, the shape and feeling of a room—these are fragments that evoke time and place and act as a talisman," says Saul.

Stephanie H. Shih
Stephanie Shih explores the diasporic nostalgia and material lineages of migration and colonization through the lens of the Asian American kitchen. Her painted ceramic sculptures examine the relationship between consumerism, cultural interchange, and identity in immigrant communities.

Alake Shilling
Alake Shilling combines her signature bubblegum pop aesthetic and curious storytelling to create ceramics and canvases of otherworldly abstraction and dynamic intrigue. Wrought with dark humor and stupefying detail, she guides her viewer through naturalistic scenes of cartoonish wild fauna and characters of her own creation.

Jessica Stoller
Working in the realm of figurative sculpture, Stoller mines the rich and complicated history of porcelain, harnessing its links to power, desire, and taste. Synthesizing the cultural, historical, and corporeal notions of the female body, Stoller expands the feminist visual vernacular and makes space for subversion, defiance, and play. Deftly employing myriad techniques over the past decade, Stoller's complex works are hand-built, thrown, carved, molded, and ultimately fired multiple times to create richly colored surfaces. The works on view marry a dizzying array of the imagined, idealized and grotesque. For Stoller, the "grotesque" becomes a powerful tool to challenge patriarchal power structures, as female figures flaunt what they are told to hide, reveling in their own pleasure and abjection.

Katie Stout
Katie Stout is an American artist and designer based in New York City. Stout creates work that combines traditional craft techniques, the legacy of female-dominated decorative arts, and contemporary and conceptual art. Her work has been described as "naive pop."

Magdalena Suarez Frimkess
Magdalena Suarez Frimkess's works have been considered unconventional in her school of ceramics, given their often sculptural as opposed functional forms. She selects her subject matter from her day's activities and encounters, which she likens to selecting a dish from a menu. Her hand-painted, rather than dipped, glazed works depict varied imaginative characters and scenes selected from history and from memory, the imagery and language of which originated in areas around the world. While one vessel may portray pre-Columbian motifs, another might assume the form of Minnie Mouse donning a Prada bag or the bust of Nefertiti. It is this diversity combined with the artist's playful poetics and humble hand that make Suarez Frimkess's stories feel so ineffably our own.

Wade Tullier
Wade Tullier's work is inspired by his unsettling experience as a forensic sculptor and researcher. The imagery that he uses traces back to the experience of working to identify the unknown, the stories he was told as a child, and growing up in southern Louisiana. As a sculptor, Tullier creates objects that draw from a history of violence, death, and destruction at the hands of natural disasters and man-made catastrophes.

Amia Yokoyama
Amia Yokoyama is a multimedia artist who focuses on experimental animation, video, sculpture, and installation. There is a thawing, muddy utopia in Yokoyama's work. Bodies are hardened in the glaze of clay and softened in the silt of the digital render.

Bari Ziperstein
Bari Ziperstein's mixed-media, ceramic-based sculpture practice engages ideas of consumerism, propaganda, and the built environment. Ziperstein is noted for her ongoing investigation of Soviet-era textile design and patterns. One such body of works is her highly technical figurative ceramic sculptures that reference 1980s propaganda posters from the Eastern Bloc, which she sourced specifically for their patronizing messages about domestic morality, alcoholism, motherhood, and the place of women in society. Ziperstein considers it to be a distinct feminist gesture that she has offered the propaganda a new tactile presence, interrogating the relationship between craft, the home, and femininity by leaning into ceramics' historical position as a craft practice.

author bios

Rahel Aima (Sharif Farrag)
Rahel Aima is a writer, editor, and critic from Dubai. She is the editor of the forthcoming *BXD: The Postwestern Review* and an associate editor at *Momus*. She was formerly a founding editor of *The State* and special projects editor at the *New Inquiry*. Her research has focused on palette and futurity; biomimicry, bugs, and ersatz surfaces; and the Khaleeji Ideology, a mode of techtopianism particular to the Arabian Gulf. She is currently at work on a book about coastal terroirs, where oil meets water on the Arabian Peninsula, and a collection of short exhibition fiction that springs from solar and lunar events. Aima was the 2018 recipient of the Andy Warhol Foundation Arts Writers Grant.

Christian Allaire (Raven Halfmoon)
Christian Allaire is an Ojibway writer from Nipissing First Nation. He earned a Bachelor of Journalism from Ryerson University in 2014, and he has since written for publications such as *Footwear News*, *Refinery29*, *Elle*, *Hazlitt*, *Mr. Porter*, and *The National Post*. Currently, he is the Fashion and Style Writer for *Vogue*.

Susan Canning (Jessica Stoller)
An independent curator and critic, Susan Canning has written features, interviews, and reviews for *Art in America*, *New Art Examiner*, and *Art Papers*, and is a contributing editor for *Sculpture* magazine.

Ivana Cruz (Joel Gaitan)
Ivana Cruz is a New York City–based Dominican writer and art director. Her work has appeared in *W* magazine, *Vogue*, *New York Times*, and *Esquire*.

Catherine Quan Damman (Candice Lin)
Catherine Quan Damman is the Linda Nochlin visiting assistant professor at the Institute of Fine Arts at New York University and a regular contributor to *Artforum* magazine. She is completing her monograph, titled *Performance: A Deceptive History*, as a 2022–2023 American Council of Learned Societies Fellow.

Dan Devening (Wade Tullier)
Dan Devening is an artist, curator, and owner/director of Devening Projects, a Chicago-based internationally focused contemporary art gallery, established in 2007. He is an adjunct professor in the Department of Painting and Drawing at the School of the Art Institute of Chicago.

Lauren Schell Dickens (Woody De Othello)
Lauren Schell Dickens is senior curator at the San José Museum of Art (SJMA). Since joining the museum in 2016 as curator, she has organized a number of major exhibitions, including *Our whole, unruly selves* (2021), *Undersoul: Jay DeFeo* (2019), *With Drawn Arms: Glenn Kaino and Tommie Smith* (2019), *Other Walks, Other Lines* (2018), and *The House Imaginary* (2018). She has organized solo exhibitions and projects with Diana Al-Hadid, Sofia Cordova, Woody De Othello, Brendan Fernandes, Aislinn Thomas, and Lara Schnitger, among

others, and co-organized the major survey of *Rina Banerjee: Make Me a Summary of the World* (2019), which toured nationally. She is currently organizing the first major exhibition of Kelly Akashi's practice, which will tour nationally. Prior to SJMA, Dickens held curatorial positions at the National Gallery of Art and Corcoran Gallery of Art in Washington, DC. She received a bachelor's degree from Yale University and a master's degree from Columbia University. Her public project with The Propeller Group and El Mac was awarded the 2018 Creative Impact Award by the city of San José. She is a 2019 Warhol Curatorial Research Fellow and recipient of the Fellows of Contemporary Art 2022 Curators Award.

Owen Duffy (Ryan Flores)
Owen Duffy is a New York City–based art historian, curator, and writer. He is currently the director of the Yeh Art Gallery at St. John's University, Queens. Duffy earned a PhD in art history from Virginia Commonwealth University. His writing has been published in *ArtReview*, *Art & Education*, *frieze*, and *BOMB* magazine, among other publications.

Michelle Loti Gonzales (Alex Becerra)
Michelle Loti Gonzales, born in 1985 and living in Berlin and Los Angeles, is a freelance writer, poet, and self-taught musician. She studied creative writing at Santa Monica College.

Gracie Hadland (Melvino Garretti)
Gracie Hadland is a Los Angeles–based writer. She writes frequently for *frieze*, *X-TRA*, and *Los Angeles Review of Books* among other publications.

Kate Mosher Hall (Seth Bogart)
Kate Mosher Hall is a Los Angeles–based artist. After graduating high school, Hall joined the L.A. punk band Mika Miko, with whom she toured the world for several years. After being kicked out of the band, she attended school at Cal Arts for her undergraduate degree and, later, UCLA for her graduate degree. Hall is represented at Hannah Hoffman Gallery in Los Angeles and Tanya Leighton Gallery in Berlin.

Chrissie Iles (Elizabeth Jaeger)
Chrissie Iles is the Anne and Joel Ehrenkranz Curator at the Whitney Museum of American Art, New York City. She is a member of the Graduate Committee at the Center for Curatorial Studies at Bard College, a faculty member of the Curatorial Studies department at the School of Visual Arts, New York, and a board member of the Julia Stoschek Foundation.

Kang Kang (Heidi Lau)
Kang Kang is a Chicago-based writer and artist. She has contributed to *The Brooklyn Rail*, *Artforum China*, *ArtReview Asia*, and *LEAP*, among other publications. She is a doctoral student in comparative literature at Northwestern University working between critical race and decolonial theory, psychoanalysis, and Sinophone ethnic minority cultures in China.

James English Leary (Keegan Monaghan)
James English Leary is a New York City–based artist.

Jason Meadows (Jennifer Rochlin)
Jason Meadows is a Los Angeles–based artist and writer.

Debbie Meniru (Lindsey Mendick)
Debbie Meniru is a London-based curator and writer. She holds a master's degree in curating from the Courtauld Institute of Art, London, and has worked on exhibitions for organizations such as the Hayward Gallery, Tate Modern, the Migration Museum, and Somerset House.

Sarah Messerschmidt (Stephanie Temma Hier)
Sarah Messerschmidt is a writer who works across anthropology, art, and critical theory. Her current research examines nonfiction and artists' films as ways of representing experience, looking at moving image practices as methods of reinvention and world-making. She has been an affiliated writer with the Maumaus School in Lisbon (2021); "The Whole Life: An Archive Project," a collaborative research initiative at the Haus der Kulturen der Welt in Berlin (2022); and the writers residency program AIR Munich at Villa Waldberta in cooperation with the Kunstverein München (2022). She regularly contributes writing to published volumes, journals, and magazines internationally.

Charles Moore (Alake Shilling)
Charles Moore is an art historian, curator, and author investigating abstraction, color theory, and social justice. He is the author of *The Black Market: A Guide to Collecting Art* (Petite Ivy Press, 2020) and *The Brilliance of the Color Black through the Eyes of Art Collectors* (Petite Ivy Press, 2021). Moore received a master's degree in museum studies from Harvard University and is currently a doctoral student at Columbia University's Teachers College.

Shinji Nanzuka (Masato Mori)
NANZUKA was founded by Shinji Nanzuka in 2005 in Tokyo, under the previous name Nanzuka Underground (2005-2011). In 2013, the gallery opened a Hong Kong branch named AISHONANZUKA as a joint gallery with Aisho Miura Arts.

Leah Ollman (Brie Ruais)
Leah Ollman has been writing criticism and features about art for the *Los Angeles Times* and *Art in America* for more than thirty years. She has written essays for books on William Kentridge, Alison Rossiter, Julie Blackmon, Michael Light, Michal Chelbin, John Brill, and Christine Corday, among others, and has contributed to numerous exhibition catalogues. Her articles and reviews have appeared in such publications as *The Brooklyn Rail*, *Sculpture*, *Paris Review Daily*, *Contemporary Art Review Los Angeles*, *Photograph*, *Art in Print*, *History of Photography*, *Art News*, *Art on Paper*, and *American Craft*. She earned her master's in art history from the Institute of Fine Arts, New York University, and graduated Phi Beta Kappa from Scripps College with a joint degree in art history and philosophy. She is currently at work on a book exploring the intersection of poetry and photography.

Corrina Peipon (Bari Ziperstein)
Corrina Peipon is a Los Angeles–based independent curator, writer, and educator. She is the founder of Continuous Project, which empowers artists and art workers through private and group consulting, teaching, and advocacy, and cofounder of Contemporary Art League, a cooperative trade organization that builds unity, solidarity, and equity within and across sectors of the contemporary art field in Los Angeles County.

Cherry Pickman (Katie Stout)
Cherry Pickman is the author of *Theory of Tides*, winner of the Poetry Society of America's Chapbook Fellowship. Her work has appeared in *32 Poems*, *American Poetry Review*, *Bennington Review*, *Boston Review*, *Dossier*, *Indiana Review*, *Jai-Alai Magazine*, and *PEN*, among others. A selection of her poems was included in the anthology *Eight Miami Poets* (Jai-Alai Book, 2015). She has been shortlisted for the Poetry Foundation's Ruth Lilly Poetry Prize, and was a finalist for the Snowbound Chapbook Award from Tupelo Press and the *Missouri Review*'s Jeffrey E. Smith Editors' Prize. Most recently, her full-length collection *Islanders* was a semifinalist for the Alice James Award. In June 2017, she received a fellowship from Artists in Residence in the Everglades. Pickman is a graduate of Columbia University's MFA program. She lives and works in Miami.

Jenelle Porter (Ruby Neri)
Jenelle Porter is a Los Angeles–based curator and writer.

Jayne Pugh (Grant Levy-Lucero)
Jayne Pugh is a writer and editor based in Los Angeles. Her essays and poems have appeared in *Maudlin House*, *Hobart*, and *Juked*, among other publications. She holds an MA in Aesthetics and Politics from the California Institute of the Arts.

Danni Shen (Dominique Fung)
Danni Shen is a curator and writer. She is currently the curatorial and public programs assistant at the Carpenter Center for the Visual Arts at Harvard University. Shen is a contributor to various exhibition catalogues as well as publications including *BOMB* magazine, *Art in America*, *Heichi* magazine, *The Brooklyn Rail*, *Hyperallergic*, *Rhizome*, and *AICA* magazine, among others.

Hanneke Skerath (Magdalena Suarez Frimkess)
Hanneke Skerath is a Los Angeles–based independent curator, cofounder of the curatorial office STUDIO LBV, and codirector of PALOMAR in Italy. She has co-organized a wide range of curatorial projects and publications such as *Luisa Lambri: Linee/Lines* at Thomas Dane Gallery, Naples; *Shio Kusaka* at the Neutra VDL Studio and Residences in Los Angeles (2020); *BLESS: Neutra Dasein* at the Neutra VDL Studio and Residences in Los Angeles (2018); *Signals* at Marc Selwyn Gallery, Los Angeles (2018); and *Concrete Islands* at Kayne Griffin Corcoran Gallery, Los Angeles (2015). She has edited numerous catalogues such as *Fausto Melotti* (2016), *Making Strange: The Chara Schreyer Collection* (2021), and *Shio Kusaka* (2021). She is currently working on a forthcoming monograph on Magdalena Suarez Frimkess.

Amy Smith-Stewart (Genesis Belanger)
Amy Smith-Stewart is chief curator at The Aldrich Contemporary Art Museum in Ridgefield, Connecticut. She has organized more than seventy exhibitions in museums, collections, galleries, and temporary spaces.

Ambika Trasi (Alex Anderson)
Ambika Trasi is a Brooklyn-based artist, curator, and writer. She has recently exhibited at Asian Arts Initiative, Philadelphia, and Heroes Gallery, New York, and has presented lecture-performances at Jack Shainman Gallery, New York, and HANGAR-Centro de Investigação Artística, Lisbon. Trasi's curatorial projects include *Salman Toor: How Will I Know* at the Whitney Museum of American Art, New York, and *A Space for Monsters* at Twelve Gates Arts, Philadelphia. Her writing has been published by the Whitney Museum of American Art, *IBRAAZ Journal for Contemporary Visual Culture in North Africa and the Middle East*, and *Arcade Project* zine.

Taylor Walsh (Trisha Baga)
Taylor Walsh is the Editorial Director at Greene Naftali Gallery, New York. She has previously worked at the Museum of Modern Art, New York and holds a PhD in art history from Harvard University.

Audrey Wollen (Amia Yokoyama)
Audrey Wollen is a writer from Los Angeles living in New York. Her criticism regularly appears in the *New York Times*, *The New York Review of Books*, *Artforum*, *Bookforum*, *The Nation*, and other publications.

Kate Wong (Narumi Nekpenekpen)
Kate Wong is a curator, writer and poet living in London, UK. Interested in the decolonial possibilities within artistic practice, she is the founder of the bi-annual journal *low theory*, a contributing writer for frieze magazine and *AnOther Magazine*, and is currently working as the Curator at MOCA Toronto.

John Yau (Jiha Moon and Stephanie H. Shih)
John Yau is a poet, critic, curator, and publisher. His reviews are published regularly in *Hyperallergic*.

First published in the United States of America in 2023 by:
Rizzoli Electa
A Division of Rizzoli International Publications, Inc.
300 Park Avenue South
New York, NY 10010
www.rizzoliusa.com

Copyright © 2023 by Jeffrey Deitch

Publisher: Charles Miers
Associate publisher: Margaret Chace
Production manager: Barbara Sadick
Editor: Loren Olson
Copy editor: Cindy Trickel
Proofreader: Richard Slovak

Designers: Polymode, Los Angeles/Raleigh: Brian Johnson, Silas Munro, and Randa Hadi

For Jeffrey Deitch:
Managing director: Alia Dahl
Image research and editorial: Sabeena Khosla
Image research: Supriya Malik
Assistant: Ellery Whaley

All rights reserved. No part of this publication may be reproduced, stored in a retrieval system, or transmitted in any form or by any means, electronic, mechanical, photocopying, recording, or otherwise, without prior consent of the publisher.

ISBN-13: 978-0-8478-9930-2
Library of Congress Control Number: 2022948168
2023 2024 2025 2026 / 10 9 8 7 6 5 4 3 2 1

Printed in Hong Kong

Visit us online:
Facebook.com/RizzoliNewYork
Twitter @Rizzoli_Books
Instagram.com/RizzoliBooks
Pinterest.com/RizzoliBooks
Youtube.com/user/RizzoliNY
Issuu.com/Rizzoli

Endpapers: Shards artwork by Pilar Almon.

Pages 7–8, 10, 14–15, 58, 60–61, 84–85, 86, 98–99, 198, 200–203: Courtesy of the artist and Jeffrey Deitch, New York. Photo by Genevieve Hanson; p. 12: Courtesy of the artist. Photo by Elon Schoenholz; pp. 13, 62: Courtesy of the artist. Photo by Grant Gutierrez; p. 16: Courtesy of the artist and Sargent's Daughters; pp. 18–21: Courtesy of the artist and GAVLAK Los Angeles | Palm Beach; pp. 22–27: Courtesy of the artist and Greene Naftali, New York. Photo by Gustavo Murillo Fernández-Valdés; pp. 28, 30–33, 31, 32: Courtesy of the artist and Karma International, Zurich. Photo by Genevieve Hanson; p. 34: Courtesy of the artist and Perrotin, New York. Photo by Guillaume Ziccarelli; pp. 36–39: Photo by Pauline Shapiro; pp. 40, 42–44: Photo by Brica Wilcox; pp. 44–45: Courtesy of the artist and FIERMAN, New York. Photo by Genevieve Hanson; p. 46: Courtesy of the artist and Jessica Silverman, San Francisco. Photo by Genevieve Hanson; pp. 48 (top), 49: Courtesy of the artist and Jessica Silverman, San Francisco. Photo by John Wilson White; pp. 48 (bottom), 50–51: Courtesy of the artist and Jessica Silverman, San Francisco. Photo by Philip Maisel; pp. 52, 54–55: Courtesy of the artist and François Ghebaly, Los Angeles and New York. Photo by Paul Salveson; pp. 56–57: Courtesy of the artist and François Ghebaly, Los Angeles. Photo by Genevieve Hanson; pp. 63, 70, 74–75: Photo by Matt Grubb, Object Studies; p. 64: Courtesy of the artist, Jeffrey Deitch, New York, and Nicodim Gallery, Los Angeles. Photo by Genevieve Hanson; pp. 66–69: Courtesy of the artist, Jeffrey Deitch, New York, and Nicodim Gallery, Los Angeles. Photo by Cooper Dodds and Genevieve Hanson; pp. 72–73: Photo by Rodrigo Gaya; p. 76: © Melvino Garretti. Courtesy of the artist and Parker Gallery, Los Angeles. Photo by Paul Salveson; pp. 78–81: © Melvino Garretti. Courtesy of the artist and Parker Gallery, Los Angeles; p. 82: Courtesy of Raven Halfmoon and Kouri + Corrao Gallery, Santa Fe; p. 87: Courtesy of Ross+Kramer Gallery, New York. Photo by John Berens; pp. 88, 90–92: Photo by Nino Mier Gallery and Charles White; p. 93: Courtesy of Bradley Ertaskiran. Photo by Lance Brewer; pp. 94, 96–97, 100: Courtesy of the artist; p. 103: Courtesy of the artist and Jack Hanley Gallery, New York. Photo by Genevieve Hanson; p. 104: Courtesy of the artist and Klemm's Berlin. Photo by Nick Ash; pp. 105, 106–107: Courtesy of the artist and Jack Hanley Gallery, New York. Photo by Brad Farwell; p. 108: © Heidi Lau. Courtesy of the artist and Matthew Brown, Los Angeles. Photo by Adam Reich; pp. 110–111: © Heidi Lau. Courtesy of the artist and Matthew Brown, Los Angeles. Photo by Gina Folly; pp. 112–113: Courtesy of the artist and Matthew Brown, Los Angeles. Photo by Genevieve Hanson; pp. 114, 116: Courtesy of the artist and Night Gallery, Los Angeles. Photo by Genevieve Hanson; pp. 117–119: Courtesy of the artist and Night Gallery, Los Angeles; pp. 120, 124–125: Courtesy of the artist and François Ghebaly, Los Angeles. Photo by Genevieve Hanson; pp. 122–123: Courtesy of the artist and François Ghebaly, Los Angeles and New York. Photo by Dario Lasagni; p. 126: Courtesy of the artist and Night Gallery, Los Angeles. Photo by Paul Salveson; pp. 128–129: Courtesy of the artist and Night Gallery, Los Angeles. Photo by Nik Massey; pp. 130–131: Courtesy of the artist and Night Gallery, Los Angeles. Photo by Marten Elder; pp. 132, 135: Courtesy of the artist and Carl Freedman Gallery, Margate; pp. 136–137: Courtesy of the artist and Carl Freedman Gallery, Margate. Photo by Genevieve Hanson; p. 142: Courtesy of the artist and James Fuentes, New York. Photo by Genevieve Hanson; pp. 144, 146–149: Courtesy of artist and Derek Eller Gallery, New York. Photo by Russell Killgore; pp. 150, 152–155: © Masato Mori. Courtesy of NANZUKA, Tokyo; pp. 156, 158–161: Courtesy of Harkawik; p. 162: © Ruby Neri. Courtesy of the artist and David Kordansky Gallery. Photo by Jeff McLane; pp. 164–165: © Ruby Neri. Courtesy of the artist, Salon 94, and Jeffrey Deitch, New York. Photo by Charles White; pp. 166, 167 (left): © Ruby Neri. Courtesy of the artist and David Kordansky Gallery. Photo by Jon DeCola; p. 167 (right): © Ruby Neri. Courtesy of the artist and Salon 94, New York; pp. 168, 170–171: Courtesy of the artist and Massimo de Carlo Gallery, London. Photo by Marten Elder; pp. 172–173: Courtesy of the artist and Massimo de Carlo Gallery, London. Photo by Genevieve Hanson; pp. 174, 176–177, 179: Courtesy of the artist and The Pit, Los Angeles. Photo by Jeff Mclane; p. 178: Courtesy of MAKI Gallery, Tokyo; p. 180: Courtesy of the artist and Albertz Benda, New York. Photo by Genevieve Hanson; p. 182: Courtesy of Night Gallery, Los Angeles. Photo by Paul Salveson; pp. 183–185: Courtesy of Albertz Benda, Los Angeles and New York, and MONA Portsmith; p. 186: Courtesy of the artist and Rachel Uffner, New York. Photo by Genevieve Hanson; pp. 188–191: Courtesy of the artist and Venus Over Manhattan, New York; pp. 192, 194–197: Photo by Robert Bredvad; pp. 204, 206–211: Courtesy of Jessica Stoller and P·P·O·W, New York; pp. 212, 214–216: Courtesy of the artist and R& Company. Photo by Genevieve Hanson; p. 217: Courtesy of the artist and Nina Johnson; pp. 218, 220–223: Courtesy of the artist and kaufmann repetto Milan/New York. Photo by Greg Carideo; pp. 224, 227 (right), 228–229: Courtesy of the artist and Primary. Photo by Tim Johnson; pp. 226, 227 (left): Courtesy of the artist; pp. 230, 232: Courtesy of the artist and Sebastian Gladstone, Los Angeles; p. 233: Courtesy of the artist and in lieu, Los Angeles. Photo by Genevieve Hanson; pp. 234–235: Courtesy of the artist and Sebastian Gladstone, Los Angeles; pp. 236, 240, 241: Photo by Thomas Barratt; pp. 238–239: Courtesy of the artist and Charles Moffett, New York. Photo by Genevieve Hanson; p. 243: © 2022 The Robert H. Colescott Separate Property Trust / Artists Rights Society (ARS), New York; p. 244: © 2022 The Robert H. Colescott Separate Property Trust / Artists Rights Society (ARS), New York. Courtesy of The Trust and Blum & Poe, Los Angeles/New York/Tokyo. Photo by Andrea Rossetti; p. 246: © 2022 Estate of Robert Arneson / Licensed by VAGA at Artists Rights Society (ARS), NY. Lee Stalsworth. Hirshhorn Museum and Sculpture Garden; p. 247: Courtesy of the artist and Pavel Zoubok Fine Art, NY; p. 248: Courtesy of the artist and Kasmin Gallery; p. 249: © Mel Casas Family Trust. Photo by Karen Baker.

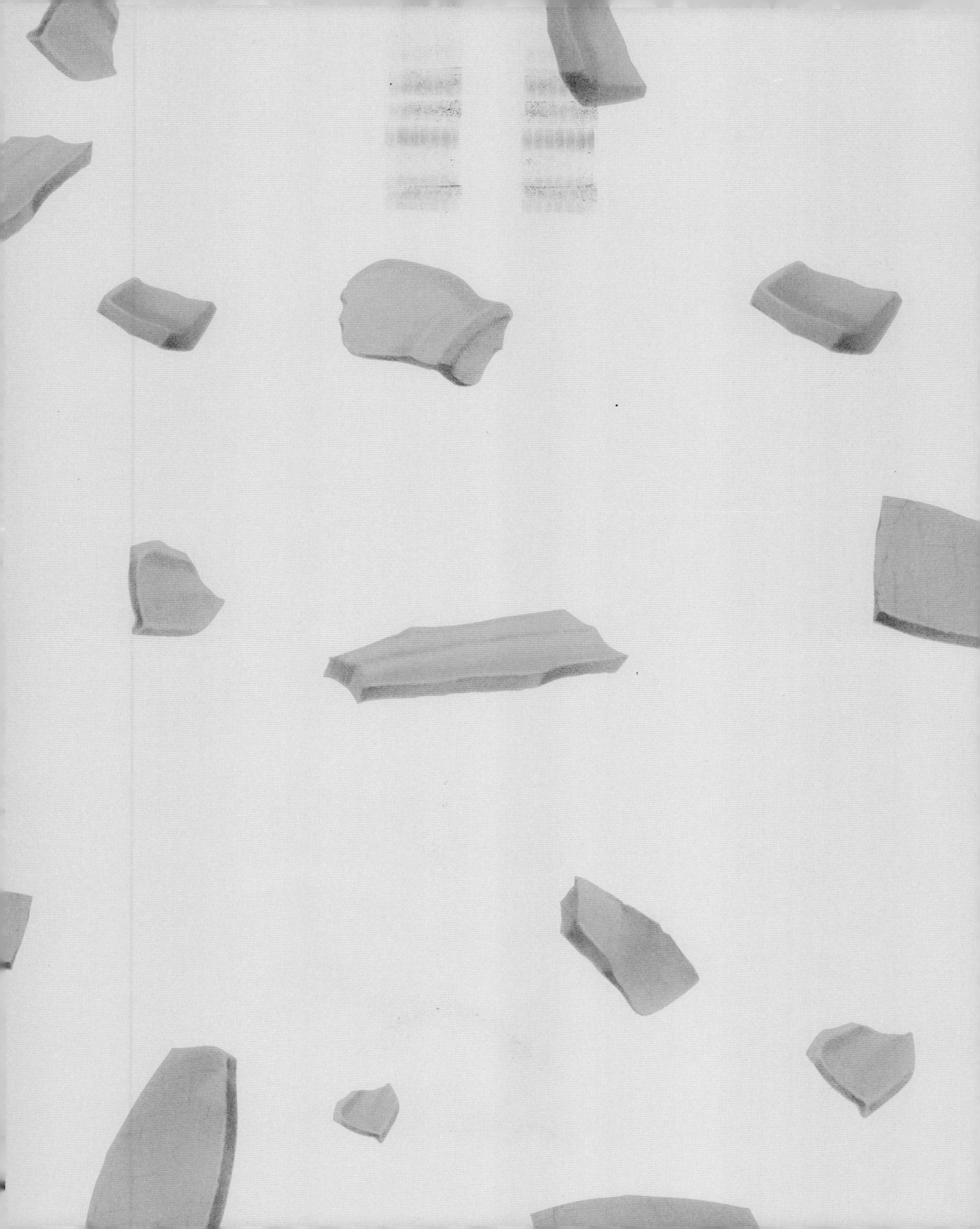